University Centre at
Blackburn
College

Telephone: 01254 292165

Please return this book on or before the last date shown

This book is destined to become a primary reference for just about anyone involved in the development of interactive products of almost any kind. It addresses both the design process and design principles and goes beyond traditional usability to address all aspects of the user experience. The authors have distilled two careers' worth of research, practice and teaching into a concise, practical and comprehensive guide for anyone involved in designing for the user experience of interactive products.—**Deborah J. Mayhew, Deborah J. Mayhew & Associates**

The UX Book covers the methods and guidelines for interaction design and evaluation that have been shown to be the most valuable to students and professionals. The students in my classes have been enthusiastic about the previous versions of this text that they used. This book will benefit anyone who wants to learn the right way to create high quality user experiences. Like good user interfaces, this text has been refined through multiple iterations and feedback with actual users (in this case, feedback from students and faculty who used earlier versions of the book in classes), and this is evident in the final result.— **Brad A. Myers, Professor, Human-Computer Interaction Institute, School of Computer Science, Carnegie Mellon University**

The UX Book takes on a big challenge: a comprehensive overview of what it takes to design great user experiences. Hartson and Pyla combine theory with practical techniques: you leave the book knowing not just what to do, but why it's important.—**Whitney Quesenbery, WQusability, author,** *Global UX: Design and research in a connected world*

The UX Book

Process and Guidelines for Ensuring
a Quality User Experience

The UX Book

Process and Guidelines for Ensuring a Quality User Experience

REX HARTSON
PARDHA S. PYLA

AMSTERDAM • BOSTON • HEIDELBERG • LONDON
NEW YORK • OXFORD • PARIS • SAN DIEGO
SAN FRANCISCO • SINGAPORE • SYDNEY • TOKYO

ELSEVIER

Morgan Kaufmann is an imprint of Elsevier

Acquiring Editor: Rachel Roumeliotis
Development Editor: David Bevans
Project Manager: André Cuello
Designer: Joanne Blank
Cover Designer: Colin David Campbell of Bloomberg L.P.

Morgan Kaufmann is an imprint of Elsevier
225 Wyman Street, Waltham, MA 02451, USA

Library of Congress Cataloging-in-Publication Data
Application submitted

British Library Cataloguing-in-Publication Data
A catalogue record for this book is available from the British Library.

ISBN: 978-0-12-385241-0

Printed in The United States of America
16 17 18 19 20   10 9 8 7 6 5

"Don't panic!"[1]

---

[1]Douglas Adams, *The Hitchhiker's Guide to the Galaxy*

Preface

GOALS FOR THIS BOOK

Our main goal for this book is simple: to help readers learn how to create and refine interaction designs that ensure a quality user experience (UX). A good user interface is like an electric light: when it works, nobody notices it. (We used to be able to use the telephone as a similar example, but now multifunction cell phones with all kinds of modalities have thrown that example under the bus.) A good user interface seems obvious, but what is not obvious is how to design it so that it facilitates a good user experience. Thus, this book addresses both what constitutes a positive user experience and the process by which it can be ensured.

Books need to be designed too, which means establishing user (reader) experience goals, requirements, user role (audience) definitions, and the like. Our goals for the reader experience include ensuring that:

- the book is easy to read
- the material is easy to learn
- the material is easy to apply
- the material is useful to students and practitioners
- the reader experience is at least a little bit fun

Our goals for the book content include:

- expanding the concept of traditional usability to a broader notion of user experience
- providing a hands-on, practical guide to best practices and established principles in a UX lifecycle
- describing a pragmatic process built on an iterative evaluation-centered UX lifecycle template for managing the overall development effort
- expanding the traditional role of design in the iterative lifecycle to embrace design thinking and ideation to address the new characteristics embodied within user experience

- providing interaction design guidelines, including in-depth discussion of affordances and other foundational concepts
- facilitating an understanding of key interaction design creation and refinement activities, such as:
  - contextual inquiry to understand user work that the design is to support
  - contextual analysis to make sense of the raw contextual inquiry data
  - requirements extraction
  - design-informing modeling
  - conceptual and detailed design
  - establishing user experience goals, metrics, and targets
  - building rapid prototypes
  - performing formative user experience evaluation
  - iterative interaction design refinement.
- describing alternative agile UX development methods
- providing pointers on how to get started with these ideas in your own work environment

Our goals for scope of coverage include:

- depth of understanding—detailed information about different aspects of the UX process (like having an expert accompanying the reader)
- breadth of understanding—as comprehensive as space permits
- range of application—the process and the design infrastructure and vocabulary, including guidelines, are not just for GUIs and the Web but for all kinds of interaction styles and devices, including ATMs, refrigerators, road signs, ubiquitous computing, embedded computing, and everyday things.

As we were wrapping up this book, the following quote from Liam Bannon (2011) came to our attention:

> *Some years ago, HCI researcher Panu Korhonen of Nokia outlined to me how HCI is changing, as follows: In the early days the Nokia HCI people were told "Please evaluate our user interface, and make it easy to use." That gave way to "Please help us design this user interface so that it is easy to use." That, in turn, led to a request: "Please help us find what the users really need so that we know how to design this user interface." And now, the engineers are pleading with us: "Look at this area of life, and find us something interesting!" This, in a nutshell, tells a story of how HCI has moved from evaluation of interfaces through design of systems and into general sense-making of our world.*

We were struck by this expressive statement of past, present, and future directions of the field of HCI. It was our goal in this book to embrace this scope of historical roots, the changing perspectives of thought, and future design directions.

USABILITY IS STILL IMPORTANT

The study of usability, a key component of ensuring a quality user experience, is still an essential part of the broad and multidisciplinary field of human–computer interaction. It is about getting our users past the technology and focusing on getting things done for work. In other words, it is about designing the technology as an extension of human capabilities to accomplish something and to be as transparent as possible in the process.

A simple example can help boost this oft-unexplained imperative, "make it transparent," into more than a nice platitude. Consider the simple task of writing with pencil and paper. The writer's focus is all about capturing expressions to convey content and meaning. Much mental energy can be directed toward organizing the thoughts and finding the right words to express them. No thought at all should be necessary toward the writing tools, the pencil and paper, or computer-based word processor. These tools are simply an extension of the writer. Until, that is, the occurrence of a breakdown, something that causes an attention shift from the task to the tools.

Perhaps the pencil lead breaks or a glitch occurs in the word processor software. The writer must turn attention away from the writing and think about how to get the software to work, making the tool that was transparent to the writer in the writing task become the focus of a breakdown recovery task (Heidegger, 1962; Weller & Hartson, 1992). Similarly, interaction designs that cause usability breakdowns for users turn attention away from the task to the computer and the user interface.

BUT USER EXPERIENCE IS MORE THAN USABILITY

As our discipline evolves and matures, more and more technology companies are embracing the principles of usability engineering, investing in sophisticated usability labs and personnel to "do usability." As these efforts are becoming effective at ensuring a certain level of usability in the products, leveling the field on that front, new factors have emerged to distinguish the different competing products.

While usability is essential to making technology transparent, in these days of extreme competition among different products and greater consumer awareness, that is not sufficient. Thus, while usability engineering is still a foundation for what we do in this book, it does not stop there. Because the focus is still on designing for the human rather than focusing on technology, "user-centered design" is still a good description. We now use a new term to express a concern beyond just usability: "user experience."

The concept of user experience conjures a broader image of what users come away with, inviting comparisons with theatre (Quesenbery, 2005), updating the old acronyms—for example, WYXIWYG, What You eXperience Is What You Get (Lee, Kim, & Billinghurst, 2005)—and spawning conferences—for example, DUX, Designing for User Experience. We will see that, in addition to traditional usability attributes, user experience entails social and cultural interaction, value-sensitive design, and emotional impact—how the interaction experience includes "joy of use," fun, and aesthetics.

A PRACTICAL APPROACH

This book takes a practical, applied, hands-on approach, based on the application of established and emerging practices, principles, and proven methods to ensure a quality user experience. The process is about practice, drawing on the creative concepts of design exploration and visioning to make designs that appeal to the emotions of users, while also drawing on engineering concepts of cost-effectiveness—making things as good as the resources permit, but not necessarily perfect.

The heart of the book is an iterative and evaluation-centered UX lifecycle template, called the Wheel, for interaction design in *Part I: Process.* Lifecycle activities are supported by specific methods and techniques spelled out in Chapters 3 through 19, illustrated with examples and exercises for you to apply yourself. The process is complemented by a framework of principles and guidelines in *Part II: Design Infrastructure and Guidelines* for getting the right content into the product. And, throughout, we try to keep our eye on the prize, the pragmatics of making it all work in your development environment.

ORDER OF THE MATERIAL

We faced the question of whether to present the process first or the design infrastructure material. We chose to start with the process because the process contains development activities that should precede design. We could just as well have started with the design infrastructure chapters, especially the interaction design guidelines, and you can read it in that order, too.

One important reason for covering the process first is a practical consideration in the classroom. In our experience, we have found it effective to teach process first so that students can get going immediately on their semester-long team project. Perhaps their designs might be a little better if they had the guidelines first, but we find that it does not matter, as their projects are about learning the process, not making the best designs. Later, when we do get into the design guidelines, the students appreciate it more because they have a process structure for where it all goes.

Use the Index

Use the index! We have tried to keep the text free of inter-section references. So, if you see a term you do not understand, use the index to find out where it is defined and discussed.

OUR AUDIENCE

This book is not a survey of human–computer interaction, usability, or user experience. Nor is it about human–computer interaction research. It is a how-to-do-it handbook, field guide, and textbook for students aspiring to be practitioners and practitioners aspiring to be better. The approach is practical, not formal or theoretical. Some references are made to the related science, but they are usually to provide context to the practice and are not necessarily elaborated.

Anyone involved in, or wishing to learn more about, creating interaction designs to ensure a quality user experience will benefit from this book. It is appropriate for a broad spectrum of readers, including all kinds of *practitioners*—interaction designers, graphic designers, usability analysts, software engineers, programmers, systems analysts, software quality-assurance specialists, human factors engineers, cognitive psychologists, cosmic psychics, trainers, technical writers, documentation specialists, marketing personnel, and project managers. Practitioners in any of these areas will find the hands-on approach of this book to be valuable and can focus mainly on the how-to-do-it parts.

Researchers in human–computer interaction will also find useful information about the current state of user interaction design and guidelines in the field. *Software engineers* will find this book easy to read and apply because it relates interaction design processes to those in software engineering.

Academic readers include teachers or instructors and students. The perspectives of student and practitioner are very similar; both have the goal of learning, only in slightly different settings and perhaps with different motivations and expectations.

We have made a special effort to support teachers and instructors for use in a college or university course at the undergraduate or graduate level. We are especially mindful that many of our teacher/instructor readers might be faced with teaching this material for the first time or without much background of their own. We have included, especially in the separate instructor's guide, much material to help them get started.

In addition to the material for course content, we have compiled a wide range of pedagogical and administrative support materials, for example, a comprehensive set of course notes, suggested course calendar, sample syllabi, project assignments, and even sample course Web pages. The exercises are adapted easily for classroom use in an ongoing, semester-long set of in-class activities to design, prototype, and evaluate an interaction design. As instructors gain the experience with the course, we expect they will tailor the materials, style, and content to the needs of their own particular setting.

We also speak to our audiences in terms of their backgrounds and needs. We want those working to develop large domain-complex systems in large-scale projects to have a sufficiently robust process for those jobs. We also want to address young "UXers" who might think the full process is overly heavy and engineering-like. We offer multiple avenues to lighter-weight processes. For many parts of the full process we offer abridged approaches.

In addition, we have added a chapter on rapid evaluation techniques and a chapter on agile UX methods, paralleling the agile software engineering processes in the literature. But we want these readers to understand that the abridged and agile processes they might use for product and small system development are grounded in full and robust processes used to develop systems with complex domains. Even if one always takes the abridged or agile path, it helps to appreciate the full process, to understand what is being abridged. Also, no matter what part of this book you need, you will find it valuable to see it set in a larger context.

Some readers will want to emphasize contextual inquiry, whereas others will want to focus on design. Although many of the process chapters have an engineering flavor, the design chapter takes on the more "designerly" essence of design thinking, sketching, and ideation. Others yet will want the heaviest coverage on evaluation of all kinds, as that is the "payoff" activity. We take the approach that the broadest coverage will reach the needs of the broadest of audiences. Each reader can customize the way of reading the book, deciding which parts are of interest and ignoring and skipping over any parts that are not.

INCREASING MATURITY OF THE DISCIPLINE AND AUDIENCE

We are approaching two decades since the first usability engineering process books, such as Nielsen (1993), Hix and Hartson (1993), and Mayhew (1999), and human–computer interaction as a discipline has since evolved and matured considerably. We have seen the World Wide Web mature to become a stock medium of commerce. The mobile communications revolution keeps users connected to one another at all times. New interaction techniques emerge and become commonplace overnight to make the users' information literally a "touch" away.

Despite all these technological advances, the need for a quality user experience remains paramount. If anything, the importance of ensuring a positive user experience keeps increasing. Given the pervasive information overload, combined with the expectation that everyone is computer savvy, the onus on designing for a quality user experience is even more critical these days.

Among all these advances, many of the concepts of existing design and development paradigms are more or less unchanged, but emerging new paradigms are stretching our understanding and definition of our primary mandate—to create an interaction design that will lead to a quality user experience. Approaches to accomplish this mandate have evolved from engineering-oriented roots in the early 1990s to more design-driven techniques today.

Although much has been added to the literature about parts of the interaction development process, the process is still unknown to many and misunderstood by many and its value is unrecognized by many. For example, many still believe it is just about "usability testing."

Since our first book (Hix & Hartson, 1993), we have conducted many short courses and university courses on this material, working with literally hundreds of students and user experience practitioners at dozens of locations in business, industry, and government. We have learned quite a bit more about what works and what does not.

It is clear that, in this same period of time, the level of sophistication among our audiences has increased enormously. At the beginning we always had to assume that most people in our classes had no user experience background, had never heard of user experience specialists, and, in fact, needed some motivation to believe in the value of user experience. As time went on, we had to adjust the short course to audiences that required no motivation and audiences increasingly knowledgeable about the need for quality user experience and what was required to achieve it. We started getting user experience specialists in the class—self-taught and graduates of other user experience courses.

WHAT WE DO NOT COVER

Although we have attempted a broad scope of topics, it is not possible to include everything in one book, nor is it wise to attempt it. We apologize if your favorite topic is excluded, but we had to draw the line somewhere. Further, many of these additional topics are so broad in themselves that they cannot be covered adequately in a section or chapter here; each could (and most do) fill a book of their own.

Among the topics not included are:

- Accessibility and the American Disabilities Act (ADA)
- Internationalization and cultural differences
- Ergonomic health issues, such as repetitive stress injury
- Specific HCI application areas, such as societal challenges, healthcare systems, help systems, training, and designing for elders or other special user populations
- Special areas of interaction such as virtual environments or 3D interaction

Additionally, our extensive discussions of evaluation, such as usability testing, are focused on formative evaluation, evaluation used to iteratively improve interaction designs. Tutorials on performing summative evaluation (to assess a level of performance with statistically significant results) are beyond our scope.

ABOUT THE EXERCISES

The Exercises Are an Integral Part of the Course Structure

A Ticket Kiosk System is used as an ongoing user interaction development example for the application of material in examples throughout the book. It provides the "bones" upon which you, the reader or student, can build the flesh of your own design for quality user experience. In its use of hands-on exercises based on the Ticket Kiosk System, the book is somewhat like a workbook. After each main topic, you get to apply the new material immediately, learning the practical techniques by active engagement in their application.

Take Them in Order

As explained earlier, we could have interchanged Part I and Part II; either part can be read first. Beyond this option, the book is designed mainly for sequential reading. Each process chapter and each design infrastructure chapter build on the previous ones and add a new piece to the overall puzzle. Because the material is cumulative, we want you to be comfortable with the material from one chapter before proceeding to the next. Similarly, each exercise builds on what you learned and accomplished in the previous stages—just as in a real-world project.

For some exercises, especially the one in which you build a rapid prototype, you may want to spread the work over a couple of days rather than the couple of hours indicated. Obviously, the more time you spend working on the exercises, the more you will understand and appreciate the techniques they are designed to teach.

Do the Exercises in a Group if You Can

Developing a good interaction design is almost always a collaborative effort, not performed in a vacuum by a single individual. Working through the exercises with at least one other interested person will enhance your understanding and learning of the materials greatly. In fact, the exercises are written for small teams because most of these activities involve multiple roles. You will get the most out of the exercises if you can work in a team of three to five people.

The teamwork will help you understand the kinds of communication, interaction, and negotiation that take place in creating and refining an interaction design. If you can season the experience by including a software developer with responsibility for software architecture and implementation, many new communication needs will become apparent.

Students

If you are a student in a course, the best way to do the exercises is to do them in teams, as in-class exercises. The instructor can observe and comment on your progress, and you can share your "lessons learned" with other teams.

Practitioners: Get buy-in to do the exercises at work

If you are a practitioner or aspiring practitioner trying to learn this material in the context of your regular work, the best way of all is an intensive short course with team exercises and projects. Alternatively, if you have a small interaction design team in your work group, perhaps a team that expects to work together on a real project, and your work environment allows, set aside some time (say, two hours every Friday afternoon) for the team exercises. To justify the extra overhead to pull this off, you will probably have to convince your project manager of the value added. Depending on whether your manager is already UX literate, your justification may have to start with a selling job for the value of a quality user experience (see Chapter 23).

Individuals

Do not let the lack of a team stop you from doing the exercises. Try to find at least one other person with whom you can work or, if necessary, get what you can from the exercises on your own. Although it would be easy to let yourself skip the exercises, we urge you to do as much on each of them as your time permits.

PROJECTS

Students

Beyond the exercises, more involved team projects are essential in a course on development for a quality user experience. The course behind this book is, and always has been, a learn-by-doing course—both as a university course and in all of our short courses for business and industry.

In addition to the small-scale, ongoing example application used by teams as a series of in-class activities in conjunction with the book exercises, we cannot emphasize enough the importance of a substantial semester-long team project outside of class, using a real client from the community—a local company, store, or organization that needs some kind of interactive software application designed. The client stands to get some free consulting and even a system prototype in exchange for serving as the project client.

Instructors: See the instructor's guide for many details on how to organize and conduct these larger team projects. The possibilities for project applications are boundless; we have had students develop interaction designs for all kinds of applications: electronic mail, an interactive Monopoly game, a personnel records system, interactive Yellow Pages, a process control system, a circuit design package, a bar-tending aid, an interactive shopping cart, a fast-food ordering system, and so on.

Practitioners

As a way of getting started in transferring this material to your real work environment, you and your existing small team can select a low-risk project. You or your co-workers may already be familiar and even experienced with some of those activities and may even already be doing some of them in your development environment. By making them part of a more complete and informed development lifecycle, you can integrate what you know with new concepts presented in the book.

For example, many development teams use rapid prototyping. Nonetheless, many teams do not know how to make a low-fidelity prototype (as opposed to one programmed on a computer) or do not know what to do with such a prototype once they have one. Many teams bring in users and have them try out the interaction design, but teams often do not know what data are most important to collect during user sessions and do not know the most effective analyses to perform once they have collected those data. Many do not know about the most effective ways to use evaluation data to get the best design improvements for the money. And very few developers know about measurable user experience targets—what they are, how to establish them, and how to use them to help improve the user experience of an interaction design and to manage the process. We hope this book will help you answer such questions.

ORIGINS OF THE BOOK

Real-World Experience

Although we have been researchers in human–computer interaction, we both have been also teachers and practitioners who have successfully used the techniques described in this book for real-world development projects, and we know of dozens, if not hundreds, of organizations that are applying this material successfully.

One of us (RH) has been teaching this material for 30 years in both a university setting and a short course delivered to hundreds of practitioners in business, industry, government, and military organizations. Obviously a much broader audience can be reached by a book than can be taught in person, which is why we have written this book. Because this book is rooted in those courses, the material has been evaluated iteratively and refined carefully through many presentations over a large number of years.

Research and Literature

In the Department of Computer Science at Virginia Tech, we (RH and colleagues) established one of the pioneering research programs in human–computer interaction back in 1979. Over the years, our work has had the following two important themes.

- Getting usability, and now UX, right in an interaction design requires an effective development process integrated within larger software and systems development processes.
- The whole point of work in this discipline, including research, is to serve effective practical application in the field.

The first point implies that human–computer interaction and designing for user experience have strong connections to software and systems engineering. Difficulties arise if human–computer interaction is treated only as a psychology or human factors problem or if it is treated as only a computer science problem. Many people who enter the HCI area from computer science do not bring to the job an appreciation of human factors and the users. Many people who work in human factors or cognitive psychology do not bring an appreciation for problems and constraints of the software engineering world.

The development of high-quality user interaction designs depends on cooperation between the roles of design and implementation. The goals of much of our work in the past decade have been to help (1) bridge the gap between the interaction design world and the software implementation world and (2) forge the necessary connections between UX and software engineering lifecycles.

The second defining theme of our work over the past years has been technology exchange between academia and the real world—getting new concepts out into the real world and bringing fresh ideas from the field of praxis back to the drawing boards of academia. Ideas from the labs of academia are just curiosities until they are put into practice, tested and refined in the face of real needs, constraints, and limitations of a real-world working environment.

Because this book is primarily for practitioners, however, it is not formal and academic. As a result, it contains fewer references to the literature than would a research-oriented book. Nonetheless, essential references have been included; after all, practitioners like to read the literature, too. The work of others is acknowledged through the references and in the acknowledgments.

AROUSING THE DESIGN "STICKLER" IN YOU

We are passionate about user experience, and we hope this enthusiasm will take hold within you, too. As an analogy, *Eats, Shoots, & Leaves: The Zero Tolerance Approach to Punctuation* by Lynn Truss (2003) is a delightful book entirely about punctuation—imagine! If her book rings bells for you, it can arouse what she calls your inner punctuation stickler. You will become particular and demanding about proper punctuation.

With this book, we hope to arouse your inner design stickler. We could think of no happier outcome in our readers than to have examples of poor interaction designs and correspondingly dreadful user experiences trigger in you a ghastly private emotional response and a passionate desire to do something about it.

This book is for those who design for users who interact with almost any kind of device. The book is especially dedicated to those in the field who get "hooked on UX," those who really care about the user experience, the user experience "sticklers" who cannot enter an elevator without analyzing the design of the controls.

FURTHER INFORMATION ON OUR WEBSITE

Despite the large size of this book, we had more material than we could fit into the chapters so we have posted a large number of blog entries about additional but related topics, organized by chapter. See this blog on our Website at TheUXBook.com. At this site you will also find additional readings for many of the topics covered in the book.

ABOUT THE AUTHORS

Rex Hartson is a pioneer researcher, teacher, and practitioner–consultant in HCI and UX. He is the founding faculty member of HCI (in 1979) in the Department of Computer Science at Virginia Tech. With Deborah Hix, he was co-author of one of the first books to emphasize the usability engineering process, *Developing User Interfaces: Ensuring Usability Through Product & Process.* Hartson has been principal investigator or co-PI at Virginia Tech on a large number of research grants and has published many journal articles, conference papers, and book chapters. He has presented many tutorials, invited lectures, workshops, seminars, and international talks. He was editor or coeditor for *Advances in Human–Computer Interaction*, Volumes 1–4, Ablex Publishing Co., Norwood, New Jersey. His HCI practice is grounded in over 30 years of consulting and user experience engineering training for dozens of clients in business, industry, government, and the military.

Pardha S. Pyla is a Senior User Experience Specialist and Lead Interaction Designer for Mobile Platforms at Bloomberg LP. Before that he was a researcher and a UX consultant. As an adjunct faculty member in the Department of

Computer Science at Virginia Tech he worked on user experience methodologies and taught graduate and undergraduate courses in HCI and software engineering. He is a pioneering researcher in the area of bridging the gaps between software engineering and UX engineering lifecycle processes.

Acknowledgments

I (RH) must begin with a note of gratitude to my wife, Rieky Keeris, who provided me with a happy environment and encouragement while writing this book. While not trained in user experience, she playfully engages a well-honed natural sense of design and usability with respect to such artifacts as elevators, kitchens, doors, airplanes, entertainment controls, and road signs that we encounter in our travels over the world. You might find me in a lot of different places but, if you want to find my heart, you have to look for wherever Rieky is.

I (PP) owe a debt of gratitude to my parents and my brother for all their love and encouragement. They put up with my long periods of absence from family events and visits as I worked on this book. I must also thank my brother, Hari, for being my best friend and a constant source of support as I worked on this book.

We are happy to express our appreciation to Debby Hix, for a careeer-long span of collegial interaction. We also acknowledge several other individuals with whom we've had a long-term professional association and friendship at Virginia Tech, including Roger Ehrich, Bob and Bev Williges, Tonya Smith-Jackson, and Woodrow Winchester. Similarly we are grateful for our collaboration and friendship with these other people who are or were associated with the Department of Computer Science: Ed Fox, John Kelso, Sean Arthur, Mary Beth Rosson, and Joe Gabbard. We are also grateful to Deborah Tatar and Steve Harrison of the Center for Human-Computer Interaction at Virginia Tech for steering us to consider more seriously the design thinking paradigm of HCI.

We are indebted to Brad Myers of Carnegie Mellon University for the use of ideas, words, examples, and figures in the contextual inquiry and modeling chapters. Brad was instrumental in the evolution of the material in this book through his patient adoption of and detailed feedback from early and incomplete trial versions.

In addition, we wish to thank Janet Davis of Grinnell College for her adoption of an early draft of this book and for her detailed and insightful feedback.

Thanks also to Jon Meads of Usability Architects, Inc. for help with ideas for the chapter on agile UX methods and to John Zimmerman of CMU for suggesting alternative graphical representations of some of the models. Additionally, one paragraph of Chapter 4 was approved by Fred Pelton.

Susan Wyche helped with discussions and introduced us to Akshay Sharma, in the Virginia Tech Department of Industrial Design. Very special thanks to Akshay for giving us personal access to the operations of the Department of Industrial Design and to his approach to teaching ideation and sketching. Akshay also gave us access to photograph the ideation studio and working environment there, including students at work and the sketches and prototypes they produced. And finally our thanks for the many photographs and sketches provided by Akshay to include as figures in design chapters.

It is with pleasure we acknowledge the positive influence of Jim Foley, Dennis Wixon, and Ben Shneiderman, with whom friendship goes back decades and transcends professional relationships.

We thank Whitney Quesenbery for discussions of key ideas and encouragement to keep writing. Thanks also to George Casaday for many discussions over a long-term friendship. We would like to acknowledge Elizabeth Buie for a long and fruitful working relationship and for helpful discussions about various topics in the book. And we must mention Bill Buxton, a friend and colleague who was a major influence on the material about sketching and ideation.

We are grateful for the diligence and professionalism of the many, many reviewers over the writing lifecycle, for amazingly valuable suggestions that have helped make the book much better than what it started out to be. Especially to Teri O'Connell and Deborah J. Mayhew for going well beyond the call of duty in detailed manuscript reviews.

We wish to thank the Department of Computer Science at Virginia Tech for all the support and encouragement.

Among those former students especially appreciated for volunteering untold hours of fruitful discussions are Terence Andre, Steve Belz, and Faith McCreary. I (RH) enjoyed my time working with you three and I appreciate what you contributed to our discussions, studies, and insights.

Susan Keenan, one of my (RH) first Ph.D. students in HCI, was the one who started the User Action Framework (UAF) work. Jose (Charlie) Castillo and Linda van Rens are two special friends and former research collaborators.

We wish to thank all the HCI students, including Jon Howarth and Miranda Capra, we have had the pleasure of working with over the years. Our discussions about research and practice with Jon and Miranda have contributed considerably to this book. We extend our appreciation to Tejinder Judge for her extensive help with studies exploring contextual inquiry and contextual analysis.

We also acknowledge all the students in classes where early drafts of this book were tested for their feedback and suggestions.

We also wish to acknowledge Mara Guimarães da Silva for very dedicated, generous, and conscientious help in gathering and formatting the references in this book.

Special thanks to Colin David Campbell of Bloomberg L.P. for the design of the book cover and many diagrams in the book.

Thanks to Mathilde Bekker and Wolmet Barendregt for discussions during my (RH) visits to Technische Universiteit Eindhoven (TU/e) in the Netherlands.

Many thanks to Phil Gray and all the other nice people in the Department of Computing Science at the University of Glasgow for hosting my (RH) wonderful sabbatical in 1989. Special thanks to Steve Draper, Department of Psychology, University of Glasgow, for providing a comfortable and congenial place to live while I was there in 1989. And thanks to Dan Olson for good memories of doing contextual studies on the Isle of Mull.

And thanks to Jeri Baker, the director of the ONE Spirit organization (www.nativeprogress.org), who has put up with my (RH) absence from my post in helping her with that organization while working on this book.

It is not possible to name everyone who has contributed to or influenced our work, professionally or personally, and it is risky to try. We have interacted with a lot of people over the years whose inputs have benefitted us in the writing. If you feel that we have missed an acknowledgement to you, we apologize; please know that we appreciate you nonetheless. Our thanks go out to you anonymous contributors.

Finally, we thank the students for the fun we have had with them at Usability Day parties and at dinners and picnics at Hartveld. In particular, we thank Terence Andre for creating the UAF hat, used at many meetings, and Miranda Capra for baking a UAF cake for one of our famous Fourth of July parties.

Finally, we are grateful for all the support from André Cuello, Dave Bevans, Steve Elliot, and all the others at Morgan Kauffman. It has been a pleasure to work with this organization.

Guiding Principles for the UX Practitioner

Be goal-directed.

Don't be dogmatic; use your common sense.

Context is everything.

The answer to most questions is "it depends."

It's about the people.

Everything should be evaluated in its own way.

Improvise, adapt, and overcome.

Contents

Introduction

Fine art and pizza delivery, what we do falls neatly in between.

– David Letterman

Objectives

After reading this chapter, you will:
1. Recognize the pervasiveness of computing in our lives
2. Be cognizant of the changing nature of computing and interaction and the need to design for it
3. Understand the traditional concept of usability and its roots
4. Have a working definition of user experience, what it is and is not
5. Understand the components of user experience, especially emotional impact
6. Recognize the importance of articulating a business case for user experience

1.1 UBIQUITOUS INTERACTION

1.1.1 Desktops, Graphical User Interfaces, and the Web Are Still Here and Growing

The "old-fashioned" desktop, laptop, and network-based computing systems are alive and well and seem to be everywhere, an expanding presence in our lives. And domain-complex systems are still the bread and butter of many business, industry, and government operations. Most businesses are, sometimes precariously, dependent on these well-established kinds of computing. Web addresses are commonplace in advertisements on television and in magazines. The foreseeable future is still full of tasks associated with "doing computing," for example, word processing, database management, storing and retrieving information, spreadsheet management. Although it is exciting to think about all the new computing systems and interaction styles, we will need to use processes for creating and refining basic computing applications and interaction styles for years to come.

1.1.2 The Changing Concept of Computing

That said, computing has now gone well beyond desktop and laptop computers, well beyond graphical user interfaces and the Web; computing has become far more ubiquitous (Weiser, 1991). Computer systems are being worn by people and embedded within appliances, homes, offices, stereos and entertainment systems, vehicles, and roads. Computation and interaction are also finding their way into walls, furniture, and objects we carry (briefcases, purses, wallets, wrist watches, PDAs, cellphones). In the 2Wear project (Lalis, Karypidis, & Savidis, 2005), mobile computing elements are combined in different ways by short-distance wireless communication so that system behavior and functionality adapt to different user devices and different usage locations. The eGadget project (Kameas & Mavrommati, 2005) similarly features self-reconfiguring artifacts, each with its own sensing, processing, and communication abilities.

Sometimes, when these devices can be strapped on one's wrist or in some way attached to a person's clothing, for example, embedded in a shoe, they are called *wearable computers*. In a project at MIT, volunteer soldiers were instrumented with sensors that could be worn as part of their clothing, to monitor heart rate, body temperature, and other parameters, to detect the onset of hypothermia (Zieniewicz et al., 2002).

"Smart-its" (Gellersen, 2005) are embedded devices containing microprocessors, sensors, actuators, and wireless communication to offer additional functionality to everyday physical world artifacts that we all "interact" with as we use them in familiar human activities. A simple example is a set of car keys that help us track them so we can find them if they are lost.

Another example of embedding computing artifacts involves uniquely tagging everyday objects such as milk and groceries using inexpensive machine-readable identifiers. It is then possible to detect changes in those artifacts automatically. For example, using this technology it is possible to remotely poll a refrigerator using a mobile phone to determine what items need to be picked up from the grocery store on the way home (Ye & Qiu, 2003). In a project at MIT that is exactly what happened, or at least was envisioned: shoes were instrumented so that, as the wearer gets the milk out for breakfast in the morning, sensors note that the milk is getting low. Approaching the grocery store on the way home, the system speaks via a tiny earphone, reminding of the need to pick up some milk (Schmandt, 1995).

Most of the user–computer interaction attendant to this ubiquitous computing in everyday contexts is taking place without keyboards, mice, or monitors. As Cooper (2004) says, you do not need a traditional user interface to have interaction.

Practical applications in business already reveal the almost unlimited potential for commercial application. Gershman and Fano (2005) cite an example of a smart railcar that can keep track of and report on its own location, state of repair, whether it is loaded or empty, and its routing, billing, and security status (including aspects affecting homeland security). Imagine the promise this shows for improved efficiency and cost savings over the mostly manual and error-prone methods currently used to keep track of railroad cars.

Proof-of-concept applications in research labs are making possible what was science fiction only a few years ago. Work at the MIT Media Lab (Paradiso, 2005), based on the earlier "Smart Matter" initiative at Xerox PARC, employs sensate media (Paradiso, Lifton, & Broxton, 2004) arranged as surfaces tiled with dense sensor networks, in the manner of biological skin, containing multimodal receptors and sensors. The goal is to use this kind of embedded and distributed computing to emulate living, sensitive tissue in applications such as robotics, telemedicine, and prosthetics. Their Tribble (Tactile Reactive Interface Built By Linked Elements) is an interesting testbed using a spherical structure of these nodes that can sense pressure, temperature, sound, illumination, and tactile stimulations and can respond with sound, vibration, and light.

More and more applications that were in research labs are now moving into commercial adoption. For example, robots in more specialized applications than just housecleaning or babysitting are gaining in numbers (Scholtz, 2005). There are robotic applications for healthcare rehabilitation, including systems to encourage severely disabled children to interact with their environment (Lathan, Brisben, & Safos, 2005), robotic products to assist the elderly (Forlizzi, 2005), robots as laboratory hosts and museum docents (Sidner & Lee, 2005), robot devices for urban search and rescue (Murphy, 2005), and, of course, robotic rover vehicles for unmanned space missions (Hamner et al., 2005).

1.1.3 The Changing Concept of Interaction

Sitting in front of a desktop or laptop usually conveys a feeling of "doing computing" to users. Users are aware of interacting with a computer and interaction is purposeful: for exchanging information, for getting work done, for learning, for play or entertainment, or just for exploring.

When we drive a car we are using the car's built-in computer and maybe even a GPS, but we do not think of ourselves as "doing computing." Tscheligi (2005) paraphrases Mark Weiser: "the world is not a desktop." Perhaps the most notable and most recognizable (by the public) example of interaction away from the desktop is seen in mobile communications. With an obviously enormous market potential, mobile communications are perhaps the fastest growing area of ubiquitous computing with personal devices and also represent one of the most intense areas of designing for a quality user experience (Clubb, 2007; Kangas & Kinnunen, 2005; Macdonald, 2004; Venkatesh, Ramesh, & Massey, 2003).

Designing for a Quality User Experience in 3D Applications

Doug A. Bowman, Department of Computer Science, Virginia Tech

Motion controls. Freehand gestures. "Natural" user interfaces. They go by many names, but interfaces involving physical interaction in 3D space are cropping up everywhere these days. Instead of pressing buttons or pushing on joysticks, gamers are swinging their arms, jumping up and down, or leaning their whole bodies to play in 3D virtual worlds. Instead of using a remote control, people are making mid-air gestures to control the components of their home theaters. Instead of looking for restaurants on a 2D map, mobile phone users look at augmented views of the real world through their phone's cameras. All this 3D interaction is certainly very cool, but does it necessarily make interfaces more "natural" or usable? How should we design 3D interaction to ensure a quality user experience?

Three-dimensional user interfaces (3D UIs) are very much an open field of research; there is much we do not yet know. What I am going to review here are a few of the major things we have learned over the last couple of decades of research in this area. For a comprehensive introduction to the field of 3D UIs, see the book *3D User Interfaces: Theory and Practice* (Addison-Wesley, 2005).

As you might expect, *3D UIs that replicate an action that people do in the real world can be very successful*. We call these "natural" or "high-fidelity" 3D UIs. For example, using physical turning and walking movements (measured by a position tracking system) to change your view of the virtual world is easy to comprehend and results in high levels of spatial understanding. Swinging your arms to make your character swing a virtual golf club is fun and engaging, requiring no special expertise. But natural 3D interaction has its limitations, as well. It can be difficult to reproduce exactly the action people use in the real world, resulting in misunderstanding. An experienced golfer might expect a slight twitch of the wrists at impact to cause the ball to draw from right to left, but it is unlikely that the interface designer included this in the technique. In fact, if an extremely realistic golf swing technique were developed, it probably would not be very fun for most players—I personally would only hit the ball 50 yards much of the time!

Another limitation of natural 3D interaction is that the user is constrained to things they can do in the real world. This leads to our second guideline, which is that *"magic" 3D interaction can allow users to perform many tasks more quickly and effectively*. It is a virtual world, after all, so why restrict ourselves to only real-world abilities? Magic techniques can be used to enhance our physical abilities (e.g., a person can pick up a 10-story building and place it somewhere else in the virtual city), our perceptual abilities (e.g., we can give the user "X-ray vision" like Superman so she can see what is on the other side of the wall), and even our cognitive abilities (e.g., the system can provide instructions to users to help them navigate through a complicated 3D world).

While we do not want to constrain the user's abilities in a 3D UI, we do want to *provide constraints that help the user to interact more easily and effectively*. For example, in an application for interior designers, even though we could allow users to place furniture anywhere in 3D space, it only makes sense to have furniture sitting upright on the floor. Therefore, 3D manipulation techniques in this case should only allow the user to control three parameters: 2D position on the floor and rotation around the vertical axis. Many 3D input devices are inherently underconstrained because they allow the user to move them freely in 3D space and do not remain in place when the user lets go. Helpful constraints can be added to the system with the use of haptic feedback, which can be passive (e.g., using a physical piece of plastic to provide a surface for 2D input) or active (based on a force feedback display, such as the Sensable Phantom).

If appropriate constraints are not provided, users not only become less precise, they may also become fatigued (imagine how tired your arm would feel if you tried to sketch 3D shapes in mid-air for 15 minutes). So the last guideline I want to highlight is to *design for user comfort*. In many computer interfaces, physical comfort is not a major issue, but 3D interaction usually involves large-scale physical movements and the use of many parts of the body (not just the hand and fingers). What is more, 3D UIs for virtual reality often involve big, surrounding 3D displays that can make users feel dizzy or even nauseated. As a result, 3D UI designers have to take special care to design interfaces that keep users feeling as comfortable as possible. For example, manipulation techniques should allow users to interact with their arms propped against their bodies or a physical surface. 3D UIs should avoid rapid movements through the virtual world or unnatural rotations of the view that can make people feel sick. And if stereoscopic displays are used, keeping virtual objects at a comfortable distance can help avoid eye strain.

Well-designed 3D UIs can make for an engaging, enjoyable, and productive user experience. Knowing the foundational principles of human–computer interaction and UX design is a great start, but using 3D-specific results and guidelines such as these will help ensure that your 3D interaction is a success.

As an aside, it is interesting that even the way these devices are presented to the public reveals underlying attitudes and perspectives with respect to user-centeredness. For example, among the synonyms for the device, "cellphone" refers to their current implementation technology, while "mobile phone" refers to a user capability.

Interaction, however, is doing more than just reappearing in different devices such as we see in Web access via mobile phone. Weiser (1991) said ". . . the most profound technologies are those that disappear." Russell, Streitz, and Winograd (2005) also talk about the disappearing computer—not computers that are departing or ceasing to exist, but disappearing in the sense of becoming unobtrusive and unremarkable. They use the example of electric motors, which are part of many machines we use daily, yet we almost never think about electric motors per se. They talk about "making computers disappear into the walls and interstices of our living and working spaces."

When this happens, it is sometimes called "ambient intelligence," the goal of considerable research and development aimed at the home living environment. In the HomeLab of Philips Research in the Netherlands (Markopoulos et al., 2005), researchers believe "that ambient intelligence technology will mediate,

Usability

Usability is the pragmatic component of user experience, including effectiveness, efficiency, productivity, ease-of-use, learnability, retainability, and the pragmatic aspects of user satisfaction.

Usefulness

Usefulness is the component of user experience to which system functionality gives the ability to use the system or product to accomplish the goals of work (or play).

Functionality

Functionality is power to do work (or play) seated in the non-user-interface computational features and capabilities.

Emotional Impact

Emotional impact is the affective component of user experience that influences user feelings. Emotional impact includes such effects as pleasure, fun, joy of use, aesthetics, desirability, pleasure, novelty, originality, sensations, coolness, engagement, novelty, and appeal and can involve deeper emotional factors such as self-expression, self-identity, a feeling of contribution to the world, and pride of ownership.

permeate, and become an inseparable common of our everyday social interactions at work or at leisure."

In these embedded systems, of course, the computer only *seems* to disappear. The computer is still there somewhere and in some form, and the challenge is to design the interaction so that the computer remains invisible or unobtrusive and interaction appears to be with the artifacts, such as the walls, directly. So, with embedded computing, certainly the need for a quality user experience does not disappear. Imagine embedded computing with a design that leads to poor usability; users will be clueless and will not have even the familiar menus and icons to find their way!

Even interaction via olfactory senses, that is, aromatic output is suggested for human–computer interaction (HCI) (Kaye, 2004), based on the claim that the sense of smell, well used in ordinary daily life, is a human sense underused in HCI.

So far, our changing concepts of interaction have involved at least some kind of computation element, even if it is embedded electronic devices that do very specialized computation. Given the many different definitions of "interaction" in the HCI literature, we turned to the English definition of the word: *mutual or reciprocal action, effect, or influence,* as adapted from Dictionary.com. So, interaction involves an exchange, but is definitely not limited to computer systems.

In the realm of user experience, this concept of mutual effect implies that interaction must be considered within a context or environment shared between system and user. User input, if accepted by the system, causes a change in the internal system state and both user and system can cause changes in the external world, for example, move a mechanical part or adjust another system.

The user's part of interaction is often expressed through explicit user actions, used to direct the interaction toward a goal. A user-related input to a system in his or her environment can also be extracted or sensed by the environment, without a deliberate or conscious action by the user. For example, a "smart wall," a wall with ambient intelligence, can proactively extract inputs it needs from a user by sensing the user's presence and identifying the user with something like radio-frequency identification technology instead of just responding to a user's input actions. It is still user–system interaction, only the system is controlling the inputs. Here the dictionary definition given earlier, relating technology to an effect or influence, definitely makes sense, with "action" being only part of that definition.

The system can also extract other inputs, absent any users, by sensing them in the state of its own environment, for example, a high-temperature warning sensor. It may then act to change its own internal state and, possibly, its external environment, for example, to adjust the temperature lower, without involving a user. This kind of automated system operation probably does not come under the aegis of human–machine interaction, although such a system would surely also involve human interaction for start-up, setting parameters, and other overall controls.

As another example of how our concept of interaction is intended to be very inclusive, consider road or highway signage. A road sign is like a computer message or user interface label in that it helps users (drivers) know what to do. In response, drivers take (driving) actions within the larger highway system. Most of the material in this book can be considered to be about interaction much more general than traditional HCI, including human–machine interaction, for example, with telephones, and ATMs, and even human–world interaction, such as interacting to navigate the structure of a museum.

1.2 EMERGING DESIRE FOR USABILITY

In the distant past, computer usage was esoteric, conducted mostly by a core of technically oriented users who were not only willing to accept the challenge of overcoming poor usability, but who sometimes welcomed it as a barrier to protect the craft from uninitiated "outsiders." Poor usability was good for the mystique, not to mention job security.

Sometimes, even more recently, we have what Cooper (2004, p. 26) calls "dancing bear" software. It is where a great idea triumphs over poor design. It is about having features just so good users cannot do without it, even if it has a terrible interaction design. Just having a bear that can dance leads one to overlook the fact that it cannot dance very well. Users are so grateful to have the functionality that they are willing to work around an interaction design that fell out of the ugly tree and hit every branch on the way down. Success despite poor interaction design can be used as a justification for resisting change and keeping the bad design ideas: "We have been doing it that way, our product is selling phenomenally, and our users love it." Think of how much better it could be with a good design.

As more people began to use computers, the general public and the press were generally slow to realize that we all can demand a better user experience. Statements of misplaced blame fail to inform or educate the public about the role of user experience in design. For example, the failure of voting machines in Florida was blamed by the press on improperly trained poll workers and confused voters. No one publicly asked the question why it takes so much training to operate a simple ballot machine or why citizens experienced with voting were confused with this system.

We are now seeing comments by people about usability of everyday situations. The very first three paragraphs of *The Long Dark Tea-Time of the Soul* (Adams, 1990, pp. 1–2) by one of our favorite authors, Douglas Adams (decidedly not a user experience specialist), open with this amazingly perspicacious observation on design of most airports:

> It can hardly be a coincidence that no language on earth has ever produced the expression "As pretty as an airport."
>
> Airports are ugly. Some are very ugly. Some attain a degree of ugliness that can only be the result of a special effort. This ugliness arises because airports are full of people who are tired, cross, and have just discovered that their luggage has landed in Murmansk (Murmansk airport is the only known exception to this otherwise infallible rule), and architects have on the whole tried to reflect this in their designs.
>
> They have sought to highlight the tiredness and crossness motif with brutal shapes and nerve-jangling colors, to make effortless the business of separating the traveler forever from his or her luggage or loved ones, to confuse the traveler with arrows that appear to point at the windows, distant tie racks, or the current position of Ursa Minor in the night sky, and wherever possible to expose the plumbing on the grounds that it is functional, and conceal the location of the departure gates, presumably on the grounds that they are not.

Poor designs can indeed look so bad to users that they are forced to assume they could not be that bad unless it was deliberate, as this character in Douglas Adams' novel did. And that is only half the story when you consider designs that look beautiful but are totally unusable. In contrast, we want to use technology to learn things, to be entertained, to connect with others, and to do good in the world. In technology now, people look beyond sheer functionality or even usability to beauty, emotional satisfaction, meaning in what they do, and for intellectual gratification.

To many, one of the most significant motivations for the field of user experience is a concern about software product quality. Unfortunately, the software industry does little to dispel concerns about quality. For example, consider this "warranty," taken verbatim from a software product and typical of what we get with most software we buy:

> This software is provided without warranty of any kind. The manufacturer does not warrant that the functions contained in the software will meet your requirements, or that the operation of the software will be uninterrupted or error-free, or that defects in the software will be corrected.

Does this not seem to say: "We do not do a good job. We do not care. And you cannot do anything about it."? Who would buy any other kind of consumer product, a TV or a car, with this kind of "warranty"? So why have we put up with this in software products?

Disastrous system development case studies give much more depth to motivating the need for usability and user experience. Marcus and Gasperini (2006) tell of an emergency-response system developed for the San Jose (CA) Police Department, a mobile, in-vehicle communication system for dispatchers and officers in cars. The police had a good working system that they had perfected and customized through years of use, but the underlying technology was too old. Unfortunately, the committee appointed to gather requirements did not include police officers and their focus was on functionality and cost, not usability. No user focus groups or contextual inquiry were considered and, not surprisingly, the mobile response functions and tasks were addressed minimally in requirements.

The resulting system had serious flaws; key information was missing while unneeded information was highlighted. Layouts were confusing and labeling was inconsistent—the typical list you would expect from an early user experience evaluation, only this was in the final system. Officer users were confused and performed poorly to the point of creating risks to their safety in the field.

The lack of feedback channels from initial users precluded fixing problems in subsequent versions. Extensive training was prescribed but could not be given due to cost. In the end, a very expensive new system had led to life-threatening perils for officer users, the situation became highly politicized, emotions ran high, and lawsuits were threatened. Much more money had to be spent in an attempt to fix major problems after the fact. This is a clear story of how a failure to take a user experience-oriented and user-centered approach to design led to truly extensive and awful consequences. A process to ensure a quality user experience that may seem to complicate things upfront can benefit everyone—customers, users, UX practitioners, designers, marketing people, and the public—in the long run.

Contextual Inquiry

Contextual inquiry is an early system or product UX lifecycle activity to gather detailed descriptions of customer or user work practice for the purpose of understanding work activities and underlying rationale. The goal of contextual inquiry is to improve work practice and construct and/or improve system designs to support it. Contextual inquiry includes both interviews of customers and users and observations of work practice occurring in its real-world context.

1.3 FROM USABILITY TO USER EXPERIENCE

1.3.1 The Traditional Concept of Usability

Human–computer interaction is what happens when a human user and a computer system, in the broadest sense, get together to accomplish something. Usability is that aspect of HCI devoted to ensuring that human–computer interaction is, among other things, effective, efficient, and satisfying for the user. So usability[1] includes characteristics such as ease of use, productivity, efficiency, effectiveness, learnability, retainability, and user satisfaction (ISO 9241-11, 1997).

1.3.2 Misconceptions about Usability

While usability is becoming more and more an established part of the technology world, some misconceptions and mischaracterizations still linger. First, usability is not what some people used to call "dummy proofing." While it might have been mildly cute the first time it was used, this term is insulting and demeaning to users and designers alike. Similarly, usability is not equivalent to being "user-friendly." This is a misdirected term; to say that it is about friendliness trivializes the scope of the interaction design process and discounts the importance of user performance in terms of user productivity, etc. As users, we are not looking for amiability; we need an efficient, effective, safe, and maybe aesthetic and fun tool that helps us reach our goals.

To many not familiar with the field, "doing usability" is sometimes thought of as equivalent to usability testing. While usability evaluation plays a very important part, maybe even a starring role, in interaction design, it is by no means all there is in the interaction design creation and refinement process, as we will see in this book.

Finally, another popular misconception about usability has to do with visual appeal. We know of cases where upper management said something to the effect that "after the software is built, I want the usability people to make it look pretty." While visual design is an integral and important part of usability, it is not the only part of interaction design.

1.3.3 The Expanding Concept of Quality in Our Designs

The field of interaction design has grown slowly, and our concept of what constitutes quality in our designs has expanded from an engineering focus on user performance under the aegis of usability into what is now widely known as user experience. As with most new concepts, it takes a while for even those who embrace the concept to agree on its definition (Dagstuhl, 2010).

Within the evolution of a growing field it is natural to see aspirations for considerable breadth. For example, Thomas and McCredie (2002) call for "new usability" to account for "new design requirements such as ambience or attention." At a CHI 2007 Special Interest Group (SIG) meeting (Huh et al.,

---

[1]Also sometimes referred to as "pragmatic quality" or "ergonomic quality" (Hassenzahl et al., 2000) and includes such attributes as simplicity and controllability.

2007), the discussion focused on "investigating a variety of approaches (beyond usability) such as user experience, aesthetic interaction, ambiguity, slow technology,[2] and various ways to understand the social, cultural, and other contextual aspects of our world."

1.3.4 Is Not Emotional Impact What We Have Been Calling User Satisfaction?

Some say the emphasis on these emotional factors is nothing new—after all, user satisfaction, a traditional subjective measure of usability, has always been a part of the concept of traditional usability shared by most people, including the ISO 9241-11 standard definition. Also, user satisfaction questionnaires are about how users feel, or at least about their opinions. As Hassenzahl et al. (2000) point out, at least in practice and as reflected in most usability questionnaires, this kind of user satisfaction has been thought of as a result of how users experience usability and usefulness.

As a result, these user satisfaction questionnaires have elicited responses that are more intellectual responses than emotional ones; they have not traditionally included much about what we call emotional impact.[3] We as a profession did not focus on those aspects as much as we did on objective user performance measures such as efficiency and error counts. Technology and design have evolved from being just productivity-enhancing tools to more personal, social, and intimate facets of our lives. Accordingly, we need a much broader definition of what constitutes quality in our designs and quality in the user experience those designs beget.

1.3.5 Functionality Is Important, but a Quality User Experience Can Be Even More So

All other things being equal, a product that affords a better user experience often outsells ones with even more functionality. For example, take the Blackberry; once a market leader in smartphones but now outclassed by the iPhone, a later entrant into the market with less functional capabilities. There are many factors governing the relative market share of each product, but given comparably capable products, user experience is arguably the most important. The iPod, iPhone, and iPad are products that represent cool high technology

---

[2]From the abstract of this workshop summary paper: slow technology [is] a design agenda for technology aimed at reflection and moments of mental rest rather than efficiency in performance.

[3]Also sometimes referred to as hedonic quality (Schrepp, Held, & Laugwitz, 2006), perceived or experienced hedonic quality (Hassenzahl, Beu, & Burmester, 2001), or emotional usability (Logan, 1994).

with excellent functionality but are also examples that show the market is now not just about the features—it is about careful design for a quality user experience as a gateway to that functionality.

Most users assume that they are getting correct and complete functional capability in their software, but the interface is their only way to experience the functionality. *To users, the interaction experience is the system.* And plain old usability still plays a role here. Users have an effort threshold beyond which they give up and are not able to access the desired functionality. Larry Marine (1994) puts it this way: "If the users can't use a feature, it effectively does not exist." He describes usability testing of a new version of a system and how users commented that they wished they had a certain feature on the current system and how frequently they would use it. But the current product *already had* that feature and designers wondered why users would ask for something they already had. The answer was clear: *the users did not have it* because it was not accessible to them.

Another instructive example once again comes from Apple. When Apple introduced the functionality for users to backup their data on the Macintosh platform, a seemingly mundane and somewhat boring task for most of us, they did so with a stellar interaction design. They introduced a cool fun metaphor, that of a time machine (also the name of this feature) that users can take to go "back in time" to retrieve files that were deleted or lost accidently. The backup procedure itself was automated for the most part and all the user needed to do was connect a backup medium to their Mac. The interesting thing here is that Microsoft, Apple's competitor, had backup capabilities in their operating systems at least since Windows 95! However, because of poor usability, most users did not know it existed and those of us who did rarely used it. The effort software engineers spent to include the feature in the application functionality was wasted, another cost of poor usability.

Hassenzahl and Roto (2007) state the case for the difference between the functional view of usability and the phenomenological view of emotional impact. People have and use technical products because "they have things to do"; they need to make phone calls, write documents, shop on-line, or search for information. Hassenzahl and Roto call these "do goals," appropriately evaluated by the usability and usefulness measures of their "pragmatic quality." Human users also have emotional and psychological needs, including needs involving self-identity, relatedness to others, and being satisfied with life. These are "be goals," appropriately evaluated by the emotional impact and phenomenological measures of their "hedonic quality."

Phenomenological Aspects of Interaction

Phenomenological aspects (deriving from phenomenology, the philosophical examination of the foundations of experience and action) of interaction are the cumulative effects of emotional impact considered over the long term, where usage of technology takes on a presence in our lifestyles and is used to make meaning in our lives.

1.3.6 A Good User Experience Does Not Necessarily Mean High-Tech or "Cool"

Often when a new cool and high-tech product is announced, technology enthusiasts and the public alike are impressed and many equate this product sizzle with amazing user experience. Much of the world culture, except the dispossessed, who are excluded from the mixed blessing of new technology, has come almost to worship high technology just because it is so cool. But for actual users the reaction can quickly shape-shift from amazement to annoyance to abomination when a failed interaction design in the cool new device becomes a barrier to its use. Clearly, while it is possible to harness new technology to serve real usability, "cool" and high technology are not intrinsic benefactors of a quality user experience.

As a case in point, in Figure 1-1 we show what was once a new Microsoft packaging design for Vista[4] and some Office products, such as this one for Office Accounting Professional 2007.

As posted in a Windows Vista blog, the Microsoft designer proudly proclaims: "With Windows Vista and 2007 Office system, we didn't just redesign the software packages themselves, but are also introducing new packaging for the two products. The packaging has been completely revised and, we hope, foreshadows the great experience that awaits you once you open it." Later in the posting, it says, "Designed to be user-friendly, the new packaging is a small, hard, plastic container that's designed to protect the software inside for life-long use. It provides a convenient and attractive place for you to permanently store both discs and documentation. The new design will provide the strength, dimensional stability and impact resistance required when packaging software today. Our plan is to extend this packaging style to other Microsoft products after the launch of Windows Vista and 2007 Office system."

Other follow-up postings by readers of that blog declare, "It looks really nice and should really stand out on the shelves. Good job folks!" and "This looks awesome, really." And "Wow! I must say, I'm very, very impressed by this; excellent job guys." But these are reactions from people who have only seen a picture of the packaging. The reaction from actual users might eventually cause Microsoft to rethink their plan of switching to this as their "standard" packaging.

A glimpse of the same design from the user's, in this case the opener's, stance can be seen in Joel Spolsky's on-line column "Joel on Software" (Spolsky, 2007).

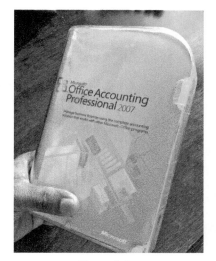

Figure 1-1

A new Microsoft software packaging design.

---

[4]Now we are delighted to see an updated version of Vista: Windows 7, otherwise known as Hasta la Vista (baby).

In an article entitled "Even the Office 2007 box has a learning curve," Spolsky says: "I simply could not figure out how to open the bizarre new packaging. It represents a complete failure of industrial design; an utter 'F' in the school of Donald Norman's Design of Everyday Things. To be technical about it, it has no true affordances and actually has some false affordances: visual clues as to how to open it that turn out to be wrong." And: "[This] is just the first of many ways that Office 2007 and Vista's gratuitous redesign of things that worked perfectly well shows utter disregard for all the time you spent learning the previous versions." Postings elsewhere by actual users contained similar sentiments.

Looking at these boxes displayed in stores, some of them actually have small instruction sheets on how to open the box taped on the outside. Upon closer inspection, this box design is a victim of a case of false affordances (Chapter 20). With what looked like hinges on one side, the box looked like a book, a shared design convention, but would not open like one—a violation of using shared conventions to explain an affordance. In our informal testing, several people with advanced degrees in computer science had significant trouble opening the box. Furthermore, the box was difficult to stack and wasteful of desk drawer space.

To give the benefit of doubt, we expect that Microsoft attempted to create an extraordinary user experience, starting from the time a user lays eyes on the software box in a store. However, the designer probably forgot that less box-savvy people will have to use this complicated design with curves and hinges. Clearly, even in just packaging, the best user experience requires a balance of functionality, usability, aesthetics, branding, identity, and so on.

In addition to user experience not just being cool, it also is not just about technology for technology's sake. Many years ago our university changed its phone system over to an all-digital exchange. At the time, the new phones seemed cool and powerful; users heard all about the different kinds of things they could do with call forwarding, paging, conference calls, and so on.

However, their initial enthusiasm for all this functionality faded quickly when they saw the 90-page "summary" user manual; no one read it, and by now almost everyone has lost it. No one ever saw or mentioned the presumably larger "full" manual. Loss of enthusiasm turned to rebellion when the university sent out word that they expected everyone to take a half-day training course on using this new phone system. One of the faculty expressed the feeling of many, "I've been using a telephone all my life and I certainly don't need a training course about a telephone now. All I want to do is make phone calls like I used to."

When many complained to the communications services department, they were actually told that they had a "low-end model" and that they might appreciate the new phones better if they had a model with even more functionality! Surely this is another case where the thing that will likely make the least improvement in ease of use is adding new technology or functionality.

Years later, we still use these same phones almost exclusively for just making and answering ordinary phone calls, and mostly ignore the other blinking lights and arrays of buttons with intimidating labels. When they need to set up the occasional conference call, they follow the button presses and sequences on a label stuck on the bottom of the phone, and those steps were passed down by word of mouth from other co-workers.

1.3.7 Design beyond Just Technology

In this book we consider technology as just one design context, a platform for certain types of design. The design itself is the focus and the reader will feel as much at home in a discussion about principles and guidelines for the design of ATMs or highway signage as about design for high-tech user interfaces.

Design is about creating artifacts to satisfy a usage need in a language that can facilitate a dialog between the creator of the artifact and the user. That artifact can be anything from a computer system to an everyday object such as a door knob.

So do not think of this book as being just about interaction design or design of user interfaces for software systems. The interaction design creation and refinement activities described herein apply more universally; they are about design to support human activities—work and play in a context. The context does not have to include software or even much technology. For example, what we say here applies equally well to designing a kitchen for two people to cook together, to the workflow of the DMV, or to the layout of an electronic voting machine.

1.3.8 Components of a User Experience

Let us start by declaring that the concept of usability has not been made obsolete by the new notions of user experience. All of the performance- and productivity-oriented usability factors, such as ease of use and learnability, are still very important in most software systems and even in many commercial products. Especially in the context of using systems associated with complex work domains, it is just as important as ever for users to get work done efficiently and effectively with minimum errors and frustration. The newer concept of user experience still embodies all these implications of usability. How much joy of use would one get from a cool and neat-looking iPad design that was very clumsy and awkward to use? Clearly there is an intertwining in that some of the joy of use can come from extremely good ease of use.

The most basic reason for considering joy of use is the humanistic view that enjoyment is fundamental to life.

– Hassenzahl, Beu, and Burmester[5]

As a result, we have expanded the scope of user experience to include:

- effects experienced due to usability factors
- effects experienced due to usefulness factors
- effects experienced due to emotional impact factors

---

[5]Hassenzahl, M., Beu, A., & Burmester, M. (2001). Engineering joy. *IEEE Software, 18*(1), pp. 70–76.

On Designing for the "Visitor Experience"[*]

Dr. Deborah J. Mayhew, Consultant, Deborah J. Mayhew & Associates[1]
CEO, The Online User eXperience Institute[2]

Here I will adopt the definition of "user experience" proposed in this book, that is, it is something entirely in the head of the user. As product designers, we do everything we can to design something that will *result* in a good user experience for our target users. As moving from designing desktop software products to designing for Websites has clarified, the user experience may be impacted by more design qualities than usability alone. As a Web user interface designer, I use the term "visitor experience" and I recognize the need to address at least five different qualities of Websites that will impact the experience of the site's visitors:

- Utility
- Functional integrity
- Usability
- Persuasiveness
- Graphic design

These I define as follows.

Utility

It is easy to overlook *utility* as a quality of a Website design that will impact visitor experience, as it is perhaps the most fundamental. The utility of a Website refers to the usefulness, importance, or interest of the site content (i.e., of

---

[1]http://drdeb.vineyard.net
[2]http://www.ouxinstitute.com

the information, products, or services offered by the site) to the visitor. It is of course relative to any particular site visitor—what is interesting or useful to you may not be to me. It is also a continuous quality, that is, some Websites will feel more or less useful or interesting to me than others. For example, many Website visitors love to use social networking sites such as YouTube or Facebook, whereas others find these a total waste of time. I will have no need for a Website that sells carpenter's tools, whereas my neighbor might visit and use that site on a regular basis. This highlights an important fact for designers to keep in mind: that a *single* design will result in *multiple* visitor experiences depending on variations in the Website visitors themselves. This is why it is always so important to design for a target audience in particular, based on solid knowledge about that audience.

Functional Integrity

A Website's *functional integrity* is simply the extent to which it works as intended. Websites may have "dead" links that go nowhere, they may freeze or crash when certain operations are invoked, they may display incorrectly on some browsers or browser versions, they may download unintended files, etc. A lack of functional integrity is the symptom of buggy or incorrect—or even malicious—code. Functional integrity is also a continuous quality—some Websites may only have a few insignificant bugs, others may be almost nonfunctional, and anything in between is possible. In addition, a visitor using one browser or browser version may experience a Website's functional integrity differently as compared to a visitor using another browser.

Usability

Usability of course refers to how easy it is to learn (for first time and infrequent visitors) and/or use (for frequent visitors) a Website. A site can have high utility and high functional integrity and still be very difficult to learn or inefficient and tedious to use. For example, the Web you use to submit your tax returns may be implemented in flawless code and be relevant to almost every adult with great potential for convenience and cost savings, but be experienced by many visitors as unacceptably hard to learn or inefficient to use. Conversely, a site might feel very usable, but not very useful to a given visitor or have low functional integrity. It might be very easy and intuitive to figure out how to perform a task, but the site may consistently crash at a certain point in the task flow so that the task can never be accomplished.

Persuasiveness

Persuasiveness refers to the extent to which the experience visitors have on a Website encourages and promotes specific behaviors, which are referred to as "conversions." What constitutes a conversion varies from site to site, and even non-eCommerce sites may be promoting some type of conversion (e.g., newsletter signup, switching to online tax filing, looking up and using medical information). But persuasiveness is a particularly important design quality on an eCommerce Website, and the primary type of conversion in this case is a sale. So in the case of eCommerce sites, persuasiveness refers mainly to the extent to which the visitor's experience encourages and promotes sales.

Two examples of persuasiveness involve the presence, quality, and location of two types of information: *vendor* information (e.g., company name, physical address and contact information, company history, testimonials of past customers, and the like) and *product* information (things such as product color, material, care instructions, and the like). Visitors look for evidence that they can trust an online vendor, especially if they have never heard of it before. Also, they are often unwilling to order a product if they cannot find all the information they need in order to judge whether it will meet their needs. This is why many people will often look for a product on Amazon.com first because it is a trusted vendor and usually provides comprehensive product information, including detailed reviews by other customers. Note that a Website may be experienced as fully functional and highly usable in terms of task completion and offer just what a visitor is looking for, but if it lacks key aspects of persuasiveness, such as adequate vendor and product information, potential sales may be lost. This is not just a loss for the Website owner, it wastes the time of the visitor and foils their goals as well, that is, it impacts their experience negatively.

Graphic Design

Finally, the "look and feel," that is, the *graphic design*, of a Website can have a significant impact on the visitor experience. The graphic design of a Website—primarily the ways colors, images, and other media are used—invoke emotional reactions in visitors that may or may not contribute to the site's goals. As with other aspects of design that impact the visitor, each visitor's reaction to a given graphic design may be different. You may be bored by soft pastel colors while I may feel reassured and calmed by them. You may find a straightforward and simple graphic design boring while to me it may feel professional and reassuring. I may be put off by sound and animation while you may find it exciting and appealing.

While utility and functional integrity are fairly independent design qualities, the lines among usability, persuasiveness, and graphic design are more blurred. Clearly usability and effective graphic design can contribute to the experience of persuasiveness, and graphic design can contribute significantly to the experience of usability. Nevertheless, it is useful to consider these design qualities separately in order to understand their importance and apply them effectively during design.

Designing for a great visitor experience requires an interdisciplinary team of experts. The age-old profession of *market research* is the relevant discipline to employ to achieve the quality of *utility*. Competent *Web development* professionals are necessary to ensure *functional integrity*. *Software and Web usability engineering* is the expertise needed to achieve *usability*. There is currently a small but growing field of experts with experience applying marketing and *persuasion psychology* to eCommerce Web design. Finally, *graphic design* professionals specializing in Website design provide the design skills and expertise in branding and target audience appeal that Websites need.

The real key here, beyond simply finding resources with the aforementioned skill sets, is to build an effective interdisciplinary design team. Often professionals with these different backgrounds and skill sets are unfamiliar with the other disciplines and how they can and must work together to design for an optimal visitor for a given target audience. At the very least, Website stakeholders need product development team members respectful of the expertise of others and with a willingness to learn to collaborate effectively to achieve the common goal of a design that results in an optimized experience for intended Website visitors. Together, specialists in these different disciplines can have the most positive impact on the success of Websites by applying their different bodies of knowledge to the site design in a way that will invoke a positive visitor experience in the target audience.

---

*This essay is a modified excerpt from a chapter called "The Web UX Design Process—A Case Study" that I have written for the forthcoming book *Handbook of Human Factors in Web Design* (2nd ed.) by Kim-Phuong L. Vu and Robert W. Proctor (Eds.), Taylor & Francis, 2011.

To illustrate the possible components of user experience, we borrow from the domain of fine dining. The usefulness of a meal can be evaluated by calculating the nutritional value, calories, and so on in comparison with the technical nutritional needs of the diner's body. The nutritional value of a meal can be viewed objectively, but can also be felt by the user insofar as the prospect of good nutrition can engender feelings of value added to the experience.

Usefulness can also be reckoned, to some extent, with respect to the diner's immediate epicurean "requirements." A bowl of chilled gefilte fish balls just will not cut it for a gourmand with a taste for a hot, juicy steak. And, when that steak is served, if it is tough and difficult to cut or chew, that will certainly impact the usability of the dining "task."

Of course, eating, especially for foodies, is a largely emotional experience. Perhaps it starts with the pleasure of anticipation. The diners will also experience a perception of and emotional response to the dining ambiance, lighting, background music, and décor, as well as the quality of service and how good the food tasted. The menu design and information about ingredients and their sources contribute to the utility and the pleasure and value of the overall experience. Part of the emotional impact analogous to the out-of-the-box experience might include the aesthetics of food presentation, which sets the tone for the rest of the dining experience.

1.3.9 User Experience Is (Mostly) Felt Internally by the User

Most in the field will agree that user experience, as the words imply, is the *totality of the effect or effects felt (experienced) internally by a user* as a result of interaction with, and the usage context of, a system, device, or product. Here, we give the terms "interaction" and "usage" very broad interpretations, as we will explain, including seeing, touching, and thinking about the system or product, including admiring it and its presentation before any physical interaction, the influence of usability, usefulness, and emotional impact during physical interaction, and savoring the memory after interaction. For our purposes, all of this is included in "interaction" and "usage context."

But is user experience entirely felt internally by the user? What about the performance-related parts of usability? Certainly the user experiences and feels internally *effects* of performance-related parts of usability, such as increased productivity. However, there are also externally observable manifestations of usability, such as time on task, that represent a component not necessarily felt internally by the user and not necessarily related to emotion. The same holds for usefulness, too. If usability and usefulness are parts of the user experience, and we feel it is useful to consider them as such, then technically not *all* user experience is felt internally by the user. It is nonetheless convenient to gloss over this exception and, as a general rule, say that:

- usability and usefulness are components of user experience
- user experience is felt internally by the user

When we use the term "usability" by itself we usually are referring to the pragmatic and non-emotional aspects of what the user experiences in usage, including both objective performance measures and subjective opinion measures, as well as, of course, qualitative data about usability problems. In contrast, when we use the broader term "user experience" we usually are referring to what the user does feel internally, including the effects of usability, usefulness, and emotional impact.

1.3.10 User Experience Cannot Be Designed

A user experience cannot be designed, only experienced. You are not designing or engineering or developing good usability or designing or engineering or developing a good user experience. There is no usability or user experience inside the design; they are relative to the user. Usability occurs within, or is revealed within, the context of a particular usage by a particular user. The same design but used in a different context—different usage and/or a different user—could lead to a different user experience, including a different level of, or kind of, usability.

We illustrate this concept with a non-computer example, the experience of enjoying Belgian chocolates. Because the "designer" and producer of the chocolates may have put the finest ingredients and best traditional processes into the making of this product, it is not surprising that they claim in their advertising a fine chocolate experience built into their confections. However, by the reasoning in the previous paragraph, the user experience resides within the consumer, not in the chocolates. That chocolate experience includes anticipating the pleasure, beholding the dark beauty, smelling the wonderful aromas, the deliberate and sensual consumption (the most important part), the lingering bouquet and after-taste, and, finally, pleasurable memories.

When this semantic detail is not observed and the chocolate is marketed with claims such as "We have created your heavenly chocolate experience," everyone still understands. Similarly, no one but the most ardent stickler protests when BMW claims "BMW has designed and built your joy!" In this book, however, we wish to be technically correct and consistent so we would have them say, "We have created sweet treats to ensure your heavenly chocolate experience" or "BMW has built an automobile designed to produce your ultimate driving experience."

To summarize our point in this section, in Figure 1-2 we illustrate how an instance of user experience occurs dynamically in time within an instance of interaction and the associated usage context between design and user. It is almost like a chemical reaction that gives off a by-product, such as caloric[6] or an extra neutron.

Almost everything in this book depends on this simple, but enormously important, notion of the user experience being the result of a user's interaction with, and usage context of, a design. Although the meaning of this diagram may not be clear at this point in your reading, we hope that these concepts will unfold as you go through this book.

Figure 1-2

User experience occurs within interaction and usage context.

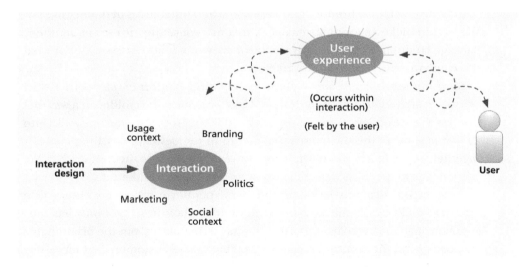

---

[6]Introduced as the very substance of heat by Lavosier in the 1770s to debunk the phlogiston theory, but you knew that.

1.3.11 Role of Branding, Marketing, and Corporate Culture

In some cases, the user experience goes even beyond the response to usability, usefulness, and joy of use. There are times when social, cultural, marketing, and political aspects, hardware choices, and the like can influence user experience. Users can get wrapped up in the whole milieu of what the manufacturer stands for, their political affiliations, how the product is marketed, and so on. What image does the brand of a product stand for? Is it a brand that uses environmentally sustainable manufacturing practices? Do they recycle? Consequently, what does the fact that someone is using a product of that particular brand say about them? These factors are more difficult to define in the abstract and more difficult to identify in the concrete.

Clearly these kinds of emotional responses are evoked by more than just product design. For some companies, many of the factors that contribute to this level of user experience may be part of the corporate DNA. For such companies, a quality user experience can be a call to action that aligns all roles toward a common mission, lived through their daily practice.

For example, consider the case of Apple. The culture of designing for user experience is so deeply engrained in their corporate culture that everything they produce has a stamp of tasteful elegance and spectacular design. This kind of fanatic emphasis on quality user experience at Apple extends beyond just the products they produce and even seeps into other areas of their company. When they make an employment offer to a new employee, for example, the package comes in a meticulously designed envelope that sets the stage for what the company stands for (Slivka, 2009b).

Similarly, when Apple sent call center technical support employees a T-shirt as a gift, it arrived in a carefully designed box with the T-shirt folded in a way that inspires a sense of design emphasis (Slivka, 2009a). From the time one walks into an Apple store to the sleek industrial design of the device, everything comes together in one harmonious whole to ensure that users love the device. (NB: We are agnostic in the PC vs. Mac religious wars, so please consider this objectively.) And, again, it is all about design for the user experience. A *New York Times* article (Hafner, 2007) extols the enchanting aura of Apple stores, "Not only has the company made many of its stores feel like gathering places, but the bright lights and equally bright acoustics create a buzz that makes customers feel more like they are at an event than a retail store." The goal of one new store in Manhattan was to make it "the most personal store ever created." This carefully designed user experience has been very successful in generating sales, return visits, and even tourist pilgrimages.

BMW embodies another corporate example of the importance of designing for emotional impact as part of a company's worldview. The makers of BMW cars have elevated the user experience to new heights in the industry. While this manufacturer could stake their reputation on the engineering aspects of these fine machines, instead their top claim to the world (BMW AG, 2010) is "Joy is BMW! More driving pleasure." And their follow-up statement really shows that it is all about user experience: "What you make people feel is just as important as what you make. And we make joy. Joy is why we built this company; joy is our inspiration. At BMW, we don't just make cars; we make joy."

We mention emotional response in the user experience as part of a corporate culture for completeness here, but it is beyond the scope of this book to say how to build this kind of emotional ambiance surrounding the company and the product. In this book we have to focus on the things we can do something about with the guidelines and processes—and that is design, mainly interaction design.

1.3.12 Why Have Such a Broad Definition?

Why do we want to include so much in our definitions of usage context and user experience? We believe that the user experience can begin well before actual usage. It can start as early as when the user beholds a system or product and its packaging or presentation. It does not necessarily end with actual usage. After usage, the pleasure, or displeasure, can persist in the user's mind. This perspective of what the user experiences about the product includes initial awareness of the product, to seeing its advertising, to visiting the store, to viewing it and buying it, to taking it out of the box, to using it, to talking with others who have used it—in other words, it is about a broad cultural and personal experience.

When we put forward this definition at conferences and workshops, sometimes we get criticism that such breadth makes it difficult to enforce, operationalize, and take ownership of user experience-related practices and responsibilities in an organization. But that is exactly the reason why the definition needs to be broad: it needs to implicitly recognize the need for multiple roles to work together, to collaborate and communicate, and to work synergistically to ensure a quality user experience. It frames the efforts toward designing for a user experience in an interdisciplinary context, where everyone from hardware engineers, to visual designers, to branding experts, to interaction designers *need* to collaborate and coordinate their efforts to define and execute a shared design vision.

1.4 EMOTIONAL IMPACT AS PART OF THE USER EXPERIENCE

The emotional aspects of user experience are just what the term implies. We are talking about pleasure, fun, aesthetics, novelty, originality, sensations, and experiential features—the affective parts of interaction. In particular, it is about the emotional impact of interaction on the user.

> *Users are no longer satisfied with efficiency and effectiveness; they are also looking for emotional satisfaction.*
>
> – Shih and Liu[7]

1.4.1 The Potential Breadth of Emotional Impact

Sometimes a user's reaction to a system or product is extremely emotional, a user experience with a deep, intimate, and personal emotional impact. At other times a user might be mildly satisfied (or dissatisfied) or just a bit pleased. Not all user experiences evoke throes of ecstasy, nor should they. Often just being well satisfied without it rising to a personally emotional level is all a user can afford in terms of emotional involvement with a software system.

But, of course, we all live for the moments when the user experience hits the high end of emotional impact range when we experience amazingly cool products (software systems almost never reach these heights). We are talking about a product for which the user experience sets the product apart from the rest in the hearts and minds of discriminating users. Have you ever had something that you really loved to use? Something that had a beauty *earned* by its amazingly beautiful design?

While other similar products may have an equally usable and useful design, they just do not have that something extra that sparks a deep emotional chord of affinity. The others do not have that indefinable something that transcends form, function, usability, and usefulness, something that elevates the usage experience to pure joy and pleasure, something akin to the appreciation of well-crafted music or art.

Buxton (2007b, p. 127) relates an entertaining and enlightening story of his experiences with personal orange juice squeezers, where subtle design differences made enormous differences in his usage experience. He really likes one above all the rest and the difference is something that, as Buxton (2007b, p. 129) puts it, "sets a whole new standard of expectation or desire." The

---

[7]Shih, Y.-H., & Liu, M. (2007). The Importance of Emotional Usability. *Journal of Educational Technology Usability, 36*(2), pp. 203–218.

differences in the product are not necessarily something you can capture in a diagram, specifications, or even photographs of the product. It is something you have to *experience*, as Buxton again puts it, you "just can't use it without a smile." But you can be sure that the difference is the result of deliberate and skillful design.

There is an interesting story from General Motors about product passion. In October 2010, the board of directors quietly discontinued the Pontiac car from the GM line of brands. Of course, the direct cause was the transition through bankruptcy, but the beginning of the end for Pontiac started 26 years earlier.

Before that, Pontiac had its own separate facilities for design, production, and manufacturing with its own people. Owners and wannabe owners were passionate about Pontiac cars and Pontiac employees had been devoted to the brand. The brand had its own identity, personality, and cachet, not to mention the notoriety from custom muscle cars such as the GTO and the Firebird TransAm in *Smokey and the Bandit.*

In 1984, however, in its great corporate wisdom, GM lumped the Pontiac works in with its other GM facilities. The economically based decision to merge facilities meant no separate ideas for design and no special attention to production. After that, there was really nothing to be devoted to and the passion was lost. Many believe that decision led to the decline and eventual demise of the brand.

So what constitutes real emotional impact in usage? While most of the emotional impact factors are about pleasure, they can be about other kinds of feelings too, including affective qualities such as love, hate, fear, mourning, and reminiscing over shared memories. Applications where emotional impact is important include social interaction (Dubberly & Pangaro, 2009; Rhee & Lee, 2009; Winchester, 2009) and interaction for cultural problem solving (Ann, 2009; Costabile, Ardito, & Lanzilotti, 2010; Jones, Winegarden, & Rogers, 2009; Radoll, 2009; Savio, 2010).

Social and cultural interactions entail emotional aspects, such as trustworthiness (especially important in e-commerce) and credibility. Design for emotional impact can also be about supporting human compassion, for example, in sites such as CaringBridge.org and CarePages.com.

Although there were earlier academic papers about emotion in the user experience, Norman (2004) was one of the first to bring the topic to light on a broad scale, relating it to his theme of everyday things. There are conferences dedicated specifically to the topic, including the biennial Conference on Design & Emotion, the goal of which is to foster a cross-disciplinary approach to design and emotion. Also, the topic is definitely blossoming in the academic literature

(Hassenzahl, 2001; Shih & Liu, 2007). Boucher and Gaver (2006) introduce the notion of ludic values, aimlessly playful qualities such as joy, surprise, delight, excitement, fun, curiosity, play, and exploration.

Attractive things make people feel good

– Donald A. Norman[8]

---

[8]Norman, D. A. (2004). *Emotional Design: Why We Love (Or Hate) Everyday Things*. New York: Basic Books.

Connections That Make "Spirit" a Part of UX

Elizabeth Buie, Luminanze Consulting

UX work speaks to the human spirit. Now, before you think I have gone all woo-woo on you, let me explain: By "human spirit," I mean the part of us that seeks connection with something larger than ourselves. This "something larger" can be different things to different people or to the same people at different times and in different contexts. It can be as mundane as nature, a cause, or being a parent; it can be as mystical as God/dess, the Universe, or even, if we stretch it, the Force. It is whatever evokes in us a sense of deep connection, and the human spirit is the part of us that feels this connection.

Let me illustrate with three stories from my own experience.

THE CONNECTEDNESS OF MUSIC

I sing in a group that performs Medieval and Renaissance polyphony—Catholic *a capella* music from the 13th to the 17th centuries. Now, I am not by any means traditionally religious (and I have never been Catholic), but this music just speaks to me. The several independent voices in these songs weave in and out to create complex harmonies that are deep, ethereal, and glorious.

For someone raised in the 20th century, learning this stuff is just plain *hard*. A month in advance of the first rehearsal for each concert, our director sends out learning files in Musical Instrument Digital Interface (MIDI) format. I import these files into music notation software, make my part a French horn played loudly, and make the other parts different instruments played more softly. This allows me to pick out my part easily and in context. I save the results as MP3s, load them onto my iPod, and play them in the car.

One morning I was driving to a client meeting, listening to my learning MP3s. The date was close enough to the performance that I knew my melodic lines fairly well (if not the words) and was singing along. In the middle of the Washington, DC rush hour (one of the worst in the United States), my spirit *soared*. I have since realized that the connection I felt that morning—that sense of oneness with everything around me—was part of my user experience of these technologies ... and so is the even deeper joy I feel when we perform this glorious music together for an audience. Creating this experience involves three pieces of equipment (four, if you count the car) and three software applications, and this soaring of spirit is part of my UX of all of them.

It is, in fact, for me their *primary* purpose.

THE DISCONNECTION OF ABSORPTION

The flip side is, of course, disconnection. These technologies can be absorbing and engrossing—to the point that if we are not careful, they can create distance and disconnection between us and those we care about. For example, I spend a lot of time in front of the computer, what with working mostly at home and not having a TV. I answer the phone that is by my desk, and it is exceedingly difficult for me to tear myself away from the screen to attend properly to a call. Most times I divide my attention somewhat, and I am sure my callers can tell.

My mother never seemed to take offense at this; she was proud of my work and always thought she was interrupting something important. One evening some years ago, she called. After a few short minutes she asked, "Are you on the computer?" I apologized and turned away from the screen; and we talked a brief while. I resolved to do better.

Three days later, however, she had an auto accident. Although she eventually regained consciousness, she had suffered a severe traumatic brain injury and was never her old self again. Seven months after the accident, she died.

So my last conversation with my mother was colored by this disconnection. I do not feel guilty about it—I did spend a lot of high-quality time with her in those months—but I do feel sad. And yet, I continue to find it inordinately difficult *not* to divide my attention between the phone and the screen.

Disconnection, too, can be part of the UX of technology.

THE SERENDIPITY OF NEW PROJECTS

In the winter of 2011 I started working on a project that provides information and exercises to support sexual health in cancer survivors. Two Websites—one for women and one for men—will supply the service. I conducted usability testing on the women's site which was still in beta and undergoing a clinical trial with cancer survivors, to see how well it helped improve their sexual health. I'm optimistic that my findings and my recommendations for design change will help both of these sites to improve their users' lives.

This project has special meaning for me. In fact, when the client told me what it was, I had to stop and catch my breath.

Ten years earlier, you see, my husband had died of prostate cancer. Antonio and I had lived with this disease for almost 10 years, and the hormone therapy that had worked so well against the cancer for several years had also destroyed his libido. You can imagine what kind of challenges *that* brings to a relationship.

So this project has a deep special meaning for me. I feel a profound connection with this user population, even though they are unaware of it. Most UX professionals can develop empathy with most user populations, but it is extra special when you have *lived* the problems that your users face. It is too late, of course, for this program to help Antonio and me, but I used my UX knowledge and skills to help make it easier for people in similar situations to address their problems.

UX IS WORK OF THE SPIRIT

Like many UX professionals, I got into this field because I want to help make people's lives better. Sure, I find the work challenging and fascinating; if I did not, I probably would have found some other work. But for me the key is knowing that what I do for a living *matters*. That it helps connect me with my users, my clients, and my best self. That it is larger than myself.

Life is about connection, and UX is no different. I submit that our work needs to nurture our own spirit and those of our users. Even when we are working on a product that has no obvious component of connection, we will serve our users best if we keep the possibility present in our minds.

Maybe the best illustration of the difference between utilitarian product usability and real user experience packed with emotional impact is demonstrated by Buxton's pictures of mountain bikes. He begins with a beautiful picture, his Figure 32, of a Trek mountain bike, just sitting there inviting you to take an exciting ride (Buxton, 2007b, pp. 98–99).

But the next picture, his Figure 33, is all about that exciting ride (Buxton, 2007b, pp. 100–101). A spray of water conveys the fun and excitement and maybe a little danger to get the blood and adrenaline pumping. In fact, you can hardly see the bike itself in this picture, but you *know* it is how we got here. The bike just sitting there is not really what you are buying; it is the breathtaking thrill of screaming through rocks, mud, and water—that is the user experience!

1.4.2 A Convincing Anecdote

David Pogue makes a convincing case for the role of emotional impact in user experience using the example of the iPad. In his *New York Times* story he explains why the iPad turned the personal devices industry upside down and started a whole new class of devices. When the iPad came out, the critics dubbed it "underwhelming," "a disappointment," and "a failure." Why would anyone want or need it?

Pogue admits that the critics were right from a utilitarian or rational standpoint: "The iPad was superfluous. It filled no obvious need. If you already had a touch-screen phone and a laptop, why on earth would you need an iPad? It did seem like just a big iPod Touch" (Pogue). And yet, as he claims, the iPad is the most successful personal electronic device ever, selling 15 million in the first months. Why? It has little to do with rational, functional, and utility appeal and has everything to do with emotional allure. It is about the personal experience of holding it in your hand and manipulating finely crafted objects on the screen.

1.4.3 Aesthetics and Affect

Zhang (2009) makes the case for aesthetics as part of an emotional or affective (about feeling or emotion) interaction. The movement from functionality and usability to aesthetics takes us from a utilitarian to an experiential orientation, from a cognitive paradigm to an affective-centric paradigm (Norman, 2002, 2004; Zhang & Li, 2004, 2005).

Interaction design can "touch humans in sensible and holistic ways" (Zhang, 2009). The term aesthetics is used to describe a sense of pleasure or beauty, including sensual perceptions (Wasserman, Rafaeli, & Kluger, 2000).

Zhang presents a theoretical linkage between aesthetics and affect. Aesthetics, a branch of philosophy and often associated with art, is considered an elusive and confusing concept (Lindgaard et al., 2006). A key issue in studies regarding aesthetics is objectivity vs. subjectivity. The objective view is that aesthetic quality is innate in the object or the design and is known by certain features or characteristics regardless of how they are perceived. This means that objective aesthetic qualities can be evaluated analytically.

The subjective view of aesthetics is that it depends on how they are perceived. Aesthetics has different effects on different people and must be evaluated with respect to users/people. It is all about perceived aesthetic quality.

However, operationally, things are still a bit fuzzy. It is difficult to state goals for aesthetic design and there is no standard for measuring aesthetics: "...there is a lack of agreement and a lack of confidence on how to measure aesthetics related concepts" (Zhang, 2009). It is typical to think of one-dimensional metrics for aesthetics, such as subjective ratings of visual appeal.

Lavie and Tractinsky (2004) draw a distinction between classical aesthetics—defined by orderliness in clean, pleasant, and symmetrical designs—and expressive aesthetics—defined by creativity, innovation, originality, sophistication, and fascinating use of special effects.

In any case, it is agreed that the result of aesthetic design can be affect, in the form of a mood, emotion, or feeling. The assessment of affect is tricky, mainly relying on subjective assessment of an individual's perception of the ability of an object or design to change his or her affect.

Zhang is interested in the relationship between aesthetics and affect. In particular how are the objective view and the subjective view connected with respect to design? How can the aesthetics of a product or system evoke a change in the person's/user's affect? Norman (2004) proposes a three-level processing model for emotional design, making connection between aesthetics and emotion explicitly:

■ Visceral processing requires visceral design—about appearance and attractiveness, appeals to "gut feeling"
■ Behavioral processing requires behavioral design—about pleasure and effectiveness (usability and performance)
■ Reflective processing requires reflective design—about self-image, identity, personal satisfaction, memories

Kim and Moon (1998) describe emotions, the immediate affective feelings about a system, in seven dimensions:

■ attractiveness
■ symmetry
■ sophistication
■ trustworthiness
■ awkwardness
■ elegance
■ simplicity

As Zhang notes, these dimensions are "non-basic" as compared to basic emotions such as joy and anger and can be domain specific. They also seem a bit arbitrary and could allow for quite a few other alternatives. In the end, it is not clear if, or how, these criteria can relate aesthetics in the design to affect in the users.

Zhang's example convinces us that the relationship is, indeed, subjective and that perceived aesthetic quality does determine affective reaction. She describes a beautiful pop-up ad on the Internet, with pleasing images and music. And you experience a feeling beyond just pleasantness. It gets your attention and activates your mind. You have an affective reaction and perceived affective quality is positive.

Now consider exactly the same ad, still *inherently* beautiful and musical, but because of other factors—for example, you are focusing on something else, trying to solve a problem—the ad is irritating and annoying. You feel distracted; your attention stolen away from the task at hand, and you try to shut it out. You might even get a little angry if you cannot shut it out. The ad has the same objective aesthetic quality but it has a different effect on your affect. Your mind's alert level is still high but you are annoyed; you have a negative effect.

The point of Zhang's example is that the same aesthetics can lead to different user experiences depending on perceived, or subjective, aesthetic quality.

1.4.4 The Centrality of Context

Context has always been important in interpreting the meaning of usability in any situation. Now, context is even more important, essential and central to the meaning of emotional and phenomenological impact in situated usage.

As an example of how anticipated usage context influences how a product is viewed, consider the Garmin GPSMAP 62st handheld GPS device. In *Field and Stream*, a hunting magazine, an advertisement stresses an impressive list of features and functionality, including such esoteric technology as "3-axis tilt-compensated 100K topo mapping, Birds-Eye Satellite imagery, and quad helix antenna." The message for hunters is that it will get you to the right place at the right time in support of the goals of hunting.

In contrast, in *Backpacker* magazine, apparently catering to the idea that the typical backpacker is more interested in the enjoyment of the outdoors, while the hunter is more mission oriented, an ad for the same device appeals strongly to emotion. In a play on words that ties the human value of self-identity with orienteering, Garmin puts presence in life style first: "Find yourself, then get back." It highlights emotional qualities such as comfort, cozy familiarity, and companionship: "Like an old pair of boots and your favorite fleece, GPSMAP 62st is the ideal hiking companion."

Because the resulting user experience for a product depends on how users view the product and strongly on the usage context, designers have to work hard. So, in general, there is no formula for creating an interaction design that can be expected to lead to a specific kind of user experience. That is a factor that adds much difficultly to designing for what we hope will be a quality user experience. However, the more designers know about users and usage context, the better they will be equipped to create a design that can lead to a desired user experience.

Presence

Presence of a product is a kind of relationship with users in which the product becomes a personally meaningful part of their lives.

1.4.5 What about Fun at Work?

Emotional impact factors such as fun, aesthetics, and joy of use are obviously desirable in personal use of commercial products, but what about in task-oriented work situations? Here usability and usefulness aspects of user experience are obvious, but the need for emotional impact is not so clear.

It is easy to think that fun and enjoyment are just not a good match to computer usage for work. Some, including most Vulcans, say that emotions interfere with the efficiency and control needed for work.

But there is evidence that fun can help at work, too, to break monotony and to increase interest and attention span, especially for repetitive and possibly boring work, such as performed in call centers. Fun can enhance the appealingness of less inherently challenging work, for example, clerical work or data entry, which can increase performance and satisfaction (Hassenzahl, Beu, & Burmester, 2001). It is easy to see how fun can lead to job satisfaction and enjoyment of some kinds of work.

It is also obvious from the fact that emotional and rational behaviors play complementary roles in our own lives that emotional aspects of interaction are not necessarily detrimental to our reasoning processes for doing work. For example, software for learning, which can otherwise be dull and boring, can be spiced up with a dose of novelty, surprise, and spontaneity.

However, fun and usability can conflict in work situations; for example, less boring means less predictable and less predictable usually goes against traditional usability attributes, such as consistency and ease of learning (Carroll & Thomas, 1988). Too simple can mean loss of attention, and consistency can translate as boring. Fun requires a balance: not too simple or boring, but not too challenging or frustrating.

Some work roles and jobs are not amenable at all to fun as part of the work practice. Consider a job that is inherently challenging, that requires full attention to the task, for example, air traffic control. It is essential for air traffic controllers to have no-nonsense software tools that are efficient and effective. Any distraction due to novelty or even slight barriers to performance due to clever and "interesting" design features will be hated and could even be dangerous. For this kind of work, task users often want less mental effort, more predictable interaction paths, and more consistent behavior. They especially do not want a system or software tool adding to the complexity.

Certainly the addition of a game-like feature is welcome in an application designed primarily for fun or recreation, but imagine an air traffic controller having to solve a fun little puzzle before the system gives access to the controls so that the air traffic controller can help guide a plane heading for a mountain top in the fog.

1.5 USER EXPERIENCE NEEDS A BUSINESS CASE

Ingenious by design; hassle-free connectivity

– On a Toshiba satellite receiver box

1.5.1 Is the Fuss over Usability or User Experience Real?

As practitioners in this field, one of the frequent challenges we face is getting buy-in toward user experience processes from upper management and business stakeholders. So what is the business case for UX?

That computer software of all kinds is in need of better design, including better user interaction design, is indisputable. Mitch Kapor, the founder of Lotus, has said publicly and repeatedly that "The lack of usability of software and the poor design of programs are the secret shame of the industry" (Kapor, 1991, 1996). Those who know the industry agree. Poor user experience is an uncontrolled source of overhead for companies using software, overhead due to lost user productivity, the need for users to correct errors, data lost through uncorrected errors, learning and training costs, and the costs of help desks and field support.

Charlie Kreitzburg, founder of Cognetics Corporation, tells of chaos, waste, and failure, which he attributes this sorry state of software development primarily to software development practices that are "techno-centric rather than user-centric." He recommends the industry to "rethink current software design practice to incorporate user-centered design" principles.

These critical assessments of the software industry are not based on personal opinion alone but on large surveys conducted by groups with strong reputations in the software industry. The Standish Group (Cobb, 1995; The Standish Group, 1994, 2001) surveyed 365 IT executive managers from companies of small, medium, and large sizes and found that the lack of attention to user inputs is one of the most important reasons why many software projects were unsuccessful. This translated to costing corporations $80 billion a year.

Some estimate that the percentage of software projects that exceed their budgets is higher than 60% (Lederer & Prasad, 1992). According to May (1998), the average software development project is 187% over budget and 222% behind schedule and implements only 61% of the specified features.

A posting by *Computer World* (Thibodeau, 2005) declared: "Badly designed software is costing businesses millions of dollars annually because it's difficult to use, requires extensive training and support, and is so frustrating that many end users underutilize applications, say IT officials at companies such as The Boeing Co. and Fidelity Investments." Keith Butler of Boeing said that usability issues can add as much as 50% to the total cost of software ownership.

Such startling reports on the dismal performance of the software development industry are not hard to find. Kwong, Healton, and Lancaster (1998) cite (among others) the Gartner Group's characterization that the state of software development is chaos: "25% of software development efforts fail outright. Another 60% produce a sub-standard product. In what other industry would we tolerate such inefficiency? As Kreitzburg has put it, imagine if 25% of all bridges fell down or 25% of all airplanes crashed."

1.5.2 No One Is Complaining and It Is Selling Like Hotcakes

It is easy to mistake other positive signs as indicators that a product has no user experience problems. Managers often say, "This system has to be good; it's selling big time." "I'm not hearing any complaints about the user interface." This is a more difficult case to make to managers because their usual indicators of trouble with the product are not working. On closer inspection, it appears that a system might be selling well because it is the only one of its kind or the strength of its marketing department or advertising obscures the problems.

And, sometimes, project managers are the only ones who do not hear the user experience complaints. Also, despite demands for an improved user experience, some users simply will not complain.

If you wonder about the user experiences with your own product, but your users are not complaining, here are some indicators to watch for, characteristics of prime candidates for having problems with usability and user experience:

- Your users are accessing only a small portion of the overall functionality your system offers
- There are a significant number of technical support calls about how to use a particular feature in the product.
- There are requests for features that already exist in the product.
- Your competitor's products are selling better even though your product has more features.

This book can help you address these issues. It is designed for those who have been struck by the importance of a good user interface and who want to find out more about what a quality user experience means, how to ensure it, and how to know when you have it. This book is especially aimed toward practitioners—people who put theory into practice in a real-world development environment.

The methods and techniques described here can be used by anyone who is involved in any part of the development of a user interaction design for a user interface.

1.5.3 A Business Strategy: Training as a Substitute for Usability in Design

"It might not be easy to use right off, but with training and practice, it will be a very intuitive design." Sounds silly and perverse, but that is what many people are really saying when they suggest training as a way to fix usability problems. Unfortunately, the following real-world example is representative of many.

A very large governmental organization serving the public sometimes attempts to solve user experience problems by "instructional bulletins" sent to all field users. These are real user experience problems that increase the time to do tasks, introduce significant opportunities for errors, and require users to remember these special-case instructions for each particular situation. Also, these bulletins are issued only once and then their complicated contents become the responsibility of the users, including those hired after they are issued and, therefore, have never received them.

In one such case, the relevant situation arises when an applicant, a client outside the organization, calls in on an 800 phone number. The call is answered by an agent working for the organization, the actual system user, acting as an information intermediary for the client/applicant. If the applicant requests certain information, to which access is not allowed, the request is denied and policy based on law requires that an explanatory written notice be sent via regular mail.

Screens referred to in the "instructional bulletin" about this kind of interaction are used to make a record of the request and the information denial decision, and to automatically generate and send out the notice. The opportunities for errors are abundant and the applicant will not receive the legally required notice if the user, the agent using the computer, fails to follow these instructions to the letter. We are told, without perceptible nodding or winking, that most agents should understand the jargon. The essence of the main part of the bulletin states:

> The 800 Number LDNY System is a 2-screen process. It issues an electronic form #101A, annotates the LPFW worksheet with a record of the closeout action, and automatically purges the lead when the closeout expires based on data propagated to the LPFW. However, the LDNY screen must be completed properly in order to propagate the current date to the REC field and "INFORMAL

DENIAL" to the REMARKS field on the LPFW screen. If this data is not propagated to the LPFW, *the applicant will not receive the notice.* IMPORTANT: To get the REC date and the REMARKS to propagate to the LPFW screen, you must remember two things:

1. On page 2 of the LDNY, you must answer YES to PRINT NOTICE, otherwise the REC date and REMARKS will not propagate to the LPFW.
2. When you press ENTER on page 2 of the LDNY screen, you are returned to the LPFP screen, a screen you have already completed. You must ENTER through this screen. This will return you to the 800 Number screen. Do NOT use the normal procedure of using the PF3 key to return to the 800 Number screen because it will prevent the appropriate "INFORMAL DENIAL" from propagating to REMARKS on the LPFW screen.

Will a user remember all this, say, a few months after it was released? Multiply this situation by many other functions, forms, situations, and "instructional bulletins" and you have a formula for massive scale errors, frustration, lost productivity, and underserved clients. Training as a substitute for usability is an ongoing per-user cost that often fails to meet the goals of increased productivity and reduced risk, errors, and cost. The question that sticks in our minds is how could someone send out this memo with a straight face? How could the memo author not see the folly of the whole situation? Perhaps that person had been part of the bureaucracy and the system for so long that he or she truly believed it had to be that way because "this is how we have always done it."

1.6 ROOTS OF USABILITY

It is a matter of debate exactly when computer usability was born. It was clearly preceded by usability work for non-computer machines in industrial design and human factors. We know that computer usability was a topic of interest to some by the late 1970s and, by the early 1980s, conferences about the topic were being established. No field exists in isolation and ours is no exception. Human–computer interaction in general and usability in particular owe much of their origin and development to influences from many other related fields.

Human factors is about making things work better for people. For example, think about building a bridge: You use theory, good design practice, and engineering principles, but you

can't really know if it will work. So you build it and have someone walk over it. Of course, if the
test fails, … well, that's one of the reasons we have graduate students.

– Phyllis Reisner

From cognitive and behavioral psychology and psychometrics, concepts such as user modeling and user performance metrics were adopted into HCI. Much of the predesign analysis, such as business process modeling, has its roots in the field of systems engineering. Also, ideas such as software architectures that could abstract the user interface and functional core concerns, rapid prototyping tools, and software environments were borrowed from the discipline of computer science (Hartson, 1998).

Our caveat to the reader: In this and similar sections on history and related work at the end of most chapters, the coverage is by no means a survey of the vast contributions on any particular topic. The topics and references included are to be taken as examples. Please forgive any omission of your favorite references and see other books on this topic for surveys that do justice.

1.6.1 A Discipline Coming of Age

Compared to venerable disciplines such as architecture or civil engineering, computer science is an infant and human–computer interaction is still an embryo. The oldest computer science departments are in their 40s or 50s, and the PC has been around only about 30 years as of this writing. As is often the case, evolution accelerates; it is safe to say that more major changes have occurred within computer science in these 40 years than in civil engineering, for example, in the past hundred or more years (Mowshowitz & Turoff, 2005). As young as it is, HCI has experienced its own accelerated evolution.

Although work was being done on "human factors in computers" in the 1970s and earlier, HCI was born at Virginia Tech and several other universities in the late 1970s and 1980s and had been going on at IBM (Branscomb, 1981), the National Bureau of Standards (now the National Institute of Standards and Technology), and other scattered locations before that. This early work mainly focused on specific topics such as ergonomics of hardware devices (CRT terminals and keyboards), training, documentation (manuals), text editors, and programming, with little general or theoretical work yet evolved.

Many believe that HCI did not coalesce into a fledgling discipline until the CHI conferences began in Boston in 1983. But it probably began a couple of years before with the "unofficial first CHI conferences" (Borman & Janda, 1986) at the May 1981 ACM/SIGSOC conference, called the Conference on Easier and

More Productive Use of Computer Systems, in Ann Arbor, Michigan, and the March 1982 Conference on Human Factors in Computer Systems in Gaithersburg, Maryland.

Also, who does not like cake and candles? So CHI (the conference) celebrated its 25th birthday in 2007 (Marcus, 2007). Marcus says, "I can remember in the mid-1980s when an HP staff member announced with amazement that the amount of code for input-output treatment had finally surpassed the amount of code that was devoted to actual data manipulation. A watershed moment." Watershed, indeed!

1.6.2 Human Factors and Industrial and Systems Engineering

Some people think that human factors got its start in "Taylorism," an early 20th-century effort to structure and manage the processes for producing a product efficiently. Through his principles of "scientific management," Frederick Winslow Taylor sought to define "best practices" of the time to reform our inefficient and wasteful, even lazy, ways of operating private and government enterprises and factories (Taylor, 1911). He is also known for helping formulate a national imperative for increased industrial efficiency.

Later, U.S. Air Force officials became concerned with airplane crashes experienced by World War II pilots. In an effort to reduce cockpit errors by pilots and to improve safety, engineers began to study critical incidents that may have led to airplane crashes. Work by Fitts and Jones (1947) is the best known in this regard. Then it grew into goals of improved production and safety in control systems for other kinds of machines, such as power plants. Eventually it has become part of the field of HCI, where it is concerned with critical incidents during interaction by computer users. This is where we got our early emphasis on simple user performance metrics (Tatar, Harrison, & Sengers, 2007).

According to Mark S. Sanders, as quoted by Christensen, Topmiller, and Gill (1988), "human factors is that branch of science and technology that includes what is known and theorized about human behavior and biological characteristics that can be validly applied to the specification, design, evaluation, operation, and maintenance of products and systems to enhance safe, effective, and satisfying use by individuals, groups, and organizations." Not far from our definition of usability, eh?

When human factors entered the computer age, it made a good fit with the emerging field of human–computer interaction. The focus on critical incidents persisted, but now the focus was on problems in HCI.

Human–computer interaction is clearly about human behavior and is used to drive system design, and human performance is the measurable outcome in using those systems (Bailey, 1996). As Bailey says, the human is the most complex part of almost any system and the most likely cause of accident or system failure, which is the reason why so much effort has gone into engineering for the performance of the human component.

We agree with all but the conclusion that the human is the most likely cause of errors or system failure; the whole point of human factors engineering is to design the system to take into account the susceptibility of the human for errors and to design the system to prevent them. So, our take on it is that the human user is what he or she is, namely human, and a design that does not take this into account is the most likely cause of errors and failures.

It is said that human factors got its start with aircraft cockpit design in World War II. The overarching assumption at that time was that *humans could be trained to fit a design*, the extent of the fit directly proportional to the amount of training. However, no matter how extensive the training and irrespective of the amount of flying experience, pilots were making dangerous mistakes while operating the controls in the cockpit. Researchers were brought in to investigate what were called "pilot errors."

Early investigators such as Fitts and Jones (1947) interviewed scores of pilots and started detecting design problems that ranged from lack of consistency among different cockpit control layouts to placement of unrelated controls together without visual or tactile differentiators to alert the pilots when wrong controls were being operated. The reports of Fitts and Jones are among the very earliest that recognized the causal connection between design flaws, rather than human errors, and mishaps in user performance.

In one such instance, as the folklore goes (not a finding of Fitts and Jones), pilots began bailing out at all the wrong times and for no apparent good reason. It seems that an update by designers included switching the locations of the ejection release and the throttle. When the finger of suspicion pointed at them, the engineers were indignant; "there were good reasons to change the design; it should have been designed that way in the first place. And pilots are very intelligent, highly trained, and already had shown that they could adapt to the changes." However, it turned out that, when under stress, the pilots sometimes involuntarily reverted to earlier learned behavior, and the result was an untimely, embarrassing, and dangerous alley-oop maneuver noted for its separation of pilot from plane.

In fact, the connection of human factors to HCI and usability is close; much of the early HCI work was referred to as "human factors in software engineering" (Gannon, 1979). In 1987 (Potosnak, 1987), for example, the place where human factors fit into the software engineering process was stated as providing a research base, models to predict human behavior, standards, principles, methods for learning about users, techniques for creating and testing systems, and tools for designing and evaluating designs.

Furthermore, many ideas and concepts from human factors laid the basis for HCI techniques later on. For example, the idea of task analysis was first used by human factors specialists in analyzing factory workers' actions on an assembly line. For many working in human factors engineering, the move to focus on HCI was a natural and easy transition.

1.6.3 Psychology and Cognitive Science

In addition to the major influence of human factors and engineering, HCI experienced a second wave of formative influence (Tatar, Harrison, & Sengers, 2007) from a special brand of cognitive science, beginning with Card, Moran, and Newell (1983), offering the first theory within HCI.

Like human factors engineering, cognitive psychology has many connections to the design for, and evaluation of, human performance, including cognition, memory, perception, attention, sense and decision making, and human behavioral characteristics and limitations, elements that clearly have a lot to do with user experience. One difference is that psychology is more about the human per se, whereas human factors engineering looks at the human as a component in a larger system for which performance is to be optimized. However, because of the influence of psychology on human factors and the fact that most human factors practitioners then were trained in psychology, the field was known at least for a while as occupational psychology.

Because the field of human factors is based on a foundation in psychology, so are HCI and user experience. Perhaps the most fundamental contribution of psychology to human–computer interaction is the standard bearer, Card, Moran, and Newell (1983), which is still today an important foundational reference.

The empiricism involved in statistical testing in human factors and HCI has especially apparent common roots in psychology; see, for example, Reisner (1977). Hammond, Gardiner, and Christie (1987) describe the role of cognitive psychology in HCI to include observing human behavior, building models of human information processing, inferring understanding of the same, and scientific, or empirical, study of human acquisition, storage, and use of knowledge/information. Cognitive psychology shares with human factors engineering the goal of system operability and, when connected to HCI, computer-based system operability.

Perhaps the most important application of psychology to HCI has been in the area of modeling users as human information processors (Moran, 1981b; Williges, 1982). Most human performance prediction models stem from Card, Moran, and Newell's Model Human Processor (1983), including the keystroke level model (Card, Moran, & Newell, 1980), the command language grammar (Moran, 1981a), the Goals, Operators, Methods, and Selections (GOMS) family of models (Card, Moran, & Newell, 1983), cognitive complexity theory of Kieras and Polson (1985), and programmable user models (Young, Green, & Simon, 1989). In the earliest books, before "usability" was a common term, "software psychology" was used to connect human factors and computers (Shneiderman, 1980).

Carroll (1990) contributed significantly to the application of psychology to HCI in fruitful ways. Carroll says, "... applied psychology in HCI has characteristically been defined in terms of the methods and concepts basic psychology can provide. This has not worked well." He goes on to explain that too much of the focus was on psychology and not enough on what it was being applied to. He provides a framework for understanding the application of psychology in the HCI domain.

As an interesting aside to the role of cognitive psychology in HCI, Digital Equipment Corporation researchers (Whiteside et al., 1985; Whiteside & Wixon, 1985) made the case for developmental psychology as a more appropriate model for interaction design than behavioral psychology and as a framework for studying human–computer interaction. The behavioral model, which stresses behavior modification by learning from stimulus–response feedback, leads to a view in which the user adapts to the user interface. Training is invoked as intervention to shape the user's behavior. The user with "wrong" behavior is importuned with error messages. Simply put, user behavior is driven by the interaction design.

In contrast, developmental psychology stresses that surprisingly complex user behavior springs from the person, not the design. The developmental view studies "wrong" user behavior with an eye to adapting the design to prevent errors. Differences between system operation and user expectations are opportunities to improve the system. "User behavior is not wrong; rather it is a source of information about the system's deficiencies (Whiteside & Wixon, 1985, p. 38)."

Finally, as even more of an aside, Killam (1991) proffers the idea that humanistic psychology, especially the work of Carl Rogers, Rogerian psychology as it is called, is an area of psychology that has been applied unknowingly, if not directly, to HCI. A client-centered approach to therapy, Rogerian psychology, as in the developmental approach, avoided the normative, directive style of prescribing "fixes" for the patient to adopt, instead listening to the patient's needs that must be met to affect healing.

The tenets of Rogerian psychology translate to some of our most well-known guidelines for interaction design, including positive feedback to encourage, especially at times when the user might be hesitant or unsure, and keeping the locus of control with the user, for example, not having the system try to second-guess the user's intentions. In sum, the Rogerian approach leads to an interaction design that provides an environment for users to find their own way through the interaction rather than having to remember the "right way."

As in the case of human factors engineering, many people moved into HCI from psychology, especially cognitive psychology, as a natural extension of their own field.

1.6.4 Task Analysis

Task analysis was being performed in human factors contexts long before HCI came along (Meister, 1985; Miller, 1953). In order to design any system to meet the needs of its users, designers must understand what tasks users will use the system for and how those tasks will be performed (Diaper, 1989b). Because tasks using machines involve manipulation of system/device objects such as icons, menus, buttons, and dialogue boxes in the case of user interfaces, tasks and objects must be considered together in design (Carroll, Kellogg, & Rosson, 1991).

The process of describing tasks (how users do things) and their relationships is called task analysis and is used to drive design and to build predictive models of user task performance. Much work was done in the 1980s and 1990s in the United Kingdom on developing task analysis to make it connect to interaction design to support users, including task analysis for knowledge description (Diaper, 1989a), the task action grammar (Payne & Green, 1986, 1989).

1.6.5 Theory

Much of the foundation for HCI has been closely related to theory in psychology, as much of it derived from adaptations of psychological theory to the human information processor known to HCI. Cognitive psychology (Barnard, 1993; Hammond, Gardiner, & Christie, 1987) and cognitive theory are the bases for much of what we do—claims analysis (Carroll & Rosson, 1992), for example.

The theory of work activity (Bødker, 1989, 1991) is embodied in techniques such as contextual inquiry.

Norman's (1986) theory of action expresses, from a cognitive engineering perspective, human task performance—the path from goals to intentions to actions (inputs to the computer) back to perception and interpretation of feedback to evaluation of whether the intentions and goals were approached or met. The study of learning in HCI (Carroll, 1984; Draper & Barton, 1993) also has obvious roots in cognitive theory. Fitts law (relating cursor travel time to distance and size of target) (MacKenzie, 1992) is clearly connected to kinesthetics and human performance.

As a prerequisite for task analysis and a significant legacy from cognitive psychology, models of humans as cognitive information processors are used to model and understand the full gamut of user cognition and physical actions needed to interact with computers (Card, Moran, & Newell, 1983). The command language grammar (Moran, 1981a) and the keystroke model (Card, Moran, & Newell, 1980), which attempt to explain the nature and structure of human–computer interaction, led directly to the Goals, Operators, Methods, and Selection (GOMS) (Card, Moran, & Newell, 1983) model. GOMS-related models, quantitative models combining task analysis and the human user as an information processor, are concerned with predicting various measures of user performance—most commonly task completion time based on physical actions in error-free expert task performance.

Direct derivatives of GOMS include Natural GOMS Language (Kieras, 1988) and cognitive complexity theory (Kieras & Polson, 1985; Lewis et al., 1990), the latter of which is intended to represent the complexity of user interaction from the user's perspective. This technique represents an interface as the mapping between the user's job-task environment and the interaction device behavior.

GOMS-related techniques have been shown to be useful in discovering certain kinds of usability problems early in the lifecycle, even before a prototype has been constructed. Studies, for example, by Gray, et al. (1990), have demonstrated a payoff in some kinds of applications where the savings of a number of user actions, for example, keystrokes or mouse movements, can improve user performance enough to have an economic impact, often due to the repetitiveness of a task.

Carroll and Rosson's task-artifact cycle (1992) elicits cognitive theories implicit in design, treating them as claims by the designer. They propose an iterative design cycle in which a scenario-based design representation depicts artifacts in different situations of use. These artifacts are then analyzed to capture design rationale via the extraction of claims (design tradeoffs), which inform the design.

1.6.6 Formal Methods

While not theory per se, formal methods have been the object of some interest and attention for supporting both theory and practice in HCI (Harrison & Thimbleby, 1990). The objectives of formal methods—precise, well-defined notations and mathematical models—in HCI are similar to those in software engineering. Formal design specifications can be reasoned about and analyzed for various properties, such as correctness and consistency. Formal specifications also have the potential to be translated automatically into prototypes or software implementation.

1.6.7 Human Work Activity and Ethnography

Work activity theory (Bødker, 1991; Ehn, 1990) has had a continuing and deep impact on HCI theory and practice. Originating in Russia and Germany and now flourishing in Scandinavia, where it has been, interestingly, related to the labor movement, this view of design based on work practice situated in a worker's own complete environment has been synthesized into several related mainstream HCI topics.

A natural progression from work activity theory to a practical tool for gathering design requirements driven by work practice in context has led to the eclectic inclusion in some HCI practices of ethnography, an investigative field rooted in anthropology (LeCompte & Preissle, 1993). Indeed, the conflux of work activity theory and ethnographic techniques was refined by many pioneers of this new direction of requirements inquiry and emerged as contextual design in the style of Beyer and Holtzblatt (1998).

1.6.8 Computer Science: Interactive Graphics, Devices, and Interaction Techniques

In parallel to, but quite different from, the human factors, psychology, and ethnography we have been describing, several related threads were appearing in the literature and practice on the computer science side of the HCI equation. This work on graphics, interaction styles, software tools, dialogue management systems, programming language translation, and interface "widgets" was essential in opening the way to practical programming techniques for bringing interaction designs to life on computers.

The origin of computer graphics is frequently attributed to pioneers such as Ivan Sutherland (1963, 1964) and solidified by masters such as Foley and colleagues (Foley & Van Dam, 1982; Foley et al., 1990; Foley & Wallace, 1974) and Newman (1968). For an insightful account of the relationship of graphics to HCI, see Grudin (2006).

The 1980s and 1990s saw a burgeoning of hardware and software developments to support the now familiar point-and-click style of interaction, including the Xerox Star (Smith et al., 1989) and the Lisa and Macintosh by Apple. This work was a rich amalgam of interaction techniques, interaction styles, user interface software tools, "dialogue management systems," and user interface programming environments.

"An *interaction technique* is a way of using a physical input/output device to perform a generic task in a human-computer dialogue" (Foley et al., 1990). A very similar term, *interaction style*, has evolved to denote the behavior of a user and an interaction object, for example, a push button or pull-down menu, within the context of task performance (Hartson, 1998). In practice, the notion of an interaction technique includes the concept of interaction style plus full consideration of internal machine behavior and software aspects.

In the context of an interaction technique, an interaction object and its supporting software is often referred to as a "widget." Libraries of widgets, software that supports programming of graphical user interfaces, are an outgrowth of operating system device handler routines used to process user input–output in the now ancient and impoverished interaction style of line-oriented, character-cell, text-only, "glass teletype" terminal interaction. Early graphics packages took interaction beyond text to direct manipulation of graphical objects, eventually leading to new concepts in displays and cursor tracking. No longer tied to just a keyboard or even just a keyboard and mouse, many unusual (then, and some still now) interaction techniques arose (Buxton, 1986; Hinckley et al., 1994; Jacob, 1993).

Myers led the field in user interface software tools of all kinds (Myers, 1989a, 1989b, 1992, 1993, 1995; Myers, Hudson, & Pausch, 2000), and Olsen is known for his work in treating the linguistic structure of human–computer dialogue from a formal computing language perspective as a means for translating the language of interaction into executable program code (Olsen, 1983).

So many people contributed to the work on User Interface Management Systems (UIMS) that it is impossible to even begin to recognize them all. Buxton and colleagues (1983) were among the earliest thinkers in this area. Others we remember are Brad Myers, Dan Olsen, Mark Green, and our researchers at Virginia Tech. Much of this kind of work was reported in the ACM Symposium on User Interface Software and Technology (UIST), a conference specifically for the software-user-interface connection.

The commercial world followed suit and we worked through quite a number of proposed "standard" interaction styles, such as OSF Motif (The Open Group). Developers had to choose from those available mainly because the styles were tied closely to software tools for generating the programming code for interaction designs using the devices and interaction styles of these approaches. Standardization, to some extent, of these interactive graphical interaction techniques led to the widgets of today's GUI platforms and corresponding style guides intended for ensuring compliance to a style, but sometimes thought of mistakenly as usability guides.

This growth of graphics and devices made possible one of the major breakthroughs in interaction styles—direct manipulation (Shneiderman, 1983; Hutchins, Hollan, & Norman, 1986)—changing the basic paradigm of interaction with computers. Direct manipulation allows opportunistic and incremental task planning. Users can try something and see what happens, exploring many avenues for interactive problem solving.

1.6.9 Software Engineering

Perhaps the closest kin of usability engineering, or interaction development, on the computer science side is the somewhat older discipline of software engineering. The development lifecycles of both these disciplines have similar and complementary structure in a development project with similar kinds of activities, such as requirements engineering, design, and evaluation. However, for the most part, these terms have different philosophical underpinnings and meanings in the two disciplines.

In an ideal world, one would expect close connections between these two lifecycles as they operate in parallel during development of a unified interactive system. For example, when usability engineers see the need for a new task, it is important to communicate that need to the software engineers in a timely manner so that they can create necessary functional modules to support that task.

However, in reality, these two roles typically do not communicate with one another until the very end when actual implementation starts. This is often too late, as many interaction design concerns have serious software architectural implications. One of the reasons for this apparent lack of connections between the two lifecycles is because of how these two disciplines grew: without either one strongly influencing the other. In fact, barring a few exceptions, the software engineering and usability engineering researchers and practitioners have mostly ignored one another over the years. We discuss this important topic of connecting with the software engineering lifecycle (Chapter 23).

The Wheel: A Lifecycle Template

He believed in love; he was married many times.

– Fred, on iteration

Objectives

After reading this chapter, you will:
1. Understand the concept of a UX lifecycle process and the need for it
2. Understand the "Wheel" UX lifecycle abstraction template
3. Appreciate the need for choosing a process instance for your own project
4. Understand how to identify project parameters and map them to process choices
5. Understand the process choice tradeoffs based on system type, domain complexity, and interaction complexity within the system complexity space
6. Know the key team roles in the UX process for producing interactive products

2.1 INTRODUCTION

The iterative, evaluation-centered UX lifecycle template described in this chapter sets the stage for the whole interaction design process part of this book. It is a map of all the choices for activities to create and refine a design that will lead to a quality user experience. These activities are where all the work products are created, including versions of the product or system being developed.

2.1.1 Flying without a Process

To set the stage, consider this all too common scenario for a misbegotten approach to interaction lifecycle activities within an interactive software development project (with many thanks to our good friend Lucy Nowell of Battelle Pacific Northwest Laboratories):

Lifecycle

A lifecycle is a structured framework consisting of a series of stages and corresponding activities—such as analysis, design, implementation, and evaluation—that characterize the course of evolution of, in this context, the full evolution of an interaction design or a complete system or product.

Iterative Process

An iterative process is one in which all or part is repeated for the purpose of exploring, fixing, or refining a design or the work product of any other lifecycle activity. It is the "wash, rinse, and repeat" characteristic of HCI.

About 25% into the project schedule, the user experience specialist is contacted and brought in to do some screen designs. *"Where is the task analysis?" "The What?" "Ok, you have done contextual inquiry and analysis and you have requirements, right?"* "Oh, yes, lots of requirements lists—we pride ourselves in gathering and documenting all the necessary functionality beforehand." *"Ummm ..., Ok, do you have any usage scenarios?"* "Uh, well, we've got a bunch of O-O use cases."

At this point the user experience specialist has the privilege of working overtime to get up to speed by poring through functional requirements documents and trying to create some usage scenarios. When the scenarios are sent out to prospective users, it is revealed that this is the first time anyone has asked them anything about the new system. The result is a deluge of feedback ("That's not how we do it!") and tons of changes suggested for the requirements ("Hey, what about this?"), including lots of brand new requirements. A very different view of the target system is emerging!

This is a critical point for management. If they are lucky or smart and there is time (a small percentage of projects), they decide to go back and do the upfront work necessary to understand the work activities and needs of users and customers. They dig into the context of real work, and users get involved in the process, helping to write usage scenarios. The requirements soon reflect real usage needs closely enough to drive a useful and fairly major redesign.

If they are not lucky or smart or do not have the time (a large percentage of product development projects), they will ignore all the commotion from users and plow ahead, confidence unshaken. The group continues on its chosen "clueless but never in doubt" path to produce yet another piece of shelfware. This project cannot be saved *by any amount* of testing, iteration, field support, or maintenance effort.

It is easy to fall into this kind of scenario in your projects. None of us are fond of the ending of this scenario. This kind of scenario is not necessarily anyone's fault; it is just about awareness of a guiding UX process that might help avoid this ending.

2.1.2 The Concept of Process
Calibration: What process means to us and others
To most people, including us:

- the term "process" connotes a set of activities and techniques
- the term "lifecycle" suggests a skeleton structure on which you can hang specific process activities, imbuing them with temporal relationships

Fine distinctions are unnecessary here, so we use the terms "process," "lifecycle," and "lifecycle process" more or less interchangeably. Here we introduce a lifecycle *template*, a skeleton representation of a basic lifecycle that you get to tailor to your needs by *instantiating it for each project.*

In your instantiation you get to determine your own process, choosing which activities to do and which techniques to use in doing them, as well as how much and how often to do each activity, and (perhaps most importantly) when to stop. Here, and in the other process chapters (Chapters 3 through 19), we offer guidelines on how to make these decisions.

What is a process?

A process is a guiding structure that helps both novices and experts deal with the complex details of a project. Process acts as scaffolding, especially for novice practitioners, to ensure that they are on track to a quality product and on the path to becoming experts. Process acts as a checklist for experts to make sure they do not miss any important aspects of the problem in the heat of productivity. A process helps designers answer questions such as "Where are we now?" and "What can/should we do next?"

A process brings to the table organizational memory from similar previous efforts by incorporating lessons learned in the past. In other words, process provides a *repeatable* formula to create a quality product. Process also alleviates risk by externalizing the state of development for observation, measurement, analysis, and control—otherwise, communication among the project roles about what they are doing is difficult because they do not have a shared concept of what they should be doing.

Why do we need a process?

Following a process is the solution recognized by software engineering folks long ago and something in which they invest enormous resources (Paulk et al., 1993) in defining, verifying, and following. On the UX side, Wixon and Whiteside were way ahead of their time while at Digital Equipment Corp in the 1980s and put it this way (Wixon & Whiteside, 1985), as quoted in Macleod et al. (1997):

> Building usability into a system requires more than knowledge of what is good. It requires more than an empirical method for discovering problems and solutions. It requires more than support from upper management and an openness on the part of all system developers. It even requires more than money and time. Building usability into a product requires an explicit engineering process. That engineering process is not logically different than any other engineering process. It involves empirical definition, specification of levels to be achieved, appropriate methods,

early delivery of a functional system, and the willingness to change that system. Together these principles convert usability from a "last minute add on" to an integral part of product development. Only when usability engineering is as much part of software development as scheduling can we expect to regularly produce products in which usability is more than an advertising claim.

Without guidance from an interaction design process, practitioners are forced to make it up as they go along. If this sounds familiar to you, you are not alone. An approach without a process will be idiosyncratic; practitioners will emphasize their own favorite process activities while other important process activities fall through the cracks. What they do is dictated and limited by their own experience. They will try to apply the activities and techniques they know as much as possible; they have hammers and everything looks like nails.

As Holtzblatt (1999) puts it, following a process for product development can work against "the relentless drive of an organization to ship 'something' by a given date." Other excuses for not following a proven approach included "we do not have time to do the whole method, so we do not do any of it," "it does not fit well with our existing methods, that we are used to," "can our designers really be trained to do this?," and "do these methods transfer well to real-world project groups?" In this and the coming chapters, we hope that we can shed some light on answers.

A process is not necessarily rigid

Remember that a process does not necessarily imply a rigid structure or even a linear one. A process can be as lightweight or heavyweight as appropriate. In other words, even an incremental and iterative lifecycle approach in the software engineering world (such as an Agile methodology) is still a process.

Lest it still sounds inflexible, we should add that experts with lots of experience can interpret a process and take appropriate shortcuts and other creative liberties with it—and we encourage that throughout the book.

2.1.3 Influences on Our Lifecycle Process

The lifecycle process described in this book is based on insight that grew out of the adaptation and extension of several existing UX and software methodologies over many years. The methods that most significantly guided our creation of our own lifecycle template are:

- the Waterfall (Royce, 1970) software engineering lifecycle
- the Spiral Model (Boehm, 1988) of software engineering

- Mayhew's usability engineering lifecycle (Mayhew, 1999b)
- the Star lifecycle of usability engineering (Hartson & Hix, 1989)
- the Wheel (Helms et al., 2006) lifecycle concept
- the LUCID framework of interaction design (Kreitzberg, 2008)

Web User Experience Design within the Usability Engineering Lifecycle[1]

Dr. Deborah J. Mayhew, Consultant, Deborah J. Mayhew & Associates [2]
CEO, The Online User eXperience Institute[3]

Within the software usability lifecycle I describe in my book *The Usability Engineering Lifecycle* (Morgan Kaufmann Publishers, 1999) is a phase consisting of a structured *top-down* iterative approach to software user interface design. Design is driven by requirements data from a requirements analysis phase. The overall design phase is divided into three levels of design as follows, with slight wording changes made here to reflect Website *user experience* (UX) design in particular. Each level includes an iterative process of design, mock-up, and evaluation, which is not addressed here.

Level 1
- Information architecture
- Conceptual model design

Level 2
- Page design standards

Level 3
- Detailed UX design

The rationale behind a *top-down* approach to UX design is that it is more efficient and effective to address distinct sets of design issues independently of one another, and in a specific order, that is, from the highest level to the most detailed level. Because the design tasks address issues that are fairly independent of one another, focusing on one level of design at a time forces designers to address *all* UX design issues explicitly and consciously. It ensures efficiency in that

---

[1]This essay is a modified excerpt from a chapter called "The Web UX Design Process—A Case Study" that I have written for the forthcoming book *Handbook of Human Factors in Web Design* (2nd ed.) by Kim-Phuong L. Vu and Robert W. Proctor (Eds.), Taylor & Francis, 2011. That chapter includes a rich case study of the top-down design process within the usability engineering lifecycle, which in turn is fully documented in *The Usability Engineering Lifecycle* by D. Mayhew, Morgan Kaufmann Publishers, 1999.

[3] (http://drdeb.vineyard.net)

[3](http://www.ouxinstitute.com)

lower level details are not revisited and reworked constantly as higher level design issues are addressed and reworked randomly. Each level of design builds on the design decisions at higher levels, which may have already been validated through iterative evaluation.

The top level in the top-down process for Web UX design includes two design foci, the first of which is **information architecture** design. The information architecture is a specification of the *navigational structure* of the Website. *It does not involve any visual design*.

Designers must design information architectures in a way that streamlines site visitor navigation *across and within tasks* and exploits the capabilities of automation (to enhance ease of *use*), while at the same time preserving familiar structures that tap into visitors' current mental models of their tasks.

While it may seem difficult at first to separate *navigational/structural* issues from *visual design* issues, it is productive to learn to do so for at least three reasons. First, the two really are *independent*. For example, you can have valid and supportive information architecture and then fail to present it clearly through an effective visual design.

Second, *different skill sets* are relevant to information architecture design as opposed to visual design. In particular, usability and persuasion skills are paramount to achieving optimal information architecture design, while in addition, graphic design skills are necessary to achieve effective appeal, atmosphere, tone, and branding, as well as help realize and support many usability and persuasion goals.

Third, the navigational structure (i.e., information architecture) is *platform independent*, whereas visual and behavioral design options will depend very much on the chosen platform. For example, a given information architecture may specify a hierarchical menu structure of categories and subcategories of products. Current Web platforms (i.e., browsers, browser versions, plug-ins) allow drop-down menus much like a traditional "GUI" menu bar structure as an option for presenting second (and even third) level navigational choices, whereas earlier browsers did not, requiring instead that different levels in a menu hierarchy be presented as sequences of pages with embedded links.

In **conceptual model design**, still within Level 1, the focus is still on navigation, but high-level design standards for *presenting the information architecture visually* are generated. Neither page content nor page design standards (i.e., visual presentation of page content) are addressed during this design task.

A good conceptual model design eliminates the need for the commonly seen "Site Map" page on Websites, that is, the user interface itself reveals the overall site structure at all times and makes it clear where you currently are in it, how you got there, and where you can go from there. A familiar example of how to achieve this is to provide a left-hand nav bar that displays an expandable/contractible set of hierarchical page links. Within this structure, the link to the current page can be cued by some sort of highlight and be inactive.

Visibility and clarity of the information architecture are large parts of what we want to achieve in Website conceptual model design. However, another key goal in a conceptual model design for a Website is *persuasion*. Also, we want the *graphic design* to be aesthetically appealing as well as appropriate to the business, to create a particular atmosphere designed to attract the target audience, and to provide strong branding.

In Level 2, **page design standards**, a second set of standards for the Website is generated for visually presenting and interacting with *page content*. This new set of standards is designed in the context of both the information architecture and the conceptual model design standards that have already been generated and (in some cases) validated.

Page design standards for a Website would typically include standards that would cover the consistent use and presentation of such things as content headers and subheaders, forms design, use of color cues, and the like. They might include a set of templates illustrating content layout standards for different categories of pages (e.g., fill-in forms, information-only pages, product description pages, pop-up dialog boxes). Consistency in the way all these things are applied in the design will again—just as it does in the case of conceptual model design standards— facilitate greatly the process of learning and remembering how to use the site. This is particularly important on Websites that will be used primarily by casual and discretionary users, as is the case with many eCommerce and other types of sites.

The standards documented during the conceptual model design and page design standards tasks, as well as the information architecture design, will dictate the detailed UX design of a large percentage of a site's functionality. Level 3, **detailed UX design**, is thus largely a matter of correctly and consistently applying standards already defined and validated to the actual detailed design of all pages and pop-up windows across the site.

However, there will always be unique details here and there across pages to which no particular established standard applies. These must still be designed, and designed well. Also, these design decisions should be driven by requirements data and evaluated.

In my 30 years of software user interface design I have found a top-down approach to user interface design to be most effective and efficient as a design process within the overall usability engineering lifecycle.

2.2 A UX PROCESS LIFECYCLE TEMPLATE

In Figure 2-1 we depict a basic abstract picture of activities for almost any kind of design, a cycle of the four elemental UX activities—Analyze, Design, Implement, and Evaluate—that we refer to generically as analysis, design, implementation, and evaluation. These four activities apply whether you are working with an architectural design, a hardware design, or a new car concept.

In the context of interaction design and UX, this abstract cycle translates to our UX lifecycle template of Figure 2-2, which we call the Wheel.

In our lifecycle concept, specific to a UX process, analysis translates to understanding user work and needs. Design translates to creating conceptual design and determining interaction behavior and look and feel. Implementation translates to prototyping, and evaluation translates to ways to see if our design is on track to meet user needs and requirements.

In a larger system view, implementation includes a final production of hardware and software, including the user interface. However, in our UX lifecycle template,

Figure 2-1

Universal abstract activity cycle of Analyze, Design, Implement, and Evaluate.

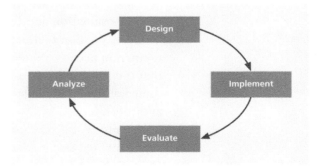

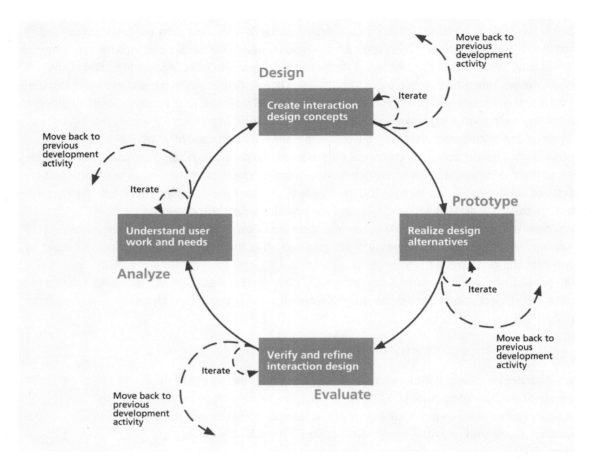

Figure 2-2

The Wheel: A lifecycle template illustrating the process part of this book.

implementation is limited to the interaction design component and prototyping is the design manifestation we use for evaluation before it is finalized for production.

The evaluation activity shown in Figure 2-2 includes both rigorous and rapid evaluation methods for refining interaction designs. Beyond that evaluation activity, the entire lifecycle is evaluation centered in the sense that the results of potentially every activity in the lifecycle are evaluated in some way, by testing, inspecting, analyzing, and taking it back to the customers and users.

The entire lifecycle, especially the prototyping and evaluation activities, is supplemented and guided by UX goals, metrics, and targets, as described in Chapter 10.

As you will see, this is not a lifecycle that must be followed arbitrarily, nor must any particular activity, sub-activity, or iteration be performed—*this is just a template showing all the possibilities*. Each of these activities and many of the more specific sub-activities correspond to one or more process-oriented chapters, among Chapters 3 through 19, of this book.

2.2.1 Lifecycle Terminology

Each of the four UX process activities in Figure 2-2 can have *sub-activities*, the major ways to do the basic activities. As an example, for the analysis activity, possible sub-activities include contextual inquiry (Chapter 3), contextual analysis (Chapter 4), requirements extraction (Chapter 5), and contextual data modeling (Chapter 6).

A *method* is a general approach to carrying out an activity or sub-activity. For example, lab-based evaluation (Chapters 12 and 14 through 17) is a method for the evaluation activity. A *technique* is a specific practice applied within a method. For example, the "think-aloud" technique is a data collection technique that can be used within the lab-based evaluation method for the evaluation activity.

2.2.2 UX Process Activities

Analyze: Understanding the business domain, user work, and user needs

The left-most of the four basic activity boxes in Figure 2-2 represents the analysis process activity. Among the many possible sub-activities to support analysis are contextual inquiry (Chapter 3) and contextual analysis (Chapter 4) for studying customer and user work practice in situ, from which we can infer user needs for a new system design.

Extracting requirements (Chapter 5) from contextual data is another analysis sub-activity. The requirements, if you choose to use them, are interaction design requirements, inputs driving the design process and helping to determine its features and the look, feel, and behavior of the interaction design. These requirements are used as a checklist to ensure that they are covered in the design, even before any UX evaluation.

Finally, synthesizing design-informing models is yet another possible analysis sub-activity. Design-informing models (Chapter 6) are abstractions of different dimensions of the work activity and design space. If you choose to use them, these include models describing how work gets done, how different roles in the work domain interact, the artifacts that are created, and so on.

Horizontal Prototype

A horizontal prototype is very broad in the features it incorporates, but offers less depth in its coverage of functionality.

Vertical Prototype

A vertical prototype contains as much depth of functionality as possible in the current stage of the project, but only for a narrow breadth of features.

T Prototype

In a "T" prototype much of the design is realized at a shallow level (the horizontal top of the T), but a few parts are done in depth (the vertical part of the T). A "T" prototype combines the advantages of both horizontal and vertical, offering a good compromise for system evaluation.

Local Prototype

A local prototype represents the small area where horizontal and vertical slices intersect. A local prototype, with depth and breadth both limited, is used to evaluate design alternatives for a particular isolated interaction detail.

Design: Creating conceptual design, interaction behavior, and look and feel

The upper-most box in Figure 2-2 represents the process activity for design, including redesign for the next version. Among the possible sub-activities to support design are design ideation and sketching (Chapter 7), where the team does creative design thinking, brainstorming, and sketching of new design ideas. Design ideation leads to the representation of mental models, conceptual design, and design storyboards. During the exploration of large numbers of design candidates, it can include physical mockups of product design ideas.

Design production is a design sub-activity involving the details of applying requirements, design-informing models, and envisioned design-informing models to drive and inform the emerging interaction design. Design production entails prototyping and iteration of the conceptual design, intermediate designs, and detailed designs.

Prototype: Realizing design alternatives

The right-most of the four basic activity boxes in Figure 2-2 represents the prototyping process activity. Prototype building is often done in parallel with, and in conjunction with, design. As designs evolve in designers' minds, they produce various kinds of prototypes as external design representations. Because prototypes are made for many different purposes, there are many kinds of prototypes, including horizontal, vertical, T, and local. Prototypes are made at many different levels of fidelity, including low fidelity (especially paper prototypes), medium fidelity, and high fidelity (programmed functional prototypes), and "visual comps" for pixel-perfect look and feel.

Evaluate: Verifying and refining the interaction design

The process activity box at the bottom of Figure 2-2 represents the UX evaluation to refine an interaction design. For evaluation to refine, you can employ rapid evaluation methods (Chapter 13) or fully rigorous methods (Chapters 12 and 14 through 17). This evaluation is where we see if we achieved the UX targets and metrics to ensure that the design "meets usability and business goals" (ISO 13407, 1999).

2.2.3 Flow among UX Process Activities
Flow not always orderly

The depiction of UX process activities in distinct boxes, as in Figure 2-2, is a convenient way to highlight each activity for discussion and for mapping to chapters in this book. These process activities, however, do not in practice have such clear-cut boundaries; there can be significant overlap. For example, most of the boxes have their own kind of evaluation, if only to evaluate the transition criterion at the exit point of each activity in the decision whether to iterate or move on.

Similarly, prototyping appears in many forms in other boxes, too. For example, the design activity entails lots of different kinds of prototypes, including sketches, which can be thought of as a kind of quick and dirty prototype to support rapid and frequent design idea exploration. In this same vein there can be a little design occurring within the analysis activity, and so on.

Managing the process with activity transition criteria

The primary objective of the overall lifecycle process is to keep moving forward and eventually to complete the design process and make the transition to production. However, for the work in a project to flow among the UX process activities, the team must be able to decide:

- when to leave an activity
- where to go after any given activity
- when to revisit a previous process activity
- when to stop making transitions and proceed to production

The answers depend on the transition criterion at the end of each process activity. There is no formula for determining transition criteria; they are generally based on whether designers have met the goals and objectives for the current iteration of that activity. Therefore, it is the job of the team, especially the project manager, to articulate those goals as transition criterion for each process activity and to decide when they are met.

For example, in the analysis activity, designers must ask themselves if they have acquired enough understanding of the work domain and user needs, usage context, workflow, and so on. Another component of any transition criterion is based on whether you have adequate resources remaining to continue. Resources limits, especially time and budget, can trump any other criteria for stopping a process activity or terminating the whole process, regardless of meeting goals and objectives.

Note in Figure 2-2 that the transition criterion coming out of each UX process activity box is a multipath exit point with three options: move forward to the next process activity, iterate some more within the current activity, or move back to a previous process activity.

The decision of where to go next after a given process activity depends on the assessed quality of the product and/or work products of the current activity and a determination of what next activity is most appropriate. For example, after an initial prototyping activity, a usability inspection might indicate that the design is ready for prototyping at a higher fidelity or that it is necessary to go back to design to fix discovered problems.

Knowing when you need inter-activity iteration depends on whether you need to pick up more information to drive or inform the design. When some of your inputs are missing or not quite right, you must revisit the corresponding process activity. However, this kind of inter-activity iteration does not mean you have to redo the whole activity; you just need to do a little additional work to get what you need.

Knowing when to stop iteration and proceed to production lies in a key process management mechanism. When UX targets (Chapter 10), often based on evaluation of user performance or satisfaction, have been employed in your process, project managers can compare evaluation results with target values and decide when to stop iterating (Genov, 2005).

Why do we even need iteration?

Iteration is a little like the doctrine of original sin in interaction design: Most interaction designs are born bad and the design teams spent the rest of their lifecycles in an iterative struggle for redemption.

– Ford Perfect

Some people may question the need for iteration. Is not that just for novice designers who cannot get it right the first time? What about expert designers carefully applying complete knowledge of design guidelines and style standards? For any nontrivial interaction design, the UX process must be, and always will need to be, iterative. The design domain is so vast and complex that there are essentially infinite design choices along many dimensions, affected by large numbers of contextual variables.

To be sure, expert designers can create a good starting point, but because it is fundamentally impossible to get it all just right the first time, we need to use the artillery approach (Figure 2-3): Ready, Fire, Aim. We need to fire off our best shot, see how it missed the mark, and make corrections to home in on the target.

Figure 2-3
Iteration: Ready, fire, aim.

Iteration is not enough

The road to wisdom? Well, it's plain and simple to express: Err and err and err again but less and less and less.

– Piet Hein, Danish poet

So, if we must always iterate, is there any motivation for trying hard to get the first design right? Why not avoid the effort upfront and let this marvel of iteration evolve it into perfection? Again, the answer is easy. You cannot just test your way to a quality user experience, you have to design for it. Iterative testing and redesign alone will not necessarily get you to a good design at the end of the day.

As Wyatt Earp once said, "Take an extra second to aim." Large interactive systems take a lot of time and money to develop; you might as well put a little more into it up front to make it right. Without an honest and earnest upfront analysis and design effort, the process tilts too heavily toward just evaluation and becomes a unidimensional diagnostic-oriented process.

To use a truly geeky example, consider a program traversing an n-dimensional surface, seeking a solution to a numerical analysis problem. If the search starts with the wrong "seed" or initial point (i.e., an initial solution that is too far from the actual solution), the algorithm might stop at a local optimum that is in a part of the search space, such as a saddle point, so remote from the optimal solution, if there is one, that you can never migrate out by any amount of iteration to get at a much better globally optimal solution. Similarly, in iterative interaction design, you can home in on the best details of a less-than-best design—honing a paring knife when you really need a butcher knife. Fixing the details of the bad design may never reveal the path to a completely new and better overall design.

So, the answer is about balance of all four process activities of Figure 2-1— analyze, design, implement, and evaluate—for a given amount of resources.

Start iteration early

The earlier the interaction design iteration begins, the better; there is no time to steer the ship when it is close to the dock. But the software implementation does not have to keep up with this iteration; instead we use interaction design prototypes, and there is no reason any production code should be committed to the interaction design until late in its lifecycle. Nevertheless, because the two roles cannot work in isolation, the software engineering people should be aware of the progression of the interaction design to ensure that their software architecture and design can support the interaction features on the user interface when it does come time to implement.

Typically, early cycles of iteration are devoted to establishing the basic underlying essentials of the design, including look and feel, and behavior, before getting into design details and their refinement. Project managers need to allow time for this explicitly in the schedule. It is an investment that pays generous dividends on everything that happens after that.

The rest of the process-related part of this book is mainly about iterating the activities in the diagram of Figure 2-2, plus a few other things in important supporting roles.

2.2.4 Lifecycle Streams

We mostly talk about complete lifecycles, where there is a clear-cut start and end to the project and where the design ideas are hatched creatively out of the imaginations of the designers. In reality that is often not the case. Often the "lifecycle" for a product never really starts or stops; it just goes on forever (or at least seems to) through multiple versions. Operating systems, such as Mac OS X and Microsoft Windows, are good examples.

The lifecycle is more of a continuous stream of reusing and, hopefully, improving ideas, designs, and deliverables or work products. In such cases the project can be heavily constrained by previously existing versions, code, and documentation. The need for stability and an orderly progression across versions makes it almost impossible to avoid the kind of inertia that works against new designs and radical rethinking. It is important for UX practitioners to make the case for at least the most important changes, changes that contribute to an eventual design evolution toward user experience improvement.

2.3 CHOOSING A PROCESS INSTANCE FOR YOUR PROJECT

Increasingly, the need to rush products to market to beat the competition is shortening development schedules and increasing the number of product versions and updates. Web applications must be developed in "Internet time." Ponderous processes and methods are abandoned in favor of lightweight, agile, and flexible approaches intended to be more responsive to the market-driven need for short product versioning cycles. Abridged methods notwithstanding, however, knowledge of the rigorous UX process is an essential foundation for all UX practitioners and it is important for understanding what is being abridged or made agile in choices for the shorter methods.

The lifecycle process diagram in Figure 2-2 is responsive to the need for many different kinds of UX processes. Because it is a template, you must instantiate it for each project by choosing the parts that best suit your project parameters. To support each of these activities, the team can pick from a variety of sub-activities, methods, techniques, and the level of rigor and completeness with which these activities are carried out. The resulting instantiation can be a heavyweight, rigorous, and complete process or a lightweight, rapid, and "just enough" process.

That choice of process can always be a point of contention—between academics and practitioners, between sponsor/customer and project team, and among team members within a project. Some say "we always do contextual inquiry" (substitute any UX process activity); they value a thorough process, even if it can sometimes be costly and impractical. Others say "we never do contextual inquiry (or whatever process activity); we just do not have the time"; they value doing it all as fast as possible, even if it can sometimes result in a lower quality product, with the idea of improving the quality in later production releases.

Much has been written about powerful and thorough processes and much has been written about their lightweight and agile counterparts. So how do we talk about UX design processes and make any sense?

2.3.1 Project Parameters: Inputs to Process Choices

In reality there are as many variations of processes as there are projects. How do you decide how much process is right for you? How do you decide the kinds of process to choose to match your project conditions? What guidance is there to help you decide? There are no set rules for making these choices. Each factor is an influence and they all come together to contribute to the choice. The lifecycle template in this chapter and the guidelines for its instantiation are a framework within which to choose the process best for you.

Among the many possible factors you could consider in choosing a process to instantiate the lifecycle template are:

- risk tolerance
- project goals
- project resources
- type of system being designed
- development organizational culture
- stage of progress within project

One of biggest goal-related factors is risk and the level of aversion to risk in a given project. The less tolerance for risks—of things going wrong, of features or requirements being missing, or not meeting the needs of users—the more need for rigor and completeness in the process.

Budget and schedule are obvious examples of the kinds of resource limitations that could hinder your process choices. Another important kind of resource is person power. How many people do you have, what project team roles can they fill, and what skills do they bring to the project? Are the types of people you have and are their strengths a good match for this type of project?

Practitioners with extensive experience and maturity are likely to need less of some formal aspects of the rigorous process, such as thorough contextual inquiry or detailed UX goals and targets. For these experienced practitioners, following the process in detail does not add much to what they can accomplish using their already internalized knowledge and honed intuition.

For example, an expert chef has much of his process internalized in his head and does not need to follow a recipe (a kind of process). But even an expert chef needs a recipe for an unfamiliar dish. The recipe helps off-load cognitive complexity so that the chef can focus on the cooking task, one step at a time.

Another project parameter has to do with the demands due to the type of system being designed. Clearly you would not use anything like the same lifecycle to design a personal mp3 music player as you would for a new air traffic control system for the FAA.

Sometimes the organization self-selects the kind of processes it will use based on its own tradition and culture, including how they have operated in the past. For example, the organization's market position and the urgency to rush a product to market can dictate the kind of process they must use.

Also, certain kinds of organizations have their culture so deeply built in that it pre-determines the kinds of projects they can take on. For example, if your organization is an innovation consulting firm such as IDEO, your natural process tools will be predisposed toward ideation and sketching. If your organization is a government contractor, such as Northrup-Grumman, your natural process tools will lean more toward a rigorous lifecycle.

Somewhat orthogonal to and overlaid upon the other project parameters is the current stage of progress within the project for which you must choose activities, methods, and techniques. All projects will go through different stages over time. Regardless of process choices based on other project parameters, the appropriateness of a level of rigor and various choices of UX methods and techniques for process activities will change as a project evolves through various stages.

For example, early stages might demand a strong focus on contextual inquiry and analysis but very little on evaluation. Later stages will have an emphasis on evaluation for design refinement. As the stage of progress keeps changing over time, it means that the need to choose a level of rigor and the methods and techniques based on the stage of product evolution is ongoing. As an example, to evaluate an early conceptual design you might choose a quick design review using a walkthrough and later you might choose UX inspection of a low-fidelity prototype or lab-based testing to evaluate a high-fidelity prototype.

2.3.2 Process Parameters: Outputs of Process Choices

Process parameters or process choices include a spectrum from fully rigorous UX processes (Chapters 3 through 17) through rapid and so-called discount methods. Choices also can be made from among a large variety of data collection techniques. Finally, an agile UX process is available as an alternative choice for the entire lifecycle process, a process in which you do a little of each activity at a time in a kind of spiral approach.

2.3.3 Mapping Project Parameters to Process Choices

To summarize, in Figure 2-4 we show the mapping from project parameters to process parameter choices. While there are some general guidelines for making these mapping choices, fine-tuning is the job of project teams, especially the project manager. Much of it is intuitive and straightforward.

In the process chapters of this book, we present a set of rather rigorous process activities, but we want the reader to understand that we know about

Figure 2-4

Mapping project parameters to process parameter choices.

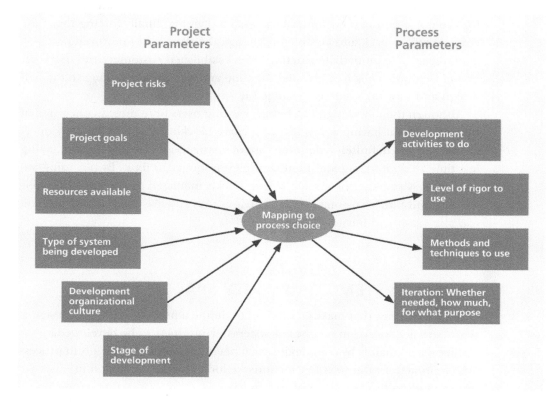

real-world constraints within tight development schedules. So, everywhere in this book, it should be understood that we encourage you to tailor your own process to each new project, picking and choosing process activities and techniques for doing them, fitting the process to your needs and constraints.

2.3.4 Choose Wisely

A real-world Web-based B2B software product company in San Francisco had a well-established customer base for their large complex suite of tools. At some point they made major revisions to the product design as part of normal growth of functionality and market focus. Operating under at least what they perceived as extreme pressure to get it to the market in "Internet time," they released the new version too fast.

The concept was sound, but the design was not well thought through and the resulting poor usability led to a very bad user experience. Because their customers had invested heavily in their original product, they had a somewhat captive market. By and large, users were resilient and grumbled but adapted. However, their reputation for user experience with the product was changing for the worse and new customer business was lagging, finally forcing the company to go back and completely change the design for improved user experience. The immediate reaction from established customers and users was one of betrayal. They had invested the time and energy in adapting to the bad design and now the company changed it on them—again.

Although the new design was better, existing users were mostly concerned at this point about having a new learning curve blocking their productivity once again. This was definitely a defining case of taking longer to do it right vs. taking less time to do it wrong and then taking even longer to fix it. By not using an effective UX process, the company had quickly managed to alienate both their existing and future customer bases. The lesson: If you live by Internet time, you can also crash and burn in Internet time!

2.4 THE SYSTEM COMPLEXITY SPACE

One of the things that makes it difficult to define a process for system design is that there is a spectrum of types of systems or products to be developed, distinguished mainly by complexity, each needing a somewhat different process and approach. In the next few sections we look at what is entailed in understanding this spectrum of system types.

Some systems are a combination of types and some are borderline cases. System or product types overlap and have fuzzy boundaries within the system complexity space. While there undoubtedly are other different ways to partition the space, this approach serves our purpose.

In Figure 2-5 we show such a "system complexity space" defined by the dimensions of interaction complexity and domain complexity. Interaction complexity, represented on the vertical axis, is about the intricacy or elaborateness of user actions, including cognitive density, necessary to accomplish tasks with the system.

Low interaction complexity usually corresponds to smaller tasks that are generally easy to do on the system, such as ordering flowers from a Website. High interaction complexity is usually associated with larger and more difficult tasks, often requiring special skills or training, such as manipulating a color image with Adobe Photoshop.

On the horizontal axis in Figure 2-5 we show work domain complexity, which is about the degree of intricacy and the technical nature of the corresponding field of work. Convoluted and elaborate mechanisms for how parts of the system work and communicate within the ecology of the system contribute to domain complexity.

MUTTS

MUTTS is the acronym for Middleburg University Ticket Transaction Service, our running example for most of the process chapters.

Photoshop, Lightroom, and Aperture

Photoshop, Lightroom, and Aperture are high-functionality software applications for managing and processing large collections of images and photographs.

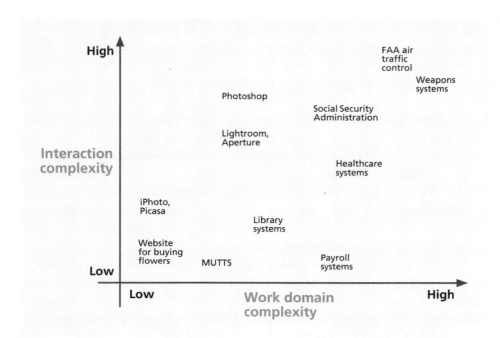

Figure 2-5

Example systems within the system complexity space (interaction complexity vs. domain complexity).

The work in domain-complex systems is often mediated and collaborative, with numerous "hand-offs" in a complicated workflow containing multiple dependencies and communication channels, along with compliance rules, regulations, and exceptions in the way work cases are handled. Examples of complex work domains include management of arcane financial instruments such as credit default swaps, geological fault analysis for earthquake prediction, and healthcare systems.

Low work domain complexity means that the way the system works within its ecology is relatively simple. Examples of work domains with low complexity include that same Website for buying flowers and a simple calendar management application.

2.4.1 The Influence of System Type on Process Choice

The location of the system or product you are designing within the system complexity space can have a major influence on process choices about the right level of rigor and the right techniques to apply. To describe the criteria UX designers can use to make the call, we look at characteristics of the four quadrants of the system complexity space in Figure 2-5.

As we move along the diagonal through this space from lower left to upper right, going from simple systems to complex systems, there is (as a generalization) a gradation of required rigor and fidelity in the corresponding processes. The quadrants are discussed in the following subsections.

Complex interaction, complex work domain

In the upper right-hand quadrant of Figure 2-5 we show the interaction-complex and domain-complex systems, which are usually large and complicated. An example of a complex interaction is an air traffic controller deciding the landing orders for an incoming airliner. An air traffic control system also has enormous domain complexity, with workflow and collaboration among a large number of work roles and user types. Another defining example for this quadrant is a large system for the Social Security Administration.

Systems appearing in this quadrant are often associated with the greatest need to manage risk. Such projects will usually entail doing all the process activity boxes in detail, along with lots of iteration. These are the development projects with the greatest compliance requirements, the most weight given to traceability, and the highest importance of error avoidance.

For example, in mission-critical systems, such as for air traffic control or for military weapons control, there is great user pressure for error avoidance. When you cannot get these things wrong and the cost of failure is unacceptable, you need the most rigorous process, the full process spelled out in great detail in Chapters 3 through 18.

Because of their sheer size and need for rigorous processes, domain-complex and interaction-complex systems are typically among the most difficult and expensive to design and develop. A decidedly engineering approach to formal requirements can be very important to help designers touch all the bases and fill in all the blanks so that no functions or features are forgotten.

This is the kind of system for which design is most likely to need full lab-based user experience evaluation and iteration to produce a well-considered and coherent overall design. This is about the design of serious systems; this sector within the system complexity space has little, if anything, to do with emotional impact factors such as aesthetics, fun, or joy of use.

For large domain-complex systems, such as military weapons systems, you are most likely to encounter resistance to innovation. Radical designs are not always welcome; conformity can be thought more important. User and operators, in some cases, commit operations to habit and perform tasks with learned behavior even if there are better ways. This might be an opportunity for you to champion change and fight against the "this is not how we do it" syndrome, but you must approach this campaign with caution.

Gaming applications can be in this quadrant but they also can span both axes throughout the space.

Usability Engineering for Bioinformatics: Decoding Biologists' and Bioinformaticians' Work Sequences

Deborah Hix and Joe Gabbard, Virginia Bioinformatics Institute and Department of Computer Science, Virginia Tech

Over a collective four decades in usability engineering (UE), we have worked in a broad variety of application domains including military (e.g., decision support systems, situational awareness applications), government (e.g., Social Security Administration), and commercial (e.g., software and hardware companies). The realm of bioinformatics is as complicated as any other single domain we have encountered. This is at least in part because of its fast-changing nature, the current explosion of genomic and related data, the complexity of the field itself, and the technology backgrounds and attitudes of biologists and bioinformaticians.

When we began working in the Virginia Bioinformatics Institute (VBI) at Virginia Tech, approximately 8 years ago, there was almost no knowledge of the existence of usability engineering, never mind any structured use of it in developing complex bioinformatics applications. During this time, we have seen a slight increase in UE efforts in this field, but many (with the exception of large government-funded) Web-based interfaces still look like they were created by graduate students!—a nonoptimal situation in a world of increasingly interactive and sophisticated Web interfaces and apps.

Designing and evaluating user interfaces for biologists and bioinformaticians are challenging in part due to the increasing availability of inexpensive genome sequencing technology, resulting in an explosion of data—in volume, complexity, and heterogeneity. Today at the lab workbench, biologists have access to a staggering flow of data of unprecedented breadth, depth, and quantity.

Further, biologists rarely use a single tool to accomplish a given task; they frequently move data across applications and tools using, for example, desktop-based applications (such as Excel) as well as Web-based resources (such as NCBI's BLAST). So, by necessity, a single technology source or tool or app cannot support their workflow, as their workflow is typically accomplished across multiple applications, Websites, and/or tools. This situation emphasizes the importance of good contextual/domain analysis and design in the UE process.

We have also seen that applications and Websites for biologists and bioinformaticians often need to support a broad variety of multiple work threads for an extensive variety of user classes. That is, the bioinformatics field intersects many specialized disciplines, and as a result, there are numerous types of user classes, each performing varied and mutually exclusive tasks. Moreover, users in this field often solve the same problem using different approaches, increasing the number of possible workflows (including specific data and tools needed) for each task. A single huge online data repository could have more than half a dozen (or even many more) very different user classes, all with different use cases and specific work flows. This situation emphasizes the importance of good user profiles in the UE process.

Finally, biologists are not necessarily early adopters of information technology. They are well versed in cutting-edge biology, but not cutting-edge computer technology. Many have, of necessity, done their own specialized application or Website development, becoming "expert enough" in tools such as scripting and Perl. This is also changing; biologists are relying less on programming- or scripting-savvy approaches. The more advanced their tools and analysis needs get, the more biologists rely on someone else's bioinformatics or software development skills to meet their needs. In today's Web 2.0 application space, most biologists want Web-based applications that support performance of very complicated user tasks without having to do (or oversee) scripting or programming themselves.

When we began in this field all those years ago, we had several approaches to introducing and promoting acceptance of UE activities into a VBI world devoid—and unaware—of them. These included immersion, "starting small," and education.

We made sure our offices were colocated with the group (of biologists and software developers) with which we were working so that we could immerse ourselves and be ever present with them. Otherwise, we might have been viewed as "a priest with a parachute," flying in to "bless" what they had done, but having little or no substantive input to either process or product. We carefully chose a small part of the UE process to perform on a small part of our product, a Web repository named PAThosystems Resource Integration Center (PATRIC), funded by the National Institutes of Health (patric.vbi.vt.edu). Choosing what part of the product with which to begin, UE should be based on a feature or function that is very important, of high visibility, and/or of high utility to users; preferably something with a "wow" factor that will make a splash. Choosing what small part of the process with which to begin should also be based on factors such as availability of appropriate users with whom to work (these may be very difficult to come by early on in an environment that has little or no UE in place, such as VBI) and current state of development of the product.

Our first substantive small UE activity was an expert evaluation (or expert inspection) of an existing in-house product that was being used to inform development of PATRIC. We chose this knowing we did not have a readily available pool of users for either domain analysis activities or a lab-based formative evaluation and that an expert evaluation did not need them. We were extremely careful in how we wrote our expert evaluation report so as not to alienate software engineers, who, to date, had designed all VBI user interfaces, with little or no interaction with users. During this time, we began to cultivate a PATRIC user group of appropriate biologists and bioinformaticians, and moved on to structured interviews and focus group-like sessions that would lead to domain analysis and user profiles. In addition to getting us much-needed information for UE, these sessions also helped expose users and developers to the UE process in a nonthreatening way. After several months, we were able to develop wireframe mockups and present them to some of our initial users, plus other stakeholders who had not been involved in domain analysis. For these earliest formative evaluations, we engaged both in-house users and remote users; for remote users, we used desktop-sharing software to present wireframes and semiworking prototypes to elicit feedback. In addition to this carefully chosen progression of UE activities, we had cooperative management who agreed to provide education; every member of the PATRIC team was required to take a 3-day intensive short course on UE.

Finally, we found that *patience* and *persistence* were nontechnical but key ingredients in this progression! It took many months to slowly and carefully insert UE practices into the PATRIC software development environment. When we encountered roadblocks, both passive aggressive and outright aggressive, we would regroup, figure out a different way to proceed, and continue moving forward. We promoted our "success stories" among the group and tried to make everyone feel continually and substantively involved in the process. We had a major breakthrough when, one day, our meeting discussion turned to some topic specifically related to user interface design, and the lead software engineer looked directly at us and announced, "That is Debby and Joe's problem!" They finally got it!

Simple interaction, complex work domain

In the lower right-hand quadrant of Figure 2-5 we show interaction-simple and domain-complex systems. In this quadrant, user tasks are relatively simple and easy to understand. The key effort for users in this quadrant is understanding the domain and its often esoteric work practice. Once that is understood, the interaction is relatively straightforward for users. Tax preparation software for average households is a good example because the underlying domain is complex but the data entry into forms can be simplified to a step-by-step process.

In the UX process, interaction simplicity means that less attention to tasks descriptions is needed, but the domain complexity calls for more attention to contextual inquiry and analysis, modeling, and requirements for insight into internal system complexity and workflow among multiple work roles. Physical modeling and the social model of Chapter 6 become more important to gain access to the essentials of how people and information interact within the system.

Simple interaction, simple work domain

The simplest quadrant is in the lower left-hand corner of Figure 2-5, where both interaction and work domain are simplest. This quadrant contains smaller Websites, certain interactive applications, and commercial products. Just because this is the simple-simple quadrant, however, does not mean that the products are simple; the products of this quadrant can be very sophisticated.

Although emotional impact factors do not apply to every system or product in this quadrant, this sector within the system complexity space has the most to do with emotional impact factors such as aesthetics or fun or joy of use. This quadrant also represents projects that are design driven, where the UX process is all about design rather than user research or user models.

There is an abundance of relatively simple systems in the world. Some, but not all, commercial software products are domain-simple and interaction-simple, at least relative to large systems of other types. An example, shown in Figure 2-5, is a Website for ordering flowers. Interaction with this Website is very simple; just one main task involving a few choices and the job is done. Work domain complexity of a Website for buying flowers is also relatively simple because it involves only one user at a time and the workflow is almost trivial.

Because of the simplicity in the work domain and interaction in this quadrant, good choices for a UX process lean toward agile approaches with a focus on design and special rapid methods for evaluation. That translates to a low level of rigor; leaving out some process activities altogether and using lightweight or specialized techniques for others.

The best designers for expert users in this case might be "dual experts," experts in HCI/UX and in the work domain. An example is a designer of Adobe Lightroom who is also deeply involved in photography as a personal hobby.

This quadrant is also where you will see innovative commercial product development, such as for an iPhone or a personal mp3 music player, and corresponding emotional impact issues and, where appropriate (e.g., for an

---

Phenomenological Aspects of Interaction

Phenomenological aspects (deriving from phenomenology, the philosophical examination of the foundations of experience and action) of interaction are the cumulative effects of emotional impact considered over the long term, where usage of technology takes on a presence in our lifestyles and is used to make meaning in our lives.

mp3 personal music player but not for a florist's Website), phenomenological aspects of interaction.

These products represent the least need for a complete rigorous lifecycle process. Designers of systems in this quadrant need not expend resources on upfront user research and analysis or requirements gathering. They can forego most of the modeling of Chapter 6 except, perhaps, specific inquiry about users and their activities, with a special interest in user personas.

Although commercial product design certainly can benefit from thorough contextual inquiry, for example, some successful products were essentially "invented" first and then marketed. The Apple iPad is a good example; the designers did not begin within a field study of existing usage patterns. They dreamed up a product that was so good that people who thought they would never be interested in such a product ended up fervently coveting one.

Projects in this quadrant are far less engineering oriented; design will be based almost entirely on a design-thinking approach. Designers are free to focus on imaginative design thinking, ideation, and sketching to make the user experience the best it can be. Processes for this type of system are usually faced with low risks, which means designers can put innovation over conformity—for example, the iPod over previous music players—and are free to envision radically new design ideas.

Early prototyping will center on multiple and disposable sketches for exploring design ideas. Later, low-fidelity prototypes will include paper prototypes and physical mockups. Subsequent evaluation will be about using rapid methods to get the conceptual design right and not being very concerned with user performance or usability problems.

Complex interaction, simple work domain

In the upper left-hand quadrant of Figure 2-5 we show interaction-complex and domain-simple systems. It is typical of an interaction-complex system to have a large volume of functionality resulting in a large number and broad scope of complex user tasks. A digital watch is an example. Its interaction complexity stems from a large variety of modal settings using overloaded and unlabeled push buttons. The domain, however, is still simple, being about "what time is it?" Workflow is trivial; there is one work role and a simple system ecology.

Attention in this quadrant is needed for interaction design—myriad tasks, screen layouts, user actions, even metaphors. Rigorous formative evaluation is needed for conceptual design and detailed interaction. The focus of modeling will be on tasks—task structure and task interaction models—and perhaps the

System Ecology

System ecology is the context provided by the surrounding parts of the world with which it interacts.

Task Structure Model

A task structure model is a hierarchical decomposition of tasks and sub-tasks showing what tasks are to be supported and the relationships among them.

Task Interaction Model

A task interaction model is a step-by-step description, including task goals, intentions, triggers, and user actions.

Artifact Model

An artifact model is a representation of how tangible elements (physical or electronic) are used and structured in the business process flow of doing the work.

artifact model, but not much attention will be given to work roles, workflow, or most of the other models of Chapter 6.

For simple work domains, regardless of interaction complexity, contextual inquiry and contextual analysis rarely result in learning something totally new that can make a difference in informing design. Rather, even more than for a simple interaction case, complex interaction requires a focus on ideation and sketching, as well as attention to emotional impact factors.

The commercial product perspective within the system complexity space

"Commercial products" is a good label for the area that spans the left-hand side of the system complexity space diagram in Figure 2-5, where you find relatively low domain complexity but variable interaction complexity. The more interaction complexity, the more sophisticated users can be.

Gradations within the system complexity space

Many systems and design projects fall across quadrants within the system complexity space. Websites, for example, can belong to multiple quadrants, depending on whether they are for an intranet system for a large organization, a very large e-commerce site, or just a small site for sharing photographs. Products such as a printer or a camera are low in domain complexity but can have medium interaction complexity.

One good illustration of complexity vs. process rigor is seen in systems for managing libraries, shown in the middle of the work domain complexity scale of Figure 2-5, near the bottom. Typical library systems have low interaction complexity because the scope of tasks and activities for any one user is fairly circumscribed and straightforward and the complexity of any one user task is low. Therefore, for a library system, for example, you do not need to model tasks too much.

However, a full library system has considerable domain complexity. The work practice of library systems can be esoteric and most UX designers will not be knowledgeable in this work domain. For example, special training is needed to handle the surprisingly important small details in cataloging procedures. Therefore, a rigorous approach to contextual inquiry and analysis may be warranted.

Because of the high work domain complexity, there is a need for thorough contextual data modeling to explain how things work in that domain. As an example, the overall workflow entails book records connected in a network, including cataloguing, circulation tracking, searching, and physical shelf location. A full flow model may be necessary to understand the flow of information among the subsystems.

Healthcare systems are another example of projects that cross system complexity space quadrants. Large healthcare systems that integrate medical instrumentation, health record databases, and patient accounting are another example of systems with somewhat complex work domains.

The healthcare domain is also saddled with more than its share of regulation, paperwork, and compliance issues, plus legal and ethical requirements—all of which lead to high work domain complexity, but not as high as air traffic control, for example. Machines in a patient's room have a fairly broad scope of tasks and activities, giving them relatively high interaction complexity.

We refer to the system complexity space throughout the rest of the process chapters in discussions about how much process is needed. For simplicity we will often state it as a tradeoff between systems with complex work domains, which need the full rigorous UX process and systems with relatively simple work domains, which need less rigor but perhaps more attention to design thinking and emotional impact.

Since simple work domains correspond roughly to the left-hand side of the system complexity space of Figure 2-5, where most commercial products are found, we will often use the term "commercial products" as a contrast to the complex domain systems, even though it is sometimes possible for a commercial product to have some complexity in the work or play domain.

2.5 MEET THE USER INTERFACE TEAM

Whatever you are, be a good one.

– Abraham Lincoln

One early stage activity in all interactive software projects is building the UX team. Someone, usually the project manager, must identify the necessary roles and match them up with available individuals. Especially in small projects, the different roles are not necessarily filled with different people; you just need to maintain the distinction and remember which role is involved in which context and discussion.

In addition to the software engineering roles, here we are mainly concerned with roles on the UX team. Roles we can envision include the following:

- ■ User researcher: involved with contextual inquiry and other work domain analysis activities. You may also need other roles even more specialized, such as a social anthropologist to perform in-depth ethnographic field studies.
- ■ Users, user representatives, customers, and subject matter experts: used as information sources in contextual inquiry and throughout the lifecycle.

- User interaction designer: involved with ideation and sketching, conceptual and detailed design, and low-fidelity prototyping activities.
- UX analyst or evaluator: involved in planning and performing UX evaluations, analyzing UX problems, and suggesting redesign solutions.
- Visual/graphic designer: involved in designing look and feel and branding and helping interaction designers with visual aspects of designs.
- Technical writer: involved in documentation, help system design, and language aspects of interaction designs.
- Interactive prototype programmer: involved in programming interactive high-fidelity UX design prototypes.
- UX manager: someone with overall responsibility for the UX process.

Figure 2-6

Example UX team roles in the context of the Wheel lifecycle template.

Some of these roles are shown with respect to the lifecycle activities in Figure 2-6.

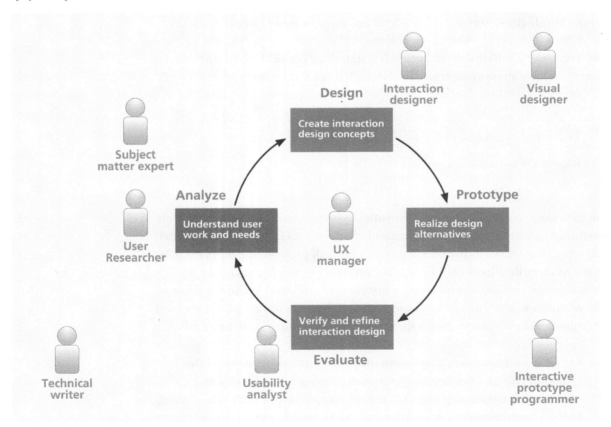

Often terms for team roles are used loosely and with overlap. For example, "UX engineer" or "UX practitioner" are catch-all terms for someone who does contextual analysis, design, and evaluation on the UX side.

As a further consideration, in many projects, team composition is not static over the whole project. For example, people may come and go when their special talents are required, and it is not unusual for the team to get smaller near the end of the lifecycle. Often near the end of the version or release cycle, much of project team gets reassigned and disappears and you get a possibly new and much smaller one, with a much shorter remaining lifecycle.

2.6 SCOPE OF UX PRESENCE WITHIN THE TEAM

In the early days of usability it was often assumed that a usability practitioner was needed only in small doses and only at certain crossroads within the project schedule, resulting in a rough and frustrating life for the usability person in the trenches. In project environments, they were treated as temp workers with narrow purviews and meager responsibilities, getting no real authority or respect.

Software developers grudgingly let the usability practitioner, who was probably a human factors engineer, look at their designs more or less after they were done. Because they were not a bona fide part of the project, they played a secondary role, something like a "priest in a parachute": The human factors engineer dropped down into the middle of a project and stayed just long enough to give it a blessing. Anything more than a few minor changes and a blessing was, of course, unacceptable at this point because the design had progressed too far for significant changes.

2.7 MORE ABOUT UX LIFECYCLES

Just as a lifecycle concept did not always exist in the software development world, the need for a separate development lifecycle for the interaction design has not always been recognized. Moreover, once a lifecycle concept was introduced, it took time for the idea to be accepted, as it had done for software in prior decades.

The Hix and Hartson book (1993) was one of the first to emphasize a separate lifecycle concept for interaction design. Among early calls to arms in this evolutionary struggle to establish acceptance of a disciplined usability process were pleas by Curtis and Hefley (1992). They argued that "interface engineering," as they called it, required an engineering discipline just like any other: "All engineering disciplines, including interface engineering, require the definition of a rigorous development process."

Hefley and friends followed this up with a CHI '96 workshop asking the question, User-centered design principles: How far have they been industrialized? (McClelland, Taylor, & Hefley, 1996). They concluded that the field was, indeed, evolving toward acceptance, but that there was still a lack of understanding of the interaction design process and a shortage of skills to carry it out. Raising awareness within management and marketing roles in the software world was a priority. Mayhew (1999b) helped solidify the concept with practitioners through a pioneering tour de force handbook-style codification of lifecycle activities and deliverables.

Usability engineering as a term and as a concept was coming into existence in the early 1990s. In his celebratory 1996 retrospective, Butler (1996) attributed the actual coining of the term "usability engineering" to John Bennett in the 1980s. Here, Butler provided a review of the discipline's state of the art as it began to mature after the first 10 years and argued for a need to integrate usability engineering using a "comprehensive integrated approach to application development."

Nielsen (1992b) had already been talking about the increasing importance of computer–user interfaces and the need to make them usable by using "a systematic usability effort using established methods." He proposed a usability engineering model that included fundamental usability tenets such as "know thy user" and advocated an iterative refinement of the interaction design.

This model proposed different phases of the UX lifecycle: pre-design, design, and post-design with corresponding activities such as understanding overall work context, understanding intended users, setting usability goals, and undertaking iterative testing. Nielsen (1993) later elaborated these ideas into one of the first usability engineering textbooks.

Whitney Quesenbery (2005) describes how the ISO 13407 standard (1999) reflected the "general industry approach to UCD" at the time. It describes four principles of user-centered design, including "active involvement of customers (or those who speak for them)," but apparently did not speak for the *users* directly.

This standard also made a strong point in favor of not just the principle of using an iterative cycle, but of the need to plan to allow time for iteration in practice. In its central focus on process, the standard prescribes five process activities, starting with planning for UCD, followed by an iterative cycle of specifying context of use, specifying requirements, producing design solutions, and evaluating designs, as seen in Figure 2-7.

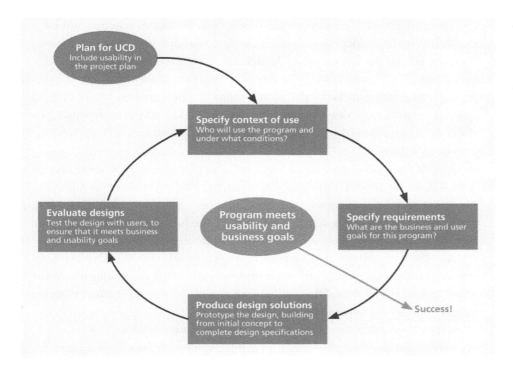

Figure 2-7

Lifecycle diagram from the ISO 13407 standard, adapted with permission.

Despite the name user-centered design, this cycle does not give much focus to design as a separate activity, but rolls it in with implementation in the "produce design solutions" box. Nonetheless, the ISO standards were timely and gave a real boost to the credentials of UCD processes to follow.

2.7.1 Much More Than Usability Testing: The Need for a Broad Lifecycle Process

As usability slowly emerged as a goal, thinking about methods to achieve it was at first slow to follow. Everyone vaguely knew you had to involve users somehow, that it helped to follow a style guide, and that you definitely had to do usability testing. Armed with just enough of this knowledge to be dangerous, the budding new usability specialists plunged in, not knowing enough to know what they did not know. But to be effective, especially cost-effective, our heroes needed help in using the right technique at the right time and place.

Without an established lifecycle concept to follow, those concerned with user experience were coming up with their own, often narrow, views of user experience methods: "silver bullet" theories that declare all you have to do is contextual inquiry, just test a lot, do everything to "empower users," be object oriented, and so on.

The most broadly fashionable of these uni-dimensional schemes was to equate the entire process with testing, setting usability in a purely diagnostic frame of reference. In response, participants in the CHI '96 workshop mentioned in the previous section felt it important to make the point: "Usability testing and evaluation make contributions to product quality, but testing alone does not guarantee quality." They contended that approaches using only post hoc testing should be expanded to incorporate other UCD activities into earlier parts of the UX process.

Outside the usability world of the time, acceptance was even more sluggish. It took time for interaction design to be recognized by others as a *full* discipline with its own rigorous lifecycle process. And it was often the software engineering people who were most resistant; oh, how soon we forget our own history! In the days when "structured programming" was just becoming the fashion (Stevens, Myers, & Constantine, 1974), development groups (often one or two programmers) without a process were often suspicious about the value added by a "process" that deflected some of the time and effort from pure programming to design and testing, etc.

And so it is with interaction design, and this time it is often the software engineers and project managers who are resisting more structure (and, therefore, more perceived overhead and cost) in parts of the overall interactive system development process not thought to contribute directly to the output of program code.

2.7.2 Fundamental Activities Involved in Building Anything

In the simplest sense, the two fundamental activities involved in (i.e., a process for) creating and building something, be it a house or a software product, are almost always the same: design and implementation. If the complexity of the task at hand is simple, say building a sand castle at the beach, it is possible to undertake design and implementation simultaneously, with minimal process, on the fly and in the head.

However, as complexity increases, each of these activities needs explicit attention and thought, leading to a more defined process. For example, in remodeling one's kitchen, some "design" activities, such as sketches for the new layout and configurations of appliances and countertops, are required before "implementing" the new kitchen.

While you have to do requirements and needs analyses for your own kitchen remodeling so that you do not end up with bells and whistles that you do not really need or use, it is even more important if you are remodeling a kitchen for someone else. You need this added process step to make sure what is being built matches the requirements.

As complexity of the target system or product increases, so does the need for additional steps in your process to manage that complexity. If we are, say, building a house instead of a kitchen, more steps are needed in the process, including consideration of "platform constraints" such as municipal regulations, geographical constraints such as the location of water lines, and, perhaps more importantly, a defined process to manage the complexity of multiple roles involved in the whole undertaking.

2.7.3 Parallel Streams of Software and Interaction Process Activities

To begin on common ground, we start with a reference point within the discipline of software engineering. Just as we discussed in the previous section, perhaps one of the most fundamental software engineering principles is the distinction between software design and software implementation, as shown in Figure 2-8.

Instead of having programmers "designing" on the fly during implementation, proper software engineering methods require software design first (after capturing requirements, of course), and the resulting design specifications are given to the programmers for implementation. Then programmers, possibly a different person or group, follow the design as documented in the specifications to implement the software.

The programmer who creates the software code to implement the design is in the best position to spot incorrect or missing parts of the specification. For example, while coding a "case statement," the programmer may notice if the specification for one of the cases is missing. At this point, the programmer has two choices: (1) save time by filling in missing parts or correcting erroneous parts of the specifications by using best judgment and experience or (2) take the extra time to send the specifications back to designers for amendments.

The first choice is tempting, especially if the schedule is tight, but the implementer has not necessarily been privy to all the prior meetings of designers about rationale, goals, design principles, and so on and may not get it right. In addition, design additions or changes made by the implementer are usually undocumented. The code written to correct the design becomes a software time bomb, later leading to a bug that can be almost impossible to find. As a result, conventional software

Figure 2-8

Distinction between software design and implementation.

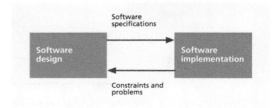

engineering wisdom requires feeding back the faulty specifications to the designers for correction and iteration back to the implementers.

Adding inquiry, requirements, and modeling plus functionality design at the beginning and testing at the end to the boxes of Figure 2-8 gives the picture of software development workflow shown in Figure 2-9.

Systems analysis involves a high-level study of the intended system, including concerns from all disciplines associated with the product. For example, if the project is to design software to manage a nuclear power plant, the systems analysis activity will include study of all component subsystems ranging from safety to software to physical plant to environmental impact.

At this stage, the key subsystems are identified and their high-level interactions specified. In the remainder of this chapter we focus on interactive software systems only and limit the discussion to creation and refinement of interaction design and the development of its software.

Design in the work domain, or application domain, in the second box from the left (Figure 2-9), is the place where the real contents of the system are crafted. If the program is a software support tool for bridge building, for example, this is where all the specialized subject matter knowledge about civil engineering, over-constrained pin joints, strength of materials, and so on is brought to bear. The software design is where algorithms, data structures, calling structures, and so on are created to represent the work design in software.

The analogous activities for user interface (this time, including the user interface software) development are shown in Figure 2-10.

Connecting the processes together and adding rapid prototyping, to get the big picture, we get the overall development workflow diagram of Figure 2-11.

Figure 2-9

Software development workflow diagram.

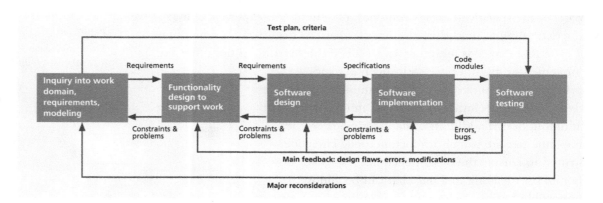

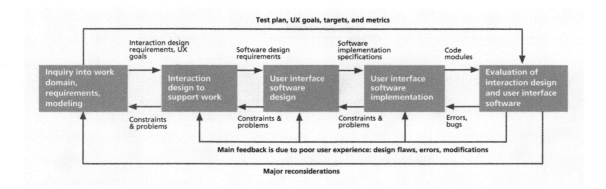

Figure 2-10

Analogous user interface development workflow.

Immediately noticeable is the lack of vertical connections, which points out the need for improved communication between the lifecycles for functional software and for the user interface component of the overall system. There is an absolute lack of formal methods to integrate these two lifecycles. This is a big hole in the practice of both sides of the picture. In practice, this communication is important to project success and all parties do their best to carry it out, relying mainly on informal channels.

The means for achieving this communication vary widely, depending on project management abilities, the size of the project, and so on. For small projects, a capable manager with a hands-on management style can function effectively as a conduit of communication between the two work domains. Larger projects, where it is impossible for one person to keep it all in his or her head, need a more structured inter-domain communication mechanism (Chapter 23).

2.7.4 Iteration for Interaction Design Refinement Can Be Very Lightweight

Figure 2-11 offers a good backdrop to the discussion of iteration within the UX lifecycle for interaction design. Management and software people often strongly resist the general idea of iteration, repetitively going back over process activities. Some team members worry that they can barely afford the time and resources to produce a system once, let alone iterate the process multiple times. This fear is due to a misconception about the nature of iteration in the overall diagram of Figure 2-11, probably because the concept has not been well explained.

In fact, if everything in the diagram of Figure 2-11 were iterated, it *would* be prohibitively burdensome and laborious. The key to understanding this kind of

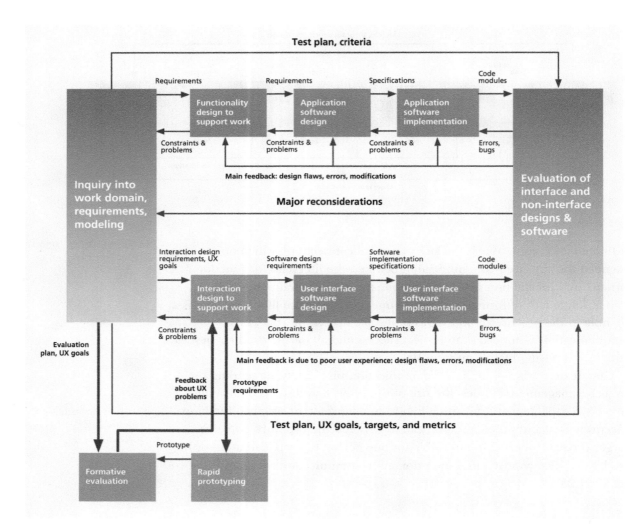

Figure 2-11

Overall interactive system development workflow diagram.

iteration needed for design refinement is in realizing that it does not mean iterating the whole process, doing everything all over again. Instead it is about only a selective part (see Figure 2-12) of the overall process, just enough to identify and fix the major UX problems.

Iterating this small sub-process is far from ponderous and costly; in fact, it:

- is only a very small and very lightweight iteration
- does not have to be expensive because it involves only a very small part of the overall process

- can occur early in the overall lifecycle when design changes cost little
- can have minimal impact on schedule because it can be done in parallel with many other parts (especially the software engineering parts) of the overall project lifecycle

These are strong reasons why iteration to refine interaction designs can be cost-effective and can lead to a high-quality user experience without being a burden to the overall software and system development budget and schedule.

The perceptive reader will see that we have come full circle; the process in Figure 2-12 is a variation of the Wheel lifecycle template of Figure 2-2. You will know more about what goes on in each part of this diagram as you go through the rest of the process part of this book (Chapters 3 through 19).

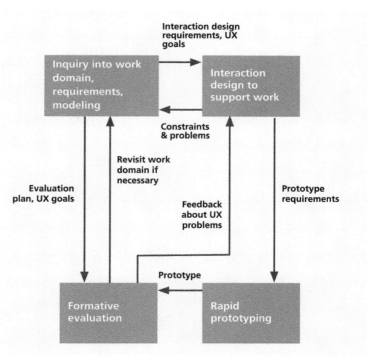

Figure 2-12

The small lightweight subprocess to be iterated for the interaction design.

The Pre-Design Part of the UX Lifecycle

Here is an overview of how contextual inquiry, contextual analysis, needs and requirements extraction, and modeling lead up to design:

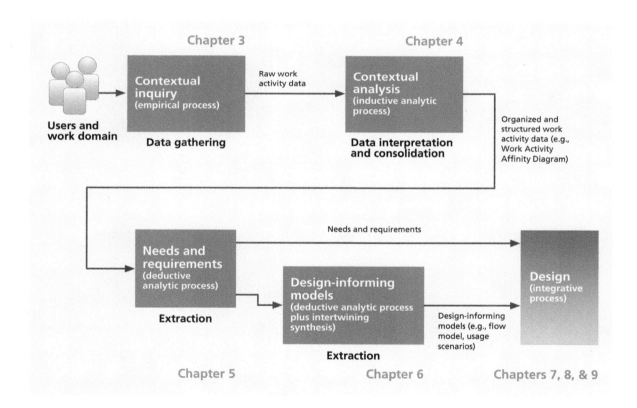

- Contextual inquiry (Chapter 3), is an *empirical* process to elicit and gather user work activity data.
- Contextual analysis (Chapter 4) is an *inductive* (bottom-up) process to organize, consolidate, and interpret the user work activity data in the next chapter.
- Chapter 5 is about a *deductive* analytic process for extracting needs and requirements.

- Chapter 6 is about a *synthesis* of various design-informing models, such as task descriptions, scenarios, and work models.
- Chapters 7, 8, and 9 are about design, an *integrative* process aided by the contextual data and their offspring, needs, requirements, and models.

The parts of the figure are not completely separable like this but, for the book, we break it up a bit to "chunk" it for easier digestion.

Contextual Inquiry: Eliciting Work Activity Data

I don't build a house without predicting the end of the present social order. Every building is a missionary[1]. . . . It's their duty to understand, to appreciate, and conform insofar as possible to the idea of the house. (Lubow, 2009)

— Frank Lloyd Wright, 1938

Objectives

After reading this chapter, you will:

1. Understand the concepts of work, work practice, and work domain
2. Understand the need to study users' work activities in the context of their work practice
3. Be prepared to write a clear and concise product or system concept statement for your envisioned system
4. Know how to prepare for undertaking user research activities
5. Be ready to conduct user research by meeting with customers and potential users to gather contextual data
6. Understand the history and roots of contextual inquiry
7. Appreciate the difference between data-driven and model-driven inquiry

3.1 INTRODUCTION

3.1.1 You Are Here

We begin each process chapter with a "you are here" picture of the chapter topic in the context of our overall Wheel lifecycle template; see Figure 3-1. The process begins with understanding user work and needs by "getting your nose in the customer's tent." To understand the users' activities in the context of

---

[1]The term "missionary" referred to his commitment to educate his customers about their own needs. While he aimed to serve his clients' needs, he felt he was the only authority on determining those needs.

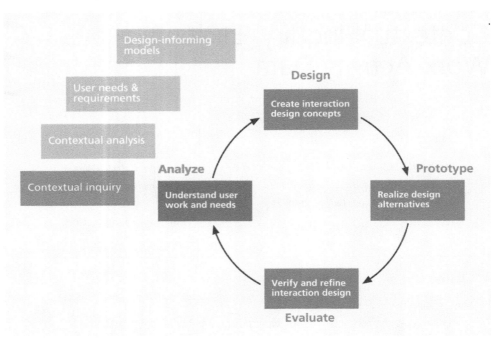

Figure 3-1

You are here; in the contextual inquiry chapter, within understanding user work and needs in the context of the overall Wheel lifecycle template.

Work

Work is the set of activities that people undertake to accomplish goals. Some of these activities involve system or product usage. This concept includes play, if play, rather than work per se, is the goal of the user.

Work Domain

The entire context of work and work practice in the target enterprise or other target usage environment.

their current work practice (or play practice), using any currently existing system or product, we do contextual inquiry (this chapter) and contextual analysis (Chapter 4). Sometimes contextual inquiry and contextual analysis are collectively called contextual studies or "user research."

3.1.2 A True Story

In southwest Virginia, somewhat remote from urban centers, when the first-time computer-based touchscreen voting machines were used, we heard that quite a few voters had difficulty in using them. Although an official gave instructions as people entered one particular voting area, a school gymnasium, he did it in a confusing way.

One of the voters in line was an elderly woman with poor eyesight, obvious from her thick eyeglasses. As she entered the voting booth, one could just imagine her leaning her head down very close to the screen, struggling to read the words, even though the font was reasonably large.

Her voice was heard floating above her voting booth, as she gave some unsolicited user feedback. She was saying that she had trouble distinguishing the colors (the screen was in primary colors: red, green, and blue). A member of another major gender nearby said aloud to himself, as if to answer the woman, that he thought there was an option to set the screen to black and white. But oddly, no one actually told this, if it was true, to the woman.

In time, the woman emerged with a huge smile, proclaiming victory over the evil machine. She then immediately wanted to tell everyone how the design should be improved. Remember, this is an elderly woman who probably knew nothing about technology or user experience but who is quite naturally willing to offer valuable user feedback.

It was easy to imagine a scenario in which the supervisors of the voting process quickly flocked about the voter and duly took notes, pledging to pass this important information on to the higher-ups who could influence the next design. But as you might guess, she was roundly humored and ignored. Call us superstitious, but that is just bad UX ju ju.

There are a few things to note in this story. First, the feedback was rich, detailed, and informative about design. This level of feedback was possible only because it occurred in real usage and real context.

Second, this woman represented a particular type of user belonging to a specific age group and had some associated visual limitations. She was also naturally articulate in describing her usage experience, which is somewhat uncommon in public situations.

So what does this have to do with contextual inquiry? If you do contextual inquiry in a real environment like this, you might get lucky and find rich user data. It is certain however that, if you do not do contextual inquiry, you will never get this kind of information about situated usage.

3.1.3 Understanding Other People's Work Practice

This chapter is where you collect data about the work domain and user's work activities. This is not about "requirements" in the traditional sense but is about the difficult task of understanding user's work in context and understanding what it would take in a system design to support and improve the user's work practice and work effectiveness.

Why should a team whose goal is to design a new system for a customer be all that interested in work practice? The answer is that you want to be able to create a design that is a fit for the work process, which may not be the same as what the designers think will fit.

So, if you must understand something about what the users do, why not just ask them? Who knows their work better than the users themselves? Many customers, including those in large and complex organizations, may wonder why you want to look at their work. "Just ask us anything about it; we have been doing it for years and know it like the back of our hands."

Work Practice

Work practice is the pattern of established actions, approaches, routines, conventions, and procedures followed and observed in the customary performance of a particular job to carry out the operations of an enterprise. Work practice often involves learned skills, decision making, and physical actions and can be based on tradition, ritualized and habituated.

Work Activity

A work activity is comprised of sensory, cognitive, and physical actions made by users in the course of carrying out the work practice.

Contextual Inquiry

Contextual inquiry is an early system or product UX lifecycle activity to gather detailed descriptions of customer or user work practice for the purpose of understanding work activities and underlying rationale. The goal of contextual inquiry is to improve work practice and construct and/or improve system designs to support it. Contextual inquiry includes both interviews of customers and users and observations of work practice occurring in its real-world context.

The answer is that what they "know" about their work practice is often biased with their own assumptions about existing tools and systems and is mostly shaped by the limitations and idiosyncrasies of these tools and practices. It is not easy for users consciously to describe what they do, especially in work that has been internalized. Humans are notoriously unreliable about this.

Also, each user has a different perspective of how the broader work domain functions. Knowledge of the full picture is distributed over numerous people. What they know about their work is like what the seven blind men "know" about an elephant.

Why not just gather requirements from multiple users and build a design solution to fit them all? You want an integrated design that fits into the "fabric" of your customer's operations, not just "point solutions" to specific problems of individual users. This can only be achieved by a design driven by contextual data, not just opinions or negotiation of a list of features.

That is why contextual inquiry has taken on importance in the UX process. It takes real effort to learn about other people's work, which is usually unfamiliar, especially the details. It can be difficult to untangle the web of clues revealed by observation of work.

Even surface observables can be complex, and the most important details that drive the work are usually hidden beneath the surface: the intentions, strategies, motivations, and policies. People creatively solve and work around their problems, making their barriers and problems less visible to them and to outsiders studying the work.

Because it is so difficult to understand user needs, much upfront time is wasted in typical projects in arguments, discussions, and conjectures about what the user wants or needs based on anecdotes, opinions, experience, etc. The processes of contextual inquiry and analysis remove the necessity for these discussions because the team ends up knowing exactly what users do, need, and think.

3.1.4 Not the Same as Task Analysis or a Marketing Survey

Oftentimes people might say, "We already do that. We do task analysis and marketing surveys." While task analysis does identify tasks, it does not give enough insight into situations where tasks were interwoven or where users needed to move seamlessly from one task to another within the work context.

Task analyses also do not work well in discovering or describing opportunistic or situated task performance. Paying attention to context in task analysis is what led us to contextual inquiry and analysis.

Similarly, you cannot substitute market research for contextual inquiry. They are just two different kinds of analysis and you may need both. Marketing data

Task Analysis

Task analysis is the investigation and deconstruction of units of work. It is the process of representing the structure of these units plus describing how they are performed, including goals, steps, and actions.

are about sales and can identify the kinds of products and even features customers want, but do not lead to any understanding about how people work or how to design for them. Customer/user data about work in context are what lead to design.

3.1.5 The Concepts of Work, Work Practice, and Work Domain

We use the term "work" to refer to the usage activities (including play) to achieve goals within a given domain. It is *what* people do to accomplish these goals. In most cases, use of the term "work" will be obvious, for example, using a CAD/CAM application to design an automobile.

"Work practice" is *how* people do their work. Work practice includes all activities, procedures, traditions, customs, and protocols associated with doing the work, usually as a result of the organizational goals, user skills, knowledge, and social interaction on the job. The context of this kind of work often includes some manual activities in association with some interactive activities.

If we are talking about the context of using a product, such as a consumer software product, then the "work" and "work activities" include all activities users are involved in while using that product. If the product is, say, a word processor, it is easy to see its usage to compose a document as work.

If the product is something like a game or a portable music player, we still refer to all activities a user undertakes while playing games or being entertained with music as "work" and "work activities." Even though the usage activities are play rather than work, we have to design for them in essentially the same way, albeit with different objectives.

Similarly we call the complete context of the work practice, including the usage context of an associated system or product, the work activity domain or simply the work domain. The work domain contains the all-important context, without which you cannot understand the work.

3.1.6 Observing and Interviewing in Situ: What They Say vs. What They Do

Okay, so we agree that we have to learn about customer/user work, but why not stay in our own offices, where we have a good working environment and lots of logistical support, such as secretaries for note-taking and transcription, and spacious comfortable conference rooms? The answer is that you cannot get all the information you need by talking with users outside their work context, which only accesses domain knowledge "in the head." Observing users and asking users to talk about their work activities *as they are doing them in their*

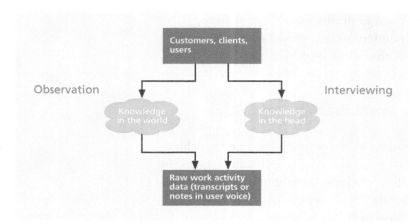

Figure 3-2

Observation and interviewing for contextual data collection.

own work context get them to speak from what they are doing, accessing domain knowledge situated "in the world" (see Figure 3-2).

Even when occurring in situ, in the user's own work environment, asking or interviewing alone is not enough. When gathering data in contextual inquiry, be sure to look beyond the descriptions of how things work, what is commonly believed, and what is told about the same. Observe the "ground truth"—the actual work practice, problems, issues, and work context. It is especially important to notice workarounds created by users when the intended system support or work practice does not support real needs.

Contextual inquiry in human–computer interaction (HCI) derives from ethnography, a branch of anthropology that focuses on the study and systematic description of various human cultures. In an article describing the transition from ethnography to contextual design, Simonsen and Kensing (1997) explain why interviews as an exclusive data-gathering technique are insufficient: "A major point in ethnographically-inspired approaches is that work is a socially organized activity where the actual behavior differs from how it is described by those who do it." You need to observe and determine for yourself how the work in question is actually done.

Just as interviewing users is not enough to uncover their unmet needs, observation without interviewing also has its potential downsides. First, if you use observation as an exclusive data-gathering technique, you could miss some important points. For example, an important problem or issue simply might not come up during any given period of observation (Dearden & Wright, 1997).

Second, observation itself can affect user behavior. This is the famous "measurement effect"[2] adapted to observation of people. The very act of observation can cause people to change the behavior being observed.

For example, when a person is subjected to new or increased attention, for example, being observed during task performance, the "Hawthorne effect"

---

[2]Study of the problem of measurement in quantum mechanics has shown that measurement of any object involves interactions between the measuring apparatus and that object that inevitably affect it in some way. – Wikipedia.com

(Dickson & Roethlisberger, 1966) can produce a temporary increase of performance due to their awareness of being observed and perceived expectations of high performance. Diaper (1989) points this out as a natural human reaction. Simply put, when users are being observed, they tend to act like they think you want them to. When we are observed at work, we all want to do our best and be appreciated.

3.1.7 The SnakeLight, an Example of How Understanding Work Practice Paid Off

Here is an anecdotal example about why it helps to understand how your users do their activities and how they use products and systems. This example of the effectiveness of in situ contextual inquiry comes to us from the seemingly mundane arena of consumer flashlights. In the mid-1990s, Black & Decker was considering getting into handheld lighting devices, but did not want to join the crowded field of ordinary consumer flashlights.

So, to get new ideas, some designers followed real flashlight users around. They observed people using flashlights in real usage situations and discovered the need for a feature that was never mentioned during the usual brainstorming among engineers and designers or in focus groups of consumers. Over half of the people they observed during actual usage under car hoods, under kitchen sinks, and in closets and attics said that some kind of hands-free usage would be desirable.

They made a flashlight that could be bent and formed and that can stand up by itself. Overnight the "SnakeLight" was the product with the largest production volume in Black & Decker history, despite being larger, heavier, and more expensive than other flashlights on the market (Giesecke et al., 2011).

3.1.8 Are We Gathering Data on an Existing System or a New System?

When gathering data and thinking about designs for a new system, analysts and designers can be strongly biased toward thinking about only the new system. Students sometimes ask, "Should we be modeling the existing way they do it or as it would be done with the new system?" This is asking whether to do modeling in the problem domain or the solution domain, the work domain or the design domain.

At the end of the day, the answer might well be "both," but the point of this particular discussion is that it must start with the existing way. Everything we do in contextual inquiry and contextual analysis in this chapter and the next is about the existing way, the existing system, and the existing work practice. Often team members get to thinking about design too early and the whole thing becomes about the new system before they have learned what they need to about work practice using the existing system.

In order for all this to work, then, there must *be* an existing system (automated, manual, or in-between), and the proposed new system would then somehow be an improvement. But what about brand new ideas, you ask, innovations so new that no such system yet exists? Our answer may be surprising: that situation happens so rarely that we are going to go out on a limb and say that there is always *some* existing system in place. Maybe it is just a manual system, but there must be an existing system or there cannot be existing work practice.

For example, many people consider the iPod to be a really innovative invention, but (thinking about its usage context) it is (mainly) a system for playing music (and/or videos). Looking at work activities and not devices, we see that people have been playing music for a long time. The iPod is another in a series of progressively sophisticated devices for doing that "work" activity, starting with the phonograph invented by Thomas Edison, or even possibly earlier ways to reproduce "recorded" sound.

If no one had ever recorded sound in any way prior to the first phonograph, then there could not have been an "existing system" on which to conduct contextual inquiry. But this kind of invention is extremely rare, a pure innovative moment. In any case, anything that happens in sound reproduction after that can be considered follow-on development and its use can be studied in contextual inquiry.

3.1.9 Introducing an Application for Examples

As a running example to illustrate the ideas in the text, we use a public ticket sales system for selling tickets for entertainment and other events. Occasionally, when necessary, we will provide other specific examples.

The existing system: The Middleburg University Ticket Transaction Service

Middleburg, a small town in middle America, is home to Middleburg University, a state university that operates a service called the Middleburg University Ticket Transaction Service (MUTTS). MUTTS has operated successfully for several years as a central campus ticket office where people buy tickets from a ticket seller for entertainment events, including concerts, plays, and special presentations by public speakers. Through this office MUTTS makes arrangements with event sponsors and sells tickets to various customers.

The current business process suffers from numerous drawbacks:

- All customers have to go to one location to buy tickets in person.
- MUTTS has partnered with Tickets4ever.com as a national online tickets distribution platform. However, Tickets4ever.com suffers from low reliability and has a reputation for poor user experience.
- Current operation of MUTTS involves multiple systems that do not work together very well.
- The rapid hiring of ticket sellers to meet periodic high demand is hampered by university and state hiring policies.

Organizational context of the existing system

The desire to expand the business coincides with a number of other dynamics currently affecting MUTTS and Middleburg University.

- The supervisor of MUTTS wishes to expand revenue-generating activities.
- To leverage their increasing national academic and athletic prominence, the university is seeking a comprehensive customized solution that includes integration of tickets for athletic events (currently tickets to athletic events are managed by an entirely different department).
- By including tickets for athletic events that generate significant revenue, MUTTS will have access to resources to support their expansion.
- The university is undergoing a strategic initiative for unified branding across all its departments and activities. The university administration is receptive to creative design solutions for MUTTS to support this branding effort.

The proposed new system: The Ticket Kiosk System

The Middleburg University Ticket Transaction Service (MUTTS) wants to expand its scope and expand to more locations, but it is expensive to rent space in business buildings around town and the kind of very small space it needs is rarely available. Therefore, the administrators of MUTTS and the Middleburg University administration have decided to switch the business from the ticket window to kiosks, which can be placed in many more locations across campus and around town.

Middleburg is home to a large public university and has reliable and well-used public transportation provided by its bus system operated by Middleburg Bus, Inc. There are several bus stops, including the library and the shopping mall, where there is space to add a kiosk for a reasonable leasing fee to the bus company.

A number of these bus stops seem good locations for kiosks; buses come and go every few minutes. Some of the major stops are almost like small bus stations with good-sized crowds getting on and off buses.

In addition to an expected increase in sales, there will be cost savings in that a kiosk requires no personnel at the sales outlets. The working title for the new system is Ticket Kiosk System, pending recommendations from our design team. The Ticket Kiosk System will have a completely new business model for the retail ticket operation.

3.2 THE SYSTEM CONCEPT STATEMENT

A system concept statement is a concise descriptive summary of the envisioned system or product stating an initial system vision or mandate; in short, it is a mission statement for the project. A system (or product) concept statement is where it all starts, even before contextual inquiry. We include it in this chapter because it describes an initial system vision or mandate that will drive and guide contextual inquiry. Before a UX team can conduct contextual inquiry, which will lead to requirements and design for the envisioned system, there has to be a system concept.

Rarely does a project team conceptualize a new system, except possibly in a "skunk-works" kind of project or within a small invention-oriented organization. The system concept is usually well established before it gets to the user experience people or the software engineering people, usually by upper management and/or marketing people. A clear statement of this concept is important because it acts as a baseline for reality checks and product scope and as something to point to in the middle of later heated design discussions.

- A system concept statement is typically 100 to 150 words in length.
- It is a mission statement for a system to explain the system to outsiders and to help set focus and scope for system development internally.
- Writing a good system concept statement is not easy.
- The amount of attention given per word is high. A system concept statement is not just written; it is iterated and refined to make it as clear and specific as possible.

An effective system concept statement answers at least the following questions:

- What is the system name?
- Who are the system users?

- What will the system do?
- What problem(s) will the system solve? (You need to be broad here to include business objectives.)
- What is the design vision and what are the emotional impact goals? In other words, what experience will the system provide to the user? This factor is especially important if the system is a commercial product.

The audience for the system concept statement is broader than that of most other deliverables in our process and includes high-level management, marketing, the board of directors, stockholders, and even the general public.

Example: System Concept Statement for the Ticket Kiosk System

Here is an example of a system concept statement that we wrote for the Ticket Kiosk System.

> The Ticket Kiosk System will replace the old ticket retail system, the Middleburg University Ticket Transaction Service, by providing 24-hour-a-day distributed kiosk service to the general public. This service includes access to comprehensive event information and the capability to rapidly purchase tickets for local events such as concerts, movies, and the performing arts.
>
> The new system includes a significant expansion of scope to include ticket distribution for the entire MU athletic program. Transportation tickets will also be available, along with directions and parking information for specific venues. Compared to conventional ticket outlets, the Ticket Kiosk System will reduce waiting time and offer far more extensive information about events. A focus on innovative design will enhance the MU public profile while Fostering the spirit of being part of the MU community and offering the customer a Beaming interaction experience. (139 words)

This statement can surely be tightened up and will evolve as we proceed with the project. For example, "far more extensive information about events" can be made more specific by saying "extensive information including images, movie clips, and reviews about events." Also, at this time we did not mention security and privacy, important concerns that are later pointed out by potential users. Similarly, the point about "focus on innovative design" can be made more specific by saying "the goal of innovative design is to reinvent the experience of interacting with a kiosk by providing an engaging and enjoyable transaction experience."

Usually a system concept statement will be accompanied by a broader system vision statement from marketing to help get a project started in the right direction. None of this yet has the benefit of information from customers or potential users. However, we do envision the customer being able to find event information, select events to buy tickets for, select seats, purchase tickets, print tickets, and get information and tickets for transportation while enjoying the overall experience interacting with the kiosk.

Upon interacting with the customers and users, some of our objectives in this system concept statement will be adjusted and assumptions corrected.

NB: All exercises are in Appendix E, near the end of the book.

Exercise

See Exercise 3-1, System Concept Statement for a System of Your Choice

3.3 USER WORK ACTIVITY DATA GATHERING

Much of the material in this chapter comes from the contextual design material existing in the literature. We do not try to reproduce these entire processes in this book, as those topics already appear in books of their own, with credit to their respective authors. What we do here is draw on these processes, adapting them to establish our own frame of reference and integrating them into the context of other requirements-related activities.

We gratefully acknowledge the sources from which we have adapted this material, mainly *Contextual Design* (Beyer & Holtzblatt, 1998) and *Rapid Contextual Design* (Holtzblatt, Wendell, & Wood, 2005). Other work we have drawn upon and which we acknowledge include Constantine and Lockwood (1999). A CHI Conference paper by Hewlett-Packard people (Curtis et al., 1999) contributed to our understanding by spelling out an excellent large-scale example of the application of contextual design.

To do your user work activity data gathering you will:

- prepare and conduct field visits to the customer/user work environment, where the system being designed will be used
- observe and interview users while they work
- inquire into the structure of the users' own work practice
- learn about how people do the work your system is to be designed to support
- take copious, detailed notes, raw user work activity data, on the observations and interviews

In these early chapters we are generally taking the perspective of domain-complex systems because it is the more "general" case. We will describe several methods and techniques that have proven successful, but you should be creative and open to including whatever techniques suit the needs of the moment. This means that you might want to use focus groups, for example, if you think they will be useful in eliciting a revealing conversation about more complex issues.

The goals of contextual inquiry are the same in both perspectives (domain-complex systems vs. interaction-complex consumer products), and most of the steps we describe apply to, or can easily be adapted for, the product perspective. Where appropriate, we will offer descriptions of how the process might differ for the product user perspective.

3.3.1 Before the Visit: Preparation for the Domain-Complex System Perspective

Learn about your customer organization before the visit

Preparation for the visit means doing upfront planning, including addressing issues such as these about the customer:

- For work activities situated in the context of a system with a complex work domain, get a feel for the customer's organizational policies and ethos by looking at their online presence—for example, Website, participation in social networks.
- Know and understand the vocabulary and technical terms of the work domain and the users.
- Learn about the competition.
- Learn about the culture of the work domain in general—for example, conservative financial domain vs. laid-back art domain.
- Be prepared to realize that there will be differences in perspectives between managers and users.
- Investigate the current system (or practices) and its history by looking at the company's existing and previous products. If they are software products, it is often possible to download trial versions of the software from the company's Website to get familiar with design history and themes.

Learn about the domain

While designing for complex and esoteric domains, working first with subject matter experts helps shorten the actual contextual inquiry process by giving you a deeper understanding of the domain, albeit from a non-user perspective. Your contextual inquiry process can now include validating this understanding. In cases where time and resources are at a premium (not an

---

Domain-Complex Systems

Domain-complex systems are systems with high degree of intricacy and technical content in the corresponding field of work. Often, characterized by convoluted and elaborate mechanisms for how parts of the system work and communicate, they usually have complicated workflow containing multiple dependencies and communication channels. Examples include an air traffic control system and a system for analyzing seismic data for oil exploration.

insignificant portion of projects in the real world), you may just have to make do with just interviewing a few subject matter experts instead of observing real users in context.

Issues about your team

In addition, there are issues to address about your team:

- Decide how many people to send on the visits.
- Decide who should go on each visit, for example, user experience people, other team members, documentation folks.
- Set your own limits on the number of visits and number of team members involved, depending on your budget and schedule.
- Plan the interview and observation strategy (who in the team does what).

Your visit-group size can depend on how many are on your initial project team, the number of different user roles you can identify, the size of the project overall, the budget, and even your project management style. Practitioners report taking as many as two to eight or more people on visits, but three to four seems to be typical.

A multidisciplinary team is more likely to capture all necessary data and more likely to make the best sense of data during subsequent analysis. We have found using two people per interview appealing; one to talk and one to take notes.

Lining up the right customer and user people

Among the things to do to prepare for a site visit for contextual inquiry, you should:

- Select and contact appropriate users or customer management and administrative people to:
  - explain the need for a visit
  - explain the purpose of the visit (to learn about their work activities)
  - explain your approach (for them actually to do the work while you are there to observe)
  - obtain permission to observe and/or interview users at work
  - build rapport and trust, for example, promise personal and corporate confidentiality
  - discuss timing—which kinds of users are doing what and when?
  - set scope: explain that you want to see the broadest representation of users and work activities, focusing on the most important and most representative tasks they do

- establish or negotiate various parameters, such as how long you will/can be there (it can be up to several intense weeks for data gathering), how often to visit (it can be up to every other day), how long for the average interview (a couple of hours maximum), and the maximum number of interviews per visit (as an example, four to six)
- Select and contact appropriate support people (determined by the management people you talk with) within the customer organization to arrange logistics for the visits.
- Select and contact appropriate people to meet, observe, and interview: customers, users (who do the work in question), especially frequent users, managers; aim for the broadest variety, cover as many usage roles as possible, plan visits to multiple sites if they exist.

This latter item, selecting the people to meet, observe, and interview, is especially important. Your fieldwork should include all work roles, selected other stakeholders who impact work directly or indirectly, and (depending on the project) possibly grand-customers (customers of the customer) outside the user's organization. You want the broadest possible sources to build a holistic and multi-perspective picture of the contextual data.

Get access to "key" people

For projects in a domain-complex system context, you might also be told by your customer that users of the system in question are scarce and generally unavailable. For example, management might resist giving access to key people because they are busy and "bothering" them would cost the organization time and money.

If you sense reluctance to give access to users, you need to step up and make the case; establish the necessity for gathering requirements that will work and the necessity for firmly basing requirements on an understanding of existing work activities. Then explain how this extra work upfront will reduce long-term costs of reworking everything if analysts do not get the right requirements. Ask for just a couple of hours with key users. Persevere.

At the other end of the spectrum, for consumer software, such as shrink-wrap word processors, users abound and you can recruit users to interview via a "help wanted" ad posted in the local grocery store.

Do not interview only direct users. Find out about the needs and frustrations of indirect users served by agents or intermediaries. And do not forget managers. Here is a quote from a team that we worked with on a project, "It was eye-opening to talk with the managers. Managers are really demanding and they have different kinds of requirements from those of the users, and they see things from a totally different viewpoint than the other users."

Sometimes you may have access to the users for only a small period of time and therefore cannot observe them doing work. In such cases, you can ask them to walk you through their typical day. You must work extra hard to ask about exceptions, special cases, and so on. This approach suffers from many of the problems we described earlier regarding not observing users in context but at least provides some insights into user's work.

What if you cannot find real users?

In the worst case, that is, when you have no access to real users (this has happened in our consulting and work experience), the last resort is to talk to user proxies. User proxies can be business experts or consultants who are familiar with the user's work.

This approach suffers from many disadvantages and often results in hearing about high-level functional needs and crude approximations of what a broad class of users need in the system. The accounts of such proxies are often tainted by their own opinions and views of the work domain. They also suffer from serious omissions and simplifications of often nuanced and complex user work activities.

Setting up the right conditions

The environment, the people, and the context of the interview should be as close a match to the usual working location and working conditions as possible. We once found ourselves being ushered into a conference room for an interview because, as the employer put it, "it is much quieter and less distracting here."

The employer had even arranged for time off from work for the worker so that he could focus his complete attention on the interview. But, of course, the conference room was not anything like the real work context and could not possibly have served as a useful source of information about the work context. We had to convince them to move the whole thing back into the active workplace.

Make sure that the observations and interviews are conducted without undue political and managerial influences. You want to create the right conditions for observation and interviews, conditions in which users feel comfortable in telling the "real" story of the everyday work practice. We once had to deal with the supervisor of a person we wanted to interview because the supervisor insisted on being present during the interview. His reason was that it was a rare opportunity to learn more about what his workers did and how.

However, we also suspected that the supervisor did not want the employee to be complaining to strangers about working conditions or the organization. However, from the worker's view, having a supervisor present looked a lot like an opportunity for the supervisor to evaluate the user's job performance. It meant not being able to be open and candid about much of anything. Instead, the employee would have to pay very close attention to doing the job and not saying anything that could be interpreted in a way that could be used against him. It would be anything but a sample of everyday work practice.

How many interviewees at a time?

It might work out that, via a group interview, multiple users can work together and produce data not accessible through a single user. However, group interviews can also mask individual thoughts. Each user may have a very different view of how things work and what the problems are, but these differences can be sublimated in an unconscious effort to reach "consensus." Additionally, group dynamics may be influenced by hidden agendas and turf battles.

Preparing your initial questions

Script your initial interview questions to get you off to a good start. There is no real secret to the initial questions; you ask them to tell you and to show you how they do their work. What actions do they take, with whom do they interact, and with what do they interact? Ask them to demonstrate what they do and to narrate it with stories of what works, what does not work, how things can go wrong, and so on.

We found that instead of asking them generally "What do you do here?" it is sometimes more helpful to ask them to walk us though what their work specifically entailed the day before and if that was typical. This kind of a specific probing gives them an easy point of reference to make their descriptions concrete.

Before the visit: Preparation for the product perspective

While the aforementioned guidelines for preparing a visit in a domain-complex system context generally also apply to a product perspective, there are a few differences. For one, the context of work in a product design perspective is usually much narrower and simpler than that in an entire organization. This is primarily because organizations contain numerous and often widely different roles, each contributing to a part of the overall work that gets accomplished.

In contrast, the work activities within a product design context are usually centered on a single user in a single role. To observe the full range of usage patterns by a single user of a product, you usually have to observe their usage over a long time. In other words, to do this kind of contextual inquiry, instead of observing several users in a work role for a relatively short time, you have to "shadow" single users over a longer time.

For example, the work, or play, activities associated with a portable music player system sometimes include searching for and listening to music. At other times the same user is trying to manage music collections. Even in cases where the design needs to support multiple users, say the user's family, the complexity of the interaction among different roles is usually much lower in the product perspective, and often more homogeneous than in a domain-complex system perspective.

Where do we start with our contextual inquiry process for such products? The best place to start is by understanding the complete usage context of this kind of product, including desirable features and limitations.

We also have to ask about things such as branding, reputation, and competition in this product segment. To find unbiased information about these issues, instead of looking online for the customer's organizational policies and culture, we need to look for user groups or blogs about using this kind of product and check out reviews for similar products.

Do some initial brainstorming to see what kinds of user communities are primary targets for this product segment. College students? Soccer moms? Amateur photographers? Then think of good places to meet people in these user classes. If necessary, use marketing firms that specialize in recruiting specific target populations.

Cross-Cultural User-Experience Design

Mr. Aaron Marcus, President, and Principal Designer/Analyst, Aaron Marcus and Associates, Inc. (AM+A)

Modern technology and commerce permit global distribution of products and services to increasingly diverse users who exist within different cultures. Culture affects every aspect of tool and sign making. Culture-centered design of user experiences seems "inevitable." Designers/analysts are aware of culture, but may not be informed of specific dimensions by which cultures can be described and measured.

Websites are one set of examples; they are immediately accessible by people worldwide and offer design challenges of "*localization*" that go beyond translation (Marcus and Gould, 2000). Some years ago, Jordanian Website Arabia.On.Line used English for North American and European visitors, but the layout read right to left as in Arabic because the local designers were too influenced by their own culture.

Localization goes beyond languages and translation. If one were to examine the home page of Yahoo.com in English and Maktoob.com, one of the Arabic world's most popular portals in Arabic, one would find not only language differences, but differences in color, imagery, organization, and topics of primary interest. There may be geographic, historical, political, aesthetic, and language differences.

Small-scale communities with preferred jargon, signs, and rituals can constitute a "cultural group." This definition is different from traditional definitions of culture that more typically refer to longstanding historical differences established over many generations and centuries. The modern cultural group may be considered more a social group or "lifestyle group," including affinity groups, social groups, and geographically dispersed groups communicating through the Internet. Today, "digital natives" vs "digital immigrants" may constitute significant differences in "culture."

The challenge for business is how to account for different user experiences that are culturally differentiated in a cost-effective manner. Developers may need to rely on market and user data to achieve short-term success and to avoid wasting money and time on too many variations. Paying attention to culture models and culture dimensions can assist.

CULTURE MODELS AND CULTURE DIMENSIONS

Analysts have written about culture for many decades. Geert Hofstede's (1997) cultural dimensions are well known and well established, although controversial for some anthropologists and ethnographers. Hofstede examined IBM employees in more than 50 countries during 1978–1983 and was able to gather data and analyze it in a statistically valid method. His definition of culture (in his model, each country has one dominant culture) concerns patterns of thinking, feeling, and acting that are "programmed" by a particular group in their children by the time they reach pubescence. The differences of culture manifest themselves in specific rituals, symbols, heroes/heroines, and values. Hofstede's five dimensions of culture are the following:

Power-distance: High vs low—differences between powerful people in the society and others

Collectivism vs individualism: being raised in a group and owing allegiance, or not

Femininity vs masculinity: roles that different sexes play within the society

Uncertainty avoidance: High vs low—the degree of discomfort about things not known

Long-term orientation vs short-term orientation: Confucian values of perseverance, virtue, etc., or other values.

For each culture dimension, Hofstede noted differences of attitudes toward work, family, and education.

CAUTIONS, CONSIDERATIONS, AND FUTURE DEVELOPMENTS

Although Hofstede's model is well established, and many studies have been based on it, there are also criticisms of the model:

- Old data, pre-postmodern (no emphasis on media, sociology of culture, politics of culture)
- Corporate subjects only, not farmers or other laborers

- Assumes one culture per country
- Assumes fixed, unchanging relationships
- Gender roles, definitions debatable
- Seems too general, stereotypical

Studies have shown that even the concept of usability may be biased. A study published in CHI 2009 Proceedings (Frandsen-Thorlacius et al., 2009) showed that Chinese users found fun and visual appeal to be related more closely to usability than for Danish users.

At the very least, awareness of culture models and culture dimensions enlarges the scope of issues. For example, these models challenge the professions of UI development to think about appropriate metaphors for different cultures, user profiles that are culture sensitive, differing mental models, and their influence on performance, not only preference, alternate navigation strategies, evaluation techniques, attitude toward emotions, etc. An additional challenge is introducing culture considerations into corporate and organization frameworks for product/service development and into centers of user-centered design. There are additional sources of insight into UX and culture, each of which has formulated models and seven plus or minus two dimensions. Each of these gives rise to further issues and interactions with culture: persuasion, trust, intelligence, personality, emotion, and cognition.

With the rise of India and China as sources of software and hardware production, innovation, and consumption, it becomes more obvious that computer-mediated communication and interaction occur in a context of culture. It is inevitable that user-experience development must account for cultural differences and similarities. Models, methods, and tools do exist, but many research issues lie ahead. Future development of tools, templates, and treasure chests of patterns will provide a body of knowledge in the future for more humane, cultured design of computer-based artifacts.

References

Hofstede, G. (1997). *Cultures and Organizations: Software of the Mind*. New York: McGraw-Hill.

Frandsen-Thorlacius, O., Hornbæk, K., Hertzum, M., & Clemmensen, T. (2009). Non-Universal Usability? A Survey of How Usability Is Understood by Chinese and Danish Users. In *Proc., CHI 2009* (pp. 41–50). 6 April 2009, Boston, MA.

Marcus, A., & Gould, E. W. (2000). Crosscurrents: Cultural Dimensions and Global Web User-Interface Design. *Interactions*, ACM Publisher, 7(4), 32–46. www.acm.org.

Data Bin

A data bin is a temporary repository—for example, a labeled pile of notes on a table—to hold data—raw contextual data at first and, later, synthesized work activity notes. Each bin corresponds to a different data category or contextual data topic.

Anticipating modeling needs in contextual inquiry: Create contextual data "bins"

There is a spectrum of approaches to contextual data collection from data driven to model driven. We draw on the best of both but lean toward the model-driven approach. A data-driven approach operates without any presuppositions about what data will be observed. There are no predefined data categories to give hints about what kind of data to expect. The data-driven approach simply relies on data encountered to guide the process of data gathering and subsequent analysis. Whatever arises in contextual inquiry observations and interviews will define the whole process.

Alternatively, a model-driven contextual inquiry process means that instead of just gathering relevant data as you encounter it in observations and interviews, you use your experience to help guide your data collection. In particular, you use the known general categories of design-informing models (Chapter 6) as a guide for kinds of data to watch for, looking forward to the data needs of modeling so that at least some of your data collection in contextual inquiry can be guided by these future needs.

From your knowledge you will have a good idea of which models will be needed for your project and what kind of data will be needed for your models. Using this knowledge, you create some initial "bins" for data categories and models into which you can start putting your contextual data, in whatever form it has at this point. A bin is a temporary place to hold data in a given category. As you collect data, you will think of other categories to add more bins.

For example, we will cover construction of what we call a physical model (Chapter 6), which includes a diagram of the physical layout of the working environment. So, if a physical model is relevant to your project, then you will need to make a sketch and/or take photos of the physical layout, where equipment is located, and so on while you are still on-site doing contextual inquiry. In order to meet those modeling needs later, you will also need to take notes about the physical layout and any problems or barriers it imposes on the work flow and work practice.

In the next chapter we will extend and complete the creation of bins for sorting and organizing your data in contextual analysis.

Data-Driven Inquiry

Data-driven inquiry is led entirely by the work activity data as it presents itself, forestalling any influence from the analyst's own knowledge, experience, or expectations. The idea is to avoid biases in data collection.

Model-Driven Inquiry

In model-driven inquiry, contextual data gathering is informed by knowledge and expectations from experience, intelligent conjecture, and knowledge of similar systems and situations. The idea is to be more efficient by using what you know, but it comes at the risk of missing data due to biases.

3.3.2 During the Visit: Collecting User Work Activity Data in the Domain-Complex System Perspective

When you first arrive

Begin your first field visit by meeting the manager, administrator, or supervisor through whom you arranged the visit. Continue with the building of trust and rapport that you started previously. Make it clear that you are doing this for the purpose of helping make a better design. It is a big advantage if, at the beginning, you can briefly meet all customer personnel who will be involved so that you can get everyone off to the same start by giving the overview of your goals and approach, explaining what will happen during your visits and why.

Remember the goal

Often in field visits for "talking with our users," people ask users what they want or need. In a contextual inquiry, we do not ask users what they want or need. We observe and interview users in their own work context about how they do their work as they are doing the work that later will be supported by the system you hope to design.

And, by all means, do not forget that we are on a quest for a quality user experience. The techniques of contextual inquiry and contextual analysis will not necessarily take care of searching out the special aspects of user experience; you have to be tuned to it. So be especially aware of user stories about particularly good or bad usage experiences and ferret out the reasons, both in design and in usage context, that contribute to those experiences.

Establish trust and rapport

The interviews with users should also start with trust building and establishing rapport. Help them understand that you have to ask many questions and "get in their face" about the work. Interviewing skills are learned; observe users doing their work and ask many questions about why they do something, how they do certain things, how they handle certain cases, and get them to tell specific stories about their work and how they feel about the work and the way it is done in the existing environment. Follow them around; do not miss a part of the work activity by staying behind if they have to move as part of their work.

Form partnerships with users

In most consulting situations the person who comes in from outside the customer organization is considered the "expert," but it is quite the opposite in contextual inquiry. The user is the expert in the domain of work practice and you are the observer trying to understand what is happening.

The process works best if you can form a partnership with each user in which you are co-investigators. Invite the user into the inquiry process where you can work together in close cooperation. You need to establish an equitable relationship with the user to support information exchange through a dialog.

As the observations and interviews proceed you can feed the partnership by sharing control of the process, using open-ended questions that invite users to talk, for example, what are you doing? Is that what you expect? Why are you doing that? Be a good listener and let the user lead the conversation. Pay attention to nonverbal communication.

Task data from observation and interview

One of the most important kinds of contextual data to collect is task data. You will need this to build your task structure models and task interaction models in Chapter 6. This is where a combination of observation and interview can work especially well. Get task-related data by observing actual sessions of users doing their own work in their own work context.

At the same time, you will interview the users, but asking only about the task they are doing, not about possible tasks or tasks that other users do. The interview component is used to interpret and assign meaning to what is observed. To have necessary data for task models later, ask questions to clarify anything not obvious in what you observe. Ask questions about the purposes and rationale for each task and each important step; why do they do certain actions?

On the observation side of things, be sure to notice the triggers for tasks and steps; what happens to cause them to initiate each task or step? For example, an incoming phone call leads to filling out an order form.

Learn about your users' task barriers by observing tasks being performed and by think-aloud verbal explanation of underlying information about the tasks, such as task goals. Notice hesitations, problems, and errors that get in the way of successful, easy, and satisfying task or step completion. Probe for what was expected and reasons why it did not turn out well. You will need these answers to model barriers in the upcoming analysis and modeling.

It takes a certain skill to key in on occurrences of critical information in the flow of observation and interviews. With practice, you will acquire an awareness and ability to detect, discern, and discriminate the wheat from the chaff of the flow.

The output of this process is raw user work activity data in the form of lengthy observation and interview notes or transcripts of recorded sessions.

Recording video

Video recording is an effective way of comprehensively capturing raw contextual data where conditions and resources permit. Video recording can help you capture important nonverbal communication cues in contextual data.

However, factors such as the time and effort to produce and review the recordings can weigh against the use of video recording in contextual inquiry data collection. Confidentiality, privacy, and other such concerns can also preclude the use of video.

In addition, video recording can interfere with a close user relationship. The feeling that what they say is permanently captured may prevent them from being forthcoming. They may not be too willing to say something negative about existing work practice or complain about policies at work. Informal note taking, however, can provide a more intimate conversational experience that may encourage honest expression. Despite all these possible barriers, video clips can provide convincing evidence, when linked to the contextual notes, that an issue is real.

Note taking

Regardless of whether you use video or audio recordings of observation and interview sessions, you should consider note taking your primary source of usable raw data. Manual paper note writing may be the most commonly used contextual inquiry data collection technique used in the real world. It is unintrusive, not intimidating to the user, and fits most naturally into what should be a more or less low-key interaction with the user. Alternatively, a laptop is acceptable for note taking, if you can do it inconspicuously.

When taking notes, you must incorporate some scheme that preserves information about the source of each note. We recommend that you use:

- quotations marks to denote what a user says
- plain text to describe observations of what users do
- parentheses to delimit your own interpretations

A small handheld digital audio recorder used inconspicuously, but not trying to be covert, might be beneficial to augment note taking, especially when things are moving fast. One way to use audio recording is as the audio equivalent of written notes.

In this mode, after hearing user comments or observing user behavior, you dictate a short summary into the recorder, much as a medical doctor dictates summaries for patient charts during daily rounds. This mode of operation has the additional benefit that if the user can hear you paraphrase and summarize the situation, it is a chance to correct any misconceptions.

Use a numbering system to identify each point in data

It is important to use a numbering system to identify uniquely each note, each point in the raw data, or each sequence in a video or audio recording or transcript. This last item is necessary to provide a way to reference each note. Later, in analysis, each conclusion must be linked to the associated raw data note or else it cannot be treated as authentic. Some of the ways to tag your raw data for reference in analysis include the following:

■ If you record sessions, you can use video frame numbers or time codes on the recording as identifiers of sequences and points in raw data.

■ If you record sessions, you definitely should assign line numbers to the transcripts, just as it is done for legal documents.

■ If you take manual notes, each note should be tagged with a note identification number tied to the person or persons who are the data source.

How to proceed

Record raw data by expressing it in the user's voice. Because these data are raw, it makes sense to express points in the interview transcripts generally as they occurred during the interview, which would usually be by using the words of the user. For example, the statement: "I like to add an extra egg when I make a cake" naturally reflects the fact that a user is speaking. If you record your interviews, the transcripts will mostly appear as the exact words of the user anyway.

Switching to an expression such as "the user likes to add an extra egg when baking a cake" unnecessarily introduces an analyst flavor that is not useful this early in the process. Moreover, the user's voice describes much closely the user's experience, and subtle use of adjectives and expressions can provide clues on designing for enhancing that experience.

It is *your* job to capture data about the user's work. Do not expect users necessarily to tell you what they want or need; this is just about how they work and how they feel about it. Your team will deduce needs later, after they understand the work. Also, do not expect users to do design, although they might occasionally suggest something they would like to see in the system.

■ Be a listener; in most cases you should not offer your opinions about what users might need.

■ Do not lead the user or introduce your own perspectives.

■ Do not expect every user to have the same view of the work domain and the work; ask questions about the differences and find ways to combine to get the "truth."

■ Capture the details as they occur; do not wait and try to remember it later.

■ Be an effective data ferret or detective. Follow leads and discover, extract, "tease out" and collect "clues." Be ready to adapt, modify, explore, and branch out.

Part of being a good detective, the latter point above, is being willing to deviate from a script when appropriate. Be prepared to follow leads and clues and take the interview and observations where you need to go, tailoring questions to meet the goal of learning all you can about their work practice, work environment, and work issues and concerns.

As an example of following leads, this is a real story told by a team doing a project for one of our classes. The client was in retail sales and the conversation of the interview had centered on that concept, including serving their customers, making the sale transaction, and recording it.

However, during this conversation the word "inventory" was mentioned once, in the context of point-of-sale data capture. No one had asked about inventory, so no one had mentioned it until now.

Our good ethnographic detectives, recognizing an entree to another area of work activities, pounced on that word and pursued a new train of thought. What about inventory? What role does it play in your point-of-sale data capture? Where does it go from there? How is it used and for what? How do you use inventory data to keep from running out of stock on items in demand? Who orders new stock and how? Once an order is sent, how do you keep track of it so it does not fall through the cracks? What happens when the new stock is delivered? How do you know when it arrives? Who works in receiving and what do they do? How do you handle partial shipments?

As an example of dialogue that violates the point above about not introducing your own perspectives, consider this user comment: "I want privacy when I am buying tickets." You might be tempted to say: "You mean, when you are looking for events and buying tickets, you do not want other people in line to know what you are doing?" To which the user might respond: "Yes, that is what I mean." A better way to handle the user's comment here would have been with a follow-up question such as "Can you elaborate what you mean by wanting privacy?"

Pay attention to information needs of users

As you talk with users in the work roles, try to identify their information needs in the context of the work activities and tasks, as they do their jobs in the work domain. Do the current work practices and the current software systems provide information needed by users to do their jobs? Is the needed information provided at the time it is needed and in the form it is needed? And beware of "information-flooding screens."

When designers do not know what users need, they often fall back on the unjustifiable excuse that the users themselves will know what they need. These designers then create designs that display all information available or all the information users *might* need, in an "information flooding screen," and let the users sort it out. The designer's assumption is that all the information needed is presented—the "it is all there" syndrome—and the users are in the best position to know which parts are needed for which functions/tasks and what format is best for the job. This is a thinly veiled copout for not doing the necessary upfront analysis to inform the design.

What about design ideas that crop up?

Contextual inquiry is not about design, but you do not want to lose any good ideas, so you should make note of design ideas from users as they come up and then get back to asking about work practice. It is normal for users to suggest design ideas, often very specific and sometimes not very practical. It is the interviewer's responsibility to take note of these suggestions, but to ask more questions to connect them back to work practice. Ask "why?" How does that suggestion fit into your workflow? What part of your work leads to a need for this?

What about analyst and designer ideas that crop up?

Similarly, make note of design ideas from your own team and tag them as such. Just as with users, it is normal for analysts to get design ideas during interviews or during subsequent analysis activities.

Because such suggestions can introduce analyst bias into what is supposed to be all about user data, "righteous" analysts may want to ignore them. But even analyst ideas generated in the action of contextual inquiry are real data and it would be a shame to lose them. So to include analyst and designer data in contextual inquiry, we suggest getting user confirmation by asking about these ideas and keeping clear the source; be sure to label or tag such notes as analyst ideas.

Questions not to ask

Do not expect you can ask customers and users for direct answers to the questions that will lead you straight to design. Remember that contextual inquiry is often called the process for discovering what users cannot tell you. In his "column" on the User Interface Engineering Website, Jared Spool (2010) advises us about three specific questions not to ask customers or users during field visits. We summarize the three no-no questions here:

- Do not ask about the future; do not ask users what they *would* do in a given circumstance. The answer will probably not reflect the reality of what they might do if in the same situation but all alone at work or at home.
- Do not ask for design advice, how they would design a given feature. Users are not designers and do not usually have a design-thinking mind-set. You are likely to get off-the-wall answers that will not fit in with the rest of your design; although their idea might work in the present situation, it might not fit other usage conditions.
- Do not ask a question by trying to state what you think is their rationale. You just put ideas in their heads and they might give answers they think you want. Users often do not think about their usage in terms of a logical rationale for each action.

Collect work artifacts

During site visits collect as many samples of work artifacts, such as paper forms, templates, work orders, and other paperwork, as you can. Work artifacts include not just paperwork, but all items used in the work practice and photos of the same.

For example, consider the keys to a customer's car in an auto repair facility. First, they may be put in an envelope with the work order, so the mechanic has the keys when needed. After repairs, the keys are hung on a peg board, separate from the repair order until the invoice is presented to the customer and the bill is paid. Artifacts include physical or electronic entities that users create, retrieve, use or reference within a task, and/or pass on to another person in the work domain. This passing of artifacts should also show up in the flow model.

Example: Work Artifacts from a Local Restaurant

One of the project teams in our user experience class designed a system to support a more efficient workflow for taking and filling food orders in a local restaurant, part of a regional chain. As part of their contextual inquiry, they gathered a set of paper work artifacts, including manually created order forms and "guest checks," shown in Figure 3-3.

These artifacts are great conversational props as we interview the different roles that use them. They provide avenues for discussion given the fact that almost every restaurant uses these artifacts over and over again. What are things that work with this kind of artifact for order taking? What are some breakdowns? How does a person's handwriting impact this part of the work activity? What is the interaction like between the wait staff and the restaurant's guests?

Other forms of data collection

Other kinds of contextual data are also essential in representing work context, including:

- Copious digital pictures of the physical environment, devices, people at work, and anything else to convey work activities and context visually. Respect the privacy of the people and ask for permission when appropriate.
- On-the-fly diagrams of workflow, roles, and relationships; have people there check them for agreement.
- On-the-fly sketches of the physical layout, floor plans (not necessary to be to scale), locations of people, furniture, equipment, communications connections, etc.
- Quantitative data—for example, how many people do this job, how long do they typically work before getting a break, or how many widgets per hour do they assemble on the average?

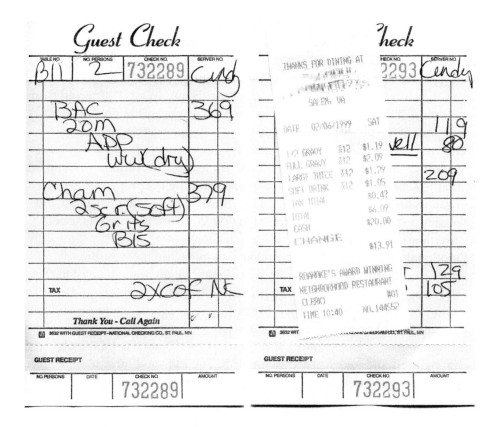

Figure 3-3
Examples of work artifacts gathered from a local restaurant.

Wrap it up

Do not overstay your welcome. Be efficient, get what you need, and get out of their way. Limit interviews to no more than two hours each; everyone is tired after that much concentrated work. At the end, you may wish to give interviewees something as a thank you. Although cash is always welcome, sometimes employers will not like you to pay their employees since in principle they are already being paid for being there. In these cases a "premium gift" is appropriate, such as a T-shirt or coffee mug inscribed with something catchy about the situation.

3.3.3 During the Visit: Collecting User Work Activity Data in the Product Perspective

Roles of users will be different with commercial products. In most cases, work in a domain-complex system context is performed by people in roles that make up the organization, which we will be calling "work roles." In the setting of a system with a complex work domain, a work role is defined and distinguished by a corresponding job title or work assignment representing an area of work responsibility. For a commercial product, a work role may just be the user.

Usage location will also be different for commercial products. The work or play by individual users of commercial products is not usually connected to an organization. This kind of work or play happens wherever the product is used. For example, if the product is a camera, the work happens pretty much anywhere.

The challenge therefore is being able to collect work activity data as it happens, in the context and location in which it happens, without influencing the user's behavior. What are the things users do when taking a photograph? With whom do they interact? What do they think about? What concerns and challenges do they have while taking pictures? What are the barriers to, or inconveniences in, doing it the way they want to?

Emotional impact and phenomenological aspects are more prominent with commercial products. A product such as a digital camera is much more likely to generate a strong emotional component within the user experience and even an emotional attachment to the device. What does it mean to the user emotionally to have a compact camera handy at all times?

A product like a digital camera also has more of a chance to be the object of long-term phenomenological acceptance into one's life and lifestyle. The more people carry the camera with them everywhere they go, the stronger the phenomenological aspects of their usage.

What does the camera's brand mean to people who carry it? How about the style and form of the device and how it intersects with the user's personality and attire? What emotions do the scratches and wearing of edges in an old camera invoke? What memories do they bring to mind? Does the user associate the camera with good times and vacations, being out taking photos with all his or her worries left behind? What does it mean to get one as a gift from someone? What about reuse and sustainability? How can we design the camera to facilitate sharing among friends and social networks?

You may have to observe longer-term usage. It usually takes longer to address these emotional and phenomenological factors in contextual inquiry because you cannot just visit once and ask some questions. You must look at long-term usage patterns, where people learn new ways of usage over time.

Example: User Data Gathering for MUTTS

We performed contextual inquiry sessions, interviewing MUTTS employees and customers. We had three analysts separately interviewing several groups of one or two users at a time and came up with a fairly rich set of raw data transcripts.

At the end, we also expanded the inquiry by asking customers about experience with other kiosks they might have used.

In most examples throughout this book, we cannot include all the details and you would not want us to. We therefore call on the reader for a kind of dramatic suspension of disbelief. The point of these examples is that it is not about content, especially completeness, which we deliberately abstracted to reduce the clutter of details. It is about simple illustrations of the process.

For simplicity, in most of our examples we will focus on MUTTS customers, whom we interviewed in the context of using the ticket office. Here are paraphrased excerpts from a typical session with a MUTTS customer:

Q: We want to begin with some questions about your usage of the ticket service, MUTTS. What do you do for a living? Tell us about your typical day.

A: I have a 9 to 5 job as a lab technician in Smyth Hall. However, I often have to work later than 5PM to get the job done.

Q: So do you use MUTTS to buy tickets for entertainment?

A: I work long hours and, at the end of the day, I usually do not have the energy to go to MUTTS for entertainment tickets. Because this is the only MUTTS location, I cannot buy tickets during normal working hours, but the MUTTS window is not open after 7PM.

Q: How often and for what have you used the MUTTS service?

A: I use MUTTS about once a month for tickets, usually for events on the same weekend.

Q: What kinds of events do you buy tickets for?

A: Mostly concerts and movies.

Q: Describe the ticket buying experience you just had here at the MUTTS ticket office.

A: It went well except that I was a little bit frustrated because I could not do the search myself for the events I might like.

Q: Can you please elaborate about that?

A: My search for something for this weekend was slow and awkward because every step had to be a series of questions and answers through the ticket seller. If I could have used her computer to browse and search, I could have found what I wanted much sooner. Also, it works better if I can see the screens myself and read the event descriptions. And I also felt I need to answer quickly because I was holding up the line.

Q: Did you know you could search for some of these events on Tickets4ever.com?

A: No, I did not know they had local events.

Q: While you were looking at the seating chart, you seemed unsure about what the ticket seller was expecting you to do with it. Can you please walk us through what you were thinking and how that fit in with the way the seating chart was laid out.

A: Yeah, that was a problem. I could see it was a seating chart but I did not understand what seats were still available and could not quite put the layout of the seats in perspective. I had to ask her what the colors meant on the chart, and what the price difference was for each of those colored regions.

Q: **Walk us through a couple of other experiences you have had at the ticket office and do not skip any details.**

A: Last week I bought two movie tickets and that was very smooth because I knew what movie I wanted to see and they are usually the same price. Generally, buying movie tickets is very easy and quick. It is only with concerts and special events that things get somewhat complicated. For example, a couple of months ago, I wanted to get tickets to a concert and I could not get to this office for a couple of days because I was working late. When I eventually got here, the tickets were sold out. I had to fill a form over there to get added to a waitlist. I do not know how the waitlist works, and that form was very confusing. Here, let me show you...

Q: **What do you like most about MUTTS?**

A: Because I am an MU employee, I get a discount on tickets. I also like that they feature the most popular and most current local events.

Q: **What do you like least about MUTTS and what concerns do you have about using MUTTS to buy tickets?**

A: MUTTS seems to have a limited repertoire of tickets. Beyond the most popular events they do not seem to handle the smaller events outside the mainstream.

Q: **What improvements, if any, would you like to see in MUTTS?**

A: It would help me if they were open later at night. It would be great if I could get football tickets here, too!

Q: **Do you buy football tickets regularly?**

A: Yes, I go to about four to five games every season.

Q: **Do you buy tickets to any other athletic events? Can you describe a typical transaction?**

A: Yes, I also get MU basketball tickets for at least a few games every season. For athletic tickets I have to be on the lookout for the dates when the lottery opens for the games I care about. I sign up for the lottery during the three days they are open and if I win, I have to go all the way to the other side of campus to the MU Athletics Tickets Office. When I am looking to buy tickets to MU basketball, I like to look at different seating options versus prices; I sometimes look for an option allowing several friends to sit together. But that process is very complicated because I have to coordinate lottery signup with some friends. We get to buy only two guest tickets if we win the lottery.

Q: **What difficulties do you experience in using MUTTS as the main source of tickets for events?**

A: The main problem is that it is too far away from where I live and work.

Because the envisioned kiosk-based ticket system is so different from the existing MUTTS ticket window, we also wanted to get their thoughts on the proposed kiosk system.

Q: **Now we want you to imagine a new service where you can buy tickets at public kiosks located across campus and the town. In particular we are planning to have ticket kiosks conveniently located at major bus stops in Middleburg. Have you had any experience with ticket kiosks in other places, other towns?**

A: That is interesting! I never bought tickets at a kiosk before.

Q: **Have you had any experience with other kinds of ticket kiosks at places like bus stops or in Metro-type commuter train stations in any big city?**

A: Yes, I lived in New York for a couple of years and I used the MTA kiosks to buy metro cards all the time.

Q: **If we were to put kiosks at places such as university parking lots, the university mall, and other public locations across campus to sell tickets that you get at this office, would you use them?**

A: I would be willing to at least try a ticket kiosk located at the Burruss Hall bus stop because I take the bus there every day. I would also try one near the University Mall because I live near there.

   Most of my free time is outside normal business hours, after many businesses are closed, so a kiosk might be convenient.

Q: **What type of information would you like to see in such a kiosk?**

A: When I look for entertainment options, I want to see the most current events (top picks for today and tomorrow) on the first screen so I can avoid searching and browsing for those.

Q: **In your transaction here at the MUTTS office today, you asked if *Unspoken Verses* is like the *Middleburg Poet Boys* band. How do you envision getting information like that at a kiosk?**

A: That is a good question! I am not sure. I guess the kiosk should have some sort of related items and good description of events. Perhaps even recommendations of some sort.

Q: **Can you envision yourself using a kiosk to do what you did today at this office?**

A: Yes, definitely. I guess I would expect some form of detailed description of the events. I should be able to look for different types of events. If there are pictures, that would help. I should be able to see a seating chart.

Exercise

See Exercise 3-2, Contextual Inquiry Data Gathering for the System of Your Choice

3.4 LOOK FOR EMOTIONAL ASPECTS OF WORK PRACTICE

Look for the impact of aesthetics and fun in work practice, and look for opportunities for more of the same. When you are visiting workplaces, observing work practice, and interviewing people in work roles, you may find that customers and users are less likely to mention emotional aspects of their work practice because they think that is about personal feelings, which they might think is inappropriate in the context of technology and functional requirements.

As a result, you must try harder to uncover an understanding about emotional and social aspects of work practice. For each different work or other role studied in contextual inquiry, try to get at how emotion might play a part. You have to be diligent and observant of little details in this regard.

Look for ways to fight job boredom. Does anyone intimate, even obliquely, that they would like their job to be less boring? What about the work is boring? Where and when are people having fun? What are they doing when they have fun? Where do people need to have fun when they are not?

Where is there stress and pressure? Where can job stress be relived with aesthetics and fun? Where would it be distracting, dangerous, or otherwise inappropriate to try to inject fun or surprise?

What are the long-term phenomenological aspects of usage? What parts of usage are learned over longer times? Where is it appropriate for users to give the system or product "presence" in their lives?

Presence

Presence of a product is a kind of relationship with users in which the product becomes a personally meaningful part of their lives.

3.5 ABRIDGED CONTEXTUAL INQUIRY PROCESS

The full rigorous process for contextual inquiry and analysis is appropriate for domain-complex systems. But the fully rigorous contextual process is not always necessary. Contextual inquiry calls for using good sense and not slavishly following a predefined process. Minimize overlap in raw data collection across interviews. Use your experience to focus on just the essentials.

Another way to abridge your contextual inquiry is to limit your scope and rigor. As an example, we were part of one small project where less than a day's worth of talking to users about their work practice made a big difference in our understanding of the work domain to inform the design.

One of the most obvious and direct ways to abridge the full contextual inquiry process to save resources is to not make audio or video recordings of the user interview sessions. This also saves resources later in contextual analysis because you do not have to transcribe the recordings.

3.6 DATA-DRIVEN VS. MODEL-DRIVEN INQUIRY

Beyer and Holtzblatt (1998) take an approach to contextual inquiry and analysis for HCI based on pure ethnographic field research. That is, their process is led entirely by work activity data. Simply stated, letting data do the driving means that if you encounter any information that seems relevant to the work practice and its milieu, collect it. This approach means forestalling any influence from your own knowledge, experience, or expectations and just gathering data as they present themselves.

Data-driven contextual inquiry results in voluminous raw data describing a wide variety of topics. To digest this mass of disparate data points, make sense of them, and put these data to work in informing design, practitioners must apply contextual analysis to extract the concise and meaningful points and issues and then sort and organize them into piles or affinity diagrams. Then the sorted categories must be converted into design-informing models such as flow models, user models, and task models. In the purely data-driven approach, these categories and models are dictated by the data content.

In effect, Beyer and Holtzblatt (1998) recommend not thinking of data categories in advance, but letting data suggest the categories and subsequent models. This will help avoid biasing the process by replacing data from users with analysts' hunches and opinions. Their "contextual design" approach to contextual inquiry and contextual analysis has proven itself effective.

However, Constantine and Lockwood (1999) show that there is more than one effective approach to gathering contextual data to inform design. They promote a method they call model driven, which is in important ways the reverse of the Beyer and Holtzblatt data-driven approach. In their "use what you know" approach, Constantine and Lockwood advocate using knowledge and expectations from experience, intelligent conjecture, knowledge of similar systems and situations, marketing analysis, mission statements, and preliminary requirements to focus your contextual inquiry data gathering to anticipate preconceived data categories and target the most useful data and to get a head start on its organization and analysis.

From this experience, most practitioners know what kinds of models they will be making and what kinds of data feed each of these models. This knowledge helps in two ways: it guides data collection to help ensure that you get the kinds of contextual data you need, but at the risk of analyst bias in those data. It also helps with analysis by giving you a head start on data categories and models.

Certainly not all of this anticipatory information will be correct for a given work practice or system, but it can provide an advantageous starting point. Experienced professional practitioners, having gone through the contextual inquiry process and having done similar analyses in other work contexts, will learn to get through the chaff efficiently and directly to the wheat.

Although their process might seem that it is about modeling and then finding just the data to support the predefined models, it really is about starting with some initial "exploratory" models to guide data collection and then focused data collection to find answers to questions and outstanding issues, to refine, redirect, and complete the models. This "model-driven inquiry" approach also has a solid real-world track record of effectiveness.

The Beyer and Holtzblatt contextual design approach works because, in the end, data will determine the truth about work practice in any specific real-world customer or user organization. However, the Constantine and Lockwood approach works because it encourages you to use your experience and what you know to anticipate data needs in contextual inquiry and contextual analysis. While data-driven inquiry assumes a "blank slate" and a completely open mind, model-driven inquiry acknowledges the reality that there is no such thing as a blank slate (Constantine & Lockwood, 1999).

The Beyer and Holtzblatt approach is rooted in real data untainted by guesswork or analyst biases. But the Constantine and Lockwood approach claims advantages in lower cost and higher efficiency; they claim the search for data is easier if you know something about what you are looking for. To them, it is about pragmatically reducing the ratio of data volume to insight yielded.

The Value of Contextual User Studies in Understanding Problem Causes

Jon Meads, President/Principal Consultant, Usability Architects, Inc.

INTRODUCTION

This is a case study that exemplifies the integration of user studies with agile development. In an agile development environment, the usability engineer may be the user's representative, part of the design team, and, often enough, both.

In order to inform the design and represent the user, the usability engineer needs to understand not only the user requirements, but also the business requirements and process. Also, it is very possible that neither the business requirements nor the current process is as well known as it should be. This case study depicts such a situation.

THE PROBLEM

I was working with an insurance claims processing company as a consultant. Their problem was that there was a high turnover of adjudicators. The adjudicators had the responsibility of reviewing all claims that the automatic processing had rejected and making a final determination on rejection or payment. The adjudicators were skilled workers and required about 6 weeks of training followed by several months of experience to get to the level of performance that the company required of them.

However, the work was both tedious and demanding, and the turnover of adjudicators was relatively high, as was the case for most of their clerical staff. The company asked me if I could redesign the user interface to make the process easier to learn so that new adjudicators could be brought on in less time.

UNDERSTANDING THE PROBLEM

As is usually the case for consultants, you work for a variety of clients in a variety of business sectors. The insurance business was completely new to me and there was a lot to learn. Management was able to explain to me what the responsibilities of the adjudicators were and what the management problem was. The company's business analysts provided me with an overview of the adjudication issues and pointed me to the policy manual, an online reference document with much more information than I could possibly absorb in a reasonable amount of time. The policy manual was the adjudicator's "bible" and becoming familiar with it was essential for them to do their work.

Management thought that something might be done to make finding the desired information in the bible easier, which would help the adjudicators. But discussions with the adjudicators did not reveal any significant problems in finding the information they needed and did not mention it as being a problem for either doing their work or in becoming proficient at their work. At this point I had no idea of what could be designed that would reduce the amount of training required.

There were two things still to do. One was to talk with the trainers to find out what they perceived to be the reason it took new adjudicators 6 months to become proficient. The other was to spend some time observing the adjudicators doing their work. Discussions with the trainers provided the first indication of what the problem really was and where the solution might lie and the observations confirmed it.

The trainers stated that the actual task of adjudicating the claims was something that was learned in a couple of weeks. The remainder of training time was spent learning where to get the information relative to the claim that would support a decision on whether to allow the claim. Watching the adjudicators doing their work showed that they were constantly pulling up new data screens, switching back and forth among the screens, and making notes on scraps of paper.

After spending some time observing the adjudicators at work, the real problem became evident. The current user interface was based on the structure of the underlying database of claims, referrals, subscribers, and providers.

To resolve an issue, adjudicators needed to immerse themselves in the database, searching for information about past claims ("encounters"), referrals, provider/clinic associations, and other pieces of data that would allow them to determine if the claim was covered or not. To do this, they were constantly navigating a complex database, pulling up screens full of data to find one or two items of interest.

It was not the training that was a problem or difficulty with the policy manual. The root problem was that they were doing the work of the computer system, sifting through large amounts of data to find those items that were pertinent to resolving the claim. Contextual research showed that the information needed to resolve a claim could be diagrammed as an object model. This model showed the needed information as well-defined objects and what the data relationships were from the perspective of the adjudicators.

I was also able to determine that the process of adjudicating a claim had three basic activities:

i. determining if a referral is needed
ii. matching a referral to a claim
iii. paying, denying, or forwarding the claim

DESIGN AND ITERATION

Although the process was usually fairly linear, the adjudicator would sometimes need to switch from one activity to another to check up on an item or resolve a minor issue. However, the recognition of these activities as constituting the process allowed for development of a simple conceptual model:

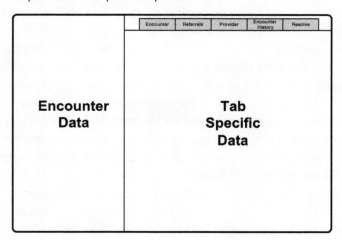

where the information the users were previously writing down as notes was consolidated and kept visible as "Encounter Data." Selecting the tabs in the upper right would bring up tools and data needed for the specific activity the adjudicator was currently engaged in.

The conceptual model, above, was validated ("tested") by several adjudicators and adjusted to make access to data being sought during the referral matching activity easier and more straightforward.

It was at this point that we entered the agile phase of development. We developed an initial working prototype that fleshed out what data should be presented along with where and how it was presented and then went through several iterations of programming and designing of the prototype, changing data that were presented, and adjusting the placement of data and the mechanisms used to present it. These intermediate prototypes were reviewed with a select group of adjudicators until we had a final version that most everyone was satisfied with. At this point, we let the graphic designer clean it up and make it more attractive. Being an in-house application, our graphic design goals were aesthetic: to provide a display that was clean in appearance and comfortable to view and work with.

SUCCESS MEASURES

The final check was to validate the design with measures on time to train and productivity. We checked expected training time by simply allowing novice adjudicators to use the new design to adjudicate a number of claims with only a simple introduction to it. We first measured their performance using the current system and then measured their performance with the new system. During the first 30 minutes of using the new system, claim resolution time was approximately 20% longer than their performance with the old system. During the second 30 minutes with the new system, they were averaging 20% less time than with the old system. By the end of 90 minutes use of the new system, adjudicators were resolving claims in about one-third of the time that they did with the old system.

Since it was the task of finding the information needed to resolve a claim that required 6 months of experience to become proficient, we were comfortable that the new system would not only improve productivity but reduce the time it took to train adjudicators and bring them to an acceptable level of proficiency.

3.7 HISTORY

3.7.1 Roots in Activity Theory

First of all, we owe a great acknowledgment to those who pioneered, developed, and promoted the concepts and techniques of contextual design. Early foundations go back to Scandinavian work activity theory (Bjerknes, Ehn, & Kyng, 1987; Bødker, 1991; Ehn, 1988). The activity theory work was conducted for quite some time in Scandinavia, in parallel with the task analysis work in Europe and the United Kingdom. More recent conferences and special issues have been devoted to the topic (Lantz & Gulliksen, 2003). Much of the initial work in this "school" was directed at the impact of computer-based systems on human labor and democracy within the organizations of the affected workers. This singular focus on human work activities shines through into contextual inquiry and analysis.

Work Activity Theory

Work activity theory in HCI stemmed from a democratic movement that flourished in Scandinavia during the 1980s. It emphasized human labor and human activities as complex, goal-directed and socially situated phenomena mediated by tool usage.

3.7.2 Roots in Ethnography

A second essential foundation for contextual inquiry is ethnography, an investigative field rooted in anthropology (LeCompte & Preissle, 1993). Anthropologists spend significant amounts of time living with and studying a particular group of humans or other possibly more intelligent animals, usually in social settings of primitive cultures. The goal is to study and document details of their daily lives and existence.

In a trend toward design driven by work practice in context, quick and dirty varieties of ethnography, along with other hermeneutic approaches (concerned with ways to explain, translate, and interpret perceived reality) (Carroll, Mack, & Kellogg, 1988), have been adapted into HCI practice as qualitative tools for understanding design requirements. Contextual inquiry and analysis are examples of an adaptation of this kind of approach as part of the evolution of requirements elicitation techniques.

The characteristics that define ethnography in anthropology are what make it just right for adaptation in HCI, where it takes place in the natural setting of the people being studied; it involves observation of user activities, listening to what users say, asking questions, and discussing the work with the people who do it; and it is based on the holistic view of understanding behavior in its context.

In contrast to long-term field studies of "pure" ethnography, with its cultural, anthropological, and social perspectives, the "quick and dirty" version of ethnography has been adapted for HCI. Although involving significantly shorter time with subjects and correspondingly less depth of analysis, this version still requires observation of subjects in their own environment and still requires attending to the sociality of the subjects in their work context (Hughes et al., 1995). For example, Hughes et al. (1994) describe application of ethnography in the area of computer-supported cooperative work (CSCW), a sub-area of HCI.

Lewis et al. (1996) describe an ethnographic-based approach to system requirements and design that parallels much of the contextual inquiry process described here. Rogers and Belloti (1997) tell how they harnessed ethnography as a research tool to serve as a practical requirements and design process. Blythin, Rouncefield, and Hughes (1997) address the adaptation of ethnography from research to commercial system development.

3.7.3 Getting Contextual Studies into HCI

The foundations for contextual design in HCI were laid by researchers at Digital Equipment Corporation (Whiteside & Wixon, 1987; Wixon, 1995; Wixon, Holtzblatt, & Knox, 1990). By 1988, several groups in academia and industry were already reporting on early contextual field studies (Good, 1989) in the United States and the United Kingdom (notably the work of Andrew Monk). Similar trends were also beginning in the software world (Suchman, 1987). Almost a decade later, Wixon and Ramey (1996) produced an edited collection of much more in-depth reports on case studies of real application of contextual studies in the field. Whiteside, Bennett, and Holtzblatt (1988) helped integrate the concept of contextual studies into the UX process.

3.7.4 Connections to Participatory Design

Contextual inquiry and analysis are part of a collection of collaborative and participatory methods that evolved in parallel courses over the past couple of decades. These methods share the characteristic that they directly involve users not trained in specialized methods, such as task analysis. Among these are participatory design and collaborative analysis of requirements and design developed by Muller and associates (1993a, 1993b) and collaborative users' task analysis (Lafrenière 1996).

Contextual Analysis: Consolidating and Interpreting Work Activity Data

4

Objectives

After you read this chapter, you will:

1. Have acquired an initial understanding of the concept of work roles
2. Know how to synthesize and manage work activity notes from raw contextual data
3. Be prepared to create an initial flow model from work activity notes to represent how work gets done
4. Consolidate large sets of user data using a work activity affinity diagram to identify unifying and underlying themes about work domains

> ### Contextual Analysis
>
> Contextual analysis is the systematic analysis—identification, sorting, organization, interpretation, consolidation, and communication—of the contextual user work activity data gathered in contextual inquiry, for the purpose of understanding the work context for a new system to be designed.

4.1 INTRODUCTION

4.1.1 You Are Here

We begin each process chapter with a "you are here" picture of the chapter topic in the context of the Wheel lifecycle template; see Figure 4-1. We have talked about eliciting work activity data (Chapter 3) and now we will analyze that data to understand the work context for the new system you are about to design.

Our source for much of this material on contextual analysis comes from Beyer and Holtzblatt (1998). The credit for this is theirs; any errors of commission or omission are ours.

Although the activities we describe for contextual inquiry and contextual analysis do occur somewhat in sequence, the sequence is not followed slavishly, allowing for reviewing or redoing a stage and, of course, for iteration.

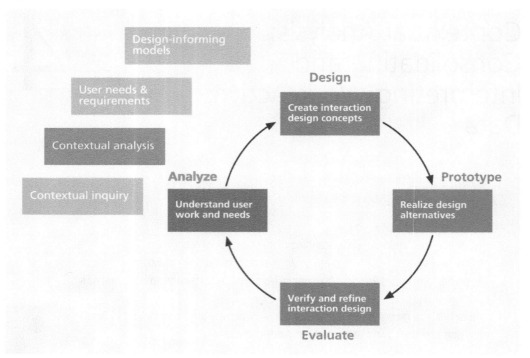

Figure 4-1

You are here; in the contextual analysis chapter, within understanding user work and needs in the context of the Wheel lifecycle template.

Flow Model

A flow model is a diagram giving the big picture or overview of work, emphasizing communication and information flow among work roles and between work roles and system components within the work practice of an organization.

4.1.2 Contextual Analysis Is Data Interpretation

Now that you have used contextual inquiry to observe and interview users about the nature of their work in context and collected corresponding contextual data, it is now time to analyze that data to understand the work domain. According to Beyer and Holtzblatt (1998), contextual analysis consists of user work activity data interpretation, consolidation, and communication. Interpretation of raw work activity data is accomplished through:

- building a flow model and
- synthesizing work activity notes

Data consolidation and communication are accomplished by, respectively:

- building a work activity affinity diagram (WAAD) from the work activity notes
- walkthroughs of all these work products

In the next few sections we will detail the phases of this analysis.

4.1.3 Overview of Data Interpretation

In Figure 4-2 we depict an overview of data interpretation, driven by user researchers who are reporting back to the rest of the team as they review and discuss their raw work activity data. As the debriefing unfolds, some team members construct the flow model as others create work activity notes (described next).

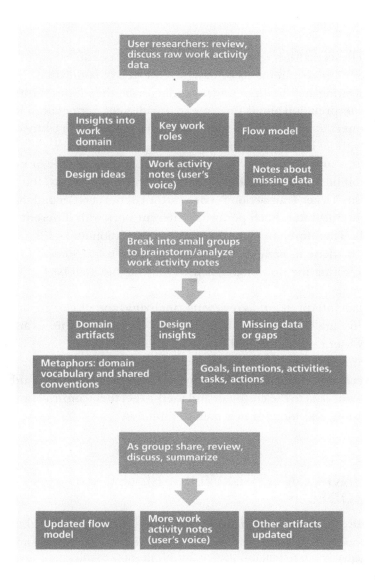

Work Activity Note

A work activity note is used to document a single point about a single concept, topic, or issue as synthesized from the raw contextual data. Work activity notes are stated as simple and succinct declarative points in the user's perspective.

Affinity Diagram

An affinity diagramming is a hierarchical technique for organizing and grouping the issues and insights across large quantities of qualitative data and showing it in a visual display, usually posted on one or more walls of a room.

Work Activity Affinity Diagram

A work activity affinity diagram (WAAD) is an affinity diagram used to sort and organize work activity notes in contextual analysis, pulling together work activity notes with similarities and common themes to highlight common work patterns and shared strategies across all users.

Figure 4-2

Data interpretation in contextual analysis.

Work Role

A work role is defined and distinguished by a corresponding job title or work assignment representing a set of work responsibilities. A work role usually involves system usage, but some work roles can be external to the organization being studied.

We also get a few notes about insights and design ideas here, as well as notes about "data holes," missing data that need to be collected in the next visit. This stage involves individual and group brainstorming and analyses with the objective of understanding user work activities as much as possible.

Two important things about contextual analysis:

■ Contextual analysis does not directly yield either requirements or design.
■ You probably have to do much of your data interpretation separately for each of the work roles.

The first point tells us that this data interpretation step is not an interpretation in terms of requirements or design. This step of contextual analysis is to pull meaning and depth of understanding from the raw user work activity data. Data interpretation allows the team to broaden the connections in raw data, which connect one or two team members with a few users, to connect all team members with all interviewees through sharing and discussion.

The second point, about work roles, reflects the fact that there is little or no overlap of responsibilities, work activities, or user concerns between, say, the Middleburg University Ticket Transaction Service (MUTTS) ticket seller and the MUTTS database administrator. Each performs different work with different concerns and needs. Therefore, much of the data interpretation and consolidation must be done in parallel for each of the work roles. Some modeling, such as creating the flow model, is used to integrate it all back together.

The essence of data interpretation is reviewing, analyzing, and discussing the raw user work activity data. A flow model is constructed. Work activity notes are produced from raw user data and tagged by source and type.

Your interpretation of data will be used in the next visits to the customer/users to check the accuracy of your understanding with the next interviews and observations. Show your data to the customer and users to get their confirmation (or not) and discussion, and look for new data to fill holes.

4.2 ORGANIZING CONCEPTS: WORK ROLES AND FLOW MODEL

As you do your contextual inquiry and analysis, there are a couple of organizing concepts: the flow model sketch and user work roles. While these technically are the beginnings of work models (Chapter 6), we include their beginnings here because they are major organizing factors that will help you maintain an understanding of the overall enterprise. Therefore, you should be aware of them throughout both contextual inquiry and contextual analysis processes.

4.2.1 Managing Complexity with Work Roles and Flow Models

We stand at the beginning of a process in which we will invest a lot of effort to understand the user's work domain for which the system is being designed and how the users of that system are best served in the design. When we are starting cold and just beginning this undertaking, the task seems enormous and daunting. We need two things to help control the complexity and wrap our heads around the problem:

- a big picture of the work domain, its components, and how information flows among them
- a way to divide the big picture into manageable pieces

Because these two things are somewhat in opposition and cannot be done by one single means, we need two complementary concepts to solve the two parts of the problem, respectively:

- a flow model to provide the big picture
- the concept of work roles as a basis to divide and conquer

We cannot overemphasize the importance of work roles and the flow model in almost everything else you do in contextual inquiry and analysis and modeling. These two notions influence almost all the UX activities that follow in this book, including contextual inquiry, contextual analysis, requirements, design, user experience goals, and UX evaluation. Because they are a major component of the flow model, we start with work roles in the next section.

4.2.2 Identify Work Roles as Early as Possible

The very first thing to start doing as you talk with customers and users is to identify work roles. A work role is defined and distinguished by a corresponding job title or work assignment representing an area of work responsibility.

As Beyer and Holtzblatt (1998, p. 163) put it, a work role is a "collection of responsibilities that accomplish a coherent part of the work." The work activities of the enterprise are carried out by individual people who act in the work roles, performing tasks to carry out the associated responsibilities. Sometimes for simplicity we will refer to a work role as a person instead of spelling out that it is a person in that work role.

A given work role may or may not involve system usage and some roles can be external to the organization, for example, a parts vendor, as long as they participate in the work practice of the organization.

Example: Initial Work Role Identification in MUTTS

The two obvious work roles in MUTTS are the ticket seller and ticket buyer. Among the other roles we discovered early in contextual inquiry are the event manager, the advertising manager, and the financial administrator. The event manager interacts with external event sponsors and venue managers to book events for which they sell tickets. The financial manager is responsible for accounting and credit card issues. The advertising manager interacts with outside sponsors to arrange for advertising, for example, ads printed on the back of tickets, posted on bulletin boards, and on the Website. In addition we discovered a few more work roles that we will introduce in later sections.

4.2.3 Start Sketching an Initial Flow Model as Early as Possible

A flow model is your picture of the work domain, its components and interconnections among them, and how things get done in that domain. A flow model captures workflow relationships among key work roles. A flow model tells who does what and how different entities communicate to get work done.

Even though your early contextual inquiry data will be incomplete and not entirely accurate, we recommend you start as early as possible acquiring an understanding of the work roles and a sketch of the flow model, refining as the picture of the work domain, the system, and its users slowly becomes clearer. You will be constantly updating this overview as you learn more via the interviews and observations. Because the flow model is a unifying representation of how the system fits into the workflow of the enterprise, it is important to understand it and get it established as early as possible.

Even the sketchiest flow model will help guide the remaining contextual inquiry. You will want to use the flow model as a reference to keep everything else in perspective as you do the research of your contextual analysis. Within the work domain and within the system, work is done by the work roles described in the previous section, which play a central part in the flow model.

Therefore, you should begin your flow model sketch by drawing icons, labeled with the work roles, which will be nodes in a connected graph that is the flow model. Include any roles external to the organization but involved in any way in the work practice. Add additional labeled nodes for any other entity, such as a database, into which and from which anything related to the work practice can flow.

We will soon refine flow models in more detail.

Example: Sketching the Flow Model for MUTTS

As we conducted contextual inquiry sessions for the MUTTS ticket-buying activity, we sketched out an initial flow model on flip charts, which we recreated here in Figure 4-3.

Later, we give more details about how to create a final flow model (Chapter 6).

Exercise

See Exercise 4-1, Flow Model Sketch for Your System

Figure 4-3

An initial flow model sketch of the MUTTS system.

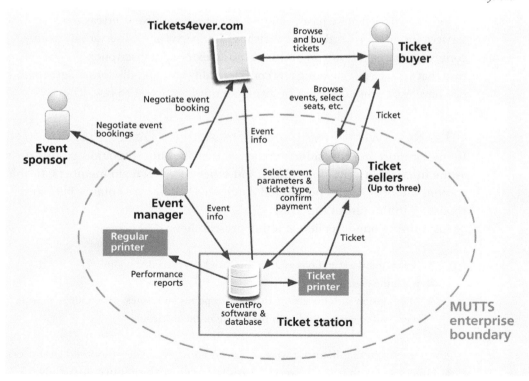

4.3 CREATING AND MANAGING WORK ACTIVITY NOTES

The main point of contextual analysis has two basic parts:

- Converting raw contextual data into work activity notes
- Converting work activity notes into a work activity affinity diagram

This section is about the former, using raw data to synthesize work activity notes.

4.3.1 Transcribing Interview and Observation Recordings

If you recorded your user and customer interviews in the contextual inquiry process, video and/or audio, you must begin contextual analysis with transcription, so you can see the raw observation and interview notes. The written notes or transcripts will of course still be just as raw as the recordings, meaning you still have to do the analysis to filter out noise and boil it down to the essentials.

In our experience we have seen people use inexpensive overseas transcription services for audio recordings of their user interviews and observations from contextual inquiry. If you do decide to use an external transcription service, make sure that you are not violating any confidentiality and non-disclosure agreements you have with your customers by giving an outsider access to raw data.

4.3.2 Reviewing Raw User Work Activity Data

In one or more interpretation sessions, gather the "interpretation group" such as the interviewers, the note takers, and other core UX team members. In this session, the people who performed contextual inquiry are coming back and reporting to the rest of the team.

Recounting one interview at a time, researchers:

- review interview and observation notes and any recorded audio
- retell the events
- in discussion with the group, capture key points and issues, design ideas, missing data, and questions arising in the course of the discussion

User researchers talk about what users said and what they observed that users did. This ensures that the team captures the real work practice and daily activities of the people the system is to support, not just the self-reported practice or official job descriptions.

- Start with one big session to help everyone get going in the same direction, then break into groups to work in parallel. Choose groupings to give an approximate balance of group size, background and skills, and distributing the user researchers across the groups.
- A moderator in each group keeps things on track, while user researchers give accounts of each interview.
- In general, people may interrupt to ask questions to clarify issues or fill gaps.
- As the interviews are reviewed, two things happen more or less in parallel: Design-informing modelers create and refine sketches of the flow model, and note takers make work activity notes.
- After the group data interpretation sessions, the groups get back together for brainstorming to tie up loose ends on the data interpretation.
- Speakers representing each group summarize their flow models, while helpers update these models, on flip charts or laptops with screen projection, in real time per discussion.
- The initial flow models from each group are consolidated into a single flow model upon which all groups can agree.
- Work activity notes are shared, discussed, and adjusted as needed and new ones that come from this discussion are added.

Finally the group engages in introspection about lessons learned. The group brainstorms to evaluate their process reflecting on what went well and what could be improved for next visit and how.

The outputs of this process of review and interpretation are:

- sets of work activity notes synthesized from raw data
- a work activity affinity diagram to organize the work activity notes

These two outputs are discussed in detail in this and the following sections.

4.3.3 Synthesizing Work Activity Notes

As each user researcher recounts interviews and observations from the transcripts of raw data, and during any subsequent discussion about these data, the group helps synthesize work activity note content from raw data and someone designated as the note taker types notes in a specific format.

Because some application domains can be unfamiliar to some team members, the work activity note synthesis should be done by people who have already been immersed in the contextual data, probably the same people who did the interviews and observations. The notes should be captured in some kind of computer-readable form, whether it is in a word processor, a spreadsheet, or directly into a database system. Ideally, the final set of synthesized work activity notes should represent raw data so well that the team never has to go back to the raw data to answer questions, fill in blanks, determine what the real point was, or to sort out context.

The step of synthesizing work activity notes from raw data of interview transcripts and observation notes is an important one. We have found from experience that this step is easy to get wrong, so we spell the process out in detail here. Work activity notes that do not work will almost surely lead you to a frustrating, time-consuming, and unsuccessful activity for building the work activity affinity diagram (WAAD).

As we proceed we will introduce guidelines for synthesizing work activity notes, starting here. (NB: the special green font used in the next line denotes such a guideline.)

As you create each new work activity note, tag it with a source ID, a unique identifier of the person being observed and/or interviewed when the note was written.

These tags are essential links to follow back to the source person in case further questions must be asked about missing data, unanswered questions, etc. Unless it will be otherwise obvious, you should also tag each work activity note with the work role with which the note is associated. Later, when we build the WAAD, we will need to know the work role referred to by each note because we often compartmentalize the WAAD by work roles.

Paraphrase and synthesize instead of quoting raw data text verbatim.

It is perfectly acceptable and often advised to paraphrase and rephrase or to condense or summarize to make your own synthesized user "statements." We want the user's perspective but not necessarily verbatim quotes of the user's words, which can be verbose and indirect. For paraphrased statements, you should maintain the user's perspective and remain true to the user's intentions.

You should not introduce any new content and keep the expression terse and to the point. It is the analyst's responsibility to abstract out a clear and concise statement conveying the substance of the issue in question.

For example:

> Raw data: "I think of sports events as social events, so I like to go with my friends. The problem is that we often have to sit in different places, so it is not as much fun. It would be better if we could sit together."

In the user's perspective: "When I am looking to buy student tickets to MU basketball, I look for an option allowing several friends to sit together." (Note that this reference to basketball games was taken from elsewhere in the raw interview data gathered from that user.)

Sometimes the paraphrasing and abstraction can lead to a simple neutral "factual" statement. For example, using the same raw data as in the previous example, we get this statement in a factual perspective: "Many students who buy MU basketball tickets want the option to sit with their friends."

Regardless of whether you write your work activity notes in the user's perspective, you should still retain *a work domain perspective*. In other words, we want to stay with observed work practice and not start moving too quickly into needs and requirements and definitely not into design.

Make each work activity note a simple declarative point instead of quoting an interviewer's question plus the user's answer.

Questions coming from the interviewer and confirmed by the user should be worded as if they came from the user.

Filter out all noise and fluff; make each note compact and concise, easily read and understood at a glance.

Raw user data are usually too verbose. You must filter out the noise and irrelevant verbiage, boiling it down to the essence.

Be brief: Keep a note to one to three succinct sentences.

Embrace breviloquence; eschew grandiloquence.

Example (how not to do it): Here is a work activity note that a student team made in a work activity note synthesis exercise for a real-world document management system. It is obviously a verbatim copy, grabbing words from raw data without any synthesis. The resulting "note" is full of noise and will require repeated readings to understand the key idea later:

U12-63 Ah, they just, they sign and mark, let me see if I have one that I can pull up, it's like that, they've changed it. But here they mark like satisfactory or unsatisfactory. It's like applied from the date that they sign. And mark satisfactory, unsatisfactory and then the date. And students can have one unsatisfactory and still pass the exam.

Here are some examples of good work activity notes for the aforementioned excerpt of the interview transcript. Note that both of these work activity notes are about what the user perceives as "factual" rather than expressing user experience:

> At the conclusion of a research defense exam each faculty member on the student's committee signs and dates an exam card to indicate if the student's performance was satisfactory or unsatisfactory.

> A student is considered to pass a research defense exam if he or she earns an assessment of "satisfactory" from all or all-but-one of the research committee.

Each note should contain just one concept, idea, or fact, with possibly one rationale statement for it. Break a long work activity note into shorter work activity notes.

An example of a rationale statement is "I do not ask for printed confirmations of my ticket transactions because I am afraid someone else might find it and use my credit card number." If there are two reasons in the rationale for the idea or concept in the note, split it into two notes.

Make each note complete and self-standing.

Be sure that each note is complete enough to stand on its own, a note that everyone can understand independently of all the others. Always resolve ambiguities and missing information as you synthesize your notes. Because the notes will be shuffled, sorted, and mixed in various ways, each note will get separated from its companions, losing any context it got from them.

Never **use an indefinite pronoun, such as "this," "it," "they," or "them" unless its referent has already been identified in the same note.**

State the work role that a person represents rather than using "he" or "she."

Add words to disambiguate and explain references to pronouns or other context dependencies.

When the antecedent is in the same work activity note, it is not a problem. However, if you separate the two sentences into two notes, you probably have to repeat the thought of the first sentence in the second note. Otherwise, the connection to the concept can be lost.

As an example of good work activity notes, consider this rather short passage of raw data in the transcript:

> U10: I think it should, I think it should go to the faculty advisor electronically because, you know, the campus mail could take a couple of days to reach.

That passage can result in several individual points as captured in these work activity notes (again, in the factual perspective), filling in some details that were established in further questioning of the user.

> Exam notecard goes to faculty advisor *before exam*.
>
> Exam notecards are currently sent to faculty advisors via campus mail, but could take a couple of days to reach them.
>
> Exam notecard should be sent to the faculty advisor electronically [design idea].

Avoid repetition of the same information in multiple places.

In general, things that go into the flow model, such as naming the work roles, do not go into the work activity notes or the WAAD. Similarly, things that go into user class definitions do not go into work activity notes.

User Class

A user class is a description of the relevant characteristics of the user population who can take on a particular work role. User class descriptions can include such characteristics as demographics, skills, knowledge, experience, and special needs—for example, because of physical limitations.

Example: Work Activity Note Synthesis for MUTTS

As inputs to this example of work activity note synthesis, we repeat selected comments from the raw data transcripts in the previous example of data gathering to show the relationship to the synthesized work activity notes. Each of these notes would be labeled with "ticket buyer" as the associated work role.

Here we show potential work activity notes that could be synthesized; others could be just as plausible. Note the cases where we had to add text (in italics) to fill in context lost due to breaking a comment into pieces. These user comments are perhaps more design oriented than typical, but that is what we got.

User comment:

> It is too difficult to get enough information about events from a ticket seller at the ticket window. For example, sometimes I want to see information about popular

events that are showing downtown this week. I always get the feeling that there are other good events that I can choose from but I just do not know which ones are available and the ticket seller usually is not willing or able to help much, especially when the ticket window is busy. Also, it is hard to judge just from the information available at the ticket window whether it has been well received by others.

Synthesized work activity notes:

It is too difficult to get enough information about events from a ticket seller at the ticket window.

I want to know about current and popular events.

I would like to be able to find my own events and not depend on the ticket seller to do all the browsing and searching.

There are potential communication gaps because the ticket seller does not always understand my needs.

During peak times, the level of personal attention from the ticket seller is minimal.

It would be nice to get reviews and other feedback from people who have already seen the show.

[Design idea] Consider including capability for people to add reviews and to rate reviews. Question: Should this capability be located at the event venues rather than the kiosk?

User comment (in response to thinking ahead about including athletic events):

When I am looking to buy student tickets to MU basketball, I like to look at different seating options vs. prices; I sometimes look for an option allowing several friends to sit together.

Synthesized work activity notes:

When I am looking to buy student tickets to MU basketball, I like to look at different seating options vs. prices.

When I am looking to buy student tickets to MU basketball, I sometimes look for an option allowing several friends to sit together.

User comment:

Last Friday, several friends and I were planning a birthday outing for our friend, Suzy. We decided to get tickets to *Juxtaposition*, the MU *a cappella* group's show, and I volunteered to pick up tickets on my way home. When I got to the ticket office there was a long line and when it was my turn I found out we could not get eight seats next to each other. I did not know if I should get tickets that are not next to each other or try for a different event. I needed to call my friends on the phone but knew I would be holding up everyone else in the line. I finally got out of the line to make the call and it took a lot more time.

Synthesized work activity notes:

Sometimes I need to coordinate events and tickets with friends who are not with me.

Sometimes I need to buy a set of tickets with adjacent seating.

[Design idea] Consider an option in the kiosk to "Find best *n* adjacent seats."

Taking time to coordinate ticket buying for groups potentially slows down everyone in the line.

[Design question] Can we add anything to the kiosk that would facilitate group collaboration and communication? How about, at least, sending confirmation of ticket purchase to group members?

4.3.4 Extending the Anticipated Data Bins to Accommodate Your Work Activity Note Categories

Here is where you capitalize on the data bins that you began to create in Chapter 3. Extend the set of existing bins to cover all the anticipated data categories for your work activity notes, as you synthesize them from the raw data.

Keep the bins as labeled stacks of notes on your work table so that the whole team can see them. The labels will denote all the useful categories plus a few generic ones for "open questions to pursue" and "issues for further discussion or debate."

Examples of typical data categories you might encounter in your raw data are:

- User and user class information
- Social aspects of work practice (how people interact with and influence each other)
- Emotional impact and long-term phenomenological aspects
- Task-specific information

> ### Data Bin
>
> A data bin is a temporary repository—for example, a labeled pile of notes on a table—to hold data—raw contextual data at first and, later, synthesized work activity notes. Each bin corresponds to a different data category or contextual data topic.

- Physical work environment
- Design inspiration ideas

4.3.5 Printing Work Activity Notes

Although you can use handwritten work activity notes, some prefer to print the notes. Beyer and Holtzblatt (1998) recommend printing the notes on yellow Post-it note stock, such as the kind that has six peel-off Post-it labels per page.

Notes printed or handwritten on colored bond printer paper formatted, say, six to a page, also work fine. If your work activity notes come from a database, you can use the "mail-merge" feature of your word processor to format each note into the table cells for either plain paper or Post-it printing.

Whichever stock you choose, print your work activity notes on plain white or yellow paper or Post-it stock to distinguish from other colors that you might use later for labels in the WAAD.

Exercise

See Exercise 4-2, Work Activity Notes for Your System

4.4 CONSTRUCTING YOUR WORK ACTIVITY AFFINITY DIAGRAM (WAAD)

This is the second of the two basic parts of contextual analysis: using work activity notes to build the work activity affinity diagram.

4.4.1 Introduction to WAAD Building

Affinity diagramming is a technique for organizing and grouping the issues and insights across all users in your contextual data and showing it in a visual display that can cover one or more walls of a room. By pulling together work activity notes with similarities and common themes, a work activity affinity diagram, guided by the emerging flow model, helps consolidate contextual data and generalizes from instances of individual user activities and issues to highlight common work patterns and shared strategies across all users.

4.4.2 What You Need to Get Started

You are going to build a hierarchical diagram of common issues and themes taken from the data. An affinity diagram is used to organize an enormous mound of individual work activity notes into a structure that yields sense, affords visualization of the user's work and, eventually, suggests ideas for designs to support it. You will need a big room with plenty of wall space, dedicated for the duration of the project. You need to be able to leave the work up on the walls over an extended period of time; it will be difficult and disruptive to have to move to another room in mid-process.

Just like having a room dedicated for user experience evaluation, having a room set aside, and labeled as such, for your contextual analysis raises awareness and gives legitimacy to your process. It establishes a real "presence" in the organization so that people might ask, "What is going on? It looks like something big here."

Here is how you should prepare the room:

- Tape up a large "belt" of butcher paper or similar around the walls of the room (Curtis et al., 1999) as a working space for posting work activity notes.
- We have found that blue "painter's tape" holds well but releases later without pulling off paint.

Make sure you have in hand the huge stack of work activity notes. Line up the players, the WAAD team. You will need about two people per 100–150 work activity notes, as the goal will be to complete the WAAD in a short time (1 to 1½ days).

Look for diversity in the WAAD team members. Definitely include the original user researchers and note takers, include analysts, designers, and other members of your broader team, and include some who would not have ordinarily gotten involved until later. If there are still empty slots on the WAAD team, spread them around among other stakeholders and others whom you would like to be exposed to the process. However, you would typically not include the rest of the design team because you will use them in the WAAD walkthrough in the next step.

Establish roles and responsibilities. Appoint one of the original interviewers or note takers as leader or moderator to manage the process and the people, and to keep the WAAD building on track. The larger the group, the more leadership and moderation needed. Sometimes other "natural" leaders emerge within the team doing the affinity diagram. This is acceptable as long as the others are allowed to take initiative and have an equal say in things. However, intervention may be required if a self-appointed leader becomes too dominating.

4.4.3 Set Rules of the Game

The moderator explains how it works. Shuffle the work activity notes so that each player gets a variety and no person in your group gets the notes from just one interviewee. Deal out a limited number of notes to each team member.

Sometimes handing out too many notes at the beginning can overwhelm novice practitioners, preventing them from getting a handle on where to start. In these cases, it can help to limit the number of notes each person gets initially, requiring them to deal with those before they get more. In our experience, 20 notes per person work well to get started.

- Allow time for each person to see what they have in their "hand."
- At the beginning, the process starts out slowly and sequentially, with the moderator explaining each step, so that everyone can see how it works and can be part of the discussion.
- Let the initial work activity notes themselves drive the organization process.
- Someone starts by "playing" one work activity note:
  - reading the note aloud
  - possibly characterizing it with some other descriptive terms
  - possibly entertaining some discussion by the group about its meaning
- Then that person posts it somewhere at the bottom of the large butcher paper working space.

Because you are just getting started, you will not know how the structure will turn out. Therefore, it is best to start as low on the butcher paper as possible, building upward and leaving room for more and more levels. It is, after all, literally a bottom-up process. When the initial "hand" is played by everyone, deal out more until all the notes are gone.

4.4.4 Avoid Inappropriate Mind-Sets in Dealing with Work Activity Notes

When your team is considering each work activity note as you build your work activity affinity diagram, having the right mind-set can help determine success. Here are some tips.

Sit on your designer and implementer instincts.

When discussing and organizing work activity notes, try to avoid too many discussions about design and any discussions about implementation. In one of our sessions, a team member rejected a work activity note by saying, "This note has a good idea but it is about something that will not be implemented in this version." How could he possibly know this early whether it could be implemented in this version? It sounded to us like unwarranted developer bias.

Because these comments were so far off base, we paused the session to remind everyone of the goals of this activity.

As an example, in one session we encountered a note about a comment from a potential Ticket Kiosk System user that it would help in transaction planning to know when the next bus is expected to arrive. Knowing that the technology for tracking buses would be out of reach, analysts rejected the note. But bus tracking is not the only way to address this still legitimate user need. At a minimum, for example, the kiosk could display information about the average arrival frequencies for buses on each route.

Do not make sweeping decisions involving technology solutions.

For example, for a student forms management system, the team was working with the mind-set of all-electronic forms. For programs of study, graduate students currently need to visit each committee member to get a signature on paper forms, leading to issues of delays and tracking down people. So, electronic forms sent via the Internet make for a better solution. However, electronic forms do not turn out to be the best solution in all cases. Because graduate student thesis defense approval forms are typically signed by the thesis committee at the time and place of the defense, paper forms are the still the simplest approach for that case.

4.4.5 Growing Clusters

After notes begin to be posted:

- Each team member in turn looks through his or her pile of notes, looking for other notes that are topically similar, for example, about the same user concern or work activity, to ones that have been posted.
- Notes that seem similar are said to "have an affinity for each other" and are read aloud and posted together in a cluster or "cloud" on the wall.
- Neatness is not essential at this point; just get birds of a feather to flock together.
- If there are two or more of essentially the same note, derived from different users, include them all in the cluster to show the "weight" of that issue.
- When no more notes can be found immediately to match the affinity of an existing cluster, someone will pick a new note from their hand to start a new cluster, and so on.

4.4.6 Compartmentalizing Clusters by Work Roles

In cases where the user interfaces and subsystems for each work role are essentially mutually exclusive (except for flow connections to other work roles), it is helpful to compartmentalize the WAAD by using work roles as the high-level group labels. This is tantamount to developing separate WAADs for each work role. You may still have to deal with an occasional work activity note that involves more than one work role, probably by splitting or duplicating the note.

4.4.7 Topical Labels for Clusters

Clusters will grow and morph like colonies of amoeba as they mature into more clearly defined bunches of notes, each related by affinity to a specific topic. This is the beginning of what Cox and Greenberg (2000) call *emergence*, "... a characteristic of the process by which the group interprets and transforms ... raw [data] fragments into rich final descriptions."

As the number of clusters grows, we have found it difficult to remember by what criterion each cluster was formed (the topic of their affinity). Work activity notes are put into the same cluster because they have an "affinity" for each other; that is, they share some common characteristic. But a quick glance at a cluster does not always reveal that characteristic.

As a solution, make a temporary label (before the cluster becomes a group with an official WAAD label) to make the "topic" of each cluster explicit, to identify the "gestalt" of the whole group, the theme that brought them together.

Temporary cluster labels allow analysts to consider the cluster as a candidate for posting further notes without having to look through the notes themselves every time. Shown in Figure 4-4 is one of the clusters for ticket-buying activities with MUTTS showing its temporary topical label.

Topical labels are *only* to help you remember what each cluster is about. When you have a new work activity note and are looking at a cluster to attach it to, topical labels serve as a cognitive-offloading technique. By offloading descriptions of the clusters from your working memory to the environment, namely to these cluster labels in the affinity diagram, you (the analyst) get support for cognition.

As clusters grow, evolve, expand, and merge, so do the topical labels. As you introduce more work activity notes, do not let topical labels determine or constrain the direction you take with a cluster; let data do the driving and change topical labels as needed to keep up. Figure 4-5 is a close-up of the topical label in Figure 4-4, again for our ticket-buying system, showing a couple of extra words added at different times to enlarge its scope during the affinity diagram-building process. Finally, a topical label is only temporary and will be removed when a real WAAD label is applied as the cluster evolves into a work activity note group.

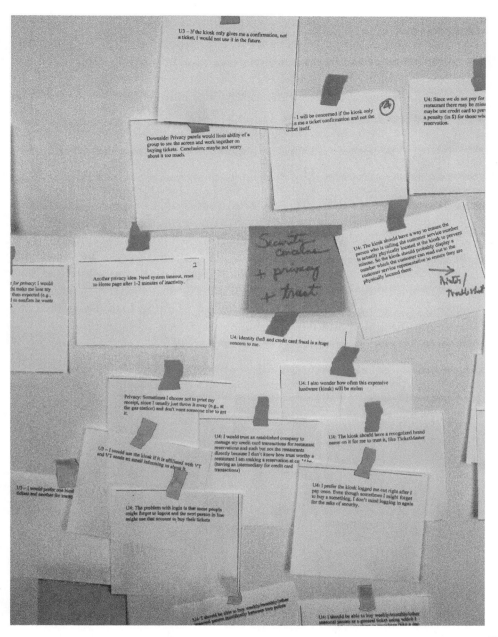

Figure 4-4
Newly hatched cluster with temporary topical label.

Figure 4-5

A topical label that has grown in scope during affinity diagram building.

4.4.8 Work Activity Note Groups

Soon clusters will mature into real affinity groups. As a cluster of work activity notes becomes a group, notes in the amorphous "cloud" of the cluster are posted in a vertical column and the group is labeled with a real group (affinity) label, in the user's perspective.

A group, for our kiosk system, with a first-level label in the user's perspective is shown in Figure 4-6.

4.4.9 Speeding It Up

Later on, when everyone is up to speed, all the players can come up to the WAAD and move things along by "playing" their work activity notes in parallel. Each one walks up to the growing WAAD and posts his or her work activity notes where appropriate, while trying to stay out of each other's way. Although each note need no longer be read aloud, talking or reading aloud is encouraged when useful to help others be aware of current thinking and new developments, such as new groups being created.

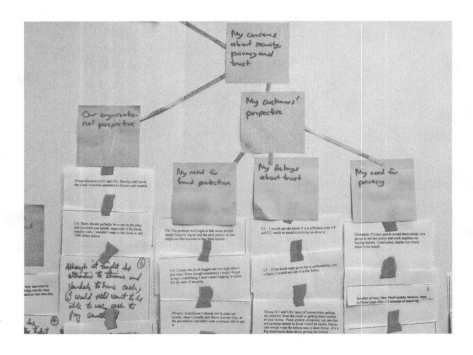

Figure 4-6

Data note group with first-level affinity label.

4.4.10 Stay Loose

Clusters are to be considered putty in the hands of analysts. They are but embryonic aggregations on the way to becoming work activity note groups. On that journey, they must remain highly malleable. As the WAAD grows, it is common, and to be expected, that clusters will move and morph into different clusters, and clusters will be split and/or merged. Labels change; notes migrate.

As work activity notes are handled, read, and posted, if a note needs explanation, clarification, or improved wording, edit it with handwriting on the spot. If needed, for example, to split a work activity note into two, handwritten notes can be added, but do not make up your own data at this point. If you think a note should or could be in more than one place in the WAAD, break it into more than one note by making copies of the note and indicating that other copies of the note exist using a label that says something like "Node-ID copy n" and place the new notes accordingly.

4.4.11 Do Not Get Invested in Data Ownership

No work activity note or group is "owned" by any team member; you just have to go with the flow and see how it develops. The success of the WAAD-building process is determined somewhat by the competence and experience of the analysts at organizing and classifying information, identifying common characteristics, and naming categories. However, there are some checks and balances. As multiple groups emerge, a work activity note may be perceived to be better placed in a different group. *Anyone* can place and/or move a note and make and/or change a label.

Just make sure that other team members are aware of the rationale and the emergence of new group or cluster definitions. There is no single correct affinity diagram for the data; many different outcomes can be equally effective.

4.4.12 Monitoring Note Groups

The goal for groups is to keep them relatively small. Your team can decide the threshold size for your situation, but anywhere from 4–5 notes to 12–15 notes defines the ballpark. As groups get to this size, you should break the group into two or more smaller groups, again based on affinity or topical similarity. Look for distinguishers as the basis for splitting.

When the work activity notes in each hand are used up, the WAAD team should look at the groups. If there are very small groups (one or two notes), review them together and see if anyone can find an existing group for those notes. Think briefly about how to handle any "mavericks" that seem hard to place, but do not spend too much time with these stragglers. They might fall into place later, especially when more work activity notes are made and posted.

4.4.13 Label Colors

The hierarchy of the WAAD has a small number of levels of labeling, usually about three. It is common practice to distinguish the levels by the color of labels. The colors are arbitrary; just be consistent.

4.4.14 Labeling Groups

The team looks through the work activity notes of a cluster and "promotes" it to a group. In Figure 4-7 you can see a team studying clusters in preparation to form groups.

The team invents a label for the group derived from the notes, representing the theme of the group, and often adapted from the cluster topical label. The label for each group is handwritten on a Post-it of the color chosen for group labels and posted at the top of the column of notes in the group.

The rules are that a group label:

- has its substance entirely derived from data in the notes, not a preconceived or predefined characterization
- is written in the customer/user perspective

Figure 4-7

Team studying clusters to form groups.

- is written in a story-telling mode (the user talking to the team telling about their work activities and thoughts)
- is understandable without reading the work activity notes in the group
- captures the collective "meanings" of the notes in the group
- is as specific and precise as possible to avoid confusion in later interpretation
- avoids wordings with low descriptive power, such as "miscellaneous" or "general"

The penultimate point above is, of course, a good guideline for almost any HCI situation. For example, a team in one of our sessions used the label "How we validate information" when they really needed the more precise label "How we validate forms." A subtle difference but important to the intended affinity for that group.

4.4.15 Grouping Groups

After all the groups have been labeled, build up the hierarchy to reduce the structure breadth and increase the depth by grouping the groups. Looking at the group labels, move them around into larger groupings (bringing the whole group with its label).

When you get groups of, again, up to about a half dozen group labels, they are supergroups or second-level (going up from the group labels at bottom) groups, which are labeled in a different color, the second-level color. In Figure 4-8, showing part of the affinity diagram for MUTTS, you can see that we used blue for group labels and pink for the second level.

Similarly, you group second-level labels to form a third level, labeled with yet another color.

As with group labels, wording of successive levels of labels has to represent their groups and subgroups so well that you do not have to read the labels or notes below them in the hierarchy to know what the group is about.

Do not spin your wheels by trying to over-refine things. It is a bit like being an artist creating a painting: use minimal and quick strokes to get a crisp and fresh effect. Overworking it can make it heavy and muddy. Do not seek the one best WAAD; as the master says, there are many paths to climb the same WAAD. You get diminishing returns soon after you start fussing over it.

4.4.16 Number of Levels

Some of the literature recommends a fixed, small number of levels in the affinity diagram. We have found, however, that some categories have more depth than others and that our ability to understand the meanings of groups is sometimes improved by more decomposition into subcategories. We recommend you let data determine the number of levels needed.

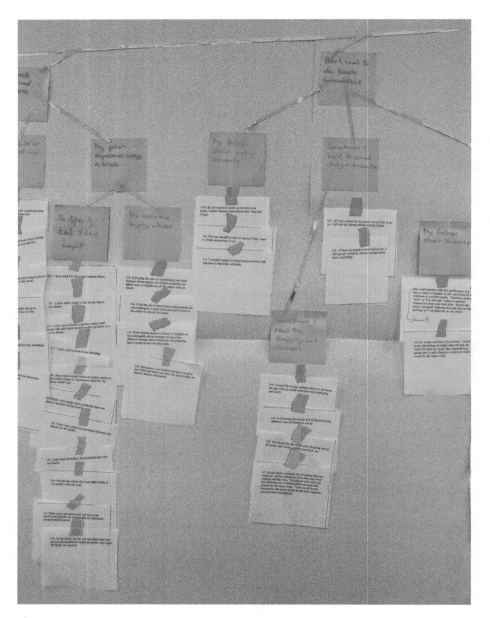

4.4.17 Representing Hierarchical and Nonhierarchical Relationships

The affinity diagram is inherently a hierarchical structure and you need to represent the arcs connecting the groups. In addition to hierarchical levels, we find occasional other relationships between categories that cut across the hierarchy. Things that happen with users or choices that users make in one part of the affinity diagram can have strong effects on choices they make in other parts. When these relationships jump out at you strongly, you can draw arcs on the butcher paper or tack on colored ribbons to represent those connections.

4.4.18 Walkthrough of the WAAD: Consolidation and Communication

One of the purposes of doing a walkthrough of the WAAD is communication, to share an appreciation of user work activities and associated issues with all stakeholders. At the same time, you can review and unify your work activity notes within the structure of the WAAD and look for data holes, work activity notes you still need.

Invite all stakeholders, including marketing, customers, potential users, engineering and development staff, and so on. Decide on a strategy for sharing and communicating the contextual inquiry and analysis results. Tell everyone upfront (before the meeting) how it will work, who is involved, what is needed, how long to plan for, etc. Explain your process in a nutshell.

Your goals will be to garner more input and discussion to help unify WAAD data and the flow model and to achieve a shared understanding of user work issues. This can also be used to brainstorm and come up with key insights as headlines for the executive summary report that may be necessary in some organizations.

- For management, emphasize high-level issues, cost justification, data integrity, security, and such corporate goals.
- Highlight the most important points and issues discovered.
- Create interest with unexpected things learned.
- Show graphical representations; flow models can be the most effective, as they show your interpretation of the flow of information and materials within their business process.

Get management engaged to show them the effectiveness of your process. Get developers engaged to obtain buy-in for the upcoming requirements and design activities.

Try to fit your process into the established methodologies of your organization; keep discussion user centered or usage centered with a user perspective, and real user quotes. Use work activity data to keep things usage centered and to deflect opinions and personal perspectives and to resolve disagreements. After you explain the overview of what the data represent and what you are hoping to accomplish, let everyone walk around and inspect the WAAD as they will.

As people walk the wall individually, taking it all in and thinking about user work and design to support it, several things can come to mind and you should ask everyone to make their own notes about these items for discussion and possibly to add them to the WAAD:

- design ideas—capture them while you can by adding them as "design idea" notes, distinguishable from the work activity notes by using a different color and/or by adding them at a different angle on the wall
- questions—to be answered by the team or by further data collection; add as "question" note in a different color or orientation
- data "holes"—missing data that you have discovered as necessary to complete the picture, used to drive further data collection in the field and added as "hole" notes in a different color or orientation

As an interesting aside, in Figure 4-9, we show a team at Virginia Tech using affinity diagram software on a high-resolution large-screen display as an alternative to paper-based work activity note shuffling (Judge et al., 2008). Each analyst can select and manipulate work activity notes on a PDA before sending them to the wall for group consideration, where they can move them around by touching and dragging.

Figure 4-9

Building a WAAD on a large touchscreen.

Example: WAAD Building for MUTTS

In Figure 4-10, you can see a photo of a large part of the overall WAAD we built for MUTTS.

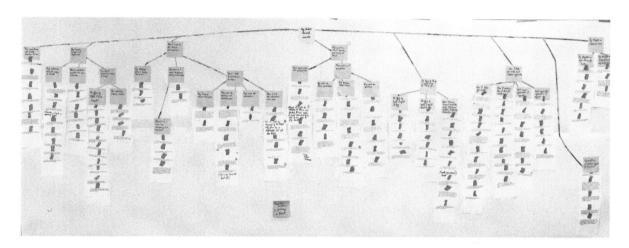

Figure 4-10

The WAAD that we built for the MUTTS example.

Figure 4-11 is a close-up photo of the MUTTS WAAD showing details for three groups having an overall label "The type of things I expect to use the kiosk for."

4.5 ABRIDGED CONTEXTUAL ANALYSIS PROCESS

4.5.1 Plan Ahead during Contextual Inquiry by Capturing One Idea per Note

The idea is to produce work activity notes without the laborious and voluminous intervening raw data transcripts. Experienced practitioners, skilled at note taking and abstracting the essence, can do some of this abstraction of detail from the real-time flow of raw data during the interviews themselves.

4.5.2 Focus on the Essence of WAAD Building

The WAAD-building process itself can also be abridged by creating clusters of all the work activity data notes without building a hierarchical abstraction of the different categories. As you get through the part of the process where you put all the work activity notes on the wall to represent the affinities as clusters, you get a

Exercise

See Exercise 4-3, WAAD Building for Your System

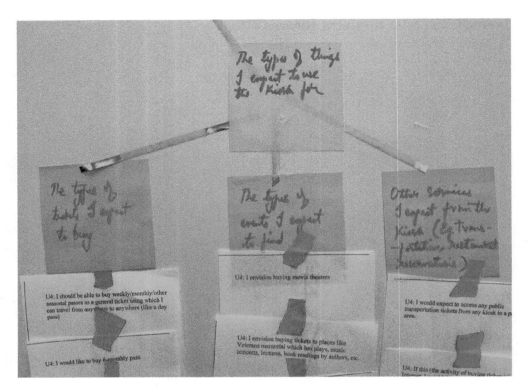

Figure 4-11

A close-up of the MUTTS WAAD.

sense of the key themes and issues in the work domain. Using the temporary labels and walking through the clusters, you can immediately start creating a list of high-level requirements for the system.

4.5.3 Use Finer-Grained Iteration to Address Pressure for Early Deliverables

It is common for a whole project team to be under constant pressure to produce deliverables. Project managers want to keep track of the direction the project is going instead of being surprised after half the project schedule has expired. Many team members think only of designs in the context of deliverables, and most customers think the same way.

Because designs do not materialize until later in the lifecycle, many people think there can be no deliverables in the early phases, such as contextual inquiry and analysis. If you set customer expectations properly for the kind of deliverables you can produce early, it can be a benefit to both of you to share your contextual inquiry and analysis results with others, including the customer. This is an important time to get feedback and reactions to your early analysis so that you can be sure you are on the right track.

Figure 4-12

Doing a full contextual inquiry and requirements extraction process upfront (Figure 4-12) means a large investment in each stage before proceeding to the next and delayed design deliverables, causing conflict with an anxious manager or customer.

Figure 4-12

Coarse-grained iteration of contextual inquiry, contextual analysis, requirements, and design.

An incremental investment in smaller and more frequent iterations is well suited for this common situation, as shown in Figure 4-13: Do a little contextual inquiry, a little contextual analysis, a little requirements extraction, and a little design and then get some feedback from users about whether you are on course.

This could mean that for contextual inquiry you do limited initial interviews with only a few people in the most important work roles. Then you can try your hand at contextual analysis, building a limited WAAD, using it to extract some requirements (Chapter 5), and maybe even doing a little design and prototyping. Then go back and do additional data gathering for contextual inquiry (with perhaps another customer or user role) and make adjustments necessary to integrate the new findings.

4.6 HISTORY OF AFFINITY DIAGRAMS

Historically, affinity diagramming has been used as an effective method for generating hierarchical categories to organize large amounts of unstructured, far-ranging, and seemingly dissimilar qualitative data about almost anything.

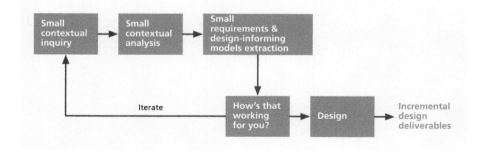

Figure 4-13

Finer-grained iteration among contextual inquiry, contextual analysis, requirements, and design.

The technique is inductive in the sense that it is a purely bottom-up process within which terms used for category labels within the organizing structure come from data themselves and not from a predefined taxonomy or pre-established vocabulary as would be in a top-down deductive approach. As Wood (2007) says, "This process exposes and makes concrete common issues, distinctions, work patterns, and needs without losing individual variation." The process also shows up missing data, to drive additional data gathering.

The affinity diagram has been called one of the most significant management and planning tools in business and has been used to organize many different kinds of ideas in brainstorming and qualitative data in studies. The original conception of affinity diagrams is attributed to Jiro Kawakita (1982) in the 1960s. Kawakita was a Japanese humanitarian who worked in areas of the ecology and rural revitalization and who received the 1984 Ramon Magsaysay Award for International Understanding. Sometimes called the KJ (Japanese people put what we call their last names first) method, the affinity diagram has become one of the most widely used of the management and planning tools coming from Japan. See Brassard (1989) for an early adaptation for business and system development.

Extracting Interaction Design Requirements

Objectives

After reading this chapter, you will:

1. Understand the nature of the gap between analysis and design
2. Understand the concept of requirements for interaction design
3. Know how to use needs and requirements as the first span to bridge this gap
4. Be able to deduce and extract requirements systematically from contextual data
5. Understand the background of interaction requirements in the context of software engineering requirements

5.1 INTRODUCTION

5.1.1 You Are Here

We begin each process chapter in the book with a "you are here" picture of the chapter topic in the context of the overall Wheel lifecycle template; see Figure 5-1. This chapter and the next are about a bridge—the bridge between contextual inquiry/analysis (Chapters 3 and 4) and design (Chapters 7, 8, and 9).

The bridge has two spans—one for needs and requirements and one for what we call design-informing models—each of which is extracted from the contextual data. This chapter is about extracting interaction design requirements within the activity of understanding user work and needs.

5.1.2 Now That We Have Done Contextual Analysis, We Have the Requirements, Right? Not

Except in those few work activity notes, perhaps, where users commented directly on a particular need or requirement, the work activity notes in your work activity affinity diagram (WAAD), not only do not represent designs, but they do not even yet represent requirements. Depending on how well you did them, the contextual inquiry and analysis you have performed so far give you an

Figure 5-1

You are here; the chapter on extracting interaction requirements, within understanding user work and needs in the context of the overall Wheel lifecycle template.

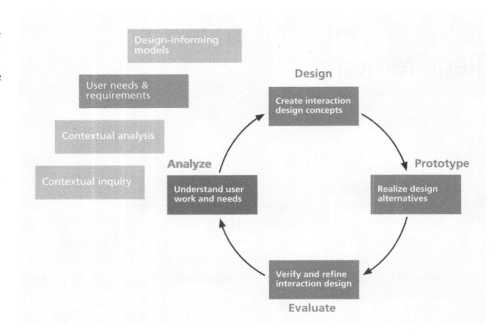

accurate and complete picture of the users' work domain, including their concerns and descriptions of their current usage.

We now are going to attempt to identify the needs and design requirements for a proposed new system to optimize, support, and facilitate work in that domain. It is now our job to comb through the WAAD and any preliminary design-informing models, such as the flow model, and deductively extract those user needs and requirements and thereby construct the first span of the bridge.

5.1.3 Gap between Analysis and Design

Contextual inquiry and analysis are about understanding existing work practice and context. Then we move on to producing designs for a new system to support possibly new ways that work gets done. But what happens in between? The output of contextual inquiry and analysis does not speak directly to what is needed as inputs to design. There is a gap.

- Information coming from contextual studies describes the work domain but does not directly meet the information needs in design.
- There is a cognitive shift between analysis-oriented thinking on one side of the gap and design-oriented thinking on the other.

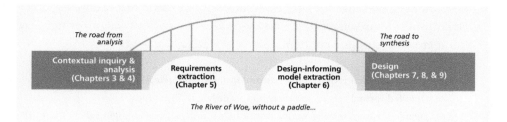

The River of Woe, without a paddle...

■ The gap is the demarcation between the old and the new—between studying existing work practice and existing systems and envisioning a new work space and new system design space.

This chapter is about how we begin to bridge this gap with requirements as shown in Figure 5-2.

Figure 5-2

Overview of the bridge to design.

5.2 NEEDS AND REQUIREMENTS: FIRST SPAN OF THE BRIDGE

5.2.1 What Are "Requirements"?

Almost everyone understands the basic meaning. The term refers to a statement of what is needed to design a system that will fulfill user and customer goals. But when you start getting specific, it is a term that can mean something different to just about everyone associated with developing interactive software systems. To one, it is about ascertaining all the functionality needed to do the job. To another it is a compilation of all the user tasks needed to do the job.

In the UX domain, interaction design requirements describe what is required to support user or customer work activity needs. To that end we are also concerned with functional requirements to ensure the usefulness component of the user experience. Finally, we will have requirements to fulfill the need for emotional impact and long-term phenomenological aspects of the user experience.

5.2.2 Requirements "Specifications"

Before we get into extracting requirements from contextual data, let us look briefly at the forms interaction design requirements can take. One term we often think of when coupled with "requirements" is "specifications."

In past software engineering traditions, a formal written requirements document was de rigueur and could even designate details about how the corresponding software is to be implemented, including such software stuff as

> ### Usability
>
> Usability is the pragmatic component of user experience, including effectiveness, efficiency, productivity, ease-of-use, learnability, retainability, and the pragmatic aspects of user satisfaction.

> ### Phenomenological Aspects of Interaction
>
> Phenomenological aspects (deriving from phenomenology, the philosophical examination of the foundations of experience and action) of interaction are the cumulative effects of emotional impact considered over the long term, where usage of technology takes on a presence in our lifestyles and is used to make meaning in our lives.

object models, pseudo-code, use cases, and software structure. However, currently in software engineering and software requirements engineering there is an increasing recognition that:

- Detailed formal requirements cannot ever be complete.
- Detailed formal requirements cannot ever be 100% correct.
- Detailed formal requirements cannot be prevented from changing throughout the lifecycle.

As a result, there appears to be a trend toward abandoning the detailed requirements specifications in favor of ascertaining the important features and capabilities.

Often people from a software engineering background expect a similar kind of requirements specification for the user interface. However, on the UX side we are talking about only *interaction design requirements*, nothing about software or implementation. Also, as we will see, it is not easy to lay down that same kind of requirements specification for the interaction design, nor is it particularly useful to try.

However we specify our requirements, there is a broad range of acceptability for completeness and detail. For domain-complex systems, with many requirements for compliance and risk avoidance, you may need a rather complete specification of requirements.

Our approach to interaction design requirements follows directly from the contextual data that we have gathered and analyzed. The result is not just a monolithic specification, but a variety of descriptions that, while not necessarily like software specifications, are each part of the whole that constitutes the interaction design requirements specification.

Therefore, at the end of the day, or more likely the end of the week, requirements extraction produces an assortment of deliverables, each of which can be thought of as a kind of "specification"—for needs and requirements and for design-informing models such as personas, tasks, user experience goals, or usage scenarios. That is why all those activities and deliverables are brought together in this chapter and the next.

5.2.3 Software and Functional Implications of Interaction Design Requirements

User needs are really not just interaction needs. Usability and UX include usefulness that we get from functionality. Often an initial requirement extracted from contextual data first appears as a requirement for a broad

Domain-Complex Systems

Domain-complex systems are systems with high degree of intricacy and technical content in the corresponding field of work. Often, characterized by convoluted and elaborate mechanisms for how parts of the system work and communicate, they usually have complicated workflow containing multiple dependencies and communication channels. Examples include an air traffic control system and a system for analyzing seismic data for oil exploration.

overall system capability—that is, it expresses a need for both functionality and user interface support.

As an example, a Ticket Kiosk System requirement might state that a user should be able to buy tickets for up to 10 different events in one session or transaction. We recommend that you devise a way to record the functional needs that correspond to user needs and requirements revealed in this process and pass them on to your software engineering counterparts. It will help them be aware of needed functionality and will help you both stay on the same page during the project.

5.3 FORMAL REQUIREMENTS EXTRACTION

This process of extracting needs and requirements is similar to data interpretation and consolidation sessions of contextual analysis in that it involves a group sitting down together and going over a large amount of data, including the WAAD and evolving design-informing models. But here it is actually easier because much of the hard work is already done.

5.3.1 Walking the WAAD for Needs and Requirements

At the end of Chapter 4 we recommended doing a "wall walk," a walkthrough of contextual data in the WAAD. It is now time for your team to get re-immersed in work activity data; this time with the focus of the walkthrough on extracting needs and requirements rather than iteratively improving the data. The general idea is to traverse the hierarchical WAAD structure and focus on extracting requirement statements from work activity notes.

5.3.2 Switching from Inductive to Deductive Reasoning

Extracting requirements from the WAAD calls for a deductive thinking process. It is deductive because each work activity note in the WAAD is treated as the major premise in a logical syllogism. The second "premise" is everything you know about UX and interaction design. The conclusion of this syllogism is a statement of user needs and requirements you deduce from the work activity note, something we capture in a "requirement statement."

To clarify with a small example from MUTTS and the Ticket Kiosk System, a WAAD note, say in node C19, that says "I am concerned about security and privacy of my transactions" can imply a design requirement (at a high level): "Shall protect security and privacy of ticket-buyer transactions." In the design, this requirement might be at least partially met by a timeout feature to clear the screen between customers. Note that at this level, requirements can be a mix of interaction and functional requirements.

5.3.3 Preparation

Select a requirements team, including people you think will be best at deductive reasoning and creativity. You will need both UX and software people represented, plus possibly system architects and maybe managers.

This team approach enhances SE-UX communication because the SE and UX roles are working together at a crucial point in their mutual lifecycles, describing and funneling the different kinds of requirements to the places they will be used. Choose a requirements team leader and a recorder, a person experienced in writing requirements.

You may need a requirements "record" template in a word processing document, a spreadsheet, or a database schema to capture the requirement statements in a consistent and structured format in an interaction design requirements document (or requirements document, for short in this context). The requirements team will work in the room where the WAAD is posted on the wall.

If there is a need for all to see each requirement statement, you can connect the recorder's computer to a screen projector and show the requirements document on an open part of the wall. The leader is responsible for walking the team through the WAAD, traversing its hierarchical structure systematically and keeping the team on track.

5.3.4 Systematic Deduction of Needs as "Hinges" to Get at Requirements

Start by letting everyone walk through the WAAD, individually and silently, to accommodate those who need to think quietly and to allow everyone to write notes about ideas for requirements. Then begin the main part of the process. As the leader walks the team through the WAAD, one node and one note at a time, the team works together to ask what user needs, if any, are reflected in this work activity note and the hierarchical labels above it.

Such user needs are still expressed in the perspective of the user and in the work domain. Although the user need is not documented in the requirements document, it is an important "hinge" in the mental process of getting from work activity notes to requirements. This interim step will become almost automatic with only a little practice.

5.3.5 Terminology Consistency

This pass through the contextual data is a chance to standardize terminology and build consistency. Your contextual data will be full of user comments about an infinitude of usage and design concepts and issues. It is natural that they will not all use exactly the same terms for the same concepts.

For example, users of a calendar system might use the terms "alarm," "reminder," "alert," and "notification" for essentially the same idea. Sometimes differences in terminology may reflect subtle differences in usage, too. So it is your responsibility to sort out these differences and act to help standardize the terminology for consistency issues in the requirements document.

5.3.6 Requirement Statements

Next, the team translates each user need into one or more interaction design requirement statements. Each requirement statement describes a way that you decide to support the user need by providing for it in the interaction design. Ask what new or more specific user interface feature you should see in the design to support the user needs implied by this WAAD note. There is not necessarily a one-to-one correspondence between work activity notes in the WAAD and needs or requirements.

A given work activity note might not generate a need or requirement. The ideas in some notes may no longer be relevant in the envisioned system design. Sometimes one work activity note can produce more than one need. A single need can also lead to more than one requirement. Examples of work activity notes, user needs, and corresponding requirements are coming soon.

Now the recorder writes the requirement statement in the requirements document by first finding the appropriate headings and subheadings. If the necessary headings are not already in the requirements document, now is the time to add them and grow the document structure as the process continues.

Interaction requirements often imply functional requirements for the system, which you may also capture here for communicating to your software people. For example:

> Interaction requirement: "Ticket buyers shall be able to see a real-time preview of available seating for a venue."

> Corresponding system requirement: "System shall have networked infrastructure to poll all kiosk transactions as they are happening and coordinate with the venue seating data to 'lock and release' selected seats."

This is a good time for the software team members to work in parallel and capture those inputs to software requirements here so that they are not lost.

These inputs will be transformed into software requirements specifications in the software requirements process, a separate process done only by the software team and not part of our scope here. Although software requirements gathering is not officially part of the interaction requirements extraction process, it is a shame to not take advantage of this opportunity to provide valuable software requirements inputs, based on real contextual data. This is also a good opportunity for you, the interaction designer, to coordinate with your software engineering teammates about your mutual requirements.

In a requirement statement it is typical to use the phrase "Users shall be able to ..." and can be followed by a rationale statement explaining the relationship of the requirement to the user need and how the requirement was determined from that need. A "notes" statement can also be part of a requirement statement. Such notes are not always necessary but they document discussion points that may have come up within the extraction process and need to be preserved for designers to consider in their process.

5.3.7 Requirement Statement Structure

A generic structure of a requirement statement that has worked for us is shown in Figure 5-3. A requirements document is essentially a set of requirement statements organized on headings at two or more levels.

For systems where risk is high and traceability is important, each requirement is tagged with the WAAD source node ID, which serves as a link back to the source of this requirement statement within the WAAD. The WAAD in turn has a link back to its source in raw work activity data.

Later, if a question arises about a particular need or requirement, the connection to original work activity data and the person who was its source can be traced to find the answers (sort of the UX lifecycle analog of a software requirements traceability matrix).

Because we use the WAAD node ID as a link this way, someone should ensure that all WAAD nodes are labeled with some identification number before the extraction process begins. We use A, B, C, ... for the highest-level nodes under the root node. Under node A, we use AA, AB, AC, ..., and for the work activity notes

Figure 5-3

Generic structure of a requirement statement.

Name of major feature or category
Name of second-level feature or category
Requirement statement [WAAD source node ID]
Rationale (if useful): Rationale statement
Note (optional): Commentary about this requirement

themselves we use the group ID plus a number, such as AB1 and AB2; this is the identifier that goes in the "WAAD source node ID" part of a requirement.

Security

Privacy of ticket–buyer transactions

Shall protect security and privacy of ticket-buyer transactions [C19]

Note: In design, consider timeout feature to clear screen between customers.

As an example, consider the work activity note that said "I am concerned about privacy and security of my transactions." In Figure 5-4 we show how the resulting requirement statement fits into the requirement statement structure of Figure 5-3.

Figure 5-4

Example requirement statement.

5.3.8 Requirements Document Structure

We show two levels of headings, but you should use as many levels as necessary for your requirements.

As an example of an extracted requirement for the Ticket Kiosk System, suppose in our contextual inquiry a user mentioned the occasional convenience of shopping recommendations from Amazon.com. The resulting requirement might look like what is shown in Figure 5-5.

Example: Extracting a Requirement Statement for the Ticket Kiosk System

Note CA9 within the WAAD for MUTTS says "I sometimes want to find events that have to do with my own personal interests. For example, I really like ice skating and want to see what kinds of entertainment events in the nearby areas feature skating of any kind." This user work activity statement implies the user need, "Ticket buyers need to find various kinds of events."

Labels on a group at a higher level imply a feature or topic of "Finding events" so we use that as the heading for this requirement in the requirements document. Lower-level labels in the WAAD narrow it down to "Direct keyword search by event description"; we will use that for our subheading.

We can then write the requirement in Figure 5-6.

Note that this comment, also in the WAAD, "I sometimes want to find events that have to do with my own personal interests," could lead to consideration of a requirement to maintain personal profiles of users.

Figure 5-5

Sample requirement statement for the Ticket Kiosk System.

Transaction flow

..... *Recommendations for buying*

Ticket-buyer purchases shall be supported by recommendations for the purchase of related items. [DE2].

Implied system requirement: During a transaction session the Ticket Kiosk System shall keep track of the kinds of choices made by the ticket buyer along with the choices of other ticket buyers who bought this item. [DE2].

Note: Amazon.com is a model for this feature.

Finding events

Direct keyword search by event description

Ticket buyers shall be able to find (e.g., search) by content to identify relevant current and future events [CA9].

Browse events by parameters

Ticket buyers shall be able to browse by category, description, location, time, rating, and price.

Figure 5-6

Example requirement statement for the Ticket Kiosk System.

5.3.9 Continue the Process for the Whole WAAD

In the Ticket Kiosk System example, you will also extract requirements for all the different ways you search and browse event information, such as requirements to search by event category, venue, date range, and so on. Take the time here to pick *all* the fruits; it is too easy to neglect the connections of rationale to user work activities and lose much of the advantage gained from the contextual analysis work.

After each requirement statement is written, it is very important for the whole team to see—for example, by projection display—or hear—for example, by the recorder reading it—the statement to ensure that the written statement represents their concept of what it was supposed to be.

Later when reviewing and finalizing the requirements document, we may find that not every "requirement" extracted from the WAAD will eventually be met because of cost, other constraints, and how our own knowledge and experience temper the process, but that kind of judgment comes later. For now, just keep cranking out the requirements.

5.3.10 Keep an Eye out for Emotional Impact Requirements and Other Ways to Enhance the Overall User Experience

When extracting requirements, most people will think of the functional requirements first, feeding usefulness. Most people might think of usability goals next, feeding UX targets. But do not forget that we are on a quest to design for a fabulous user experience and this is where you will find opportunities for that, too.

In addition to getting at routine requirements for tasks, functions, and features, seek out those indefinable evolving characteristics essential to a quality usage experience. Because factors related to emotional impact or phenomenological aspects may not be as clear-cut or explicit as functional or other interaction requirements, you have to be alert for the indicators.

Work activity notes with user concerns, frustration, excitement, and likings offer opportunities to design a system to address emotional issues. Especially look out for work activity notes that make even an oblique reference to "fun" or "enjoyment" or to things like data entry being too boring or the use of colors being unattractive. Any of these could be a clue to ways to provide a more rewarding user experience. Also, be open minded and creative in this phase; even if a note implies a need that is technologically difficult to address, record it. You can revisit these later to assess feasibility and constraints.

5.3.11 Extrapolation Requirements: Generalization of Contextual Data

User statements in a WAAD can be quite narrow and specific. You may need to generate extrapolation requirements to broaden existing contextual data to cover more general cases.

For example, ticket buyers using MUTTS, in anticipation of a kiosk, might have expressed the need to search for events based on a predetermined criterion but said nothing about browsing events to see what is available. So you might write an extrapolation requirement about the obvious need also to browse events (as we did in Figure 5-6).

As another example, in our WAAD for MUTTS, a ticket buyer speaks about the desirability of being able to post an MU football ticket for exchange with a ticket in another location in the stadium to be able to sit with their friends. In our extrapolation requirement statement we broadened this to "Ticket buyer shall be able to post, check status of, and exchange student tickets." And we added a relationship note: "Will require ticket-buyer user 'accounts' of some kind where they can login using their MU Passport IDs."

In another work activity note a user mentioned it would be nice to be able to select seats from all available seats in a given price category. This translates to a requirement to display seating availability and to be able to filter that list of available seats (such as by price categories). Seat selection *assumes* the existence of a lock and release mechanism of some sort, something we perhaps did not yet have in the requirements document. This is a technical requirement to give the buyer a temporary option on the selected seats until the transaction is completed or abandoned. So we added an extrapolation requirement to cover it:

> Shall have a default time interval for locking available seating while the ticket buyer is making a choice.

> Rationale: If a ticker buyer has not performed any actions with the interface in a certain amount of time, we assume the ticket buyer has left the kiosk or at least abandoned the current transaction.

The timeout will release those seats back to an available pool for others to access from other kiosks.

Another work activity note said, "I often plan to attend entertainment events with friends." At first, we thought this comment was just a passing remark about how he would use it. It did not seem to imply a requirement because it did not say anything directly about a feature.

On reflection, however, we could easily broaden it slightly to imply a possible need to communicate with those friends and, with a bit more extrapolation, maybe facilitate sending tickets or event information to them via email. This extrapolation could well be beyond the scope of the user's intent and it could be beyond the scope of the current project, but it should be saved as an input about a potential future feature and, more importantly, as a chance to provide a great user experience.

This example is a good one because it starts with a statement about usage. And that is what contextual data are about, so we should not have missed seeing an implied requirement because "it did not say anything about a feature." It is our job to come up with requirements implied by usage statements.

In balance, while extrapolation requirement statements may be necessary and valuable, we should be careful with them. To be sure, we distinguish them by calling them (and tagging them as) extrapolation requirements, which must be taken back to users for confirmation as real needs or requirements. This validation can result in a thumbs up and you can include it in your requirements document or it can result in a thumbs down and you can eliminate that requirement.

5.3.12 Other Possible Outputs from the Requirements Extraction Process

In addition to requirement statements, a work activity note in a WAAD can lead to certain other outputs, discussed in the following subsections.

Questions about missing data

Sometimes, as you go deeper into the implications of contextual data, you realize there are still some open questions. For example, in our contextual inquiry for MUTTS, while we were putting together requirements for the accounting system to aggregate sales at the end of the day, we had to face the fact that the existing business manages tickets from two independent systems. One is the local ticket office sales and the other is from the national affiliate, Tickets4ever .com. During our contextual inquiry and analysis we neglected to probe the interaction between those two and how they reconciled sales across those two systems.

System support needs

You may also occasionally encounter system requirements for issues outside the user experience or software domains, such as expandability, reliability, security, and communications bandwidth. These are dealt with in a manner similar to that used for the software requirements inputs. A few examples from the MUTTS WAAD illustrate:

> Work activity note: "Identity theft and credit card fraud are huge concerns for me."

> System requirement: "System shall have specific features to address protecting ticket buyers from identity theft and credit card fraud." (This "requirement" is vague but it is really only a note for us to contact the systems people to figure out potential solutions to this problem.)

> Work activity note: "When I am getting tickets for, say, a controversial political speaker, I do not want people in line behind me to know what I am doing."

> System requirement: "Physical design of kiosk shall address protecting privacy of a ticket buyer from others nearby."

Marketing inputs

Sometimes a comment made by a user during contextual inquiry might make a good input to the marketing department as a candidate sound bite that can be adapted into advertising copy. This is a good opportunity to communicate with the marketing people and help cement your working relationship with them.

Example: Requirements Extraction for the Ticket Kiosk System

Here are a few selected requirements extracted from the MUTTS WAAD that we are using to inform requirements for the Ticket Kiosk System.

Shopping cart

Existence of feature

> Ticket buyer shall have a shopping cart concept with which they can buy multiple items and pay only once [BBA1-4]

Accessibility of shopping cart

> Ticket buyer shall be able to view and modify shopping cart at all times [BBA3]

Shopping cart versatility

Ticket buyer shall be able to add different kinds/types of items (example, different events, sets of tickets for the same event) [BBA4]

Note: This requirement is important because it has implications on how to display shopping cart contents with dissimilar types of objects in it.

Transaction flow

Timeouts

Extrapolation: Ticket buyer shall be supported by a timeout feature [BCA] Rationale: To protect ticket buyer privacy

Extrapolation: Ticket buyer shall be made aware of the existence and status of timeout, including progress indicator showing remaining time and audible beep near the end of the timeout period [BCA] [BCA1]

Extrapolation: Ticket buyer shall have control to reset the timeout and keep the transaction alive

Extrapolation: Ticket buyer's need to keep transaction alive shall be supported by automation, timer reset triggered by ticket buyer activity

Immediate exit

Ticket buyer shall be able to make a quick exit and reset to the home screen [BCB1]

Rationale: Important for kiosks in bus stations where user may have to quit in the middle of a transaction and to protect their privacy

Ticket buyer shall have a way to quickly return to a specific item they were viewing just prior to an immediate exit [BCB1]

Note: Ticket buyer shall be able to use an event ID number for direct access next time or the system can potentially do it using an "account" and restore state.

Recommendations for buying

Extrapolation: Ticket buyer purchases shall be supported by recommendations for related items [BCB2]

Extrapolation: Ticket buyer shall be able to say no to recommendations easily [BCB2]

Transaction progress awareness

Ticket buyer shall be able to track the progress of the entire transaction (what is done and what is left to do) using, for example, a "bread crumb" trail [BCB3-4]

Ticket buyer reminders

Ticket buyer shall receive reminders to take the ticket and MU Passport/credit card at the end of each transaction [BCC1-2]

Checkout

Ticket buyer shall have, before making a payment, a confirmation page showing exactly what is being purchased [BCD1]

Ticket buyer shall receive actual ticket and not just confirmation [BCD2]
Rationale: For maintaining ticket buyer trust
Note: This is a huge issue involving marketing, high-level business decisions, and hardware (printer) reliability and kiosk maintenance

Ticket buyer shall be able to use cash, credit cart, debit card, or MU Passport for payment [BCD3]

Note: For cash transaction it is difficult to recognize and dispense change [BCD4], and attracts vandals and thieves [BCD5]

System requirements

Performance

The system shall have a good response time to make transactions fast (so ticket buyers do not miss the bus) [BCB5]

Exercise

See Exercise 5-1, Extracting Requirement Statements for Your System

5.3.13 Constraints as Requirements

Constraints, such as from legacy systems, implementation platforms, and system architecture, are a kind of requirements in real-world development projects. Although, as we have said, much of the interaction design can and should be done independently from concerns about software design and implementation, your interaction design must eventually be considered as an input to software requirements and design.

Legacy System

A legacy system is a system with maintenance problems that date back possibly many years.

Therefore, eventually, you and your interaction design must be reconciled with constraints coming from systems engineering, hardware engineering, software engineering, management, and marketing. Not the least of which includes development cost and schedule, and profitability in selling the product.

What restrictions will these constraints impose on product scope? Are product, for example, a kiosk, size and/or weight to be taken into account if, for example, the product will be on portable or mobile equipment? Does your system have to be integrated with existing or other developing systems? Are there compliance issues that mandate certain features? Constraints arise from the problems of legacy systems, limitations of implementation platforms, demands of hardware and software, budgets, and schedules.

Example: Constraints for MUTTS

A hardware constraint for the existing working environment of MUTTS is the necessity of keeping the secure credit card server continuously operational. An inability of the ticket office to process credit card transactions would essentially bring their business to a halt. They have only one "general purpose" technician on staff to care for this server plus all the other computers, network connections, printers, scanners, and so on.

In addition, the physical space of the MUTTS office is constrained, a constraint that should also show up in the physical model (Chapter 6), and work areas can become cramped on busy days. Their office space is leased, a fact that is not likely to change in the near future, so a more efficient work flow is desirable. Sometimes the air conditioning is inadequate.

The constraints will show significant differences in going from MUTTS to the Ticket Kiosk System. Here are some example constraints that might be anticipated in the Ticket Kiosk System, mostly about hardware (systems engineering people would probably add quantitative standards to be met in some cases):

- Special-purpose hardware for the kiosk
- Rugged, "hardened" vandal-proof outer shell
- All hardware to be durable, reliable
- Touchscreen interaction, no keyboard
- Network communications possibly specialized for efficiency and reliability
- If have a printer for tickets (likely), maintenance must be an extremely high priority; cannot have any customers pay and not get tickets (e.g., from paper or ink running out)
- Need a "hotline" communication feature as backup, a way for customers to contact company representatives in case this does happen

Exercise

See Exercise 5-2, Constraints for Your System

5.3.14 Prioritizing Requirements

A drawback of affinity diagrams is that they do not contain priority information, so every note has the same weight as any other note. A note about a major task has the same significance as a passing comment. As a result, the extracted requirements are also unprioritized. To remedy this, as part of the validation process, ask your customer and users to prioritize the requirements.

At a minimum they can point out the key requirements and the requirements that are "also-rans." These can be separated into different sections of a requirements document or distinguished by a color-coding scheme.

With a bit more effort you can tag each requirement with an importance rating. Later, you will use these priority ratings to decide which design-informing models to focus on. For example, important tasks will be the ones chosen as the basis for representative scenarios.

Often, as the result of prioritizing, you and your customer achieve a realization of, and mutual understanding about, the fact that some requirements cannot be met realistically in the current product version and must be set aside for consideration in the future.

5.3.15 Taking Requirements Back to Customers and Users for Validation

After your own review, it is time to take the requirements document or requirements WAAD back to the customer and users for validation. This is a critical step for them because it gives them a chance to offer inputs and correct misconceptions before you get into design. It also helps solidify your relationship as partners in the process.

For each work role, schedule a meeting with the representative users, preferably some from the ones you have interviewed or otherwise interacted with before, and some new users. Walk them through the requirements to make sure your interpretation of requirements from the work activity notes is accurate.

Pay close attention to feedback from new users who are looking at the requirements for the first time. They may provide valuable feedback on anything you missed or new insights into the needs. Remember that these users are experts in the work domain, but probably not in the domains of interaction design or software development, so protect them from technical jargon.

5.3.16 Resolve Organizational, Sociological, and Personal Issues with the Customer

When you take your requirements to the customer for validation, it is also a good opportunity to resolve organizational, social, and personal issues. Because your requirements reflect what you intend to put into the design, if heeded, they can flash early warning signs to customers and users about issues of which your team

Work Role

A work role is defined and distinguished by a corresponding job title or work assignment representing a set of work responsibilities. A work role usually involves system usage, but some work roles can be external to the organization being studied.

may be unaware, even after thorough contextual inquiry. Especially if your requirements are pointing toward a design that changes the work environment, the way work is done, or the job descriptions of workers, your requirements may give rise to issues of territoriality, fear, and control.

Changes in the workflow may challenge established responsibilities and authorities. There may also be legal requirements or platform constraints for doing things in a certain way, a way you cannot change, regardless of your arguments for efficiency or better user experience. Organizational, social, and personal issues can catch your team by surprise because they may well be thinking mostly about technical aspects and design at this point.

Work Activity Affinity Diagram

A work activity affinity diagram (WAAD) is an affinity diagram used to sort and organize work activity notes in contextual analysis, pulling together work activity notes with similarities and common themes to highlight common work patterns and shared strategies across all users.

5.4 ABRIDGED METHODS FOR REQUIREMENTS EXTRACTION

5.4.1 Use the WAAD Directly as a Requirements Representation

To save time and cost, the WAAD itself can be taken as a set of implicit requirements, without formally extracting them. On the WAAD you created in contextual analysis, highlight (e.g., using a marker pen) all groups or individual work activity notes that imply requirements and design ideas directly or indirectly. The way a WAAD note can represent a requirement is: you must cover, include, or accommodate (in the interaction design) the issue, idea, or concept expressed in the note.

To use the Ticket Kiosk System example of customer security and privacy again, the work activity note says, "I am concerned about the security and privacy of my transactions." Instead of rewriting this as a formal requirement statement in a requirements document as we did previously, you just interpret it directly as you read it to "shall protect security and privacy of ticket-buyer transactions."

This requirement may immediately generate ideas about how to solve the problem in the design, such as by automatic timeout and and/or a limited viewing angle on the physical kiosk. You should also document these design ideas immediately, while you can, as notes directly on the WAAD.

You will acquire the ability to look at the WAAD with an interpretative eye and see the work activity notes as more explicit requirements. Clear and crisply written work activity notes will help make this mental step of interpretation easier.

5.4.2 Anticipating Needs and Requirements in Contextual Analysis

In anticipation of the need to extract requirements here, we can introduce a shortcut in contextual analysis, adjusting the process for work activity note synthesis and saving some cost. The shortcut involves doing some interpretation of the raw data, on the fly, to move it more rapidly to reflect requirements.

For example, consider a work activity note from the MUTTS interviews that says: "After the lottery results for an MU football game are out, students who won try to exchange tickets with others so they and their friends can sit together." From this, you can move more rapidly toward needs and requirements by restating it as: "Some MU football ticket lottery winners need an ability to go to a kiosk and trade tickets with other winners so they can sit with their friends."

5.4.3 Use Work Activity Notes as Requirements (Eliminate the WAAD Completely)

Another efficient abridgement technique, for experienced practitioners, is eliminating the WAAD altogether and using the bins of sorted work activity notes as requirements. Building a WAAD is about organizing large amounts of data to identify underlying themes and relationships.

If your contextual inquiry did not result in a huge number of work activity notes (a likely case in an abridged approach), you can identify relationships by just manipulating the work activity notes themselves. But you still have to make the mental step of interpretation to deduce requirements on the fly.

Constructing Design-Informing Models

Objectives

After reading this chapter, you will:

1. Know how to construct design-informing models as the second span to bridge the gap between analysis and design
2. Understand user models such as work roles, user classes, social models, and user personas
3. Understand usage models such as flow model, task models, and the information object model
4. Understand work environment models such as the artifact model and physical model
5. Understand the role of barriers (to work practice) within models

6.1 INTRODUCTION

6.1.1 You Are Here

We begin each process chapter in the book with a "you are here" picture of the chapter topic in the context of the overall Wheel lifecycle template; see Figure 6-1. We have now made it across the first of two spans of the bridge between contextual analysis and design. We have extracted requirements and are now on our way to constructing some design-informing models.

6.2 DESIGN-INFORMING MODELS: SECOND SPAN OF THE BRIDGE

In crossing the second span of our bridge on the way to design (Figure 5-2), we take what we learned in contextual analysis and build "design-informing models," evolving work products that we can use to bridge the rest of the gap toward design. Just as we did in the previous chapter for requirements

Figure 6-1

You are here; the chapter on constructing design-informing models, within understanding user work and needs in the context of the overall Wheel lifecycle template.

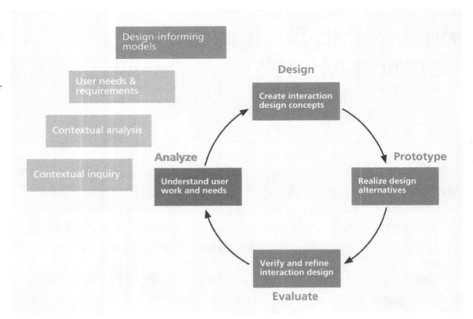

extraction, in this chapter we introduce another kind of deductive data extraction: from the work activity affinity diagram (WAAD) or your bins of sorted work activity notes and other contextual data to these design-informing models.

We wish to acknowledge upfront the ample influence of Holtzblatt and colleagues (Beyer & Holtzblatt, 1998; Holtzblatt, Wendell, & Wood, 2005), who have led the way in bringing ethnographic studies of work practice into the human–computer interaction context, in this chapter. In their book, *Contextual Design* (Beyer & Holtzblatt, 1998), Beyer and Holtzblatt use five models: flow, physical, artifact, sequence, and cultural.

In the book *Rapid Contextual Design* (Holtzblatt, Wendell, & Wood, 2005), the authors use mainly the physical, sequential, and artifact models. We have built on their work here, adapting and modifying it for our own needs. We also feature flow, artifact, and physical models. Their cultural model has been adapted to form our social model, and we have expanded their sequence model into a number of different task models.

We also acknowledge the influence of Constantine and Lockwood (1999). Much of our model-driven approach is based loosely on their "use what you know" technique.

6.2.1 What Are Design-Informing Models and How Are They Used?

Design-informing models are not building blocks that appear directly in a design but are artifacts that embody, drive, inform, and inspire the design. They are design-oriented constructs, such as task descriptions or user personas, that turn raw data into actionable items as design ideas, as elements to consider or take into account in the design.

Like WAADs and requirements, design-informing models:

- help integrate and summarize the contextual data
- point back to the data, to maintain the "chain of custody" to ensure that the design is based on real contextual data
- provide a shared focus for analysis now and, later, design
- provide intermediate deliverables, which can be important to your working relationship with the customer

6.2.2 Envisioned Design-Informing Models

Even though this chapter is about modeling existing work practice, the purpose of the models is to inform design. So, as we get closer to design in Chapters 7, 8, and 9, we need to make a transition with our models from existing to envisioned work practice. To this end, after we construct each kind of model, we also look at the envisioned version of that model for the new design.

Use these models as springboards to your design scenarios, sketches, and storyboarding. Using the flow model and physical model as guides, look for ways to make flows more efficient and to avoid redundant data entry and unnecessary physical motions. From the task interaction models, try to reduce and automate steps.

Using the social model as a guide, find ways to increase communication, reinforce positive values, address concerns of people in work roles, and accommodate influences. One important way to use each kind of model to inform design is to look at all the barriers identified in the models and solve the problems they represent.

When the new work practice and supporting system are quite different from the existing ones, the transition from modeling to design begins with a transition from the models of existing work practice by envisioning how each model will make the transition to the new work practice and supporting design.

Each model directly informs its envisioned counterpart. Envisioned design-informing models are a step closer toward design from analysis. Most of

Persona

A persona, as used in contextual data representation and interaction design, is a hypothetical but specific "character" in a specific work role, with specific user class characteristics. As a technique for making users real to designers, a persona is a story and description of a realistic individual who has a name, a life, and a personality, allowing designers to limit design focus to something very specific.

Barrier

A barrier, in contextual modeling, is a problem that interferes with normal operations of user work practice. Anything that impedes user activities, interrupts work flow or communications, or interferes with the performance of work responsibilities is a barrier to the work practice.

Scenario

A scenario is a design input in the form of a story about specific people performing work activities in a specific work situation within a specific work context, told in a concrete narrative style, as if it were a transcript of a real usage occurrence. Scenarios are deliberately informal, open-ended, and fragmentary narrative depictions of key usage situations happening over time.

the envisioned design-informing models can be very brief, addressing only the differences from the existing models.

In cases where the new work practice and new system are only incrementally improved versions of the old work practice and system, envisioned design-informing models are probably of little value and usually can be skipped.

6.3 SOME GENERAL "HOW TO" SUGGESTIONS

6.3.1 Maintain Connections to Your Data

It is important to label everything you put in a model with an identifier tag that points directly back to the place in the raw data that was the source of this item in the model. This tag can be the line number in the raw data transcript, a time code in a recording, or a note number in your manually recorded notes. It can also be a node-ID in your WAAD, which indirectly takes you to raw data source tags. This tagging allows your analysis team to get back to the raw data immediately to resolve questions, disagreements, or interpretations of the data. If any element of a model has no pointer back to the data, it must then be considered an unsupported assumption and is subject to additional scrutiny.

6.3.2 Extract Inputs to Design-Informing Models

The business of extracting inputs for design-informing models is not the "next step" after requirements extraction, but you do this in conjunction with requirements extraction. We discuss it separately here for clarity, but usually you would not want to take the time and energy to make another pass through the contextual data at this point. As you "walk the wall" and traverse the WAAD for extracting requirements, take notes on design-informing models, too.

References to design-informing models just come out naturally; you'll see references to task descriptions, references to user types, references to social concerns, and so on. In WAAD notes and other contextual data, references to design-informing models will often be indirect or implied and sometimes oblique. These work activity notes will seldom be complete descriptions of any component of a design-informing model, but will be hints and clues and pieces of the puzzle that you, the detective, will assemble as you compile each model deductively.

6.3.3 Use Your "Bins" of Sorted Work Activity Notes from Contextual Inquiry and Contextual Analysis

It is hoped, as a result of anticipating in contextual analysis your current needs for modeling, that you will have separate work activity note bins sorted out for each kind of model. For example, you might have bins of user-related notes for user class definitions and personas. Separate your task-related work activity notes into sub-bins for hierarchical task inventory (HTI), task sequences, scenarios, and so on.

These ordered and structured bins of notes for each resulting model type provide the inputs to drive your synthesis of the corresponding design-informing models. The user models bin will contain notes revealing major work roles. The social models bin might contain notes (perhaps through a user concern) about how people in those roles relate. Similarly, the flow model bin may contain notes about and inputs to workflow-related descriptions. Task-related work activity notes in your task model bin are obvious sources of inputs to task descriptions for task modeling, storyboarding, and scenarios.

> **User Class**
>
> A user class is a description of the relevant characteristics of the user population who can take on a particular work role. User class descriptions can include such characteristics as demographics, skills, knowledge, experience, and special needs—for example, because of physical limitations.

Example: Bins of Inputs to Design-Informing Models from MUTTS

Here are a few examples of items found in the personas bin and the task descriptions bin, as inputs to corresponding design-informing models. References in square brackets at the end of each input item are tags, tracing the input item back to the data. In this case, the combination of letters and numbers reflects a node within the hierarchical structure of a WAAD.

- Personas
    - I usually work long hours in the lab, on the other side of campus [from BA1-4]
    - I like classical music concerts, especially from local artists [from CE3-4]
    - I love the sense of community in Middleburg [from BC2-1]
- Task descriptions
    - Sometimes I need to buy a set of tickets with adjacent seating [from EB5-6]
    - After the lottery results for an MU football game are out, students who won try to exchange tickets with others so that they and their friends can sit together [from EA3-14]

6.3.4 Represent Barriers to Work Practice

In most of the models you will want to represent problems that interfere with normal operations of the users. These barriers to usage are of special interest because they point out where users have difficulties in the work practice. These barriers also represent key opportunities for improvement in the design.

Barriers include what Beyer and Holtzblatt call "breakdowns," but are a bit more general. Anything that impedes user activities, interrupts workflow or communications, or interferes with the performance of work responsibilities is a barrier to the work practice. Any time you observe users having difficulties at various steps in their work or experiencing confusion or awkwardness in the work role or task performance, even if it does not cause a full breakdown, is a candidate for being labeled as a barrier.

Especially in the flow model, barriers can include problems with coordination, slips of communication, forgetting to do things, getting the timing of steps wrong, failure to pass along needed information, and so on. We will use the Beyer and Holtzblatt symbology of a graphical red lightning bolt ($\nearrow$) in various ways to indicate barriers in our design-informing models.

6.4 A NEW EXAMPLE DOMAIN: SLIDESHOW PRESENTATIONS

In addition to our running MUTTS and Ticket Kiosk System example, in this chapter we will use examples from a contextual inquiry study of slideshow presentations performed at Carnegie Mellon University (Cross, Warmack, & Myers, 1999) to illustrate some of the models in this chapter. Many thanks to Brad Myers for permission to use it here.

These examples about slideshow presentations were chosen because the domain is easy to understand, the models are relatively straightforward, and the models are supported with real contextual data. A small group of user researchers analyzed a set of pre-existing videotapes of nine academic presentations representing a variety of subject matter, audience sizes, audience location (some local and remote, some local only), presentation styles, and audience reaction styles (listen-only, questions, criticism). The objective of the study was to find design improvements to the slide presentation process, possibly through a technology solution.

This example illustrates a creative adaptation of contextual inquiry to make use of available video data, unbiased data because it was not taken with contextual inquiry in mind but just to create a record of the presentations. Although the existing videotapes allowed observation of work as it occurs in its own context, they did not permit interaction with users and questioning of users during the observations. Nonetheless, their adaptation of the contextual inquiry method did yield observational data, which did lead to some design-informing models; we use them here as real-world examples.

6.5 USER MODELS

User models are a set of models that define who the users are, including everything about work roles, sub-roles, user class definitions, and personas. Perhaps the most important of the design-informing models are the user models of this section and the usage models of the next.

6.5.1 Work Roles

A work role corresponds to the duties, functions, and work activities of a person with a certain job title or job responsibility. For Constantine and Lockwood (1999), a role is a set of responsibilities assumed by a human within an activity in relation to a focal system. In other words, work roles are "hats" that people wear when they take on the corresponding job responsibilities and perform the associated activities.

As an integral part of contextual analysis, we got an early start at identifying work roles (Chapter 4). Now, in this section, we follow up on this step as part of the modeling.

A work role can involve:

- System usage or not (meaning the person in the role may or may not be a direct user)
- Internal or external to the organization, as long as the job entails participation in the work practice of the organization

Sub-roles

For some work roles, there are obvious sub-roles distinguished by different subsets of the tasks the work role does. See the MUTTS example after the next section.

Mediated work roles

For many systems, your contextual data will show you that there are "users" in roles that do not use the system, at least not directly, but still play a major part in the usage context. These mediated users, whom Cooper (2004) calls "served users," have true work roles in the enterprise and are true stakeholders in the system requirements and design and definitely play roles in contextual analysis, scenarios, user class definitions, and even personas.

The ticket-buyer role for MUTTS is a prime example of a user role whose interaction with the computer system is mediated; that is, someone else acts as an agent (the ticket seller) or intermediary between this kind of user and the computer system. It turns out, of course, that ticket buyers will become direct user roles in the envisioned Ticket Kiosk System. The ticket buyer is still a very important role and indirect user of MUTTS and is, therefore, important to interview in contextual inquiry.

The ticket buyer will be the main role considered in subsequent examples. These mediated roles are often customers and clients of the enterprise on whose behalf direct users such as clerks and agents conduct transactions with the computer system. They might be point-of-sale customers or clients needing services from a retail outlet, a government agency, a bank, or an insurance agency. They have needs that reflect on user tasks directly and that are mapped into the interaction design. The working relationship between the mediated users and the agent is critical.

Example: Work Roles and Sub-roles for MUTTS

MUTTS work roles include:

- ticket buyer, with further sub-roles as described later, who interacts with the ticket seller to learn about event information and buy event tickets [from AA-3-6]
- ticket seller, who serves ticket buyers and uses the system to find and buy tickets on behalf of ticket buyers [from AL-11-16]
- event manager, who negotiates with event promoters about event information and tickets to be sold by the MUTTS ticket office [from AF-7-13]
- advertising manager, who negotiates advertising to be featured via MUTTS [from AB-5-18]
- maintenance technician, who maintains the MUTTS ticket office computers, Website, ticket printers, and network connections [from AC-3-10]
- database administrator, who tends the reliability and data integrity of the database [from AG-2-17]
- financial administrator, who is responsible for financial and accounting-related affairs [from AH-1-6]
- administrative supervisor, who oversees the entire MU services department [from AE-6-6]
- office manager, who is in charge of the daily MUTTS operation [from AF-2-15]
- assistant office manager, who assists the office manager [from AC-1-8]

We also identified sub-roles for the ticket-buyer role: student, general public, faculty/staff, alumni, seniors, and children. People in the ticket-buyer role for MUTTS are associated with the main goal of ticket buying. However, a student of Middleburg University, in what we might call the MU-student sub-role, is associated predominantly with the goal of picking up athletic tickets reserved for students.

In contrast, nonstudent sports fans want to buy more publicly available sporting tickets. Similarly, town residents and Middleburg visitors, who may be more interested in buying concert and other event tickets, can comprise two other sub-roles. Finally, ticket buyers in the MU-alumni sub-role are buyers of tickets for university-hosted alumni events.

The administrative supervisor has overall responsibility for daily operations, success of the program, and planning for the future. Because she is charged with responsibility for more than one such program, she is definitely not involved in the daily operation.

There are also some work roles external to MUTTS, but who interact with people in MUTTS work roles, including:

- event promoters, who interact with the event manager to book events
- venue managers, who interact with the event manager to establish seat selection charts
- advertisers, who interact with the advertising manager to book advertising

Exercise

See Exercise 6-1, Identifying Work Roles for Your System

Envisioned work roles

The basic work itself, *what* has to be done, usually does not change much from the old system to the new system. For example, for MUTTS, even with the introduction of kiosks, the goals of most work roles are still the same. Much of the change from old to new shows up in envisioned work roles and an envisioned flow model. For example, the responsibilities and tasks of some roles may change.

As we move from the existing system and existing work practice to the design of the new work process, work roles can be expanded and changed. Some old work roles are no longer necessary; for example, the ticket seller may no longer exist as a role. Some new roles are introduced and we now spotlight some roles that were previously only in the murky background. Along with new roles, we get new issues and concerns in the envisioned social model, new work activities and constraints. The new roles come alive in the new workflow of the envisioned flow model.

Because you might have some new roles in the new design, you may not have contextual data from them. If you have not already interviewed people who might serve in these roles, now is the time to do just a little bit more contextual inquiry to see if there are any new considerations for design arising from the new roles.

Example: Envisioned New Work Roles for Ticket Kiosk System

The major difference between the new Ticket Kiosk System and the old MUTTS is that public kiosks are being used instead of a computer in the ticket office to find and sell tickets. With ticket kiosks come changes in work roles.

In the most significant role transformation, the ticket-seller role disappears and the ticket-buyer role becomes a direct user through the kiosk, now becoming what is perhaps the central role in the design. The ticket-buyer role includes all people who use the kiosk in a public manner, for example, for buying tickets and/or looking for information. The same sub-roles and user classes generally still apply.

Relationship of work roles to other concepts

Work roles are distinguished by the kinds of work they use the system to accomplish. For example, the MUTTS ticket seller who helps customers buy tickets does entirely different tasks with the system than, say, the event manager who, behind the scenes, enters entertainment event information into the system so that tickets can be offered, printed, and purchased.

In Figure 6-2, we show the relationship of work roles to other key concepts. Work roles are central to flow models.

User Class

A user class is a description of the relevant characteristics of the user population who can take on a particular work role. User class descriptions can include such characteristics as demographics, skills, knowledge, experience, and special needs—for example, because of physical limitations.

Work Role

A work role is defined and distinguished by a corresponding job title or work assignment representing a set of work responsibilities. A work role usually involves system usage, but some work roles can be external to the organization being studied.

Flow Model

A flow model is a diagram giving the big picture or overview of work, emphasizing communication and information flow among work roles and between work roles and system components within the work practice of an organization.

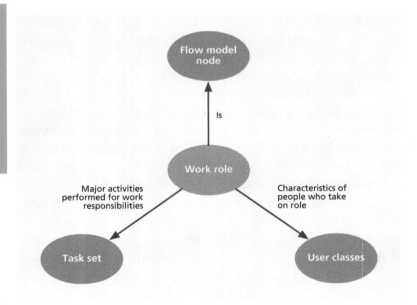

Figure 6-2

Concepts defining and related to work roles.

6.5.2 User Classes

A user class is defined by a description of the relevant characteristics of people who might take on a particular work role. Every work role will have at least one accompanying description of potential user community who can perform that role. Sometimes a work role can have such a broad user population that it requires more than one user class definition to describe all the different kinds of people who can assume that role.

User class definitions document the general characteristics of these groups of people who can take on a given role in terms of such characteristics as demographics, skills, knowledge, and special needs. Some specialized user classes, such as "soccer mom," "yuppie," "metrosexual," or "elderly citizen," may be dictated by marketing (Frank, 2006).

Knowledge- and skills-based characteristics

User class definitions can include background, experience, training, education, and/or skills expected in a user performing a work role. For example, a given class of users must be trained in X and must have Y years experience in Z.

User class characteristics can include user knowledge of computers—both in general and with respect to specific systems. Some knowledge- and skills-based characteristics of user class definitions can be mandated by organizational policies or even legal requirements, especially for work roles that affect the public.

For example, organizational policy might require a specific kind of training for anyone to take on a given role or no one is allowed to take on the role of an air traffic controller until they have met rather strict requirements for levels of experience and background training mandated by federal law.

In Figure 6-3 we show relationships among work roles, sub-roles, and user class characteristics.

User class characteristics can include user knowledge of the work domain—knowledge of and experience with the operations, procedures, and semantics of the various aspects of the application area the system being designed is trying to address.

For example, a medical doctor might be an expert in domain knowledge for an MRI system, but may have novice-to-intermittent knowledge in the area of related computer applications. In contrast, a secretary in the hospital may be a novice in the domain of MRI but may have more complete knowledge regarding the use of related computer applications.

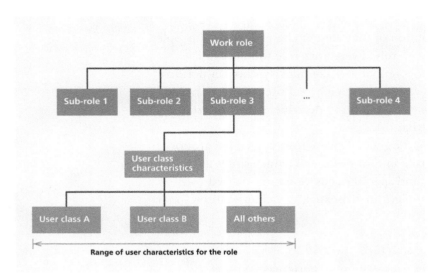

Figure 6-3

Relationships among work roles, sub-roles, and user class characteristics.

Physiological characteristics

Physiological factors include impairments and limitations. Age can imply physiological factors in user class characteristics. If older adults are expected to take on a given work role, they may have known characteristics to be accommodated in design. Beyond the popular but often inaccurate characterization of having cognitive rigor mortis, older adults can be susceptible to sensory and motor limitations that come naturally with age.

The older adult population in our country is growing rapidly, mainly due to aging baby boomers. A study of potential usability barriers for older adults in 50 state and 50 federal e-government Websites (Becker, 2005) revealed a huge amount of easily correctable flaws in the form of distractions, poor use of color, nonstandard use of links, nonstandard search boxes and mechanisms, requirements for precise motor movements with the mouse, font size, and Web page lengths. Also, electronic voting machines, although not online, are certainly part of the concept of e-government.

Physiological characteristics are certainly one place where accessibility issues can be found. Within usage roles you may also find subclasses of users based on special characteristics such as special needs and disabilities, such as the woman voter mentioned in Chapter 3.

Web Accessibility

Dr. Jonathan Lazar

Department of Computer and Information Sciences and Universal Usability Laboratory, Towson University

Why are not more Websites accessible for people with disabilities when there are guidelines and tools available to help developers make their Websites accessible? This is a question that fascinates me. I am a professor of computer and information sciences at Towson University, founder and director of the Universal Usability Laboratory, and author of the book *Web Usability: A User-Centered Design Approach*, editor of the book *Universal Usability: Designing Computer Interfaces for Diverse User Populations*, and coauthor of the book *Research Methods in Human-Computer Interaction*.

I first became fascinated with this research question when the World Wide Web Consortium, and their Web Accessibility Initiative, came out with the Web Content Accessibility Guidelines (WCAG) version 1.0 in May 1999, which provide guidance to developers on how to design Web pages that are accessible to people with motor and perceptual impairments. People with impairments often use alternative input or output devices, for instance, people with motor impairments (such as limited use of hands) may not use a pointing device or may use an alternative keyboard or speech recognition for input. People with visual impairment may use a screen reader (such as JAWS, Window-Eyes, or VoiceOver), which provides computer-synthesized speech output of what appears on the screen, as well as back-end textual equivalents and labels in the code. To make a Website accessible does not mean changing the visual appearance. Web accessibility means to make sure that the Web page uses appropriate coding standards, such as making sure that all graphics and forms have meaningful text labels (such as name, address, rather than form1, form2), making sure that links make sense when heard out of context ("information about the history of Wal-Mart" rather than "click here"), making sure that any scripts, applets, or plug-ins have accessible equivalent content, and captioning and/or transcripts for any multimedia. And, of course, a Website is a living, breathing entity that changes on a daily basis. A Website that was accessible last week may be inaccessible this week, and accessible again next week. Accessibility must be maintained and monitored through organizational processes. A very common approach for this is for companies and government agencies to run a monthly report using automated accessibility tools (such as Deque WorldSpace or SSB Bart InFocus). While usability testing, involving users with disabilities, is the best way to evaluate Websites, automated accessibility testing (using some of the tools described previously) is used commonly for ongoing evaluation.

The WCAG 1.0 guidelines influenced laws around the world that were created that require that government information on the Web be accessible. Most laws are based on WCAG 1.0 or are strongly influenced by it. For instance, the Section 508 regulations in the United States, in subsection 1194.22 (the section addressing Websites), specifically notes that paragraphs a–k were based on WCAG 1.0. The Section 508 guidelines (which apply to both Websites and many other forms of technology) have been legally, in effect, since June 2001. However, there has been a gap between existing law and actual compliance. Most U.S. federal Websites are not currently accessible, and the Justice Department, which is in charge of reporting on Section 508 compliance to the U.S. Congress and the president every 2 years, has not done so since 2003. A July 2010 memo from the CIO of the U.S. federal government states that compliance activities will begin again soon. The Canadian national government has not fared any better. In November 2010, a Canadian federal court ruled that the Canadian national government has not followed their own laws related to Web accessibility and has set a 15-month deadline for the Canadian federal government to bring their Websites into compliance with the accessibility law.

Not only is accessibility policy changing, but the accessibility guidelines themselves are changing as well. In December 2008, version 2.0 of the WCAG was approved. Governments around the world are working on updating their regulations to match more closely with the new WCAG 2.0. In the United States, the Section 508 regulations have already been under review, and a new draft of Section 508 regulations (which is still waiting final approval) was released in March 2010.

Accessibility is not just important for government Websites, but also for Websites of companies, transportation providers, education, and nonprofit organizations. When Websites are inaccessible, it can lead to unemployment, discriminatory pricing, and lack of access to education. For instance, in one study from my research group, we determined that when Websites of airlines are not accessible, the airfares quoted to people who are calling the airlines on the phone are often higher, despite the callers noting that they have a disability and the law requires that they receive the same fares (and that they cannot be charged the call center fee). In November 2010, Pennsylvania State University was sued by the National Federation of the Blind, who claimed that the course management software, the department Websites, and even the online library catalog were inaccessible, prohibiting access to education. eBay has recently made their Website accessible, providing more employment and revenue opportunities for people with impairment. Currently, the U.S. Justice Department is working toward clarifying the Americans with Disabilities Act so that Websites of public accommodations (such as state government, education, and stores) would be addressed more clearly in the law.

I urge everyone to learn more about Web accessibility. Some great suggestions: start by trying to navigate a Website using only a keyboard, without using a pointing device. Then either download a free demo version of the screen reader JAWS (http://www.freedomscientific.com/jaws-hq.asp) or use a free Web-based screen reader such as WebAnywhere (http://webanywhere.cs.washington.edu). Read up on the Web Content Accessibility Guidelines (http://www.w3.org/TR/WCAG20) and check in to see what is currently happening in the public policy area related to Web accessibility. Web accessibility is a goal that can be achieved. As usability engineers, we play an important role in making this happen.

Suggested reading

Ebay. (2010). *EBay for users with special needs access*. Downloaded fromhttp://pages.ebay.com/help/account/accessibility.html.

Lazar, J., Jaeger, P., & Adams, A., et al. (2010). Up in the air: Are airlines following the new DOT rules on equal pricing for people with disabilities when websites are inaccessible? *Government Information Quarterly*, *27*(4), 329–336.

Loriggio, P. (2010). *Court Orders Ottawa to Make Websites Accessible to the Blind*. Downloaded fromhttp://www.theglobeandmail.com/news/national/ontario/court-orders-ottawa-to-make-websites-accessible-to-blind/article1817535/?cmpid=rss1.

Parry, M. (2010). *Penn State Accused of Discriminating Against Blind Students*. Downloaded fromhttp://chronicle.com/blogs/wiredcampus/penn-state-accused-of-discriminating-against-blind-students/28154.

Web Accessibility Initiative. (2010). *Web Content Accessibility Guidelines 2.0*. Downloaded from http://www.w3.org/TR/WCAG20/.

Experience-based characteristics

Experience-based characteristics can also contribute to user class or subclass definitions. Also, you should remember that experienced users for some systems are novices for others. Considerations include:

- novice or first-time user: may know application domain but not specifics of the application

- intermittent user: uses several systems from time to time; knows application domain but not details of different applications
- experienced user: "power" user, uses application frequently and knows both application and task domain very well

Example: User Class Definitions for MUTTS

Even though the ticket-seller role will be eliminated in the Ticket Kiosk System, it is instructive to look at user classes for the ticket seller work role for MUTTS. What characteristics are needed for this role? What training, background, or experience is required? Minimum requirements include point-and-click computer skills with typical Windows-based applications. Probably some simple training is called for. They had a manual explaining the job responsibilities, but over time it has become lost [from CJ2-17].

Because ticket sellers are often hired as part-time student employees, there can be considerable turnover with time. So, as a practical matter, much of the ticket seller training is picked up as on-the-job training or while "apprenticing" with someone more experienced in the role, with some mistakes occurring along the way [from DF1-9]. This variability of competence in the work role, which is the main interface with the public, is not always the best for customer satisfaction, but there does not seem to be a way around that [from HA2-12].

Other roles, such as the event manager or advertising manager, require some specific training because the work involves some complexity and must be done consistently from one client to another. The event manager must have knowledge and experience with the general domain of entertainment, events, and ticket selling. The advertising manager must have a certain level of knowledge and experience with promotions, sales, and the advertising aspects of business.

As we move from MUTTS to the Ticket Kiosk System, we will see user class definitions that relate more directly to kiosk usage. For example, you might be expected to include inexperienced (first-time) users from the general public, as well as senior citizens with limited motor skills and some visual impairment. Because the database administrator role includes tasks that involve technical issues, such as database structures and data integrity, a user class appropriate for the database administrator role would include requirements for professional training in database management functions. Finally, an additional work role, maintenance technician, is also introduced to maintain the kiosks. More new work roles will arise as they are encountered during the creation of the envisioned flow model and the envisioned social models.

Exercise

See Exercise 6-2, User Class Definitions for Your System

6.5.3 Social Models

Work does not happen in a vacuum; it occurs within a social setting, in the broadest sense. The social model is a design-informing model that captures the communal aspects of the users' organizational workplace, including the overall flavor, philosophy, ambiance, and environmental factors.

The social model highlights what is important to the organization. It characterizes the norms of behavior, influences, attitudes, and pressures that affect users within the work and usage context. Social models are about thought processes, mind-sets, policies, feelings, attitudes, and terminology that occur in the work environment. They include the concerns and influences of Beyer and Holtzblatt's cultural model. They include social ambiance and the social milieu, which define explicit or implicit social interaction in the workplace.

We call it a social model because it is mainly about the feelings, issues, and concerns of people in the workplace and the forces that influence those feelings and concerns, which often have a significant influence on how people approach and do their work.

Other factors involved include position or influence within the political structure of the organization, user goals, job-related factors, for example, job description, location, and level of responsibility, motivational factors, and attitudes toward the system such as "I hate this system because it will add to my work."

The social model contains nodes connected with arcs. Nodes represent active roles and arcs represent social relationships, such as influence by role on another. We describe how to create a social model diagram in the following sections.

Identify active entities and represent as nodes

In the social model, different entities—especially work roles— with concerns or influences within the work practice are represented as nodes. The active entities can also include any non-individual agent or force that participates in, influences, or is impacted by the work practice, internal to or external to the immediate work environment.

Examples of external roles that interact with work roles include outside vendors, customers, "the government," "the market," or "the competition." Perhaps the project team depends on an external vendor to supply a certain part in order to build a design prototype. Or an external regulatory agency may have put a rule in effect that limits the way a product can be marketed.

Alternatively, the enterprise may be limited by union policy regarding the number of people who can take on a given work role. Some workers in a large government agency may feel bound up by government rules and policies, by federal and state legislation, and by working in a union shop. Finally, generic roles in the broader business process model, such as "management," "the government," "the market," and "the competition," can be roles in a social model.

Groups and subgroups of roles. Work roles and other roles can be grouped into generalized roles that represent common concerns or influences. Group roles can be very informal with respect to the official organization chart. For example, you can refer to "those people in shipping" or "management" as groups.

System-related roles. There can be a number of different kinds of nonhuman roles in a social model, including databases, systems, external signals, and devices.

Workplace ambiance. The workplace ambiance is another nonhuman social model entity, one that represents the prevailing organizational identity and organizational attitudes, and any pervasive organizational personality. Ambiance includes the milieu, the atmosphere of the workplace, and the general "air" or "way of life" in the workplace.

Ambiance is part of the social model rather than a working environment model because of the psychological impact on users. Sometimes the ambiance of a workplace reflects stress and pressure.

As an example, consider a typical doctor's office. The general mood or work climate is rushed, chronically overbooked, and behind schedule. Emergencies and walk-ins add to the already high workload. The receptionist is under pressure to make appointments correctly, efficiently, and without errors. Everyone feels the constant background fear of mistakes and the potential of resulting lawsuits.

Work domain. The work domain itself can be an entity in a social model, possibly containing constraints and influences on the work practice. Examples include conventions and traditions in the work domain and legal and business policy constraints.

Create nodes to represent social model entities. Each node in a social model diagram represents an entity in the work practice of the enterprise. Start with sketching a node, as a circle for example, for each of the entities, of the kinds described in previous sections, in your broadly viewed existing working environment. Label each node with the name of the entity. Use circles within circles, in a Venn diagram approach, to represent groups and subgroups.

> ### Work Environment Model
>
> A work environment model is a model that defines the milieu in which work gets done, including constraints and artifact and physical models.

Example: Entities in the Slideshow Presentation Social Model

In Figure 6-4 we show the beginnings of a social model. We start by identifying the entities. In the social models for the cases studied in contextual inquiry for the Slideshow Commander, there were two main roles: one or more people in the presenter role and a group called the audience. In turn, the audience was sometimes composed of subgroups, local audience and remote audience(s).

To represent these entities as nodes in our diagram of Figure 6-4, we have drawn a circle labeled "Presenter" on the left and a large circle for "Audience" on the right. Two smaller circles inside the main audience circle are labeled for the subgroups "Local Audience" and "Remote Audience." We also added "Ambiance" as a nonhuman entity.

Each presentation potentially included one or more other subsidiary roles in the social model (not shown in Figure 6-4 for the sake of readability), including technical support, the host (to welcome the audience and introduce the speaker), advisory committees (in the case of student presentations), and members of the presenter's immediate research team. All of the people filling

Figure 6-4

Depiction of entities in the slideshow presentation social model. Thanks to Brad Myers, Carnegie Mellon University, and his colleagues for their case study (Cross, Warmack, & Myers, 1999) on which this example is based.

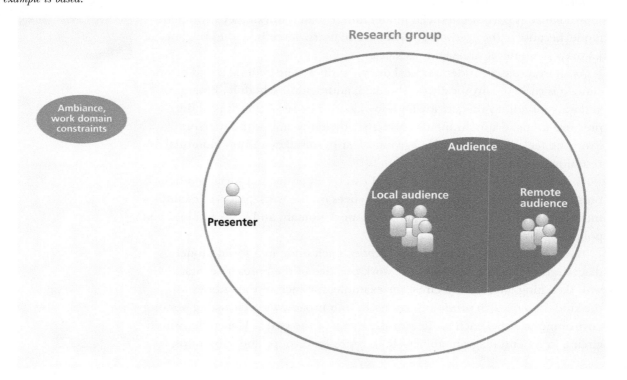

these roles worked toward making the communication between presenter and audience as smooth and as informative as possible.

Identify concerns and perspectives and represent as attributes of nodes

Often managers treat concerns of their employees as "intangibles," yet they can have a very tangible effect on how people work. Workers often have concerns about other workers, issues connected to their work roles, work goals, and how things get done in the work domain. The concerns show what people care about in the work place and how they think about their work, the tools they use, the people they work with, and the organization they work for.

They may (and are likely to) share overall work goals with other work roles, but each work role has a different perspective on the work and the workplace and on the other work roles. Groups and subgroups can have their own set of common concerns, just as any other entity. Many concerns are hidden and must be teased out in contextual inquiry.

For example, while the primary intents of people in work roles are to get the job done, people also have secondary intents driven by their own personal and possibly tacit agenda or concerns. Those concerns in turn motivate user behavior in doing the work and, if a system is used to do the work, in using the system.

For example, a manager might be concerned with capturing very complete documentation of each business transaction, whereas the person in the work role that has to compile the documentation may have as a goal to minimize the work involved. If our analysis does not capture this secondary user goal, in design we may miss an opportunity to streamline that task and the two goals may remain in conflict.

Finally, there is another kind of concern, personal concerns that relate to the user as a person rather than to the work. For example, most workers want to do almost anything to avoid being embarrassed or being made to look stupid. It is natural not to want to lose face publicly. Designs that emphasize worker production can be broadened to take these more personal concerns into account. Satisfied workers are more productive.

The point here is that information about this kind of personal concerns cannot be obtained from any requirements document, task analysis, or other engineering method. You must do the contextual inquiry and analysis and social modeling.

Label nodes with associated concerns. Summaries of user concerns are represented as text in "thought bubbles" connected to human roles and expressed in the perspective of users. We are showing what goes on inside the head of the person in the role in the style of a cartoon.

Example: Concerns in the Slideshow Presentation Social Model

In Figure 6-5 we have added the concerns of several roles of Figure 6-4. Because a member of the local audience was selected to set up the software and equipment for the presentation, we added "Selected Member" as a subgroup of "Local Audience." Note the feelings and concerns of the presenter and those of the audiences.

Identify influences and represent as relationships among entities

Each entity type can exert different kinds of influences on other entities.

Personal and professional inter-role influences. Individuals in work roles have different kinds of influence on individuals in other work roles that affect behavior within the work practice. There are personal feelings about the work and about

Figure 6-5

Depiction of concerns in the slideshow presentation social model.

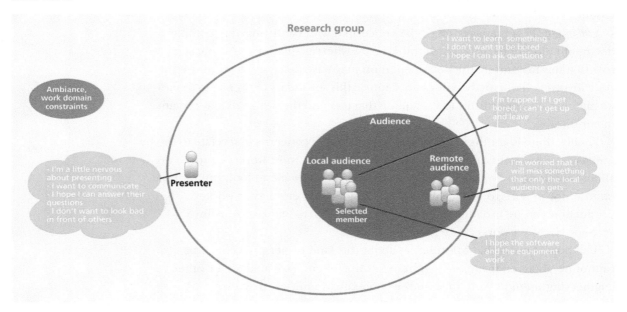

co-workers that influence how well people work together. The model may also reflect plain old interpersonal or inter-role frictions and animosities.

In an enterprise that counts on teamwork, there will be dependencies of people in certain roles on others in other roles—the ability to do one's job well can depend on others doing theirs equally well. As an example, consider a case in which one person gathers data from machines in the field and someone else analyzes these data. The analyst depends on getting accurate and timely data from the data gatherer.

Power influences. There are many kinds of power within most organizations. Power relationships between roles can stem from having different official ranks. As an example of influence built into the professional hierarchy, in our consulting with the U.S. Navy we often encountered a strong professional imperative that sometimes put rank above reason. It often meant to those of lower rank that it is better (for your career, if not for the task at hand) to follow orders and keep your opinions to yourself, for example, opinions about what might be a better way to do things.

Alternatively, nonmilitary employees can "pull rank" based on official job titles. Influence stemming from this kind of power relationship can be exerted in many ways. However, in a social model, power influence is not always based on power that comes with a given job title in an organization chart; it can be leverage or clout that exists as a practical matter and often comes from people who proactively take on leadership roles.

Influence comes from the strength or authority a person exerts in a work role. In meetings, to whom does everyone listen the most? When the chips are down, who gets the job done, even it if means working outside the box?

For systems with complex work domains, territorial boundaries are important to some people and can have a profound effect on how work is done. Interaction designers must take all these influences into account if they are to come up with a design that works in the target environment.

System-related influences. People in various roles can feel influences, including pressure or stress, from system-related entities, including the computer system. For example, a slow server can frustrate a data entry clerk and cause job stress.

Influences from ambiance. The general atmosphere of the workplace can exert powerful influences on work practice and behavior, including the values on which daily work practice is based, and the implied expectations that underlie the "way of life" in an organization.

Influences from work domain constraints. Constraints imposed by legal requirements and regulations, as well as organizational policies and politics, can frustratingly tie your hands as barriers to accomplishing your work goals.

Another source of influence on enterprise work practice has to do with whether system usage is discretionary or captive. This parameter, dictated by work domain constraints, indicates whether users in a particular work role have a choice in deciding to adopt or use the system being designed or whether political or organizational policies or business needs mandate the use of the system.

Discretionary users can walk away from the system if they do not like it. If a discretionary user does choose to use the system, that user is usually a receptive user, one who is favorably inclined toward adopting the system being designed. In contrast, captive users may feel trapped and may see the new system merely as adding to their work.

Barriers as influences. Barriers to successful work practice are a type of influence in the social model. One of the most common kinds of barrier to consider when redesigning work practice within a complex-domain system is rooted in people's attitude toward change.

Just because new ways of getting work done, new technology, and new systems may have obvious advantages to you, the designer, does not mean that they will not be upsetting to, and resisted by, the people whose jobs are affected. The attitude toward change can vary across an organization, from top management all the way down to the worker bees.

We have labored in organizations in which legacy systems thrive long beyond their useful lives because old-timers are bound up in a struggle to hang on to the old ways within an ancient "stove pipe" management structure. It is all but impossible to sell new ideas in these bastions of tradition.

It may sound like a trite observation, but the "we have never done it that way" mentality can be a huge and real barrier to creativity in a social work environment. Dissatisfied workers can also present real barriers within a work environment. In your contextual inquiry and analysis be sensitive to indicators of job dissatisfaction and do your best to glean insight on the underlying causes.

Be sure to include in your social model how people think and act negatively in response to dissatisfaction. Is the watercooler or the break room the center of subversive coordination? Is subversion or passive-aggressive behavior a common answer to power and authority? How strong is the "whistle-blower" mentality? Does the organization thrive on a culture of guerilla activity?

As in the other models, barriers, or potential barriers, in relationships between entities are represented as a red bolt of lightning (⚡), in this case on influence arcs. See examples of these barriers in Figure 6-6.

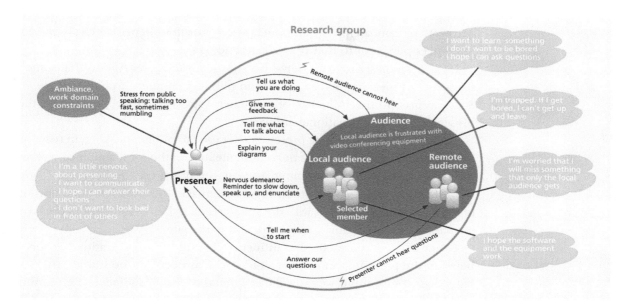

Figure 6-6

*Depiction of influences in
the slideshow presentation
social model.*

Consequences of and reactions to influence. People react to pressures and influences. Backlash reactions to influences are what Beyer and Holtzblatt call "push-back." For example, a person in a particular work role feels pressure to deliver but barriers to performing on the job have combined to produce frustration.

Users can react to this kind of job frustration by "pulling in their wings" and hunkering down to "endure" the job or they can react by causing further stress for everyone. This kind of situation needs a solution that will restore everyone's ability to contribute to the success of the enterprise while enjoying satisfaction on the job.

Create arcs to represent influences. Influences by one entity upon another are represented by an arrow, or directed arc, from the influencer to the influencee in the style of "influence: consequence/reaction". An arc can be bidirectional, shown as a two-headed arrow, if, for example, the two entities depend on each other in the same way. Arcs are labeled to denote the specific influence being represented.

Example: Arcs Representing Influences in the Slideshow Presentation Social Model

In Figure 6-6, we have added arcs representing some selected influences in the slideshow presentation social model. Note that arrows to and from the outer "Audience" circle correspond to influences common to both kinds of audience.

Arrows to or from an inner circle, such as the "Local Audience" circle, represent influences pertinent to that type of audience only.

In their studies, the team noted the mostly obvious observation that some stress due to speaking before a group in public is common to most people. So, we represent this influence of the general stress of public speaking on the presenter from the situational ambiance.

The team noted that some presenters not used to public speaking, in reaction to this influence, will display a nervous demeanor to the local audience, talking too fast and sometimes mumbling. You can see this presenter behavior represented as an influence on the local audience in the lower left-hand portion of the diagram in Figure 6-6, with the added reaction by the audience in the form of reminders to slow down, speak up, and enunciate.

Other barriers represented as influences include communication barriers between the presenter and remote audiences, as noted in the studies. In Figure 6-6, for example, we show the fact that the remote audience often cannot hear the presenter as a barrier, with a red lightning bolt, to the "influence" labeled "Tell me what you're doing."

Similarly, another red lightning bolt shows that the presenter cannot always hear questions from remote audiences. As an example of another barrier, when source material references were given verbally, they could not be remembered by audience members; this caused a barrier to pursuing the topic further after the talk.

Limited space in this one small figure precludes completeness, but you can imagine other influences. For example, the presenter desires feedback, support, and interesting questions from the audience. The audience desires clear and organized information. The presenter wants to impress everyone and wants to stimulate interesting discussion and help the audience understand the material. The audience wants clear and complete information.

An additional influence related to work domain constraints might arise with hierarchical audiences, as opposed to peers only. Their studies found a strong element of influence (again, not shown in Figure 6-6, for simplicity) due to the presence of faculty and thesis supervisors at a student presentation.

Because it is their job to do so, this kind of audience often exhibited a more critical tone and a more "demanding" (of explanations and rationale) and stressful ambiance for the presenter as compared to the more collaborative, sharing, and supportive ambiance of peer audiences that usually offered suggestions in a two-way exchange.

Example: A Social Model for MUTTS

In the example social model for MUTTS shown in Figure 6-7, we present selected parts of what is an even larger model. Starting with the roles, we identify the ticket seller and ticket buyer as the main ones, represented as two nearby circles near the top. Almost always you will want to include the ambiance and work domain as nonhuman entities.

The administrative supervisor, database administrator, and office manager are shown, and a full representation of the model would also show all other roles that appear in the upcoming flow model, such as the event manager, the advertising manager, and the financial administrator.

The diagram shows a few examples of concerns, including mutual concerns between the ticket buyer and the ticket seller about possible negative consequences of going to a kiosk-based system. The administrative supervisor is also shown as concerned about insufficient revenues from

Figure 6-7

Example social model for MUTTS.

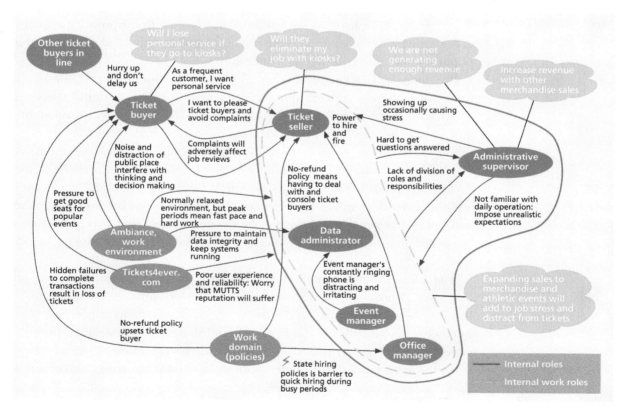

tickets alone. Note for clarity of narrative reading that we have omitted tags to the data sources.

The bulk of the diagram is devoted to influences. For example, the ticket seller wants to please ticket buyers and especially wants to avoid complaints from ticket buyers, complaints that could have a negative effect on the ticket seller's job reviews. You can also see pressure, when the ticket window is busy, from other ticket buyers in line for the current ticket buyer to hurry up and not delay the rest of them.

The ambiance exerts certain pressures on ticket buyers, too, because the environment is public and can be noisy, distracting the ticket buyer and impeding the ability to make event choices, seating choices, and other decisions needed to buy tickets.

The database administrator works in a relatively quiet office but could be faced with daily pressure to maintain data integrity and to keep the systems up and running continuously. Because of sharing a fairly small office with the event manager, whose phone is ringing constantly, the database administrator can, at times, find it hard to concentrate. When faced with the pressure of things going wrong with the computer, the ringing phone and constant chatter on the phone can become enormously irritating.

Problems with Tickets4ever.com are a negative influence on all internal work roles. There is concern that the poor quality usage experience users get on Tickets4ever.com will cast a shadow on MUTTS's reputation for reliability and service. Because ticket buyers do not necessarily make the distinction between Tickets4ever.com and MUTTS, they can all be painted with the same brush. For big concerts, a large online demand can sometimes overwhelm the Tickets4ever.com server and it goes down. If a transaction fails for any reason and the order does not go through and the ticket buyer starts over, he or she can sometimes get charged twice. If he or she does not start over, sometimes the order does not go through and the ticket buyer fails to get the expected tickets.

The administrative supervisor has influence on all the internal work roles, out of proportion to her real role in the work practice. Because she is not involved directly in the day-to-day operations, employees perceive her as unfamiliar with the work practice and therefore unrealistic in her expectations for performance. The staff then feels obligated to explain when the expectations are not met. And, when the workers have questions, it is hard for them to get answers from her.

To make things worse, the administrative supervisor tends to show up occasionally, causing stress for everyone. So she has an impact on people in other work roles and makes all their jobs harder, producing more on-the-job stress.

As another example of her influence, because the administrative supervisor's concerns that the enterprise is not generating enough revenue on contracts, ticket sales, and advertising, she has aspirations to increase total revenues by selling many items in addition to tickets, including over-the-counter commodities such as candy, gum, and aspirin, plus merchandise souvenirs, T-shirts, hats, and banners. But the people currently in other work roles are resisting this kind of change, saying that these merchandising activities will distract their focus on actual ticket operations. Plus their main sales software, Event Pro, is not set up for event-independent merchandise sales.

An example of work domain influence on both ticket buyers and ticket sellers is seen in the organizational policy not to give refunds for tickets. Tickets can be exchanged, but for a $3 fee. This policy causes a public relations problem because the staff has to deal with and console disappointed ticket buyers.

Another influence from the work domain, this one on the office manager, stems from the fact that MUTTS uses up to three ticket sellers to operate their three ticket stations. They often have just one ticket seller but in periods of high demand they need to hire additional ticket sellers quickly, which they later lay off. However, university hiring policies make it difficult to hire and fire temporary ticket sellers on a timely basis to match workload demands.

Ticket buyers exert various influences on the ticket seller. For example, many repeat customers want a "small-town" relationship with the ticket seller. They want them to remember the ticket buyer by name and, in some cases, provide recommendations based on what the ticket buyer likes.

Among the influences from the work domain is pressure on the ticket buyer to buy tickets for popular events before all the good seats are gone. For season tickets, it is especially important to get good seats because you will have the same seats for the whole season.

As an example of influence of the work domain on all roles, when the workload is high, over-the-counter sales get hectic and there is pressure on everyone to get things right. Errors and problems will upset ticket buyers.

Finally, through contextual inquiry interviews, we discovered an influence on all work roles that can be traced indirectly to the administrative supervisor. In some cases there is a lack of a clear division of roles and responsibilities,

Exercise

See Exercise 6-3, A Social
Model for Your System

Exercise

See Exercise 6-4, A Social
Model for a Smartphone

making it uncertain who is authorized to do what and who is not. This influence can lead to hand tying and, because of it, sometimes things do not get done.

Social models in the commercial product perspective

Social Model for a SmartphoneSocial models about usage of a commercial product can be very illuminating to designers. What is the context of usage? When do people use it? Are other people around? What does the product look like—is the impression cool or is it dorky? What are the users' feelings about having and using the product? Are they proud or embarrassed to own it? What does it say about them as individuals? What influenced them to buy it as opposed to a competing product?

The envisioned social model

As new work roles arise, so do concerns and influences experienced by people in those roles.

Example: An Envisioned Social Model for the Ticket Kiosk System

As we introduce the concept of ticket kiosks all around town, new roles, concerns, and influences arise in the social model. Venue managers may see the potential for greatly increased ticket sales but may wonder if they can handle the additional logistics. Advertisers might be thinking about how they can monitor the effects of the additional advertising. How can they determine if their kiosk ads are cost-effective?

The working environment for the ticket buyer now will be quite different. Instead of standing at the ticket office window, the ticket buyer will be at a kiosk in a public place that could be noisy and distracting. Also, now that the ticket seller is replaced with a kiosk, the ticket buyer interacts with a machine instead of a human; the issue of trust may become more important.

The ticket buyer will still need to communicate with friends and other individuals to discuss event information—only now the ticket buyer is at the kiosk. A cellphone would still work, but also maybe this need to communicate might inspire designers to consider a possible future feature requirement for including a way to send event information from the kiosk, via the Internet, to email addresses. This need for outside communication could also show up in the flow model.

Another example of a concern is that of a customer who uses the kiosk located at a bus stop: "If my bus arrives when I am only partway through a transaction to buy tickets, will I be able to get out quickly and safely and resume later, for example, after work tomorrow, without losing too much progress in my search for entertainment events?"

Because many of the kiosks will be placed near bus stops, the Middleburg Bus Authority, although not a direct user of the Ticket Kiosk System, becomes a stakeholder. And this new stakeholder has concerns about whether crowds at the kiosks will interfere with Middleburg Bus operations or introduce a safety hazard to bus riders.

Also, if the kiosks are actually on Middleburg Bus property, how much income can be expected from leasing the space for the kiosk? Middleburg Bus may also be worried about the added exposure to public liability, whether bus stop lighting is adequate, and will there be any added public safety issues? By the same token, the local police may be concerned about the potential for vandalism and whether a kiosk poses an "attractive nuisance."

6.5.4 User Personas

Technically, personas are a type of user models, but they are tied so closely to design that we discuss them in Chapter 7.

6.6 USAGE MODELS

Usage models are a set of models that define how work gets done, including flow models, task structure models, and task interaction models.

6.6.1 Flow Model

Different authors place different relative values on different kinds of models, but we believe that if you had to pick the single most valuable design-informing model, the flow model is it. The flow model is a picture of existing work processes in the work domain being analyzed for a new design.[1]

The flow model is like a plan view in architecture—it shows a bird's-eye view of the entire workflow of the enterprise humming along below. It should show territorial boundaries, especially the separation between enterprise and non-enterprise work roles.

Initial sketches of the enterprise flow model are begun from customer and user data early in contextual inquiry. Now we follow up on the flow model sketches and complete the flow model.

---

[1]Our approach to the flow model was influenced by Monk and Howard's (1998) rich picture model, which in turn has its roots in the Checkland's Soft Systems Methodology (Checkland & Scholes, 1990), which itself connects to roots common to those of work activity theory, contextual design, and other ethnographic and sociotechnical techniques in system design (Bjerknes, Ehn, & Kyng, 1987).

The focus of a flow model is on the issue of with whom and with what do the users in each work role interact. Specify whether the system supports inter-role communication or users must do it on their own, for example, via a shared database or through a telephone conversation. What information is exchanged when entities communicate? Describe the different types of information that are exchanged among work roles and other entities.

For example, in a financial institution, a loan officer may need to speak with customers over the phone as part of a home loan application. Such details provide valuable insights to designing for their work activities. For instance, in this case, the user interface of the loan officer user class could have an option to dial the customer's primary phone number as and when required at the touch of a button.

Creating a flow model diagram

Since early contextual analysis, you will have already been creating a flow model, representing workflow and other flow within the enterprise. We introduced this with a quick sketch in Chapter 4. Structurally, a flow model is a graph of nodes and directed arcs (arrows).

Nodes for entities. Labeled nodes represent entities in the enterprise workflow. Be sure you have represented as nodes all the work roles, including individuals or groups, direct or mediated users, potential users of all kinds, and all other entities that interact to get work done within the work practice.

"Other entities" include people outside the enterprise and entities such as systems, software, and devices. Most work domains in a domain-complex system context have a central database that users in all kinds of roles use to store, update, and retrieve work data. Draw entity nodes for information systems and databases that, like the work roles, are usually central in the workflow. Label each node with the corresponding entity name. Instead of using labeled circles for work role nodes, you can make your flow model more expressive by representing work roles as icons or stick figures depicting one or more people in those roles. You can make your flow model even more compelling by representing entity nodes with pictures of the corresponding personas labeled with their persona names, where they exist.

Having the user work roles visually in the center of a flow model also will help maintain user-centered thinking. Also, focusing on their workflow will help maintain usage-centered thinking.

Arcs for flow. Add labeled arcs or arrows to connect the entity nodes, showing who talks with whom and who gives what to whom, both internal to the enterprise and externally in the rest of the world. The arcs represent communication and coordination necessary to do the work of the enterprise—via email, phone calls, letters, memos, and meetings. Arrows show the flow of information, goods, services, workflow, work products, and artifacts during the execution of work practice.

If flow from one work role or piece of equipment in the system branches to more than one place, it can be helpful to know about how often it goes each way. Sellers (1994, p. 62, Figure 67) suggests labeling flow lines with percentages representing frequency of flow, if you have data to support it. Along with the label naming each arc, as much as possible, add a tag or identifier back to the relevant associated part of the raw data, using the tagging we did in Chapter 3.

If physical equipment contributes to flow, for example, information is communicated via telephones or email, label arcs accordingly. Flow model components should reveal how people get help in their work and make it clear where each artifact comes from and where it goes in the work process. Flow models also include non-UI software functionality, too, when it is part of the flow; for example, the payroll program must be run before printing and then issuing paychecks.

If you make a flow model of how a Website is used in work practice, do not use it as a flowchart of pages visited, but it should represent how information and command flow among the sites, pages, and users.

Example: A Flow Model for Slideshow Presentations

Separate flow models for slideshow presentation cases showed that the flow of information was often interrupted, either briefly or significantly, for almost 10 minutes during one presentation. The flow in some presentations, particularly ones with remote audiences, was overwhelmed with the need for the speaker and technicians to manipulate multiple electronic devices.

Barriers to flow were revealed most frequently when information flow to the presenter or the audience was interrupted, such as when extraneous application windows blocked part of the presentation screen or when sound controls were not adjusted properly. In Figure 6-8 we show an example flow model for slideshow presentations. Note the red lightning bolts representing barriers to flow.

Barrier

A barrier, in contextual modeling, is a problem that interferes with normal operations of user work practice. Anything that impedes user activities, interrupts work flow or communications, or interferes with the performance of work responsibilities is a barrier to the work practice.

Example: A Flow Model for MUTTS

The early sketch of the ticket-buying flow model for MUTTS shown in Figure 4-3 evolved into the diagram shown in Figure 6-9.

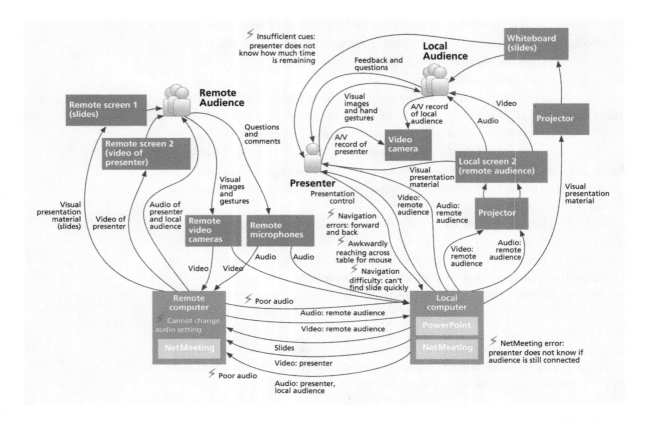

Figure 6-8

Example flow model from the slideshow presentation contextual inquiry. Thanks to Brad Myers, Carnegie Mellon University, and his colleagues for their case study (Cross, Warmack, & Myers, 1999) on which this is based.

This flow model shows flow of goods, services, and significant internal flow of information, for example, tickets and event information for customer, for running the business of MUTTS. The flow model is also a model of the enterprise organization business process, as it includes information transformations that occur as part of the flow as a component of the work process.

You may note that some of the important roles in the work process are within the MUTTS enterprise boundary (shown as an oval outline in Figure 6-9) and some are external. Some of the internal roles are, in fact, paired with external (to the MUTTS enterprise) roles in order to accomplish the flow of work.

For example, the internal role of event manager pairs up with the external role of the event promoter to carry out the work of booking and entering information for particular events. Note also interactions among roles not involved directly in ticket buying or selling, such as friends and/or family of

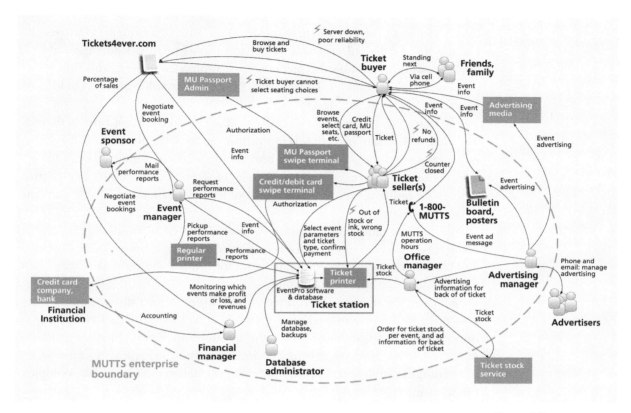

Figure 6-9

Flow model of our version of MUTTS.

ticket buyer in the upper right-hand corner of the diagram, standing there with the ticket buyer or on the cell phone, communicating about choices of events, dates, seats, and prices.

Flow models in the product perspective

In the perspective of a system with a complex work domain, the flow model is a complex enterprise representation. In the product perspective, the flow model can still be useful but is usually much simpler because there is usually no "organization" involved.

Flow models in the product perspective usually have fewer work roles than their domain-complex counterparts. The nature of work in the product perspective is different because of the fact that it does not happen in a fixed place. In an organization the workflow is somewhat fixed, although usually complex.

For a product, the workflow and context have much more variation from somewhat defined usage to connections with other users and devices for a

Exercise

See Exercise 6-5, Creating a Flow Model for Your System

large number of purposes. For example, in the case of a camera, most people just use it to take pictures, but if we expand the scope of consideration of workflow we get into how the pictures are downloaded, stored, and further processed and exchanged. Those parts of the photographic process could have implications for camera design.

For example, the need for easy physical access to the flash card, tethered-use picture transfer by cable, remote transfer by WiFi or infrared connections, sharing with friends and family, and streaming directly to printers or the Internet. The flow models of work in the product perspective tend to be much less connected than the typically established work patterns in an organization.

As another example, if the product being designed is a midrange laser printer, you need to model work activities in different types of homes, offices, and businesses, including all the activities for finding the right cartridge when one runs out and where to buy one.

Similarly, the amount of information exchanged among different work roles associated with a commercial product tends to be less structured and more opportunistic in nature. Also, given that the adoption of most end user products tends to be discretionary, it is much more important to capture and model a broad range of subjective and emotional impact factors than in domain-complex system contexts.

The envisioned flow model

Holtzblatt and colleagues (Beyer & Holtzblatt, 1998, pp. 275–285; Holtzblatt, Wendell, & Wood, 2005, Chapter 11) use the term "visioning" to describe their creation of an envisioned flow model. Through structured and focused brainstorming, the team creates a new design for work practice. The resulting vision is a story about the future, a new flow model of what the new work practice will be like and how the new system will support it.

To sketch out your envisioned flow model, you can start by reviewing, if necessary, relevant parts of your WAAD (Chapter 4) and any relevant design-informing models including, of course, your existing flow model. Brainstorm the flow of information and physical work artifacts among work roles and other parts of the system, such as external data sources and any central databases, as needed to carry out the high-level tasks in your HTI. Look for where work is handed off between roles, as these are places where things can fall through the cracks.

Hierarchical Task Inventory (HTI)

Hierarchical task inventory (HTI) is the process of cataloguing and representing the hierarchical relationships among the tasks and sub-tasks that must be supported in the system design.

Example: Envisioned Flow Model for the Ticket Kiosk System

The early sketch of the ticket-buying flow model in Figure 4-3 evolved into the diagram shown in Figure 6-9, which captured the viewpoints of the ticket-buying customer of MUTTS and the internal and external work roles required to run the business.

This flow model evolved into the envisioned flow model of Figure 6-10, which captures the viewpoints of the ticket-buying customer of the kiosk and some of the roles internal to the kiosk enterprise organization required to run the business, including the marketing manager, the event information manager, the database administrator, the financial administrator, and kiosk maintenance. This envisioned flow model shows several additional new work roles not identified previously for the Ticket Kiosk System.

Figure 6-10

Envisioned flow model for the Ticket Kiosk System.

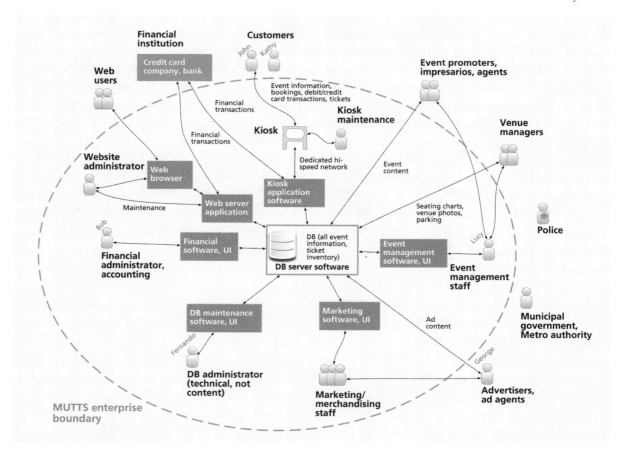

6.6.2 Task Models

Task models represent what users do or need to do in the work practice and work environment, using system or not. Task models include both task structure and task interaction models. The primary task structure model is the hierarchical task inventory, similar to the idea of hierarchical task analysis. There are several different task interaction models, each with its own way to represent the interaction.

Tasks vs. functions

In order to understand task modeling, one must appreciate the distinction between a task and a function. Informally, we may use the terms more or less interchangeably when talking about the features of a system, but when we wish to avoid confusion, we use the term "task" to refer to things a user does and the term "function" to things the system does.

When the point of view is uncertain, we sometimes see a reference to both. For example, if we talk about a situation where information is "displayed/viewed," the two terms represent two views of the same phenomenon. It is clear that "display" is something the system does and "view" is something the user does, as the user and system collaborate to perform the task/function. Within contextual analysis, of course, the user, or task, view is paramount.

6.6.3 Task Structure Models—Hierarchical Task Inventory

Task structure modeling, such as hierarchical task inventory modeling, is the process of cataloguing the tasks and subtasks that must be supported in the system design. Like functional decompositions, hierarchical task inventories capture relationships among tasks that need to be supported in a new system design.

Task inventories

A hierarchical task inventory, in which tasks are broken down into a series of subtasks and steps, is used:

- to show what user tasks and actions are possible
- to guide overall design
- as a checklist for keeping track of task coverage in your design (Constantine & Lockwood, 1999, p. 99)
- for matching that coverage to your inventory of scenarios and other task representations

Also, the accounting of the scope of tasks in hierarchical task inventory can serve as feedback about completeness in the contextual inquiry data, highlighting task-related areas of missing or inadequate contextual data to pursue in subsequent data-gathering activities. A hierarchical inventory of tasks is also a good source from which to select tasks for usage and design scenarios.

Figure 6-11

Hierarchical relationship of task A, the super-task, and tasks B and C, subtasks.

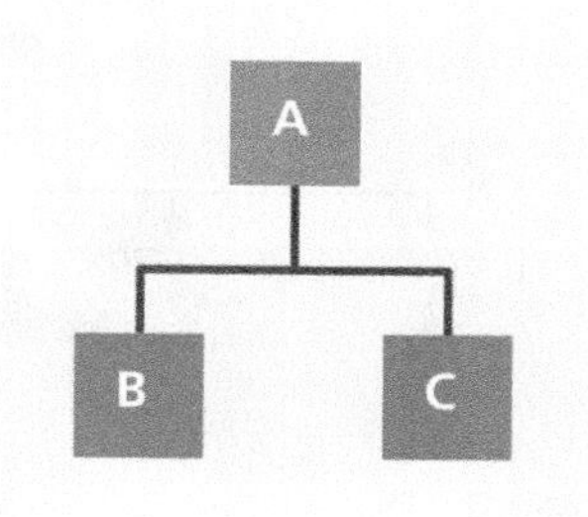

Task naming in hierarchical task inventories

In hierarchical task decomposition, each task is named and task names are usually of the form "action object," such as "add appointment" or "configure parameters." Task names require usage-centered wording rather than system-centered wording. For example, "view appointment" is a task name, but "display appointment" would be a system function name.

Hierarchical relationships are represented graphically by the usual tree-like structure, as in Figure 6-11. If task A is drawn above task B, it means A is a super-task of B, or B is a subtask of A. Exactly the same relationship exists between A and C. B and C are "sibling" tasks.

The litmus test characteristic for the meaning of this hierarchical relationship is that *doing B is part of doing A*. Another way to put it is: if the user is doing task B, then that user is also doing task A. As an example, if the user is filling out the name field in a form (task B), then that user is also filling out a form (task A).

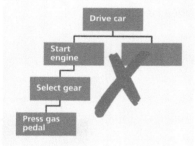

Figure 6-12

An incorrect hierarchical relationship attempting to show temporal sequencing.

Avoid temporal implications in hierarchical task inventories

The hierarchical relationship does not show temporal sequencing. So, in Figure 6-12 we depict an incorrect attempt at a hierarchical relationship because selecting a gear is not part of starting the engine.

Example: Hierarchical Task Inventory for MUTTS

Starting at the very highest level of tasks for MUTTS, you have the major task sets performed by each of the work roles, such as the financial administrator, the database administrator, the event manager, the advertising manager, and the ticket buyer. Using an "action-object" approach to task naming, these major task sets might be called "manage finances," "manage database," and so on, as shown in Figure 6-13.

> **Work Role**
>
> A work role is defined and distinguished by a corresponding job title or work assignment representing a set of work responsibilities. A work role usually involves system usage, but some work roles can be external to the organization being studied.

The full HTI diagram for MUTTS is enormous. Because the work roles often represent mutually exclusive task sets, often leading to separate interaction designs, it is convenient to treat them in separate HTI diagrams. In this example,

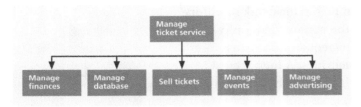

Figure 6-13

Sketch of the top levels of a possible hierarchical task inventory diagram for MUTTS.

we focus on the ticket-seller role and the corresponding most obvious task: "sell tickets."

How does this break down into subtasks? This is where our design-informing model notes about tasks come in. If we organize them in a hierarchical structure, we will see notes about big tasks at the top, subtasks in the middle, and individual user actions (if any) at the bottom. Looking at the top-level notes, we see that "sell tickets" involves a number of potential user activities to find and decide on an appropriate event before the actual ticket purchase is made.

We intend the "sell tickets" task to encompass all event searching and other subtasks that necessarily go into making a final ticket sale. In Figure 6-14, we show a few more details for under the "sell tickets."

Figure 6-14

Partial HTI for MUTTS "sell tickets" task.

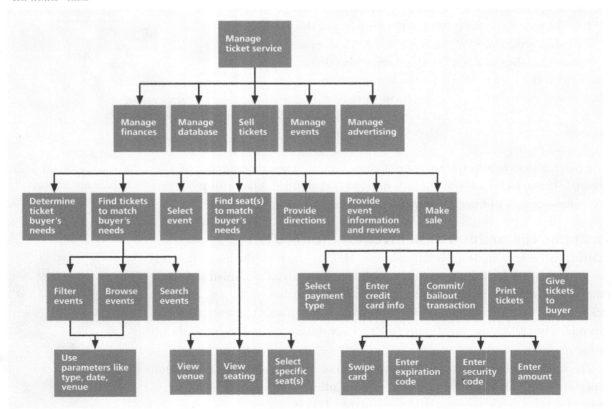

As we work with tasks we try to organize by adding logical structure. For example, there may not be task-related work activity notes explicitly about "finding information" in the contextual data, but there are references to work activities that imply the need for searching, browsing, and filtering event information. So we have pulled these together and synthesized the general heading of "find information."

Exercise

See Exercise 6-6,
Hierarchical Task Inventory
for Your System

Envisioned task structure model

If the task structure changes in your new vision of work practice, then it is important to update the HTI representation to reflect your envisioned task structure. The HTI also shows the new vision of how all the subtasks fit together under the tasks.

Example: Envisioned Hierarchical Task Inventory for the Ticket Kiosk System

The envisioned HTI diagram for the Ticket Kiosk System is very similar to the HTI diagram of MUTTS. The essential difference is that finding and ticket buying tasks are now done by the ticket buyer instead of the ticket seller, and they are done on a kiosk instead of a computer. New work roles and corresponding tasks will be added for kiosk monitoring and maintenance.

6.6.4 Task Interaction Models

In addition to modeling task structure, and much more important for understanding user work, we must model the interaction part of tasks, steps, and user actions required to perform tasks.

Usage scenarios as narrative task interaction models

Scenarios are a task description technique that offers powerful tools for gaining insight about user needs and activities, supporting almost every phase of the interaction design lifecycle. In this chapter the term "scenario" refers to a "usage scenario" because these scenarios are extracted from contextual data that reflect actual usage that stems from real work practice in the existing work domain. When we get to design, we will talk about "design scenarios" because those scenarios are stories of what usage will look like using the new design.

Like other design-informing models, scenarios are threads that link various interaction design process activities. Scenarios begin in contextual inquiry and requirements analysis and later will play an obviously important role in design. Real contextual data provide the necessary richness to avoid superficiality

(Nardi, 1995). Even after transitioning to a product, scenarios can be updated and used for usability evaluation and in training to show users examples of how to do various tasks.

What are scenarios, how do they work? Usage scenarios are stories about specific people performing work activities in a specific existing work situation within a specific work context, told in a concrete narrative style, as if it were a transcript of a real usage occurrence. However, as Go and Carroll (2004) point out, scenarios are many things to many people. In addition to their obvious value in requirements and design, Go and Carroll (2004) demonstrate their use as a brainstorming tool for planning, a decision-making tool for stakeholders, requirements engineering support, and a tool for object-oriented analysis and design.

Scenarios describe key usage situations happening over time, being deliberately informal, open-ended, and fragmentary. Interaction designers use these scenarios to gain a better understanding of the system usage in the context of the user's actual experience. Tasks defined in task modeling become the heart of each scenario, which attempts to capture a representative description of the actual task performance.

Because scenarios are work oriented, they focus on needs, goals, and concerns of users. Scenarios reveal and facilitate agreement on requirements and evoke thought and discussion about requirements, design, user experience goals, and testing strategy.

Elements of scenarios. Scenarios typically capture these kinds of elements:

- Agents (users, people in work roles, often in personas, system, sensors)
- User goals and intentions
- User background, training, needs, etc.
- Reflections on work practice, including user planning, thoughts, feelings, and reactions to system
- User actions and user interface artifacts
- System responses, feedback
- User tasks, task threads, workflows, including common, representative, mission critical, and error and recovery situations
- Environmental and work context (e.g., phone ringing)
- Barriers, difficulties encountered in usage
- And, of course, a narrative, a story that plays out over time

Usage scenarios should be annotated, as meta-data, with comments about what you have observed that works and what does not, what the problems are with the way things are done currently. We represent a barrier or difficulty in a usage scenario with the usual red lightning bolt (⚡) added at a strategic place in the text.

Scenarios are not for everyone. The efficacy of scenarios as models to inform design is not universally lauded. In a CHI 2003 tutorial, Constantine and Lockwood (2003) claim that scenarios suffer from a few drawbacks, which we quote verbatim here:

- coarse-grained model muddles distinct tasks
- rarely feasible to model entire task domain
- superfluous details distract from essentials
- exceptional, uncommon, or unimportant actions can assume undue prominence in story line
- concreteness does not facilitate innovative thinking

Example: Usage Scenario for MUTTS

Here is a fairly detailed usage scenario about a group of students using MUTTS.

On cellphone and email over a day or two, Priya and a group of her friends plan an evening out together on the coming weekend. They agree to meet at the MUTTS ticket window on Friday afternoon. Some walk to MUTTS, while others take the bus.

With the work week behind them, the group is in a festive mood, looking for entertainment over the weekend. They decide to check out events for Saturday night. After waiting in line, Priya asks the ticket seller what kinds of events have tickets available for Saturday night. The agent looks through her computer listings of movies, concerts, plays, fairs, carnivals, and special events and tells the group about their options. After talking among themselves, they decide they want to go to a concert. The agent asks, "Which kind, classical or pop?" They choose to go with a pop concert. Again, she tells them their options. They finally decide on a concert playing at The Presidium.

There is some unease within the group, though, because they feel that the agent did not give them enough information to make the best choice (⚡) and they felt some pressure to decide in a hurry (⚡), as the agent was standing there and waiting.

They ask about what seats are available and the agent goes back to her computer and brings up a graphical seating map of the hall. However, the tickets the agent has on hand are for only a subset of the seats actually available, forcing the group to pick from these, knowing they had not seen all the real

Exercise

See Exercise 6-7, Usage
Scenarios for Your System

options (⋏). They choose their seats based on price and seat location and the agent requests an option to buy the tickets, locking out others until the transaction is either completed or given up. The group agrees on the purchase and then discusses the matter of paying. They decide to give Priya cash and she will pay on her credit card, so Priya swipes her credit card through the slot on the counter. The transaction is authorized by the credit card company, the sale is committed, and the agent gives them the tickets. The group is happy, but they leave with a nagging feeling that there must be a better way to buy tickets.

Envisioned usage scenarios or design scenarios

One of the most effective kinds of design-informing model for facilitating connections between requirements and design is the design scenario. In the envisioned transition to design, these scenarios are stories of what usage will look like in the new design, stories that inform design in a detailed and concrete way.

Design scenarios are the best way to visualize early the consequences of design choices and to share and communicate design ideas at the task level. Scenarios are an excellent medium for discussion of design alternatives and are easy to change as the design evolves. Much of your early design can be informed by design scenarios, starting with the key task set you have chosen to lead the design effort.

In creating a design informed by a scenario, you do not want your design to be too specialized for *just* that one scenario, but you want to be general enough to *cover* the scenario. However, do not overgeneralize the design to cover every user's needs in a big potpourri of functions, either. As your personas evolve (next section), you can feature them in design scenarios. This will help show clearly how your designs are aimed at particular personas. Soon you will also be extending your scenarios by interspersing the narrative with graphic presentations of storyboards.

Example: Design Scenario for the Ticket Kiosk System

A local movie theater, The Bijou, has a standing contract with the Ticket Kiosk System Company, and every time a new movie comes up, all of the information about showings, trailers, and advertising blurbs get sent automatically to the kiosk event manager in the right format so that most of it can be posted automatically.

Many different local and other advertisers have contacted the marketing manager and sent graphics and text advertising for their products and companies. For example, the Back Country Provisions has a beautiful advertisement about tents, backpacks, hiking boots, and so on. Plus, they have an agreement to associate their advertisement with any event, for example, a movie about Alaska, that has to do with hiking, camping, or traveling into any kind of wilderness or camping situation.

On a Friday night, Joe drives his pickup into the parking lot next to a bus stop with a Ticket Kiosk System kiosk. Joe is looking for some entertainment for the evening, something to take his mind off the busy past week. He is thinking about a fun sporting event on this Friday night, maybe basketball game or a hockey game.

At the "Welcome" screen Joe, touches the button labeled "Sports" from the main menu and looks under the current date. But the ones that are available that night really do not appeal to him, so he starts browsing for other events. He touches the "Main menu" button and returns to the "Welcome" screen.

Joe is tired after a hard week of work, and he does not think he has the energy to go to a concert, so he thinks he might like to just sit back and see a movie. He touches the "Movies" button and browses casually through some of the movies that are currently showing and sees *Into the Wild* and gets excited. He has never been to Alaska and he has always wanted to go. In fact, this would be a great movie for him to take a date.

Joe has been secretly dating a woman named Jane, who lived in Alaska before moving to this area. Joe calls Jane on his cellphone and, although she too would prefer to attend a hockey game, she agrees to meet him at The Bijou.

While Joe is standing there on the phone in front of the kiosk, he sees an advertisement for Back Country Provisions, which is showing on the far right-hand side of the screen, as it is automatically associated with this movie. As he looks at it, he imagines himself off in the wilderness, escaping his busy work life. He dreams of himself on this nice trip to Alaska. He makes a note to stop by at Back Country Provisions and see what kinds of hiking boots they have.

Joe then pays for the tickets with a credit card, and the transaction goes by wire to the financial company. The transaction is approved and the tickets are printed. The printer ink is getting a little low, which triggers a sensor, and a warning is sent to the kiosk maintenance person. Joe is so excited about pulling this all off (the transaction and the date) that he almost forgets to take the tickets from the slot, but he sees the reminder message on the screen that says "Thank you. Do not forget to take your credit card and your tickets."

Exercise

See Exercise 6-8, Design Scenarios for Your System

Step-by-step task interaction models

A more direct and less story-oriented way to describe task interaction is by a step-by-step task interaction model. Beyer and Holtzblatt (1998) call this kind of model a "sequence" or a "sequence model."

A step-by-step task interaction model contains a detailed description of task performance observed in users or as told by users. Remember that task interaction modeling is all about current work practice, not (yet) an envisioned way to do things with a new system. So, any references to specific systems or technology necessary in describing the task steps will always be to existing technology and existing task-supporting systems.

The task interaction model of work also shows the detailed steps of task performance, including temporal ordering of actions and activities. Like usage scenarios, task interaction models capture instances of possibilities ("go paths" or representative paths), not complete task specifications. At the beginning, individual task interaction models will be mostly linear paths without branching. Later you can add the most important branching or looping.

So, for example, an initial task interaction model for an online purchase might not show a decision point where the user can pay with either a credit card or PayPal. It would just be a linear set of steps for the task of buying a ticket with a credit card. Later, as task interaction models are consolidated, a separate linear path for the alternative of paying with PayPal is merged, introducing a decision-making point and branching (see sub-section later).

Task and step goals. A task or step goal is the purpose, reason, or rationale for doing the task or taking the step. Called the user "intent" by Beyer and Holtzblatt (1998), the goal is a user intention, in the sense of being "what the user wants to accomplish" by doing the task. Each task interaction model will include a goal statement at the top. Goals and subgoals, as well as multiple goals, are possible for the same task and for each step in a task.

The goal of a task, being the "what" of a task interaction model, is often more important to understanding work than the way a task is performed or the steps of the "how." If the work stays the same in the transition to a new system, the task goal usually stays the same, regardless of the operational steps in the way of doing the task. In fact, a list of the goals can stand alone without the task steps, as a "to-do" list for the user.

Task triggers. A task trigger (Beyer & Holtzblatt, 1998) is an event or activation condition that leads that user to initiate a given task. For example, when a user makes a phone call, it might be because something came up that presented an information need that can be resolved by the call. If the user logs into a system, it is because a need arose, maybe from an incoming call, to access that system.

If a user sends a "heads-up" message to a user in another role, it is because of a desire or need to inform that user of something important to the work process. Triggers are easy to identify in your contextual inquiry observations.

New work arrives in the user's in-box, a new aircraft appears on the air traffic controller's screen, an email request arrives, or the calendar says a report is due soon.

Information and other needs in tasks. One of the most important components of a task description is the identification of user information and other needs at any step. Unmet information needs constitute one of the largest sources of barriers in task performance. The contextual inquiry and analysis processes and modeling can help you identify these needs and eventually design to meet them.

Information and other needs of people in work roles at certain points within task performance are represented by specific annotations to the graphical diagram of a step-by-step task interaction model. Just before the step in which the need occurs, we add an indented line beginning with a red block "N," like this, N, followed by a description of the need.

Barriers within task interaction models. These are things that happen or difficulties encountered that present impediments to task performance, including things that slow the user down and make a task more difficult than necessary. The symbol for a barrier in a task interaction model is, you guessed it, a red lightning bolt ($\mathcal{N}$), which you should put at the beginning of an indented line explaining the barrier.

Something that requires the user's attention to be divided might be a task barrier or an intervening manual step that interrupts the flow of using the system. Task barriers also include interruptions and having to "stack" one task in the middle to go off and do something else before coming back and trying to remember where things were in the original task. For example, suppose a key input to a task is unavailable, delayed, or difficult to dig out. Perhaps the user has to stop in the middle of the task and go to a different system to get the needed information. That kind of task detour is a barrier.

If the user's reaction or response to a barrier is known through the contextual data, add a brief description of that right after the barrier description among the task steps.

Creating a step-by-step task interaction model. Step-by-step task interaction models are mostly textual. Write the initial task interaction model as a linear task thread, as a model of one instance of how a task happened with a user, not a general model of how all users perform the task. Sequential steps can be written as an ordered list without the need for flowchart-style arrows to show the flow. Linear lines of text are less cluttered and easier to read.

Start with some structural components, a label for the task name and a contextual data identifier, a tag identifying the source of the specific data used for this instance of the model.

The task description is labeled at the top with one or more task goals and the task trigger, followed by the steps at whatever granularity of detail is needed to help everyone understand it. Lines describing breakdowns and information needs are indented to set them off, interspersed with the steps, and labeled, respectively with a ⩕ or an **N**. Include responses or reactions to barriers, if known, and label as such. In addition, each task step can be labeled with its own step goal(s) and step trigger.

It can help analysis and discussion to number the steps so that you can refer to, for example, step 5 of the send email task interaction model. Note cases of multitasking, where the user is juggling more than one task thread at once. The increased cognitive load to keep track of multiple tasks can be a barrier to ease of use.

Example: Step-by-Step Task Interaction Model for MUTTS

This is an example of a step-by-step task interaction model for the task of ticket buying by the ticket seller work role. People often have something specific in mind when they go to buy tickets but, to illustrate a rich step-by-step interaction model, we are using an example in which the ticket buyer starts by wanting to know what is available.

> **Task name:** Finding entertainment for a given date (performed by ticket seller on behalf of ticket buyer)
>
> **Task goal:** Helping a ticket buyer choose and buy a ticket for entertainment for this coming Friday night
>
> **Task trigger:** Ticket buyer arrives at the MUTTS ticket window on the way home from work on a Thursday evening, thinking ahead to the weekend

Ticket Buyer	Ticket Seller
1. Tells ticket seller about general goal of wanting to find an entertainment event for the next night (Friday night)	
2. Asks agent about available types of entertainment	3. "There are plays, concerts, movies, and sports"
4. Not enough information yet to decide on the category. Asks to see examples of different types.	

Step goal: Consider examples of entertainment events

5. Asks what events are available for Friday night	

Barrier ⚡: Agent sees that the number of results is too large to sort through or tell the customer about

Response to barrier:

	6. Ask customer how to filter results or narrow it down (e.g., "Tell me more about what you like")
7. "How about something within reasonable walking distance downtown or near a Middleburg bus stop?	8. Tells about some possibilities

Task continues:

9. Thinks about the list of possibilities

⚡: It is difficult to think about specific events while remembering all the others given orally on the list

Response to barrier:

10. Makes a few sketchy notes by hand

Trigger: Movies seem attractive to ticket buyer

Goal: Find a movie to see

11. Tells agent about switching focus to just movies	
12. Tells agent to use the same criterion about being within reasonable walking distance downtown or near a Middleburg bus stop	13. Tells about possibilities
14. Considers possibilities and finds a few he likes	
15. Writes choices down on paper	

Trigger for interrupt to embedded task: Thinks a friend might also like these movies

N: Needs to know friend's opinion of the selections

Goal: Contact a friend to help narrow these last few choices down and pick something together

16. Asks agent to please wait

17. Calls friend on cellphone

18. Makes choice with friend

Trigger: Choice made, ready to buy two tickets

Goal: To buy tickets

19. Tells agent to buy two tickets to selected movie	20. Sets up transaction in computer
	21. Cash or credit card?
22. Gives agent credit card	23. Swipes card
24. Signs credit transaction	25. Prints tickets and receipt
	26. Gives printed tickets and returns credit card and receipt

Branching and looping. Although step-by-step task interaction models are primarily for capturing linear sequences of representative task steps, sometimes you encounter a point in the work practice where there is a choice. You observe some doing A and other users B. You can generalize the task sequence representation by showing this choice in both observed paths using branching, as shown with arrows on the left-hand side of Figure 6-15. Note the conditions for branching on the diagram.

Similarly, if you observe iteration of a set of tasks or task steps, you can represent that as shown on the right-hand side of Figure 6-15. For sets of steps that are repeated or iterated, note the number of iterations or the condition for termination.

Example: Task Interaction Branching and Looping for MUTTS

In Figure 6-16 we show a sketch of task interaction representation for selling tickets with MUTTS. Note several instances of looping to iterate parts of the task and, in the bottom box, branching to accommodate two different cases.

Essential use case task interaction models

By combining the best characteristics of step-by-step task descriptions and software use cases, Constantine and Lockwood (1999, p. 100 ff) created essential use cases as an alternative task interaction modeling technique.

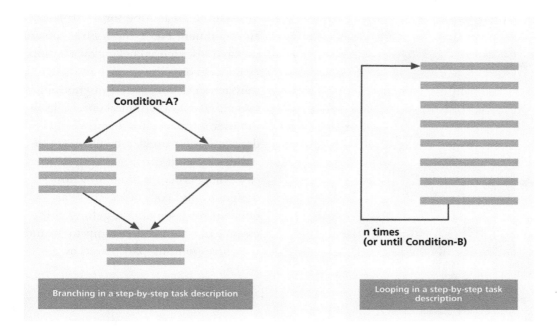

Condition-A?

Branching in a step-by-step task description

**n times
(or until Condition-B)**

Looping in a step-by-step task
description

Figure 6-15

*Branching and looping
structures within step-by-
step task interaction
models.*

An essential use case is a structured narrative, in the language of users in the work domain, that describes a single user intention or goal, a complete, well-defined task description that is meaningful to a user in a role (Constantine & Lockwood, 2003).

An essential use case is a kind of step-by-step task description but, being more abstract and less specific than step-by-step task interaction models of the previous section, it is not a complete story, nor is it a scenario, but rather a task skeleton on which a scenario story could be woven. An essential use case is a simple, general, and abstract task description, independent of technology or implementation. Just as it does in task interaction models, the importance of the task goals underlying an interaction greatly overshadows that of specific steps or user actions to carry them out.

In the classic style of using columns, or "swim lanes," to represent collaborative task performance between user and system, an essential use case has two columns: one for user interactions and one for corresponding system responsibilities. The inclusion of system responsibilities clearly connects user actions to requirements for what the system must do in response.

Each essential use case is named with a "continuing verb" to indicate an ongoing intention, plus a fully qualified object, for example, "buying a movie ticket." Essential use cases capture what users intend to do and why, but not how,

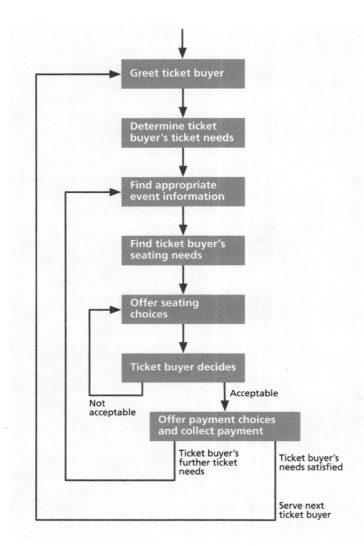

Figure 6-16

Task interaction branching and looping for MUTTS.

for example, searching for a particular entertainment event, but nothing about user actions, such as clicking on a button.

Because only the essence of the transaction is represented and nothing is said about how the transaction looks in the user interface, it is an easy description for users and customers to understand and confirm. Essential use cases help structure the interaction design around core tasks. These are efficient representations, getting at the essence of what the user wants to do and the corresponding part played by the system.

The term "essential" refers to abstraction. An essential use case contains only steps essential to the user and the task. The representation is a further abstraction in that it represents only one possible task thread, usually the simplest thread without all the alternatives or special cases. Each description is expressed as a pure work-domain representation, not a system domain or design-oriented expression.

To illustrate, in Constantine and Lockwood's ATM example, the user's first step is expressed as an abstract purpose, the "what" of the interaction: "identify self." They do not express it in terms of a "how"; for example, they do not say the first step is to "insert bank card." This is a deceptively simple example of a very important distinction.

The abstraction of essential use cases is the opposite of the concreteness of usage scenarios. Usage scenarios read like real stories because they contain specific names of people and specific details about the context. These concrete details make the story easy to read and easy to understand, but when they are generalized as essential use cases, they serve better as inputs to interaction design.

Many of the details, although they add interest, are not essential to the general understanding of a task and how users perceive and perform it. In usage scenarios, those names and details are placeholders for more general attributes and information. The user's name is a stand-in for all such users. A specific usage scenario describes an instance of the task, an instance of an essential use case.

Task cases are simplified and technology and implementation independent, traits that bring them close to the essence of work activities. Essential use cases are descriptions of what users do, not about design.

Example: Essential Use Case for MUTTS

Table 6-1 contains an example, cast in the same fashion as Constantine and Lockwood (2003). This is a task that the ticket seller does with the computer using the ticket buyer's credit card.

Your contextual data can indicate focal points for expanding and elaborating task details. As an example, there are some possible alternative cases following step 6, when the system reads the credit card. Perhaps the system could not read the card successfully or maybe there is a problem with the credit or debit account associated with the card—the card has been reported stolen, the account has been cancelled, or payment is overdue.

While these detailed alternative task paths are important to capture, they are not usually put directly in the task description, as they would interfere with its abstract simplicity. You can create new essential use cases for these ancillary

User Intention	System Responsibility
1. Ticket seller to computer: Express intention to pay	2. Request to insert card
3. Ticket seller or ticket buyer: Insert card	4. Request to remove card quickly
5. Withdraw card	6. Read card information
	7. Summarize transaction and cost
	8. Request signature (on touch pad)
9. Ticket buyer: Write signature	10. Conclude transaction
	11. Issue receipt
12. Take receipt	

Table 6-1

Example essential use case: Paying for a ticket purchase transaction (with a credit or debit card)

task threads or you can put the alternate cases and exceptions in a list that goes with the basic task description to remind designers that these special cases have to be dealt with in the design.

Envisioned task interaction models

Individual task descriptions in your envisioned task interaction models are exactly what you need as inputs to scenario and storyboard content. Begin your envisioned task descriptions by selecting a set of key tasks that will serve to focus the initial design effort and help you control complexity. Remember that task triggers are pivotal and must be represented in the envisioned models, too; otherwise the same task will not get done when using the new design.

Also, do not forget to design for task threads. It is relatively easy to design for single user tasks isolated from the workflow. In fact, HTI can lead you to think that tasks can be boxed up and addressed separately.

But, of course, tasks are woven into a fabric of user workflow. Real work occurs as task threads, and you have to design for the continuity of likely next tasks within the workflow. Your contextual data are key for understanding where you find these "go paths" or "happy paths" that users like to slide through.

6.6.5 Information Object Model

Information objects are work domain objects shared by users and the system. As internally stored application objects, information objects are hugely important in the operation and design of a system. These are mainly the entities that move through the workflow in the flow model. These are the entities within an application that are operated on by users; they are searched and browsed for, accessed and displayed, modified and manipulated, and stored back again.

In action-object task names, such as "add appointment," the object (appointment) is often an information object. They are connected directly to the design ontology that drives the bread and butter of most domain-complex system designs. They show up as objects of user actions in usage scenarios and other task descriptions and drive design questions such as how will users access the objects and how will we represent them to users in displays, as well as how will users do the operations to manipulate these application objects?

In a calendar application, for example, appointments will be objects that are created and manipulated by users. As another simple example, suppose a user draws a circle with a graphics-drawing package. Data representing the circle

Design Ontology

Design ontology is a description of all the objects and their relationships, users, user actions, tasks, everything surrounding the existence of a given aspect of a design.

are stored by the system, the user can call it up and the system will display it, and the user can manipulate and modify it and save it back in the system.

Most information objects have defining attributes. A calendar appointment has date, time, subject, and so on; a graphical circle has a radius, location, color, and so on. Start the information object model by compiling information objects identified in the contextual data. Sketch an outline or list of information objects, their attributes, and the relationships among them.

Example: Identifying Information Objects and Attributes in MUTTS

The two-word goal of the main task of the ticket seller work roles is "sell tickets." Within this goal, the term "tickets" identifies a principal information object in the system. We know that a ticket is associated with an event, another information object, which in turn is linked to attributes, such as event date, time, venue, and so on. We also know that each event object is associated with descriptive attributes, such as genre, to support customer user searching and browsing.

Analyzing scenarios to identify ontology

As usage stories, scenarios tie together many kinds of design-informing models. They help you identify information objects and how they are manipulated and by which work roles. To see links with other design-informing models, you can tag or highlight words and phrases occurring in scenarios with the type of design element they represent. You can identify and label the components of design scenarios, such as tasks, actions, user interface objects, user roles, user experience goals, user classes, user characteristics, application information objects, system data objects, and work context.

Example: Scenario Analysis to Help Identify Ontological Elements of the Ticket Kiosk System

We have highlighted (with italics and color) some of the ontological elements of the example scenario for the Ticket Kiosk System given earlier.

On *cellphone* and *email* over a day or two, *Priya* and *a group of her friends* agree to take in some entertainment together on the coming weekend. They agree to meet at the Ticket Kiosk System kiosk at the *library bus stop* at *5:30 PM on Friday.* Some walk to the kiosk from nearby, while others avail themselves of the convenience of the bus. The group is in a *festive mood, looking forward to sharing some fun over the weekend.*

Priya steps up to the kiosk and sees a *"Welcome" screen with an advertisement for a movie scrolling at the top* and text that says "What kind of even information would you like to see?," followed by several *touchscreen buttons* with labels on the left-hand side such as "Browse by event type," "*Browse by venue/location*," and "Event calendar: Browse by date." On the right-hand side there are buttons for specific types of events, such as "Sports," "Concerts," "Movies," "Special features," etc.

Because they are *looking for something specifically for the next night*, she touches the "Event calendar" button, *looking for events such as movies, concerts, plays, fairs, or even a carnival for Saturday night*. After browsing for a while and talking among themselves, they want to go to a concert. Priya touches the "*Concerts*" button, and they are presented with the subcategories *Rock, Classical, Folk, and Pop*. They choose to go with pop concerts and Priya touches that button. From among several choices, they finally decide on a concert called "Saturday Night at the Pops" playing at The Presidium.

- *Cellphone* and *email* refer to methods of communicating with family and friends outside the system
- *Priya* is the name of a person in the customer/user role
- *a group of her friends* refers to other roles, customers who are probably not direct users
- *library bus stop* refers to a location of use (of a kiosk), part of the work context
- *5:30 PM on Friday* refers to a time of use (a time when the kiosk is open but the old MUTTS would not have been open), also part of the work context
- *festive mood, looking forward to sharing some fun over the weekend* refers to an emotional state of mind of the users, expressing an expectation to be met by the product, a subtle part of the work context
- *"Welcome" screen with an advertisement for a movie scrolling at the top* is a design idea for user interface objects
- *touchscreen buttons* are possible user interface objects
- *"Browse by venue/location"* is a suggested button label, which also indicates a user task
- *looking for something specifically for the next night* is a user task
- *looking for events such as movies, concerts, plays, fairs, or even a carnival for Saturday night* is a combination of user tasks
- *"Concerts," Rock, Classical, Folk, and Pop* are names of categories of information/application objects

And so on. Can you identify others? The idea of identifying these different entities within scenarios is that they help pick out types and instances of design-informing models and help identify ontological objects and tie them together in the threads of design scenarios in ways that directly inform designing.

Exercise

See Exercise 6-9, Identifying Information Objects for Your System

6.7 WORK ENVIRONMENT MODELS

Working environment models are a set of models that define the milieu in which work gets done, including constraints, artifact models, and physical models.

These models capture how the related work environment factors affect tasks in real usage. Of the work environment models, the physical model is probably the most important. Factors such as the layout of work space, proximity of printers or scanners, and the inability to hold a device with a keyboard while standing up will have a direct impact on UX and work practice.

In the slideshow presentation example presented earlier, the physical model indicates where people in the different roles will be standing or seated, the presentation room layout, and the ability to control light from windows and to control selectively the artificial lighting in the room. Sound and other attributes of the space will contribute to the physical model, as do the availability and locations of electrical outlets and Internet connections.

6.7.1 Artifact Model

An artifact model shows how tangible elements (physical or electronic) are used and structured in the business process flow of doing the work. Work artifacts are one of the most important entities that get passed from one work role to another within the flow model. Examples include paper memos, email messages, correspondence templates, product change orders, and other things people create and use while working. Sometimes artifacts are work products, information objects used in daily operation of the enterprise, for example, an order form being filled out, that reveal traces of people's work practices. The contextual inquiry team must pay close attention to how these artifacts are created, communicated, and used. What are those notes scribbled on those forms? Why are some fields in this form left blank? Why is there a sticky note on this form? Perhaps a signature is required for approval on other kinds of documents. This model is one reason why observers and interviewers must collect as many artifacts as possible during their contextual inquiry field visits to users.

Example: Artifact Model from a Restaurant

It is easy to think of artifacts associated with a restaurant. In Chapter 3 we mentioned collecting artifacts from a restaurant, examples of which are shown in Figure 3-3. The first artifact encountered by a person in the customer work role, delivered by the person in the wait-staff work role, is a menu, used by the customer work role to decide on something to order.

Other usual restaurant work artifacts include the order form on which the wait-staff person writes the original order and the guest check, which can be the same artifact or a printed check if the order is entered into a system. Finally, there might be a regular receipt and, if a credit card is used, a credit card signature form and a credit card receipt. Artifacts in restaurants, as they do in most enterprises, are the basis for at least part of the flow model. In Figure 6-17 you can see how restaurant artifacts help show the workflow from order to serving to concluding payment.

Figure 6-17

Part of a restaurant flow model with focus on work artifacts derived from the artifact model.

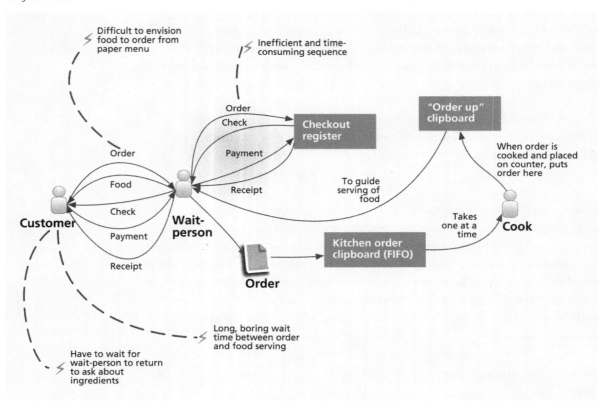

The artifacts, especially when arranged as part of a flow model, can help make a connection from contextual data to thinking ahead about design. For example, the waiting and boredom shown in Figure 6-17 pose a "barrier" to the customer.

This leads us to ask questions such as: How can we make that experience for the customer placing the order more fun, engaging, and informed? This kind of question posed now will later provide a great starting point for design brainstorming later: Would not it be cool if each dining table contained an embedded interactive touch tablet. Users could pass time by playing games, doing email, or surfing the Web.

Another barrier shown in Figure 6-17 is the difficulty of ordering food from a textual description in a paper menu. Interviewing restaurant customers about their experiences, you find that many people, when they order a dish and then see something else someone has ordered, wish to get that dish instead.

Paper menus do not leverage this rich human sensual connection to the food! However, this discussion of restaurant artifacts does help us ask questions that will later inspire design: If the table contained an interactive display, then why not let the customer use it to interact with the kitchen, ask questions about ingredients, and see images of the dish being served? In fact, why not let the customers place their orders themselves?

Constructing the artifact model

How do you make the model? Well, the artifact model is mainly a collection of artifacts, but you can organize it for analysis and use. In contextual inquiry you will have collected the artifacts, usually visual, by making a drawing, a copy, or a photograph or by having collected a real example of the artifact. An example of a tangible work artifact is a guest check from a restaurant. If an artifact is more aural than visual, a recording of the sound could be an artifact.

Next, the team should make "artifact posters." Attach samples of each artifact to a separate flip chart page. Add annotation to your "exhibits" to provide more information about your observations of them in the work practice. Add explanations of how each artifact is used in the work practice and workflow.

Annotate artifacts with stick-on notes associating them with tasks, user goals, and task barriers. Each poster drives discussion to explain the artifact's use while trying to tease out associated issues and user needs. As usual, the process can generate additional user work activity notes from what is learned about the artifacts and how they are used.

Example: Artifact Model for Slideshow Presentations

The artifact model for slideshow presentations did not turn up anything unexpected, but it is informative. It includes physical devices such as laser pointers for pointing to the screen and a timer or watch for keeping track of time, bottled water for the speaker and/or the audience members, possible paper handouts with copies of the slides, and a PC and mouse. Because the artifacts, especially the various pieces of equipment, are physical, there is some overlap with the physical model.

6.7.2 Physical Model

The physical model gives the roles, activities, and artifacts of other models a physical setting, showing the physical environment as it supports (or not) the work. The physical model shows physical dimensions of the work spaces, buildings, walls, rooms, workstations, all physical equipment, and collaboration spaces, but does not have to be an exact to-scale floor plan. The physical model includes computing and communications and other work devices, for example, copy machines, telephones, FAX machines, printers, and network connections.

Because a physical model shows the placement and paths of movement of people and objects within this work space layout diagram, it can be used to assess the proximities of task-related equipment and artifacts and task barriers due to distances, awkward layouts, and physical interference among roles in a shared work space.

The latter is helped by showing movement lines of each user role within the space, including multiple lines for multiuser movement in doing a collaborative task. If the physical locations or devices associated closely with the same tasks or related tasks are located at a distance from each other, it can result in wasted time and effort for workers.

For example, in the design for her house, a friend did this kind of physical model and workflow analysis and found that the traditional American proclivity for putting the clothes washer and dryer in the basement gave a very poor proximity-to-task-association ratio for the task of doing laundry. Enlarging the dressing room and putting the washer and dryer in there improved this ratio enormously.

Similarly, the flow of fresh vegetables from the car to the kitchen led to moving the garage from the basement level to the living floor level (aided by a steep grade). In both cases, the changes brought the physical model elements much closer to their location of use in the design.

Looking further at the veggie flow in the physical model led to an efficient design of a kitchen island as a shared food preparation and cooking area—cleaning at the veggie sink, flowing over to slicing and dicing, and then flowing to sautéing under a bright light and a vent hood.

When creating physical models, also think of all the physical characteristics of a workplace that can affect work activities and add them as annotations. For example, a steel mill floor is about noise, dust, hot temperatures, and safety concerns, making it more difficult to think. A system with a terminal on a factory floor means dirty conditions and no place to hold manuals or blueprints. This may result in designs where the use of audio could be a problem, needing more prominent visual design elements, such as blinking lights.

Other concerns by people in the physical working environment might include room lighting, air quality and ventilation, room temperature, and how to set all these parameters to suit everyone. Note the red lightning bolts representing barriers to work practice in the physical model.

Example: Physical Model for Slideshow Presentations

The physical model of the presentation room described the arrangement of physical structures that limit or define the work space and usage and movement within the space. These physical models showed the room, equipment and other artifacts used, positioning of the presenter and audience within the environment, and barriers that arose due to limitations of these physical layouts.

The physical models fell into two cases: presentations that included remote audience members required a different physical arrangement than for local-only presentations. In particular, remote presentations used more devices, including cameras, screens, and sound control boards.

All presentations, however, used a seated local audience, a standing presenter, and at least one screen that showed the slides to the audience and served as a display for some of the interaction used to control the slideshow.

Most physical barriers in the social models occurred when the desires of the presenter to give information, and the audience to receive information, were obstructed. For example, the behavior of several presenters indicated a desire to be near the audience physically, but their movement toward and among the audience often blocked the audience's view of the slides on the screen. Also, presentations with multiple presenters had difficulty with transitions between presenters because of physical barriers to handing off the presentation.

Other barriers to smooth task performance included cords over which presenters sometimes tripped and difficult-to-reach controls for videos and slide advancement. In Figure 6-18 we show a physical model for one of the presentation cases.

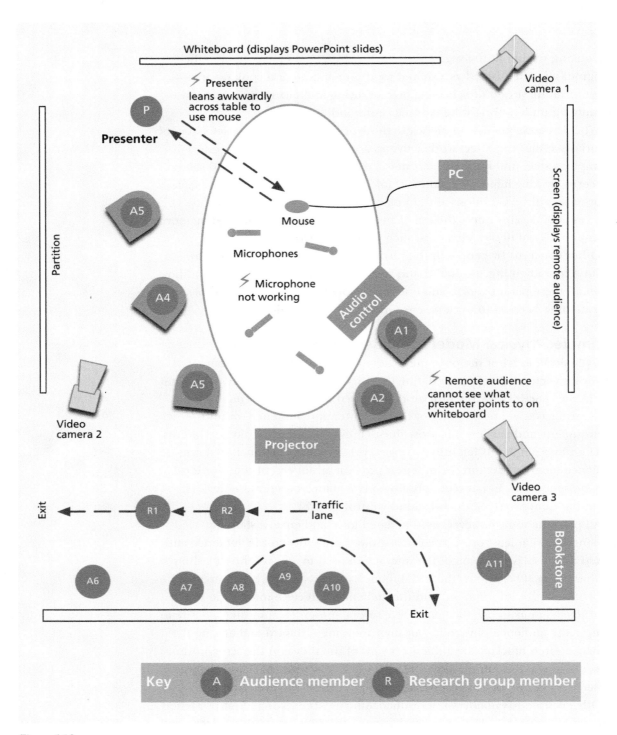

Figure 6-18

Physical model for one slideshow presentation case. Thanks to Brad Myers, Carnegie Mellon University, and his colleagues for their example (Cross, Warmack, & Myers, 1999) on which this is based.

As an aside, you might think that this physical model would not be very useful since it is very specific to one presentation room and one work space in one presentation case. Surely other presentation rooms will be quite different in size and layout.

But it is exactly the point of contextual inquiry: that you can take work practice data from a very specific existing working environment and learn things that apply to the more general case. This team was able to do just that in discovering the problem of presenters having to stay near the computer during the presentation, needing to lean awkwardly across tables to use the PC mouse to change slides. This is a barrier to quality presentations and could be true in most settings, regardless of room layout details.

Example: Physical Model for MUTTS

In Figure 6-19 we show the physical model for MUTTS. The center of workflow is the ticket counter, containing up to three active ticket seller terminals. On the back wall, relative to ticket sellers, are the credit card and MU Passport swiping stations. This central ticket-selling area is flanked with the manager's and assistant manager's administrative offices.

Barriers not shown in Figure 6-19 include a barrier to the ticket buyer lines: At peak times, customers may have to wait in long lines outside the ticket window.

Figure 6-19

A physical model for MUTTS.

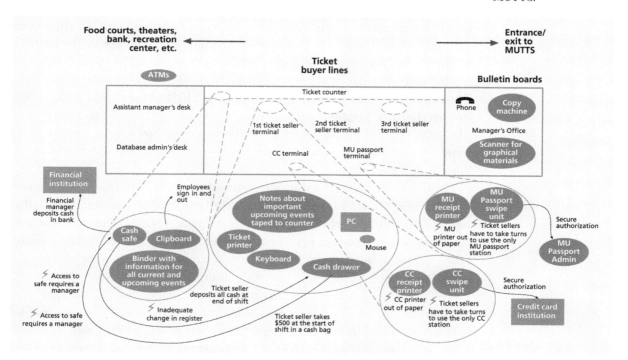

The scanner in the manager's office, used to digitize graphical material such as posters or advertisements for Website content, presents barriers to usage: It is very slow and is not in a convenient location for all to share.

The ticket printers can also introduce barriers to workflow. Because they are specialized printers for ticket stock, when one goes down or runs out of paper or ink, the employees cannot just substitute another printer. They have to wait until the technician can get it serviced or, worse, until it can be sent out for service.

Envisioned physical model

As much as possible, try to describe the physical model of the new work practice and new system. In many cases, the physical model will not change that much in the transition. Our Ticket Kiosk System is an exception; the physical model will change completely.

6.8 BARRIER SUMMARIES

Many of the models tell partial stories from different perspectives, but no one model highlights all the barriers discovered in contextual inquiry and analysis. Yet it is the barriers to work practice and user performance that most directly inform design ideas for the new system. So it can be helpful and informative to extract barrier-related information from the models and summarize the barriers in one place.

Example: Barrier Summaries for the Slideshow Presentation System

The team that did the slideshow presentation contextual inquiry summarized some selected barriers found in their step-by-step task interaction model as follows, in Table 6-2.

Further, in Table 6-3 the team summarized the most frequently encountered barriers. The "% of talks" column is the percentage of presentations in which the barrier occurred at least once. "Count" is the total number of instances of the barrier observed across all presentation cases. "Severity" is the average severity rating across all instances of the barriers. "Average duration" is the average length of time of a single instance of the interruption due to the barrier.

The single most frequent barrier to slide presentation was the physical awkwardness of changing slides. Six out of nine presenters walked to one spot to talk, but then had to turn and walk to a location typically 3 feet away, position themselves, advance the slides using the mouse on their PC, and then return to their original location to talk.

Table 6-2

Summary of selected barriers discovered within the step-by-step task interaction models for slideshow presentations[a]

#	Trigger	Goal	Barrier
18	Question from remote audience member	Answer questions	Audio unintelligible. Local members instruct remote members to adjust audio setting.
19	Comment from remote member	Respond to comment	Audio unintelligible. Local members instruct remote members to reconnect.
20	Comments from local members	Respond to comments by referring to slide from earlier in presentation	Presenter tries to return to slide. Presenter searches through slides rapidly but cannot find it.
21	Question from local member	Answer question	Presenter tries again and eventually finds slide.
22	Local member asks presenter to bring up previous slide.	Go backward one slide	Presenter tries to go back one slide but goes forward one slide instead.
23	Remote audience reconnected	Continue discussion	
24	Question from remote member	Answer question	
25	Comment from local member	Respond to question	Presenter flips through slides searching for "system architecture" slide.

[a]Thanks to Brad Myers, Carnegie Mellon University, and his colleagues for their case study (Cross, Warmack, & Myers, 1999) on which this is based.

Table 6-3

Summary of most frequent barriers observed in presentation cases[a]

Description	Model	% of Talks	Count (Over all Talks)	Average Severity	Average Duration (Each Time)
1. Changing slides is difficult and awkward because of the placement of the mouse or laptop.	Physical	67	166	1.2	2 sec
2. Presenter loses track of time, must ask for verbal update.	Sequence	44	6	1.5	55 sec
3. Reference provided is incomplete or skimmed over, audience members would be unable to find it after the talk.	Cultural	44	6	1	19 sec
4. Camera view is unclear or pointed at wrong information.	Flow	33	3	1.7	60 sec
5. Audio level for demos is not set correctly.	Flow	33	3	2	46 sec

[a]Thanks to Brad Myers, Carnegie Mellon University, and his colleagues for their case study (Cross, Warmack, & Myers, 1999) on which this is based.

Often, the PC was on a low table, or otherwise difficult to reach, further compounding the problem. This behavior wasted a significant amount of time during presentations. One presenter found a solution that wasted less time: stay next to the slide control throughout the lecture part of the presentation, but move to a spot away from behind the podium and closer to the audience for the duration of the discussion period.

The second-most frequent barrier to a smooth presentation was an inability of presenters to keep track of time or be aware of how much time they had remaining. Six of the presenters asked an audience member for a time check at some point during their lectures.

None of the barriers reached the highest severity rating used by the study group—causing a permanent and premature end to the presentation. However, three different presentations did encounter barriers with major severity, requiring significant portions of the talk to be skipped. One had a demo that could not be shown because the PC lacked Shockwave software. Two of the presentations with remote audiences contained significant periods of time when the remote audience could not read the presentation slides because of an unfocused camera and problems with the settings of the NetMeeting software.

6.9 MODEL CONSOLIDATION

If you constructed your models with multiple subteams working in parallel, you will get multiple models of the same type. Now is the time to consolidate the model versions by merging, uniting, and combining them into one model. The key idea is to induce generalizations, that is, a bottom-up process to build a general model from pieces of specific data.

It is a little like eliminating the unimportant details and taking the union of the important ones over all the versions of the model.

As an example, start with representations of single user stories of task steps in the existing work practice. Merge the description of essentially the same task created with data from several users, and factor out the differences in details. The result is a more abstract or more general representation of the interaction, representing how most or all users do the task.

Example: Flow Model Consolidation for MUTTS

When flow modeling that was begun in contextual inquiry is continued during contextual analysis by different subteams, each may model things differently; for example, the same work role might get modeled in different ways, yielding different work role descriptions and work role names. Because these various versions of the flow model are about the same workflow, they can be consolidated essentially by merging them.

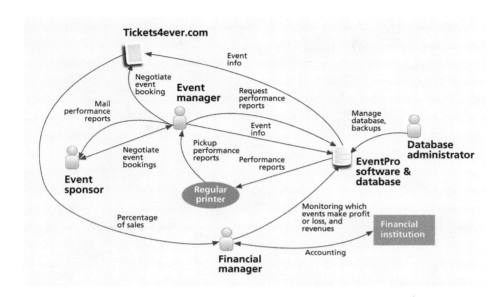

Figure 6-20

Flow model from a group who observed and interviewed the event manager, event sponsors, the financial manager, and the database administrator.

For example, Figures 6-20, 6-21, and 6-22 are partial flow models constructed by groups who observed and interviewed different parts of the overall organization and work practice.

See, in Figure 6-9, how the three parts of the overall flow model came together in model consolidation.

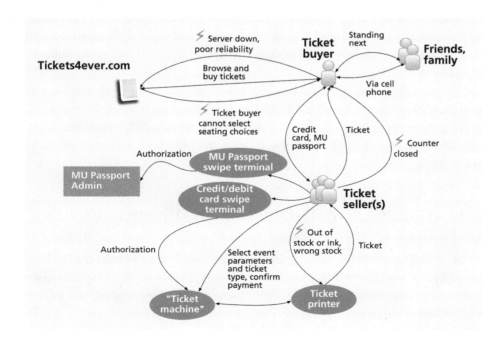

Figure 6-21

Flow model from a group who mainly observed and interviewed ticket buyers and ticket sellers.

Figure 6-22

Flow model from a group who observed and interviewed the office manager, the advertising manager, and external advertisers.

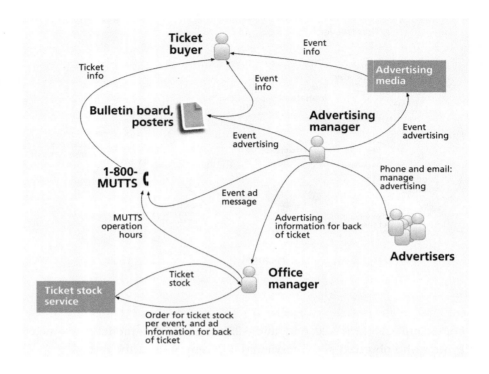

6.10 PROTECTING YOUR SOURCES

One of the things to watch out for throughout the process, especially when dealing with design-informing models, is confidentiality. This is important in all cases where you have observed, synthesized, deduced, or were given insights that were about problems and breakdowns arising due to social and political issues in the work practice.

Situations involving breakdowns due to bad management or flawed work practices (modeled in social models) are especially dangerous if there is a chance the sources will be revealed. Make this your unbreakable rule: When you take data and models back to anyone, users or management, everything must be anonymous.

6.11 ABRIDGED METHODS FOR DESIGN-INFORMING MODELS EXTRACTION

6.11.1 Be Selective about the Modeling You Need to Do

Do not be bound by the exact models we discuss in this chapter. Depending on the work domain and your design goals, some kinds of models will not be important, while others will take on much more importance.

6.11.2 Designer-Ability-Driven Modeling

In the real world, designers use design-informing modeling to understand and control the complexity of the work domain in the context of designing the next generation of system support. To be efficient, each designer chooses the amount of modeling necessary to meet his or her own needs, which in turn depend on the designer's individual skills, knowledge, and experience.

Less experienced designers will need to work out models in more detail to manage complexity and be sure that all the complexity of the work domain is accounted for. Expert designers, who perhaps have experience in a similar kind of system or a similar work domain, already know things that will propel their process forward more rapidly. Often it is not necessary to develop all the models fully and formally along the way. Experienced analysts or designers do not build models that will tell them something they already know.

The models are a way of cognitively off-loading details so that there is room in the analyst's head for other analysis. Experienced designers have abstractions for some of the models mentally built in, leaving room for further analysis. Of course such ability-driven approaches run the risk of missed details and issues falling through the cracks, but the practical bottom line is that, in most real-world projects, designers rarely develop a complete set of full models, but just the key aspects of the models they feel they need the most.

So, students entering the professional workforce and novice practitioners should make all the complete models but should also be aware of this reality and not come across as impractical to the more experienced analysts by insisting on constructing every model in full before moving on to design.

6.11.3 Use a Hybrid of WAAD and Relevant Models

Mix and match the modeling best suited for your needs. Add different models of your own creation. Combine simple models into a hybrid model, for example, combine workflow superimposed upon a physical model.

Another effective way of abridging the process for creating design-informing models is by creating a hybrid of a WAAD and relevant models on the same wall. We recommended using large strips of butcher paper to create your WAAD; you can capture the essence of the different models right next to the clusters of work activity notes on the WAAD. This canvas affords a fluid medium to represent relationships among the different themes in the work domain; you can draw on the WAAD and annotate it with ideas that you would otherwise capture in different formal models while using a full rigorous process.

For example, any interpersonal concerns that you would usually capture in a social model will now just become annotations on the cluster of notes organized under the corresponding work roles. In our experience we found a hybrid of a WAAD and flow model to be the most useful.

6.11.4 Create Design-Informing Models on the Fly during Interviews

Another abridged technique we have used in the field with great success is on-the-fly modeling during the actual contextual inquiry process. Experienced practitioners can create or add to models as they are interviewing and observing users during contextual inquiry.

Any information that can be captured as a model is done so as rough sketches, and the remaining information is captured as regular work activity notes. For example, during our interview with a MUTTS ticket seller, she mentioned the need for all ticket sellers to enter the amount of money taken from the safe into a ledger at the start of a shift, a need for recording the total deposit at the end of the shift, and to attach a printout of all sales in that shift generated by the ticketing software system. Instead of capturing this information as a series of work activity notes, we can capture this in a flow model diagram on the fly.

6.12 ROOTS OF ESSENTIAL USE CASES IN SOFTWARE USE CASES

A use case is not a user experience lifecycle artifact, but a software engineering and systems engineering artifact for documenting functional requirements, especially for object-oriented development, of a system. "Use-cases, stated simply, allow description of sequences of events that, taken together, lead to a system doing something useful" (Bittner & Spence, 2003). They include outside roles—end users and external entities such as database servers or bank authorization modules—and internal system responses to outside actions.

Although a use case can represent the user view, the bottom-line focus is on functional, not interaction, requirements. Sometimes use cases are thought of as an object-oriented approach to user modeling, but in practice they are usually created by developers and systems analysts without any contextual data from users.

Use cases are formalized usage scenarios, narratives of "black box" functionality in the context of user–system interaction (Constantine & Lockwood, 1999, p. 101). Use cases are often used as a component of software requirements. Their strong software orientation means that use cases lean in the direction of software implementation and away from user interaction design.

As Meads says (2010), in use cases, the user is an external object, not a person with human needs and limitations. This view leads to system requirements, but not to usage or UX requirements.

Use cases describe the major business requirements, features, and functions that the envisioned system must support. A use case "describes a sequence of actions that are performed by a human in work roles or other entities such as a machine or another system as they interact with the software" (Pressman, 2009); "use cases help to identify the scope of the project and provide a basis for project planning" (Pressman, 2009).

In answer to the need for something more effective than use cases in identifying interaction design requirements, Constantine (1994a, 1995) created a variation he calls "essential use cases."

Design Thinking, Ideation, and Sketching

7

A common mistake that people make when trying to design something completely foolproof is to underestimate the ingenuity of complete fools.

– Douglas Adams

Objectives

After you read this chapter, you should be able to:
1. Understand the evolution of design paradigms
2. Appreciate the design-thinking philosophy
3. Understand the ecological, interaction, and emotional design perspectives
4. Undertake ideation and sketching and appreciate their close relationship

7.1 INTRODUCTION

7.1.1 You Are Here

We begin each process chapter with a "you are here" picture of the chapter topic in the context of the overall Wheel lifecycle template; see Figure 7-1. We have noted that contextual inquiry (Chapter 3) is empirical, contextual analysis (Chapter 4) is inductive, requirements extraction (Chapter 5) is deductive, and design is integrative.

Chapters 3 and 4 are about existing work practice and any existing system. Chapters 5 and 6 are the bridge connecting analysis and design. This chapter and the next two are about designing the new work practice and the new system.

7.1.2 Design vs. Development

The entire field of system development uses the term "design" in a very broad sense, often connoting the entire lifecycle process. People refer to the "system design lifecycle" or "the interaction design process." People say "you cannot do design without including evaluation." And, of course, we agree.

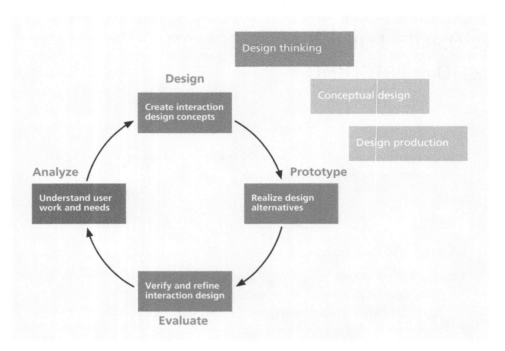

Figure 7-1

You are here; the first of three chapters on creating an interaction design in the context of the overall Wheel lifecycle template.

The problem is that "design" is also used narrowly to refer to the creative human activity by which new ideas are synthesized and put together to make up parts of an interaction design, that is, to the box labeled "Design" in Figure 7-1, the topic of this chapter. In this usage, design is just one process activity and does not include the others; it specifically does not include analysis or evaluation.

There is really no effective term to distinguish the overall process from just synthesis activity. We would love to use the terms "develop" and "development" for the entire lifecycle process, calling it a "development lifecycle process." However, "develop," "development," and "developer" are terms used almost universally to denote software engineering concepts tied strongly to programming and coding. A developer is someone who writes or develops implementation code.

Our path to happiness regarding this terminology trap is to follow the loose conventions of the field and use "design" with both narrow and broad meanings, hoping that context will provide clarity. In addition, we avoid "develop," "developer," or "development" as much as possible unless we are talking about software implementation. Instead, we will refer to the entire UX lifecycle process as a process for creating and refining interaction designs and will refer to activities in the lifecycle as process activities. On a rare occasion, we might lapse into using "development" to mean the creation and refinement of something, such as the development of a flow model. In those cases we are counting on context to avoid ambiguity.

7.2 DESIGN PARADIGMS

In a seminal paper that we think should have received more exposure, Harrison, Tatar, and Sengers (2007) paint the history of the focus of design in human–computer interaction (HCI) as a series of paradigms: engineering, human information processing (HIP), and phenomenological. They get credit for identifying the phenomenological perspective as a major design paradigm within the three major intellectual waves that have formed the field of HCI:

- Engineering and human factors: deconstruct work with the objective of designing the machine for optimum human performance.
- Cognitive science: the theory of what is happening in the human mind during and with respect to interaction by treating human minds as information processors.
- The phenomenological paradigm (they call it the phenomenological matrix): emphasis in interaction is about making meaning (more on this later).

The increasing importance of social and situated actions in HCI was at odds with both the usability-oriented engineering paradigm and the cognitive logic of the human information processor approach. The initial reluctance of HCI as a field to recognize and embrace the phenomenological paradigm spawned a parallel exploration in computer-supported cooperative work.

Activity theory helped explain the situated actions in work practice but did not do much to help design and evaluation. The paper by Harrison, Tatar, and Sengers (2007) is an evangelical wake-up call to include the phenomenological paradigm in mainstream HCI.

7.2.1 Engineering Paradigm

With some of its roots in software engineering, the HCI engineering paradigm prescribed starting with an inventory of the functionality envisioned for a new system and proceeding to build an interaction design of the best quality possible given available resources.

With recognition that user interaction deserved attention on its own, usability engineering emerged as a practical approach to usability with a focus on improving user performance, mainly through evaluation and iteration. The engineering approach casts design as just another lifecycle phase, a systematic approach that often works well for building systems with complex work domains.

Phenomenological Aspects of Interaction

Phenomenological aspects (deriving from phenomenology, the philosophical examination of the foundations of experience and action) of interaction are the cumulative effects of emotional impact considered over the long term, where usage of technology takes on a presence in our lifestyles and is used to make meaning in our lives.

Domain-Complex Systems

Domain-complex systems are systems with high degree of intricacy and technical content in the corresponding field of work. Often, characterized by convoluted and elaborate mechanisms for how parts of the system work and communicate, they usually have complicated work flow containing multiple dependencies and communication channels. Examples include an air traffic control system and a system for analyzing seismic data for oil exploration.

The engineering paradigm also had strong roots in human factors, where work was studied, deconstructed, and modeled. Here, the goal was user productivity and eliminating user errors. An example is the study of an assembly line where each action required to do work efficiently was described carefully. These descriptions were then more or less translated into requirements.

Designs focused on how to support these requirements and to automate where desirable. It was a purely utilitarian and requirements-driven approach. Success was measured by how much the user could accomplish, and alternative methods and designs were compared with statistical summative studies.

7.2.2 Human Information Processing (HIP) Paradigm

The human information processing approach to HCI is based on the metaphor of "mind and computer as symmetrically coupled information processors" (Tatar, Harrison, & Sengers, 2007). This paradigm, which at its base is about models of how information is sensed, accessed, and transformed in the human mind and, in turn, how those models reflect requirements for the computer side of the information processing, was defined by Card, Moran, and Newell (1983) and well explained by Williges (1982).

The HIP paradigm has its roots in psychology and human factors, from which it gets an element of cognitive theory. Especially as psychology is used in the discipline of human factors, it is about human mental states and processes; it is about modeling human sensing, cognition, memory, information understanding, decision making, and physical performance in task execution. The idea was that once these human parameters were codified, it is possible to design a product that "matches" them. Guidelines, such as not having more than seven plus or minus two items on transient lists on a user interface because of limits on human short-term memory, were a result of this type of thinking.

Human–Computer Interaction Design and the Three Paradigms

**Deborah Tatar, Department of Computer Science, and, by courtesy, Psychology; Member, Center for Human-Computer Interaction; Member, Program for Women and Gender Studies; Virginia Tech
Steve Harrison, Department of Computer Science and School of Visual Arts, Virginia Tech.**

Methods are like toothbrushes. Everyone uses them, but nobody wants to use somebody else's. John Zimmerman

As you learn the methods in this book, you will adopt them for your own, and as you adopt them, you will adapt them to the situation that you are working in. Learning this well will allow you to design how you design.

However, some changes are particularly difficult to understand and encompass. These are shifts across paradigms. You are unlikely to do this often, but sometimes it may be important to know when a shift is important or to recognize that someone else is working in a different paradigm.

In this sidebar, we define design as making something new that fits with reality. A design idea is a proposal for action in the world, burdened with the responsibility to solve problems or create delight. These definitions are cross-cutting. But the outcomes of design work are not as general as these definitions because any given design problem is approached within the particular way of seeing the world held by the designers. Such world views consist of a set of practices, expectations, and values sometimes called *paradigms*. Some world views value "thinking outside the box." In fact, they may value this so much that one criterion for success is to break out of whatever assumptions are seen to be in place! Others may value the most refined interface that perfectly fits a heavily researched user. Paradigms suggest the kinds of questions that the designer should care about, what factors are important to consider, and what factors are outside the scope of the endeavor. The notion of paradigms differs a bit in its use in linguistics, in science, and in computation. What is really important here is that, in design, there is no absolute best for all circumstances. It depends on the paradigm. Identifying the paradigms in design helps us understand the intended value of the work more clearly.

The three paradigms we identify in human–computer interaction (HCI) are human factors, classical cognitivism/information processing, and the third/phenomenologically situated paradigm. Each of these paradigms represents a world view. Each encompasses a set of practices and expectations for the value and contribution of research. Each contributes to HCI, but in different ways. Some people might argue that there are more than three paradigms, whereas some might argue that there are fewer. But these have substantial claim to both history and utility. Human factors focus on optimizing man–machine fit. Classical cognitivism/information processing emphasizes (ideally predictive) models and theories about the relationship between what is in the computer and in the human mind. The third paradigm, with its base in phenomenology, focuses on the experiential quality of interaction, primarily the ways that users experience meaning in the artifact and its use. The third paradigm, unlike the other two, emphasizes the ways in which individuals and individual experiences in the moment may differ from one another.

To orient you, we will cartoon the nature of each of the paradigms through a simple and well-known interface example.

In the 1960s, the U.S. Air Force developed automated cockpit warning systems to alert pilots to hazardous conditions. The systems used recorded voices to tell pilots to turn, climb, or dive to avoid head-on collisions, among other things. Each of the three paradigms contributes a different kind of thinking to the formulation of the problem and the range of solutions.

1. Situations that drove the initial system design were classic examples of human factors "critical incidents" (Flanagan, 1954). That is, pilots were crashing more often than they needed to. The Air Force realized that they needed to gain the pilots' attention quickly to avert these problems. At the time, all pilots and flight controllers were male, so someone had the bright idea of using a woman's voice so that it would be immediately identified as the "emergency voice." This was clever and worked well to reduce pilot errors.

2. The use of women's voices was a particular design solution. However, it worked for reasons of interest to the classical cognitivism/information processing paradigm; women's voices effectively differentiated signal from noise in the system interface's interaction

with the pilot. They allowed the efficient transmission of information, an important factor in any model of (i) human, (ii) computer, and (iii) interaction. Instead of simply saying "we are using women's voices because they are different from men's voices," in this paradigm, we describe a model in which women's voices vs men's voices is an instance of the critical, generalizable parameter of signal/noise differentiation. This description suggests other design solutions. For example, a taxonomy of voice types, based on cognitive load and desired response times, could be created. Indeed, experimentation using this approach revealed that familiar women's voices (i.e., wives, girlfriends) further improved pilot performance over nonspecific women's voices. This approach optimized communication and pilot mental workload. This kind of characterization also continued to be useful once women became pilots and flight controllers. It predicted that their voices would no longer have the crucial properties and that another design solution needed to be sought.

3. However, starting with the first paradigm finding, there is still more to be said. A pilot's wife's voice might be most familiar, but might lead to unpredictable pilot response when the couple was on the verge of divorce. In the third/phenomenologically situated paradigm, we include construction of meaning in our description of the situation, including social and emotional meaning. This leads to different design implications and explorations than those that emerge in the design solutions of the other two approaches. In fact, the original female voice was reputed to have been selected for its sultry and seductive tone.[1] This quality reinforced the idea of the space of the cockpit being "male," echoed in movies such as *Top Gun*. However this appeared originally to pilots, it became palpably inappropriate in creating a comfortable workplace as women became pilots and flight controllers. An important aspect of the third paradigm is that it is as concerned with the variety of human behaviors as with their prevalence. That is, suppose you find that voices with certain properties work well for 98% of pilots. In the third paradigm, you might decide that you have to account for what makes the other 2% different, whereas in the first two paradigms, one is more likely to dismiss these as statistical aberrations or error.

We picked this example because the boundaries to generalizability have changed so palpably that it is relatively easy to perceive all three paradigms. Most of the time that is not the case, even retrospectively. People make arguments based on unarticulated positions, allegiances, and values, often dismissing thinking in other paradigms as uninteresting, unimportant, dull, or frivolous.

We advance the idea of the three paradigms not as an absolute truth to last for the ages, but as an important heuristic that helps explain important differences of opinion about what constitutes good design in HCI. This perspective is useful in understanding what is happening in contemporary HCI. It may also be helpful in scoping particular design problems, in understanding the concerns of a particular client, and in working across organizational and institutional team boundaries.

---

[1]One interesting side effect was to gender popular media representations of flight control automata as female. Particularly notable is the original StarTrek computer.

7.2.3 Design-Thinking Paradigm

Harrison, Tatar, and Sengers (2007) propose a third HCI design paradigm that they call the "phenomenological matrix." We call it the design-thinking paradigm because our use of that concept goes a bit beyond their description of a "pure" phenomenological approach. This third design paradigm brings a vision of the desired user experience and product appeal and how the design of a product can induce that experience and appeal.

For Bødker and Buur (2002), the third paradigm for HCI design is motivated by a desire to "reframe usability practice." The heavy priority for usability testing in traditional usability methods meant that usability concerns were being brought into the process too late and that emphasis was on refining a design but not on getting the right design in the first place [as Buxton (2007b) would say it]. They used participatory design techniques to experiment with and explore design through early prototypes as design sketches.

Another of their reasons for reframing usability practice is the fact that the usual usability techniques focused on snapshots of usage, user performance evaluated during single tasks. But they wanted to include emergence of use. They also wanted to *overlap* the four basic process activities—analysis, design, implementation, and evaluation—instead of "pipelining" them in an iterative process.

As a contrast to the other two paradigms, the third one is not about the utilitarian aspects but more about the emotional and phenomenological ones. The design-thinking paradigm is about social and cultural aspects of interaction and the design of "embodied interaction" because it is about interaction involving our whole bodies and spirit, not just our fingertips on a keyboard. It is also about "situated" design because it is about the notion of "place" with respect to our interaction with technology.

Malcolm McCullough (2004) espoused this idea in the context of pervasive, embedded, and ubiquitous computing surrounding us in our lives and in our architecture, connecting interaction design with psychology, cultural anthropology, and technology. A primary characteristic of the design-thinking paradigm is the importance of emotional impact derived from design—the pure joy of use, fun, and aesthetics felt in the user experience.

To put the paradigms in perspective, consider the concept of a new car design. In the first paradigm, the engineering view, a car is built on a frame that holds all the parts. The question of its utility is about how it all fits together and whether it makes sense as a machine for transportation. It is also about performance, horsepower, handling, and fuel mileage. The second paradigm will see the car design as an opportunity to develop ergonomic seating and maybe new steering control concepts, as well as placement of controls to react quickly to emergency driving situations.

The design-thinking view of the third paradigm will also encompass many of the things necessary to produce a car that works, but will emphasize emotional

Participatory Design

Participatory design is a democratic process for design entailing user participation in design for work practice. Underlying participatory design is the arguments that users should be involved in designs they will be using, and that all stakeholders, including and especially users, have equal inputs into interaction design.

impact, "coolness" of the ride, and how to optimize the design to best appeal to the joy of driving and feelings of ownership pride. The design-thinking paradigm will also highlight the phenomenological aspects of how a car becomes more than just transportation from A to B, but how it becomes an integral part of one's life.

The third paradigm, our design-thinking paradigm, is about designing for the user experience. Architects have long known that the physical building is not really the target of the design; they are designing for the experience of being in and using that building. Similarly, we are not designing products to sell; we are selling the experience that the product engenders, encourages, and supports.

Sometimes the design-thinking approach can be in opposition to what contextual inquiry and requirements might say a design should have. Frank Lloyd Wright was a master at envisioning a concept and an experience for his clients, often ignoring their inputs. You can see similarities in the design of the iPad. Popular criticism of the iPad cited the lack of so-called connection features, the ability to write free-form notes, and so on, making this a gadget that would not appeal to people. The argument was that this will be just another gadget without a clearly defined utility because it lacked the features to replace a laptop or a desktop computer.

However, the overwhelming success of this device goes to the fact that it is not about utility but the intimate experience of holding a beautiful device and accessing information in a special way. Before the iPad, there were email, digital newspapers such as CNN.com, book readers, and photo viewers, but this device introduced an experience in doing these same things that was unprecedented. With the design-thinking approach, often the outcome is an intangible something that evokes a deeper response in the user.

7.2.4 All Three Paradigms Have a Place

These paradigms are just frameworks within which to think about design. The paradigms are not necessarily mutually exclusive; they do overlap and can be complementary. In most real system or product development, there is room for more than one approach.

To read some of the new literature on design thinking, you might think that the old engineering approach to interaction design is on its way out (Nilsson & Ottersten, 1998), but a utilitarian engineering approach is still effective for systems with complex work domains. Just because a methodical and systematic approach to contextual inquiry, requirements, and modeling is a characteristic of the engineering paradigm does not mean that we do not pay attention to such things in the other paradigms.

Even the most innovative design thinking can benefit from being grounded in a real understanding of user work practice and user needs that comes from contextual inquiry and analysis. And even creative design thinking must still be directed and informed, and informing design can mean doing contextual inquiry and analysis, modeling, requirements extraction, prototyping, and so on. Further, there is no reason why the rich approach of design thinking, using ideation and sketching, should not be followed with iterative refinement.

Similarly, there is need for creativity and innovation in all three paradigms. Just because we single out design thinking as the main place we discuss innovation and creativity does not mean there is no call for creativity in the other paradigms.

Further, even when the engineering paradigm or design-thinking paradigm is dominant in a project, designing from HIP-like inputs is still effective for leading to an interaction that is consistent with human cognitive capabilities and limitations. A consideration of ergonomics, human factors, and carefully studied workflow can still have a valid place in almost any kind of design.

7.3 DESIGN THINKING

The "design" box in the lifecycle template is usually a placeholder for an unknown or unspecified process. The usual UX lifecycle glosses over the whole subject of what is in the box labeled "design" (Buxton, 2007b). Design should be more than just a box within a larger lifecycle; it is a separate discipline on its own.

What some call design is applied only after functionality and interaction design are completed, when the product needs a shell or skin before going to market and everyone wants to know what color the device will be. This might help make an existing product attractive and perhaps more marketable, but this is cosmetic design, not essential design built into the product from the start.

Design Thinking

Design thinking is a mind-set in which the product concept and design for emotional impact and the user experience are dominant. It is an approach to creating a product to evoke a user experience that includes emotional impact, aesthetics, and social- and value-oriented interaction. As a design paradigm, design thinking is an immersive, integrative, and market-oriented eclectic blend of art, craft, science, and invention.

Ideation

Ideation is an active, creative, exploratory, highly iterative, fast-moving collaborative group process for forming ideas for design. With a focus on brainstorming, ideation is applied design thinking.

Sketching

Sketching is the rapid creation of free-hand drawings expressing preliminary design ideas, focusing on concepts rather than details. Multiple sketches of multiple design ideas are an essential part of ideation. A sketch is a conversation between the sketcher or designer and the artifact.

Fortunately, this emerging mind-set that we call design thinking turns that around and puts a focus on design up front. The design-thinking paradigm is an approach to creating an experience that includes emotional impact, aesthetics, and social- and value-oriented interaction. The design of the product concept and design for emotional impact and the user experience comes first; it is a design-driven process.

Designers are called upon to create a new vision, taking customers and users to a profound and satisfying user experience. After the design concept emerges, then engineers can follow up by providing the functionality and interaction design to make the vision a reality.

Design thinking is immersive; everything is about design. Design thinking is integrative; you pull many different inputs, inspiration, and ideas together to focus on a design problem. Design thinking is human centered, requiring a thorough understanding of the needs, especially the emotional needs, of human users.

Design thinking is market oriented, requiring a thorough understanding of the market, trends in usage and technology, and the competition. As such, design thinking is not just the world of dreamers and geeks; it has become an essential business tool for decision making and marketing. Design thinking is broadly attentive to the product, packaging, presentation, and customer support. Design thinking is an eclectic blend of art, craft, science, and invention.

In the traditional engineering view, we use terms such as plan, analyze, build, evaluate, and optimize. In the design-thinking perspective, you are more likely to hear terms such as create, ideate, craft, envision, interpret, excite, provoke, stimulate, and empathize.

The Apple iPod Touch is an example of a product resulting from design thinking. The device has superb usability; its soft buttons have precise and predictable labels. The physical device itself has a marvelous design with great emotional impact. Much design effort went into aspects that had nothing to do with performance or functionality.

The packaging, gift-wrapping, and engraving appeal to a personal and social desirability. It is attractive; it is delightful. The user experience is everything and everything is about design. In fact, the label on the device does not say, "Made by Apple"; it says, "Designed by Apple!" "You buy it for what it can do, but you love it because it is so cool." Apple's senior vice president of industrial design, Jonathan Ive, says (Salter, 2009) "With technology, the function is much more abstract to users, so the product's meaning is almost entirely defined by the designer."

7.4 DESIGN PERSPECTIVES

We describe three design perspectives as filters through which we view design and design representations to guide thinking, scoping, discussing, and doing design. They are easy to understand and do not require much explanation.

7.4.1 Ecological Perspective

The ecological design perspective is about how the system or product works within its external environment. It is about how the system or product is used in its context and how the system or product interacts or communicates with its environment in the process. This is a work role and workflow view, which includes social interaction and long-term phenomenological aspects of usage as part of one's lifestyle.

System infrastructure (Norman, 2009a) plays an important role in the ecological perspective because the infrastructure of a system, the other systems and devices with which it interacts in the world, is a major part of its ecology. Infrastructure leads you to think of user activities, not just isolated usage. Norman (2009b) states it in a way that designers should take to heart, "A product is actually a service."

7.4.2 Interaction Perspective

The interaction design perspective is about how users operate the system or product. It is a task and intention view, where user and system come together. It is where users look at displays and manipulate controls, doing sensory, cognitive, and physical actions.

7.4.3 Emotional Perspective

The emotional design perspective is about emotional impact and value-sensitive aspects of design. It is about social and cultural implications, as well as the aesthetics and joy of use. System infrastructure (Norman, 2009b) can also play a role in the emotional perspective because the infrastructure of a system provides scaffolding for the phenomenological aspects of usage, which are about broader usage contexts over longer periods of time.

A product is not just a product; it is an experience (Buxton, 2007a). People do not usually use a product in isolation from other activities. People use products as part of an activity, which can include many different kinds of usage of many different things. And that starts with the out-of-the-box experience, which is not enhanced by difficult hard plastic encasing, large user manuals, complex installation procedures, and having to consent to a legal agreement that you cannot possibly read.

The Delicate Balance among Visual Appeal, Emotion, and Usability

Gitte Lindgaard, Distinguished Research Professor, Carleton University, Ottawa, Canada
Professor, Neuro affective psychology, Swinburne University of Technology, Melbourne, Australia

"Yellow sox → nice guy!" We know that many snap decisions, such as assessing the suitability of a person to a particular job, are often based on less than credible, if not entirely irrelevant, information. Still, whether we are sizing up another person or deciding to stay on a given Website, first impressions are instant, effortless, powerful, and based on affect, that is, on "what my body tells me to feel." Even decisions that should involve serious contemplation, additional information, and evidence from different sources are made instantly. Worse, once we have made a decision, we set out to "prove" to ourselves that our decision was "right."

Thus, when encountering an ugly, cluttered Website, we will be out of there on the next click, before gleaning the quality of the information, goods, or services it offers. However, if we have decided a priori to buy a given product from a certain vendor, we will persevere and complete our purchase, hating every step of the interaction. In our annoyed, even angry, state, we go out of our way to identify every trivial usability flaw simply to justify that initial decision.

Yet, we are much more likely to hang around and enjoy the ride on a pretty site even if its products are of a lower quality and the usability issues more serious and more numerous than on the ugly site so unceremoniously discarded. When given a choice, even the most unusable, but very pretty, site will typically be preferred over a less appealing, more usable site. In some studies, people, well aware of the site's poor usability, have vigorously defended and justified their choice.

Numerous other studies have shown that beauty matters and that the first impression "sets the scene" for further action, at least in a Web environment where the next site is but a click away; visual appeal is simply used as a screening device. Quality of content will only be evaluated on sites that pass that initial step.

This rather uncompromising instant approach to decide on staying or leaving a Website could suggest that being pretty is all that matters. Not so! When the Canadian government wanted to attract masses of new graduates, they designed a vibrantly colorful Website with lots of animation in the belief that "this is what young people like." They then took their beautiful Website around the country for feedback from the target audience. "Yeah, we like lots of bright color and movement" was the response, "but not when looking for a job in the Government!"

For an application to appeal to users, then, their judgmental criteria depend on the usage context. Even a neutral, relative boring gray color may occasionally be very appealing, pleasant to use, and highly usable. Figure 1 shows a telecommunications network alarm management system. In earlier versions of the software it was almost impossible to identify the problem nodes, making the operator's job extremely stressful. If a blockage between two nodes is not detected and rectified within a few minutes, the problems spread so quickly that the entire network may break down, blocking *all* communication and making it almost impossible to fix.

The gray background on the left shows a map of a recognizable part of a certain city with a network problem. The rough-looking color indicates land surrounding a small (outlined) river, shown with a smooth surface and overlaid with the network nodes currently in alarm mode. This facilitates the geographical identification of the location. The red rectangles indicate the most serious problem nodes and the seriousness of these.

In the present example, there is no communication between the two red nodes; the yellow node is affected, but is still able to communicate. Callout balloons with the letters "C" (critical, circled in green), "M", and "m" (both

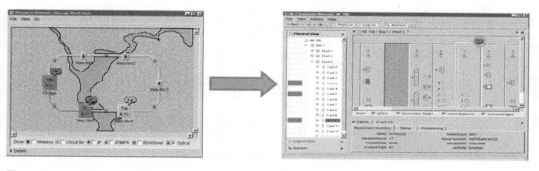

Figure 1

Example of an alarm management system relying on a simple visual language

medium) show where to start fixing the problem. Clicking on the red "C" takes the operator directly to the faulty equipment, shown on the right, where clicking again on the red C shows the affected equipment.

This example takes us back to Mark Weiser's notion of "calm computing" aiming to ensure that the user feels good and "in control" at all times. There are no design gimmicks, no fun or attempt to "jazz up" the displays with smart icons or pretty colors in this user interface; it just "feels right." This simple, very effective visual language presented on a consistent, bland background has removed most of the stress previously experienced by network operators. It has been adopted by the International Telecommunications Union as a standard for network management systems.

These examples contradict the currently sexy assumption in the human–computer interaction community that even serious tasks should be couched in a colorful gaming model. Apparently, appropriateness also features prominently when deciding how much to like a Website or an application. Judgments of appropriateness are based largely on culturally constructed expectations. The domain and the purpose of an interactive product determine our expectations and hence influence how we feel about it. This emotional effect underlies our situated judgment of appeal. Indeed, in our collective quest to create great user experiences, we must be careful not to lose sight of the traditional, often sneezed at, utilitarian brand of usability.

The example in Figure 2 is from a high-pressure petrochemical plant-management system. The plant produces many types of plastic, from purified, highly compressed gas injected under high pressure into reactor vessels operating at 200°+ C. The gas is mixed with chemical catalysts, which eventually turn the mix into tiny plastic pellets. The left side of Figure 2 shows how the pressure (red pen) and temperature (green pen) were plotted automatically on a constantly scrolling paper roll before automation. The variation in each parameter is shown in rows, and time is given in columns, with each row representing 30 minutes in elapsed time. The range of movement of those two pens enabled the team leader to easily monitor four reactor vessels simultaneously.

Three minor changes in the management system are shown on the right: (1) time is now shown in rows, (2) each column represents 10 minutes (instead of 30) of lapsed time, and (3) the two indicators are shown on different screens. These apparently minor changes paralyzed production completely. The highly experienced team with over 20 years of practice was unable to achieve the required quality of product; they continually overadjusted either the pressure or the temperature.

Consequently, the company nearly lost its main customer who bought 60% of the products, and an engineer had to be on duty with the team 24/7 for the next 6 months. The screen display was just as visually appealing as the original paper roll, but relearning the system rendered the system unusable. Thus, aesthetics alone did not ensure usability; the

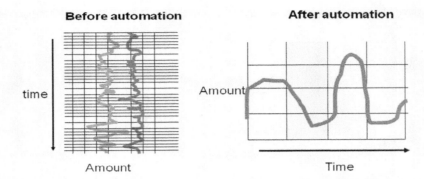

Figure 2
A before- and after-automation display shows minor changes to a mission-critical system

Before automation

time

Amount

After automation

Amount

Time

operators disliked the system intensely, and violation of the long-established expectations of what and how information should be displayed turned out to be a very costly oversight.

Evidently, the relationship among visual appeal, emotion, and usability is much more complex than may be assumed. To date, relatively little attention has been paid to the power of expectation, to our sense of appropriateness, and to our decisions concerning the "fitness for purpose" of interactive products. However, these do profoundly affect the appeal and hence our acceptance of such products. As user interface designers, we simply cannot afford to ignore the context in, and purpose for, which our products will be seen and used.

7.5 USER PERSONAS

For the Latin sticklers, we prefer the easy-going "personas" over the pedantic but probably more correct "personae." Personas are a powerful supplement to work roles and user class definitions. Storytelling, role-playing, and scenarios go hand in hand with personas.

We have leaned heavily on Cooper (2004) for our descriptions of personas with additional ideas on connecting to contextual data from Holtzblatt, Wendell, and Wood (2005, Chapter 9) and we gladly acknowledge their contributions here. Personas are an excellent way of supporting the design thinking and design perspectives of this chapter.

7.5.1 What Are Personas?

A persona is not an actual user, but a pretend user or a "hypothetical archetype" (Cooper, 2004). A persona represents a specific person in a specific work role and sub-role, with specific user class characteristics. Built up from contextual data, a persona is a story and description of a specific individual who has a name, a life, and a personality.

Personas are a popular and successful technique for making your users *really real*. Personas have an instant appeal through their concreteness and personal engagement that makes them ideal for sharing a visualization of the design target across the whole UX team.

Stories Are at the Center of User Experience

Whitney Quesenbery, WQusability, Coauthor, *Storytelling in User Experience: Crafting Stories for Better Design* **(Rosenfeld Media)**

Perhaps you think that stories and storytelling are out of place in a book about methodology and process. Once, you might have been right. As recently as 2004, a proposal for a talk about writing stories and personas as a way of understanding the people who use our systems was rejected out of hand with, "Personas? Stories!? We are *engineers*!"

They were wrong.

Stories have always been part of how human beings, including engineers, come up with new ideas and share those ideas with others. Stories may be even more important for innovative ideas. It is not very hard to explain an incremental change: "It is just like it is now, but with this one difference." But when you are trying to imagine an entirely new concept or a design that will change basic processes, you need a story to fill in the gaps and make the connections between *how it is now* and *how it might be.*

To see what I mean, try this experiment. Close your eyes and try to explain to your 1995 self why you might want to use Twitter, Yelp, or Foursquare. There are just too many steps between the world then and the world now.

Sometimes it is easy because the context is familiar. Yelp's story is like that: You are standing somewhere—the lobby of a building or a street corner—and you are hungry. Where can you go eat? Is it open *right now*? The idea is easy; the product is new because we could not pull off the technology, even just a few years ago.

Sometimes it is hard because the idea meets a need you did not know you even had. When Twitter first launched, people said "Why would I want to know *that much* about someone else's daily life?" CommonCraft's video, Twitter in Plain English[2] takes up this challenge by showing how the system works in 2 minutes and 23 seconds. Not in technical terms, but in the human actions and human relationships it is based on.

Could you have predicted that (for a few years) a FAX would be the easiest way to order lunch from the local deli? It does not make sense until you think about the entire user experience.

One place to start an innovation story is with a frustrating situation. Tell a story that explains that point of pain. Maybe your story starts with how annoying it is to take sandwich orders from a room full of people. Include context and imagery and a realistic situation. Or it might be about the noise and craziness of lunch hour in a busy city deli, with people all yelling at once and at least three different languages in the kitchen.

---

[2]www.commoncraft.com/twitter

Now change that story to give it a better ending. That is your innovation story.

You have people, in a situation, with a problem, and a solution, along with what will make it work.

Before you decide that your story is ready to share, ask yourself, "Did it all seem too easy? Did the story seem a little too perfect?" If so, take a 10-minute timeout and start over. Back in the deli, did you decide that the solution would be a laptop on the deli counter? Did you think about the people standing behind a counter, wiping mustard off their hands? It is easy to fall into the trap of writing stories about the users we wish we had.

Stories in user experience are not made up fairy tales; they are grounded in good user research and other data. They are like personas in this way. Personas start with data, organized into user profiles. It is the stories that turn a good user profile into a persona, that is, adding the emotions, detailed personal characteristics, and specific background or goals that make a persona come alive. You cannot tell much of a story about a stick figure. However, if you imagine Jason, who is leaving high school, is interested in computers, and loves his local sports team, you can begin to think about what kind of experiences will work well for Jason and how he might interact with the product you are designing.

Similarly, you can start with a task or goal. Use your favorite method to model the task. That gives you the analysis. Put that together into a sequence of actions, and you have a scenario. Add character into that narrative, with all their context and personal goals. Let their emotions be part of it; they are not robots. Are they frustrated, eager, happy, or sad? Now you are starting to craft a story.

Both personas and stories rely on data. They are the raw material. Scenarios and profiles are the skeleton—the basic shape and size of it. But it is when you add emotion and imagery that you have a story. If you understand the human and technical context, your stories will have believable characters and narratives.

The next time you want to help someone understand a design or how it will be used, try a story instead of a technical explanation. The really great thing about stories is that they make people want to tell more stories, which will get everyone engaged with the idea and its impact on our lives. All of a sudden, you are all talking about user experience.

7.5.2 What Are Personas Used For? Why Do We Need Them?

Common sense might dictate that a design for a broad user population should have the broadest possible range of functionality, with maximum flexibility in how users can pick the parts they like the most. But Cooper (2004, p. 124) tells us this thinking is wrong. He has shown that, because you simply cannot make a single design be the best for everyone, it is better to have a small percentage of the user population completely satisfied than the whole population half-satisfied.

Cooper extends this to say it can be even better to have an even smaller percentage be ecstatic. Ecstatic customers are loyal customers and effective marketing agents. The logical extreme, he says, is to design for one user. This is where a persona comes in, but you have to choose that one user very carefully.

It is not an abstract user with needs and characteristics averaged across many other kinds of users. Each persona is a single user with very concrete characteristics.

Edge cases and breadth

Personas are a tool for controlling the instinct to cover everything in a design, including all the edge cases. This tool gives us ways to avoid all the unnecessary discussion that comes with being "edge-cased to death" in design discussions.

Personas are essential to help overcome the struggle to design for the conflicting needs and goals of too many different user classes or for user classes that are too broad or too vaguely defined. In situations where users for one work role come from different user classes, but all have to take on the same work role, a persona lets us focus on designing literally for a single person and liberates them from having to sort through all the conflicting details of multiple user classes.

As Cooper (2004) put it, personas can help end feature debates. What if the user wants to do X? Can we afford to include X? Can we afford to not include X? How about putting it in the next version? With personas, you get something more like this: "Sorry, but Noah will not need feature X." Then someone says "But someone might." To which you reply, "Perhaps, but we are designing for Noah, not 'someone.'"

A specific persona makes clear what functionality or features must be included and what can be omitted. It is much easier to argue whether a person represented by a specific persona would like or use a given design feature.

Designers designing for themselves

Designing to "meet the needs of users" is a vague and ill-defined notion giving designers the slack to make it up as they go. One common way designers do stray from thinking about the user is when they design for themselves. In most project environments, it is almost impossible for designers to not think of the design in terms of how they would use it or react to it.

One of the strengths of personas is that they deflect this tendency of designers to design for themselves. Because of their very real and specific characteristics, personas hold designers' feet to the fire and help them think about designs for people other than themselves. Personas help designers look outward instead of inward. Personas help designers ask "How would Rachel use this feature?," forcing them to look at the design from Rachel's perspective. The description of a persona needs to make it so well defined as a real and living being that it is impossible for a designer or programmer to substitute themselves or their own characteristics when creating the design.

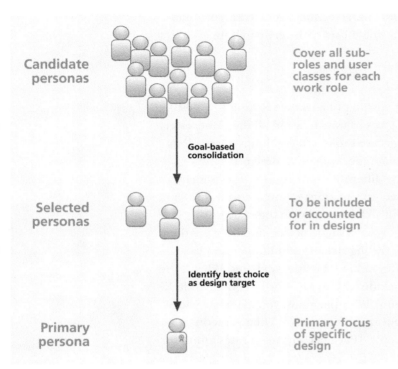

Figure 7-2

Overview of the process of creating a persona for design.

7.5.3 How Do We Make Them?

As in most other things we do in analysis and design, we create a separate set of personas for each work role. For any given work role, personas are defined by user goals arising from their sub-roles and user classes. Different sub-roles and associated user classes have different goals, which will lead to different designs.

Identifying candidate personas

Although personas are hypothetical, they are built from contextual data about real users. In fact, candidate personas are identified on the fly as you interview potential users. When you encounter a user whose persona would have different characteristics than any of the existing ones, add it to the list of candidates.

This means that you will create multiple candidate personas generally corresponding to a major sub-role or user class, as shown in the top part of Figure 7-2. How many candidate personas do you need? As many as it takes to cover all the users. It could be in the dozens.

Goal-based consolidation

The next step is to merge personas that have similar goals. For example, in the Ticket Kiosk System we have a persona of an undergraduate student ticket buyer sub-role who lives on campus and is interested in MU soccer tickets. Another persona in the same work role, this time a graduate student who lives off campus, is interested in MU tennis tickets.

These two personas have different backgrounds, defining characteristics, and perhaps personal interests. But in the context of designing the kiosk system, they are similar in their goals: get tickets for medium popularity athletic events at MU.

This step reduces the number of personas that you must consider, as shown in the middle part of Figure 7-2. But you still cannot design for a whole group of personas that you may have selected, so we choose one in the next section.

Selecting a primary persona

Choose one of the personas selected in the previous step as the one primary persona, the single best design target, the persona to which the design will be made specific.

Making this choice is the key to success in using the persona in design. The idea is to find common denominators among the selected personas. Sometimes one of the selected personas represents a common denominator among the others and, with a little adjusting, that becomes the primary persona.

The way you get the primary persona right is to consider what the design might look like for each of the selected personas. The design specifically for the right primary persona will at least work for the others, but a design specifically for any of the other selected personas may not work for the primary persona.

An example of the primary persona for the student sub-role in the Ticket Kiosk System could be that of Jane, a biology major who is a second-generation MU attendee and a serious MU sports fan with season tickets to MU football. This persona is a candidate to be primary because she is representative of most MU students when it comes to MU "school spirit."

Another persona, that of Jeff, a music major interested in the arts, is also an important one to consider in the design. But Jeff is not a good candidate as a primary persona because his lack of interest in MU athletics is not representative of a majority of MU students.

In constructing the primary persona, making it precise and specific is paramount. Specificity is important because that is what lets you exclude other cases when it comes to design. Accuracy (i.e., representing a particular real user) is not as important because personas are hypothetical.

Do not choose a mixture of users or an "average" user; that will be a poor choice and the resulting design will probably not work well for any of the personas. Averaging your users just makes your persona a Mr. Potato Head, a conglomeration that is not believable and not representative of a single user.

7.5.4 Mechanics of Creating Personas

Your persona should have a first and last name to make it personal and real. Always, of course, use fictitious names for personas to protect the anonymity of the real users upon which they may be based. Mockup a photo of this person. With permission, take one of a volunteer who is a visual match to the persona or use a photo from a noncopyrighted stock collection. Write some short textual narratives about their work role, goals, main tasks, usage stories, problems encountered in work practice, concerns, biggest barriers to their work, etc.

Whenever a persona is developed for a work role, if there is enough space in the flow and social model diagrams, you can show the association of your personas to work roles by adding the persona represented as a "head shot" photo or drawing of a real person attached with lines to the work role icon. Label each with the persona's name.

7.5.5 Characteristics of Effective Personas

Make your personas rich, relevant, believable, specific, and precise

The detail of a persona has to be a rich part of a life story. It has to be specific and precise; this means lots of details that all fit together. Give your persona a personality and a life surrounded with detailed artifacts.

Personas are relevant and believable. Every persona must be a complete and consistent picture of a believable person. Personas excel in bringing out descriptions of user skills.

Unlike aggregate categories (e.g., user classes), a persona can be a frequent user without being an expert (because they still do not understand how it works).

Make your personas "sticky"

Some practitioners of the persona technique go far beyond the aforementioned minimal descriptions of their creations. The idea is to get everyone thinking in terms of the personas, their needs, and how they would use a given system.

Personas need to get lots of visibility, and their personalities need to be memorable or "sticky" in the minds of those who encounter them (Nieters, Ivaturi, & Ahmed, 2007). To this end, UX teams have created posters, trading cards, coffee mugs, T-shirts, screen "wallpaper," and full-sized cardboard stand-up figures to bring their personas alive and give them exposure, visibility, and memorability to keep them on the minds of all stakeholders.

At Cisco in San Jose, designers have gone so far as to invent "action figures" (à la Spiderman), little dolls that could be dressed and posed in different ways and photographed (and sometimes further "developed" via Photoshop) in various work contexts to represent real usage roles (Nieters, Ivaturi, & Ahmed, 2007). To us, that may be going beyond what is necessary.

Where personas work best

When personas are used in designing commercial products or systems with relatively simple work domains (i.e., projects on the left-hand side of the system complexity space of Figure 2.5), they help account for the nuances and the activities in personal lives outside organizations. Social networking and other phenomenological behavior come into play.

For example, you may have the kind of person who always carries a phone but does not always carry a camera. This might help in design discussions about whether to combine a camera in a cellphone design.

As you move toward the right-hand side of the system complexity space of Figure 2.5, toward systems for more complex work domains, the work practice often becomes more firmly defined, with less variation in goals. Individual users in a given work role become more interchangeable because they have almost the same exact goals. For example, the work goals of an astronaut are established by the mission, not by the person in the astronaut role and usage is prescripted carefully.

In this kind of project environment, personas do not offer the same advantages in informing design. Roles such as astronaut or air traffic controller are defined very restrictively with respect to background, knowledge, skills, and training, already narrowing the target for design considerably. People who take on that role face stiff user class specifications to meet and must work hard and train to join the user community defined by them. All users in the population will have similar characteristics and all personas for this kind of role will look pretty much alike.

Figure 7-3

Adjusting a design for the primary persona to work for all the selected personas

7.5.6 Goals for Design

As Cooper (2004) tells us, the idea behind designing for a persona is that the design must make the primary persona very happy, while not making any of the selected personas unhappy. Buster will love it and it still works satisfactorily for the others.

7.5.7 Using Personas in Design

Team members tell "stories" about how Rachel would handle a given usage situation. As more and more of her stories are told, Rachel becomes more real and more useful as a medium for conveying requirements.

Start by making your design as though Rachel, your primary persona, is the only user. In Figure 7-3, let us assume that we have chosen persona P3 as the primary persona out of four selected personas.

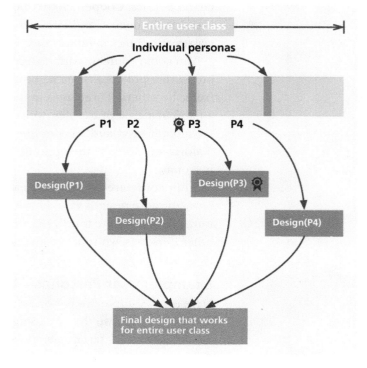

Because D(P3) is a design specific to just P3, D(P3) will work perfectly for P3. Now we have to make adjustments to D(P3) to make it suffice for P1.

Then, in turn, we adjust it to suffice for P2 and P4. The final resulting design will retain the essence of D(P3), plus it will include most of the attributes that make D(P1), D(P2), and D(P4) work for P1, P2, and P4, respectively.

As you converge on the final design, the nonprimary personas will be accounted for, but will defer to this primary persona design concerns in case of conflict. If there is a design trade-off, you will resolve the trade-off to benefit the primary persona and still make it work for the other selected personas.

7.5.8 Example: Cooper's In-Flight Entertainment System

Cooper (2004, p. 138) describes the successful use of personas in a Sony design project for an in-flight entertainment system called P@ssport. In addition to the work roles for system maintenance and the flight attendants who set up and operate the entertainment system, the main users are passengers on flights. We call this main work role the Traveler.

The user population that takes on the role of Traveler is just about the broadest possible population you can imagine, including essentially all the people who travel by air—almost everyone. Like any general user population, users might represent dozens of different user classes with very diverse characteristics. Cooper showed how the use of personas helped mitigate the breadth, vagueness, and openness of specification of the various Traveler user classes and their characteristics.

You could come up with dozens or more personas to represent the Traveler, but in that project the team got it down to four personas, each very different from the others. Three were quite specialized to match the characteristics of a particular type of traveler, while the fourth was an older guy who was not technology savvy and was not into exploring user interface structures or features—essentially the opposite of most of the characteristics of the other personas.

They considered designs for each of the first three personas, but because none of those designs would have worked for the fourth, they came up with an initial design for the fourth persona and then adapted it to work well for all the other personas, without sacrificing its effectiveness for the target persona.

Example: User Personas—Lana and Cory

Here is an example of a persona derived from the interviews of the couple, Lana and Cory, whom we treat as a single composite persona because they share an approach to entertainment events. (NB: The interspersed comments in parentheses are not part of the personas, but possibly design-related observations related to various aspects of the personas.)

Lana is a young 20-something manager and yoga instructor in the Dirk Gently Holistic Yoga Studio and enjoys using her laptop during off-work hours. Cory works as a graphic designer at Annals of Myth-information, a small-sized company of creative people.

Lana does not own a car, a smart option in Middleburg, so she takes the bus for distances beyond walking or biking. Cory has to drive to work but bikes or takes public transportation to other places on weekends. Lana and Cory work hard, play hard, and are ready for entertainment on the weekends. (Because they both spend time occasionally at bus stops, it would be a good place for them to peruse the entertainment possibilities and buy tickets while waiting for the bus.)

In addition to pursuing Middleburg entertainment, Lana and Cory have also been known to skip over to Washington, DC, or New York City to visit friends and take in some world-class entertainment. (Therefore, they would love to see information about events in other cities included in the kiosk.)

They occasionally take time out on weekday evenings to do something different, to get away from the routine, which can include seeing a movie, visiting a museum, going out with friends, or traveling in the immediate area. As a balance to the routine of their jobs, they both crave opportunities for learning and personal growth so they often seek entertainment that is sophisticated and interesting, entertainment that challenges intellectually.

However, there are some days they want to rest their minds and they seek something more like mindless entertainment, often something that will make them laugh. They hear about a lot of events and places to visit through word of mouth, but they wonder about how many other interesting events do not come to their attention.

Cory, being influenced by his work in designing social Websites, wonders if sources of entertainment information could also provide a special kind of social networking. He would like to see mediated discussions about events and entertainment-related issues or at least a way to post and read reviews and opinions of various movies and other performances.

Similarly, Lana would like a way to share event information. "Like maybe this weekend there is going to be a jazz festival at a certain sculpture garden and I want Cory to know about it. It would be nice to have a button to touch to cause some kind of link or download to my iPhone or iPod." It is easy to copy information from an entertainment Website and send it via email, but sharing is not as easy from a ticket office or kiosk.

To sum up the characteristics of their joint persona, they:

Exercise

See Exercise 7-1, Creating a User Persona for Your System

- lead busy lives with a need for cooling off once or twice a week
- are sophisticated, educated, and technology savvy
- are civic minded and care about sustainability and environment
- like the outdoors
- have a good group of friends with whom they sometimes like to share entertainment

7.6 IDEATION

Ideation is an active, fast-moving collaborative group process for forming ideas for design. It is an activity that goes with design thinking; you might say that ideation is a tool of design thinking; *ideation is applied design thinking.*

Ideation is where you start your conceptual design. This is a hugely creative and fun phase. Ideation is where you brainstorm to come up with ideas to solve design problems. Ideation is inseparable from sketching and evaluation aimed at exploration of design ideas.

7.6.1 Essential Concepts
Iterate to explore
Ideation involves exploration and calls for extensive iteration (Buxton, 2007b). Be ready to try, try, try, and try again. Think about Thomas Edison and his more than 10,000 experiments to create a usable and useful light bulb. Make sketches and physical mockups early and often, and expose customers and users to your designs; involve them in their creation, exploration, and iteration.

The evaluation part of this kind of exploratory iteration is never formal; there are no established "methods." It is a fast, furious, and freewheeling comparison of many alternatives and inspiration for further alternatives. If you are starting out with only two or three alternatives, you are not doing this right.

Idea creation vs. critiquing
In the active give-and-take of design, there are two modes of thinking: idea creation and critiquing. Idea creation is about the generation of new ideas and throwing them out for discussion and inspiration. Critiquing is review and judgment.

Although you will interweave idea creation and critiquing throughout the design process, you should know which mode you are in at any given time and not mix the modes. That especially means not to mix critiquing into idea creation. Idea creation should result in a pure flow of ideas regardless of feasibility, in the classic tradition of brainstorming. Although we know that, at the end of the day, practical implementation constraints must be considered and allowed to carry weight in the final overall design, saying "Hey, wait a minute!" too early can stifle innovation.

Mason (1968) calls this separation of idea creation and critiquing "go-mode and stop-mode thinking."[3] Sodan (1998) calls it the yin and yang of computer science. In idea-creation mode you adopt a freewheeling mental attitude that will permit ideas to flourish. In critiquing you revert to a cold-blooded, critical attitude that will bring your judgment into full play.

Idea creation gives a new creative idea time to blossom before it is cut at the stem and held up to the scale. Idea creation gives you permission to be radical; you get to play outside the safe zone and no one can shoot you down. Allowing early cries of "that will never work," "they have already tried that," "it will cost too much," "we do not have a widget for that," or "it will not work on our implementation platform" will unfairly hobble and frustrate this first step of creativity.

We once experienced an interesting example of this tension between innovation and implementation constraints with a consulting client, an example that we call the *implementation know-it-all*. The interaction designers in a cross-disciplinary team that included software folks were being particularly innovative in scenario and prototype sketching but the software team member was not going along.

He was doubtful whether their implementation platform could support the design ideas being discussed and he got his team to stop designing, start talking about technical feasibility, and explore implementation solutions. When we threw a "premature critiquing" penalty flag, he defended his position with the rationale that there was no sense spending time on an interaction design if you are only to discover that it cannot be implemented.

This might sound like a reasonable stance, but it is actually the other way around! You do not want to spend time working on technical solutions for an interaction design feature that can change easily as you evaluate and iterate. That is the whole point of low-fidelity prototypes; they are inexpensive, fast, and easy to make without concerns about implementation platforms. Wait and see how the design turns out before worrying about how to implement it.

---

[3]Thanks to Mark Ebersole, long ago, for this reference.

Beyond this, early stifling of a design idea prevents a chance to explore parts of the idea that are practical. Even when the idea does turn out to be infeasible, the idea itself is a vehicle for exploring in a particular direction that can later be used to compare and contrast with more feasible ideas.

The design teams at IDEO (ABC News Nightline, 1999) signal premature critiquing by ringing a wrist-mounted bicycle bell to signal the foul of being judgmental too early in design discussions. To help engender an idea creation attitude in early design discussions, Cooper, Reimann, and Dubberly (2003, p. 82) suggest that team members consider the user interface as all-powerfully magical, freeing it from implementation-bound concerns up front. When you do not have to consider the nuts and bolts of implementation, you might find you have much more creative freedom at the starting point.

7.6.2 Doing Ideation

If the roof doesn't leak, the architect hasn't been creative enough

—Frank Lloyd Wright (Donohue, 1989)

Set up work spaces

Set aside physical work spaces for ideation, individual work, and group work. Establish a place for design collaboration (Bødker & Buur, 2002). If possible, arrange for dedicated ideation studio space that can be closed off from outside distractions, where sketches and props can be posted and displayed, and that will not be disturbed by time-sharing with other meetings and work groups.

Figure 7-4

The Virginia Tech ideation studio, the "Kiva" (photo courtesy of Akshay Sharma, Virginia Tech Department of Industrial Design).

In Figure 7-4 we show the collaborative ideation studio, called the Kiva, in the Virginia Tech Department of Industrial Design. The Kiva was originally designed and developed by Maya Design in Pittsburgh, Pennsylvania, and is used at Virginia Tech with their permission.

The Kiva is a cylindrical space in which designers can brainstorm and sketch in isolation from outside distractions. The space inside is large enough for seating and work tables. The inner surface of most of the space is a metallic skin. It is painted so it serves an enveloping whiteboard that can hold magnetic "push pins." The large-screen display on the outside can be used for announcements, including group scheduling for the work space.

In Figure 7-5 we show individual and group work spaces for designers.

Assemble a team

Why a team? The day of the lone genius inventor is long gone, as is the die-hard misconception of the disheveled genius inventor flailing about in a chaotic frenzy in a messy and cluttered laboratory (picture the professor in *Back to the Future*) (Brown, 2008).

Thomas Edison, famous not just for his inventions but for processes to create inventions, broke with the single genius inventor image and was one of the first to use a team-based approach to innovation. Thomas Edison "made it a profession that blended art, craft, science, business savvy, and an astute understanding of customers and markets" (Brown, 2008, p. 86). Today, design thinking is a direct descendant of Edison's tradition, and in this design thinking, teamwork is essential for bouncing ideas around, for collaborative brainstorming and sketching, and for potentiating each other's creativity.

Figure 7-5

Individual and group designer work spaces (photos courtesy of Akshay Sharma, Virginia Tech Department of Industrial Design).

So, gather a creative and open-minded team. You might think that only a talented few brilliant and inventive thinkers could make ideation work successfully. However, we all have the innate ability to think freely and creatively; we just have to allow ourselves to get into the mode—and the mood—for a free-thinking flow of ideas without inhibition and without concern that we will be criticized.

Try to include people with a breadth of knowledge and skills, cross-disciplinary people who have experience in more than one discipline or area. Include customer representatives and representative users. If you are going to be thinking visually, it helps to have a visual designer on the team to bring ideas from graphic design.

Use ideation bin ideas to get started

If you gathered ideation inputs into a "bin" of work activity notes back in contextual analysis, now is the time to use them. An ideation input bin is an unconstrained and loosely organized place to gather all the work activity notes and other ideas for sparking and inspiring design.

You should also include emotional impact factors in your ideation inputs because ideation is most likely where these factors will get considered for incorporation into the design. In your contextual data, look for work activity notes about places in the work practice that are dreaded, not fun, kill joy, or drudgery so you can invent fun ways to overcome these feelings.

Shuffle the notes around, form groups, and add labels. Use the notes as points of departure in brainstorming discussions.

Conceiving and Informing the Magitti Context Aware Leisure Guide

Dr. Victoria Bellotti, Principal Scientist, and Dr. Bo Begole, PARC, a Xerox Company

In the realm of new product and service innovation, it is rare that a business places such importance on the idea of utility that it is willing to invest heavily in user-centered research before investing in design and implementation of any kind. It is especially rare before even determining who the user should be or what the product or service should do. When this happened at PARC in 2003–2006, we were delighted to participate in an extraordinary collaboration with Dai Nippon Printing (DNP), the highest-revenue printing technologies and solutions company in the world. DNP executives wished to respond to the widespread transition from printed to electronic media. So they asked PARC, with its reputation for user-centered technology innovation, to discover a new rich media technology-based business opportunity and to develop an innovative solution for the Japanese market. They wanted the solution to be centered on leisure content, as that was most compatible with the bulk of the content in their traditional media printing business.

Initially the most important thing we needed to do was to search broadly for an ideal target user. A method we call "Opportunity Discovery" was developed to handle the situation where one wants to brainstorm and eliminate possible market opportunities in a systematic manner. Many different problem statements representing a demographic plus some activity, problem, or desire were compared side by side in terms of preagreed criteria, which represented the properties of an ideal opportunity for DNP. The most promising three were selected for further, deeper exploration.

Representatives of those target markets were interviewed about their receptiveness to new technology and finally the youth market was chosen as the most likely to adopt a novel technology solution.

Using surveys, interviews, and shadowing, we determined that the 19- to 25-year-old age group had the most leisure, as they were between cram school and a demanding career. These were therefore chosen as the ideal target for our leisure technology. After engaging in some persona explorations, we brainstormed about 500 ideas for possible technology solutions and subsequently clustered them into more coherent concepts. The concepts were evaluated by a team of PARC and DNP representatives for their intuitive appeal, their match to DNP's business competencies, and their potential to generate intellectual property, which could be used to protect any business endeavor built around the technology against competitors. The five best ideas were then sketched out in a deliberately rough scenario form to elicit criticism and improvement. They were then taken to Tokyo and exposed to representatives of the target market for feedback, refinement, and an indication as to which was the most compelling.

In the end, two scenarios were neck and neck—Magic Scope (a system for viewing virtual information) and Digital Graffiti (a system for creating virtual information). These scenarios were combined into the Magitti city leisure guide concept, which was then elaborated in a much more detailed format. We crystallized the idea of recommending venues where leisure activities could be pursued that became the heart of the final system. A mockup was built out of cardboard and plastic with switchable paper screens that matched the storyline in the scenario. This was taken back to Japan for in situ evaluation on the streets of Tokyo with target market representatives. We also held focus group evaluations using just the paper screens where more penetrating questions could be asked of large groups who outnumbered the researchers and were more confident in this context.

As Magitti was taking shape, we continued our field investigations, involving more interviews, observations, and a mobile phone diary, which led to useful insights that informed the system design. One phenomenon that we noticed was that people in the city tended to travel a long way to meet friends half-way between their widely dispersed homes. The half-way points were often unfamiliar and indeed most young people we interviewed on the street reported being moderately to extremely unfamiliar with the location they were in. A second phenomenon we noticed was that our young prospective users tended not to plan everything in advance, sometimes only the meeting place was preagreed. Both of these phenomena constituted good evidence of the receptivity toward or need for a leisure guide.

We surfaced a strong requirement for one-handed operation, as most Japanese people use public transit and carry bags with only one hand free in the context of use that Magitti was intended for. We also discovered a need for photos that convey ambiance inside a venue, as it is hard to see inside many Japanese businesses, even restaurants, because they are often above ground floor level. Finally, the fact that our target users trusted the opinions of people more than businesses and advertisers led us to believe that end user-generated content would be important.

Our extensive fieldwork and user-centered design activities allowed us to develop a well-grounded idea of what we needed to build and how it should work before we ever wrote a line of code for DNP. It is quite extraordinary that this happens so rarely, given that a lot of wasted development effort can be saved in technology innovation by good user-centered work. We can use observation to drive insights and focus our efforts on solving real problems, and we can elicit feedback from target users about simple scenarios and mockups early on to elicit crucial feedback. This approach was responsible for the fact that the Magitti system concept was very appealing to representatives of its target market. The working prototype we subsequently developed was also well received and found to be helpful in leisure outings in Tokyo. The commercial solution based off the Magitti prototype is now initially available in Japan as an iPhone application called MachiReco (meaning city recommender).

REFERENCE

Bellotti, V., Begole, B., Chi, E. H., Ducheneaut, N., Fang, J., & Isaacs, E., et al. (2008). Activity-based serendipitous recommendations with the Magitti mobile leisure guide. In *Proceeding of the twenty-sixth annual SIGCHI conference on Human factors in computing systems (CHI '08)* (pp. 1157–1166). New York, NY, USA: ACM.

Brainstorm

Is it wrong to cry "Brainstorm!" in a crowded theater?

—Anonymous

Ideation is not just sketching, it is brainstorming. According to Dictionary.com, brainstorming is a "conference technique of solving specific problems, amassing information, stimulating creative thinking, developing new ideas, etc., by unrestrained and spontaneous participation in discussion." Ideation is classic brainstorming applied to design.

Setting the stage for ideation. Part of brainstorming involves the group deciding for itself how it will operate. But for groups of any size, it is a common activity to start with an overview discussion in the group as a whole.

The initial overview discussion establishes background and parameters and agreement on goals of the design exercise. Post major issues and concepts from your ideation bin (see earlier discussion). The ideation team leader must be sure that everyone on the team is in tune with the same rules for behavior (see subsection on rules of engagement later).

Next, divide up the team into pairs or small sub-teams and go to breakout groups to create and develop ideas. The goal of breakout groups is to have intense rapid interactions to spawn and accumulate large numbers of ideas about characteristics and features. Use marking pens on flip charts and/or write on whiteboards. Put one idea per sheet of paper so that you have maximum freedom to move each around independently.

Use sketches (imperative, not optional) annotated with short phrases to produce quick half-minute representations of ideas. You can include examples of other systems, conceptual ideas, considerations, design features, marketing ideas, and experience goals. Get all your whacky, creative, and off-the-wall ideas out there. The flow should be a mix of verbal and visual.

Reconvene when the sub-teams have listed all the ideas that they can think of or when the allotted time is up. In turn, each sub-team reports on their work to the whole group. First posting their annotated sketches around the room, the sub-teams walk the group through their ideas and explain the concepts. The sub-teams then lead a group discussion to expand and elaborate the ideas, adding new sketches and annotations, but still going for essentials, not completeness of details.

When the font of new ideas seems to have run dry for the moment, the group can switch to critiquing mode. Even in critiquing, the focus is not to shoot down ideas but to take parts that can be changed or interpreted differently and use them in even better ways.

Figure 7-6

Ideation brainstorming within the Virginia Tech ideation studio, Kiva (photo courtesy of Akshay Sharma, Department of Industrial Design).

In Figure 7-6 we show an example of ideation brainstorming in mid-process within the Virginia Tech ideation studio.

The mechanics of ideation. Use outlining as verbal sketching. An outline is easier to scan for key ideas than bulk text. An outline is an efficient way to display ideation results on flip charts or in projected images.

Immerse your sketching and ideation within a design-support ecology, a "war room" of working artifacts as inputs and inspiration to ideation. Get it all out there in front of you to point to, discuss, and critique. Fill your walls, shelves, and work tables with artifacts, representations of ideas, images, props, toys, notes, posters, and materials.

Make the outputs of your ideation as visual and tangible as possible; intersperse the outline text with sketches, sketches, and more sketches. Post and display everything all around the room as your visual working context. Where appropriate, build physical mockups as embodied sketches.

Use teamwork and play off of each other's ideas while "living the part of the user." Talk in scenarios, keeping customers and users in the middle, telling stories of their experience as your team weaves a fabric of new ideas for design solutions.

In IDEO's "deep dive" approach, a cross-disciplinary group works in total immersion without consideration of rank or job title. In their modus operandi of focused chaos (not organized chaos), "enlightened trial and error succeeds over the planning of lone genius." Their designing process was illustrated in a well-known *ABC News* documentary with a new design for supermarket shopping carts, starting with a brief contextual inquiry where team members visit different

> ## Physical Mockup
>
> A physical mockup is a tangible, three-dimensional, physical prototype or model of a device or product, often one that can be held in the hand, and often crafted rapidly out of materials at hand, and used during exploration and evaluation to at least simulate physical interaction.

stores to understand the work domain of shopping and issues with existing shopping cart designs and use.

Then, in an abbreviated contextual analysis process, they regrouped and engaged in debriefing, synthesizing different themes that emerged in their contextual inquiry. This analysis fed parallel brainstorming sessions in which they captured all ideas, however unconventional. At the end of this stage they indulged in another debriefing session, combining the best ideas from brainstorming to assemble a design prototype. This alternation of brainstorming, prototyping, and review, driven by their "failing often to succeed sooner" philosophy, is a good approach for anyone wishing to create a good user experience.

Rules of engagement. The process should be democratic; this is not a time for pulling rank or getting personal. Every idea should be valued the same. Ideation should be ego free, with no ownership of ideas; all ideas belong to the group; all are equally open to critiquing (when the time comes). It is about the ideas, not the people. There is to be no "showboating" or agendas of individuals to showcase their talent.

The leader should be especially clear about enforcing "cognitive firewalling" to prevent incursions of judgment into the idea-creation mode. If the designers are saying they need a particular feature that requires an interstellar ion-propulsion motor and someone says "wait, we cannot make that out of Tinkertoys," you will have to throw out a penalty flag.

Example: Ideation for the Ticket Kiosk System

We brainstormed with potential ticket buyers, students, MU representatives, and civic leaders. Here we show selected results of that ideation session with our Ticket Kiosk System design team as a consolidated list with related categories in the spirit of "verbal sketching." As in any ideation session, ideas were accompanied with sketches. We show the idea part of the session here separately to focus on the topic of this section.

Thought questions to get started:

What does "an event" mean? How do people treat events in real life?

An event is more than something that happens and maybe you attend

An event can have emotional meanings, can be thought provoking, can have meaning that causes you to go out and do something

Ontological artifacts:

Tickets, events, event sponsors, MU student ID, kiosk

Things people might want to do with tickets:

   People might want to email tickets to friends

Possible features and breadth of coverage:

   We might want to feature customized tickets for keepsake editions

   Homecoming events

   Parents weekend events

   Visiting speakers on current topics

   Visitor's guide to what's happening in town and the university

   Christmas tour of Middleburg

   View Christmas decorations on historic homes

   Walk Main Street to see decorations and festive shops

Types of events:

   Action movies, comedy (plays, stand-up), concerts, athletic events, specials

Special themes and motifs:

   Motif for the Ticket Kiosk System could be "Adventures in Entertainment," which would show up in the physical design (the shape, images and colors, the aesthetic appearance) of the kiosk itself and would carry through to the metaphor pervading the screen, dialogue, buttons, and so on in the interaction design

   Complete theme package: Football game theme: brunch, tailgating parties, game tickets, post-game celebrations over drinks at select places in town, followed by a good football movie

   Date night theme: Dinner and a movie, restaurant ads with movie/event tickets, proximity information and driving/public transportation directions, romantic evening, flowers from D'Rose, dinner at Chateau Morrisette, tour some of the setting of the filming of *Dirty Dancing*, stroll down Draper Road under a full moon (calendar and weather driven), watch *Dirty Dancing* at The Lyric Theater, tickets for late-night wine tasting at The Vintage Cellar, wedding planner consultation (optional)

Business consideration:

   Because it is a college town, if we make a good design, it can be reused in other college towns

   Competition: Because we are up against ubiquitous Websites, we have to make the kiosk experience something way beyond what you can get on a Website

Emotional impact:

   Emotional aspect about good times with good friends

   Emphasize MU team spirit, logos, etc.

   Entertainment event tickets are a gateway to fun and adventure

   Combine social and civic participation

   Indoor locations could have immersive themes with video and surround sound

Immersive experience: For example, indoor kiosk (where security is less of a problem) at The University Mall, offer an experience "they cannot refuse," support with surrounding immersive visuals and audio, ATM-like installation with wrap-around display walls and surround sound, between ticket buyers, run preview of theme and its mood

Minority Report style UIs

Rock concerts for group euphoria

Monster trucks or racing: ambiance of power and noise, appeals to the more primal instincts and thrill-seeking

Other desired impact:

Part of university and community "family"

Ride on the emerging visibility of and talent at MU

Collective success and pride

Leverage different competencies of MU and community technologies

Patron-of-the-arts feeling: classiness, sophistication, erudition, feeling special

Community outreach:

Create public service arrangements with local government (e.g., could help advertise and sell T-shirts for annual street art fair)

Advertise adult education opportunities, martial arts classes, kids camps, art and welding courses

Ubiquitous locations:

Bus stops

Library

Major dorms

Student center

City Hall building

Shopping malls

Food courts

Inside busses

Major academic and administrative buildings

7.7 SKETCHING

We have already mentioned sketching several times. Sketching is the rapid creation of freehand drawings expressing preliminary design ideas, focusing on concepts rather than details. To start with, we credit Bill Buxton (2007b) as the champion for sketching; much of what we say about sketching can be credited to him.

7.7.1 Essential Concepts

Sketching is essential to ideation and design

Design is a process of creation and exploration, and sketching is a visual medium for that exploration. Sketching for design goes back at least to the Middle Ages. Consider da Vinci and all his famous sketch books. Nilsson and Ottersten (1998) describe sketching as an essential visual language for brainstorming and discussion.

By adding visualization to ideation, sketching adds cognitive supercharging, boosting creativity by bringing in more human senses to the task (Buxton, 2007a). Clearly sketching supports communication within ideation and, as Nilsson and Ottsersten (1998) point out, sketches also serve as an important longer-term design documentation. This helps other team members and designers retain understanding of the design and its details as they get into prototyping and implementation. The evolution of your sketches provides a history of your thinking.

What sketching is and is not

Sketching is not about putting pen to paper in the act of drawing. A sketch is not about making a drawing or picture of a product to document a design. A sketch is not just an artifact that you look at; *a sketch is a conversation* between the sketcher or designer and the artifact. A sketch is a medium to support a conversation among the design team members.

In a talk at Stanford, Buxton (2007a) challenges his audience to draw his mobile phone. But he does not mean a drawing of the phone as a product. He means something much harder—a sketch that reveals the interaction, *the experience* of using the phone in a situated context, where the product and its physical affordances encourage one type of behavior and experience over another.

Sketches are not the same as prototypes

Sketches are not prototypes, at least not in the usual UX process sense (Buxton, 2007b). Sketches are not used to refine a design that has been chosen. Sketches are for exploring the possibilities for creating a design. Sketching *is* designing, whereas prototyping in the usual sense is implementation to build a concrete design representation for testing.

In Figure 7-7, based on Buxton's Figure 52 (2007b), we show how sketches and prototypes are different in almost every way.

Sketches evoke thinking and ideas to arrive at a design. Prototypes illustrate an instance of a design. While sketches suggest possibilities, prototypes describe

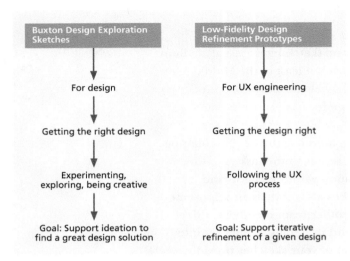

Figure 7-7

Comparison between Buxton design exploration sketches and traditional low-fidelity refinement prototypes.

designs already decided upon. Sketches are to explore and raise questions. Prototypes are to refine and provide answers.

The lifecycle iteration of sketching is a divergence of discovery, an expansion of ideas and possibilities. In contrast, the lifecycle iteration of the HCI engineering process is intended to be a convergence, a closing-up of ideas and possibilities. Sketches are deliberately tentative, noncommittal, and ambiguous. Prototypes, however detailed, are depictions of specific designs.

Sketching is embodied cognition to aid invention

Sketching is not intended to be a tool for documenting designs that are first created in one's head and then transferred to paper. In fact, the sketch itself is far less important than the process of making it. The process of sketching is a kind of cognitive scaffolding, a rich and efficient way to off-load part of the cognition, especially the mental visualization, to physical artifacts in the world.

A sketch is not just a way to represent your thinking; the act of making the sketch is part of the thinking. Sketching is a direct part, not an after-the-fact part, of the process of invention. *Designers invent while sketching.* Sketching embraces one's whole being: the hands, the mind, and all the senses.

The kinesthetics of sketching, pointing, holding, and touching bring the entire hand-eye-brain coordination feedback loop to bear on the problem solving. Your physical motor movements are coupled with visual and cognitive activity; the designer's mind and body potentiate each other in invention.

In Figure 7-8 you can see an example of a sketch to think about design.

7.7.2 Doing Sketching

Stock up on sketching and mockup supplies

Stock the ideation studio with sketching supplies such as whiteboards, blackboards, corkboards, flip chart easels, Post-its™ of all sizes, tape, and marking pens. Be sure to include supplies for constructing physical mockups, including scissors, hobby knives, cardboard, foam core board, duct tape, Scotch™ tape, wooden blocks, push pins, thumb tacks, staples, string, bits of cloth, rubber, other flexible materials, crayons, and spray paint.

Use the language of sketching

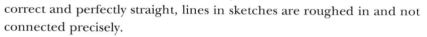

To be effective at sketching for design, you must use a particular vocabulary that has not changed much over the centuries. One of the most important language features is the vocabulary of lines, which are made as freehand "open" gestures. Instead of being mechanically correct and perfectly straight, lines in sketches are roughed in and not connected precisely.

Figure 7-8

A sketch to think about design (photo courtesy of Akshay Sharma, Virginia Tech Department of Industrial Design).

In this language, lines overlap, often extending a bit beyond the corner. Sometimes they "miss" intersecting and leave the corner open a little bit. Further, the resolution and detail of a sketch should be low enough to suggest that it is a concept in the making, not a finished design. It needs to look disposable and inexpensive to make. Sketches are deliberately ambiguous and abstract, leaving "holes" for the imagination.

They can be interpreted in different ways, fostering new relationships to be seen within them, even by the person who drew them. In other words, avoid the appearance of precision; if everything is specified and the design looks finished, then the message is that you are telling something, "this is the design," not proposing exploration, "let us play with this and see what comes up." You can see this unfinished look in the sketches of Figures 7-9 and 7-10.

Here are some defining characteristics of sketching (Buxton, 2007b; Tohidi et al., 2006):

- Everyone can sketch; you do not have to be artistic
- Most ideas are conveyed more effectively with a sketch than with words
- Sketches are quick and inexpensive to create; they do not inhibit early exploration
- Sketches are disposable; there is no real investment in the sketch itself
- Sketches are timely; they can be made just-in-time, done in-the-moment, provided when needed

Figure 7-9

Freehand gestural sketches for the Ticket Kiosk System (sketches courtesy of Akshay Sharma, Virginia Tech Department of Industrial Design).

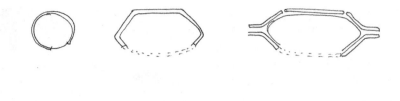

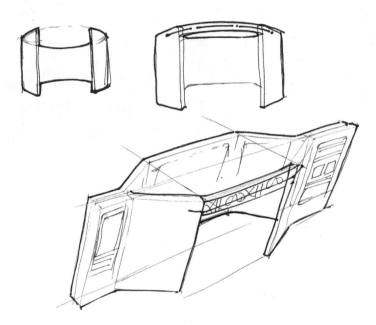

- Sketches should be plentiful; entertain a large number of ideas and make multiple sketches of each idea
- Textual annotations play an essential support role, explaining what is going on in each part of the sketch and how

Exercise

See Exercise 7-2, Practice in Ideation and Sketching

Exercise

See Exercise 7-3, Ideation and Sketching for Your System

In Figure 7-11, we show examples of designers doing sketching.

Example: Sketching for a Laptop/Projector Project

The following figures show sample sketches for the K-YAN project (K-yan means "vehicle for knowledge"), an exploratory collaboration by the Virginia Tech Industrial Design Department and IL&FS.[4] The objective is to develop a combination laptop and projector in a single portable device for use in rural India. Thanks to Akshay Sharma of the Virginia Tech Industrial Design Department for these sketches. See Figures 7-12 through 7-15 for different kinds of exploratory sketches for this project.

---

[4]http://kyan.weebly.com

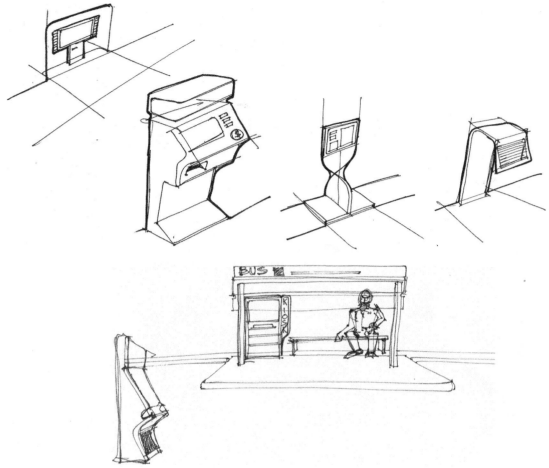

Figure 7-10

Ideation and design exploration sketches for the Ticket Kiosk System (sketches courtesy of Akshay Sharma, Virginia Tech Department of Industrial Design).

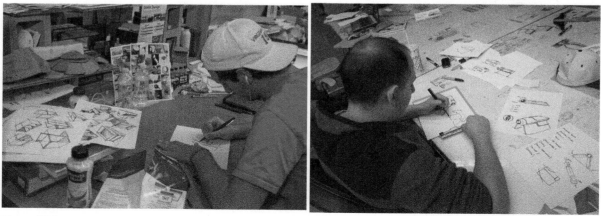

Figure 7-11

Designers doing sketching (photos courtesy of Akshay Sharma, Virginia Tech Department of Industrial Design).

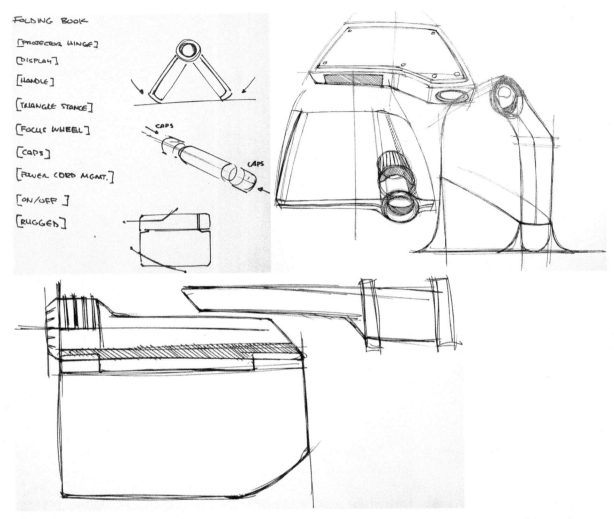

Figure 7-12

Early ideation sketches of K-YAN (sketches courtesy of Akshay Sharma, Department of Industrial Design).

7.7.3 Physical Mockups as Embodied Sketches

Just as sketches are two-dimensional visual vehicles for invention, a physical mockup for ideation about a physical device or product is a three-dimensional sketch. Physical mockups as sketches, like all sketches, are made quickly, highly disposable, and made from at-hand materials to create tangible props for exploring design visions and alternatives.

A physical mockup is an embodied sketch because it is an even more physical manifestation of a design idea and it is a tangible artifact for touching, holding, and acting out usage (see Figures 7-16 and 7-17).

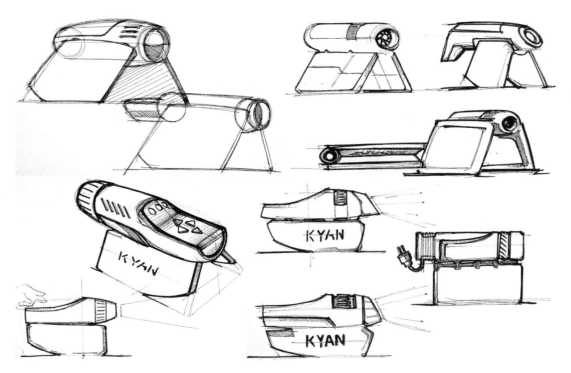

Where appropriate in your ideation, you can do the same. Build many different mockups, each as creative and different as possible. Tell stories about the mockup during ideation and stretch it as far as you can.

For later in the process, after design exploration is done and you want a 3D design representation to show clients, customers, and implementers, there are services to produce finished-looking, high-fidelity physical mockups.

Figure 7-13

Mid-fidelity exploration sketches of K-YAN (sketches courtesy of Akshay Sharma, Virginia Tech Department of Industrial Design).

7.8 MORE ABOUT PHENOMENOLOGY

7.8.1 The Nature of Phenomenology

Joy of use is an obvious emotional counterpart to ease of use in interaction. But there is a component of emotional impact that goes much deeper. Think of the kind of personal engagement and personal attachment that leads to a product being invited to become an integral part of the user's lifestyle. More than functionality or fun—this is a kind of companionship. This longer-term situated kind of emotional impact entails a phenomenological view of interaction (Russell, Streitz, & Winograd, 2005, p. 9).

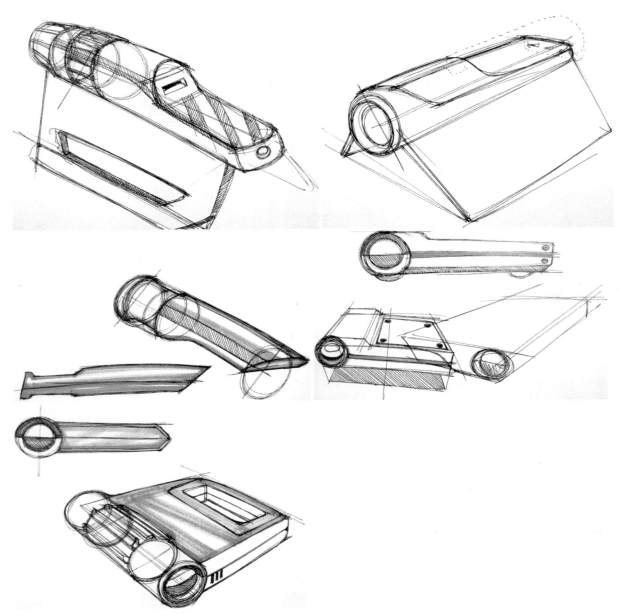

Figure 7-14
Sketches to explore flip-open mechanism of K-YAN (sketches courtesy of Akshay Sharma, Virginia Tech Department of Industrial Design).

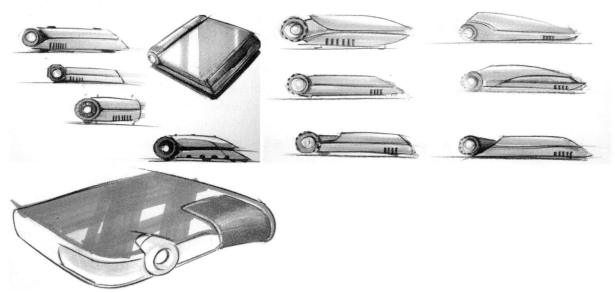

Figure 7-15
Sketches to explore emotional impact of form for K-YAN (sketches courtesy of Akshay Sharma, Virginia Tech Department of Industrial Design).

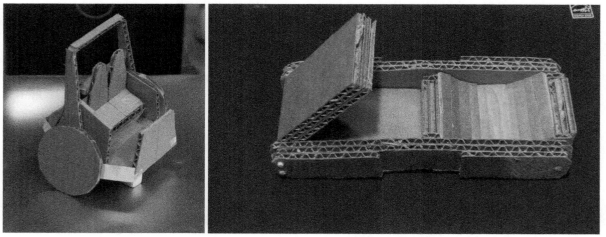

Figure 7-16
Examples of rough physical mockups (models courtesy of Akshay Sharma, Virginia Tech Department of Industrial Design).

Figure 7-17

Example of a more finished looking physical mockup (model courtesy of Akshay Sharma, Virginia Tech Department of Industrial Design).

Emerging from humanistic studies, phenomenology[5] is the philosophical examination of the foundations of experience and action. It is about phenomena, things that happen and can be observed. But it is not about logical deduction or conscious reflection on observations of phenomena; it is about individual interpretation and intuitive understanding of human experience.

Phenomenology is part of the "modern school of philosophy founded by Edmund Husserl. Its influence extended throughout Europe and was particularly important to the early development of existentialism. Husserl attempted to develop a universal philosophic method, devoid of presuppositions, by focusing purely on phenomena and describing them; anything that could not be seen, and thus was not immediately given to the consciousness, was excluded."[6]

"The phenomenological method is thus neither the deductive method of logic nor the empirical method of the natural sciences; instead it consists in realizing the presence of an object and elucidating its meaning through intuition. Husserl considered the object of the phenomenological method to be the immediate seizure, in an act of vision, of the ideal intelligible content of the phenomenon" (Husserl, 1962). His key and defining work from the early 20th century is now reprinted in an English translation.

However, it was Martin Heidegger who translated it into "the most thorough, penetrating, and radical analysis of everyday experience" (Winograd & Flores, 1986, p. 9). Heidegger, quoted often in human–computer interaction contexts, was actually a student of Professor Husserl and, although they had collaborated closely, they had a falling out during the 1940s over the social politics of World War II.[7] "Writers like Heidegger challenge the dominant view of mind, declaring that cognition is not based on the systematic manipulation of representations" (Winograd & Flores, 1986, p. 10). This view is in opposition to the human-as-information-processor paradigm discussed earlier in this chapter.

---

[5]Dictionary.com says phenomenology is: 1. the movement founded by Husserl that concentrates on the detailed description of conscious experience, without recourse to explanation, metaphysical assumptions, and traditional philosophical questions; 2. the science of phenomena as opposed to the science of being.

[6]http://www.reference.com/browse/Phenomenology+

[7]http://en.wikipedia.org/wiki/Edmund_Husserl

Because phenomenology is about observables, it enjoys a relationship with hermeneutics, the theory of interpretation (Winograd & Flores, 1986, p. 27), to fill the need to explain what is observed. Historically, hermeneutics was about interpretation of artistic and literary works, especially mythical and sacred texts and about how human understanding of those texts has changed over time. However, "one of the fundamental insights of phenomenology is that this activity of interpretation is not limited to such situations, but pervades our everyday life" (Winograd & Flores, 1986, p. 27).

7.8.2 The Phenomenological View in Human–Technology Interaction

When translated to human–computer interaction, phenomenological aspects of interaction represent a form of emotional impact, an affective state arising within the user. It is about emotional phenomena within the interaction experience and the broadest interpretation of the usage context. It is about a social role for a product in long-term relationships with human users. It is about a role within human life activities. In that regard, it is related to activity theory (Winograd & Flores, 1986) because activity theory also emphasizes that the context of use is central to understanding, explaining, and designing technology (Bødker, 1991).

7.8.3 The Phenomenological Concept of Presence

The phenomenological paradigm is central to Harrison, Back, and Tatar (2007), who make it clear that HCI is no longer just about usability and user performance, but that it is about presence of technology as part of our lives: "We argue that the coming ubiquity of computational artifacts drives a shift from efficient *use* to meaningful *presence* of information technology." This is all about moving from the desktop to ubiquitous, embedded, embodied, and situated interaction.

Presence

Presence of a product is a kind of relationship with users in which the product becomes a personally meaningful part of their lives.

Hallnäs and Redström (2002) also describe the "new usability" as a shift from use to "presence." To them, a key characteristic of phenomenological concepts is that the product or system that is the target of design or evaluation is *present in the user's life*, not just being used for something. That certainly rules out almost all desktop software, for example, but calls to mind favorite portable devices, such as the iPhone and iPod, that have become a part of our daily lives.

Use or functional descriptions are about what you do with the product. Presence is about what it means to you. A description of presence is an existential description, meaning that the user has given the product a place to exist in the user's life; it is about being known within the user's human experience rather than a theoretical or analytical description.

So, presence is about a relationship we have with a device or product. It is no longer just a device for doing a task, but we feel emotional ties. In Chapter 8, the Garmin handheld GPS is described as a haven of comfort, coziness, familiarity, and companionship, like a familiar old pair of boots or your favorite fleece. The device has been invited into the user's emotional life, and that is presence.

As Hallnäs and Redström put it, "... 'presence' refers to existential definitions of a thing based on how we invite and accept it as part of our *lifeworld*." Winograd and Flores (1986, p. 31) allude to the same relationship, as expressed by Heidegger, "He [Heidegger] argues that the separation of subject and object denies the more fundamental unity of *being-in-the-world*." Here subject means the person having the user experience, and the object is everything they perceive and experience. You cannot separate the user, the context, and the experience.

Presence, or the potential for presence, cannot necessarily be detected directly in design or evaluation. Acceptance is usually accompanied by a "disappearance" (Weiser, 1991) of the object as a technological artifact. Hallnäs and Redström use, as a simple but effective example, a chair. If your description of the chair simply refers to the fact that you sit in it without reference to why or what you do while sitting in it, you have removed the user and the usage context; it is more or less just a functional description. However, if the user describes this chair as the place where she seeks comfort each evening in front of the fire after a long day's work, then the chair has an emotional presence in that user's life.

7.8.4 The Importance of Phenomenological Context over Time

From the discussion so far, it should be abundantly clear that the kind of emotional context found in the phenomenological paradigm is a context that must unfold over time. Usage develops over time and takes on its own life, often apart from what designers could envision. Users learn, adapt, and change during usage, creating a dynamic force that gives shape to subsequent usage (Weiser, 1991).

Short-term studies will not see this important aspect of usage and interaction. So, while users can experience snapshot episodes of good or bad usability, good or bad usefulness, and even good or bad emotional impact, the phenomenological aspects of emotional impact are about a deeper and longer-term concept. It is not just about a point in time within usage, but it speaks to a whole style and presence of the product over time. The realization of this fact is essential in both design and evaluation for emotional impact within the phenomenological context.

Mental Models and Conceptual Design

Objectives

After reading this chapter, you will:

1. Understand designers' and users' mental models and the mapping between them
2. Be able to create conceptual designs from ecological, interaction, and emotional perspectives
3. Know what storyboards are and how to produce them
4. Understand the background aspects of embodied, ubiquitous, and situated interactions

8.1 INTRODUCTION

8.1.1 You Are Here

We begin each process chapter with a "you are here" picture of the chapter topic in the context of the overall Wheel lifecycle template; see Figure 8-1. This chapter is a continuation of design, which we started in Chapter 7 and will conclude in Chapter 9, for designing the new work practice and the new system.

8.2 MENTAL MODELS

8.2.1 What Is a Mental Model?

According to Wikipedia.org, "a mental model is an explanation of someone's thought process about how something works in the real world." A designer's mental model is a vision of how a system works as held by the designer. A user's mental model is a description of how the system works, as held by the user. It is the job of conceptual design (coming up soon) to connect the two.

Figure 8-1

You are here; the second of three chapters on creating an interaction design in the context of the overall Wheel lifecycle template.

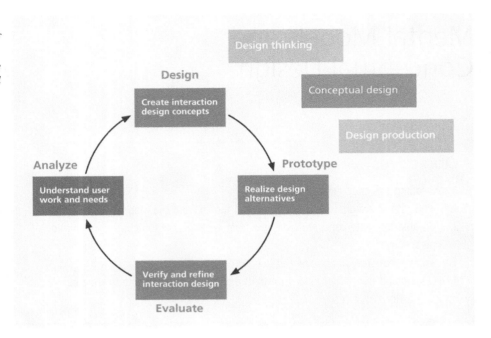

8.2.2 Designer's Mental Model

Sometimes called a conceptual model (Johnson & Henderson, 2002, p. 26), the designer's mental model is the designer's conceptualization of the envisioned system—what the system is, how it is organized, what it does, and how it works. If anyone should know these things, it is the designer who is creating the system. But it is not uncommon for designers to "design" a system without first forming and articulating a mental model.

The results can be a poorly focused design, not thought through from the start. Often such designs proceed in fits and starts and must be retraced and restarted when missing concepts are discovered along the way. The result of such a fuzzy start can be a fuzzy design that causes users to experience vagueness and misconceptions. It is difficult for users to establish a mental model of how the system works if the designer has never done the same.

As shown in Figure 8-2, the designer's mental model is created from what is learned in contextual inquiry and analysis and is transformed into design by ideation and sketching.

Johnson and Henderson (2002, p. 26) include metaphors, analogies, ontological structure, and mappings between those concepts and the task domain or work practice the design is intended to support. The closer the designer's mental model orientation is to the user's work domain and work

Metaphor

A metaphor is an analogy used in design to communicate and explain unfamiliar concepts using familiar conventional knowledge. Metaphors control complexity by allowing users to adapt what they already know in learning how to use new system features.

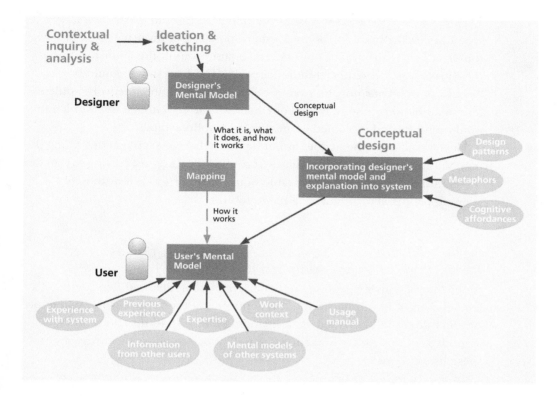

Figure 8-2

*Mapping the designer's
mental model to the user's
mental model.*

practice, the more likely users will internalize the model as their own. To paraphrase Johnson and Henderson's rule for relating the designer's mental model to the final design: if it is not in the designer's mental model, the system should not require users to be aware of it.

Designer's mental model in the ecological perspective: Describing what the system is, what it does, and how it works within its ecology

Mental models of a system can be expressed in any of the design perspectives of Chapter 7. In the ecological perspective, a designer's mental model is about how the system or product fits within its work context, in the flow of activities involving it and other parts of the broader system. In Norman's famous book, *The Design of Everyday Things*, he describes the use of thermostats (Norman, 1990, pp. 38–39) and how they work. Let us expand the explanation of thermostats to a description of what the system is and what it does from the perspective of its ecological setting.

First, we describe what it is by saying that a thermostat is part of a larger system, a heating (and/or cooling) system consisting of three major parts: a heat source, a heat distribution network, and a control unit, the latter being the thermostat and some other hidden circuitry. The heat source could be gas, electric, or wood burning, for example. The heat distribution network would use fans or air blowers to send heated or cooled air through hot air ducts or a pump would send heated or cooled water through subfloor pipes.

Next, we address what it does by noting that a thermostat is for controlling the temperature in a room or other space. It controls heating and cooling so that the temperature stays near a user-settable value—neither too hot or too cold—keeping people at a comfortable temperature.

Designer's mental model in the interaction perspective: Describing how users operate it

In the interaction perspective, a designer's mental model is a different view of an explanation of how things work; it is about how a user operates the system or product. It is a task-oriented view, including user intentions and sensory, cognitive, and physical user actions, as well as device behavior in response to these user actions.

In the thermostat example, a user can see two numerical temperature displays, either analog or digital. One value is for the current ambient temperature and the other is the setting for the target temperature. There will be a rotatable knob, slider, or other value-setting mechanism to set the desired target temperature. This covers the sensory and physical user actions for operating a thermostat. User cognition and proper formation of intentions with respect to user actions during thermostat operation, however, depend on understanding the usually hidden explanation of the behavior of a thermostat in response to the user's settings.

Most thermostats, as Norman explains (1990, pp. 38–39), are binary switches that are simply either on or off. When the sensed ambient temperature is below the target value, the thermostat turns the heat on. When the temperature then climbs to the target value, the thermostat turns the heat source off. It is, therefore, a false conceptualization, or false mental model, to believe that you can make a room warm up faster by turning the thermostat up higher.

The operator's manual for a particular furnace unit would probably say something to the effect that you turn it up and down to make it warmer or cooler, but would probably fall short of the full explanation of how a thermostat works. But the user is in the best position to form effective usage strategies, connecting user actions with expected outcomes, if in possession of this knowledge of thermostat behavior.

There are at least two possible design approaches to thermostats, then. The first is the common design containing a display of the current temperature plus a knob to set the target temperature. A second design, which reveals the designer's mental model, might have a display unit that provides feedback messages such as "checking ambient temperature," "temperature lower than target; turning heat on," and "temperature at desired level; shutting off." This latter design might suffer from being more complex to produce and the added display might be a distraction to experienced users. However, this design approach does help project the designer's mental model through the system design to the user.

Designer's mental model in the emotional perspective: Describing intended emotional impact

In the emotional perspective, the mental model of a design it about the expected overarching emotional response. Regarding the thermostat example, it is difficult to get excited about the emotional aspects of thermostats, but perhaps the visual design, the physical design, how it fits in with the house décor, or the craftsmanship of its construction might offer a slight amount of passing pleasure.

8.2.3 User's Mental Model

A user's mental model is a conceptualization or internal explanation each user has built about how a particular system works. As Norman says (1990), it is a natural human response to an unfamiliar situation to begin building an explanatory model a piece at a time. We look for cause-and-effect relationships and form theories to explain what we observe and why, which then helps guide our behavior and actions in task performance.

As shown in Figure 8-2, each user's mental model is a product of many different inputs including, as Norman has often said, knowledge in the head and knowledge in the world. Knowledge in the head comes from mental models of other systems, user expertise, and previous experience. Knowledge in the world comes from other users, work context, shared cultural conventions, documentation, and the conceptual design of the system itself. This latter source of user knowledge is the responsibility of the system designer.

Few, if any, thermostat designs themselves carry any knowledge in the world, such as a cognitive affordance that conveys anything like Norman's explanation of a thermostat as a binary switch. As a result, thermostat users depend on knowledge in the head, mostly from previous experience and shared conventions. Once you have used a thermostat and understand how it works, you pretty much understand all thermostats.

But sometimes mental models adapted from previous encounters with similar systems can work against learning to use a new system with a different conceptual design. Norman's binary switch explanation is accurate for almost every thermostat on the planet, but not for one in the heater of a mid-1960s Cadillac. In a fascinating departure from the norm, you could, in fact, speed up the heating system in this car, both the amount of heat and the fan speed, by setting the thermostat to a temperature higher than what you wanted in steady state.

Since cars were beginning to have more sophisticated (in this case, read more failure prone) electronics, why not put them to use? And they did. The output heat and fan speed were proportional to the difference between the ambient temperature and the thermostat setting. So, on a cold day, the heater would run wide open to produce as much heat as possible, but it would taper off its output as it approached the desired setting.

Lack of a correct user mental model can be the stuff of comedy curve balls, too. An example is the scene in the 1992 movie, *My Cousin Vinny*, where Marisa Tomei—as Vinny's fiancée, Mona Lisa Vito—tries to make a simple phone call. This fish-out-of-water scene pits a brash young woman from New York against a rotary dial telephone. You cannot help but reflect on the mismatch in the mapping between her mental model of touch-tone operation and the reality of old-fashioned rotary dials as she pokes vigorously at the numbers through the finger holes.

But, lest you dismiss her as a ditzy blond, we remind you that it was she who solved the case with her esoteric knowledge in the head, proving that the boys' 1964 Buick Skylark could not have left the two tire tracks found outside the convenience store because it did not have a limited-slip differential.

8.2.4 Mapping and the Role of Conceptual Design

The mapping in Figure 8-2 is an abstract and objective ideal transformation of the designer's mental model into the user's mental model (Norman, 1990, p. 23). As such the mapping is a yardstick against which to measure how closely the user's mental model matches the reality of the designer's mental model.

The conceptual design as it is manifest in the system is an implementation of this mapping and can be flawed or incomplete. A flawed conceptual design leads to a mismatch in the user's mental model. In reality, each user is likely to have a different mental model of the same system, and mental models can be incomplete and even incorrect in places.

8.3 CONCEPTUAL DESIGN

8.3.1 What Is a Conceptual Design?

A conceptual design is the part of an interaction design containing a theme, notion, or idea with the purpose of communicating a design vision about a system or product. A conceptual design is the manifestation of the designer's mental model within the system, as indicated in Figure 8-2. It is the part of the system design that brings the designer's mental model to life within the system. A conceptual design corresponds to what Norman calls the "system image" of the designer's mental model (Norman, 1990, pp. 16, 189–190), about which he makes the important point: this is the only way the designer and user can communicate.

Conceptual design is where you innovate and brainstorm to plant and first nurture the user experience seed. You can never iterate the design later to yield a good user experience if you do not get the conceptual part right up front. Conceptual design is where you establish the metaphor or the theme of the product—in a word, the concept.

8.3.2 Start with a Conceptual Design

Now that you have done your contextual inquiry and analysis, requirements, and modeling, as well as your ideation and sketching, how do you get started on design? Many designers start sketching out pretty screens, menu structures, and clever widgets.

But Johnson and Henderson (2002) will tell you to start with conceptual design before sketching any screen or user interface objects. As they put it, screen sketches are designs of "how the system *presents itself* to users. It is better to start by designing what the system *is* to them." Screen designs and widgets will come, but time and effort spent on interaction details can be wasted without a well-defined underlying conceptual structure. Norman (2008) puts it this way: "What people want is usable devices, *which translates into understandable ones*" (final emphasis ours).

To get started on conceptual design, gather the same team that did the ideation and sketching and synthesize all your ideation and sketching results into a high-level conceptualization of what the system or product is, how it fits within its ecology, and how it operates with users.

For most systems or products, especially domain-complex systems, the best way to start conceptual design is in the ecological perspective because that captures the system in its context. For product concepts where the emotional impact is paramount, starting with that perspective is obvious. At other times the "invention" of an interaction technique like that of the iPod Classic scroll wheel might be the starting point for a solution looking for a problem and is best visualized in the interaction perspective.

8.3.3 Leverage Metaphors in Conceptual Design

One way to start formulating a conceptual design is by way of metaphors— analogies for communication and explanations of the unfamiliar using familiar conventional knowledge. This familiarity becomes the foundation underlying and pervading the rest of the interaction design.

What users already know about an existing system or existing phenomena can be adapted in learning how to use a new system (Carroll & Thomas, 1982). Use metaphors to control complexity of an interaction design, making it easier to learn and easier to use instead of trying to reduce the overall complexity (Carroll, Mack, & Kellogg, 1988).

One of the simple and oldest examples is the use of a typewriter metaphor in a word processing system. New users who are familiar with the knowledge, such as margin setting and tab setting in the typewriter domain, will already know much of what they need to know to use these features in the word processing domain.

Metaphors in the ecological perspective

Find a metaphor that can be used to describe the broader system structure. An example of a metaphor from the ecological perspective could be the description of iTunes as a mother ship for iPods, iPhones, and iPads. The intention is that all operations for adding, removing, or organizing media content, such as applications, music, or videos, are ultimately managed in iTunes and the results are synced to all devices through an umbilical connection.

Metaphors in the interaction perspective

An example of a metaphor in the interaction perspective is a calendar application in which user actions look and behave like writing on a real calendar. A more modern example is the metaphor of reading a book on an iPad. As the user moves a finger across the display to push the page aside, the display takes on the appearance of a real paper page turning. Most users find it comfortingly familiar.

Another great example of a metaphor in the interaction perspective can be found in the Time Machine feature on the Macintosh operating system. It is a backup feature where the user can take a "time machine" to go back to older backups—by flying through time as guided by the user interface—to retrieve lost or accidentally deleted files.

One other example is the now pervasive desktop metaphor. When the idea of graphical user interfaces in personal computers became an economic feasibility, the designers at Xerox Parc were faced with an interesting interaction design challenge: How to communicate to the users, most of whom were going to see this kind of computer for the first time, how the interaction design works?

In response, they created the powerful "desktop" metaphor. The design leveraged the familiarity people had with how a desktop works: it has files, folders, a space where current work documents are placed, and a "trash can" where documents can be discarded (and later recovered, until the trash can itself is emptied). This analogy of a simple everyday desk was brilliant in its simplicity and made it possible to communicate the complexity of a brand new technology.

As critical components of a conceptual design, metaphors set the theme of how the design works, establishing an agreement between the designer's vision and the user's expectations. But metaphors, like any analogy, can break down when the existing knowledge and the new design do not match.

When a metaphor breaks down, it is a violation of this agreement. The famous criticism of the Macintosh platform's design of ejecting an external disk by dragging its icon into the trashcan is a well-known illustration of how a metaphor breakdown attracts attention. If Apple designers were faithful to the desktop metaphor, the system should probably discard an external disk, or at least delete its contents, when it is dragged and dropped onto the trashcan, instead of ejecting it.

Metaphors in the emotional perspective

An example of a metaphor from the emotional perspective is seen in advertising in *Backpacker* magazine of the Garmin handheld GPS as a hiking companion. In a play on words that ties the human value of self-identity with orienteering, Garmin uses the metaphor of companionship: "Find yourself, then get back." It highlights emotional qualities such as comfort, cozy familiarity, and companionship: "Like an old pair of boots and your favorite fleece, GPSMAP 62ST is the ideal hiking companion."

8.3.4 Conceptual Design from the Design Perspectives

Just as any other kind of design can be viewed from the three design perspectives of Chapter 7, so can conceptual design.

Conceptual design in the ecological perspective

The purpose of conceptual design from the ecological perspective is to communicate a design vision of how the system works as a black box within its environment. The ecological conceptual design perspective places your system or product in the role of interacting with other subsystems within a larger infrastructure.

As an example, Norman (2009) cites the Amazon Kindle™—a good example of a product designed to operate within an infrastructure. The product is for reading books, magazines, or any textual material. You do not need a computer to download or use it; the device can live as its own independent ecology. Browsing, buying, and downloading books and more is a pleasurable flow of activity. The Kindle is mobile, self-sufficient, and works synergistically with an existing Amazon account to keep track of the books you have bought through Amazon.com. It connects to its ecology through the Internet for downloading and sharing books and other documents. Each Kindle has its own email address so that you and others can send lots of materials in lots of formats to it for later reading.

As discussed previously, the way that iPods and iTunes work together is another example of conceptual design in the ecological perspective. Norman calls this designing an infrastructure rather than designing just an application. Within this ecosystem, iTunes manages all your data. iTunes is the overall organizer through which you buy and download all content. It is also where you create all your playlists, categories, photo albums, and so on. Furthermore, it is in iTunes that you decide what parts of your data you want on your "peripherals," such as an iPod, iPad, or iPhone. When you connect your iDevice to the computer and synchronize it, iTunes will bring it up to date, including an installation of the latest version of the software as needed.

Usability of an Ecology of Devices: A Personal Information Ecosystem

Manuel A. Pérez-Quiñones, Department of Computer Science, Virginia Tech
The world of ubiquitous computing imagined by Mark Weiser (1991) is upon us. The computational power of small devices is enabling new uses of computing away from the desktop or office. Networking and communication abilities of devices make it possible to use computing in mobile settings. Storage and display improvements make difficult

tasks now possible on small devices. For example, one can do photo and video editing on an iPhone. The "cloud" is tying all of these together and providing access to computing and information anytime, anywhere.

In this new environment, the biggest challenge for usability engineers is that all of these devices are used together to accomplish user's information needs and goals. Whereas before we had tools dedicated to particular tasks (e.g., email programs), now we have a set of devices, each with a set of tools to support the same tasks. The usability of these tasks must be evaluated as a collection of devices working together, not as the sum of the usability of individual tools. Some tasks, on the surface, can be done on any of our many devices. Take email, for example. You can read, reply, forward, and delete emails in your phone, tablet device, laptop, desktop, game console, or even TV or entertainment center. However, managing email sometimes entails more than that. Once you get to filing and refinding previous email messages, the tasks gets very complicated on some of these devices. And opening some attachments might not be possible in other devices. Also, even though we have connectivity to talk to anyone in the world, you do not quite have enough connectivity to print an email remotely at home or at the office. The result is that not all devices support all the tasks required to accomplish our work, but the collection of devices together do, while allowing mobility and 24/7 access to information.

The challenge comes on how to evaluate a system of coordinated device usage that spans multiple manufacturers, multiple communication capabilities, and multiple types of activities. The experience of using (and configuring and managing) multiple devices together is very different than using only one device. As a matter of fact, the usability of just one device is barely a minimum fit for it to work within the rest of devices used in our day-to-day information management. Furthermore, the plethora of devices creates a combinatorial explosion of device choices that make assessing the usability of the devices together practically impossible.

Part of the problem is that we lack a way to understand and study this collection of devices. To alleviate this need, we have proposed a framework, called a personal information ecosystem (PIE) (Pérez-Quiñones et al., 2008), that at least helps us characterize different ecologies that emerge for information management. The idea of ecosystems in information technology is not new, but our approach is most similar to Spinuzzi's (2001) ecologies of genre. Spinuzzi argues that usability is not an attribute of a single product or artifact, but that instead it is best studied across the entire ecosystem used in an activity. His approach borrows ideas from distributed cognition and activity theory.

At the heart of the ecology of devices is an information flow that is at its optimum point (i.e., equilibrium) when the user is exerting no extra effort to accomplish his/her tasks. At equilibrium, the user rarely needs to think of the devices, the data format, or the commands to move information to and from devices. This equilibrium, however, is disrupted easily by many situations: introduction of a new device, disruption in service (wifi out of range), changes in infrastructure, incompatibility between programs, etc. It is often quite a challenge to have all of your devices working together to reach this equilibrium. The usability of the ecosystem depends more on the equilibrium and ease of information flow than on the individual usability of each device.

However, having a terminology and understanding the relationships between devices are only the beginning. I would claim that designing and assessing user experience within an ecology of devices is what Rittel (1972) calls a "wicked problem." A wicked problem, according to Rittel, is a problem that by its complexity and nature cannot have a definitive formulation. He even states that a formulation of the problem itself corresponds to a particular solution of the problem. Often, wicked problems have no particular solution, instead we judge a solution as good or bad. We often cannot even test a solution to a wicked problem, we can only indicate to a degree to which a given solution is good. Finally, in wicked problems, according to Rittel, there are many explanations for the same discrepancy and there is no way to test which of these explanations is the best one. In general, every wicked problem can be considered a symptom of another problem.

Why is designing and assessing usability of an ecology a wicked problem? First, different devices are often designed by different companies. We do not really know which particular combination of devices a given user will own. Evaluating all combinations is prohibitively expensive, and expecting one company to provide all the devices is not ideal either, as monopolies tend to stifle innovation. As a result, the user is stuck in an environment that can at best provide a local optimum—"if you use this device with this other device, then your email will work ok."

Second, while some problems are addressed easily by careful design of system architecture, eventually new uses emerge that were not anticipated by the designers. For example, if a user is using IMAP as the server protocol for his/her email, then all devices are "current" with each other as the information about her/his email is stored in a central location. But even this careful design of network protocols and systems architecture cannot account for all the uses that evolve over time. The email address autocompletion and the signature that appears at the bottom of your email are both attributes of the clients and are not in the IMAP protocol. Thus, a solution based on standards can only support agreed common tasks from the past but does not support emergent behavior.

Third, the adoption of a new device into the ecology often breaks other parts that were already working effectively. As a result, whatever effort has gone into solving a workflow problem is lost when a different combination of devices is present. For example, I use an Apple MacBook Pro as my main computer, an iPad for most of my home use, and an Android phone for my communication needs. At times, finding a good workflow for these three devices is a challenge. I have settled on using GMail and Google Calendar in all three devices because there is excellent support for all three. But other genres are not as well supported. Task management, for example, is one where I currently do not have a good solution that works in my phone, the most recent addition to my PIE. New devices upset the equilibrium of the ecosystem; the problem that I am addressing (task management) is a symptom of another problem I introduced.

Fourth, the impact of the changes in an ecosystem is highly personalized. I know users whose email management and information practices improved when they obtained a smartphone. For them, most of their email traffic was short and for the purpose of coordinating meetings or upcoming events. Introduction of a smartphone allowed them to be more effective in their email communication. For me, for example, the impact was the opposite. As most knowledge workers, I do a lot of work over email with discussions and document exchanges. The result is that I tag my email and file messages extensively. But because my phone and tablet device provide poor support for filing messages, I now leave more messages in my inbox to be processed when I am back on my laptop. Before I added my smartphone to my ecosystem, my inbox regularly contained 20 messages. Now, my inbox has pending tasks from when I was mobile. The result is that I have 50 to 60 messages regularly in my inbox. Returning to my laptop now requires that I "catch-up" on work that I did while mobile. The impact of adding a smartphone has been negative to me, in some respects, whereas for other users it had a positive effect.

Finally, a suitable solution to a personal ecosystem is one that depends on the user doing some work as a designer of his or her own information flow. Users have to be able to observe their use, identify their own inefficiencies, propose solutions, and design workflows that implement those solutions. Needless to say, not every user has the skills to be a designer and to even be able to self-assess where their information flow is disrupted. Spinuzzi (2001) discusses this point using the Bødker (1991) concept of breakdowns. Paraphrasing Spinuzzi, breakdowns are points at which a person realizes that his or her information flow is not working as expected and thus the person must devote attention to his or her tools/ecosystem instead of his or her work. Typically this is what a usability engineer would consider a usability problem, but in the context of a PIE, this problem is so deeply embedded in the particular combination of devices, user tasks, and user information flows that it is practically impossible for a usability engineer to identify this breakdown. We are left with the user as a designer as the only option of improving the usability of a PIE.

As usability engineers, we face a big challenge on how to study, design, and evaluate user experience of personal information ecosystem that have emerged in today's ubiquitous environments.

References

Bødker, S. (1991). *Through the Interface: A Human Activity Approach to User Interface Design*. Hillsdale, New Jersey: Erlbaum.

Pérez-Quiñones, M. A., Tungare, M., Pyla, P. S., & Harrison, S. (2008). Personal Information Ecosystems: Design Concerns for Net-Enabled Devices. In *Proceedings of Latin American-WEB'2008 Conference*, (pp. 3–11). October 28–30, Vila Velha, Espírito Santo, Brasil.

Rittel, H. (1972). On the planning crisis: Systems Analysis of the 'first and Second Generations'. *Bedriftskonomen*, *8*, 390–396.

Spinuzzi, C. (2001). Grappling with Distributed Usability: A Cultural-Historical Examination of Documentation Genres over Four Decades. *Journal of Technical Writing and Communication*, *31*(1), 41–59.

Weiser, M. (1991). The Computer for the 21st Century. *Scientific American*, 94–100, September.

Conceptual design in the interaction perspective

The conceptual design from the interaction perspective is used to communicate a design vision of how the user operates the system. A good example of conceptual design from an interaction perspective is the Mac Time Machine backup feature discussed previously. Once that metaphor is established, the interaction design can be fleshed out to leverage it.

The designers of this feature use smooth animation through space to represent traveling through the different points in time where the user made backups. When the user selects a backup copy from a particular time in the past, the system lets the user browse through the files from that date. Any files from that backup can be selected and they "travel through time" to the present, thereby recovering the lost files.

As an example of designers leveraging the familiarity of conceptual designs from known applications to new ones, consider a well-known application such as Microsoft Outlook. People are familiar with the navigation bar on the left-hand side, list view at the top right-hand side, and a preview of the selected item below the list. When designers use that same idea in the conceptual design of a new application, the familiarity carries over.

Conceptual design in the emotional perspective

Conceptual design from the emotional perspective is used to communicate a vision of how the design elements will evoke emotional impact in users. Returning to the car example, the design concept could be about jaw-dropping performance and how your heart skips a beat when you see its aerodynamic form or it could be about fun and being independent from the crowd. Ask any MINI driver about what their MINI means to them.

In Figure 8-3 we summarize conceptual design in the three perspectives.

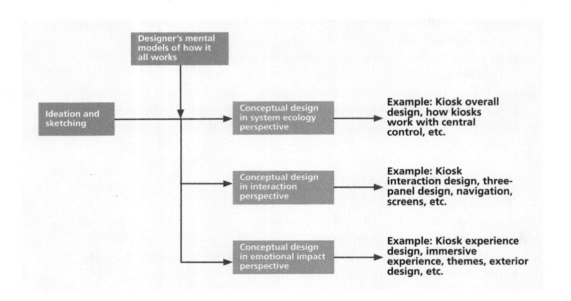

Figure 8-3

Designer workflow and connections among the three conceptual design perspectives.

Example: Conceptual Design for the Ticket Kiosk System

There is a strong commonly held perception of a ticket kiosk that includes a box on a pedestal and a touchscreen with colorful displays showing choices of events. If you give an assignment to a team of students, even most HCI students, to come up with a conceptual design of a ticket kiosk in 30 minutes, 9 times out of 10 you will get something like this.

But if you teach them to approach it with design thinking and ideation, they can come up with amazingly creative and varied results.

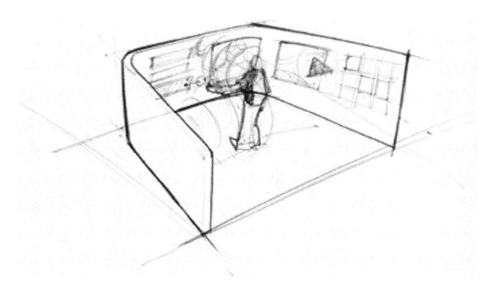

Figure 8-4

Part of a conceptual design showing immersion in the emotional perspective (sketch courtesy of Akshay Sharma, Virginia Tech Department of Industrial Design).

In our ideation about the Ticket Kiosk System, someone mentioned making it an immersive experience. That triggered more ideas and sketches on how to make it immersive, until we came up with a three-panel overall design. In Figure 8-4 we show this part of a conceptual design for the Ticket Kiosk System showing immersion in the emotional perspective.

Here is a brief description of the concept, in outline form.

- The center screen is the interaction area, where immersion and ticket-buying action occur.
- The left-hand screen contains available options or possible next steps; for example, this screen might provide a listing of all required steps to complete a transaction, including letting user access these steps out of sequence.
- The right-hand screen contains contextual support, such as interaction history and related actions; for example, this screen might provide a summary of the current transaction so far and related information such as reviews and ratings.
- The way that the three panels lay out context as a memory support and for consistent use is a kind of human-as-information-processor concept.
- Using the sequence of panels to represent the task flow is a kind of engineering concept.
- Each next step selection from the left-hand panel puts the user in a new kind of immersion in the center screen, and the previous immersion situation becomes part of the interaction history on the right-hand panel.

■ Addressing privacy and enhancing the impression of immersion: When the ticket buyer steps in, rounded shields made of classy materials gently wrap around. An "Occupied" sign glows on the outside. The inside of the two rounded half-shells of the shield become the left-hand-side and right-hand-side interaction panels.

In Figure 8-5 we show ideas from an early conceptual design for the Ticket Kiosk System from the ecological perspective.

In Figure 8-6 we show ideas from an ecological conceptual design for the Ticket Kiosk System focusing on a feature for a smart ticket to guide users to seating.

In Figure 8-7 we show ecological conceptual design ideas for the Ticket Kiosk System focusing on a feature showing communication connection with a smartphone. You can have a virtual ticket sent from a kiosk to your mobile device and use that to enter the event.

In Figure 8-8 we show ecological conceptual design ideas for the Ticket Kiosk System focusing on the features for communicating and social networking.

Exercise

See Exercise 8-1, Conceptual Design for Your System

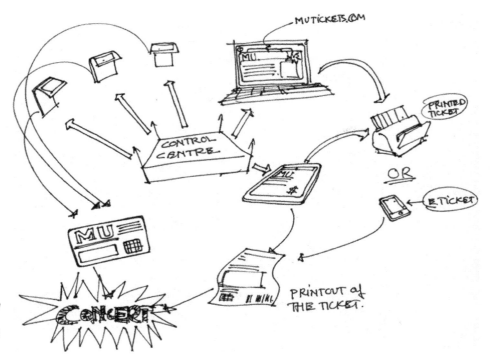

Figure 8-5

Early conceptual design ideas from the ecological perspective (sketch courtesy of Akshay Sharma, Virginia Tech Department of Industrial Design).

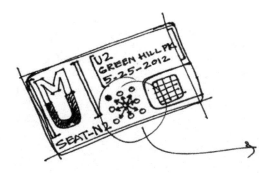

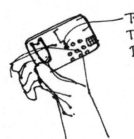

SEAT FINDING ASSISTANCE SYSTEM.

THE LIGHT BLINKS TO INDICATE THE DIRECTION OF YOUR SEAT.

Figure 8-6

Ecological conceptual design ideas focusing on a feature for a smart ticket to guide users to seating (sketch courtesy of Akshay Sharma, Virginia Tech Department of Industrial Design).

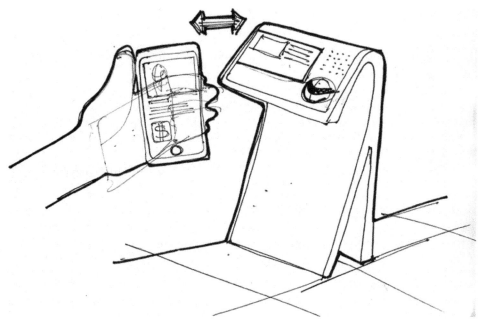

Figure 8-7

Ecological conceptual design ideas focusing on a feature showing communication connection with a smartphone (sketch courtesy of Akshay Sharma, Virginia Tech Department of Industrial Design).

Figure 8-8

Ecological conceptual design ideas focusing on the features for communicating and social networking (sketch courtesy of Akshay Sharma, Virginia Tech Department of Industrial Design).

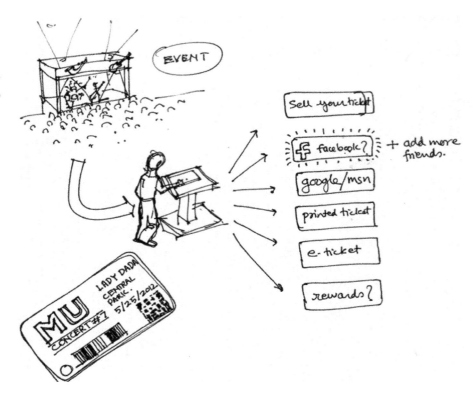

In Figure 8-9 we show part of a conceptual design for the Ticket Kiosk System in the interaction perspective.

8.4 STORYBOARDS

8.4.1 What Are Storyboards?

A storyboard is a sequence of visual "frames" illustrating the interplay between a user and an envisioned system. Storyboards bring the design to life in graphical "clips," freeze-frame sketches of stories of how people will work with the system. This narrative description can come in many forms and at different levels.

Storyboards for representing interaction sequence designs are like visual scenario sketches, envisioned interaction design solutions. A storyboard might be thought of as a "comic-book" style illustration of a scenario, with actors, screens, interaction, and dialogue showing sequences of flow from frame to frame.

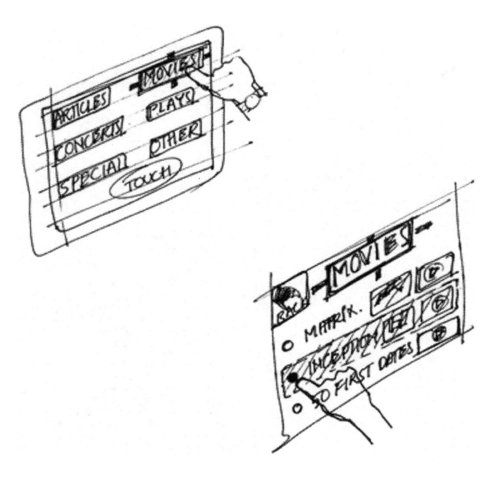

Figure 8-9

Part of a conceptual design in the interaction perspective (sketch courtesy of Akshay Sharma, Virginia Tech Department of Industrial Design).

8.4.2 Making Storyboards to Cover All Design Perspectives

From your ideation and sketches, select the most promising ideas for each of the three perspectives. Create illustrated sequences that show each of these ideas in a narrative style.

Include things like these in your storyboards:

- Hand-sketched pictures annotated with a few words
- All the work practice that is part of the task, not just interaction with the system, for example, include telephone conversations with agents or roles outside the system
- Sketches of devices and screens
- Any connections with system internals, for example, flow to and from a database
- Physical user actions

■ Cognitive user actions in "thought balloons"

■ Extra-system activities, such as talking with a friend about what ticket to buy

For the ecological perspective, illustrate high-level interplay among human users, the system as a whole, and the surrounding context. Look at the envisioned flow model for how usage activities fit into the overall flow. Look in the envisioned social model for concerns and issues associated with the usage in context and show them as user "thought bubbles."

As always in the ecological perspective, view the system as a black box to illustrate the potential of the system in a context where it solves particular problems. To do this, you might show a device in the hands of a user and connect its usage to the context. As an example, you might show how a handheld device could be used while waiting for a flight in an airport.

In the interaction perspective, show screens, user actions, transitions, and user reactions. You might still show the user, but now it is in the context of user thoughts, intentions, and actions upon user interface objects in operating the device. Here is where you get down to concrete task details. Select key tasks from the HTI, design scenarios, and task-related models to feature in your interaction perspective storyboards.

Use storyboards in the emotional perspective to illustrate deeper user experience phenomena such as fun, joy, and aesthetics. Find ways to show the experience itself—remember the excitement of the mountain bike example from Buxton (Chapter 1).

Figure 8-10

Example of a sequence of sketches as a storyboard in the ecological perspective (sketches courtesy of Akshay Sharma, Virginia Tech Department of Industrial Design).

Example: Ticket Kiosk System Storyboard Sketches in the Ecological Perspective

See Figure 8-10 for an example of a sequence of sketches as a storyboard depicting a sequence using a design in the ecological perspective.

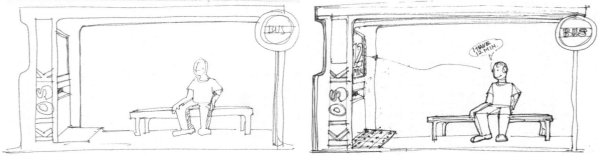

Continued

Figure 8.10, cont'd

Example: More Ticket Kiosk System Storyboard Sketches in the Ecological Perspective

In Figure 8-11 we show part of a different Ticket Kiosk System storyboard in the ecological perspective.

Figure 8-11

Part of a different Ticket Kiosk System storyboard in the ecological perspective (sketches courtesy of Akshay Sharma, Virginia Tech Department of Industrial Design).

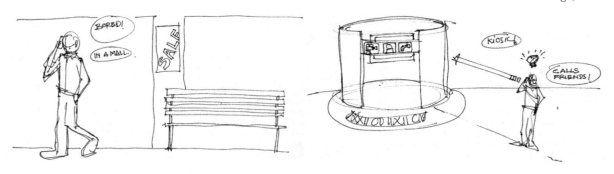

Example: Ticket Kiosk System Storyboard Sketches in the Interaction Perspective

The following is one possible scenario that came out of an ideation session for an interaction sequence for a town resident buying a concert ticket from the Ticket Kiosk System. This example is a good illustration of the breadth we intend for the scope of the term "interaction," including a person walking with respect to the kiosk, radio-frequency identification at a distance, and audio sounds being made and heard. This scenario uses the three-screen kiosk design, where LS = left-hand screen, CS = center screen, RS = right-hand screen, and SS = surround sound.

- Ticket buyer walks up to the kiosk
- Sensor detects and starts the immersive protocol
- Provides "Occupied" sign on the wrap-around case
- Detects people with MU passports
- Greets buyer and asks for PIN
- [CS] Shows recommendations and most popular current offering based on buyer's category
- [RS] Shows buyer's profile if one exists on MU system
- [LS] Lists options such as browse events, buy tickets, and search
- [CS] Buyer selects "Boston Symphony at Burruss Hall" from the recommendations
- [RS] "Boston Symphony at Burruss Hall" title and information and images
- [SS] Plays music from that symphony
- [CS] Plays simulated/animated/video of Boston Symphony in a venue that looks like Burruss Hall. Shows "pick date and time"
- [LS] Choices, pick date and time, go back, exit.
- [CS] Buyer selects "pick date and time" option
- [CS] A calendar with "Boston Symphony at Burruss Hall" is highlighted, with other known events and activities with clickable dates.
- [CS] Buyer selects date from the month view of calendar (can be changed to week)
- [RS] The entire context selected so far, including date
- [CS] A day view with times, such as Matinee or evening. The rest of the slots in the day show related events such as wine tasting or special dinner events.
- [LS] Options for making reservations at these special events
- [CS] Buyer selects a time
- [RS] Selected time
- [CS] Available seating chart with names for sections/categories aggregate number of available seats per each section

- ■ [LS] Categories of tickets and prices
- ■ [CS] Buyer selects category/section
- ■ [RS] Updates context
- ■ [CS] Immerses user from a perspective of that section. Expands that section to show individual available seats. Has a call to action "Click on open seats to select" and an option to specify number of seats.
- ■ [LS] Options to go back to see all sections or exit
- ■ [CS] Buyer selects one or more seats by touching on available slots. A message appears "Touch another seat to add to selection or touch selected seat to unselect."
- ■ [CS] Clicks on "Seat selection completed"
- ■ [RS] Updates context
- ■ [CS] Shows payment options and a virtual representation of selected tickets
- ■ [LS] Provides options with discounts, coupons, sign up for mailing lists, etc.
- ■ [CS] Buyer selects a payment option
- ■ [CS] Provided with a prompt to put credit card in slot
- ■ [CS] Animates to show a representation of the card on screen
- ■ [CS] Buyer completes payment
- ■ [LS] Options for related events, happy hour dinner reservations, etc. These are contextualized to the event they just bought the tickets just now.
- ■ [CS] Animates with tickets and CC coming back out of their respective slots

In Figure 8-12 we have shown sample sketches for a similar storyboard.

8.4.3 Importance of Between-Frame Transitions

Storyboard frames show individual states as static screenshots. Through a series of such snapshots, storyboards are used to show the progression of interaction over time. However, the important part of cartoons (and, by the same token, storyboards) is the space between the frames (Buxton, 2007b). The frames do not reveal how the transitions are made.

For cartoons, it is part of the appeal that this is left to the imagination, but in storyboards for design, the dynamics of interaction in these transitions are where the user experience lives and the actions between frames should be part of what is sketched. The transitions are where the cognitive affordances in your design earn their keep, where most problems for users exist, and where the challenges lie for designers.

We can augment the value of our storyboards greatly to inform design by showing the circumstances that lead to and cause the transitions and the context,

Cognitive Affordance

A cognitive affordance is a design feature that helps users with their cognitive actions: thinking, deciding, learning, remembering, and knowing about things.

Exercise

See Exercise 8-2, Storyboard for Your System

situation, or location of those actions. These include user thoughts, phrasing, gestures, reactions, expressions, and other experiential aspects of interaction. Is the screen difficult to see? Is the user too busy with other things to pay attention to the screen? Does a phone call lead to a different interaction sequence?

In Figure 8-13 we show a transition frame with a user thought bubble explaining the change between the two adjacent state frames.

Figure 8-12

Sample sketches for a similar concert ticket purchase storyboard in the interaction perspective (sketches courtesy of Akshay Sharma, Virginia Tech Department of Industrial Design).

Continued

Figure 8.12, cont'd

Figure 8.12, cont'd

Figure 8-13

Storyboard transition frame with thought bubble explaining state change (sketches courtesy of Akshay Sharma, Virginia Tech Department of Industrial Design).

8.5 DESIGN INFLUENCING USER BEHAVIOR

Beale (2007) introduces the interesting concept of slanty design. "Slanty design is an approach that extends user-centered design by focusing on the things people should (and should not) be able to do with the product(s) behind the design." Design is a conversation between designers and users about both desired and undesired usage outcomes. But user-centered design, for example, using contextual inquiry and analysis, is grounded in the user's current behavior, which is not always optimal. Sometimes, it is desirable to change, or even control, the user's behavior.

The idea is to make a design that works best for all users taken together and for the enterprise at large within the ecological perspective. This can work against what an individual user wants. In essence, it is about controlling user behavior through designs that attenuate usability from the individual user's interaction perspective, making it difficult to do things not in the interest of other users or the enterprise in the ecological perspective, but still allowing the individual users to accomplish the necessary basic functionality and tasks.

One example is sloped reading desks in a library, which still allow reading but make it difficult to place food or drink on the desk or, worse, on the documents. Beale's similar example in the domain of airport baggage claims is marvelously simple and effective. People stand next to the baggage conveyor belt and many people even bring their carts with them. This behavior increases usability of the system for them because the best ease of use occurs when you can just pluck the baggage from the belt directly onto the cart.

However, crowds of people and carts cause congestion, reducing accessibility and usability of other users with similar needs. Signs politely requesting users to remain away from the belt except at the moment of luggage retrieval are regrettably ineffective. A slanty design for the baggage carousel, however, solves the problem nicely. In this case, it involves something that is physically slanty; the surrounding floor slopes down away from the baggage carousel.

This interferes with bringing carts close to the belt and significantly reduces the comfort of people standing near the belt, thus reducing individual usability by forcing people to remain away from the carousel and then make a dash for the bags when they arrive within grasping distance. But it works best overall for everyone in the ecological perspective. Slanty design includes evaluation to eliminate unforeseen and unwanted side effects.

There are other ways that interaction design can influence user behavior. For example, a particular device might change reading habits. The Amazon Kindle device, because of its mobility and connectedness, makes it possible for users to access and read their favorite books in many different environments. As another example, interaction design can influence users to be "green" in their everyday activities. Imagine devices that detect the proximity of the user, shutting themselves down when the user is no longer there, to conserve power.

The Green Machine User-Experience Design: An Innovative Approach to Persuading People to Save Energy with a Mobile Device That Combines Smart Grid Information Design Plus Persuasion Design

Aaron Marcus, President, and Principal Designer/Analyst, Aaron Marcus and Associates, Inc. (AM+A)
In past decades, electric meters in homes and businesses were humble devices viewed primarily by utility company service technicians. Smart Grid developments to conserve energy catapult energy data into the forefront of high-technology innovation through information visualization, social media, education, search engines, and even games and entertainment. Many new techniques of social media are transforming society and might incorporate Smart Grid data. These techniques include the following:

- **Communication:** Blogs, microblogging, social networking, soc net aggregation, event logs/tracking
- **Collaboration:** wikis, social bookmarking (social tagging), social news, opinions, Yelp
- **Multimedia:** photo/video sharing, livecasting, audio/music sharing
- **Reviews and opinions:** product/business reviews, community Q+As
- **Entertainment:** platforms, virtual worlds, game sharing

Prototypes of what might arise are to be found in many places around the Internet. As good as these developments are, they do not go far enough. Just showing people information is good, but not sufficient. What seems to be missing is persuasion.

We believe that one of the most effective ways in which to reach people is to consider mobile devices, in use by more than three billion people worldwide. Our Green Machine mobile application prototype seeks to persuade people to save energy.

Research has shown that with feedback, people can achieve a 10% energy-consumption reduction without a significant lifestyle change. In the United States, this amount is significant, equal to the total energy provided by wind and solar resources, about 113.9 billion kwh/year. President Obama allocated more than $4 billion in 2010 Smart Grid funding to help change the context of energy monitoring and usage. Most of the Smart Grid software development has focused on desktop personal computer applications. Relatively few have taken the approach of exploring the use of mobile devices, although an increasing number are being deployed.

For our Green Machine project, we selected a home-consumer context to demonstrate in an easy-to-understand example how information design could be merged with persuasion design to change users' behavior. The same principles can be reapplied to the business context, to electric vehicle usage, and to many other contexts. For our use scenario, we assumed typical personas, or user profiles: mom, dad, and the children, who might wish to see their home energy use status and engage with the social and information options available on their mobile devices.

We incorporated five steps of behavior-changing process: increasing frequency of use of sustainability tools, motivating people to reduce energy consumption, teaching them how to reduce energy consumption, persuading them to make short-term changes, and persuading them to make long-term changes in their behavior. This process included, for example, the following techniques: rewards, using user-centered design, motivating people via views into the future, motivating them through games, providing tips to help people get started and to learn new behaviors, providing visual feedback, and providing social interaction.

We tested the initial designs with about 20 people, of varying ages (16–65), both men and women, students, professionals, and general consumers. We found most were quite positive about the Green Machine to be effective in motivating them and changing their behavior in both the short and the long term. A somewhat surprising 35% felt a future view of the world in 100 years was effective even though the news was gloomy based on current trends. We made improvements in icon design, layout, and terminology based on user feedback.

The accompanying two figures show revised screen designs for comparison of energy use and tips for purchasing green products. The first image shows how the user compares energy use with a friend or colleague. Data charts can appear, sometimes with multiple tracks, to show recent time frames; all of which can be customized, for example, a longer term can show performance over a month's time, or longer. The second image shows data about a product purchase that might lead the user to choose one product/company over another because of their "green" attributes. A consumption meter at the top of each screen is a constant reminder of the user's performance. Other screens offer a view into the future 100 years from now to show an estimate of what the earth will be like if people behave as the user now does. Still other screens show social networking and other product evaluation screens to show how a user might use social networks and product/service data to make smarter choices about green behavior.

The Green Machine concept design proved sturdy in tests with potential users. The revised version stands ready for further testing with multicultural users. The mental model and navigation can be built out further to account for shopping, travel, and other energy-consuming activities outside the home. The Green Machine is ready to turn over to companies or governmental sponsors of commercial products and services based on near-term Smart Grid technology developments, including smart-home management and electric/hybrid vehicle management. Even more important, the philosophy, principles, and techniques are readily adapted to other use contexts, namely that of business, both enterprise and small-medium companies, and with contexts beyond ecological data, for example, healthcare. Our company has already developed a follow-on concept design modeled on the Green Machine called the Health Machine.

Coupled with business databases, business use contexts, and business users, the Green Machine for Business might provide another example of how to combine Smart Grid technology with information design and persuasion design for desktop, Web, and mobile applications that can more effectively lead people to changes in business, home, vehicle, and social behavior in conserving energy and using the full potential of the information that the Smart Grid can deliver.

Acknowledgment

This article is based on previous publications (Jean and Marcus, 2009, 2010; Marcus 2010a,b); it includes additional/newer text and newer, revised images.

References

Jean, J., & Marcus, A. (2009). The Green Machine: Going Green at Home. *User Experience (UX)*, *8*(4), 20–22ff.
Marcus, A. (2010a). Green Machine Project. *DesignNet*, *153*(6) June 2010, 114–115 (in Korean).
Marcus, A. (2010b). The Green Machine. *Metering International*, (2), July 2010, South Africa, 90–91.
Marcus, A., & Jean, J. (2010). Going Green at Home: The Green Machine. *Information Design Journal*, *17*(3), 233–243.

8.6 DESIGN FOR EMBODIED INTERACTION

Embodied interaction refers to the ability to involve one's physical body in interaction with technology in a natural way, such as by gestures. Antle (2009) defines embodiment as "how the nature of a living entity's cognition is shaped by the form of its physical manifestation in the world." As she points out, in contrast to the human as information processor view of cognition, humans are primarily active agents, not just "disembodied symbol processors." This means bringing interaction into the human's physical world to involve the human's own physical being in the world.

Embodied interaction, first identified by Malcolm McCullough in *Digital Ground* (2004) and further developed by Paul Dourish in *Where the Action Is* (2001) is central to the idea of phenomenological interaction. Dourish says that embodied interaction is about "how we understand the world, ourselves, and interaction comes from our location in a physical and social world of embodied factors." It has been described as moving the interaction off the screen and into the real world. Embodied interaction is action situated in the world.

To make it a bit less abstract, think of a person who has just purchased something with "some assembly required." To sit with the instruction manual and just think about it pales in comparison to supplementing that thinking with physical actions in the working environment—holding the pieces and moving them around, trying to fit them this way and that, seeing and feeling the spatial relations and associations among the pieces, seeing the assembly take form, and feeling how each new piece fits.

This is just the reason that physical mockups give such a boost to invention and ideation. The involvement of the physical body, motor movements, visual connections, and potentiation of hand–eye–mind collaboration lead to an embodied cognition far more effective than just sitting and thinking.

Simply stated, embodiment means having a body. So, taken literally, embodied interaction occurs between one's physical body and surrounding technology. But, as Dourish (2001) explains embodiment does not simply refer to physical reality but "the way that physical and social phenomena unfold in real time and real space as a part of the world in which we are situated, right alongside and around us."

As a result, embodiment is not about people or systems per se. As Dourish puts it, "embodiment is not a property of systems, technologies, or artifacts; it is a property of interaction. Cartesian approaches separate mind, body, and thought from action, but embodied interaction emphasizes their duality."

Although tangible interaction (Ishii & Ullmer, 1997) seems to have a following of its own, it is very closely related to embodied interaction. You could say that they are complements to each other. Tangible design is about interactions between human users and physical objects. Industrial designers have been dealing with it for years, designing objects and products to be held, felt, and manipulated by humans. The difference now is that the object involves some kind of computation. Also, there is a strong emphasis on physicality, form, and tactile interaction (Baskinger & Gross, 2010).

More than ever before, tangible and embodied interaction calls for physical prototypes as sketches to inspire the ideation and design process. GUI interfaces emphasized seeing, hearing, and motor skills as separate, single-user, single-computer activities. The phenomenological paradigm emphasizes other senses, action-centered skills, and motor memory. Now we collaborate and communicate and make meaning through physically shared objects in the real world.

In designing for embodied interaction (Tungare et al., 2006), you must think about how to involve hands, eyes, and other physical aspects of the human body in the interaction. Supplement the pure cognitive actions that designers have considered in the past and take advantage of the user's mind and body as they potentiate each other in problem solving.

Design for embodied interaction by finding ways to shape and augment human cognition with the physical manifestations of motor movements, coupled with visual and other senses. Start by including the environment in the interaction design and understand how it can be structured and physically manipulated to support construction of meaning within interaction.

Embodied interaction takes advantage of several things. One is that it leverages our innate human traits of being able to manipulate with our hands. It also takes advantage of humans' advanced spatial cognition abilities—laying things on the ground and using the relationships of things within the space to support design visually and tangibly.

If we were to try to make a digital version of a game such as Scrabble (example shown later), one way to do it is by creating a desktop application where people operate in their own window to type in letters or words. This makes it an interactive game but not embodied.

Figure 8-14

The Scrabble Flash Cube game.

Another way to make Scrabble digital is the way Hasbro did it in Scrabble Flash Cubes (see later). They made the game pieces into real physical objects with built-in technology. Because you can hold these objects in your hands, it makes them very natural and tangible and contributes to emotional impact because there is something fundamentally natural about that.

Example: Embodied and Tangible Interaction in a Parlor Game

Hasbro Games, Inc. has used embedded technology in producing an electronic version of the old parlor game Scrabble. The simple but fun new Scrabble Flash Cubes game is shown in Figure 8-14. The fact that players hold the cubes, SmartLink letter tiles, in their hands and manipulate and arrange them with their fingers makes this a good example of embodied and tangible interaction.

At the start of a player's turn, the tiles each generate their own letter for the turn. The tiles can read each other's letters as they touch as a player physically shuffles them around. When the string of between two and five letters makes up a word, the tiles light up and beep and the player can try for another word with the same tiles until time is up.

The tiles also work together to time each player's turn, flag duplicates, and display scores. And, of course, it has a built-in dictionary as an authority (however arbitrary it may be) on what comprises a real word.

8.7 UBIQUITOUS AND SITUATED INTERACTION

8.7.1 Ubiquitous, Embedded, and Ambient Computing

The phenomenological paradigm is about ubiquitous computing (Weiser, 1991). Since the term "computing" can conjure a mental image of desktop computers or laptops, perhaps the better term would be ubiquitous interaction with technology, which is more about interaction with ambient computer-like technology worn by people and embedded within appliances, homes, offices, stereos and entertainment systems, vehicles, and roads.

Kuniavsky (2003) concludes that ubiquitous computing requires extra careful attention to design for the user experience. He believes ubiquitous computing devices should be narrow and specifically targeted rather than multipurpose or general-purpose devices looking more like underpowered laptops. And he emphasizes the need to design complete systems and infrastructures instead of just devices.

The concept of embedded computing leans less toward computing in the living environment and more toward computing within objects in the environment. For example, you can attach or embed radio-frequency identification chips and possibly limited GPS capabilities in almost any physical object and connect it wirelessly to the Internet. An object can be queried about what it is and where it is. You can ask your lost possessions where they are (Churchill, 2009).

There are obvious applications to products on store or warehouse shelves and inventory management. More intelligence can be built into the objects, such as household appliances, giving them capabilities beyond self-identification to sensing their own environmental conditions and taking initiative to communicate with humans and with other objects and devices. As example is ambient computing as manifest in the idea of an aware and proactive home.

Ubiquitous Interaction

Ubiquitous interaction is interaction occurring not just on computers and laptops but potentially everywhere in our environment. Interactive devices are being worn by people; embedded within appliances, homes, offices, stereos and entertainment systems, vehicles, and roads; and finding their way into walls, furniture, and objects that we carry.

8.7.2 Situated Awareness and Situated Action

The phenomenological paradigm is also about situated awareness in which the technology and, by the same token, the user are aware of their context. This includes awareness of the presence of others in one's own activity space and their awareness of your virtual presence in their activity spaces. In a social interaction setting, this can help find other people and can help cultivate a feeling of community and belonging (Sellen et al., 2006).

Being situated is all about a sense of "place," the place of interaction within the broader usage context. An example of situated awareness (credit not ours) is a cellphone that "knows" it is in a movie theater or that the owner is in a nonphone conversation; that is, the device or product encompasses knowledge of the rules of human social politeness.

Design Production

9

After reading this chapter, you will:
1. Know how to use requirements to drive design
2. Understand the macro view of lifecycle iteration for design
3. Be able to unpack conceptual designs and explore strategies for realization in intermediate design
4. Understand wireframes and how to make and use them
5. Be prepared to use annotated scenarios, prototypes, and wireframes to represent screens and navigation in detailed design
6. Know how to maintain a custom style guide in design
7. Understand the concept of interaction design specifications for software implementation

9.1 INTRODUCTION

9.1.1 You Are Here

We begin each process chapter with a "you are here" picture of the chapter topic in the context of the overall Wheel lifecycle template; see Figure 9-1. This chapter is a continuation of the previous one about designing the new work practice and the new system.

In Chapter 7 we did ideation and sketching and in Chapter 8 we conceptualized design alternatives. Now it is time to make sure that we account for all the requirements and envisioned models in those designs. This is especially important for domain-complex systems where it is necessary to maintain connections to contextual data.

The translation from requirements to design is often regarded as the most difficult step in the UX lifecycle process. We should expect it to be difficult because now that we have made the cognitive shift from analysis-mode thinking to synthesis-mode thinking, there are so many possible choices for design to meet any one given requirement and following requirements does not guarantee an integrated overall solution.

Figure 9-1

You are here; the third of three chapters on creating an interaction design in the context of the overall Wheel lifecycle template.

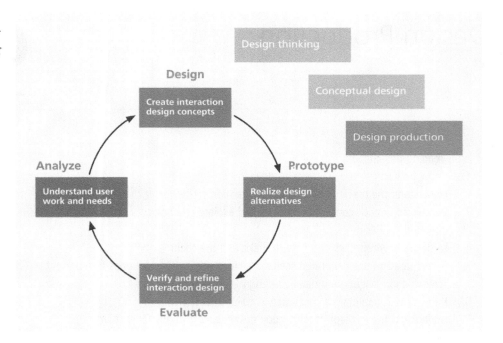

Beyer, Holtzblatt, and Wood (2005, p. 218) remind us that "The design isn't explicit in the data." "The data guides, constrains, and suggests directions" that design "can respond to." The requirements, whether in a requirements document or as an interpretation of the work activity affinity diagram (WAAD), offer a large inventory of things to be supported in the design.

9.2 MACRO VIEW OF LIFECYCLE ITERATIONS FOR DESIGN

In Figure 9-2 we show a "blow up" of how lifecycle iteration plays out on a macroscopic scale for the various types of design. Each type of design has its own iterative cycle with its own kind of prototype and evaluation. Among the very first to talk about iteration for interaction design were Buxton and Sniderman (1980).

The observant reader will note that the progressive series of iterative loops in Figure 9-2 can be thought of as a kind of spiral lifecycle concept. Each loop in turn addresses an increasing level of detail. For each different project context and each stage of progress within the project, you have to adjust the amount of and kind of design, prototyping, and evaluation to fit the situation in each of these incarnations of that lifecycle template.

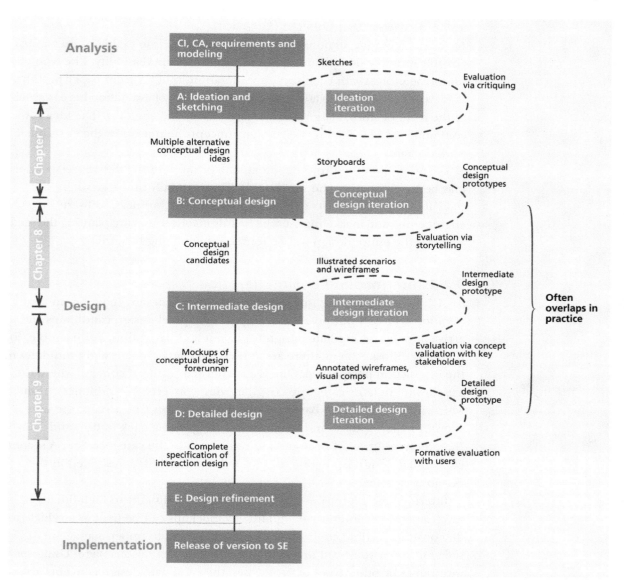

Figure 9-2

Macro view of lifecycle iterations in design.

9.2.1 Ideation Iteration

At "A" in Figure 9-2, iteration for ideation and sketching (Chapter 7) is a lightning-fast, loosely structured iteration for the purpose of exploring design ideas. The role of prototype is played by sketches, and the role of evaluation is carried out by brainstorming, discussion, and critiquing. Output is possibly multiple alternatives for conceptual designs, mostly in the form of annotated rough sketches.

9.2.2 Conceptual Design Iteration

At "B" in Figure 9-2, iteration for conceptual design is to evaluate and compare possibly multiple design concepts and weigh concept feasibility. The type of prototype evolves with each successive iteration, roughly from paper prototype to low-fidelity wireframes and storyboards. The type of evaluation here is usually in the form of storytelling via storyboards to key stakeholders. The idea is to communicate how the broader design concepts help users in the envisioned work domain.

Depending on the project context, one or more of the design perspectives may be emphasized in the storyboards. This is usually the stage where key stakeholders such as users or their representatives, business, software engineering, and marketing must be heavily involved. You are planting the seeds for what the entire design will be for the system going forward.

9.2.3 Intermediate Design Iteration

At "C" in Figure 9-2, the purpose of intermediate design (coming up soon) iteration is to sort out possible multiple conceptual design candidates and to arrive at one intermediate design for layout and navigation. For example, for the Ticket Kiosk System, there are at least two conceptual design candidates in the interaction perspective. One is a traditional "drill-in" concept where users are shown available categories (e.g., movies, concerts, MU athletics) from which they choose one. Based on the choice on this first screen, the user is shown further options and details, navigating with a back button and/or "bread crumb" trail, if necessary, to come back to the category view. A second conceptual design is the one using the three-panel idea described in the previous chapter.

Intermediate prototypes might evolve from low-fidelity to high-fidelity or wireframes. Fully interactive high-fidelity mockups can be used as a vehicle to demonstrate leading conceptual design candidates to upper management stakeholders if you need this kind of communication at this stage. Using such wireframes or other types of prototypes, the candidate design concepts are validated and a conceptual design forerunner is selected.

9.2.4 Detailed Design Iteration

At "D" in Figure 9-2, iteration for detailed design is to decide screen design and layout details, including "visual comps" (coming up soon) of the "skin" for look and feel appearance. The prototypes might be detailed wireframes and/or high-fidelity interactive mockups. At this stage, the design will be fully specified with complete descriptions of behavior, look and feel, and information on how all workflows, exception cases, and settings will be handled.

9.2.5 Design Refinement Iteration

At "E" in Figure 9-2, a prototype for refinement evaluation and iteration is usually medium to high fidelity and evaluation is either a rapid method (Chapter 13) or a full rigorous evaluation process (Chapters 12 and 14 through 18).

9.3 INTERMEDIATE DESIGN

For intermediate design, you will need the same team you have had since ideation and sketching, plus a visual designer if you do not already have one. Intermediate design starts with your conceptual design and moves forward with increasing detail and fidelity. The goal of intermediate design is to create a logical flow of intermediate-level navigational structure and screen designs. Even though we use the term screen here for ease of discussion, this is also applicable to other product designs where there are no explicit screens.

9.3.1 Unpacking the Conceptual Design: Strategies for Realization

At "C" in Figure 9-2, you are taking the concepts created in conceptual design, decomposing them into logical units, and expanding each unit into different possible design strategies (corresponding to different conceptual design candidates) for concept realization. Eventually you will decide on a design strategy, from which spring an iterated and evaluated intermediate prototype.

9.3.2 Ground Your Design in Application Ontology with Information Objects

Information Object

An information object is an internally stored work object shared by users and the system. Information objects are often data entities central to work flow, being operated on by users; they are searched and browsed for, accessed and displayed, modified and manipulated, and stored back again.

Per Johnson and Henderson (2002, p. 27), you should begin by thinking in terms of the ontological structure of the system, which will now be available in analyzed and structured contextual data. This starts with what we call information objects that we identified in modeling (Chapter 6).

As these information objects move within the envisioned flow model, they are accessed and manipulated by people in work roles. In a graphics-drawing application, for example, information objects might be rectangles, circles, and other graphical objects that are created, modified, and combined by users.

Identify relationships among the application objects—sometimes hierarchical, sometimes temporal, sometimes involving user workflow. With the help of your physical model, cast your ontological net broadly enough to identify other kinds of related objects, for example, telephones and train tickets, and their physical manipulation as done in conjunction with system operation.

In design we also have to think about how users access information objects; from the user perspective, accessing usually means getting an object on the screen so that it can be operated on in some way. Then we have to think about what kinds of operations or manipulation will be performed.

For example, in the Ticket Kiosk System, events and tickets are important information objects. Start by thinking about how these can be represented in the design. What are the best design patterns to show an event? What are the design strategies to facilitate ways to manipulate them?

In your modeling you should have already identified information objects, their attributes, and relationships among them. In your conceptual design and later in intermediate design, you should already have decided how information objects will be represented in the user interaction design. Now you can decide how users get at, or access, these information objects.

Typically, because systems are too large and complex to show all information objects on the screen at once initially, how do your users call up a specific information object to operate on it? Think about information seeking, including browsing and searching.

Decide what operations users will carry out on your information objects. For example, a graphics package would have an operation to create a new rectangle object and operations to change its size, location, color, etc. Think about how users will invoke and perform those operations.

Add these new things to your storyboards. The design of information object operations goes hand in hand with design scenarios (Chapter 6), personas (Chapter 7), and storyboards (Chapter 8), which can add life to the static wireframe images of screens.

9.3.3 Illustrated Scenarios for Communicating Designs

One of the best ways to describe parts of your intermediate interaction design in a document is through illustrated scenarios, which combine the visual communication capability of storyboards and screen sketches with the capability of textual scenarios to communicate details. The result is an excellent vehicle for sharing and communicating designs to the rest of the team, and to management, marketing, and all other stakeholders.

Making illustrated scenarios is simple; just intersperse graphical storyboard frames and/or screen sketches as figures in the appropriate places to illustrate the narrative text of a design scenario. The storyboards in initial illustrated scenarios can be sketches or early wireframes (coming up later).

9.3.4 Screen Layout and Navigational Structure

During this phase, all layout and navigation elements are fully fleshed out. Using sequences of wireframes, key workflows are represented while describing what happens when the user interacts with the different user interface objects in the design. It is not uncommon to have wireframe sets represent part of the workflow or each task sequence using click-through prototypes.

9.4 DETAILED DESIGN

At "D" in Figure 9-2, for detailed design you will need the same team you had for intermediate design, plus documentation and language experts, to make sure that the tone, vocabulary, and language are accurate, precise and consistent, both with itself and with terminology used in the domain.

9.4.1 Annotated Wireframes

To iterate and evaluate your detailed designs, refine your wireframes more completely by including all user interface objects and data elements, still represented abstractly but annotated with call-out text.

9.4.2 Visual Design and Visual Comps

As a parallel activity, a visual designer who has been involved in ideation, sketching, and conceptual design now produces what we call visual "comps," meaning variously comprehensive or composite layout (a term originating in the printing industry). All user interface elements are represented, now with a very specific and detailed graphical look and feel.

A visual comp is a pixel-perfect mockup of the graphical "skin," including objects, colors, sizes, shapes, fonts, spacing, and location, plus visual "assets" for user interface elements. An asset is a visual element along with all of its defining characteristics as expressed in style definitions such as cascading style sheets for a Website. The visual designer casts all of this to be consistent with company branding, style guides, and best practices in visual design.

Custom Style Guide

A custom style guide is a document that is fashioned and maintained by designers to capture and describe details of visual and other general design decisions that can be applied in multiple places. Its contents can be specific to one project or an umbrella guide across all projects on a given platform, or over a whole organization.

Exercise

See Exercise 9-1, Intermediate and Detailed Design for Your System

9.5 WIREFRAMES

In Figure 9-3 we show the path from ideation and sketching, task interaction models, and envisioned design scenarios to wireframes as representations of your designs for screen layout and navigational flow.

Along with ideation and sketching, task interaction models and design scenarios are the principal inputs to storytelling and communication of designs. As sequences of sketches, storyboards are a natural extension of sketching. Storyboards, like scenarios, represent only selected task threads. Fortunately, it is a short and natural step from storyboards to wireframes.

To be sure, nothing beats pencil/pen and paper or a whiteboard for the sketching needed in ideation (Chapter 7), but, at some point, when the design concept emerges from ideation, it must be communicated to others who pursue the rest of the lifecycle process. Wireframes have long been the choice in the field for documenting, communicating, and prototyping interaction designs.

9.5.1 What Are Wireframes?

Wireframes, a major bread-and-butter tool of interaction designers, are a form of prototype, popular in industry practice. Wireframes comprise lines and outlines (hence the name "wire frame") of boxes and other shapes to represent emerging interaction designs. They are schematic diagrams and "sketches" that define a Web page or screen content and navigational flow. They are used to illustrate high-level concepts, approximate visual layout, behavior, and sometimes even look and feel for an interaction design. Wireframes are embodiments of maps of screen or other state transitions during usage, depicting envisioned task flows in terms of user actions on user interface objects.

The drawing aspects of wireframes are often simple, offering mainly the use of rectangular objects that can be labeled, moved, and resized. Text and graphics

Figure 9-3

The path from ideation and sketching, task interaction models, and envisioned design scenarios to wireframes.

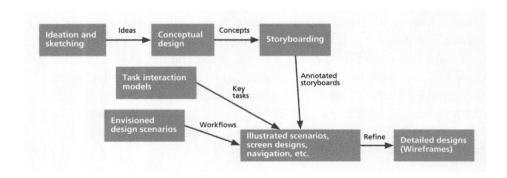

representing content and data in the design is placed in those objects. Drawing templates, or stencils, are used to provide quick means to represent the more common kinds of user interface objects (more on this in the following sections).

Wireframes are often deliberately unfinished looking; during early stages of design they may not even be to scale. They usually do not contain much visual content, such as finished graphics, colors, or font choices. The idea is to create design representations quickly and inexpensively by just drawing boxes, lines, and other shapes.

As an example of using wireframes to illustrate high-level conceptual designs, see Figure 9-4. The design concept depicted in this figure is comprised of a three-column pattern for a photo manipulation application. A primary navigation pane (the "nav bar") on the left-hand side is intended to show a list of all the user's photo collections. The center column is the main content display area for details, thumbnail images and individual photos, from the collection selected in the left pane.

The column on the right in Figure 9-4 is envisioned to show related contextual information for the selected collection. Note how a simple wireframe using just boxes, lines, and a little text can be effective in describing a broad

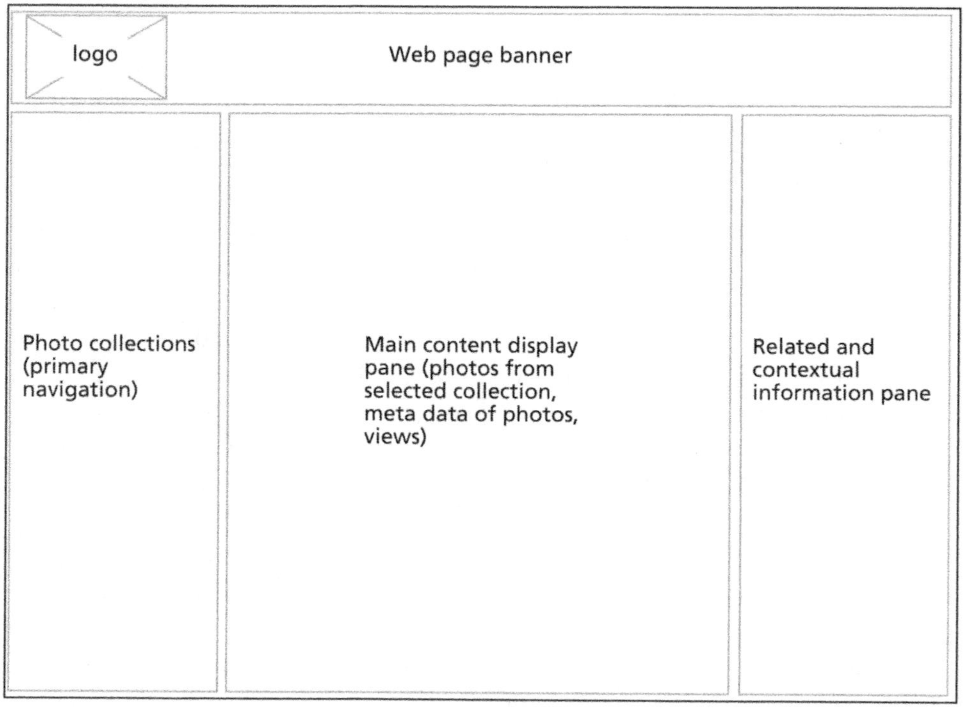

Figure 9-4

An example wireframe illustrating a high-level conceptual design.

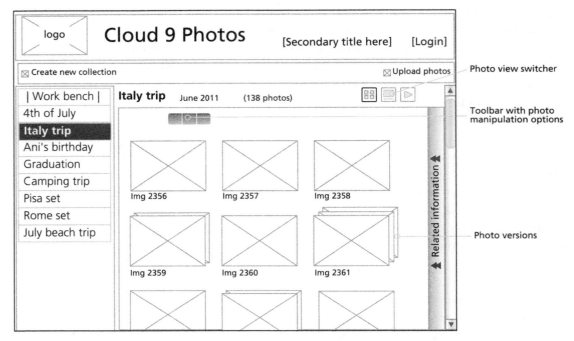

Figure 9-5

Further elaboration of the conceptual design and layout of Figure 9-4.

interaction conceptual design pattern. Often these kinds of patterns are explored during ideation and sketching, and selected sketches are translated into wireframes.

While wireframes can be used to illustrate high-level ideas, they are used more commonly to illustrate medium-fidelity interaction designs. For example, the idea of Figure 9-4 is elaborated further in Figure 9-5. The navigation bar in the left column now shows several picture collections and a default "work bench" where all uploaded images are collected. The selected item in this column, "Italy trip," is shown as the active collection using another box with the same label and a fill color of gray, for example, overlaid on the navigation bar. The center content area is also elaborated more using boxes and a few icons to show a scrollable grid of thumbnail images with some controls on the top right. Note how certain details pertaining to the different manipulation options are left incomplete while showing where they are located on the screen.

Wireframes can also be used to show behavior. For example, in Figure 9-6 we show what happens when a user clicks on the vertical "Related information" bar in Figure 9-5: a pane with contextual information for this collection (or individual photo) slides out. In Figure 9-7 we show a different view of the content

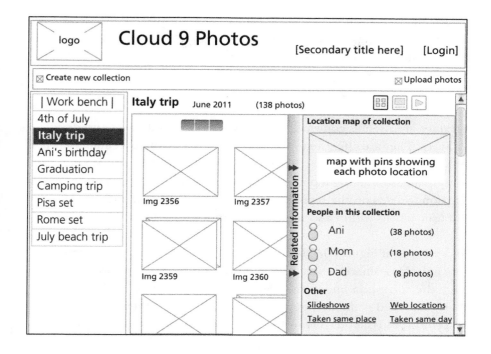

Figure 9-6

The display that results when a user clicks on the "Related information" bar.

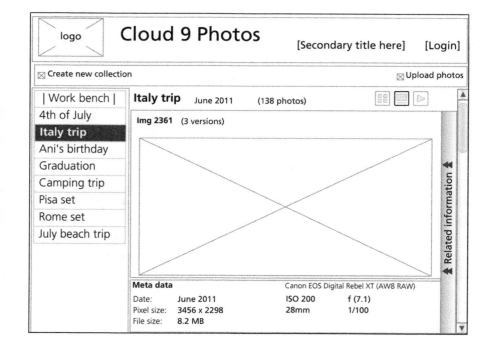

Figure 9-7

The display that results when a user clicks on the "One-up" view button.

pane, this time as a result of a user clicking on the "One-up" view switcher button in Figure 9-5 to see a single photo in the context pane. Double-clicking a thumbnail image will also expand that image into a one-up view to fill the content pane.

9.5.2 How Are Wireframes Used?

Wireframes are used as conversational props to discuss designs and design alternatives. They are effective tools to elicit feedback from potential users and other stakeholders. A designer can move through a deck of wireframes one slide at a time, simulating a potential scenario by pretending to click on interaction widgets on the screen. These page sequences can represent the flow of user activity within a scenario, but cannot show all possible navigational paths.

For example, if Figures 9-5, 9-6, and 9-7 are in a deck, a designer can narrate a design scenario where user actions cause the deck to progress through the corresponding images. Such wireframes can be used for rapid and early lab-based evaluation by printing and converting them into low-fidelity paper prototypes (Chapter 11). A rough low- to medium-fidelity prototype, using screens like the ones shown in Figures 9-5, 9-6, and 9-7, can also be used for design walkthroughs and expert evaluations. In the course of such an evaluation, the expert can extrapolate intermediate states between wireframes.

What we have described so far is easy to do with almost all wireframing tools. Most wireframing tools also provide hyperlinking capabilities to make the deck a click-through prototype. While this takes more effort to create, and even more to maintain as the deck changes, it provides a more realistic representation of the envisioned behavior of the design. However, the use of this kind of prototype in an evaluation might require elaborating all the states of the design in the workflow that is the focus of the evaluation.

Finally, after the design ideas are iterated and agreed upon by relevant stakeholders, wireframes can be used as interaction design specifications. When wireframes are used as inputs to design production, they are annotated with details to describe the different states of the design and widgets, including mouse-over states, keyboard inputs, and active focus states. Edge cases and transition effects are also described. The goal here is completeness, to enable a developer to implement the designs without the need for any interpretation. Such specifications are usually accompanied by high-fidelity visual comps, discussed previously in this chapter.

9.5.3 How to Build Wireframes?

Wireframes can be built using any drawing or word processing software package that supports creating and manipulating shapes, such as iWork Pages, Keynote, Microsoft PowerPoint, or Word. While such applications suffice for simple wireframing, we recommend tools designed specifically for this purpose, such as OmniGraffle (for Mac), Microsoft Visio (for PC), and Adobe InDesign.

Many tools and templates for making wireframes are used in combination—truly an invent-as-you-go approach serving the specific needs of prototyping. For example, some tools are available to combine the generic-looking placeholders in wireframes with more detailed mockups of some screens or parts of screens. In essence they allow you to add color, graphics, and real fonts, as well as representations of real content, to the wireframe scaffolding structure.

In early stages of design, during ideation and sketching, you started with thinking about the high-level conceptual design. It makes sense to start with that here, too, first by wireframing the design concept and then by going top down to address major parts of the concept. Identify the interaction conceptual design using boxes with labels, as shown in Figure 9-4.

Take each box and start fleshing out the design details. What are the different kinds of interaction needed to support each part of the design, and what kinds of widgets work best in each case? What are the best ways to lay them out? Think about relationships among the widgets and any data that need to go with them. Leverage design patterns, metaphors, and other ideas and concepts from the work domain ontology. Do not spend too much time with exact locations of these widgets or on their alignment yet. Such refinement will come in later iterations after all the key elements of the design are represented.

As you flesh out all the major areas in the design, be mindful of the information architecture on the screen. Make sure the wireframes convey that inherent information architecture. For example, do elements on the screen follow a logical information hierarchy? Are related elements on the screen positioned in such a way that those relationships are evident? Are content areas indented appropriately? Are margins and indents communicating the hierarchy of the content in the screen?

Next it is time to think about sequencing. If you are representing a workflow, start with the "wake-up" state for that workflow. Then make a wireframe representing the next state, for example, to show the result of a user action such as clicking on a button. In Figure 9-6 we showed what happens when a user clicks on the "Related information" expander widget. In Figure 9-7 we showed what happens if the user clicks on the "One-up" view switcher button.

Once you create the key screens to depict the workflow, it is time to review and refine each screen. Start by specifying all the options that go on the screen (even those not related to this workflow). For example, if you have a toolbar, what are all the options that go into that toolbar? What are all the buttons, view switchers, window controllers (e.g., scrollbars), and so on that need to go on the screen? At this time you are looking at scalability of your design. Is the design pattern and layout still working after you add all the widgets that need to go on this screen?

Think of cases when the windows or other container elements such as navigation bars in the design are resized or when different data elements that need to be supported are larger than shown in the wireframe. For example, in Figures 9-5 and 9-6, what must happen if the number of photo collections is greater than what fits in the default size of that container? Should the entire page scroll or should new scrollbars appear on the left-hand navigation bar alone? How about situations where the number of people identified in a collection are large? Should we show the first few (perhaps ones with most number of associated photos) with a "more" option, should we use an independent scrollbar for that pane, or should we scroll the entire page? You may want to make wireframes for such edge cases; remember they are less expensive and easier to do using boxes and lines than in code.

As you iterate your wireframes, refine them further, increasing the fidelity of the deck. Think about proportions, alignments, spacing, and so on for all the widgets. Refine the wording and language aspects of the design. Get the wireframe as close to the envisioned design as possible within the constraints of using boxes and lines.

9.5.4 Hints and Tips for Wireframing

Because the point of wireframing is to make quick prototypes for exploring design ideas, one of the most important things to remember about wireframing is modularity. Just as in paper prototyping, you want to be able to create multiple design representations quickly.

Being modular means not having too many concepts or details "hard coded" in any one wireframe. Build up concepts and details using "layers." Most good wireframing tools provide support for layers that can be used to abstract related design elements into reusable groups. Use a separate layer for each repeating set of widgets on the screen. For example, the container "window" of the application with its different controls can be specified once as a layer and this layer can be reused in all subsequent screens that use that window control.

Similarly, if there is a navigation area that is not going to change in this wireframe deck, for example, the left-hand collections pane in Figure 9-5, use one shared layer for that. Layers can be stacked upon one another to construct a slide. This stacking also provides support for ordering in the Z axis to show overlapping widgets. Selection highlights, for example, showing that "Italy trip" is the currently selected collection in Figure 9-5, can also created using a separate "highlight" layer.

Another tip for efficient wireframing is to use stencils, templates, and libraries of widgets. Good wireframing tools often have a strong community following of users who share wireframing stencils and libraries for most popular domains— for example, for interaction design—and platforms—for example, Web, Apple iOS, Google's Android, Microsoft's Windows, and Apple's Macintosh. Using these libraries, wireframing becomes as easy as dragging and dropping different widgets onto layers on a canvas.

Create your own stencil if your design is geared toward a proprietary platform or system. Start with your organization's style guide and build a library of all common design patterns and elements. Apart from efficiency, stencils and libraries afford consistency in wireframing.

Some advanced wireframing tools even provide support for shared objects in a library. When these objects are modified, it is possible to automatically update all instances of those objects in all linked wireframe decks. This makes maintenance and updates to wireframes easier.

Sketchy wireframes

Sometimes, when using wireframes to elicit feedback from users, if you want to convey the impression that the design is still amenable to changes, make wireframes look like sketches. We know from Buxton (2007a) that the style or "language" of a sketch should not convey the perception that it is more developed than it really is. Straight lines and coloring within the lines give the false impression that the design is almost finished and, therefore, constructive criticism and new ideas are no longer appropriate.

However, conventional drawing tools, such as Microsoft Visio, Adobe Illustrator, OmniGraffle, and Adobe inDesign, produce rigid, computer-drawn boxes, lines, and text. In response, "There is a growing popularity toward something in the middle: Computer-based sketchy wireframes. These allow computer wireframes to look more like quick, hand-drawn sketches while retaining the reusability and polish that we expect from digital artifacts" (Travis, 2009).

Fortunately, there are now a number of templates and tools such as Balsamic Mockups[1] that let you use the standard drawing packages to draw user interface objects in a "sketchy" style that makes lines and text have a look as if done by hand.

9.6 MAINTAIN A CUSTOM STYLE GUIDE

9.6.1 What Is a Custom Style Guide?

A custom style guide is a document that is fashioned and maintained by designers to capture and describe details of visual and other general design decisions that can be applied in multiple places. Its contents can be specific to one project or an umbrella guide across all projects on a given platform or over a whole organization.

A custom style guide is a kind of internal documentation integral to the design process. Every project needs one. Your custom style guide documents all the design decisions you make about style issues in your interaction design, especially your screen designs.

Because your design decisions continue to be made throughout the project and because you sometimes change your mind about design decisions, the custom style guide is a living document that grows and is refined along with the design. Typically this document is private to the project team and is used only internally within the development organization.

Although style guides and design guidelines (Chapter 22) both give guidance for design, they are otherwise almost exact opposites. Guidelines are usually suggestions to be interpreted; compliance with style guides is often required.

Guidelines are very general and broad in their applicability and usually independent of implementation platforms and interaction styles. Style guides are usually very specific to a platform and interaction style and even to a particular device.

9.6.2 Why Use a Custom Style Guide?

Among the reasons for designers to use a custom style guide within a project are:

- It helps with project control and communication. Without documentation of the large numbers of design decisions, projects—especially large projects—get out of control. Everyone invents and introduces his or her own design ideas, possibly different each day. The result almost inevitably is poor design and a maintenance nightmare.

---

[1]http://balsamiq.com/products/mockups

■ It is a reliable force toward design consistency. An effective custom style guide helps reduce variations of the details of widget design, layout, formatting, color choices, and so on, giving you consistency of details throughout a product and across product lines.

■ A custom style guide is a productivity booster through reuse of well-considered design ideas. It helps avoid the waste of reinvention.

9.6.3 What to Put in a Custom Style Guide?

Your custom style guide should include all the kinds of user interface objects where your organization cares the most about consistency (Meads, 2010). Most style guides are very detailed, spelling out the parameters of graphic layouts and grids, including the size, location, and spacing of user interface elements. This includes widget (e.g., dialogue boxes, menus, message windows, toolbars) usage, position, and design. Also important are the layouts of forms, including the fields, their formatting, and their location on forms.

Your style guide is the appropriate place to standardize fonts, color schemes, background graphics, and other common design elements. Other elements of a style guide include interaction procedures, interaction styles, message and dialogue fonts, text styles and tone, labeling standards, vocabulary control for terminology and message wording, and schemes for deciding how to use defaults and what defaults to use. It should be worded very specifically, and you should spell out interpretations and conditions of applicability.

You should include as many sample design sketches and pictures taken from designs on screens as possible to make it communicate visually. Supplement with clear explanatory text. Incorporate lots of examples of good and bad design, including specific examples of UX problems found in evaluation related to style guide violations.

Your style guide is also an excellent place to catalog design "patterns" (Borchers, 2001), your "standard" ways of constructing menus, icons, dialogue boxes, and so on. Perhaps one of the most important parts of a style guide are rules for organizational signature elements for branding.

Example: Make up Your Minds

At the Social Security Administration (SSA), we encountered a design discussion about whether to put the client's name or the client's social security number first on a form used in telephone interviews. The current system had the social security number first, but some designers changed it because they thought it would be friendlier to ask the name first.

Later, another group of designers had to change it back to social security number first because the SSA's policy for contact with clients requires first asking the social security number in order to retrieve a unique SSA record for that person. Then the record is used to verify all the other variables, such as name and address. This policy, in fact, was the reason it had been done this way in the beginning, but because that first design group did not document the design decision about field placement in this type of form or the rationale behind it in their custom style guide, others had to reinvent and redesign—twice.

9.7 INTERACTION DESIGN SPECIFICATIONS

9.7.1 What Is an Interaction Design Specification?

Interaction design specifications are descriptions of user interface look and feel and behavior at a level of completeness that will allow a software programmer to implement it precisely.

Discussions of "specifications" often lead to a diversity of strongly felt opinions. By definition, a specification is a complete and correct description of something. Specifications play an indispensable role in software engineering. However, because it is difficult or impossible to construct complete and correct descriptions of large complex systems, it is not uncommon to find incomplete and ambiguous specifications in the software development world. Also, there are no standards for interaction design specifications.

As a result, this connection between the two domains persists as one of the great mysteries in the trade, one of the things people on both sides seem to know the least about. In each organization, people in project roles on both sides figure out their own ways to handle this communication, to varying degrees of effectiveness, but there is no one general or broadly shared approach. See Chapter 23 for a more in-depth discussion about this communication problem.

In human–computer interaction (HCI), some argue that it is not practical to create a design specification because as soon as they invest the effort, the specification is more or less rendered useless by changes in the design due to our iterative lifecycle concept. However, there is no reason that a design specification cannot be just as dynamic as the design itself. In fact, a series of versions of a design specification can be valuable in tracking the trajectory of the evolving design and as a way to reflect on the process. In addition, by maintaining the interaction design specifications as the design progresses, it is possible to give the SE team periodic previews, avoiding surprises at the end.

9.7.2 Why Should We Care about Interaction Design Specifications?

Well, when we have devoted our resources to design and iterative refinement of the interaction part of a system, we would really like to get that design into the software of the system itself. To do that, we have to tell the SE people, the ones who will implement our designs, what to build for the interaction part. The user interaction design on the UX side becomes the user interface software requirements for the user interface software design on the SE side.

In simple terms, we UX folks need a design representation because the SE folks need a requirements specification for the user interface software. You want it to be a very specific specification so there is no room for the SE people to do interaction design on their own.

Without some kind of interaction design specifications, the software result could be almost anything. However, in practice, it is prohibitively expensive to produce specifications that are "complete." Designers usually infuse enough graphical and textual details for a programmer to understand design intent, and issues that are not clear in the specification are handled on the social back channels. If programmers are part of the process early on, they will have a better understanding on the design as it evolved and therefore have less need for explanations outside of the specification.

9.7.3 What about Using a Prototype as a Design Specification?

The case for prototypes as interaction design representations is built on the fact that prototypes already exist naturally as concrete, living design representations. Abstract textual design specifications do not lend themselves to visualization of the design, whereas a prototype can be "touched" and manipulated to examine the design in action. Plus, prototypes capture all that design detail in a way that no descriptive kind of representation can.

It is especially easy to view an iteratively refined and relatively complete high-fidelity prototype as a wonderfully rich and natural way to represent an interaction design. And it looks even better when compared to the enormous, tedious, and cumbersome additional task of writing a complete specification document describing the same design in text. For example, just one dialogue box in an interaction would typically require voluminous narrative text, including declarative definitions of all objects and their attributes. The resulting long litany of descriptor attributes and values, which when read (or if read), would fail to convey the simple idea conveyed by seeing and "trying" the dialogue box itself.

However, while prototypes make for good demonstrations of the design, they are not effective as reference documents. A prototype cannot be "searched" to find where a specific design point or requirement is addressed. A prototype does not have an "index" with which to look up specific concepts. A prototype cannot be treated as a list of features to be implemented. Some say there is no substitute for having a formal document that spells everything out and that can be used to resolve arguments and answer questions about the requirements.

Also, some prototypes are not complete or even 100% accurate in all details. Taken as a specification, this kind of prototype does not reveal which parts are incomplete or only representative.

A prototype requires interpretation as a specification. There is still a great deal about a dialogue box, for example, not necessarily conveyed by a picture. Is it every detail that you see, including the text on the labels, the font and colors, and so on? For example, is the font size of a particular button label within a complicated dialogue box the exact font style and size that *shall* be used or just something used because they had to use *some* font. It does not say. Of course, the more high fidelity it is, the more literally it is to be taken, but the dividing line is not always explicit.

9.7.4 Multiple, Overlapping Representation Techniques as a Possible Solution

Because no single representation technique serves all purposes as a interaction design specification, we must do our best to compile sets of representations to include as much of the interaction design as possible. In the current state of the art this can mean coalescing descriptions in multiple and sometimes overlapping dimensions, each of which requires a different kind of representation technique.

These multiple descriptions come from the many work products that have evolved in parallel as we moved through the formulation of requirements and early design-informing models (Chapter 6), including hierarchical task inventory (HTI) diagrams, usage scenarios, screen designs, user interface object details (graphical user interface objects, not the OO software kind), wireframes, lists of pull-down menu options, commands, dialogue boxes, messages, and behaviors, and of course the prototype.

9.8 MORE ABOUT PARTICIPATORY DESIGN

Although we do not describe participatory design as a specific technique in the main part of this chapter, users certainly can and should participate in the entire design process, starting from ideation and sketching to refinement. Because the specific technique of participatory design is an important part of HCI history and literature, we touch on it here.

9.8.1 Basics of Participatory Design

At the very beginning of a design project, you often have the user and customers on one side and system designers on the other. Participatory design is a way to combine the knowledge of work practice of the users and customers with the process skills of system designers.

It is interesting that although participatory design has a lot in common with, including its origins, contextual inquiry and contextual analysis, many applications of participatory design have been in the absence of upfront contextual inquiry or contextual analysis processes. Regardless of how it gets started, many design teams end up realizing that although participatory design is a good way to get at real user needs by involving users in design, it is not a substitute for involving users in defining requirements, the objective of contextual inquiry and contextual analysis.

A participatory design session usually starts with reciprocal learning in which the users and the designers learn about each others' roles; designers learn about work practices and users learn about technical constraints (Carmel, Whitaker, & George, 1993). The session itself is a democratic process. Rank or job title has no effect; anyone can post a new design idea or change an existing feature. Only positive and supportive attitudes are tolerated. No one can criticize or attack another person or their ideas. This leads to an atmosphere of freedom to express even the farthest out ideas; creativity rules.

In our own experience, we have found participatory design very effective for specific kinds of interaction situations. For example, we think it could be a good approach, especially if used in conjunction with design scenarios, to sketching out the first few levels of screens of the Ticket Kiosk System interaction. These first screens are very important to the user experience, where first impressions formed by users and where we can least afford to have users get lost and customers turn away. However, in our experience, the technique sometimes does not scale up well to complete designs of large and complex systems.

9.8.2 PICTIVE[2]—An Example of an Approach to Participatory Design

Inspired by the mockup methods of the Scandinavian project called UTOPIA (Bødker et al., 1987), which provided opportunities for workers to give inputs to workplace technology and organizational work practices, PICTIVE (Muller, 1991; Muller, Wildman, & White, 1993) is an example of how participatory design has been operationalized in HCI. PICTIVE supports rapid group

---

[2]Plastic Interface for Collaborative Technology Initiatives through Video Exploration.

prototype design using paper and pencil and other "low technology" materials on a large table top in combination with video recording.

The objective is for the group to work together to find technological design solutions to support work practice and, sometimes, to redesign the work practice in the process. Video recording is used to chronicle and communicate the design process and to record walkthroughs used to summarize the designs.

PICTIVE is, as are most participatory design approaches, a hands-on design-by-doing technique using low-tech tools, such as those used for paper prototyping: blackboards, large sheets of paper, bulletin boards, push pins, Post-it notes, colored marking pens, index cards, scissors, and tape. PICTIVE deliberately uses these low-tech (noncomputer, nonsoftware) representations to level the playing field between users and technical design team members. Otherwise using even the most primitive programming tools for building prototypes on the fly can cast the users as outsiders and the design practitioners as intermediaries through whom all user ideas must flow. It then is no longer a collaborative storytelling activity.

After the mutual introduction to each others' backgrounds and perspectives, the group typically discusses the task at hand and the design objectives to get on the same page for doing the design. Then they gather around a table on which there is a large paper representation of a generic computer "window." Anyone can step forward and "post" a design feature, for example, button, icon, menu, dialogue box, or message, by writing or drawing it on a Post-it note or similar piece of paper, sticking it on the "window" working space, and explaining the rationale. The group can then discuss refinements and improvements. Someone else can edit the text on the object, for example, and change its location in the window.

The group works collaboratively to expand and modify, adding new objects, changing objects, and moving objects to create new layouts and groupings and changing wording of labels and messages, and so on, all the while communicating their thinking and reasons behind each change. The results can be evaluated immediately as low-fidelity prototypes with walkthroughs (usually recorded as video for further sharing and evaluation). In most project environments that use this kind of participatory design, it is often used in the consultative design mode, where users participate in forming parts of the design but the professional design practitioners have the final responsibility for the overall design.

PICTIVE has been evaluated informally in the context of several real product design projects (Muller, 1992). User participants report getting enjoyment from the process and great satisfaction in having a receptive audience for their own design ideas and, especially, in seeing those design ideas included in the group's output.

9.8.3 History and Origins

Participatory design entails user participation in design for work practice. Participatory design is a democratic process for design (social and technological) of systems involving human work, based on the argument that users should be involved in designs they will be using, and that all stakeholders, including and especially users, have equal inputs into interaction design (Muller & Kuhn, 1993).

The idea of user participation in system design harkens back (as does the work on contextual studies) at least to a body of effort called work activity theory (Bødker, 1991; Ehn, 1990). Originating in Russia and Germany, it flourished in Scandinavia in the 1980s where it was closely related to the workplace democracy movement. These early versions of participatory design embraced a view of design based on work practice situated in a worker's own complete environment, but also espoused empowerment of workers to "codetermine the development of the information system and of their workplace" (Clement & Besselaar, 1993).

Going back to the 1980s and earlier, probably the most well-known participatory design project was the Scandinavian project called UTOPIA (Bødker et al., 1987). A main goal of Project UTOPIA was to overcome limitations on opportunities for workers to affect workplace technology and organizational work practices. UTOPIA was one of the first such projects intended to produce a commercial product at the end of the day.

Participatory design has been practiced in many different forms with different rules of engagement. In some projects, participatory design limits user power to creating only inputs for the professional designers to consider, an approach called consultative design by Mumford (1981). Other approaches give the users full power to share in the responsibility for the final outcome, in what Mumford calls consensus design.

Also beginning in the 1970s and 1980s, an approach to user involvement in design (but probably developed apart from the participatory design history in Scandinavia) called Joint Application Design was emerging from IBM in the United States and Canada (August 1991). Joint Application Design falls between consultative design and consensus design in the category of representative design (Mumford, 1981), a commonly used approach in industry in which user representatives become official members of the design teams, often for the duration of the project. In comparison with participatory design, Joint Application Design is often a bit more about group dynamics, brainstorming, and organized group meetings.

In the early 1990s, the Scandinavian approach to democratic design was adapted and extended within the HCI community in the form of participatory design. Muller's (1991) vision of participatory design as embodied in his PICTIVE approach is the most well-known adaptation of the general concept specifically to HCI. The first Participatory Design Conference met in 1990 and it has been held biannually ever since. Participatory design has since been codified for practice (Greenbaum & Kyng, 1991), reviewed (Clement & Besselaar, 1993), and summarized (Muller, 2003a,b).

Summary of the Flow of Actitives in Chapters 3 through 9

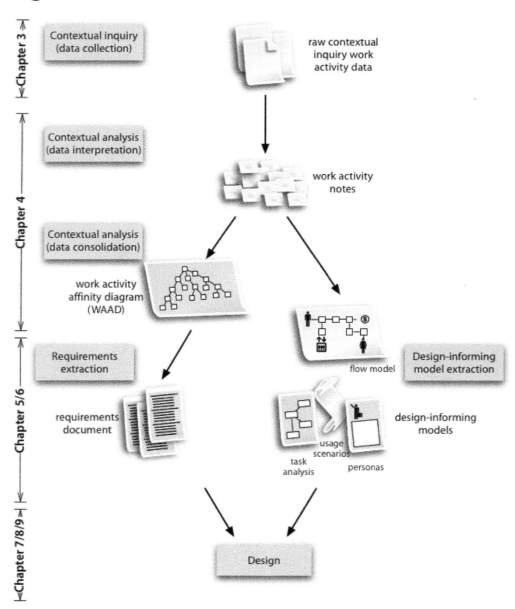

Chapter 3

Contextual inquiry (data collection)

raw contextual inquiry work activity data

Chapter 4

Contextual analysis (data interpretation)

work activity notes

Contextual analysis (data consolidation)

work activity affinity diagram (WAAD)

Design-informing model extraction

flow model

Chapter 5/6

Requirements extraction

requirements document

design-informing models

task analysis

usage scenarios

personas

Chapter 7/8/9

Design

UX Goals, Metrics, and Targets

10

Objectives

After reading this chapter, you will:
1. Understand the concepts of UX goals, metrics, and targets
2. Appreciate the need for setting UX target values for the envisioned system
3. Understand the influence of user classes, business goals, and UX goals on UX targets
4. Be able to create UX target tables, including identifying measuring instruments and setting target values
5. Know how UX targets help manage the UX lifecycle process

10.1 INTRODUCTION

10.1.1 You Are Here

We are making splendid progress in moving through the Wheel UX lifecycle template. In this chapter we establish operational targets for user experience to assess the level of success in your designs so that you know when you can move on to the next iteration. UX goals, metrics, and targets help you plan for evaluation that will successfully reveal the user performance and emotional satisfaction bottlenecks. Because UX goals, metrics, and targets are used to guide much of the process from analysis through evaluation, we show it as an arc around the entire lifecycle template, as you can see in Figure 10-1.

10.1.2 Project Context for UX Metrics and Targets

In early stages, evaluation usually focuses on qualitative data for finding UX problems. In these early evaluations the absence of quantitative data precludes the use of UX metrics and targets. But you may still want to establish them at this point if you intend to use them in later evaluations.

However, there is another need why you might forego UX metrics and targets. In most practical contexts, specifying UX metrics and targets and following up with

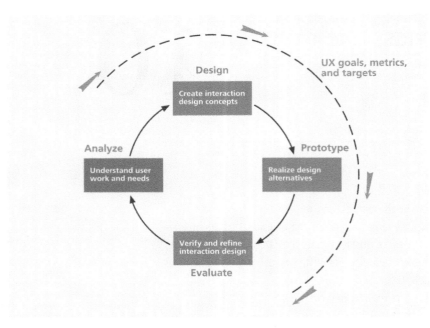

Figure 10-1

You are here; the chapter on UX goals, metrics, and targets in the context of the overall Wheel lifecycle template.

Benchmark Task

A benchmark task is a description of a task performed by a participant in formative evaluation so that UX measures such as time-on-task and error rates can be obtained and compared to a baseline value across the performances of multiple participants.

them may be too expensive. This level of completeness is only possible in a few organizations where there are established UX resources. In most places, one round of evaluation is all one gets. Also, as designers, we can know which parts of the design need further investigation just by looking at the results of the first round of evaluation. In such cases, quantitative UX metrics and targets may not be useful but benchmark tasks are still essential as vehicles for driving evaluation.

Regardless, the trend in the UX field is moving away from a focus on user performance and more toward user satisfaction and enjoyment. We include the full treatment of UX goals, metrics, and targets here and quantitative data collection and analysis in the later UX evaluation chapters for completeness and because some readers and practitioners still want coverage of the topic.

In any case, we find that this pivotal interaction design process activity of specifying UX goals, metrics, and targets is often overlooked, either because of lack of knowledge or because of lack of time. Sometimes this can be unfortunate because it can diminish the potential of what can be accomplished with the resources you will be putting into user experience evaluation. This chapter will help you avoid that pitfall by showing you techniques for specifying UX goals, metrics, and targets.

Fortunately, creating UX metrics and targets, after a little practice, does not take much time. You will then have specific quantified UX goals against which to test rather than just waiting to see what happens when you put users in front of your interaction design. Because UX metrics and targets provide feasible objectives for formative evaluation efforts, the results can help you pinpoint where to focus on redesign most profitably.

And, finally, UX goals, metrics, and targets offer a way to help manage the lifecycle by defining a quantifiable end to what can otherwise seem like endless iteration. Of course, designers and managers can run out of time, money, and patience before they meet their UX targets—sometimes after just one round of evaluation—but at least then they know where things stand.

10.1.3 Roots for UX Metrics and Targets

The concept of formal UX measurement specifications in tabular form, with various metrics operationally defining success, was originally developed by Gilb (1987). The focus of Gilb's work was on using measurements in managing software development resources. Bennett (1984) adapted this approach to usability specifications as a technique for setting planned usability levels and managing the process to meet those levels.

These ideas were integrated into usability engineering practice by Good et al. (1986) and further refined by Whiteside, Bennett, and Holtzblatt (1988). Usability engineering, as defined by Good et al. (1986), is a process through which quantitative usability characteristics are specified early and measured throughout the lifecycle process.

Carroll and Rosson (1985) also stressed the need for quantifiable usability specifications, associated with appropriate benchmark tasks, in iterative refinement of user interaction designs. And now we have extended the concept to UX targets. Without measurable targets, it is difficult to determine, at least quantitatively, whether the interaction design for a system or product is meeting your UX goals.

10.2 UX GOALS

UX goals are high-level objectives for an interaction design, stated in terms of anticipated user experience. UX goals can be driven by business goals and reflect real use of a product and identify what is important to an organization, its customers, and its users. They are expressed as desired effects to be experienced in usage by users of features in the design and they translate into a set of UX measures. A UX measure is a usage attribute to be assessed in evaluating a UX goal.

You will extract your UX goals from user concerns captured in work activity notes, the flow model, social models, and work objectives, some of which will be market driven, reflecting competitive imperatives for the product. User experience goals can be stated for all users in general or in terms of a specific work role or user class or for specific kinds of tasks.

Examples of user experience goals include ease-of-use, power performance for experts, avoiding errors for intermittent users, safety for life-critical systems, high customer satisfaction, walk-up-and-use learnability for new users, and so on.

Example: User Experience Goals for Ticket Kiosk System

We can define the primary high-level UX goals for the ticket buyer to include:

- Fast and easy walk-up-and-use user experience, with absolutely no user training
- Fast learning so new user performance (after limited experience) is on par with that of an experienced user [from AB-4-8]
- High customer satisfaction leading to high rate of repeat customers [from BC-6-16]

Some other possibilities:

- High learnability for more advanced tasks [from BB-1-5]
- Draw, engagement, attraction
- Low error rate for completing transactions correctly, especially in the interaction for payment [from CG-13-17]

Exercise

See Exercise 10-1,
Identifying User Experience
Goals for Your System

10.3 UX TARGET TABLES

Through years of working with real-world UX practitioners and doing our own user experience evaluations, we have refined the concept of a UX target table, in the form shown in Table 10-1, from the original conception of a usability specification table, as presented by Whiteside, Bennett, and Holtzblatt (1988). A spreadsheet is an obvious way to implement these tables.

For convenience, one row in the table is called a "UX target." The first three columns are for the work role and related user class to which this UX target applies, the associated UX goal, and the UX measure. The three go together because each UX measure is aimed at supporting a UX goal and is specified with respect to a work role and user class combination. Next, we will see where you get the information for these three columns.

As a running example to illustrate the use of each column in the UX target table, we will progressively set some UX targets for the Ticket Kiosk System.

Table 10-1

Our UX target table, as evolved from the Whiteside, Bennett, and Holtzblatt (1988) usability specification table

Work Role: User Class	UX Goal	UX Measure	Measuring Instrument	UX Metric	Baseline Level	Target Level	Observed Results

10.4 WORK ROLES, USER CLASSES, AND UX GOALS

Because UX targets are aimed at specific work roles, we label each UX target by work role. Recall that different work roles in the user models perform different task sets.

So the key task sets for a given work role will have associated usage scenarios, which will inform benchmark task descriptions we create as measuring instruments to go with UX targets. Within a given work role, different user classes will generally be expected to perform to different standards, that is, at different target levels.

Example: A Work Role, User Class, and UX Goal for the Ticket Kiosk System

In Table 10-1, we see that the first values to enter for a UX target are work role, a corresponding user class, and related UX goal. As we saw earlier, user class definitions can be based on, among other things, level of expertise, disabilities and limitations, and other demographics.

For the Ticket Kiosk System, we are focusing primarily on the ticket buyer. For this work role, user classes include a casual town resident user from Middleburg and a student user from the Middleburg University. In this example, we feature the casual town user.

Translating the goal of "fast-and-easy walk-up-and-use user experience" into a UX target table entry is straightforward. This goal refers to the ability of a typical occasional user to do at least the basic tasks on the first try, certainly without training or manuals. Typing them in, we see the beginnings of a UX target in the first row of Table 10-2.

> **Measuring Instrument**
>
> A measuring instrument is the means for providing values for a particular UX measure; it is the vehicle through which values are generated and measured. A typical measuring instrument for generating objective UX data is a benchmark task—for example, user performance of a task gives time and error data—while a typical measuring instrument for generating subjective UX data is a questionnaire.

Table 10-2

Choosing a work role, user class, and UX goal for a UX target

Work Role: User Class	UX Goal	UX Measure	Measuring Instrument	UX Metric	Baseline Level	Target Level	Observed Results
Ticket buyer: Casual new user, for occasional personal use	Walk-up ease of use for new user						

10.5 UX MEASURES

Within a UX target, the UX measure is the general user experience characteristic to be measured with respect to usage of your interaction design. The choice of UX measure implies something about which types of measuring instruments and UX metrics are appropriate.

UX targets are based on quantitative data—both objective data, such as observable user performance, and subjective data, such as user opinion and satisfaction.

Some common UX measures that can be paired with quantitative metrics include:

- Objective UX measures (directly measurable by evaluators)
    - Initial performance
    - Long-term performance (longitudinal, experienced, steady state)
    - Learnability
    - Retainability
    - Advanced feature usage
- Subjective UX measures (based on user opinions)
    - First impression (initial opinion, initial satisfaction)
    - Long-term (longitudinal) user satisfaction

Initial performance refers to a user's performance during the very first use (somewhere between the first few minutes and the first few hours, depending on the complexity of the system). Long-term performance typically refers to performance during more constant use over a longer period of time (fairly regular use over several weeks, perhaps). Long-term usage usually implies a steady-state learning plateau by the user; the user has become familiar with the system and is no longer constantly in a learning state.

Initial performance is a key UX measure because any user of a system must, at some point, use it for the first time. Learnability and retainability refer, respectively, to how quickly and easily users can learn to use a system and how well they retain what they have learned over some period of time.

Advanced feature usage is a UX measure that helps determine user experience of more complicated functions of a system. The user's initial opinion of the system can be captured by a first impression UX measure, whereas long-term user satisfaction refers, as the term implies, to the user's opinion after using the system for some greater period of time, after some allowance for learning.

Initial performance and first impression are appropriate UX measures for virtually every interaction design. Other UX measures often play support roles to address more specialized UX needs. Conflicts among UX measures are not unheard of. For example, you may need both good learnability and good expert performance. In the design, those requirements can work against each other. This, however, just reflects a normal kind of design trade-off. UX targets based on the two different UX measures imply user performance requirements pulling in two different directions, forcing the designers to stretch the design and face the trade-off honestly.

Example: UX Measures for the Ticket Kiosk System

For the walk-up ease-of-use goal of our casual new user, let us start simply with just two UX measures: initial performance and first impression. Each UX measure will appear in a separate UX target in the UX target table, with the user class of the work role and UX goal repeated, as in Table 10-3.

10.6 MEASURING INSTRUMENTS

Within a UX target, the measuring instrument is a description of the method for providing values for the particular UX measure. The measuring instrument is how data are generated; it is the vehicle through which values are measured for the UX measure.

Although you can get creative in choosing your measuring instruments, objective measures are commonly associated with a benchmark task—for example, a time-on-task measure as timed on a stopwatch, or an error rate measure made by counting user errors—and subjective measures are commonly associated with a user questionnaire—for example, the average user rating-scale scores for a specific set of questions.

Table 10-3

Choosing initial performance and first impression as UX measures

Work Role: User Class	UX Goal	UX Measure	Measuring Instrument	UX Metric	Baseline Level	Target Level	Observed Results
Ticket buyer: Casual new user, for occasional personal use	Walk-up ease of use for new user	Initial user performance					
Ticket buyer: Casual new user, for occasional personal use	Initial customer satisfaction	First impression					

For example, we will see that the objective "initial user performance" UX measure in the UX target table for the Ticket Kiosk System is associated with a benchmark task and the "first impression" UX measure is associated with a questionnaire. Both subjective and objective measures and data can be important for establishing and evaluating user experience coming from a design.

10.6.1 Benchmark Tasks

According to Reference.com, the term "benchmark" originates in surveying, referring to:

> Chiseled horizontal marks that surveyors made in stone structures, into which an angle-iron could be placed to form a "bench" for a leveling rod, thus ensuring that a leveling rod could be accurately repositioned in the same place in future. These marks were usually indicated with a chiseled arrow below the horizontal line.

As a measuring instrument for an objective UX measure, a benchmark task is a representative task that you will have user participants perform in evaluation where you can observe their performance and behavior and take qualitative data (on observations of critical incidents and user experience problems) and quantitative data (user performance data to compare with UX targets). As such, a benchmark task is a "standardized" task that can be used to compare (as an engineering comparison, not a rigorous scientific comparison) performance among different users and across different design versions.

Address designer questions with benchmark tasks and UX targets

As designers work on interaction designs, questions arise constantly. Sometimes the design team simply cannot decide an issue for themselves and they defer it to UX testing ("let the users decide"). Perhaps the team does not agree on a way to treat one design feature, but they have to pick something in order to move forward.

Maybe you do agree on the design for a feature but you are very curious about how it will play out with real users. Perchance you do not believe an input you got in your requirements from contextual analysis but you used it, anyway, and now you want to see if it pans out in the design.

We have suggested that you keep a list of design questions as they came up in design activities. Now they play a role in setting benchmark tasks to get feedback from users regarding these questions. Benchmark tasks based on designer issues are often the only way this kind of issue will get considered in evaluation.

Selecting benchmark tasks

In general, of course, the benchmark tasks you choose as measuring instruments should closely represent tasks real users will perform in a real work context. Pick tasks where you think or know the design has weaknesses. Avoiding such tasks violates the spirit of UX targets and user experience evaluation; it is about finding user experience problems so that you can fix them, not about proving you are the best designer. If you think of UX targets as a measure of how good you are as a designer, you will have a conflict of interest because you are setting your own evaluation criteria. That is not the point of UX targets at all.

Here are some guidelines for creating effective benchmark tasks.

Create benchmark tasks for a representative spectrum of user tasks.
Choose realistic tasks intended to be used by each user class of a work role across the system. To get the best coverage for your evaluation investment, your choices should represent the cross section of real tasks with respect to frequency of performance and criticality to goals of the users of the envisioned product. Benchmark tasks are also selected to evaluate new features, "edge cases" (usage at extreme conditions), and business-critical and mission-critical tasks. While some of these tasks may not be performed frequently, getting them wrong could cause serious consequences.

Start with short and easy tasks and then increase difficulty progressively.
Because your benchmark tasks will be faced by participant users in a sequence, you should consider their presentation order. In most cases, start with relatively easy ones to get users accustomed to the design and feeling comfortable in their role as evaluators. After building user confidence and engagement, especially with the tasks for the "initial performance" UX measure, you can introduce more features, more breadth, variety, complexity, and higher levels of difficulty.

In some cases, you might have your user participants repeat a benchmark task, only using a different task path, to see how users get around in multiple ways. The more advanced benchmark tasks are also a place to try your creativity by introducing intervening circumstances. For example, you might lead the user down a path and then say "At this point, you change your mind and want to do such and such, departing from where you are now."

For our ticket kiosk system, maybe start with finding a movie that is currently playing. Then follow with searching for and reserving tickets for a movie that is to be showing 20 days from now and then go to more complex tasks such as purchasing concert tickets with seat and ticket type selection.

Include some navigation where appropriate. In real usage, because users usually have to navigate to get to where they will do the operations specific to performing a task, you want to include the need for this navigation even in your earliest benchmark tasks. It tests their knowledge of the fact that they do need to go elsewhere, where they need to go, and how to get there.

Avoid large amounts of typing (unless typing skill is being evaluated). Avoid anything in your benchmark task descriptions that causes large user performance variation not related to user experience in the design. For example, large amounts of typing within a benchmark task can cause large variations in user performance, but the variations will be based on differences in typing skills and can obscure performance differences due to user experience or usability issues.

Match the benchmark task to the UX measure. Obviously, if the UX measure is "initial user performance," the task should be among those a first-time user realistically would face. If the UX measure is about advanced feature usage, then, of course, the task should involve use of that feature to match this requirement. If the UX measure is "long-term usage," then the benchmark task should be faced by the user after considerable practice with the system. For a UX measure of "learnability," a set of benchmark tasks of increasing complexity might be appropriate.

Adapt scenarios already developed for design. Design scenarios clearly represent important tasks to evaluate because they have already been selected as key tasks in the design. However, you *must* remember to remove information about how to perform the tasks, which is usually abundant in a scenario. See guideline "Tell the user *what* task to do, but not *how* to do it" in the next section for more discussion.

Use tasks in realistic combinations to evaluate task flow. To measure user performance related to task flow, use combinations of tasks such as those that will occur together frequently. In these cases, you should set UX targets for such combinations because difficulties related to user experience that appear during performance of the combined tasks can be different than for the same tasks performed separately. For example, in the Ticket Kiosk System, you may wish to measure user performance on the task thread of searching for an event and then buying tickets for that event.

As another example, a benchmark task might require users to buy four tickets for a concert under a total of $200 while showing tickets in this price range for the upcoming few days as sold out. This would force users to perform the task of searching through other future concert days, looking for the first available day with tickets in this price range.

Do not forget to evaluate with your power users. Often user experience for power users is addressed inadequately in product testing (Karn, Perry, & Krolczyk, 1997). Do your product business and UX goals include power use by a trained user population? Do they require support for rapid repetition of tasks, complex and possibly very long tasks? Does their need for productivity demand shortcuts and direct commands over interactive hand-holding?

If any of these are true, you must include benchmark tasks that match this kind of skilled and demanding power use. And, of course, these benchmark tasks must be used as the measuring instrument in UX targets that match up with the corresponding user classes and UX goals.

To evaluate error recovery, a benchmark task can begin in an error state. Effective error recovery is a kind of "feature" that designers and evaluators can easily forget to include. Yet no interaction design can guarantee error-free usage, and trying to recover from errors is something most users are familiar with and can relate to. A "forgiving" design will allow users to recover from errors relatively effortlessly. This ability is definitely an aspect of your design that should be evaluated by one or more benchmark tasks.

Consider tasks to evaluate performance in "degraded modes" due to partial equipment failure. In large interconnected, networked systems such as military systems or large commercial banking systems, especially involving multiple kinds of hardware, subsystems can go down. When this happens, will your part of the system give up and die or can it at least continue some of its intended functionality and give partial service in a "degraded mode?" If your application fits this description, you should include benchmark tasks to evaluate the user's perspective of this ability accordingly.

Do not try to make a benchmark task for everything. Evaluation driven by UX targets is only an engineering sampling process. It will not be possible to establish UX targets for all possible classes of users doing all possible tasks. It is often stated that about 20% of the tasks in an interactive system account for 80% of the usage and vice versa. While these figures are obviously folkloric guesses, they carry a grain of truth to guide in targeting users and tasks in establishing UX targets.

Constructing benchmark task content

Here we list a number of tips and hints to consider when creating benchmark task content.

Remove any ambiguities with clear, precise, specific, and repeatable instructions. Unless resolving ambiguity is what we want users to do as part of the task, we must make the instructions in benchmark task descriptions clear and not confusing. Unambiguous benchmark tasks are necessary for consistent results; we want differences in user performance to be due to differences in users or differences in designs but usually not due to different interpretations of the same benchmark task.

As a subtle example, consider this "add appointment" benchmark task for the "initial performance" UX measure for an interdepartmental event scheduling system. Schedule a meeting with Dr. Ehrich for a month from today at 10 AM in 133 McBryde Hall concerning the HCI research project.

For some users, the phrase "1 month from today" can be ambiguous. Why? It can mean, for example, on the same date next month or it can mean exactly 4 weeks from now, putting it on the same day of the week. If that difference in meaning can make a difference in user task performance, you need to make the wording more specific to the intended meaning.

You also want to make your benchmark tasks specific so that participants do not get sidetracked on irrelevant details during testing. If, for example, a "find event" benchmark task is stated simply as "Find an entertainment event for sometime next week," some participants might make it a long, elaborate task, searching around for some "best" combination of event type and date, whereas others would do the minimum and take the first event they see on the screen. To mitigate such differences, add specific information about event selection criteria.

Tell the user *what* task to do, but not *how* to do it. This guideline is very important; the success of user experience evaluation based on this task will depend on it. Sometimes we find students in early evaluation exercises presenting users with task instructions that spell out a series of steps to perform. They should not be surprised when the evaluation session leads to uninteresting results.

The users are just giving a rote performance of the steps as they read them from the benchmark task description. If you wish to test whether your interaction design helps users discover how to do a given task on their own, you must avoid giving any information about *how* to do it. Just tell them *what* task to do and let them figure out how.

> Example (to do): "Buy two student tickets for available adjacent seats as close to the stage as possible for the upcoming Ben King concert and pay with a credit card."
>
> Example (not to do): "Click on the Special Events button on the home screen; then select More at the bottom of the screen. Select the Ben King concert and click on Seating Options. . . ."
>
> Example (not to do): "Starting at the Main Menu, go to the Music Menu and set it as a Bookmark. Then go back to the Main Menu and use the Bookmark feature to jump back to the Music Menu."

Do not use words in benchmark tasks that appear specifically in the interaction design. In your benchmark task descriptions, you must avoid using any words that appear in menu headings, menu choices, button labels, icon pop-ups, or any place in the interaction design itself. For example, do not say "Find the first event (that has such and such a characteristic)" when there is a button in the interaction design labeled "Find." Instead, you should use words such as "Look for . . ." or "Locate . . ."

Otherwise it is very convenient for your users to use a button labeled "Find" when they are told to "Find" something. It does not require them to think and, therefore, does not evaluate whether the design would have helped them find the right button on their own in the course of real usage.

Use work context and usage-centered wording, not system-oriented wording. Because benchmark task descriptions are, in fact, descriptions of user tasks and not system functionality, you should use usage-centered words from the user's work context and not system-centered wording. For example, "Find information about xyz" is better than "Submit query about xyz." The former is task oriented; the latter is more about a system view of the task.

Have clear start and end points for timing. In your own mind, be sure that you have clearly observable and distinguishable start and end points for each benchmark task and make sure you word the benchmark task description to use these end points effectively. These will ensure your ability to measure the time on task accurately, for example.

At evaluation time, not only must the evaluators know for sure when the task is completed, but *the participant must know when the task is completed*. For purposes of evaluation, the task cannot be considered completed until the user experiences closure.

The evaluator must also know when the user knows that the task has been completed. Do not depend on the user to say when the task is done, even if you explicitly ask for that in the benchmark task description or user instructions. Therefore, rather than ending task performance with a mental or sensory state (i.e., the user knowing or seeing something), it is better to incorporate a user action confirming the end of the task, as in the (to do) examples that follow.

> Example (not to do): "Find out how to set the orientation of the printer paper to "landscape." Completion of this task depends on the user knowing something and that is not a directly observable state. Instead, you could have the user actually set the paper orientation; this is something you can observe directly.
>
> Example (not to do): "View next week's events." Completion of this task depends on the user seeing something, an action that you may not be able to confirm. Perhaps you could have the user view and read aloud the contents of the first music event next week. Then you know whether and when the user has seen the correct event.
>
> Example (to do): "Find next week's music event featuring Rachel Snow and add it to the shopping cart."
>
> Example (to do): Or, to include knowing or learning how to select seats, "Find the closest available seat to the stage and add to shopping cart."
>
> Example (to do): "Find the local weather forecast for tomorrow and read it aloud."

Keep some mystery in it for the user. Do not always be too specific about what the users will see or the parameters they will encounter. Remember that real first-time users will approach your application without necessarily knowing how it works. Sometimes try to use benchmark tasks that give approximate values for some parameters to look for, letting the rest be up to the user. You can still create a prototype in such a way that there is only one possible "solution" to this task if you want to avoid different users in the evaluation ending in a different state in the system.

> Example (to do): "Purchase two movie tickets to *Bee Movie* within 1.5 hours of the current time and showing at a theatre within 5 miles of this kiosk location."

Annotate situations where evaluators must ensure pre-conditions for running benchmark tasks. Suppose you write this benchmark task: "Your dog, Mutt, has just eaten your favorite book and you have decided that he is not worth spending money on. Delete your appointment with the vet for Mutt's annual checkup from your calendar."

Every time a user performs this task during evaluation, the evaluator must be sure to have an existing appointment already in your prototype calendar so that each user can find it and delete it. You must attach a note in the form of rubrics (next point later) to this benchmark task to that effect—a note that will be read and followed much later, in the evaluation activity.

Use "rubrics" for special instructions to evaluators. When necessary or useful, add a "rubrics" section to your benchmark task descriptions as special instructions to evaluators, not to be given to participants in evaluation sessions. Use these rubrics to communicate a heads-up about anything that needs to be done or set up in advance to establish task preconditions, such as an existing event in the kiosk system, work context for ecological validity, or a particular starting state for a task.

Benchmark tasks for addressing designer questions are especially good candidates for rubrics. In a note accompanying your benchmark task you can alert evaluators to watch for user performance or behavior that might shed light on these specific designer questions.

Put each benchmark task on a separate sheet of paper. Yes, we want to save trees but, in this case, it is necessary to present the benchmark tasks to the participant only one at a time. Otherwise, the participant will surely read ahead, if only out of curiosity, and can become distracted from the task at hand.

If a task has a surprise step, such as a midtask change of intention, that step should be on a separate piece of paper, not shown to the participant initially. To save trees you can cut (with scissors) a list of benchmark tasks so that only one task appears on one piece of paper.

Write a "task script" for each benchmark task. You should write a "task script" describing the steps of a representative or typical way to do the task and include it in the benchmark task document "package." This is just for use by the evaluator and is definitely not given to the participant. The evaluator may not have been a member of the design team and initially may not be too familiar with how to perform the benchmark tasks, and it helps the evaluator to be able to

---

Ecological Validity

Ecological validity refers to the realism with which a design of evaluation setup matches the user's real work context. It is about how accurately the design or evaluation reflects the relevant characteristics of the ecology of interaction, i.e., its context in the world or its environment.

anticipate a possible task performance path. This is especially useful in cases where the participant cannot determine a way to do the task; then, the evaluation facilitator knows at least one way.

Example: Benchmark Tasks as Measuring Instruments for the Ticket Kiosk System

For the Ticket Kiosk System, the first UX target in Table 10-3 contains an objective UX measure for "Initial user performance." An obvious choice for the corresponding measuring instrument is a benchmark task. Here we need a simple and frequently used task that can be done in a short time by a casual new user in a walk-up ease-of-use situation. An appropriate benchmark task would involve buying tickets to an event. Here is a possible description to give the user participant:

> "BT1: Go to the Ticket Kiosk System and buy three tickets for the Monster Truck Pull on February 28 at 7:00 PM. Get three seats together as close to the front as possible. Pay with a major credit card."

In Table 10-4 we add this to the table as the measuring instrument for the first UX target.

Let us say we want to add another UX target for the "initial performance" UX measure, but this time we want to add some variety and use a different benchmark task as the measuring instrument—namely, the task of buying a movie ticket. In Table 10-5 we have entered this benchmark task in the second UX target, pushing the "first impression" UX target down by one.

Table 10-4

Choosing "buy special event ticket" benchmark task as measuring instrument for "initial performance" UX measure in first UX target

Work Role: User Class	UX Goal	UX Measure	Measuring Instrument	UX Metric	Baseline Level	Target Level	Observed Results
Ticket buyer: Casual new user, for occasional personal use	Walk-up ease of use for new user	Initial user performance	BT1: Buy special event ticket				
Ticket buyer: Casual new user, for occasional personal use	Initial customer satisfaction	First impression					

Table 10-5

Choosing "buy movie ticket" benchmark task as measuring instrument for second initial performance UX measure

Work Role: User Class	UX Goal	UX Measure	Measuring Instrument	UX Metric	Baseline Level	Target Level	Observed Results
Ticket buyer: Casual new user, for occasional personal use	Walk-up ease of use for new user	Initial user performance	BT1: Buy special event ticket				
Ticket buyer: Casual new user, for occasional personal use	Walk-up ease of use for new user	Initial user performance	BT2: Buy movie ticket				
Ticket buyer: Casual new user, for occasional personal use	Initial customer satisfaction	First impression					

How many benchmark tasks and UX targets do you need?

As in most things regarding human–computer interaction, it depends. The size and complexity of the system should be reflected in the quantity and complexity of the benchmark tasks and UX targets. We cannot even give you an estimate of a typical number of benchmark tasks.

You have to use your engineering judgment and make enough benchmark tasks for reasonable, representative coverage without overburdening the evaluation process. If you are new to this, we can say that we have often seen a dozen UX targets, but 50 would probably be too much—not worth the cost to pursue in evaluation.

How long should your benchmark tasks be (in terms of time to perform)? The typical benchmark task takes a range of a couple of minutes to 10 or 15 minutes. Some short and some long are good. Longer sequences of related tasks are needed to evaluate transitions among tasks. Try to avoid really long benchmark tasks because they may be tiring to participants and evaluators during testing.

Ensure ecological validity

The extent to which your evaluation setup matches the user's real work context is called *ecological validity* (Thomas & Kellogg, 1989). One of the valid criticisms of lab-based user experience testing is that a UX lab can be kind of a sterile environment, not a realistic setting for the user and the tasks. But you can take steps to add ecological validity by asking yourself, as you write your benchmark task descriptions, how can the setting be made more realistic?

- What are constraints in user or work context?
- Does the task involve more than one person or role?
- Does the task require a telephone or other physical props?
- Does the task involve background noise?
- Does the task involve interference or interruption?
- Does the user have to deal with multiple simultaneous inputs, for example, multiple audio feeds through headsets?

As an example for a task that might be triggered by a telephone call, instead of writing your benchmark task description on a piece of paper, try calling the participant on a telephone with a request that will trigger the desired task. Rarely do task triggers arrive written on a piece of paper someone hands you. Of course, you will have to translate the usual boring imperative statements of the benchmark task description to a more lively and realistic dialogue: "Hi, I am Fred Ferbergen and I have an appointment with Dr. Strangeglove for a physical exam tomorrow, but I have to be out of town. Can you change my appointment to next week?"

Telephones can be used in other ways, too, to add realism to work context. A second telephone ringing incessantly at the desk next door or someone talking loudly on the phone next door can add realistic task distraction that you would not get from a "pure" lab-based evaluation.

Example: Ecological Validity in Benchmark Tasks for the Ticket Kiosk System

To evaluate use of the Ticket Kiosk System to manage the work activity of ticket buying, you can make good use of physical prototypes and representative locations. By this we mean building a touchscreen display into a cardboard or wooden kiosk structure and place it in the hallway of a relatively busy work area. Users will be subject to the gawking and questions of curiosity seekers. Having co-workers join the kiosk queue will add extra realism.

10.6.2 User Satisfaction Questionnaires

As a measuring instrument for a subjective UX measure, a questionnaire related to various user interaction design features can be used to determine a user's satisfaction with the interaction design. Measuring a user's satisfaction provides a subjective, but still quantitative, UX metric for the related UX measure.

As an aside, we should point out that objective and subjective measures are not always orthogonal.

As an example of a way they can intertwine, user satisfaction can actually affect user performance over a long period of time. The better users like the system, the more likely they are to experience good performance with it over the long term. In the following examples we use the QUIS questionnaire (description in Chapter 12), but there are other excellent choices, including the System Usability Scale or SUS (description in Chapter 12).

Example: Questionnaire as Measuring Instrument for the Ticket Kiosk System

If you think the first two benchmark tasks (buying tickets) make a good foundation for assessing the "first-impression" UX measure, then you can specify that a particular user satisfaction questionnaire or a specific subset thereof be administered following those two initial tasks, stipulating it as the measuring instrument in the third UX target of the growing UX target table, as we have done in Table 10-6.

Example: Goals, Measures, and Measuring Instruments

Before moving on to UX metrics, in Table 10-7 we show some examples of the close connections among UX goals, UX measures, and measuring instruments.

Table 10-6

Choosing questionnaire as measuring instrument for first-impression UX measure

Work Role: User Class	UX Goal	UX Measure	Measuring Instrument	UX Metric	Baseline Level	Target Level	Observed Results
Ticket buyer: Casual new user, for occasional personal use	Walk-up ease of use for new user	Initial user performance	BT1: Buy special event ticket				
Ticket buyer: Casual new user, for occasional personal use	Walk-up ease of use for new user	Initial user performance	BT2: Buy movie ticket				
Ticket buyer: Casual new user, for occasional personal use	Initial customer satisfaction	First impression	Questions Q1–Q10 in the QUIS questionnaire				

Table 10-7

Close connections among UX goals, UX measures, and measuring instruments

UX Goal	UX Measure	Potential Metrics
Ease of first-time use	Initial performance	Time on task
Ease of learning	Learnability	Time on task or error rate, after given amount of use and compared with initial performance
High performance for experienced users	Long-term performance	Time and error rates
Low error rates	Error-related performance	Error rates
Error avoidance in safety critical tasks	Task-specific error performance	Error count, with strict target levels (much more important than time on task)
Error recovery performance	Task-specific time performance	Time on recovery portion of the task
Overall user satisfaction	User satisfaction	Average score on questionnaire
User attraction to product	User opinion of attractiveness	Average score on questionnaire, with questions focused on the effectiveness of the "draw" factor
Quality of user experience	User opinion of overall experience	Average score on questionnaire, with questions focused on quality of the overall user experience, including specific points about your product that might be associated most closely with emotional impact factors
Overall user satisfaction	User satisfaction	Average score on questionnaire, with questions focusing on willingness to be a repeat customer and to recommend product to others
Continuing ability of users to perform without relearning	Retainability	Time on task and error rates re-evaluated after a period of time off (e.g., a week)
Avoid having user walk away in dissatisfaction	User satisfaction, especially initial satisfaction	Average score on questionnaire, with questions focusing on initial impressions and satisfaction

10.7 UX METRICS

A *UX metric* describes the kind of value to be obtained for a UX measure. It states what is being measured. There can be more than one metric for a given measure. As an example from the software engineering world, software complexity is a measure; one metric for the software complexity measure (one way to obtain values for the measure) is "counting lines of code."

Most commonly, UX metrics are objective, performance-oriented, and taken while the participant is doing a benchmark task. Other UX metrics can be subjective, based on a rating or score computed from questionnaire results. Typical objective UX metrics include time to complete task[1] and number of errors made by the user. Others include frequency of help or documentation use; time spent in errors and recovery; number of repetitions of failed commands (what are users trying to tell us by repeating an action that did not work before?); and the number of commands, mouse-clicks, or other user actions to perform task(s).

If you are feeling adventurous you can use a count of the number of times the user expresses frustration or satisfaction (the "aha and cuss count") during his or her first session as an indicator of his or her initial impression of the interaction design. Of course, because the number of remarks is directly related to the length of the session, plan your levels accordingly or you can set your levels as a count per unit time, such as comments per minute, to factor out the time differences. Admittedly, this measuring instrument is rather participant dependent, depending on how demonstrative a participant feels during a session, whether a participant is generally a complainer, and so on, but this metric can produce some interesting results.

Typically, subjective UX metrics will represent the kind of numeric outcome you want from a questionnaire, usually based on simple arithmetic statistical measures such as the numeric average. Remember that you are going only for an engineering indicator of user experience, not for statistical significance.

Interestingly, user perceptions of elapsed time, captured via a questionnaire or post-session interview, can sometimes be an important UX measure. We know of such a case that occurred during evaluation of a new software installation procedure. The old installation procedure required the user to perform repeated disk (CD-ROM) swaps during installation, while the new installation procedure required only one swap. Although the new procedure took less time, users *thought* it took them longer because they were not kept busy swapping disks.

And do not overlook a combination of measures for situations where you have performance trade-offs. If you specify your UX metric as some function, such as a sum or an average, of two other performance-related metrics, for

---

[1] Although the time on task often makes a useful UX metric, it clearly is not appropriate in some cases. For example, if the task performance time is affected by factors beyond the user's control, then time on task is not a good measure of user performance. This exception includes cases of long and/or unpredictable communication and response-time delays, such as might be experienced in some Website usage.

example, time on task and error rate, you are saying that you are willing to give up some performance in one area if you get more in the other.

We hope you will explore many other possibilities for UX metrics, extending beyond what we have mentioned here, including:

- percentage of task completed in a given time
- ratio of successes to failures
- time spent moving cursor (would have to be measured using software instrumentation, but would give information about the efficiency of such physical actions, necessary for some specialized applications)
- for visibility and other issues, fixations on the screen, cognitive load as indicated by correlation to pupil diameter, and so on using eye-tracking

Finally, be sure you match up your UX measures, measuring instruments, and metrics to make sense in a UX target. For example, if you plan to use a questionnaire in a UX target, do not call the UX measure "initial performance." A questionnaire does not measure performance; it measures user satisfaction or opinion.

Example: UX Metrics for the Ticket Kiosk System

For the initial performance UX measure in the first UX target of Table 10-6, as already discussed in the previous section, the length of time to buy a special event ticket is an appropriate value to measure. We specify this by adding "time on task" as the metric in the first UX target of Table 10-8.

Table 10-8

Choosing UX metrics for UX measures

Work Role: User Class	UX goal	UX Measure	Measuring Instrument	UX Metric	Baseline Level	Target Level	Observed Results
Ticket buyer: Casual new user, for occasional personal use	Walk-up ease of use for new user	Initial user performance	BT1: Buy special event ticket	Average time on task			
Ticket buyer: Casual new user, for occasional personal use	Walk-up ease of use for new user	Initial user performance	BT2: Buy movie ticket	Average number of errors			
Ticket buyer: Casual new user, for occasional personal use	Initial customer satisfaction	First impression	Questions Q1–Q10 in the QUIS questionnaire	Average rating across users and across questions			

As a different objective performance measure, you might measure the number of errors a user makes while buying a movie ticket. This was chosen as the value to measure in the second UX target of Table 10-8. You will often want to measure both of these metrics during a participant's single performance of the same single task. A participant does not, for example, need to perform one "buy ticket" task while you time performance and then do a different (or repeat the same) "buy ticket" task while you count errors.

Finally, for the UX metric in the third UX target of Table 10-8, the subjective UX target for the first impression UX measure, let us use the simple average of the numeric ratings given across all users and across all the questions for which ratings were given (i.e., Q1 to Q10).

10.8 BASELINE LEVEL

The baseline level is the benchmark level of the UX metric; it is the "talking point" level against which other levels are compared. It is often the level that has been measured for the current version of the system (automated or manual). For example, the Ticket Kiosk System might be replacing the ticket counter in the ticket office.

The baseline level for time on task can be an average of measured times to do the task in person over the ticket counter. That might be quite different from what you expect users will be able to achieve using our new system, but it is a stake in the sand, something for comparison. Measuring a baseline level helps ensure that the UX metric is, in fact, measurable.

10.9 TARGET LEVEL

A UX target is a quantitative statement of an aimed-at or hoped-for value for a UX metric. Thus, a UX target is an operationally defined criterion for success of user experience stemming from an interaction design, an engineering judgment about the quality of user experience expected from an interactive system.

The target level for a UX metric is the value indicating attainment of user experience success. It is a quantification of the UX goal for each specific UX measure and UX metric. UX metrics for which you have not yet achieved the target levels in evaluation serve as focal points for improvement by designers.

Just barely meeting a target level is the minimum performance acceptable for any UX measure; it technically meets the UX goals—but only barely. In theory, you hope to achieve better than the target level on most UX measures; in reality, you are usually happy to pass regardless of by how much.

Because "passing" the user experience test means meeting all your target levels simultaneously, you have to ensure that the target levels for all UX measures in the entire table must be, in fact, simultaneously attainable. That is, do not build in trade-offs of the kind where meeting one target level goal might make it much more difficult to meet another related target level.

So how do you come up with reasonable values for your target levels? As a general rule of thumb, a target level is usually set to be an improvement over the corresponding baseline level. Why build a new system if it is not going to be better? Of course, improved user performance is not the only motivation for building a new system; increased functionality or just meeting user needs at a higher level in the design can also be motivating factors. However, the focus here is on improving user experience, which often means improved user performance and satisfaction.

For initial performance measures, you should set target levels that allow enough time, for example, for unfamiliar users to read menus and labels, think a bit, and look around each screen to get their bearings. So do not use levels for initial performance measures that assume users are familiar with the design.

10.10 SETTING LEVELS

The baseline level and target level in the UX target table are key to *quantifying user experience metrics*. But sometimes setting baseline and target levels can be a challenge. The answer requires determining what level of user performance and user experience the system is to support.

Obviously, level values are often "best guesses" but with practice UX people become quite skilled at establishing reasonable and credible target levels and setting reasonable values. This is not an exact science; it is an engineering endeavor and you get better at it with experience.

Among the yardsticks you can use to set both baseline and target levels are:

■ an existing system or previous version of the new system being designed
■ competing systems, such as those with a large market share or with a widely acclaimed user experience

What if there are no existing or competing systems? Be creative and use your problem-solving skills. Look at manual ways of doing things and adjust for automation. For example, if there were no calendar systems, use a paper calendar. Start with some good educated engineering estimates and improve with experience from there.

Although it may not always be explicitly indicated in a UX target table, the baseline and target *levels shown are the mean over all participants* of the corresponding measure. That is, the levels shown do not have to be achieved by every participant in the formative evaluation sessions. So, for example, if we specify a target level of four errors for benchmark task BT 2 in the second UX target of Table 10-8 as a worst acceptable level of performance, there must be no more than *an average of* four errors, as averaged across all participants who perform the "buy movie ticket" task.

Example: Baseline Level Values for the Ticket Kiosk System

To determine the values for the first two UX target baseline levels for the Ticket Kiosk System, we can have someone perform the benchmark tasks for buying a ticket for a special event and a movie using MUTTS. Suppose that buying a ticket for a special event takes about 3 minutes. If so, this value, 3 minutes, makes a plausible baseline level for the first UX target in Table 10-9. Because most people are already experienced with ticket offices, this value is not really for initial performance, but it gives some idea for that value.

To set a baseline value for the second UX target, for buying a movie ticket, it can be assumed that almost no one should make any errors doing this at a ticket counter, so let us set the baseline level as less than 1, as in Table 10-9.

To establish a baseline value for the first impression UX measure in the third UX target, we could administer the questionnaire to some users of MUTTS. Let us say we have done that and got an average score of a 7.5 out of 10 for the first impression UX measure (a value we put in Table 10-9).

Example: Target Level Values for the Ticket Kiosk System

In Table 10-10, for the first initial performance UX measure, let us set the target level to 2.5 minutes. In the absence of anything else to go on, this is a reasonable choice with respect to our baseline level of 3 minutes. We enter this

Table 10-9

Setting baseline levels for UX measures

Key User Role: User Class	UX goal	UX Measure	Measuring Instrument	UX Metric	Baseline Level	Target Level	Observed Results
Ticket buyer: Casual new user, for occasional personal use	Walk-up ease of use for new user	Initial user performance	BT1: Buy special event ticket	Average time on task	3 minutes		
Ticket buyer: Casual new user, for occasional personal use	Walk-up ease of use for new user	Initial user performance	BT2: Buy movie ticket	Average number of errors	<1		
Ticket buyer: Casual new user, for occasional personal use	Initial customer satisfaction	First impression	Questions Q1–Q10 in questionnaire XYZ	Average rating across user and across questions	7.5/10		

value into the "Target level" column for the first UX target of the UX target table in Table 10-10.

With a baseline level of less than one error for the "Buy movie ticket" task, it would again be tempting to set the target level at zero, but that does not allow for *anyone ever* to commit an error. So let us retain the existing level, <1, as the target level for error rates, as entered into the second UX target of Table 10-10.

For the first impression UX measure, let us be somewhat conservative and set a target level of a mean score of 8 out of 10 on the questionnaire. Surely 80% is passing in most anyone's book or course. This goes in the third UX target of Table 10-10.

Just for illustration purposes, we have added a few additional UX targets to Table 10-10. The UX target in the fourth row is for a regular music patron's task of buying a concert ticket using a frequent-customer discount coupon. The UX measure for this one is to measure experienced usage error rates using the "Buy concert ticket" benchmark task, with a target level of 0.5 (average).

Additional benchmark tasks used in the last two UX targets of the table are:

BT5: You want to buy a ticket for the movie *Almost Famous* for between 7:00 and 8:00 PM tonight at a theater within a 10-minute walk from the Metro station. First check to be sure this movie is rated PG-13 because you will be with your 15-year-old son. Then

Table 10-10

Setting target levels for UX metrics

Work Role: User Class	UX Goal	UX Measure	Measuring Instrument	UX Metric	Baseline Level	Target Level	Observed Results
Ticket buyer: Casual new user, for occasional personal use	Walk-up ease of use	Initial user performance	BT1: Buy special event ticket	Average time on task	3 min, as measured at the MUTTS ticket counter	2.5 min	
Ticket buyer: Casual new user, for occasional personal use	Walk-up ease of use for new user	Initial user performance	BT2: Buy movie ticket	Average number of errors	<1	<1	
Ticket buyer: Casual new user, for occasional personal use	Initial customer satisfaction	First impression	Questions Q1–Q10 in questionnaire XYZ	Average rating across users and across questions	7.5/10	8/10	
Ticket buyer: Frequent music patron	Accuracy	Experienced usage error rate	BT3: Buy concert ticket	Average number of errors	<1	<1	
Casual public ticket buyer	Walk-up ease of use for new user	Initial user performance	BT4: Buy Monster Truck Pull tickets	Average time on task	5 min (online system)	2.5 min	
Casual public ticket buyer	Walk-up ease of use for new user	Initial user performance	BT4: Buy Monster Truck Pull tickets	Average number of errors	< 1	<1	
Casual public ticket buyer	Initial customer satisfaction	First impression	QUIS questions 4–7, 10, 13	Average rating across users and across questions	6/10	8/10	
Casual public ticket buyer	Walk-up ease of use for user with a little experience	Just post-initial performance	BT5: Buy *Almost Famous* movie tickets	Average time on task	5 min (including review)	2 min	
Casual public ticket buyer	Walk-up ease of use for user with a little experience	Just post-initial performance	BT6: Buy Ben Harper concert tickets	Average number of errors	<1	<1	

go to the reviews for this movie (to show us you can find the reviews, but you do not have to spend time reading them now) and then buy two general admission tickets.

BT6: Buy three tickets to the Ben Harper concert on any of the nights on the weekend of September 29th–October 1st. Get the best seats you can for up to $50 per ticket. Print out the directions for taking the Metro to the concert.

10.11 OBSERVED RESULTS

The final column in Table 10-10 is for *observed results*, a space reserved for recording values measured while observing users performing the prescribed tasks during formative evaluation sessions. As part of the UX target table, this column affords direct comparisons between specified levels and actual results of testing.

Because you typically will have more than one user from which observed results are obtained, you can either record multiple values in a single observed results column or, if desired, add more columns for observed results and use this column for the average of the observed values. If you maintain your UX target tables in spreadsheets, as we recommend, it is easier to manage observed data and results (Chapter 16).

Exercise

See Exercise 10-2, Creating Benchmark Tasks and UX Targets for Your System

10.12 PRACTICAL TIPS AND CAUTIONS FOR CREATING UX TARGETS

Here we present some hints about filling out your UX target table, some of which were adapted from Whiteside, Bennett, and Holtzblatt (1988). These suggestions are not intended to be requirements, but rather to show the range of possibilities.

Are user classes for each work role specified clearly enough?

User class definitions are important in identifying representative users who will serve as participants in evaluation sessions (Chapter 15). As already mentioned, the characteristics of users playing a work role may affect the setting of UX targets, resulting in different measuring instruments and UX metrics for different user classes while performing the same task. If there are several user classes for which different UX targets are appropriate, you will address them with separate and different UX targets in the table.

Have you taken into account potential trade-offs among user groups? For example, you must consider the trade-offs between learnability for new users and the possibility that "help" for these new users might get in the way of power performance by experienced users.

Are the values for the various levels reasonable? This may be one of the hardest questions to answer. In fact, the first few times you create UX targets, you will probably be making a lot of guesses. You do get better at it with practice.

Be prepared to adjust your target level values, based on initial observed results. Sometimes in evaluation you observe that users perform dramatically differently than you had expected when you set the levels. These cases can help you refine the target levels in UX targets, too. While it is possible to set the levels too leniently, it is also possible that you make your initial UX targets too demanding, especially in early cycles of iteration.

When your observed results are much worse than specified levels, there typically are two possibilities. In the first (and preferable) case, the process of evaluation and refinement is working just as it should; the UX targets are reasonable, and evaluation has shown that there are serious UX problems with the design. When these problems are solved, the design will meet the specified UX goals.

In the second case, the UX targets have been set for an unrealistically high level of expectation, and no matter how much you improve the design and its user experience, the UX goals might never be met. Sometimes, for example, a task simply takes longer than its designers first anticipated, even with a good design.

If you are not meeting your levels, especially after a few rounds of iteration, you will need to assess them to see whether they are simply too difficult to attain or whether the design just needs a great deal of work. Determining which of these cases you have is, of course, not always easy. You will have to rely on your knowledge of interaction design, experience, intuition, and ultimately your best judgment to decide where the problem lies—with the UX target levels or with the design.

Remember that the target level values are averages. So do not set impossible average goals such as zero errors.

How well do the UX measures capture the UX goals for the design? Again, this can be elusive. It is entirely possible to establish UX targets that have little or nothing to do with assessing the real user experience of a design. For example, a benchmark task might be very non-representative, leading to design improvements in parts of the application that will rarely be used.

It is equally easy to omit inadvertently UX targets that are critical to assessing user experience. Again, with experience, you will gain a better understanding of when you have established UX measures and levels that capture the user experience of the design.

What if the design is in its early stages and you know the design will change significantly in the next version, anyway? Will it be a waste of time to create benchmark tasks and UX targets if the system is expected to undergo major changes in the near future? A UX representative of one project team we worked with sent email saying "We spent 2 days evaluating the XXX tool (first version) only to discover that the more recent version was significantly different and many of the issues we identified were no longer valid."

Our answer: As long as the tasks have not changed significantly, as long as users would still do those same tasks with the new design (even if they are now done in a different way), your work in creating benchmark tasks and UX targets should not have been wasted. Benchmark tasks and level settings are supposed to be independent of the design details.

What about UX goals, metrics, and targets for usefulness and emotional impact? Quantitative measures and metrics for UX goals about usefulness and emotional impact, including phenomenological aspects and social or cultural impact, and value-sensitive design are more limited. The principal measuring instrument for these measures is the questionnaire and, possibly, post-session interviews.

And, of course, there are experimental data collection techniques for detecting and/or measuring emotional responses (Chapter 12). You can use the number of smiles per interaction as a UX metric if you can detect, and therefore, count, smiles. Phenomenological aspects require longer term measures (also in Chapter 12).

Questionnaires and interviews can also be used to assess branding issues. For example, you can ask if the user thinks this product is "on-brand" or you can show two variations and ask which is better associated with the brand and why. Although this kind of data collection leans more toward qualitative, you can find ways to quantify it, if desired.

10.13 HOW UX TARGETS HELP MANAGE THE USER EXPERIENCE ENGINEERING PROCESS

First of all, the end of evaluation activity in each iteration of the lifecycle is a good time to evaluate your benchmark task descriptions and UX targets. How well did they work for you? If you think they should be improved, do it now.

Also, after each iteration of evaluation, we have to decide whether to continue iterating. But we cannot keep iterating forever. So how do we know when to stop? We tell how the project manager can use the evaluation results in conjunction with UX targets to decide when to stop iterating in Chapter 16.

10.14 AN ABRIDGED APPROACH TO UX GOALS, METRICS, AND TARGETS

As in most of the other process chapters, the process here can be abridged, trading completeness for speed and lower cost. Possible steps of increasing abridgement include:

- Eliminate objective UX measures and metrics, but retain UX goals and quantitative subjective measures. Metrics obtained with questionnaires are easier and far less costly than metrics requiring empirical testing, lab based or in the field.
- Eliminate all UX measures and metrics and UX target tables. Retain benchmark tasks as a basis for user task performance and behavior to observe in limited empirical testing for gathering qualitative data (UX problem data).
- Ignore UX goals, metrics, and targets altogether and use only rapid evaluation methods later, producing only qualitative data.

Prototyping

11

Objectives

After reading this chapter, you will:

1. Be able to articulate what prototyping is and why it is needed
2. Understand how to choose the appropriate depth and breadth, level of fidelity, and amount of interactivity of prototypes
3. Understand special types of prototypes, such as physical mockups and Wizard of Oz prototypes
4. Understand the appropriate type of prototype for a given stage of design evolution
5. Understand the role of prototypes in the transition to a product
6. Know how to make effective paper prototypes

11.1 INTRODUCTION

11.1.1 You Are Here

We begin each process chapter with a "you are here" picture of the chapter topic in the context of the overall Wheel lifecycle template; see Figure 11-1. Although prototyping is a kind of implementation, design and prototyping in practice often overlap and occur simultaneously. A prototype in that sense is a design representation.

So, as you create the design and its representation, you are creating the prototype. Therefore, although in Figure 11-1 it might seem that prototyping is limited to a particular place within a cycle of other process activities, like all other activities, prototyping does not happen only at some point in a rigid sequence.

11.1.2 A Dilemma, and a Solution

Have you ever rushed to deliver a product version without enough time to check it out? Then realized the design needed fixing? Sorry, but that ship has already left the station. The sooner you fail and understand why, the sooner you can succeed. As Frishberg (2006) tells us, "the faster you go, the sooner you know." If only you had made some early prototypes to work out the design changes before

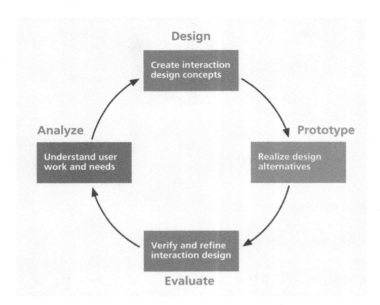

Figure 11-1

You are here; the chapter on prototyping in the context of the overall Wheel lifecycle template.

releasing it! In this chapter we show you how to use prototyping as a hatching oven for partially baked designs within the overall UX lifecycle process.

Traditional development approaches such as the waterfall method were heavyweight processes that required enormous investment of time, money, and personnel. Those linear development processes have tended to force a commitment to significant amounts of design detail without any means for visualizing and evaluating the product until it was too late to make any major changes.

Construction and modification of software by ordinary programming techniques in the past have been notoriously expensive and time-consuming activities. Little wonder there have been so many failed software development projects (Cobb, 1995; The Standish Group, 1994, 2001)—wrong requirements, not meeting requirements, imbalanced emphasis within functionality, poor user experience, and so much customer and user dissatisfaction.

In thinking about how to overcome these problems, we are faced with a dilemma. The only way to be sure that your system design is the right design and that your design is the best it can be is to evaluate it with real users. However, at the beginning you have a design but no system yet to evaluate. But after it is implemented, changes are much more difficult.

Enter the prototype. A prototype gives you something to evaluate before you have to commit resources to build the real thing. Because prototyping provides an early version of the system that can be constructed much faster and is less expensive, something to stand in stead of the real system to evaluate and inform refinement of the design, it has become a principal technique of the iterative lifecycle.

Universality of prototyping

The idea of prototyping is timeless and universal. Automobile designers build and test mockups, architects and sculptors make models, circuit designers use "bread-boards," artists work with sketches, and aircraft designers build and fly experimental designs. Even Leonardo da Vinci and Alexander Graham Bell made prototypes.

Thomas Edison sometimes made 10,000 prototypes before getting just the right design. In each case the concept of a prototype was the key to affording the design team and others an early ability to observe something about the final product—evaluating ideas, weighing alternatives, and seeing what works and what does not.

Alfred Hitchcock, master of dramatic dialogue design, is known for using prototyping to refine the plots of his movies. Hitchcock would tell variations of stories at cocktail parties and observe reactions of his listeners. He would experiment with various sequences and mechanisms for revealing the story line. Refinement of the story was based on listener reactions as an evaluation criterion. *Psycho* is a notable example of the results of this technique.

Scandinavian origins

Like a large number of other parts of this overall lifecycle process, the origins of prototyping, especially low-fidelity prototyping, go back to the Scandinavian work activity theory research and practice of Ehn, Kyng, and others (Bjerknes, Ehn, & Kyng, 1987; Ehn, 1988) and participatory design work (Kyng, 1994). These formative works emphasized the need to foster early and detailed communication about design and participation in understanding the requirements for that design.

11.2 DEPTH AND BREADTH OF A PROTOTYPE

The idea of prototypes is to provide a fast and easily changed early view of the envisioned interaction design. To be fast and easily changed, a prototype must be something less than the real system. The choices for your approach to prototyping are about *how* to make it less. You can make it less by focusing on just the breadth or just the depth of the system or by focusing on less than full fidelity of details in the prototype (discussed later in this chapter).

11.2.1 Horizontal vs. Vertical Prototypes

Horizontal and vertical prototypes represent the difference between slicing the system by breadth and by depth in the features and functionality of a prototype (Hartson & Smith, 1991). Nielsen (1987) also describes types of prototypes based on how a target system is sliced in the prototype. In his usability

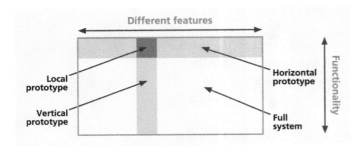

Figure 11-2

Horizontal and vertical prototyping concepts, from Nielsen (1993), with permission.

engineering book (1993), Nielsen illustrates the relative concepts of horizontal and vertical prototyping, which we show as Figure 11-2.

A horizontal prototype is very broad in the features it incorporates, but offers less depth in its coverage of functionality. A vertical prototype contains as much depth of functionality as possible in the current state of progress, but only for a narrow breadth of features.

A horizontal prototype is a good place to start with your prototyping, as it provides an overview on which you can base a top-down approach. A horizontal prototype is effective in demonstrating the product concept and for conveying an early product overview to managers, customers, and users (Kensing & Munk-Madsen, 1993) but, because of the lack of details in depth, horizontal prototypes usually do not support complete workflows, and user experience evaluation with this kind of prototype is generally less realistic.

A horizontal prototype can also be used to explore how much functionality will really be used by a certain class of users to expose typical users to the breadth of proposed functionality and get feedback on which functions would be used or not.

A vertical prototype allows testing a limited range of features but those functions that are included are evolved in enough detail to support realistic user experience evaluation. Often the functionality of a vertical prototype can include a stub for or an actual working back-end database.

A vertical prototype is ideal for times when you need to represent completely the details of an isolated part of an individual interaction workflow in order to understand how those details play out in actual usage. For example, you may wish to study a new design for the checkout part of the workflow for an e-commerce Website. A vertical prototype would show that one task sequence and associated user actions, in depth.

11.2.2 "T" Prototypes

A "T" prototype combines the advantages of both horizontal and vertical, offering a good compromise for system evaluation. Much of the interface is realized at a shallow level (the horizontal top of the T), but a few parts are done in depth (the vertical part of the T). This makes a T prototype essentially a horizontal prototype, but with the functionality details filled out vertically for some parts of the design.

In the early going, the T prototype provides a nice balance between the two extremes, giving you some advantages of each. Once you have established a system overview in your horizontal prototype, as a practical matter the T prototype is the next step toward achieving some depth. In time, the horizontal foundation supports evolving vertical growth across the whole prototype.

11.2.3 Local Prototypes

We call the small area where horizontal and vertical slices intersect a "local prototype" because the depth and breadth are both limited to a very localized interaction design issue. A local prototype is used to evaluate design alternatives for particular isolated interaction details, such as the appearance of an icon, wording of a message, or behavior of an individual function. It is so narrow and shallow that it is about just one isolated design issue and it does not support any depth of task flow.

A local prototype is the solution for those times when your design team encounters an impasse in design discussions where, after a while, there is no agreement and people are starting to repeat themselves. Contextual data are not clear on the question and further arguing is a waste of time. It is time to put the specific design issue on a list for testing, letting the user or customer speak to it in a kind of "feature face-off" to help decide among the alternatives.

For example, your design team might not be able to agree on the details of a "Save" dialogue box and you want to compare two different approaches. So you can mockup the two dialogue box designs and ask for user opinions about how they behave.

Local prototypes are used independently from other prototypes and have very short life spans, useful only briefly when specific details of one or two particular design issues are being worked out. If a bit more depth or breadth becomes needed in the process, a local prototype can easily grow into a horizontal, vertical, or T prototype.

11.3 FIDELITY OF PROTOTYPES

The level of fidelity of a prototype is another dimension along which prototype content can be controlled. The fidelity of a prototype reflects how "finished" it is perceived to be by customers and users, not how authentic or correct the underlying code is (Tullis, 1990).

11.3.1 Low-Fidelity Prototypes

Low-fidelity prototypes are, as the term implies, prototypes that are not faithful representations of the details of look, feel, and behavior, but give rather high-level, more abstract impressions of the intended design. Low-fidelity prototypes are appropriate when design details have not been decided or when they are likely to change and it is a waste of effort and maybe even misleading to try and flesh out the details.

Because low-fidelity prototypes are sometimes not taken seriously, the case for low-fidelity prototyping, especially using paper, bears some explaining. In fact, it is perhaps at this lowest end of the fidelity spectrum, paper prototypes, that dwells the highest potential ratio of value in user experience gained per unit of effort expended. A low-fidelity prototype is much less evolved and therefore far less expensive. It can be constructed and iterated in a fraction of the time it takes to produce a good high-fidelity prototype.

But can a low-fidelity prototype, a prototype that does not look like the final system, really work? The experience of many has shown that despite the vast difference between a prototype and the finished product, low-fidelity prototypes can be surprisingly effective.

Virzi, Sokolov, and Karis (1996) found that people, customers, and users do take paper prototypes seriously and that low-fidelity prototypes do reveal many user experience problems, including the more severe problems. You can get your project team to take them seriously, too. Your team may be reluctant about doing a "kindergarten" activity, but they will see that users and customers love them and that they have discovered a powerful tool for their design projects.

But will not the low-fidelity appearance bias users about the perceived user experience? Apparently not, according to Wiklund, Thurrott, and Dumas (1992), who concluded in a study that aesthetic quality (level of finish) did not bias users (positively or negatively) about the prototype's perceived user experience. As long as they understand what you are doing and why, they will go along with it.

Sometimes it takes a successful personal experience to overcome a bias against low fidelity. In one of our UX classes, we had an experienced software developer who did not believe in using low-fidelity prototypes. Because it was a requirement in the project for the course, he did use the technique anyway, and it was an eye-opener for him, as this email he sent us a few months later attests:

> After doing some of the tests I have to concede that paper prototypes are useful.
> Reviewing screenshots with the customer did not catch some pretty obvious
> usability problems and now it is hard to modify the computer prototype. Another

problem is that we did not get as complete a coverage with the screenshots of the system as we thought and had to improvise some functionality pretty quickly. I think someone had told me about that . . . .

Low-fidelity prototyping has long been a well-known design technique and, as Rettig (1994) says, if your organization or project team has not been using low-fidelity prototypes, you are in for a pleasant surprise; it can be a big breakthrough tool for you.

11.3.2 Medium-Fidelity Prototypes

Sometimes you need a prototype with a level in between low fidelity and high fidelity. Sometimes you have to choose one level of fidelity to stick with because you do not have time or other resources for your prototype to evolve from low fidelity to high-fidelity. For teams that want a bit more fidelity in their design representations than you can get with paper and want to step up to computer-based representations, medium-fidelity prototypes can be the answer.

In Chapter 9, for example, this occurs about when you undertake intermediate design and early detailed design. As a mechanism for medium-fidelity prototypes, wireframes (also in Chapter 9) are an effective way to show layout and the breadth of user interface objects and are fast becoming the most popular approach in many development organizations.

11.3.3 High-Fidelity Prototypes

In contrast, high-fidelity prototypes are more detailed representations of designs, including details of appearance and interaction behavior. High-fidelity is required to evaluate design details and it is how the users can see the complete (in the sense of realism) design. High-fidelity prototypes are the vehicle for refining the design details to get them just right as they go into the final implementation.

As the term implies, a high-fidelity prototype is faithful to the details, the look, feel, and behavior of an interaction design and possibly even system functionality. A high-fidelity prototype, if and when you can afford the added expense and time to produce it, is still less expensive and faster than programming the final product and will be so much more realistic, more interactive, more responsive, and so much more representative of a real software product than a low-fidelity prototype. High-fidelity prototypes can also be useful as advance sales demos for marketing and even as demos for raising venture capital for the company.

An extreme case of a high-fidelity prototype is the fully-programmed, whole-system prototype, discussed soon later, including both interaction design and non-user-interface functionality working together. Whole system prototypes can be as expensive and time-consuming as an implementation of an early version of the system itself and entail a lot of the software engineering management issues of non-prototype system development, including UX and SE collaboration about system functionality and overall design much earlier in the project than usual.

11.4 INTERACTIVITY OF PROTOTYPES

The amount of interactivity allowed by a prototype is not independent of the level of fidelity. In general, high interactivity requires high-fidelity. Here we discuss various ways to accomplish interactivity within a prototype.

11.4.1 Scripted and "Click-Through" Prototypes

The first prototypes to have any "behavior," or ability to respond to user actions, are usually scripted prototypes, meaning programmed with a scripting language. Scripting languages are easy to learn and use and, being high-level languages, can be used to produce some kinds of behavior very rapidly. But they are not effective tools for implementing much functionality. So scripted prototypes will be low or medium fidelity, but they can produce nice live-action storyboards of screens.

A "click-through" prototype is a medium-fidelity prototype with some active links or buttons that allow sequencing through screens by clicking, but usually with no more functionality than that. Wireframes can be used to make click-through prototypes by adding links that respond in simple ways to clicking, such as moving to the next screen.

11.4.2 A Fully Programmed Prototype

Even the prototypes of large systems can themselves be large and complex. On rare occasions and in very special circumstances, where time and resources permit and there is a genuine need, a project team is required to produce a high-fidelity full-system operational prototype of a large system, including at least some back-end functionality.

One such occasion did occur in the early 1990s when the FAA sought proposals from large development organizations for a big 10-year air traffic control system development project. Bidders successful in the first phase of proposals would be required to design and build a full-function proof-of-concept prototype in a project that itself took nearly 2 years and cost millions of dollars. On the basis of this prototype phase, even larger multiyear contracts would be awarded for construction of the real system.

Such large and fully functional prototypes call for the power of a real programming language. Although the resulting prototype is still not intended to be the final system, a real programming language gives the most flexibility to produce exactly the desired look and feel. And, of course, a real programming language is essential for implementing extensive functionality. The process, of course, will not be as fast, low in cost, or easy to change.

11.4.3 "Wizard of Oz" Prototypes: Pay No Attention to the Man Behind the Curtain

The Wizard of Oz prototyping technique is a deceptively simple approach to the appearance of a high degree of interactivity and highly flexible prototype behavior in complex situations where user inputs are unpredictable. The setup requires two connected computers, each in a different room. The user's computer is connected as a "slave" to the evaluator's computer. The user makes input actions on one computer, which are sent directly to a human team member at the evaluator's computer, hidden in the second room.

The human evaluator sees the user inputs on the hidden computer and sends appropriate simulated output back to the user's computer. This approach has particular advantages, one of which is the apparently high level of interactivity as seen by the user. It is especially effective when flexible and adaptive "computer" behavior is of the essence, as with artificial intelligence and other difficult-to-implement systems. Within the limits of the cleverness of the human evaluator, the "system" should never break down or crash.

In one of the earliest uses of the Wizard of Oz technique that we know of, Good and colleagues (1984) designed empirically a command-driven email interface to accommodate natural novice user actions. Users were given no menus, help, no documentation, and no instruction.

Users were unaware that a hidden operator was intercepting commands when the system itself could not interpret the input. The design was modified iteratively so that it would have recognized and responded to previously intercepted inputs. The design progressed from recognizing only 7% of inputs to recognizing about 76% of user commands.

The Wizard of Oz prototyping technique is especially useful when your design ideas are still wide open and you want to see how users behave naturally in the course of simulated interaction. It could work well, for example, with a kiosk.

You would set up the general scope of usage expected and let users at it. You will see what they want to do. Because you have a human at the other end, you do not have to worry about whether you programmed the application to handle any given situation.

11.4.4 Physical MockUps for Physical Interactivity

If a primary characteristic of a product or system is physicality, such as you have with a handheld device, then an effective prototype will also have to offer physical interactivity. Programming new applications on physical devices with real software means complex and lengthy implementation on a challenging hardware and software platform. Prototypes afford designers and others insight into the product look and feel without complicated specialized device programming.

Some products or devices are "physical" in the sense that they are something like a mobile device that users might hold in their hands. Or a system might be "physical" like a kiosk. A physical prototype for such products goes beyond screen simulation on a computer; the prototype encompasses the whole device. Pering (2002) describes a case study of such an approach for a handheld communicator device that combines the functionality of a PDA and a cellphone.

If the product is to be handheld, make a prototype from cardboard, wood, or metal that can also be handheld. If the product, such as a kiosk, is to sit on the floor, put the prototype in a cardboard box and add physical buttons or a touchscreen.

You can use materials at hand or craft the prototype with realistic hardware. Start off with glued-on shirt buttons and progress to real push-button switches. Scrounge up hardware buttons and other controls that are as close to those in your envisioned design as possible: push buttons, tilt buttons, sliders, for example, from a light dimmer, knobs and dials, rocker switch, or a joystick from an old Nintendo game.

Even if details are low fidelity, these are higher fidelity in some ways because they are typically 3D, embodied, and tangible. You can hold them in your hands. You can touch them and manipulate them physically. Also, physical prototypes are excellent media for supporting evaluation of emotional impact and other user experience characteristics beyond just usability.

And just because physical product prototyping usually involves a model of physical hardware does not rule out being a low-fidelity prototype. Designers of the original Palm PDA carried around a block of wood as a physical prototype of the envisioned personal digital assistant. They used it to explore the physical feel and other requirements for such a device and its interaction possibilities (Moggridge, 2007, p. 204).

Physical prototyping is now being used for cellphones, PDAs, consumer electronics, and products beyond interactive electronics, employing found objects, "junk" (paper plates, pipe cleaners, and other playful materials) from the recycle bin, thrift stores, dollar stores, and school supply shops (N. Frishberg, 2006). Perhaps IDEO[1] is the company most famous for its physical prototyping for product ideation; see their shopping cart project video (*ABC News Nightline*, 1999) for a good example.

Wright (2005) describes the power of a physical mockup that users can see and hold as a real object over just pictures on a screen, however powerful and fancy the graphics. Users get a real feeling that this *is* the product. The kind of embodied user experience projected by this approach can lead to a product that generates user surprise and delight, product praise in the media, and must-have cachet in the market.

Paper-in-device mockup prototype, especially for mobile applications

The usual paper prototype needs an "executor," a person playing computer to change screens and do all the other actions of the system in response to a user's actions. This role of mediator between user and device will necessarily interfere with the usage experience, especially when a large part of that experience involves, holding, feeling, and manipulating the device itself.

Bolchini, Pulido, and Faiola (2009) and others devised a solution by which they placed the paper prototype inside the device, leveraging the advantages of paper prototyping in evaluating mobile device interfaces with the real physical device. They drew the prototype screens on paper, scanned them, and loaded them into the device as a sequence of digital images that the device can display. During evaluation, users can move through this sequential navigation by making touches or gestures that the device already can recognize.

This is an agile and inexpensive technique, and the authors reported that their testing showed that even this limited amount of interactivity generated a lot of useful feedback and discussion with evaluation users. Also, by adding page annotations about user interactions, possible user thoughts, and other behind-the-scenes information, the progression of pages can become like a design storyboard of the usage scenario.

---

[1]http://www.ideo.com

11.4.5 Animated Prototypes

Most prototypes are static in that they depend on user interaction to show what they can do. Video animation can bring a prototype to life for concept demos, to visualize new interaction designs, and to communicate design ideas. While animated prototypes are not interactive, they are at least active.

Löwgren (2004) shows how video animations based on a series of sketches can carry the advantages of low-fidelity prototypes to new dimensions where a static paper prototype cannot tread. Animated sketches are still "rough" enough to invite engagement and design suggestions but, being more like scenarios or storyboards, animations can convey flow and sequencing better in the context of usage.

HCI designers have been using video to bring prototypes to life as early as the 1980s (Vertelney, 1989). A simple approach is to use storyboard frames in a "flip book" style sequence on video or, if you already have a fairly complete low-fidelity prototype, you can film it in motion by making a kind of "claymation" frame-by-frame video of its parts moving within an interaction task.

11.5 CHOOSING THE RIGHT BREADTH, DEPTH, LEVEL OF FIDELITY, AND AMOUNT OF INTERACTIVITY

There are two major factors to consider when choosing the right breadth, depth, level of fidelity, and amount of interactivity of your prototypes: the stage of progress you are in within the overall project and the design perspective in which you are prototyping. These two factors are interrelated, as stages of progress occur within each of the design perspectives.

11.5.1 Using the Right Level of Fidelity for the Current Stage of Progress

Choosing your audience and explaining the prototype

In general, low-fidelity prototypes are a tool to be used within the project team. Low-fidelity prototypes are shown to people outside the team only to get feedback on very specific aspects of the design. If low-fidelity prototypes are shown casually around to users and customer personnel without careful explanation, they can be misinterpreted. To someone not familiar with their use, a paper prototype can look like the product of an inexperienced amateur.

Even if they do get beyond the rough appearance, without guidance as to what kind of feedback you want, "sophisticated" users and customers will immediately see missing features and think that you do not know what you are doing, possibly creating a credibility gap. Therefore, low-fidelity prototypes are often considered "private" to the project team and reserved for your own use for early exploration and iterative refinement of the conceptual design and early workflow.

Therefore, when a project is deliverable-oriented and the customer expects to evaluate your progress based on what they see developing as a product, a medium- or high-fidelity prototype can be used as a design demo. Practitioners often construct pixel-perfect representations of envisioned designs for these prototypes to show off designs to customers, users, and other non-team stakeholders. Such realistic-looking demos, however, carry the risk of being interpreted as complete designs, as versions of the final product. If something is wrong or missing, the designers are still blamed. Explaining everything in advance can head off these complications.

A progression of increasing fidelity to match your stage of progress

As a general rule, as you move through stages of progress in your project, you will require increasing levels of fidelity in your prototypes. For example, the goal in an early stage might be to determine if your design approach is even a good idea or a feasible one.

The goal of a later stage might simply be to show off: "Look at what a cool design we have!" In Table 11-1 we describe the appropriate time and place to use each kind of prototype in terms of various kinds of iteration within design production (Chapter 9). The types of prototypes mentioned in Table 11-1 are described in various places, mostly in this chapter.

11.5.2 Using the Right Level of Fidelity for the Design Perspective Being Addressed

For each design perspective in which you make a prototype, you must decide which kind of prototype, horizontal or vertical and at what fidelity, is needed, requiring you to consider what aspects of the design you are worried about and what aspects need to be tested in that perspective. In large part, this means asking about the audience for and the purpose of your prototype in the context of that perspective. What do you hope to accomplish with a prototype in the design perspective being addressed? What questions will the prototype help you answer?

Table 11-1

Summary of the uses for various levels of fidelity and types of prototypes

Kind of Iteration	Purpose	Types of Prototypes
Ideation and sketching	To support exploring ideas, brainstorming, and discussion (so design details are inappropriate)	Sketches, fast and disposable mockups, ultralow fidelity
Conceptual design	To support exploration and creation of conceptual design, the high-level system structure, and the overall interaction metaphor	Evolution from hand-drawn paper, computer-printed paper, low-fidelity wireframes, high-fidelity wireframes, to pixel-perfect interactive mockups (to communicate with customer)
Intermediate design	To support interaction design for tasks and task threads	Evolution from paper to wireframes
Detailed design	Support for deciding navigation details, screen design and layout, including pixel-perfect visual comps complete specification for look and feel of the "skin"	Detailed wireframes and/or pixel-perfect interactive mockups
Design refinement	To support evaluation to refine a chosen design by finding and removing as many UX problems as possible	Medium to high fidelity, lots of design detail, possibly a programmed prototype

Ecological Perspective

The ecological design perspective is about how the system or product works within its external environment. It is about how the system or product is used in its context and how the system or product interacts or communicates with its environment in the process.

Prototyping for the ecological perspective

To support exploration of the high-level system structure, a prototype in the ecological perspective is a kind of concept map to how the different parts of the system will work at the conceptual level and how it fits in with the rest of the world—other systems and products and other users.

As you evaluate the conceptual design, remember that you are looking at the big picture so the prototypes do not need to be high fidelity or detailed. If evaluation with early conceptual prototypes shows that users do not get along well with the basic metaphor, then the designers will not have wasted all the time it takes to work out design details of interaction objects such as screen icons, messages, and so on.

The development of IBM's Olympic Message System (Gould et al., 1987) was an avant garde example of product prototyping with emphasis on the ecological setting. IBM was tasked to provide a communications system for the 1984 Olympics in Los Angeles to keep athletes, officials, families, and friends in immediate contact during the games. For their earliest concept testing they used a "Wizard of Oz" technique whereby participants pressed keys on a computer terminal and spoke outgoing messages. The experimenter read aloud the incoming messages and gave other outputs as the interaction required.

For enhanced ecological validity they used a "hallway methodology" that started with a hollow wooden cylinder set in IBM building hallways, with pictures of screens and controls pasted on. They quickly learned a lot about the best height, location, labeling, and wording for displays. Real interactive displays housed in more finished kiosk prototypes led to even more feedback from visitors and corporate passersby. The resulting system was a big success at the Olympics.

Prototyping for the interaction perspective

For conceptual design, support early exploration with ideation and sketching using rapid and disposable low-fidelity prototypes. As you evaluate the conceptual design, remember that you are looking at the big picture so the fidelity of prototypes can be low. Use many rapid iterations to refine candidate conceptual design ideas.

As you move into intermediate design iteration, start by choosing a few tasks that are the most important and prototype them fairly completely. Mockup a typical task so that a user can follow a representative task thread.

Use medium-fidelity prototypes, such as wireframes, to flesh out behavior, including sequencing and responses to user actions. As we will see in later chapters on formative evaluation, a great deal can be learned from an incomplete design in a prototype.

For detailed design, after you have exhausted possibilities in evaluating the conceptual model and early screen design ideas with your low-fidelity, possibly paper, prototype, you will move on. You might next use a computer-printed paper prototype or a computer-based mockup to test increasing amounts of design detail.

You will flesh out your prototype with more complete task threads, well-designed icons, and carefully worded messages. Representing and evaluating full design details require high-fidelity prototypes, possibly programmed and possibly connected with some working functionality, such as database functions.

Prototyping for the emotional perspective

A prototype to support evaluation of emotional impact needs certain kinds of details. High fidelity and high interactivity are usually required to support this perspective. Although full details at the interaction level may not always be required, you do need details relating to fun, joy of use, and user satisfaction. Further, the emotional perspective for physical devices more or less demands physical mockups for a real feeling of holding and manipulating the device.

Ecological Validity

Ecological validity refers to the realism with which a design of evaluation setup matches the user's real work context. It is about how accurately the design or evaluation reflects the relevant characteristics of the ecology of interaction, i.e., its context in the world or its environment.

Interaction Perspective

The interaction design perspective is about how users operate the system or product. It is a task and intention view, where user and system come together. It is where users look at displays and manipulate controls, doing sensory, cognitive, and physical actions.

Emotional Perspective

The emotional design perspective is about emotional impact and value-sensitive aspects of design. It is about social and cultural implications, as well as the aesthetics and joy of use.

11.5.3 Managing Risk and Cost within Stages of Progress and within Design Perspectives

There has been much debate over the relative merits of low-fidelity prototypes vs. high-fidelity prototypes, but Buxton (2007a) has put it in a better light: It is not so much about high-fidelity prototypes vs. low-fidelity prototypes as it is about getting the right prototype. But, of course, part of getting it right is in determining the right level of abstraction for the purpose.

One way to look at the horizontal vs. vertical and low-fidelity vs. high-fidelity question is with respect to the three design perspectives (Chapter 7). For each of these perspectives, it is about managing risk, particularly the risk (in terms of cost) of getting the design wrong (with respect to the corresponding perspective) and the cost of having to change it.

A user interaction design can be thought of in two parts:

- the appearance, especially the visual aspects of the user interface objects
- the behavior, including sequencing and responses to user actions

Of these, which has the biggest risk in terms of cost to change late in the schedule? It is the behavior and sequencing. The behavior is the part that corresponds roughly to the design metaphor envisioned to support the user workflow. Therefore, we should try to get the best design we can for the behavior before we worry about details of appearance. That means our earliest and easiest to change prototypes should represent interaction design behavior and that means having a low-fidelity prototype first. This interaction structure and sequencing is very easy to change with paper screens, but becomes increasingly more difficult to modify as it is committed to programming code.

In low-fidelity prototypes it can even be a disadvantage to show too many details that appear refined. As Rettig (1994) points out, if you have a nice slick look and feel, you will naturally get most of your feedback on the look and feel details rather than on high-level issues such as workflow, task flow, overall layout, and the metaphor. Also, some users may be less willing to suggest changes for a prototype that even appears to be high fidelity because of the impression that the design process is completed and that any feedback they provide is probably too late (Rudd, Stern, & Isensee, 1996).

Later, however, increasingly higher fidelity prototypes can be used to establish and refine the exact appearance, the visual and manipulation aspects of interface objects such as colors, fonts, button design, highlighting an object, and so on, and eventually to bring in some depth in terms of functionality, for example, more detail about checking and handling errors in user inputs. As shown in Table 11-2, there is a place for both low-fidelity and high-fidelity prototypes in most design projects.

Type of Prototype	"Strength"	When in Lifecycle to Apply "Strength"	Cost to Fix Appearance	Cost to Fix Sequencing	Table 11-2
Low fidelity (e.g., paper)	Flexibility; easy to change sequencing, overall behavior	Early	Almost none	Low	
High fidelity (e.g., computer)	Fidelity of appearance	Later	Intermediate	High	

Table 11-2

Summary of comparison of low-fidelity and high-fidelity prototypes

Finally, and just as an aside, prototyping is a technique that can help manage and reduce risks on the software engineering side as well on the UX side of a project.

11.5.4 Summary of the Effects of Breadth, Depth, and Fidelity Factors

In the graph in Figure 11-3 we show roughly how scope (vertical vs. horizontal) and fidelity issues play out in the choice of prototyping approaches based on what the designer needs.

11.6 PAPER PROTOTYPES

Soon after you have a conceptual design mapped out, give it life as a low-fidelity prototype and try out the concept. This is the time to start with a horizontal prototype, showing the possible breadth of features without much depth. The facility of paper prototypes enables you, in a day or two, to create a new design idea, implement it in a prototype, evaluate it with users, and modify it.

Low fidelity usually means paper prototypes. You should construct your early paper prototypes as quickly and efficiently as possible. Early versions are just about interaction, not functionality. You do not even have to use "real" widgets.

Sometimes a paper prototype can act as a "coding blocker" to prevent time wasted on coding too early. At this critical juncture, when the design is starting to come together,

Figure 11-3

Depth, breadth, and fidelity considerations in choosing a type of prototype.

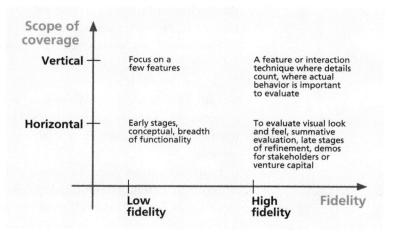

programmers are likely to suffer from the WISCY syndrome (Why Isn't Sam Coding Yet?). They naturally want to run off and start coding.

You need a way to keep people from writing code until we can get the design to the point where we should invest in it. Once any code gets written, there will be ownership attached and it will get protected and will stay around longer than it should. Even though it is just a prototype, people will begin to resist making changes to "their baby"; they will be too invested in it. And other team members, knowing that it is getting harder to get changes through, will be less willing to suggest changes.

11.6.1 Paper Prototypes for Design Reviews and Demos

Your earliest paper prototypes will have no functionality or interaction, no ability to respond to any user actions. You can demonstrate some predefined sequences of screen sketches as storyboards or "movies" of envisioned interaction. For the earliest design reviews, you just want to show what it looks like and a little of the sequencing behavior. The goal is to see some of the interaction design very quickly—in the time frame of hours, not days or weeks.

11.6.2 Hand-Drawn Paper Prototypes

The next level of paper prototypes will support some simulated "interaction." As the user views screens and pretends to click buttons, a human "executor" plays computer and moves paper pieces in response to those mock user actions.

11.6.3 Computer-Printed Paper Prototypes

Paper prototypes, with user interface objects and text on paper printed via a computer, are essentially the same as hand-drawn paper prototypes, except slightly higher fidelity in appearance. You get fast, easy, and effective prototypes with added realism at very low cost. To make computer-printable screens for low-fidelity prototypes, you can use tools such as OmniGraffle (for the Mac) or Microsoft Visio.

Berger (2006) describes one successful case of using a software tool not intended for prototyping. When used as a prototyping tool, Excel provides grid alignment for objects and text, tabbed pages to contain a library of designs, a hypertext feature used for interactive links, and a built-in primitive database capability.

Cells can contain graphical images, which can also be copied and pasted, thus the concept of templates for dialogue box, buttons, and so on can be thought of as native to Excel. Berger claimed fast turnarounds, typically on a daily basis.

11.6.4 Is not paper just a stopgap medium?

Is not paper prototyping a technique necessary just because we do not yet have good enough software prototyping tools? Yes and no. There is always hope for a future software prototyping tool that can match the fluency and spontaneity afforded by the paper medium. That would be a welcome tool indeed and perhaps wireframing is heading in that direction but, given the current software technology for programming prototypes even for low-fidelity prototypes, there is no comparison with the ease and speed with which paper prototypes can be modified and refined, even if changes are needed on the fly in the midst of an evaluation session.

Therefore, at least for the foreseeable future, paper prototyping has to be considered as more than just a stopgap measure or a low-tech substitute for that as yet chimerical software tool; it is a legitimate technology on its own.

Paper prototyping is an embodied effort that involves the brain in the creative hand–eye feedback loop. When you use any kind of programming, your brain is diverted from the design to the programming. When you are writing or drawing on the paper with your hands and your eyes and moving sheets of paper around manually, you are thinking about design. When you are programming, you are thinking about the software tool.

Rettig (1994) says that with paper, "... interface designers spend 95% of their time thinking about the design and only 5% thinking about the mechanisms of the tool. Software-based tools, no matter how well executed, reverse this ratio."

11.6.5 Why Not Just Program a Low-Fidelity Prototype?

At "run-time" (or evaluation time), it is often useful to write on the paper pages, something you cannot do with a programmed prototype. Also, we have found that paper has much broader visual bandwidth, which is a boon when you want to look at and compare multiple screens at once. When it comes time to change the interaction sequencing in a design, it is done faster and visualized more easily by shuffling paper on a table.

Another subtle difference is that a paper prototype is always available for "execution," but a software prototype is only intermittently executable—only between sessions of programming to make changes. Between versions, there is a need for fast turnaround to the next version, but the slightest error in the code will disable the prototype completely. Being software, your prototype is susceptible to a single bug that can bring it crashing down and you may be caught in a position where you have to debug in front of your demo audience or users.

The result of early programmed prototypes is almost always slow prototyping, not useful for evaluating numerous different alternatives while the trail to interaction design evolution is still hot. Fewer iterations are possible, with more "dead time" in between where users and evaluators can lose interest and have correspondingly less opportunity to participate in the design process. Also, of course, as the prototype grows in size, more and more delay is incurred from programming and keeping it executable.

Because programmed prototypes are not always immediately available for evaluation and design discussion, sometimes the prototyping activity cannot keep up with the need for fast iteration. Berger (2006) relates an anecdote about a project in which the user interface software developer had the job of implementing design sketches and design changes in a Web page production tool. It took about 2 weeks to convert the designs to active Web pages for the prototype and in the interim the design had already changed again and the beautiful prototypes were useless.

11.6.6 How to Make an Effective Paper Prototype

Almost all you ever wanted to know about prototyping, you learned in Kindergarten.

Get out your paper and pencil, some duct tape, and WD-40. Decide who on your team can be trusted with sharp instruments, and we are off on another adventure. There are many possible approaches to building paper prototypes. The following are some general guidelines that have worked for us and that we have refined over many, many iterations.

Start by setting a realistic deadline. This is one kind of activity that can go on forever. Time management is an important part of any prototyping activity. There is no end to the features, polishing, and tweaking that can be added to a paper prototype. And watch out for design iteration occurring before you even get the first prototype finished. You can go around in circles before you get user inputs and it probably will not add much value to the design. Why polish a feature that might well change within the next day anyway?

Gather a set of paper prototyping materials. As you work with paper prototypes, you will gather a set of construction materials customized to your approach. Here is a starter list to get you going:

- Blank plastic transparency sheets, 8½ × 11; the very inexpensive write-on kind works fine; you do not need the expensive copier-type plastic
- An assortment of different colored, fine-pointed, erasable and permanent marking pens

- A supply of plain copier-type paper (or a pad of plain, unlined, white paper)
- Assorted pencils and pens
- Scissors
- "Scotch" tape (with dispensers)
- A bottle of Wite-out or other correction fluid
- Rulers or straight edges
- A yellow and/or pink highlighter
- "Sticky" (e.g., Post-it) note pads in a variety of sizes and colors

Keep these in a box so that you have them handy for the next time you need to make a paper prototype.

Work fast and do not color within the lines. If they told you in school to use straight lines and color only within the boxes, here is a chance to revolt, a chance to heal your psyche. Change your personality and live dangerously, breaking the bonds of grade school tyranny and dogmatism, something you can gloat about in the usual postprototype cocktail party.

Draw on everything you have worked on so far for the design. Use your conceptual design, design scenarios, ideation, personas, storyboards, and everything else you have created in working up to this exciting moment of putting it into the first real materialization of your design ideas.

Make an easel to register (align) your screen and user interface object sheets of paper and plastic. Use an "easel" to register each interaction sheet with the others. The simple foam-core board easels we make for our short courses are economical and serviceable. On a piece of foam-core board slightly larger than 8½ × 11, on at least two (of the four) adjacent sides add some small pieces of additional foam-core board as "stops," as seen in Figures 11-4 and 11-5, against which each interaction sheet can be pushed to ensure proper positioning. When the prototype is being "executed" during UX evaluation, the easel will usually be taped to the tabletop for stability.

Figure 11-4

Foam-core board paper prototype easel with "stops" to align the interaction sheets.

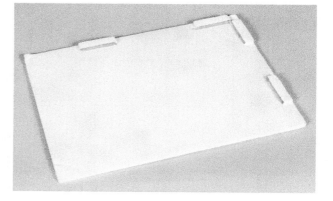

Make underlying paper foundation "screens." Start with simplest possible background for each screen in pencil or pen

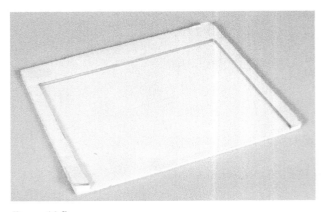

Figure 11-5

Another style of "stops" on a foam-core board paper prototype easel.

on full-size paper (usually 8½ × 11) as a base for all moving parts. Include only parts that never change. For example, in a calendar system prototype, show a monthly "grid," leaving a blank space for the month name). See Figure 11-6.

Use paper cutouts taped onto full-size plastic "interaction sheets" for all moving parts. Everything else, besides the paper foundation, will be taped to transparent plastic sheets. Draw everything else (e.g., interaction objects, highlights, dialogue boxes, labels) in pencil, pen, or colored markers on smaller pieces of paper and cut them out. Tape them onto separate full-size 8½ × 11 blank plastic sheets in the appropriate position aligned relative to objects in the foundation screen and to objects taped to other plastic sheets.

We call this full-size plastic sheet, with paper user interface object(s) taped in position, an "interaction sheet." The appearance of a given screen in your prototype is made up of multiple overlays of these interaction sheets. See Figure 11-7.

When these interaction sheets are aligned against the stops in the easel, they appear to be part of the user interface, as in the case of the pop-up dialogue box in Figure 11-8.

Figure 11-6

Underlying paper foundation "screen."

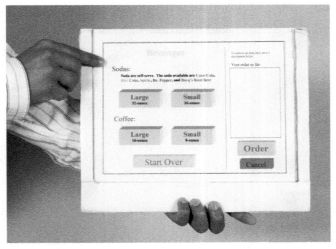

Be creative. Think broadly about how to add useful features to your prototype without too much extra effort. In addition to drawing by hand, you can use simple graphics or paint programs to import images such as buttons, and resize, label, and print them in color. Fasten some objects such as pull-down lists to the top or side of an interaction sheet with transparent tape hinges so that they can "flap down" to overlay the screen when they are selected. See Figure 11-9.

Scrolling can be done by cutting slits in your paper menu, which is taped to a plastic sheet. Then a slightly smaller slip

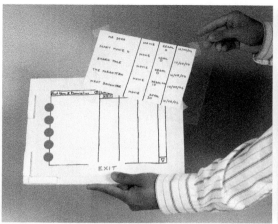

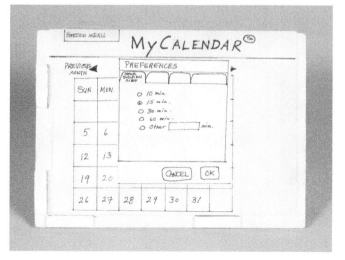
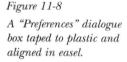

Figure 11-7

Paper cutouts taped to full-size plastic for moving parts.

of paper with the menu choices can be slid through the slots. See Figure 11-10.

Use any creative techniques to demonstrate motion, dynamics, and feedback.

Do not write or mark on plastic interaction sheets. The plastic interaction sheets are almost exclusively for mounting and positioning the paper pieces. The plastic is supposed to be transparent; that is how layering works. Do not write or draw on the plastic. The only exception is for making transparent objects such as highlights or as an input medium on which users write input values. Later we will discuss completely blank sheets for writing inputs.

Figure 11-8

A "Preferences" dialogue box taped to plastic and aligned in easel.

Make highlights on plastic with "handles" for holding during prototype execution. Make a highlight to fit each major selectable object. Cut out a plastic square or rectangle with a long handle and color in the highlight (usually just an outline so as not to obscure the object or text being highlighted) with a permanent marking pen. See Figure 11-11.

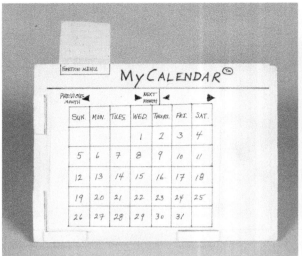

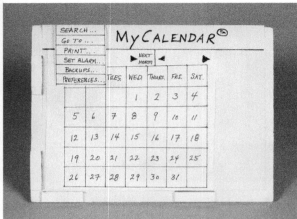

Figure 11-9

Pull-down menu on a tape "hinge."

Figure 11-10

Paper sliding through a slit for scrolling.

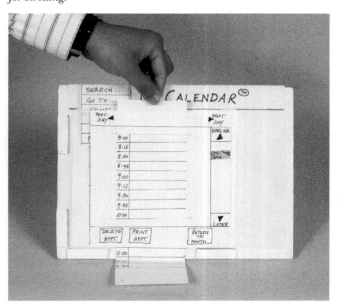

Make your interaction sheets highly modular by including only a small amount on each one. Instead of customizing a single screen or page, build up each screen or display in layers. The less you put on each layer, the more modular and, therefore, the more reuse you will get. With every feature and every variation of appearance taped to a different sheet of plastic, you have the best chance at being able to show the most variation of appearances and user interface object configurations you might encounter. Be suspicious of a lot of writing/drawing on one interaction sheet. When a prototype user gives an input, it usually makes a change in the display. Each possible change should go on a separate interaction sheet.

Get modularity by thinking about whatever needs to appear by itself. When you make an interaction sheet, ask yourself: *Will every single detail on here always appear together?* If there is a chance two items on the same interaction sheet will ever appear separately, it is best to put them on separate interaction sheets. They come back together when you overlay them together, but they can still be used separately, too. See Figure 11-12.

Do lots of sketching and storyboarding before making interaction sheets. This will save time and work.

Use every stratagem for minimizing work and time. Focus on design, not writing and paper cutting.

Reuse at every level. Make it a goal to not draw or write anything twice; use templates for the common parts of similar objects. Use a copy machine or scanner to reproduce common parts of similar interaction objects and write in only the differences. For example, for a calendar, use copies of a blank month template, filling in the days for each month. The idea is to capture in a template everything that does not have to change from one instance to another.

Cut corners when it does not hurt things. Always trade off accuracy (when it is not needed) for efficiency (that is always needed). As an example, if it is not important to have the days and dates be exactly right for a given month on a calendar, use the same date numbers for each month in your early prototype. Then you can put the numbers in your month template and not have to write any in.

Make the prototype support key tasks. Prototype at least all benchmark tasks from your UX target table, as this prototype will be used in the formative evaluation exercise.

Make a "this feature not yet implemented" message. This is the prototype's response to a user action that was not anticipated or that has not yet been included in the design. You will be surprised

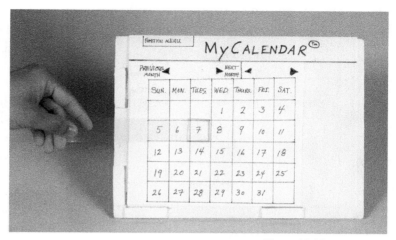

Figure 11-11
Selection highlight on plastic with a long handle.

Figure 11-12
Lots of pieces of dialogue as paper cutouts aligned on plastic sheets.

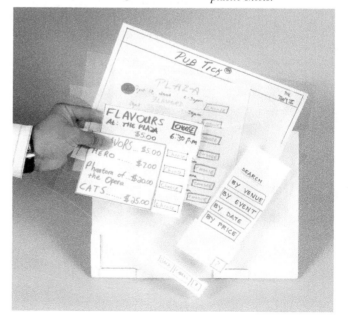

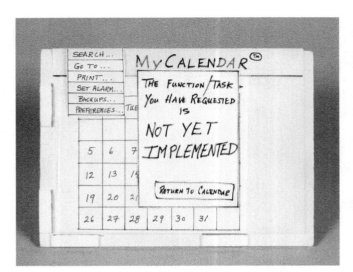

Figure 11-13

"Not yet implemented" message.

Figure 11-14

Data entry on clear plastic overlay sheet.

how often you may use this in user experience evaluation with early prototypes. See Figure 11-13.

Include "decoy" user interface objects.

If you include only user interface objects needed to do your initial benchmark tasks, it may be unrealistically easy for users to do just those tasks. Doing user experience testing with this kind of initial interaction design does not give a good idea of the ease of use of the design when it is complete and contains many more user interface objects to choose from and many more other choices to make during a task.

Therefore, you should include many other "decoy" buttons, menu choices, etc., even if they do not do anything (so participants see more than just the "happy path" for their benchmark tasks). Your decoy objects should look plausible and should, as much as possible, anticipate other tasks and other paths. Users performing tasks with your prototype will be faced with a more realistic array of user interface objects about which they will have to think as they make choices about what user actions are next. And when they click on a decoy object, that is when you get to use your "not implemented" message. (Later, in the evaluation chapters, we while discuss probing the users on why they clicked on that object when it is not part of your envisioned task sequence.)

Accommodate data value entry by users.

When users need to enter a value (e.g., a credit card number) into a paper prototype, it is usually sufficient to use a clear sheet of plastic (a blank interaction sheet) on top of the layers and let them write the value in with a marking pen; see Figure 11-14. Of course, if your design requires them to enter that number using a touchscreen on an iPad, for example, you have to create a "text input" interaction sheet.

Create a way to manage complex task threads. Before an evaluation session, the prototype "executor" will have all the paper sheets and overlays all lined up and ready to put on the easel in response to user actions. When the number of prototype pieces gets very large, however, it is difficult to know what stack of pieces to use at any point in the interaction, and it is even more difficult to clean it all up after the session to make it ready for the next session.

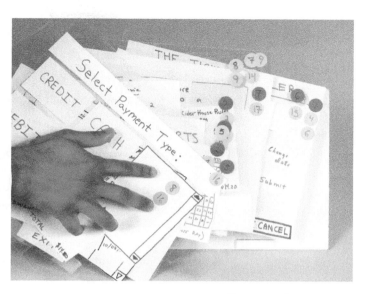

Figure 11-15
Adhesive-backed circles for color coding task threads on prototype pieces.

As an organizing technique that works most of the time, we have taken to attaching colored dots to the pieces, color coding them according to task threads. Sheets of adhesive-backed colored circles are available at most office supply stores. See Figure 11-15. Numbers written on the circles indicate the approximate expected order of usage in the corresponding task thread, which is the order to sort them in when cleaning up after a session.

Pilot test thoroughly. Before your prototype is ready to be used in real user experience evaluation sessions, you must give it a good shake-down. Pilot test your prototype to be sure that it will support all your benchmark tasks. You do not want to make the rookie mistake of "burning" a user participant (subject) by getting them started only to discover the prototype "blows up" and prevents benchmark task performance.

Simulate user experience evaluation conditions by having one member of your team "execute" the prototype while another member plays "user" and tries out all benchmark tasks. The user person should go through each task in as many ways as anyone thinks possible to head off the "oh, we never thought they would try *that*" syndrome later in testing. Do not assume error-free performance by your users; try to have appropriate error messages where user errors might occur. When you think your prototype is ready, get someone from outside your group and have them play the user role in more pilot testing.

Exercise

See Exercise 11-1, Building a Low-Fidelity Paper Prototype for Your System

11.7 ADVANTAGES OF AND CAUTIONS ABOUT USING PROTOTYPES

11.7.1 Advantages of Prototyping

In sum, prototypes have these advantages:

- Offer concrete baseline for communication between users and designers
- Provide conversational "prop" to support communication of concepts not easily conveyed verbally
- Allow users to "take the design for a spin" (who would buy a car without taking it for a test drive or buy a stereo system without first listening to it?)
- Give project visibility and buy-in within customer and developer organizations
- Encourage early user participation and involvement
- Give impression that design is easy to change because a prototype is obviously not finished
- Afford designers immediate observation of user performance and consequences of design decisions
- Help sell management an idea for new product
- Help affect a paradigm shift from existing system to new system

11.7.2 Potential Pitfalls of Prototyping

Prototyping, however, is not without potential drawbacks that, with some caution, can be avoided.

Get cooperation, buy-in, and understanding

To ensure your best chances of success with a process based on prototyping, especially if your organization is not experienced with the technique, the UX team must first secure cooperation and buy-in from all parties involved, including management.

Be sure you sell prototyping as the vehicle through which you will apply an iterative process and eventually come to an acceptable level of user experience in the design. Otherwise, managers may view allocation of resources to building a prototype, especially a throw-away one, as wasteful.

In a small contract we had many years ago with a nationally known retail chain, we were asked to help redesign the in-store point-of-sale software. The process was discussed only generally because the UX people did not think others needed to know much about what, after all, *they* would be doing. So when there seemed to be agreement upfront, it seemed like the client had bought into the process. But it turned out to not be a real buy-in.

When we presented the first prototype, one that had never been evaluated or iterated, the client's software people immediately took over the prototype and the interaction designers were powerless to apply their process further to arrive at a better design. Later, when the design proved inferior, the interaction designers were blamed, validating the software people's view that a UX process does not add value. "We just implemented what you designed."

If at least project management, if not the SE people, had understood the process and the place of the prototype within that process, and if the UX people had been empowered to carry out their process, this unfortunate scenario could have been avoided.

Be honest about limitations and do not overpromise

However, you must present a design prototype to any audience—management, customers, users, other professionals—with the utmost of professional honesty. It is your responsibility not even passively to allow your audience to assume or believe that it is the real product, especially for design exploration prototypes and prototypes promising features that do not yet exist and, possibly, cannot be delivered.

The ease of making a low-fidelity prototype makes it easy to add bells and whistles that you may not be able to deliver in the final product. Remember that a prototype can be perceived to make promises about features and functionality. And a slick prototype can cause management to believe that you are further along in development than you really are in the project schedule.

Do not overwork your prototype

The engineering maxim to "make it good enough" applies particularly to prototypes. A programmed prototype can seduce designers into the trap of overdesign or wasting resources on overworking a prototype, only eventually to have it scrapped.

Do not "fall in love" with your prototype and continue to expand and polish it after it has served its usefulness. Establish formative evaluation goals for prototyping and stick to them.

Finally, it may not be you, but your boss or manager who falls in love with your prototype. You might be expected to "baby sit" the prototype and keep it updated to the minute so you can trot it out without notice to demonstrate it to the next visiting dignitary or visitor. Our advice is to find a way to be busy on something more important.

11.8 PROTOTYPES IN TRANSITION TO THE PRODUCT

If you have a high-fidelity prototype near the end of the iterative UX lifecycle, you will be thinking next about making the transition from prototype to real product. Do you keep the prototype or do you scrap it and start over? The answer often is that you do some of each.

Perhaps the most important consideration is the investment you have made in the iterative refinement of your design. To protect that investment, you should do everything possible to preserve the details of the user interface objects, the "look" or appearance part of the design—the layout and design of all screens and the exact wording of all labels, menus, and text. If a single detail changes in the transition, it could impact the user experience—user experience that you bought and paid for during evaluation and iteration.

Similarly, you will want to preserve the feel and sequencing behavior of your well-tested prototype. However, this will require careful recoding from the ground up. Your prototype code for the sequencing always was "spaghetti" code and was never intended to be anything else.

11.8.1 Graduation Day in the Trenches: The Sacred Passing of the Prototype

After all your iteration, the day will arrive in each project where all attention will "graduate" from prototypes to the current version or release of the final software product. There is no longer an independent UX lifecycle, and all the action in this "tail" of the lifecycle will be on the SE side because they own the code.

Some formative evaluation can still be done, but it will be with the real software system and not the prototype. Further changes on either side will be much slower and more expensive. As marketing circles in, and perhaps after a little bubbly for celebration/commiseration, the UX team will either disband or start working on their next great design.

What happens to the prototype code?

If you do, as we suggest you might, use your interaction design prototype as part or all of your interaction design specifications. What are the conditions that determine how you offer it to the SE folks? How much of the prototype software, especially for a high-fidelity prototype, is to be thrown away and how much is reused? In most cases, the technical answer is that it all should be thrown away; the design is what you reuse.

You cannot just keep the prototype

Despite the urge to say "Hey, we have a prototype that works, let us just use that as the first version of the product," in almost all cases the prototype cannot be gussied up into the final product, for a number of reasons. Rarely is the best software platform for fast mockups and flexibility of cut-and-try changes to prototypes the best platform for production software. Furthermore the prototype code is never production quality; if it is, you were doing prototyping wrong.

How do you reuse the interaction design of the prototype?

Expectations for the implementation of your prototype in production software are that it will be generally faithful to the intent and behavior of the prototype, including sequencing and connections to functionality, and literally and absolutely faithful to every detail of the look, feel, and design of the user interface objects.

The need for faithfulness of conversion in the second point just given is paramount. Details such as font size or location of a dialogue box have been finely honed through significant investment in iterative design and evaluation. These details are to be treated as sacrosanct and taken literally to an extreme; they are too valuable to risk being "lost in translation" at this point in the project.

One way that many practitioners get this result is to use a prototype that is a wireframe plus a visual comp "skin," a graphical appearance created by visual designers and often constrained to an exacting visual style guide dictating color choices (often with great precision down to the RGB increments), branding, and so on.

An important tool for capturing and communicating much of the interaction design detail is the custom project style guide (Chapter 9). Your project style guide, if maintained to capture detailed design decisions, can serve as a reference to enforce consistency in similar other designs and will go a long way toward preventing loss of details in the transition from one platform to another.

The need for UX and SE collaboration and respect

At this point of the overall project, the process requires even more collaboration across the UX–SE aisle. The UX people "own" the interaction design but not the software that implements it. It is a little like owning a home but not the land upon which it sits. The "hand-off" point is a serious nexus in the two lifecycles. As the hand-off occurs across the boundaries of the two domains, there is a tendency on both sides to think that full responsibility has passed from one team to another. But a successful hand-off has to be much more of a collaborative event. Both sides face the challenge of connecting the interaction design representations to existing software development processes.

UX interests are vested in the design, and SE interests are vested in what will become the implementation code. Mutual preservation of those interests demands careful collaboration, tempered with mutual respect (Chapter 23).

Do not think the UX team is now done

There are no standards governing the translation from prototype to product implementation. Because preserving quality user experience in the design is not in the purview of the SE people, the UX people have a strong responsibility to ensure that their interaction design comes through with fidelity. If the SE people are the sole interpreters of this process, there is no way to predict the assiduousness at the task.

There are important reasons why the UX team cannot just hand it off and walk away, confident that it is now entirely within the SE bailiwick. There are currently no major software development lifecycle concepts that include adequate support for including the UX lifecycle or its work products, such as interaction design specifications, as a serious part of the overall system development process.

The SE people do not have, and should not be expected to have, the UX skills and knowledge to interpret the interaction design specifications thoroughly and accurately enough to get a perfect translation to software requirements specifications. The SE people did not participate in the interaction requirements and design processes and, therefore, do not know its inner details, boundaries, and supporting rationale.

The SE people cannot know all of what is contained in and communicated by the prototype (as part of the interaction design specifications) without guidance from the UX people who created and refined it. Anyway, if your interaction design matriculates from prototype to implementation successfully, congratulations!

11.9 SOFTWARE TOOLS FOR PROTOTYPING

In a previous section we mentioned a hope for the future about tools that would allow us to replace paper prototypes with low-fidelity programmed prototypes, but with the same ease of building, modifying, and executing low-fidelity prototypes as we had in the paper medium. The human–computer interaction (HCI) research community has not been unaware of this need and has tried to address it over the years (Carey & Mason, 1989; Gutierrez, 1989; Hix & Schulman, 1991; Landay & Myers, 1995). However, the technical challenges of designing and building such a software tool have been steep. We are not there yet, but such a software tool would certainly be valuable.

In the 1990s, user interface management systems (UIMSs), broad tool suites for defining, implementing, and executing interaction designs and prototypes (Myers, 1989, 1993, 1995; Myers, Hudson, & Pausch, 2000), and software prototyping tools were hot topics. Hix and Schulman (1991) also did some work on software tool evaluation methods.

There were different and competing looks, feels, and interaction styles built into many of these tools, such as CUA (IBM), OpenLook (Next), Toolbook (Asymetrix), Altia design (Altia, Inc.), Delphi (Borlund), Visual Basic (Microsoft Windows), and Dreamweaver (from Macromedia, for Web-based interaction). Some were not available commercially but were developed by the organizations that used them (e.g., TAE Plus by NASA). And some tools depended on a variety of different "standards," such as OSF Motif, not to mention Windows vs. Macintosh.

Many of the first tools for prototyping of interactive systems required a great deal of programming. Thus, interaction designers lacking programming skills could not use them directly, and "compiling" a new design iteration into executable form could be lengthy, complex, and fraught with bugs. Because many of the early UIMSs had a strong connection to computer graphics, resulting prototypes could be very realistic and could exhibit rather complex graphical behavior.

Some tools were, and some still are, based on interpretable interface definitions of the design entered declaratively, possibly along with some behavior structuring code. The interpretive approach offered more speed and flexibility in accommodating changes but, because of early hardware limitations, almost always caused the prototype execution to suffer slow performance. As the ability to produce user interface façades advanced in the tools, provision was made to program or at least stub non-interface functionality, moving the technology slowly toward whole system prototypes.

There is still no single prototyping platform capable of facilitating rapid prototype construction while meeting requirements to simulate today's complex interaction paradigms. This has been a persistent problem in HCI, where the prototyping tools are always a little behind on the state of the art of interaction possibilities.

For example, in a study we conducted with eight student teams working on building a real-world software system, we observed a situation where the interaction designers in the team needed an autocomplete feature in a pull-down menu as a core feature of their prototype. But because they could not get autocompletion in a prototype without a database, the software engineers in the team ended up having to build the database to support this one interaction design feature.

That software investment could not be used in the product itself, however, because it was on the wrong platform. We have to keep repeating the difficult prototype programming it takes to provide the functional behaviors that are becoming expected in any interactive software system, such as log-in sequences, auto-completion functions, or data entry validation sequences. Nowadays more and more of these complex interaction patterns are being communicated using static or click-through wireframes. We hope the state of the art in prototyping tools will soon evolve to support such patterns more effectively.

11.9.1 Desiderata for Prototyping Tools

As we have said, prototyping tools so far have almost always shared the same downside: it takes too long to make changes, as even the smallest amount of programming distracts from the purpose of a low-fidelity prototype and, as the prototype grows in size, it becomes less amenable to changes. Therefore, we (especially the user interface software community) continue on a quest for the perfect software prototyping tool, among the desired features of which are:

- Fast and effortless changes
  - Ease on the order of that of paper prototypes: as natural as changing a paper prototype
  - Tool transparency: Needs so little focus on the software that it does not distract from the design and prototype building
  - Fast turnaround to executability so there is almost no wait before it can be executed again
- Non-programmer ease of prototype definition and use
  - Non-programmers must be able to define and modify design features
- Built-in common behaviors and access to large varieties of other behaviors via a library of plug-ins
  - Easily include realism of features and behavior commensurate with expectations for modern interaction styles
- Supports a wide variety of interaction styles and devices, including various pointing and selecting devices, touchscreens, speech/audio, tactile/haptic, and gesture

- Ease of creating and modifying links to various points within the interaction design (e.g., buttons, icons, and menu choices to particular screens) to simulate user navigational behavior
- Communication with external procedures and programs (e.g., calls, call-backs, data transfer) to include some functionality and additional application behavior
- Capability to import text, graphics, and other media from other sources
- Capability to export look and feel components for eventual transition to final product code

UX Evaluation Introduction

Objectives

After reading this chapter, you will:

1. Understand the difference between formative and summative evaluation and the strengths and limitations of each
2. Understand the difference between analytic and empirical methods
3. Understand the difference between rigorous and rapid methods
4. Know the strengths and weaknesses of various data collection techniques, such as critical incident identification, thinking aloud, and questionnaires
5. Distinguish evaluation techniques oriented toward usability and emotional impact
6. Understand the concept of the evaluator effect and its impact on evaluation results

12.1 INTRODUCTION

12.1.1 You Are Here

We begin each process chapter with a "you are here" picture of the chapter topic in the context of the overall Wheel lifecycle template; see Figure 12-1. This chapter is an introduction that will lead us into the types and parts of UX evaluation of the following chapters.

12.1.2 Evaluate with a Prototype on Your Own Terms

Users will evaluate the interaction design sooner or later, so why not have them do it sooner—working with your team, using the proper techniques, and under the appropriate conditions—or you can wait until it is in the field, where you cannot control the outcome—visualize bad rumors about your product and huge costs to fix the problems because you have already committed the design to software.

12.1.3 Measurability of User Experience

But can you evaluate usability or user experience? This may come as a surprise, but neither usability nor user experience is directly measurable. In fact, most interesting phenomenon, such as teaching and learning, share the same

Figure 12-1

You are here, at the evaluation activity in the context of the overall Wheel lifecycle template.

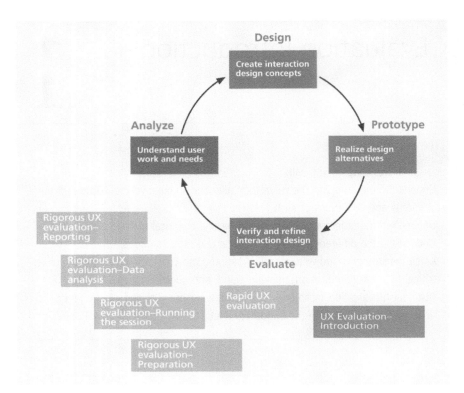

difficulty. So we resort to measuring things we *can* measure and use those measurements as *indicators* of our more abstract and less measurable notions.

For example, we can understand usability effects such as productivity or ease of use by measuring observable user performance-based *indicators* such as time to task completion and error counts. You can design a feature so that the performance of a certain task in a usability lab will yield a desirable objective measurement of, say, time on task. In almost any work context this translates to good user performance.

Questionnaires also provide indicators of user satisfaction from their answers to questions we think are closely related to satisfaction. Similarly, emotional impact factors such as user satisfaction and joy of use also cannot be measured directly but only through indirect indicators.

12.1.4 User Testing? No!

Before we get into the different types of evaluation, let us first calibrate our perspective on what we are testing here. Ask yourself honestly: Do you use the term "user testing?" If you do, you are not alone: the term appears in many books and papers on human–computer interaction (HCI) as it does in a large volume of online discussions and practitioner conversations.

You know what it means and we know what it means, but no user will like the idea of being tested and, thereby, possibly made to look ridiculous. No, we are not testing users, so let us not use those words. We might be testing or evaluating the design for usability or the full user experience it engenders in users, but *we are not testing the user*. We call it UX evaluation or even UX testing, but not "user testing!"

It might seem like a trivial PC issue, but it goes beyond being polite or "correct." When you are working with users, projecting the right attitude and making them comfortable in their role can make a big difference in how well they help you with evaluation. UX evaluation must be an ego-free process; you are improving designs, not judging users, designers, or developers.

We know of a case where users at a customer location were forced to play the user role for evaluation, but were so worried that it was a ruse to find candidates for layoffs and staff reductions that they were of no real value for the evaluation activities. If your user participants are employees of the customer organization, it is especially important to be sure they know you are not testing them. Your user participants should be made to feel they are part of a design process partnership.

12.2 FORMATIVE VS. SUMMATIVE EVALUATION

In simplest terms, formative evaluation helps you form the design and summative evaluation helps you sum up the design. A cute, but apropos, way to look at the difference: "When the cook tastes the soup, that's formative; when the guests taste the soup, that's summative" (Stake, 2004, p. 17).

The earliest reference to the terms formative evaluation and summative evaluation we know of stems from their use by Scriven (1967) in education and curriculum evaluation. Perhaps more well known is the follow-up usage by Dick and Carey (1978) in the area of instructional design. Williges (1984) and Carroll, Rosson, and Singley (1992) were among the first to use the terms in an HCI context.

Formative evaluation is primarily diagnostic; it is about collecting qualitative data to identify and fix UX problems and their causes in the design. *Summative evaluation* is about collecting quantitative data for assessing a level of quality due to a design, especially for assessing improvement in the user experience due to formative evaluation.

Qualitative Data

Qualitative data are non-numeric and descriptive data, usually describing a UX problem or issue observed or experienced during usage.

Quantitative Data

Quantitative data are numeric data, such as user performance metrics or opinion ratings.

Formal summative evaluation is typified by an empirical competitive benchmark study based on formal, rigorous experimental design aimed at comparing design hypothesis factors. Formal summative evaluation is a kind of controlled hypothesis testing with an m by n factorial design with y independent variables, the results of which are subjected to statistical tests for significance. Formal summative evaluation is an important HCI skill, but we do not cover it in this book.

Informal summative evaluation is used, as a partner of formative evaluation, for quantitatively summing up or assessing UX levels using metrics for user performance (such as the time on task), for example, as indicators of progress in UX improvement, usually in comparison with pre-established UX target levels (Chapter 10).

However, informal summative evaluation is done without experimental controls, with smaller numbers of user participants, and with only summary descriptive statistics (such as average values). We include informal summative evaluation in this book as a companion activity to formative evaluation.

12.2.1 Engineering Evaluation of UX: Formative Plus Informal Summative

Life is one big, long formative evaluation.

– Anonymous

Try as you might in the design phase, the first version of your interaction design is unlikely to be the best it can be in meeting your business goals of pleasing customers and your UX goals of pleasing users. Thus the reason for iteration and refinement cycles, to which evaluation is central.

You do not expect your first design to stand for long. Our friend and colleague, George Casaday calls it: "Waffle Wisdom" or "Pancake Philosophy"— like the first waffle or pancake, you expect from the start to throw away the first design, and maybe the next few. Formative evaluation is how you find out how to make the next ones better and better.

In UX engineering, formative UX evaluation includes any method that meets the definition of helping to form the design. Most, if not all, rapid UX evaluation methods (Chapter 13) have only a formative UX evaluation component and do not have a summative component. In lab-based UX testing sessions we also often use only formative evaluation, especially in early cycles of iteration when we are defining and refining the design and are not yet interested in performance numbers.

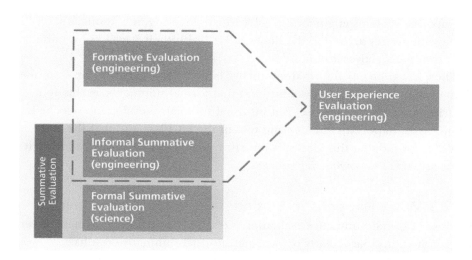

In rigorous UX evaluation we often add an informal summative evaluation component to formative evaluation, the combination being used to improve an interaction design and to assess how well it has been improved. We call this combination "UX engineering evaluation" or just "UX evaluation," as shown in Figure 12-2.

At the end of each iteration for a product version, the informal summative evaluation is used as a kind of acceptance test to compare with our UX targets and ensure that we meet our UX and business goals with the product design.

12.2.2 Engineering vs. Science

It's all very well in practice but it will never work in theory.

– French management saying

Sometimes empirical lab-based UX testing that includes quantitative metrics is the source of controversy with respect to "validity." Sometimes we hear "If you do not include formal summative evaluation, are you not missing an opportunity to add some science?" "Since your informal summative evaluation was not controlled testing, why should we not dismiss your results as too 'soft'?" "Your informal studies just are not good science. You cannot draw any conclusions."

These questions ignore the fundamental difference between formal and informal summative evaluation and the fact that they have completely different goals and methods. This may be due, in part, to the fact that the fields of HCI and UX were formed as a melting pot of people from widely varying backgrounds. From their own far-flung cultures in psychology, human factors engineering, systems engineering, software engineering, marketing, and management they arrived at the docks of HCI with their baggage containing their own perspectives and mind-sets.

Thus, it is known that formal summative evaluations are judged on a number of rigorous criteria, such as validity, and that formal summative evaluation contributes to our *science* base. But informal summative evaluation may be less known as an important engineering tool in the HCI bag and that the *only* criterion for judging this kind of summative evaluation method is whether it works as part of an *engineering* process.

12.2.3 What Happens in Engineering Stays in Engineering

Because informal summative evaluation is engineering, it comes with some very strict limitations, particularly on sharing informal summative results.

Informal summative evaluation results are only for internal use as engineering tools to do an engineering job by the project team and cannot be shared outside the team. Because of the lack of statistical rigor, these results especially cannot be used to make any claims inside or outside the team. To make claims about UX levels achieved, for example, from informal summative results, would be a violation of professional ethics.

We read of a case where a CEO of a company got a UX report from a project team, but discounted the results because they were not statistically significant. This problem could have been avoided by following our simple rules and not distributing formative evaluation reports outside the team or by writing the report with careful caveats.

But what if you are required to produce a formative evaluation report for consumption beyond the team or what if you need results to convince the team to fix the problems you find in a formative evaluation? We address those questions and more in Chapter 17, evaluation reporting.

12.3 TYPES OF FORMATIVE AND INFORMAL SUMMATIVE EVALUATION METHODS

12.3.1 Dimensions for Classifying Formative UX Evaluation Methods

In practice, there are two orthogonal dimensions for classifying types of formative UX evaluation methods:

- empirical method vs. analytic method
- rigorous method vs. rapid method

12.3.2 Rigorous Method vs. Rapid Method

Formative UX evaluation methods can be either rigorous or rapid. We define rigorous UX evaluation methods to be those methods that maximize effectiveness and minimize the risk of errors regardless of speed or cost, meaning to refrain from shortcuts or abridgements.

Rigorous empirical UX evaluation methods entail a full process of preparation, data collection, data analysis, and reporting (Chapters 12 and 14 through 18). In practical terms, this kind of rigorous evaluation is usually conducted in the UX lab. Similarly, the same kind of evaluation can be conducted at the customer's location in the field.

Rigorous empirical methods such as lab-based evaluation, while certainly not perfect, are the yardstick by which other evaluation methods are compared. Rigorous and rapid methods exist mainly as quality vs. cost trade-offs.

> ### Ecological Validity
>
> Ecological validity refers to the realism with which a design of evaluation setup matches the user's real work context. It is about how accurately the design or evaluation reflects the relevant characteristics of the ecology of interaction, i.e., its context in the world or its environment.

- Choose a rigorous empirical method such as lab-based testing when you need effectiveness and thoroughness, but expect it to be more expensive and time-consuming.
- Choose the lab-based method to assess quantitative UX measures and metrics, such as time-on-task and error rates, as indications of how well the user does in a performance-oriented context.
- Choose lab-based testing if you need a controlled environment to limit distractions.
- Choose empirical testing in the field if you need more realistic usage conditions for ecological validity than you can establish in a lab.

However, UX evaluation methods can be faster and less expensive.

- Choose a rapid evaluation method for speed and cost savings, but expect it to be (possibly acceptably) less effective.
- Choose a rapid UX evaluation method for early stages of progress, when things are changing a lot, anyway, and investing in detailed evaluation is not warranted.
- Choose a rapid method, such as a design walkthrough, an informal demonstration of design concepts, as a platform for getting initial reactions and early feedback from the rest of the design team, customers, and potential users.

12.3.3 Analytic Method vs. Empirical Method

On a dimension orthogonal to rapid vs. rigorous, formative UX evaluation methods can be either empirical or analytic (Hix & Hartson, 1993; Hartson, Andre, & Williges, 2003). Empirical methods employ data observed in the performance of real user participants, usually data collected in lab-based testing.

Analytical methods are based on looking at inherent attributes of the design rather than seeing the design in use. Many of the rapid UX evaluation methods (Chapter 13), such as design walkthroughs and UX inspection methods, are analytic methods.

Some methods in practice are a mix of analytical and empirical. For example, expert UX inspection can involve "simulated empirical" aspects in which the expert plays the role of the users, simultaneously performing tasks and "observing" UX problems.

Empirical methods are sometimes called "payoff methods" (Carroll, Singley, & Rosson, 1992; Scriven, 1967) because they are based on how a design or design change pays off in terms of real observable usage. Examples of the kind of data collected in empirical methods include quantitative user performance data, such as time on task and error rates, and qualitative user data derived from usage observation, such as UX problem data stemming from critical incident identification and think-aloud remarks by user participants. Analytical methods are sometimes called "intrinsic methods" because they are based on analyzing intrinsic characteristics of the design rather than seeing the design in use.

In describing the distinction between payoff and intrinsic approaches to evaluation, Scriven wrote an oft-quoted (Carroll, Singley, & Rosson, 1992; Gray & Salzman, 1998, p. 215) analogy featuring an axe (Scriven, 1967, p. 53): "If you want to evaluate a tool, say an axe, you might study the design of the bit, the weight distribution, the steel alloy used, the grade of hickory in the handle, etc., or you might just study the kind and speed of the cuts it makes in the hands of a good axeman," speaking of intrinsic and payoff evaluation, respectively. In Hartson, Andre, and Williges (2003) we added our own embellishments, which we paraphrase here.

Although this example served Scriven's purpose well, it also offers us a chance to make a point about the need to identify UX goals carefully before establishing evaluation criteria. Giving a UX perspective to the axe example, we note that user performance observation in payoff evaluation does not necessarily require an *expert* axeman (or axeperson). Expert usage might be one component of the vision in axe design, but it is not an exclusive requirement in payoff evaluation. UX goals depend on expected user classes of key work roles and the expected kind of usage.

For example, an axe design that gives optimum performance in the hands of an expert might be too dangerous for a novice user. For the weekend wood whacker, safety might be a UX goal that transcends firewood production, calling for a safer design that might necessarily sacrifice some efficiency. One hesitates to contemplate the metric for this case, possibly counting the number of 911 calls from a cellphone in the woods near Newport, Virginia, or the number of visits to the ER. Analogously, UX goals for a novice user of a software accounting system (e.g., TurboTax), for example, might place ease of use and data integrity (error avoidance) above sheer expert productivity.

Emotional impact factors can also be evaluated analytically. For example, a new axe in the hands of an expert might elicit an emotional response. Perhaps the axe head is made of repurposed steel from the World Trade Center—what patriotic and emotional impact that could afford! A beautiful, gleaming polished steel head, a gorgeously finished hickory wood handle, and a fine leather scabbard could elicit a strong admiration of the craftsmanship and aesthetics, as well as great pride of ownership.

Emotional impact factors can also be evaluated empirically. One need only observe the joy of use of a finely made, exquisitely sharpened axe. In a kind of think-aloud technique, the user exclaims with pleasure about the perfect balance as he or she hits the "sweet spot" with every fast-cutting stroke.

12.3.4 Where the Dimensions Intersect

Some example UX evaluation methods are shown in Figure 12-3 at the various intersections between the two dimensions empirical vs. analytic and rigorous vs. rapid.

We usually associate the rigorous empirical category with lab-based evaluation (Chapters 14 through 17), but empirical UX evaluation in a conference room or field setting can also be rigorous. The rapid evaluation methods (Chapter 13) are mostly analytic methods but at least one rapid empirical method (RITE) exists, designed to pick the low-hanging fruit at relatively low cost.

In addition, most practitioners in the field have their own versions of the lab-based method that might qualify as rapid because of severe abridgements but also still qualify as empirical because they involve data collection using participants. Rigorous analytic methods are beyond the scope of this book.

Figure 12-3

Sample UX evaluation methods at intersections between the dimensions of UX evaluation method types.

12.4 TYPES OF EVALUATION DATA

Fundamentally, UX data can be objective or subjective and it can be quantitative or qualitative. Because the two dimensions are orthogonal, you can see all four combinations,

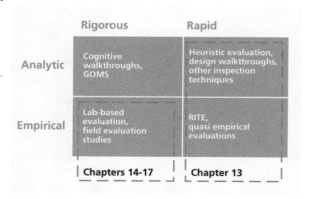

	Rigorous	Rapid
Analytic	Cognitive walkthroughs, GOMS	Heuristic evaluation, design walkthroughs, other inspection techniques
Empirical	Lab-based evaluation, field evaluation studies	RITE, quasi empirical evaluations
	Chapters 14-17	Chapter 13

objective and quantitative, subjective and quantitative, and so forth. When your rigorous evaluation is driven by benchmark tasks, the kinds of data collected in the process will mirror what is specified in UX targets and metrics.

12.4.1 Objective Data vs. Subjective Data

Objective UX data are data observed directly by either the evaluator or the participant. Subjective UX data represent opinions, judgments, and other subjective feedback usually from the user, concerning the user experience and satisfaction with the interaction design.

12.4.2 Quantitative Data vs. Qualitative Data

Quantitative data are numeric data, such as data obtained by user performance metrics or opinion ratings. Quantitative data are the basis of an informal summative evaluation component and help the team assess UX achievements and monitor convergence toward UX targets, usually in comparison with the specified levels set in the UX targets (Chapter 10). The two main kinds of quantitative data collected most often in formative evaluation are objective user performance data measured using benchmark tasks (Chapter 10) and subjective user-opinion data measured using questionnaires (coming up later).

Qualitative data are non-numeric and descriptive data, usually describing a UX problem or issue observed or experienced during usage. Qualitative data are usually collected via critical incident (also coming up later) and/or the think-aloud technique (see later) and are the key to identifying UX problems and their causes. Both objective and subjective data can be either qualitative or quantitative.

12.5 SOME DATA COLLECTION TECHNIQUES

12.5.1 Critical Incident Identification

The key objective of formative evaluation is to identify defects in the interaction design so that we can fix them. But during an evaluation session, you cannot always see the interaction design flaws directly. What we can observe directly or indirectly are the effects of those design flaws on the users. We refer to such effects on the users during interaction as critical incidents. Much of the attention of evaluators in evaluation sessions observing usage is spent looking for and identifying critical incidents.

Critical incidents

Despite numerous variations in procedures for gathering and analyzing critical incidents, researchers and practitioners agree about the definition of a critical incident. A critical incident is an event observed within task performance that is a significant indicator of some factor defining the objective of the study (Anderssona & Nilsson, 1964).

In the UX literature (Castillo & Hartson, 2000; del Galdo, et al., 1986), critical incidents are indicators of "something notable" about usability or the user experience. Sometimes that notable indication is about something good in the user experience, but the way we usually use it is as an indicator of things that go wrong in the stream of interaction details, indicators of UX problems or features that should be considered for redesign.

The best kind of critical incident data are detailed, observed during usage, and associated closely with specific task performance. The biggest reason why lab-based UX testing is effective is that it captures exactly that kind of detailed usage data as it occurs.

Critical incidents are observed directly by the facilitator or other observers and are sometimes expressed by the user participant. Some evaluators wait for an obvious user error or task breakdown to record as a critical incident. But an experienced facilitator can observe a user hesitation, a participant comment in passing, a head shaking, a slight shrugging of the shoulders, or drumming of fingers on the table. A timely facilitator request for clarification might help determine if any of these subtle observations should be considered a symptom of a UX problem.

Critical incident data about a UX problem should contain as much detail as possible, including contextual information, such as:

- the user's general activity or task
- objects or artifacts involved
- the specific user intention and action that led immediately to the critical incident
- expectations of the user about what the system was supposed to do when the critical incident occurred
- what happened instead
- as much as possible about the mental and emotional state of the user
- indication of whether the user could recover from the critical incident and, if so, a description of how the user did so
- additional comments or suggested solutions to the problem

Relevance of critical incident data

Critical incident identification is arguably the single most important source of qualitative data in formative evaluation. These detailed data, perishable if not captured immediately and precisely as they arise during usage, are essential for isolating specific UX problems within the user interaction design.

History of critical incident data

The origins of the critical incident technique can be traced back at least to studies performed in the Aviation Psychology Program of the U.S. Army Air Forces in World War II to analyze and classify pilot error experiences in reading and interpreting aircraft instruments. The technique was first formally codified by the work of Fitts and Jones (1947). Flanagan (1954) synthesized the landmark critical incident technique.

Mostly used as a variation

When Flanagan designed the critical incident technique in 1954, he did not see it as a single rigid procedure. He was in favor of modifying this technique to meet different needs as long as original criteria were met. The variation occurring over the years, however, may have been more than Flanagan anticipated. Forty years after the introduction of Flanagan's critical incident technique, Shattuck and Woods (1994) reported a study that revealed that this technique has rarely been used as originally published. In fact, numerous variations of the method were found, each suited to a particular field of interest. In HCI, we have continued this tradition of adaptation by using our own version of the critical incident technique as a primary UX evaluation technique to identify UX problems and their causes.

Critical incident reporting tools

Human factors and human–computer interaction researchers have developed software tools to assist identifying and recording critical incident information. del Galdo et al. (1986) investigated the use of critical incidents as a mechanism to collect end-user reactions for simultaneous design and evaluation of both online and hard-copy documentation. As part of this work, del Galdo et al. (1986) designed a software tool to collect critical incidents from user subjects.

Who identifies critical incidents?

One factor in the variability of the critical incident technique is the issue of who makes the critical incident identification. In the original work by Fitts and Jones (1947), the user (an airplane pilot) reported the critical incidents after task performance was completed. Flanagan (1954) used trained observers to collect critical incident information while observing users performing tasks.

del Galdo et al. (1986) involved users in identifying their own critical incidents, reporting during task performance. The technique was also used as a self-reporting mechanism by Hartson and Castillo (1998, 2000) as the basis for remote system or product usability evaluation. Further, Dzida, Wiethoff, and Arnold (1993) and Koenemann-Belliveau et al. (1994) adopted the stance that identifying critical incidents during task performance can be an individual process by either the user or an evaluator or a mutual process between the user and an evaluator.

Timing of critical incident data capture: The evaluator's awareness zone

While users are known to report major UX problems in alpha and beta testing (sending software out for comments on how well it worked), one reason these methods cannot be relied upon for thorough identification of UX problems to fix is the retrospective nature of that kind of data collection. Lab-based UX evaluation has the advantage of having the precious and volatile details right in front of you as they happen. The key to this kind of UX data is in the details, and details of these data are perishable; they must be captured immediately as they arise during usage.

As a result, do not lose this advantage; capture and document the details while they are fresh (and not just by letting the video recorder run). If you capture them as they happen, we call it concurrent data capture. If you capture data immediately after the task, we call it contemporaneous data capture. If you try to capture data after the task is well over, through someone trying to remember the details in an interview or survey after the session, this is retrospective data capture and many of the once-fresh details can be lost.

It is not as easy, however, as just capturing critical incident data immediately upon its occurrence. A critical incident is often not immediately recognized for what it is. In Figure 12-4, the evaluator's recognition of a critical incident will

Figure 12-4

Critical incident description detail vs. time after critical incident.

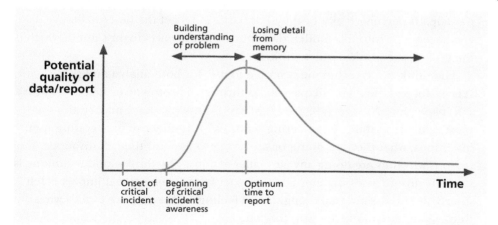

necessarily occur sometime after it begins to occur. And following the point of initial awareness, after confirming that it is a critical incident, the evaluator requires some time and thought in a kind of "awareness zone" to develop an understanding of the problem, possibly through discussion with the participant.

The optimum time to report the problem, the time when the potential for a quality problem report is highest, is at the peak of this problem understanding, as seen in Figure 12-4. Before that point, the evaluator has not yet established a full understanding of the problem. After that optimum point, natural abstraction due to human memory limitations sets in and details drop off rapidly with time, accelerated by proactive interference from any intervening tasks.

12.5.2 The Think-Aloud Technique

Also called "think-aloud protocol" or "verbal protocol," the think-aloud technique is a qualitative data collection technique in which user participants, as the name implies, express verbally their thoughts about their interaction experience, including their motives, rationale, and perceptions of UX problems. By this method, participants let us in on their thinking, giving us access to a precious understanding of their perspective of the task and the interaction design, their expectations, strategies, biases, likes, and dislikes.

Why use the think-aloud technique?

General observational data are important during an evaluation session with a participant attempting to perform a task. You can see what parts of a task the user is having trouble with, you can see hesitations about using certain widgets, and so on. But the bulk of real UX problem data is hidden from observation, in the mind of the participant. What is really causing a hesitation and why does this participant perceive it as a problem or barrier? To get the best qualitative data, you have to tap into this hidden data, buried in the participant's mind, which is the goal of the think-aloud technique.

The think-aloud technique is simple to use, for both analyst and participant. It is useful for when a participant walks through a prototype or helps you with a UX inspection. Nielsen (1993, p. 195) says "thinking aloud may be the single most valuable usability engineering method." It is effective in accessing user intentions, what they are doing or are trying to do, and their motivations, the reasons why they are doing any particular actions. The think-aloud technique is also effective in assessing emotional impact because emotional impact is felt internally and the internal thoughts and feelings of the user are exactly what the think-aloud technique accesses for you.

The think-aloud technique can be used in both rigorous empirical methods (lab-based) and rapid empirical methods (quasi-empirical and RITE)—that is, any UX evaluation method that involves a user "participant." Variations of this simple technique are rooted in psychological and human factors experimentation well before it was used in usability engineering (Lewis, 1982).

What kind of participant works best?

Some participants can talk while working; get them if you can. The usual participant for think-aloud techniques is someone who matches the work role and user class definitions associated with the tasks you will use to drive the evaluation. This kind of participant will not be trained as a UX practitioner, but that usually will not deter them from offering opinions and theories about UX problems and causes in your design, which is what you want.

You must remember, however, that it is *your* job to accept their comments as inputs to your process and it is still up to you to filter and interpret all think-aloud data in the context of your design. Participants and think-aloud techniques are not a substitute for you doing your job.

So, if think-aloud participants are not typically trained UX practitioners, what about using participants who are? You can use trained UX practitioners as participants, if they are not stakeholders in your project. They will give a different perspective on your design, often reflecting a better and deeper understanding and analysis. But their analysis may not be accurate from a work-domain or task perspective, so you are still responsible for filtering and interpreting their comments.

Is thinking aloud natural for participants?

It depends on the participant. Some people find it natural to talk while they work. Some people are able and only too willing to share their thoughts while working or while doing anything. Others are naturally quiet or contemplative and must be prompted to verbalize their thoughts as they work.

Some people, in the cannot-walk-and-chew-gum category, have difficulty expressing themselves while performing a physical task—activities that require help from different parts of the brain. For these people, you should slow things down and let them "rest" and talk only between actions. Even the most loquacious of participants at times will need prompting, "what are you thinking about?" or "what do you think you should do next?"

Also, sometimes participants ask questions, such as "what if I click on this?," to which your reply should encourage them to think it through themselves, "what do you think will happen?" When an interaction sequence leads a participant to surprise, confusion, or bewilderment—even fleetingly—ask them, "was that what you expected?" or "what *did* you expect?"

How to manage the think-aloud protocol?

The think-aloud technique is intended to draw out cognitive activity, not to confirm observable behavior. Therefore, your instructions to participants should emphasize telling you what they are thinking, not describing what they are doing. You want them to tell you why they are taking the actions that you can observe.

Once your participants get into thinking aloud, they may tend to keep the content at a chatty conversational level. You may need to encourage them to get past the "it is fine" stage and get down into real engagement and introspection. And sometimes you have to make an effort to keep the think-aloud comments flowing; some participants will not naturally maintain thinking aloud while they work and will have to be prodded gently.

Seeing a participant sit there silently struggling with an unknown problem tells us nothing about the problem or the design. Because we are trying to extract as much qualitative data as possible from each participant, elicitation of participant thoughts is a valuable facilitator skill. You might even consider a brief practice lesson on thinking aloud with each participant before you start the session itself.

Retrospective think-aloud techniques

If, as facilitator, you perceive that the think-aloud technique, when used concurrently with task performance, is interfering in some way with task performance or task measurements, you can wait until after task completion (hence the name "retrospective") and review a video recording of the session with the participant, asking for more complete "thinking aloud" during this review of his or her own task performance. In this kind of retrospective think-aloud technique, the participant is acting less as a task performer and more as an observer and outside "commentator," but with detailed inside information. The audio of this verbal review can be recorded on a second track in synchronism with the video, for even further later analysis, if necessary.

This approach has the advantage of capturing the maximum amount of think-aloud data but has the obvious downside of requiring a total of at least twice as much time as just the session itself. It also suffers from the time lag after the actual events. While better than a retrospective review even later, some details will already be fading from the participant's memory.

Co-discovery think-aloud techniques

Using a single participant is the dominant paradigm in usability and UX testing literature. Single users often represent typical usage and you want to be sure that single users can work their way through the tasks. However, you may also wish to try the increasingly common practice of using two or more participants in a team approach, a technique that originated with O'Malley, Draper, and Riley (1984). Kennedy (1989) named it "co-discovery" and that name has stuck.

While it can seem unnatural and inhibiting for a lone participant to be thinking aloud, essentially talking to oneself, there is more ease in talking in a natural conversation with another person (Wildman, 1995). A single individual participant can have trouble remembering to verbalize, but it is just natural with a partner. When the other person is also verbalizing in a problem-solving context, it amounts to a real and natural conversation, making this approach increasingly popular with practitioners and organizations.

Hackman and Biers (1992) found that multiple participants, while slightly more expensive, resulted in more time spent in verbalizing and, more importantly, participant teams spent more time verbalizing statements that had high value as feedback for designers.

Co-discovery is an especially good method for early low-fidelity prototypes; it gets you more viewpoints. And there is less need for the facilitator to interact, intervene, or give hints. The participants ask each other the questions and give themselves the guidance and prodding. When one participant gets stuck, the other can suggest things to try. When two people act as a real team, they are more willing to try new things and less intimidated than if they had been working solo.

Co-discovery pays off best when their thinking aloud becomes an interactive conversation between the participants, but this can produce qualitative data at a prodigious rate, at times more than twice as fast as from one participant. Two co-participants can bounce thoughts and comments back and forth. You may have to switch from zone defense, where each data collector does their best to catch what comes their way, to a person-to-person arrangement where each data collector is assigned to focus on comments by just one of the participants. This is where video capture makes for a good back-up to review selectively if you think you might have missed something.

There are many ways for a co-discovery session to play out. The scenarios often depend on participant personalities and who takes the lead. You should let them take turns at driving; both still have to pay attention. In cases where one participant has a dominant personality to the point where that person wants to run things and perhaps thinks he or she knows it all, try to get the other participant to drive as much as possible, to give them some control. If one person seems to drift off and lose attention or interest, you may have to use the usual techniques for getting school children re-engaged in an activity, "Johnny, what do *you* think about that problem?"

Finally, as a very practical bonus from planning a co-discovery session, if one participant does not show up, you can still do the session. You avoid the cost of an idle slot in the lab and having to reschedule.

Does thinking aloud affect quantitative task performance metrics in lab-based evaluation?

It depends on the participant. Some participants can naturally chat about what they are doing as they work. For these participants, the concurrent think-aloud technique usually does not affect task performance when used with measured benchmark tasks.

This is especially true if the participant is just thinking aloud and not engaged with questions and answers by the facilitator. But for some participants, the think-aloud protocol does affect task performance. This is especially true for non-native speakers because their verbalizations just take longer.

12.5.3 Questionnaires

A questionnaire is the primary instrument for collecting subjective data from participants in all types of evaluations. It can be used to supplement objective (directly observable) data from lab-based or other data collection methods or as an evaluation method on its own. A questionnaire can contain probing questions about the total user experience. Although post-session questionnaires have been used primarily to assess user satisfaction, they can also contain effective questions oriented specifically toward evaluating broader emotional impact and usefulness of the design.

Questionnaires are a self-reporting data collection technique and, as Shih and Liu (2007) say, semantic differential questionnaires (see next section) are used most commonly because they are a product-independent method that can yield reliable quantitative subjective data. This kind of questionnaire is inexpensive to administer but requires skill to produce so that data are valid and reliable.

In the days of traditional usability, questionnaires were used mostly to assess self-reported user satisfaction. And they were "seen as a poor cousin to [measures of] efficiency" (Winograd & Flores, 1986), but Lund (2001, 2004), points out that subjective metrics, such as the kind one gets from questionnaire results, are often effective at getting at the core of the user experience and can access "aspects of the user experience that are most closely tied to user behavior and purchase decisions."

Semantic differential scales

A semantic differential scale, or Likert scale (1932), is a range of values describing an attribute. Each value on the scale represents a different level of that attribute. The most extreme value in each direction on the scale is called an anchor. The scale is then divided, usually in equal divisions, with points between the anchors that divide up the difference between the meanings of the two anchors.

The number of discrete points we have on the scale between and including the anchors is the granularity of the scale, or the number of choices we allow users in expressing their own levels of the attribute. The most typical labeling of a point on a scale is a verbal label with an associated numeric value but it can also be pictorial.

For example, consider the following statement for which we wish to get an assessment of agreement by the user: "The checkout process on this Website was easy to use." A corresponding semantic differential scale for the "agreement" attribute to assess the user's level of agreement might have these anchors: strongly agree and strongly disagree. If the scale has five values, including the anchors, there are three points on the scale between the anchors. For example, the agreement scale might include strongly agree, agree, neutral, disagree, and strongly disagree with the associated values, respectively, of $+2, +1, 0, -1,$ and -2.

The Questionnaire for User Interface Satisfaction (QUIS)

The QUIS, developed at the University of Maryland (Chin, Diehl, & Norman, 1988) is one of the earliest available user satisfaction questionnaires for use with usability evaluation. It was the most extensive and most thoroughly validated questionnaire at the time of its development for determining subjective interaction design usability.

The QUIS is organized around such general categories as *screen, terminology and system information, learning,* and *system capabilities.* Within each of these general categories are sets of questions about detailed features, with Likert scales from which a participant chooses a rating. It also elicits some demographic information, as well as general user comments about the interaction design being evaluated. Many practitioners supplement the QUIS with some of their own questions, specific to the interaction design being evaluated.

The original QUIS had 27 questions (Tullis & Stetson, 2004), but there have been many extensions and variations. Although developed originally for screen-based designs, the QUIS is resilient and can be extended easily, for example, by replacing the term "system" with "Website" and "screen" with "Web page."

Practitioners are free to use the results of a QUIS questionnaire in any reasonable way. In much of our use of this instrument, we calculated the average scores, averaged over all the participants and all the questions in a specified subset of the questionnaire. Each such subset was selected to correspond to the goal of a UX target, and the numeric value of this score averaged over the subset of questions was compared to the target performance values stated in the UX target table.

Although the QUIS is quite thorough, it can be administered in a relatively short time. For many years, a subset of the QUIS was our own choice as the questionnaire to use in both teaching and consulting.

The QUIS is still being updated and maintained and can be licensed[1] for a modest fee from the University of Maryland Office of Technology Liaison. In Table 12-1 we show a sample excerpted and adapted with permission from the QUIS with fairly general applicability, at least to desktop applications.

---

[1]http://lap.umd.edu/quis/

Table 12-1

An excerpt from QUIS, with permission

User Evaluation of Interactive Computer Systems

For each question, please circle the number that most appropriately reflects your impressions about this topic with respect to using this computer system or product.

1. Terminology relates to task domain	[distantly]	0 1 2 3 4 5 6 7 8 9 10	[closely] NA
2. Instructions describing tasks	[confusing]	0 1 2 3 4 5 6 7 8 9 10	[clear] NA
3. Instructions are consistent	[never]	0 1 2 3 4 5 6 7 8 9 10	[always] NA
4. Operations relate to tasks	[distantly]	0 1 2 3 4 5 6 7 8 9 10	[closely] NA
5. Informative feedback	[never]	0 1 2 3 4 5 6 7 8 9 10	[always] NA
6. Display layouts simplify tasks	[never]	0 1 2 3 4 5 6 7 8 9 10	[always] NA
7. Sequence of displays	[confusing]	0 1 2 3 4 5 6 7 8 9 10	[clear] NA
8. Error messages are helpful	[never]	0 1 2 3 4 5 6 7 8 9 10	[always] NA
9. Error correction	[confusing]	0 1 2 3 4 5 6 7 8 9 10	[clear] NA
10. Learning the operation	[difficult]	0 1 2 3 4 5 6 7 8 9 10	[easy] NA
11. Human memory limitations	[overwhelmed]	0 1 2 3 4 5 6 7 8 9 10	[are respected] NA
12. Exploration of features	[discouraged]	0 1 2 3 4 5 6 7 8 9 10	[encouraged] NA
13. Overall reactions	[terrible]	0 1 2 3 4 5 6 7 8 9 10	[wonderful] NA
	[frustrating]	0 1 2 3 4 5 6 7 8 9 10	[satisfying] NA
	[uninteresting]	0 1 2 3 4 5 6 7 8 9 10	[interesting] NA
	[dull]	0 1 2 3 4 5 6 7 8 9 10	[stimulating] NA
	[difficult]	0 1 2 3 4 5 6 7 8 9 10	[easy] NA

The System Usability Scale (SUS)

The SUS was developed by John Brooke while at Digital Equipment Corporation (Brooke, 1996) in the United Kingdom. The SUS questionnaire contains 10 questions. As an interesting variation from the usual questionnaire, the SUS alternates positively worded questions with negatively worded questions to prevent quick answers without the responder really considering the questions.

The questions are presented as simple declarative statements, each with a five-point Likert scale anchored with "strongly disagree" and "strongly agree" and with values of 1 through 5. These 10 statements are (used with permission):

- I think that I would like to use this system frequently
- I found the system unnecessarily complex
- I thought the system was easy to use
- I think that I would need the support of a technical person to be able to use this system
- I found the various functions in this system were well integrated
- I thought there was too much inconsistency in this system
- I would imagine that most people would learn to use this system very quickly
- I found the system very cumbersome to use
- I felt very confident using the system
- I needed to learn a lot of things before I could get going with this system

The 10 items in the SUS were selected from a list of 50 possibilities, chosen for their perceived discriminating power.

The bottom line for the SUS is that it is robust, extensively used, widely adapted, and in the public domain. It has been a very popular questionnaire for complementing a usability testing session because it can be applied at any stage in the UX lifecycle and is intended for practical use in an industry context. The SUS is technology independent; can be used across a broad range of kinds of systems, products, and interaction styles; and is fast and easy for both analyst and participant. The single numeric score (see later) is easy to understand by everyone. Per Usability Net (2006), it is the most highly recommended of all the publically available questionnaires.

There is theoretical debate in the literature about the dimensionality of SUS scoring methods (Bangor, Kortum, & Miller, 2008; Borsci, Federici, & Lauriola, 2009; J. Lewis & Sauro, 2009). However, the practical bottom line for the SUS, regardless of these formal conclusions, is that the unidimensional approach to scoring of SUS (see later) has been working well for many practitioners over the years and is seen as a distinct advantage. The single score that this questionnaire yields is understood easily by almost everyone.

The analysis of SUS scores begins with calculating the single numeric score for the instance of the questionnaire marked up by a participant. First, for any unanswered items, assign a middle rating value of 3 so that it does not affect the outcome on either side.

Next we calculate the adjusted score for positively worded items. Because we want the range to begin with 0 (so that the overall score can range from 0), we shift the scores for positively worded items down by subtracting 1, giving us a new range of 0 to 4.

To calculate the adjusted score for negatively worded items, we must compensate for the fact that these scales go in the opposite direction of positively worded scales. We do this by giving the negatively worded items an adjusted score of 5 minus the rating value given, also a giving us a range of 0 to 4.

Next, add up the adjusted item scores for all 10 questions, giving a range of 0 to 40. Finally, multiply by 2.5 to get a final SUS score in the range of 0 to 100.

What about interpreting the SUS score? Often a numerical score yielded by any evaluation instrument is difficult to interpret by anyone outside the evaluation team, including project managers and the rest of your project team. Given a single number out of context, it is difficult to know what it means about the user experience. The score provided by the SUS questionnaire, however, has the distinct advantage of being in the range of zero to 100.

By using an analogy with numerical grading schemes in schools based on a range of 0 to 100, Bangor, Kortum, and Miller (2008) found it practical and feasible to extend the school grading interpretation of numeric scores into letter grades, by the usual 90 to 100 being an "A", and so on (using whatever numeric to letter grade mapping you wish). Although this translation has no theoretical or empirical basis, this simple notion does seem to be an effective way to communicate the results, and using a one-number score normalized to a base of 100 allows you even to compare systems that are dissimilar.

Clearly, an evaluation grade of "A" means it was good and an evaluation of "D" or lower means the need for some improvement is indicated. At the end of the day, each project team will have to decide what the SUS scores mean to them.

The Usefulness, Satisfaction, and Ease of Use (USE) Questionnaire

With the goal of measuring the most important dimensions of usability for users across many different domains, Lund (2001, 2004) developed USE, a questionnaire for evaluating the user experience on three dimensions:

usefulness, satisfaction, and ease of use. USE is based on a seven-point Likert scale.

Through a process of factor analysis and partial correlation, the questions in Table 12-2 were chosen for inclusion in USE per Lund. As the questionnaire is still under development, this set of questions is a bit of a moving target.

The bottom line for USE is that it is widely applicable, for example, to systems, products, and Websites, and has been used successfully. It is available in the public domain and has good face validity for both users and practitioners, that is, it looks right intuitively and people agree that it should work.

Other questionnaires

Here are some other questionnaires that are beyond our scope but might be of interest to some readers.

		Table 12-2
Usefulness	It helps me be more effective.	
	It helps me be more productive.	*Questions in USE*
	It is useful.	*questionnaire*
	It gives me more control over the activities in my life.	
	It makes the things I want to accomplish easier to get done.	
	It saves me time when I use it.	
	It meets my needs.	
	It does everything I would expect it to do.	
Ease of use	It is easy to use.	
	It is simple to use.	
	It is user-friendly.	
	It requires the fewest steps possible to accomplish what I want to do with it.	
	It is flexible.	
	Using it is effortless.	
	I can use it without written instructions.	
	I do not notice any inconsistencies as I use it.	
	Both occasional and regular users would like it.	
	I can recover from mistakes quickly and easily.	
	I can use it successfully every time.	
Ease of learning	I learned to use it quickly.	
	I easily remember how to use it.	
	It is easy to learn to use it.	
	I quickly became skillful with it.	
Satisfaction	I am satisfied with it.	
	I would recommend it to a friend.	
	It is fun to use.	
	It works the way I want it to work.	
	It is wonderful.	
	I feel I need to have it.	
	It is pleasant to use.	

General-purpose usability questionnaires:

- ■ Computer System Usability Questionnaire (CSUQ), developed by Jim Lewis (1995, 2002) at IBM, is well-regarded and available in the public domain.
- ■ Software Usability Measurement Inventory (SUMI) is "a rigorously tested and proven method of measuring software quality from the end user's point of view" (Human Factor Research Group, 1990).[2] According to Usability Net,[3] SUMI is "a mature questionnaire whose standardization base and manual have been regularly updated." It is applicable to a range of application types from desk-top applications to large domain-complex applications.
- ■ After Scenario Questionnaire (ASQ), developed by IBM, is available in the public domain (Bangor, Kortum, & Miller, 2008, p. 575).
- ■ Post-Study System Usability Questionnaire (PSSUQ), developed by IBM, is available in the public domain (Bangor, Kortum, & Miller, 2008, p. 575).

Web evaluation questionnaires:

- ■ Website Analysis and MeasureMent Inventory (WAMMI) is "a short but very reliable questionnaire that tells you what your visitors think about your web site" (Human Factor Research Group, 1996b).

Multimedia system evaluation questionnaires:

- ■ Measuring the Usability of Multi-Media Systems (MUMMS) is a questionnaire "designed for evaluating quality of use of multimedia software products" (Human Factor Research Group, 1996a).

Hedonic quality evaluation questionnaires:

- ■ The Lavie and Tractinsky (2004) questionnaire
- ■ The Kim and Moon (1998) questionnaire with differential emotions scale

Modifying questionnaires for your evaluation

As an example of adapting a data collection technique, you can make up a questionnaire of your own or you can modify an existing questionnaire for your own use by:

- ■ choosing a subset of the questions
- ■ changing the wording in some of the questions
- ■ adding questions of your own to address specific areas of concern
- ■ using different scale values

---

[2]Human Factors Research Group (http://www.ucc.ie/hfrg/) questionnaires are available commercially as a service, on a per report basis or for purchase, including scoring and report-generating software.
[3]http://www.usabilitynet.org/tools/r_questionnaire.htm

comprehensive list of verbal and non-verbal behaviors to be noted during observation, see Tullis and Albert (2008, p. 170).

Indicators of emotional impact are usually either self-reported via verbal techniques, such as questionnaires, or physiological responses observed and measured in participants with non-verbal techniques.

Self-reported indicators of emotional impact

While extreme reactions to a bad user experience can be easy to observe and understand, we suspect that the majority of emotional impact involving aesthetics, emotional values, and simple joy of use may be perceived and felt by the user but not necessarily by the evaluator or other practitioner. To access these emotional reactions, we must tap into the user's subjective feelings; one effective way to do that is to have the user or participant do the reporting. Thus, verbal participant self-reporting techniques are a primary way that we collect emotional impact indicators.

Participants can report on emotional impact within their usage experience during usage via their direct commentary collected with the think-aloud technique. The think-aloud technique is especially effective in accessing the emotional impact within user experience because users can describe their own feelings and emotional reactions and can explain their causes in the usage experience.

Questionnaires, primarily those using semantic differential scales, are also an effective and frequently used technique for collecting self-reported retrospective emotional impact data by surveying user opinions about specific predefined aspects of user experience, especially emotional impact.

Other self-reporting techniques include written diaries or logs describing emotional impact encounters within usage experience. As a perhaps more spontaneous alternative to written reports, participants can report these encounters via voice recorders or phone messages.

Being subjective, quantitative, and product independent, questionnaires as a self-reporting technique have the advantages of being easy to use for both practitioners and users, inexpensive, applicable from earliest design sketches and mockups to fully operational systems, and high in face validity, which means that intuitively they seem as though they should work (Westerman, Gardner, & Sutherland, 2006).

However, self-reporting can be subject to bias because human users cannot always access the relevant parts of their own emotions. Obviously, self-reporting techniques depend on the participant's ability for conscious awareness of subjective emotional states and to articulate the same in a report.

Questionnaires as a verbal self-reporting technique for collecting emotional impact data (AttrakDiff and others)

Questionnaires about emotional impact allow you to pose to participants probing questions based on any of the emotional impact factors, such as joy of use, fun, and aesthetics, offering a way for users to express their feelings about this part of the user experience.

AttrakDiff, developed by Hassenzahl, Burmester, and Koller (2003), is an example of a questionnaire especially developed for getting at user perceptions of emotional impact. AttrakDiff (now AttrakDiff2), based on Likert (semantic differential) scales, is aimed at evaluating both pragmatic (usability plus usefulness) and hedonic[4] (emotional impact) quality in a product or system.

Reasons for using the AttrakDiff questionnaire for UX data collection include the following:

- AttrakDiff is freely available.
- AttrakDiff is short and easy to administer, and the verbal scale is easy to understand (Hassenzahl, Beu, & Burmester, 2001; Hassenzahl, et al., 2000).
- AttrakDiff is backed with research and statistical validation. Although only the German-language version of AttrakDiff was validated, there is no reason to believe that the English version will not also be effective.
- AttrakDiff has a track record of successful application.

With permission, we show it in full in Table 12-3 as it appears in Hassenzahl, Schöbel, and Trautman (2008, Table 1).

Across the many versions of AttrakDiff that have been used and studied, there are broad variations in the number of questionnaire items, the questions used, and the language for expressing the questions (Hassenzahl et al., 2000). Table 12-4 contains a variation of AttrakDiff developed by Schrepp, Held, and Laugwitz (2006), shown here with permission.

For a description of using AttrakDiff in an affective evaluation of a music television channel, see Chorianoipoulos and Spinellis (2004).

Once an AttrakDiff questionnaire has been administered to participants, it is time to calculate the average scores. Begin by adding up all the values given by the participant, excluding all unanswered questions. If you used a numeric scale of 1 to 7 between the anchors for each question the total will be in the range of 1 to 7 times the number of questions the participant answered.

---

[4]"Hedonic" is a term used mainly in the European literature that means about the same as emotional impact.

Scale Item	Semantic Anchors	
Pragmatic Quality 1	Comprehensible	Incomprehensible
Pragmatic Quality 2	Supporting	Obstructing
Pragmatic Quality 3	Simple	Complex
Pragmatic Quality 4	Predictable	Unpredictable
Pragmatic Quality 5	Clear	Confusing
Pragmatic Quality 6	Trustworthy	Shady
Pragmatic Quality 7	Controllable	Uncontrollable
Hedonic Quality 1	Interesting	Boring
Hedonic Quality 2	Costly	Cheap
Hedonic Quality 3	Exciting	Dull
Hedonic Quality 4	Exclusive	Standard
Hedonic Quality 5	Impressive	Nondescript
Hedonic Quality 6	Original	Ordinary
Hedonic Quality 7	Innovative	Conservative
Appeal 1	Pleasant	Unpleasant
Appeal 2	Good	Bad
Appeal 3	Aesthetic	Unaesthetic
Appeal 4	Inviting	Rejecting
Appeal 5	Attractive	Unattractive
Appeal 6	Sympathetic	Unsympathetic
Appeal 7	Motivating	Discouraging
Appeal 8	Desirable	Undesirable

Table 12-3

AttrakDiff emotional impact questionnaire as listed by Hassenzahl, Schöbel, and Trautman (2008), with permission

For example, because there are 22 questions in the sample in Table 12-3, the total summed-up score will be in the range of 22 to 154 if all questions were answered. If you used a scale from -3 to $+3$ centered on zero, the range for the sum of 22 question scores would be -66 to $+66$. The final result for the questionnaire is the average score per question.

Modifying AttrakDiff. In applying the AttrakDiff questionnaire in your own project, you can first make a choice among the different existing versions of AttrakDiff. You can then choose how many of those questions or items, and which ones, you wish to have in your version.

Table 12-4

A variation of the AttrakDiff emotional impact questionnaire, as listed in Appendix A1 of Schrepp, Held, and Laugwitz (2006), reordered to group related items together, with permission

Scale	Item	English Anchor 1	English Anchor 2
Pragmatic quality	PQ1	People centric	Technical
Pragmatic quality	PQ2	Simple	Complex
Pragmatic quality	PQ3	Practical	Impractical
Pragmatic quality	PQ4	Cumbersome	Facile
Pragmatic quality	PQ5	Predictable	Unpredictable
Pragmatic quality	PQ6	Confusing	Clear
Pragmatic quality	PQ7	Unmanageable	Manageable
Hedonic – identity	HQI1	Isolates	Connects
Hedonic – identity	HQI2	Professional	Unprofessional
Hedonic – identity	HQI3	Stylish	Lacking style
Hedonic – identity	HQI4	Poor quality	High quality
Hedonic – identity	HQI5	Excludes	Draws you in
Hedonic – identity	HQI6	Brings me closer to people	Separates me from people
Hedonic – identity	HQI7	Not presentable	Presentable
Hedonic – stimulation	HQS1	Original	Conventional
Hedonic – stimulation	HQS2	Unimaginative	Creative
Hedonic – stimulation	HQS3	Bold	Cautious
Hedonic – stimulation	HQS4	Innovative	Conservative
Hedonic – stimulation	HQS5	Dull	Absorbing
Hedonic – stimulation	HQS6	Harmless	Challenging
Hedonic – stimulation	HQS7	Novel	Conventional
Attractiveness	ATT1	Pleasant	Unpleasant
Attractiveness	ATT2	Ugly	Pretty
Attractiveness	ATT3	Appealing	Unappealing
Attractiveness	ATT4	Rejecting	Inviting
Attractiveness	ATT5	Good	Bad
Attractiveness	ATT6	Repulsive	Pleasing
Attractiveness	ATT7	Motivating	Discouraging

You then need to review the word choices and terminology used for each of the anchors and decide on the words that you think will be understood most easily and universally. For example, you might find "Pretty – Ugly" of the Schrepp et al. (2006) version a better set of anchors than "Aesthetic –

Unaesthetic" of the Hassenzahl version or you may wish to add "Interesting – Boring" to "Exciting – Dull" as suggested in Hassenzahl, Beu, and Burmester (2001).

Note also that the questions in AttrakDiff (or any questionnaire) represent strictly operational definitions of pragmatic and hedonic quality, and because you may have missed some aspects of these measures that are important to you, you can add your own questions to address issues you think are missing.

Alternatives to AttrakDiff. As an alternative to the AttrakDiff questionnaire, Hassenzahl, Beu, and Burmester (2001) have created simple questionnaire of their own for evaluating emotional impact, also based on semantic differential scales. Their scales have the following easy-to-apply anchors (from their Figure 1):

- outstanding vs. second rate
- exclusive vs. standard
- impressive vs. nondescript
- unique vs. ordinary
- innovative vs. conservative
- exciting vs. dull
- interesting vs. boring

Like AttrakDiff, each scale in this questionnaire has seven possible ratings, including these end points, and the words were originally in German.

Verbal emotion measurement instruments, such as questionnaires, can assess mixed emotions because questions and scales in a questionnaire or images in pictorial tools can be made up to represent sets of emotions (Desmet, 2003). PrEmo, developed by Desmet, uses seven animated pictorial representations of pleasant emotions and seven unpleasant ones. Desmet concludes that "PrEmo is a satisfactory, reliable emotion measurement instrument in terms of applying it across cultures."

There is a limitation, however. Verbal instruments tend to be language dependent and, sometimes, culture dependent. For example, the vocabulary for different dimensions of a questionnaire and their end points are difficult to translate precisely. Pictorial tools can be the exception, as the language of pictures is more universal. Pictograms of facial expressions can sometimes express emotions elicited more effectively than verbal expression, but the question of how to draw the various pictograms most effectively is still an unresolved research challenge.

An example of another emotional impact measuring instrument is the Self-Assessment Manikin (SAM) (Bradley & Lang, 1994). SAM contains nine symbols indicating positive emotions and nine indicating negative emotions. Often used for Websites and print advertisements, the SAM is administered during or immediately after user interaction. One problem with application after usage is that emotions can be fleeting and perishable.

Observing physiological responses as indicators of emotional impact

In contrast to self-reporting techniques, UX practitioners can obtain emotional impact indicator data through monitoring of participant physiological responses to emotional impact encounters as usage occurs. Usage can be teeming with user behaviors, including facial expressions, such as ephemeral grimaces or smiles, and body language, such as tapping of fingers, fidgeting, or scratching one's head, that indicate emotional impact.

Physiological responses can be "captured" either by direct behavioral observation or by instrumented measurements. Behavioral observations include those of facial expressions, gestural behavior, and body posture.

The emotional "tells" of facial and bodily expressions can be fleeting and subliminal, easily missed in real-time observation. Therefore, to capture facial expressions data and other similar observational data reliably, practitioners usually need to make video recordings of participant usage behavior and do frame-by-frame analysis. Methods for interpreting facial expressions have been developed, including one called the Facial Action Coding System (Ekman & Friesen, 1975).

Kim et al. (2008) remind us that while we can measure physiological effects, it is difficult to connect the measurements with specific emotions and with causes within the interaction. Their solution is to supplement with traditional synchronized video-recording techniques to correlate measurements with usage occurrences and behavioral events. But this kind of video review has disadvantages: the reviewing process is usually tedious and time-consuming, you may need an analyst trained in identifying and interpreting these expressions often within a frame-by-frame analysis, and even a trained analyst cannot always make the right call.

Fortunately, software-assisted recognition of facial expressions and gestures in video images is beginning to be feasible for practical applications. Software tools are now becoming available to automate real-time recognition and interpretation of facial expressions. A system called "faceAPI"[5] from Seeing Machines is advertised to both track and understand faces. It comes as a software

---

[5]http://www.seeingmachines.com/product/faceapi/

module that you embed in your own product or application. An ordinary Webcam, focused on the user's face, feeds both faceAPI and any digital video-recording program with software-accessible time stamps and/or frame numbers.

Facial expressions do seem to be mostly culture independent, and you can capture expressions without interruption of the usage. However, there are limitations that generally preclude their use. The main limitation is that they are useful for only a limited set of basic emotions such as anger or happiness, but not mixed emotions. Dormann (2003) says it is, therefore, difficult to be precise about what kind of emotion is being observed.

In order to identify facial expressions, faceAPI must track the user's face during head movement that occurs in 3D with usage. The head-tracking feature outputs X, Y, Z position and head orientation coordinates for every video frame. The facial feature detection component of faceAPI tracks three points on each eyebrow and eight points around the lips.

The detection algorithm is "robust to occlusions, fast movements, large head rotations, lighting, facial deformation, skin color, beards, and glasses." This part of faceAPI outputs a real-time stream of facial feature data, time coordinated with the recorded video, that can be understood and interpreted via a suite of image-processing modules. The faceAPI system is a commercial product, but a free version is available to qualified users for non-commercial use.

Bio-metrics to detect physiological responses to emotional impact

The use of instrumented measurement of physiological responses in participants is called biometrics. Biometrics are about detection and measurement of autonomic or involuntary bodily changes triggered by nervous system responses to emotional impact within interaction events. Examples include changes in heart rate, respiration, perspiration, and eye pupil dilation. Changes in perspiration are measured by galvanic skin response measurements to detect changes in electrical conductivity.

Such nervous system changes can be correlated with emotional responses to interaction events. Pupillary dilation is an autonomous indication especially of interest, engagement, and excitement and is known to correlate with a number of emotional states (Tullis & Albert, 2008).

The downside of biometrics is the need for specialized monitoring equipment. If you can get some good measuring instruments and are trained to use them to get good measures, it does not get more "embodied" than this. But most equipment for measuring physiological changes is out of reach for the average UX practitioner.

It is possible to adapt a polygraph or lie detector, for example, to detect changes in pulse, respiration, and skin conductivity that could be correlated with emotional responses to interaction events. However, the operation of most of this equipment requires skills and experience in medical technology, and interpretation of raw data can require specialized training in psychology, all beyond our scope. Finally, the extent of culture independence of facial expressions and other physiological responses is not entirely known.

12.5.5 Data Collection Techniques to Evaluate Phenomenological Aspects of Interaction

Long-term studies required for phenomenological evaluation

Phenomenological aspects of interaction involve emotional impact, but emotional impact over time not emotional impact in snapshots of usage as you might be used to observing in other kinds of UX evaluation. The new perspective that the phenomenological view brings to user experience requires a new kind of evaluation (Thomas & Macredie, 2002).

Phenomenological usage is a longitudinal effect in which users invite the product into their lives, giving it a presence in daily activities. As an example of a product with presence on someone's life, we know someone who carries a digital voice recorder in his pocket everywhere he goes. He uses it to capture thoughts, notes, and reminders for just about everything. He keeps it at his bedside while sleeping and always has it in his car when driving. It is an essential in his lifestyle.

Thus, phenomenological usage is not about tasks but about human activities. Systems and products with phenomenological impact are understood through usage over time as users assimilate them into their lifestyles (Thomas & Macredie, 2002). Users build perceptions and judgment through exploration and learning as usage expands and emerges.

The timeline defining the user experience for this kind of usage starts even before first meeting the product, perhaps with the desire to own or use the product, researching the product and comparing similar products, visiting a store (physical or online), shopping for it, and beholding the packaging and product presentation. By the time long-term physiological studies are done, they really end up being case studies. The length of these studies does not necessarily mean large amounts of person-hours, but it can mean significant calendar time. Therefore, the technique will not fit with an agile method or any other approach based on a very short turnaround time.

It is clear that methods for studying and evaluating phenomenological aspects of interaction must be situated in the real activities of users to encounter a broad range of user experience occurring "in the wild." This means that you cannot just schedule a session, bring in user participants, have them "perform," and take your data. Rather, this deeper importance of context usually means collecting data in the field rather than in the lab.

The best raw phenomenological data would come from constant attention to the user and usage, but it is seldom, if ever, possible to live with a participant 24/7 and be in all the places that a busy life takes a participant. Even if you could be with the participant all the time, you would find that most of the time you will observe just dead time when nothing interesting or useful is happening or when the participants are not even using the product. When events of interest do happen, they tend to be episodic in bursts, requiring special techniques to capture phenomenological data.

But, in fact, the only ones who can be there all the times and places where usage occurs are the participants. Therefore, most of the phenomenological data collection techniques are self-reporting techniques or at least have self-reporting components—the participants themselves report on their own activities, thoughts, problems, and kinds of usage. Self-reporting techniques are not as objective as direct observation, but they do offer practical solutions to the problem of accessing data that occur in your absence.

These longer term user experience studies are, in some ways, similar to contextual inquiry and even approach traditional ethnography in that they require "living with the users." The Petersen, Madsen, and Kjaer (2002) study of two families' usage of TV sets over 4 to 6 months is a good example of a phenomenological study in the context of HCI and UX.

The iPod is an example of a device that illustrates how usage can expand over time. At first it might be mostly a novelty to play with and to show friends. Then the user will add some applications, let us say the *iBird Explorer: An Interactive Field Guide to Birds of North America.*[6] Suddenly usage is extended out to the deck and perhaps eventually into the woods. Then the user wants to consolidate devices by exporting contact information (address book) from an old PDA.

Finally, of course, the user will start loading it up with all kinds of music and books on audio. This latter usage activity, which might come along after several months of product ownership, could become the most fun and the most enjoyable part of the whole usage experience.

Goals of phenomenological data collection techniques

Regardless of which technique is used for phenomenological data collection, the objective is to look for occurrences within long-term usage that are indicators of:

---

[6] http://www.ibird.com/

- ways people tend to use the product
- high points of joy in use, revealing what it is in the design that yields joy of use and opportunities to make it even better
- problems and difficulties people have in usage that interfere with a high-quality user experience
- usage people want but is not supported by the product
- how the basic mode of usage changes, evolves, or emerges over time
- how usage is adapted; new and unusual kinds of usage people come up with on their own

The idea is to be able to tell stories of usage and emotional impact over time.

Diaries in situated longitudinal studies

In one kind of self-reporting technique, each participant maintains a "diary," documenting problems, experiences, and phenomenological occurrences within long-term usage. There are many ways to facilitate this kind of data capture within self-reporting, including:

- paper and pencil notes
- online reporting, such as in a blog
- cellphone voice-mail messages
- pocket digital voice recorder

We believe that the use of voice-mail diaries for self-reporting on usage has importance that goes well beyond mobile phone studies. In another study (Petersen, Madsen, & Kjaer, 2002), phone reporting proved more successful than paper diaries because it could occur in the moment and had a much lower incremental effort for the participant. The key to this success is readiness at hand.

A mobile phone is, well, very mobile and can be kept ready to use at all times. Participants do not need to carry paper forms and a pen or pencil and can make the calls any time day or night and under conditions not conducive to writing reports by hand. Cellphones keep users in control during reporting; they can control the amount of time they devote to each report.

As Palen and Salzman (2002) learned, the mobile phone voice-mail method of data collection over time is also low in cost for analysts. Unlike paper reports, recorded voice reports are available immediately after their creation and systematic transcription is fairly easy. They found that unstructured verbal data supplemented their other data very well and helped explain some of the observations or measurements they made.

Users often expressed subjective feelings, bolstering the phenomenological aspects of the study and relating phone usage to other aspects of their daily lives. These verbal reports, made at the crucial time following an incident, often mentioned issues that users forgot to bring up in later interviews, making voice-mail reports a rich source of issues to follow up on in subsequent in-person interviews.

If a mobile phone is not an option for self-reporting, a compact and portable handheld digital voice recorder is a viable alternative. If you can train the participants to carry it essentially at all times, a dedicated personal digital recorder is an effective and low-cost tool for self-reporting usage phenomena in a long-term study.

Evaluator triggered reporting for more representative data

Regardless of the reporting medium, there is still the question of when the self-reporting is to be done during long-term phenomenological evaluation. If you allow the participant to decide when to report, it could bias reporting toward times when it is convenient or times when things are going well with the product, or the participant might forget and you will lose opportunities to collect data.

To make the reporting a bit more randomly timed and according to your choice of frequency, thereby possibly being more likely to capture representative phenomenological activity, you can be proactive in requesting reports. Buchanan and Suri (2000) suggest that the participant be given a dedicated pager to carry at all times. You can then use the pager to signal randomly timed "events" to the participant "in the wild." As soon as possible after receiving the pager signal, the participant is to report on current or most recent product usage, including specific real-world usage context and any emotional impact being felt.

Periodic questionnaires over time

Periodically administered questionnaires are another self-reporting technique for collecting phenomenological data. Questionnaires can be used efficiently with a large number of participants and can yield both quantitative and qualitative data. This is a less costly method that can get answers to predefined questions, but it cannot be used easily to give you a window into usage in context to reveal growth and emergence of use over time. As a last resort, you can use a series of questionnaires spaced over time and designed to elicit understanding of changes in usage over those time periods.

Direct observation and interviews in simulated real usage situations

The aforementioned techniques of self reporting, triggered reporting, and periodic questionnaires are ways of sampling long-term phenomenological usage activity. As another alternative, the analyst team can simulate real long-term usage within a series of direct observations and interviews. The idea is to meet with participant(s) periodically, each time setting up conditions to encourage episodes of phenomenological activity to occur during these observational periods. The primary techniques for data collection during these simulated real usage sessions are direct observation and interviews.

We described an example of using this technique in Chapter 15. Petersen, Madsen, and Kjaer (2002) conducted a longitudinal study of the use of a TV and video recorder by two families in their own homes. During the time of usage, analysts scheduled periodic interviews within which they posed numerous usage scenarios and had the participants do their best to enact the usage, while giving their feedback, especially about emotional impact. The idea is to set up conditions so you can capture the essence of real usage and reflect real usage in a tractable time-frame.

12.6 VARIATIONS IN FORMATIVE EVALUATION RESULTS

Before we conclude this chapter and move on to rapid and rigorous evaluation methods, we have to be sure that you do not entertain unrealistically high expectations for the reliability of formative evaluation results. The reality of formative evaluation is that, if you repeat an evaluation of a design, prototype, or system applying the same method but different evaluators, different participants, different tasks, or different conditions, you will get different results. Even if you use the same tasks, or the same evaluators, or the same participants, you will get different results. And you certainly get even more variation in results if you apply different methods. It is just not a repeatable process. When the variation is due to using different evaluators, it is called the "evaluator effect" (Hertzum & Jacobsen, 2003; Vermeeren, van Kesteren, & Bekker, 2003).

Reasons given by Hertzum and Jacobsen (2003) for the wide variation in results of "discount" and other inspection methods include:

- vague goals (varying evaluation focus)
- vague evaluation procedures (the methods do not pin down the procedures so each application is a variation and an adaptation)
- vague problem criteria (it is not clear how to decide when an issue represents a real problem)

The most important reason for this effect is due to the individual differences among people. Different people see usage and problems differently. Different people have different detection rates. They naturally see different UX problems in the same design. Also in most of the methods, issues found are not questioned for validity. This results in numerous false positives, and there is no approach for scrutinizing and weeding them out. Further, because of the vagueness of the methods, intra-evaluator variability can contribute as much as inter-evaluator variability. The same person can get different results in two successive evaluations of the same system.

As said earlier, much of this explanation of limited effectiveness applies equally well to lab-based testing, too. That is because many of the phenomena and principles are the same and the working concepts are not that different.

In our humble opinion, the biggest reason for the limitations of our current methods is that the problem—evaluating UX in large system designs—is very difficult. The challenge is enormous—picking away at a massive application such as MS Word or a huge Website with our Lilliputian UX tweezers. And this is true regardless of the UX method, including lab-based testing. Of course, for these massive and complex systems, everything else is also more difficult and more costly.

How can you ever hope to find your way through it all, let alone do a thorough job of UX evaluation? There are just so many issues and difficulties, so many places for UX problems to hide. It brings to mind the image of a person with a metal detector, searching over a large beach. There is no chance of finding all the detectable items, not even close, but often the person does find many things of value.

No one has the resources to look everywhere and test every possible feature on every possible screen or Web page in every possible task. You are just not going to find all the UX problems in all those places. One evaluator might find a problem in a place that other evaluators did not even look. Why are we surprised that each evaluator does not come up with the same comprehensive problem list? It would take a miracle.

Rapid Evaluation Methods

13

Objectives

After reading this chapter, you will:

1. Understand design walkthroughs, demonstrations, and reviews as early rapid evaluation methods
2. Understand and apply inspection techniques for user experience, such as heuristic evaluation
3. Understand and apply rapid lab-based UX evaluation methods, such as RITE and quasi-empirical evaluation
4. Know how to use questionnaires as a rapid UX evaluation method
5. Appreciate the trade-offs involved with "discount" formative UX evaluation methods

13.1 INTRODUCTION

13.1.1 You Are Here

We begin each process chapter with a "you are here" picture of the chapter topic in the context of the overall Wheel lifecycle template; see Figure 13-1. This chapter, about rapid UX evaluation methods, is a very important side excursion along the way to the rest of the fully rigorous evaluation chapters.

Some projects, especially large domain-complex system projects, require the rigorous lab-based UX evaluation process (Chapters 14 through 17). However, many smaller fast-track projects, including those for developing commercial products, often demand techniques that are faster and less costly than lab-based evaluation in the hope of achieving much of the effectiveness but at a lower cost. We call these techniques "rapid" because they are about being fast, which means saving cost.

Here are some of the general characteristics of rapid evaluation methods:

- Rapid evaluation techniques are aimed almost exclusively at finding qualitative data—finding UX problems that are cost-effective to fix.
- Seldom, if ever, is attention given to quantitative measurements.

Figure 13-1

You are here, the chapter on rapid evaluation, within the evaluation activity in the context of the overall Wheel lifecycle template.

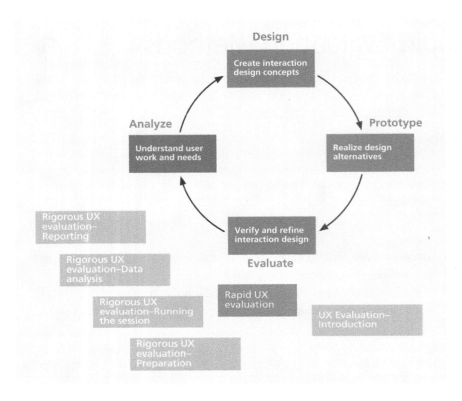

- There is a heavy dependency on practical techniques, such as the "think-aloud" technique.
- Everything is less formal, with less protocol and fewer rules.
- There is much more variability in the process, with almost every evaluation "session" being different, tailored to the prevailing conditions.
- This freedom to adapt to conditions creates more room for spontaneous ingenuity, something experienced practitioners do best.

In early stages of a project you will have only your conceptual design, scenarios, storyboards, and maybe some screen sketches or wireframes—usually not enough for interacting with customers or users. Still, you can use an informal rapid evaluation method to get your design on track. You can use interaction design demonstrations, focus groups, or walkthroughs where you do the driving.

Beyond these early approaches, when you have an interactive prototype—either a low-fidelity paper prototype or a medium-fidelity or high-fidelity prototype—most rapid evaluation techniques are abridged variations of what have generally been known as inspection techniques or of the lab-based approach. If you employ participants, engage in a give and take of questions and answers, comments, and feedback. In addition, you can be proactive with prescripted interview questions, which you can ask in a kind of structured think-aloud data-gathering technique during or after a walkthrough.

Very few practitioners or teams today use any one "pure" rapid evaluation method; they adapt and combine to suit their own processes, schedules, and resource limitations. We highlight some of the most popular techniques, the suitability of which for your project depends on your design and evaluation context. Inspection is probably the primary rapid evaluation technique, but quasi-empirical methods, abridged versions of lab-based evaluation, are also very popular and effective.

13.2 DESIGN WALKTHROUGHS AND REVIEWS

A design walkthrough is an easy and quick evaluation method that can be used with almost any stage of progress but which is especially effective for early interaction design evaluation before a prototype exists (Bias, 1991). Memmel, Gundelsweiler, and Reiterer (2007, Table 8) declare that user and expert reviews are less time-consuming and more cost-effective than participant-based testing and that their flexibility and scalability mean the effort can be adjusted to match the needs of the situation. Even early lab-based tests can include walkthroughs (Bias, 1991). Sometimes the term is used to refer to a more comprehensive team evaluation, more like a team-based UX inspection.

Who is involved? Design walkthroughs usually entail a group working collaboratively under the guidance of a leader. The group can include the design team, UX analysts, subject-matter experts, customer representatives, and potential users.

The goal of a design walkthrough is to explore a design on behalf of users to simulate the user's view of moving through the design, but to see it with an expert's eye. The team is trying to anticipate problems that users might have if they were the ones using the design.

What materials do you need upfront? You should prepare for a design walkthrough by gathering at least these items:

- Design representation(s), including storyboards, screen sketches, illustrated scenarios (scenario text interspersed with storyboard frames and/or screen sketches), paper prototypes, and/or higher fidelity prototypes
- Descriptions of relevant users, work roles, and user classes
- Usage or design scenarios to drive the walkthrough

Inspection (UX)

A UX inspection is an analytical evaluation method in which a UX expert evaluates an interaction design by looking at it or trying it out, sometimes in the context of a set of abstracted design guidelines. Expert evaluators are both participant surrogates and observers, asking themselves questions about what would cause users problems and giving an expert opinion predicting UX problems.

Quasi-Empirical Evaluation

Quasi-empirical UX evaluation methods are empirical because they involve taking some kind of data using volunteer participants, but they are quick and dirty versions of empirical methods, being very informal and not following a strict protocol. Quasi-empirical methods focus on qualitative data to identify UX problems that can be fixed and usually do not involve quantitative data.

Here is how it works. It is usually more realistic and engaging to explore the design through the lens of usage or design scenarios. The leader walks the group through key workflow patterns that the system is intended to support. A characteristic that distinguishes design walkthroughs from various kinds of user-based testing is that the practitioner in charge does the "driving" instead of the customer or users.

As the team follows the scenarios, looking systematically at parts of the design and discussing the merits and potential problems, the leader tells stories about users and usage, user intentions and actions, and expected outcomes. The leader explains what the user will be doing, what the user might be thinking, and how the task fits in the work practice, workflow, and context. As potential UX problems arise, someone records them on a list for further consideration.

Walkthroughs may also include considerations of compliance with design guidelines and style guides as well as questions about emotional impact, including aesthetics and fun. Beyond just the details of UX and other design problems that might emerge, it is a good way to communicate about the design and keep on the same page within the project.

13.3 UX INSPECTION

When we use the term "UX inspection," we are aware that you cannot inspect UX but must inspect a design for user experience issues. However, because it is awkward to spell it out that way every time, we use "UX inspection" as a short-hand for the longer phrase. As an analogy, if you hire someone to do a safety inspection of your house, you want them to "inspect the house for safety issues" just as we want a UX inspection to be an inspection of the design for user experience issues. This is consistent with our explanation of how we use the term "UX" in a broader denotation than that of the term "user experience."

13.3.1 What Is UX Inspection?

A UX inspection is an "analytical" evaluation method in that it involves evaluating by looking at and trying out the design yourself as a UX expert instead of having participants exercise it while you observe. Here we generalize the original concept of usability inspection to include inspection of both usability characteristics and emotional impact factors and we call it UX inspection.

The evaluator is both participant surrogate and observer. Inspectors ask themselves questions about what would cause users problems. So, the essence of these methods is the inspector giving an expert opinion predicting UX problems.

Because the process depends on the evaluator's judgment, it requires an expert, a UX practitioner or consultant, which is why this kind of evaluation method is also sometimes called "expert evaluation" or "expert inspection." These evaluation methods are also sometimes called "heuristic evaluation (HE)" but that term technically applies only to one particular version, "the heuristic evaluation method" (Nielsen, 1994b), in which "heuristics" or generalized design guidelines are used to drive an inspection (see later).

> **Heuristic**
>
> A heuristic is an informal maxim, rule of thumb, or generalized guideline about interaction design.

13.3.2 Inspection Is a Valuable Tool in the UX Toolbox

Not all human–computer interaction (HCI) literature is supportive of inspection as an evaluation tool, but practitioners in the field have been using it for years with great success. In our own practice, we definitely find value in inspection methods and highly recommend their use in cases (for example):

> **Heuristic Evaluation**
>
> A heuristic evaluation is a kind of UX evaluation involving expert inspection guided by a set of heuristics.

- Where they are applied in early stages and early design iterations. It is an excellent way to begin UX evaluation and pick the low-hanging fruit and clear out the mass of obvious problems.
- Where you should save the more expensive and more powerful tools, such as lab-based testing, for later to dig out the more subtle and difficult problems. Starting with lab-based testing on an immature and quickly evolving design can be like using a precision shovel on a large snow drift.
- Where you have not yet done any other kind of evaluation. It is especially appropriate when you are brought in to evaluate an existing system that has not undergone previous UX evaluation and iterative redesign.
- Where you cannot afford or cannot do lab-based testing for some reason but still want to do *some* evaluation. UX inspection can still do a good job for you when you do not have the time or other resources to do a more thorough job.

13.3.3 How Many Inspectors Are Needed?

In lab-based UX testing, you can improve evaluation effectiveness by adding more participants until you get diminishing returns. Similarly, in UX inspection, to improve effectiveness you can add more inspectors. But does it help? Yes, for inspections, a team approach is beneficial, maybe even necessary, because low individual detection rates preclude finding enough problems by one person.

Experience has shown that different experts find different problems. But this diversity of opinion is valuable because the union of problems found over a group of inspectors is much larger than the set of problems found by any individual. Most heuristic inspections are done by a team of two or more usability inspectors, typically two or three inspectors.

But what is the optimal number? It depends on conditions and a great deal on the system you are inspecting. Nielsen and Landauer (1993) found that, under some conditions, a small set of experts, in the range of 3 to 5, is optimal before diminishing returns. See the end of Chapter 14 for further discussion about the "3 to 5 users" rule and its limitations. As with almost any kind of evaluation, some is better than none and, for early project stages, we often are satisfied with a single inspection by one or two inspectors working together.

13.3.4 What Kind of Inspectors Are Needed?

Not surprisingly, Nielsen (1992a) found that UX experts (practitioners or consultants) make the best inspection evaluators. Sometimes it is best to get a fresh view by using an expert evaluator who is not on the project team. If those UX experts also have knowledge in the subject-matter domain of the interface being evaluated, all the better. Those people are called dual experts and can evaluate through both a design guidelines perspective and a work activity, workflow, and task perspective. The equivalent of having a dual expert can be approximated by a team approach—pairing up a UX expert with a work domain expert.

13.4 HEURISTIC EVALUATION, A UX INSPECTION METHOD

13.4.1 Introduction to Heuristic Evaluation

For most development projects in the 1990s, the "default usability person," the unqualified software developer pressed into usability service, was the rule. Few trained UX specialists actually worked in design projects. Now the default practitioner is slowly moving toward becoming the exception. As more people specifically prepared for the UX practitioner role became available, the definition of "novice evaluator" has shifted from the default practitioner who perhaps had an SE day job to a trained practitioner, just with less experience than an expert.

But in reality there still is, and will be for some time, a shortage of good UX practitioners, and the heuristic method is intended to help these novices perform acceptably good usability inspections. It has been described as a method that novices can grab onto and use without a great deal of training. The effectiveness of a rule-based method used by a novice, of course, cannot be expected to be on a par with a more sophisticated approach or by any approach used by an expert practitioner.

As Nielsen (1992a; Nielsen & Molich, 1990) states, the heuristic evaluation (HE) method has the advantages of being inexpensive, intuitive, and easy to motivate practitioners to do, and it is effective for use early in the UX process. Therefore, it is no surprise that of all the inspection methods, the HE method is the best known and the most popular. Another important point about the heuristics is that they teach the designers about criteria to keep in mind while doing their own designs so they will not violate these guidelines.

A word of caution, however: Although the HE method is popular and successful, there will always be some UX problems that show up in real live user-based interaction that you will not see in a heuristic, or any other, inspection or design review.

13.4.2 How-to-Do-It: Heuristic Evaluation

Heuristics

Following publication of the original heuristics, Nielsen (1994a) enhanced the heuristics with a study based on factor analysis of a large number of real usability problems. The resulting new heuristics (Nielsen, 1994b) are given in Table 13-1.

Visibility of System Status

The system should always keep users informed about what is going on through appropriate feedback within reasonable time.

Match Between System and The Real World

The system should speak the users' language, with words, phrases, and concepts familiar to the user rather than system-oriented terms. Follow real-world conventions, making information appear in a natural and logical order.

User Control and Freedom

Users often choose system functions by mistake and will need a clearly marked "emergency exit" to leave the unwanted state without having to go through an extended dialogue. Support undo and redo.

Consistency and Standards

Users should not have to wonder whether different words, situations, or actions mean the same thing. Follow platform conventions.

Continued

Table 13-1

Nielsen's refined heuristics, quoted with permission from www.useit.com

Error Prevention

Even better than good error messages is a careful design that prevents a problem from occurring in the first place. Either eliminate error-prone conditions or check for them and present users with a confirmation option before they commit to the action.

Recognition Rather Than Recall

Minimize the user's memory load by making objects, actions, and options visible. The user should not have to remember information from one part of the dialogue to another. Instructions for use of the system should be visible or easily retrievable whenever appropriate.

Flexibility and Efficiency of Use

Accelerators—unseen by the novice user—may often speed up the interaction for the expert user such that the system can cater to both inexperienced and experienced users. Allow users to tailor frequent actions.

Aesthetic and Minimalist Design

Dialogues should not contain information that is irrelevant or rarely needed. Every extra unit of information in a dialogue competes with the relevant units of information and diminishes their relative visibility.

Help Users Recognize, Diagnose, and Recover from Errors

Error messages should be expressed in plain language (no codes), indicate the problem precisely, and suggest a solution constructively.

Help and Documentation

Even though it is better if the system can be used without documentation, it may be necessary to provide help and documentation. Any such information should be easy to search, focused on the user's task, list concrete steps to be carried out, and not be too large.

The procedure

Despite the large number of variations in practice, we endeavor to describe what roughly represents the "plain" or "standard" version. These inspection sessions can take from a couple of hours for small systems to several days for larger systems. Here is how to do it:

- The project team or manager selects a set of evaluators, typically three to five.
- The team selects a small, tractable set, about 10, of "heuristics," generalized and simplified design guidelines in the form of inspection questions, for example, "Does the

interaction design use the natural language that is familiar to the target user?" The set of heuristics given in the previous section are a good start.

- Each inspector individually browses through each part of the interaction design, asking the heuristic questions about that part:
  - assesses the compliance of each part of the design
  - notes places where a heuristic is violated as candidate usability problems
  - notes places where heuristics are supported (things done well)
  - identifies the context of each instance noted previously, usually by capturing an image of the screen or part of the screen where the problem or good design feature occurs
- All the inspectors get together and, as a team, they:
  - merge their problem lists
  - select the most important ones to fix
  - brainstorm suggested solutions
  - decide on recommendations for the designers based on the most frequently visited screens, screens with the most usability problems, guidelines violated most often, and resources available to make changes
  - issue a group report

A heuristic evaluation report should:
  - start with an overview of the system being evaluated
  - give an overview explanation of inspection process
  - list the inspection questions based on heuristics used
  - report on potential usability problems revealed by the inspection, either:
    - by heuristic—for each heuristic, give examples of design violations and of ways the design supports the heuristic
    - by part of the design—for each part, give specific examples of heuristics violated and/or supported
  - include as many illustrative screen images or other visual examples as possible.

The team then puts forward the recommendations they agreed on for design modifications, using language that will motivate others to want to make these changes. They highlight a realistic list of the "Top 3" (or 4 or 5) suggestions for modifications and prioritize suggestions, to give the biggest improvement in usability for the least cost (perhaps using the cost-importance analysis of Chapter 16).

Reporting

We have found it best to keep HE reporting simple. Long forms with lots of fields can capture more information, but tend to be tedious for practitioners who have to report large numbers of problems. Table 13-2 is a simple HE reporting

Table 13-2

Simple HE reporting form, adapted from Brad Myers

Heuristic Evaluation Report

Dated:

MM/DD/YYYY

Prepared By:

NAME:

SIGNATURE:

Evaluation Of:

Name of system being evaluated: XYZ Website

Other information about the system being evaluated:

Problem #: 1

Prototype screen, page, location of problem:

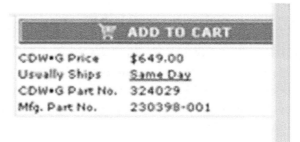

Name of heuristic: Consistency

Reason for reporting as negative or positive: Inconsistent placement of "Add to Cart" buttons: The "Add to Cart" button is below the item in CDW but above in CDW-G.

Scope of problem: Every product page

Severity of problem (high/medium/low): Low—minor, cosmetic problem

Justification for severity rating: Unlikely that users will have trouble with finding or recognizing the button

Suggestions to fix: Move the button on one of the sites to be in the same place as on the other site.

Possible trade-offs (why fix might not work): This may result in an inconsistency with something else, but unknown what that might be.

form that we have adapted, with permission, from one developed by Brad Myers. You can make up a Word document or spreadsheet form to put these headings in columns as an efficient way to report multiple problems, but they do not fit that way in the format of our book.

Description of columns in Table 13-2 is as follows:

Prototype screen, page, location of problem: On which screen and/or which location on a screen of the user interface was critical incident or problem located?

Name of heuristic: Which of the 10 heuristics is being referenced? Enter the full name of the heuristic.

Reason for reporting as negative or positive: Explain reasons why the interface violates or upholds this heuristic. Be sure to be clear about *where* in the screen you are referencing.

Scope of problem: Describe the scope of the feedback or the problem; include whether the scope of the issue is throughout the product or within a specific screen or screens. If the problems are specific to a page, include the appropriate page numbers.

Severity of problem (high/medium/low): Your assessment as to whether the implication of the feedback is *high, medium,* or *low* severity.

Justification of severity rating: The reason why you gave it that rating.

Suggestions to fix: Suggestion for the modifications that might be made to the interaction design to address the issue or issues.

Possible trade-offs (why fix might not work): Mentioning trade-offs adds to your credibility.

Be specific and insightful; include subtlety and depth. Saying "the system does not have good color choices because it does not use color" is pretty trivial and is not helpful. Also, if you evaluated a prototype, saying that functions are not implemented is obvious and unhelpful.

Variations abound

The one "constant" about the HE method and most other related rapid and inspection methods is the variation with which they are used in practice. These methods are adapted and customized by almost every team that ever uses them usually in undocumented and unpublished ways.

Task-based or heuristic-based expert UX inspections can be conducted with just one evaluator or with two or more evaluators, each acting independently or all working together. Other expert UX inspections can be scenario based, persona based, checklist based, or as a kind of "can you break it?" test.

As an example of a variation that was described in the literature, participatory heuristic evaluation extends the HE method with additional heuristics to address broader issues of task and workflow, beyond just the design of user

Critical Incident

A critical incident is a UX evaluation event that occurs during user task performance or other user interaction, observed by the facilitator or other observers or sometimes expressed by the user participant, that indicates a possible UX problem. Critical incident identification is arguably the single most important source of qualitative data.

interface artifacts to "consider how the system can contribute to human goals and human experience" (Muller et al., 1998, p. 16). The definitive difference in participatory HE is the addition of users, work domain experts, to the inspection team.

Sears (1997) extended the HE method with what he calls heuristic walkthroughs. Several lists are prepared and given to each practitioner doing the inspection: user tasks, inspection heuristics, and "thought-focusing questions." Each inspector performs two inspections, one using the tasks as a guide and supported by the thought-focusing questions. The second inspection is the more traditional kind, using the heuristics. Their studies showed that "heuristic walkthroughs resulted in finding more problems than cognitive walkthroughs and fewer false positives than heuristic evaluations."

Perspective-based usability inspection (Zhang, Basili, & Shneiderman, 1999) is another published variation on the HE method. Because a large system can present a scope too broad for any given inspection session, Zhang et al. (1999) proposed "perspective-based usability inspection," allowing inspectors to focus on a subset of usability issues in each inspection. The resulting focus of attention afforded a higher problem detection rate within that narrower perspective.

Examples of perspectives that can be used to guide usability inspections are novice use, expert use, and error handling. In their study, Zhang et al. (1999) found that their perspective-based approach did lead to significant improvement in detection of usability problems in a Web-based application. Persona-based UX inspection is a variation on the perspective-based inspection in that it includes consideration of context of use via the needs of personas (Wilson, 2011).

As our final example, Cockton et al. (2003) developed an extended problem-reporting format that improves heuristic inspection methods by finding and eliminating many of the false positives typical of the usability inspection approach. Traditional heuristic methods poorly support problem discovery and analysis. Their Discovery and Analysis Resource (DARe) model allows analysts to bring distinct discovery and analysis resources to bear to isolate and analyze false negatives as well as false positives.

Limitations

While a helpful guide for inexperienced practitioners, we find that heuristics usually get in the way of the experts. To be fair to the heuristic method, the heuristic method was intended as a kind of "scaffolding" to help novice practitioners do usability inspections so it should not really be compared with expert usability inspection methods anyway.

It was perhaps self-confirming when we read that others found the actual heuristics to be similarly unhelpful (Cockton, Lavery, & Woolrych, 2003; Cockton & Woolrych, 2001). In their studies, Cockton et al. (2003) found that it is experts who find problems with inspection, not experts using heuristics. Cockton and Woolrych (2002, p. 15) also claim that the "inspection methods do not encourage analysts to take a rich or comprehensive view of interaction." While this may be true for heuristic methods, it does not have to be true for all inspection methods.

A major drawback with any inspection method, including the HE method, is the danger that novice practitioners will get too comfortable with it and think the heuristics are enough for any evaluation situation. There are few indications in its usage that let the novice practitioner know when it is not working well and when a different method should be tried.

Also, like all UX inspection methods, the HE method can generate a lot of false negatives, situations in which inspectors identified "problems" that turned out to be not real problems or not very important UX problems. Finally, like most other rapid UX evaluation methods, the HE method is not particularly effective in finding usability problems below the surface—problems about sequencing and workflow.

13.5 OUR PRACTICAL APPROACH TO UX INSPECTION

We have synthesized existing UX inspection methods into a relatively simple and straightforward method that, unlike the heuristic method, is definitely for UX experts and not for novices. Sometimes we have novices sit in and observe the process as a kind of apprentice training, but they do not perform these inspections on their own.

13.5.1 The Knock on Your Door

It is the boss. You, the practitioner, are being called in and asked to do a quick UX assessment of a prototype, an early product, or an existing product being considered for revision. You have 1 or 2 days to check it out and give feedback. You feel that if you can give some valuable feedback on UX flaws, you will gain some credibility and maybe get a bigger role in the project next time.

What method should you use? No time to go to the lab, and even the "standard" inspection techniques will take too long, with too much overhead. What you need is a practical, fast, and efficient approach to UX inspection. As a solution, we offer an approach that evolved over time in our own practice. You can apply this approach at almost any stage of progress, but it usually works better in the early stages. We believe that most real-world UX inspections are more like our approach than like the somewhat more elaborate techniques to inspection described in the literature.

13.5.2 Driven by Experience, Not Heuristics or Guidelines

We should say upfront that we do not explicitly use design guidelines or even "heuristics" to drive or guide this kind of UX inspection. In our own industry and consulting experience, we have just not found specific heuristics as useful as we would like.

To be clear, we are saying that we do not employ user design guidelines to *drive* the inspection process. The driving perspective is usage. We focus on tasks, work activities, and work context. We do insist, however, that an expert working and practical knowledge of design guidelines is essential to support the rapid analysis used to decide what issues are real problems and to understand the underlying nature of the problems and potential solutions. For this analysis, intertwined with inspection activities, we depend on our knowledge of design guidelines and their interpretation within the design.

We like a usage-based approach because it allows the practitioner to take on the role of user better, taking the process from purely analytic to include at least a little "empirical" flavor. Using this approach, and our UX intuition honed over the years, we can see, and even anticipate, UX problems, many of which might not have been revealed under the heuristic spotlight.

13.5.3 Use a Co-Discovery or Team Approach in UX Inspection

Expert UX practitioners as inspectors are in the role of "UX detectives." To aid the detective work, it can help to use two practitioners, working together as mutual sounding boards in a give-and-take interplay, potentiating each other's efforts to keep the juices flowing, to promote a constant flow of think-aloud comments from the inspectors, and to maintain a barrage of problem notes flying.

It is also often useful to have a non-UX person with you to look at the design from a global point of view. Teaming up with customers, users, designers, and other people familiar with the overall system can help make up for any lack of system knowledge you may have, especially if you have not been with the team during the entire project. Teaming up with users or work domain experts (which you might already have on your team) can reinforce your user-surrogate role and bring in more work-domain expertise (Muller et al., 1998).

13.5.4 Explore Systematically with a Rich and Comprehensive Usage-Oriented View

As an inspector, you should not just look for individual little problems associated with individual tasks or functions. Use all your experience and knowledge to see the big picture. Keep an expert eye on the high-level view of workflow, the overall integration of functionality, and emotional impact factors that go beyond usability.

For example, how are the three design perspectives covered in Chapter 8 accounted for by the system? Does the system ecology make sense? Is the conceptual design for interaction appropriate for envisioned workflows? What about the conceptual design for emotional impact?

Representative user tasks help us put ourselves in the users' shoes. By exploring the tasks ourselves and taking our own think-aloud data, we can imagine what real users might encounter in their usage. This aspect of our inspections is driven as systematically as possible by two things: the task structure and the interaction design itself. A hierarchical task inventory (Chapter 6) is helpful in attaining a good understanding of the task structure and to ensure broad coverage of the range of tasks.

If the system is highly specialized and complex and you are not a work domain expert, you might not be able to comprehend it in a short time so get help from a subject-matter expert. Usage scenarios and design scenarios (Chapter 6) are fruitful places to look to focus on key user work roles and key user tasks that must be supported in the design.

Driving the inspection with the interaction design itself means trying all possible actions on all the user interface artifacts, trying out all user interface objects such as buttons, icons, and menus. It also means being opportunistic in following leads and hunches triggered by parts of the design.

The time and effort required for a good inspection are more or less proportional to the size of the system (i.e., the number of user tasks, choices, and system functions). System complexity can have an even bigger impact on inspection time and effort.

The main skill you need for finding UX problems as you inspect the design is your detective's "eagle eye" for curious or suspicious incidents or phenomena. The knowledge requirement centers on design guidelines and principles and your mental inventory of typical interaction design flaws you have seen before. You really have to know the design guidelines cold, and the storehouse of problem examples helps you anticipate and rapidly spot new occurrences of the same types of problems.

Soon you will find the inspection process blossoming into a fast-moving narration of critical incidents, UX problems, and guidelines. By following various threads of UX clues, you can even uncover problems that you do not encounter directly within the tasks.

13.5.5 Emotional Impact Inspection

In the past, inspections for evaluating interaction designs have been almost exclusively usability inspections. But this kind of evaluation can easily be extended to a more complete UX inspection by addressing issues of emotional impact, too. The process is essentially the same, but you need to look beyond a task view to the overall usage experience. Ask additional questions.

Among the emotional impact questions to have in mind in a UX inspection are:

- Is usage fun?
- Is the visual design attractive (e.g., colors, shapes, layout) and creative?
- Will the design delight the user visually, aurally, or tactilely?
- If the target is a product:
  - Is the packaging and product presentation aesthetic?
  - Is the out-of-the-box experience exciting?
  - Does the product feel robust and good to hold?
  - Can the product add to the user's self-esteem?
  - Does the product embody environmental and sustainable practices?
  - Does the product convey the branding of the organization?
  - Does the brand stand for progressive, social, and civic values?
- Are there opportunities to improve emotional impact in any of the aforementioned areas?

Most of the questions in a questionnaire for assessing emotional impact are also applicable as inspection questions here. As an example, using attributes from AttrakDiff:

- Is the system or product interesting?
- Is it exciting?
- Is it innovative?
- Is it engaging?
- Is it motivating?
- Is it desirable?

13.5.6 Use All Your Personalities

Roses are red;
Violets are blue.
I'm schizophrenic, . . .
And I am, too.

You need to be at least a dual personality, with a slightly schizophrenic melding of the UX expert perspective and a user orientation. As a surrogate for users, you must think like a user and act like a user. But you must simultaneously think and act like an expert, observing and analyzing yourself in the user role.

Your UX expert credentials have never been in doubt, but demands of the user surrogate role can take you outside your comfort zone. You have to shed the designer and analyst mind-sets in favor of design-informing views of the world. You must immerse yourself in the usage-oriented perspective; become the user and live usage!

If you have doubts about your ability to play the user-surrogate role, as we said in a previous section, you should recruit an experienced user (hopefully one who is familiar with UX principles) or user representative to sit with you and help direct the interaction, informing the process with their work domain, user goal, and task knowledge.

13.5.7 Take Good Notes

As you do your inspection and play user, good note taking is essential for capturing precious critical incidents and UX problem data in the moment that they occur. Just as prompt capture of critical incidents is essential in lab-based testing to capture the perishable details while they are still fresh, you need to do the same during your inspections. You cannot rely on your memory and write it all down at the end. Once you get going, things can happen fast, just as they do in a lab-based evaluation session.

We often take our notes orally, dictating them on a handheld digital recorder. Because we can talk much faster than we can write or type, we can record our thoughts with minimal interruption of the flow or of your intense cognitive focus. Try to include as much analysis and diagnosis as you can, stating causes in the design in terms of design guidelines violated. As with most skill-based activities, you get better with practice.

You may not be able to suggest immediate solutions for more complex problems (e.g., reorganizing workflow) that require significant thought and discussion. However, you can usually suggest a cause and a fix for most problems. Given enough detail in the problem description, the solutions are often self-suggesting. For example, if a label has low color contrast between the text and the background, the solution is to increase the color contrast.

Dumas and Redish (1999) suggest that you should be more specific in suggesting this kind of solution, including what particular colors to use. It is a good idea to capture these design solution ideas, but treat them only as points of departure. Those decisions still need to be thought out carefully by someone with the requisite training in the use of colors and with knowledge of organizational style standards concerning color, branding, and so on. If you give an example of some colors that might work, you need to ensure that the designers do not take those colors as the exact solution without thinking about it further.

13.5.8 Analyze Your Notes

Sort out your inspection notes and organize them by problem type or design feature. If necessary, you can use a fast affinity diagram approach (see Chapter 4) on the top of a large work table. Print all notes on small pieces of paper and organize them by topic. Prioritize your recommendations for fixing, maybe with cost-importance analysis (Chapter 16).

13.5.9 Report Your Results

Your inspection report (Chapter 17) will be a lot like the one we described for the heuristic method earlier in this chapter, only you will not refer to heuristics. Tell about how you did the process in enough detail for your audience to understand the evaluation context.

Sometimes UX inspection, as does any evaluation method, raises questions. In your report, you should include recommendations for further evaluation, with specific points to look for and specific questions to answer.

Exercise

See Exercise 13-1, Formative UX Inspection

13.6 DO UX EVALUATION RITE

13.6.1 Introduction to the Rapid Iterative Testing and Evaluation (RITE) UX Evaluation Method

There are many variations of rapid UX evaluation techniques. Most are some variation of inspection methods, but one in particular that stands out is not based on inspection: the approach that Medlock, Wixon, and colleagues (Medlock et al., 2002, 2005; Wixon, 2003) call RITE, for "rapid iterative testing and evaluation," is an empirical rapid evaluation method and is one of the best.

RITE employs user-based UX testing in a fast collaborative (team members and participants) test-and-fix cycle designed to pick the low-hanging fruit at relatively low cost. In other methods, the rest of the team is usually not present to see the process, so problems found by UX evaluators in the mystical methods are sometimes not believed. This is solved by the collaborative evaluation process in RITE; the whole team is involved in arriving at the results.

The key feature of RITE is the fast turnaround. UX problems are analyzed right after the product is evaluated with a number of user participants and the whole project team decides on which changes to make. Changes are then implemented immediately. If warranted, another iteration of testing and fixing might ensue.

Because changes are included in all testing that occurs after that point, further testing can determine the effectiveness of the changes—whether the problem is, in fact, fixed and whether the fix introduces any new problems. Fixing a problem immediately also gives access to any aspects of the product that could not be tested earlier because they were blocked by that problem.

In his inimitable Wixonian wisdom, our friend Dennis reminds us that, "In practice, the goal is to produce, in the quickest time, a successful product that meets specifications with the fewest resources, while minimizing risk" (Wixon, 2003).

13.6.2 How-to-Do-It: The RITE UX Evaluation Method

This description of the RITE UX evaluation method is based mainly on Medlock et al. (2002).

The project team starts by selecting a UX practitioner, whom we call the facilitator, to direct the testing session. The UX facilitator and the team prepare by:

- identifying the characteristics needed in participants
- deciding on which tasks they will have the participants perform
- agreeing on critical tasks, the set of tasks that every user must be able to perform
- constructing a test script based on those tasks
- deciding how to collect qualitative user behavior data
- recruiting participants (Chapter 14) and scheduling them to come into the lab

The UX facilitator and the team conduct the evaluation session for one to three participants, one at a time:

- gathering the entire project team and any other relevant project stakeholders, either in the observation room of a UX lab or around a table in a conference room
- bringing in the participant playing the role of user

- introducing everyone and setting the stage, explaining the process and expected outcomes
- making sure that everyone knows the participant is helping evaluate the system and the team is not in any way evaluating the participant
- having the participant perform a small number of selected tasks, while all project stakeholders observe silently
- having the participants think aloud as they work
- working together with the participants to find UX problems and ways the design should be improved
- taking thorough notes on problem indicators, such as task blocking and user errors
- focusing session notes on finding usability problems and noting their severity

The UX facilitator and other UX practitioners:

- identify from session notes the UX problems observed and their causes in the design
- give everyone on the team the list of UX problems and causes

The UX practitioner and the team address problems:

- identifying problems with obvious causes and obvious solutions, such as those involving wording or labeling, to be fixed first
- determining which other problems can also reasonably be fixed
- determining which problems need more discussion
- determining which problems require more data (from more participants) to be sure they are real problems
- sorting out which problems they cannot afford to fix right now
- deciding on feasible solutions for the problems to be addressed
- implementing fixes for problems with obvious causes and obvious solutions
- starting to implement other fixes and bringing them into the current prototype as soon as feasible

The UX practitioner and the team immediately conduct follow-up evaluation:

- bringing in new participants
- having them perform the tasks associated with the fixed problems, using the modified design
- working with the participants to see if the fixes worked and to be sure the fixes did not introduce any new UX problems

The entire process just described is repeated until you run out of resources or the team decides it is done (all major problems found and addressed).

13.6.3 Variations in RITE Data Collection

Although RITE is unusual as a rapid evaluation method that employs UX testing with user participants, what really distinguishes RITE is the fast turnaround and tight coupling of testing and fixing. As a result, it is possible to consider alternative data collection techniques within the RITE method. For example, instead of testing with user participants, the team could employ a UX inspection method, heuristic evaluation or otherwise, for data collection while retaining the fast analysis and fixing parts of the cycle.

13.7 QUASI-EMPIRICAL UX EVALUATION

13.7.1 Introduction to Quasi-Empirical UX Evaluation

Quasi-empirical UX evaluation methods are empirical because they involve taking some kind of data using volunteer participants. Beyond that, their similarities to other empirical methods fade rapidly. Most empirical methods are characterized by formal protocols and procedures; rapid methods are anything but formal or protocol bound. Thus, the qualifier "quasi."

Most empirical methods have at least some focus on quantitative data; quasi-empirical approaches have none. The single paramount mission is qualitative data to identify UX problems that can be fixed efficiently.

Although formal empirical evaluations often take place in a UX lab or similar setting, quasi-empirical testing can occur almost anywhere, including UX lab space, a conference room, an office, a cafeteria, or in the field. Like other rapid evaluation methods, practitioners using quasi-empirical techniques thrive on going with what works. While most empirical methods require controlled conditions for user performance, it is now not only acceptable but recommended to interrupt and intervene at opportune moments to elicit more thinking aloud and to ask for explanations and specifics.

Quasi-empirical methods are defined by the freedom given to the practitioner to innovate, to make it up as they go. Quasi-empirical evaluation sessions mean being flexible about goals and approaches. When conducted by the best practitioners, quasi-empirical evaluation is punctuated with impromptu changes of pace, changes of direction, and changes of focus—jumping on issues as they arise and milking them to get the most information about problems, their effects on users, and potential solutions.

This innovation in real time is where experience counts. Because of the ingenuity required and the need to adapt to each situation, experienced practitioners are usually more effective at quasi-empirical techniques, as they are with all rapid evaluation techniques. Each quasi-empirical session is different and can be tailored to the project conditions. Each session participant is different—some are more knowledgeable whereas some are more helpful. You must find ways to improvise, go with the flow, and learn the most you can about the UX problems.

Unlike other empirical methods, there are no formal predefined "benchmark tasks," but a session can be task driven, drawing on usage scenarios, essential use cases, step-by-step task interaction models, or other task data or task models you collected and built up in contextual inquiry and analysis and modeling. Quasi-empirical sessions can also be driven by exploration of features, screens, widgets, or whatever suits.

13.7.2 How-to-Do-It: Quasi-Empirical UX Evaluation
Prepare

Begin by ensuring that you have a set of representative, frequently used, and mission-critical tasks for your participants to explore. Draw on your contextual data and task models (structure models and interaction models). Have some exploratory questions ready (see next section).

Assign your UX evaluation team roles effectively, including evaluator, facilitator, and data collectors. If necessary, use two evaluators for co-discovery. Further prepare for your quasi-empirical session the same way you would for a full empirical session, only less formally and less thoroughly, to match the more rapid and more opportunistic nature of the quasi-empirical approach.

Thus preparation includes lightweight selection and recruiting of participants, preparation of materials such as the informed consent form, and establishment of protocols and procedures for the sessions. You should also do pilot testing to shake down the prototype and the procedures, but getting the prototype bug-free is a little less important for quasi-empirical evaluation, as you can be very flexible during the session.

Conduct session and collect data

As you, the facilitator, sit with each participant:

- Cultivate a partnership; you get the best results from working closely in collaboration.
- Make extensive use of the think-aloud data collection technique. Encourage the participant by prompting occasionally: "Remember to tell us what you are thinking as you go."
- Make sure that the participant understands the role as that of helping you evaluate the UX.

■ Although recording audio or video is sometimes helpful in rigorous evaluation methods, to retain a rapidness in this method, it is best not to record audio or video; just take notes. Keep it simple and lightweight.

■ Encourage the participant to explore the system for a few minutes and get familiarized with it. This type of free-play is important because it is representative of what happens when users first interact with a system (except in cases where walk up and use is an issue).

■ Use some of the tasks that you have at hand, from the preparation step given earlier, more or less as props to support the action and the conversation. You are not interested in user performance times or other quantitative data.

■ Work together with the participant to find UX problems and ways the design should be improved. Take thorough notes; they are sole raw data from the process.

■ Let the user choose some tasks to do.

■ Be ready to follow threads that arise rather than just following prescribed activities.

■ Listen as much as you can to the participant; most of the time it is your job to listen, not talk.

■ It is also your job to lead the session, which means saying the right thing at the right time to keep it on track and to switch tracks when useful.

At any time during the session, you can interact with the participant with questions such as:

■ Ask participants to describe initial reactions as they interact with this system.

■ Ask questions such as "How would you describe this system to someone who has never seen it before? What is the underlying "model" for this system? Is that model appropriate? Where does it deviate? Does it meet your expectations? Why and how? These questions get to the root of determining the user's mental model for the system.

■ Ask what parts of the design are not clear and why.

■ Inquire about how the system compares with others they have used in the past.

■ Ask if they have any suggestions for changing the designs.

■ To place them in the context of their own work, ask them how they would use this system in their daily work. In other words, ask them to walk you through some tasks they would perform using this system in a typical workday.

Analyze and report results

Because the UX data analysis procedure (Chapter 16) pretty much applies regardless of how you got data, use the parts of that chapter about analyzing qualitative data.

13.8 QUESTIONNAIRES

A questionnaire, discussed at length in Chapter 12, is a fast and easy way to collect subjective UX data, either as a supplement to any other rapid UX evaluation method or as a method on its own.

Questionnaires with good track records, such as the Questionnaire for User Interface Satisfaction (QUIS), the System Usability Scale (SUS), or Usefulness, Satisfaction, and Ease of Use (USE), are all easy and inexpensive to use and can yield varying degrees of UX data. Perhaps the AttrakDiff questionnaire might be the best choice for a rapid stand-alone method, as it is designed to address both pragmatic (usability and usefulness) and hedonic (emotional impact) issues.

For a general discussion of modifying questionnaires for your particular evaluation session, see Chapter 12 about modifying the AttrakDiff questionnaire.

13.9 SPECIALIZED RAPID UX EVALUATION METHODS

13.9.1 Alpha and Beta Testing and Field Surveys

Alpha and beta testing are useful post-deployment evaluation methods. After almost all development is complete, manufacturers of software applications sometimes send out alpha and beta (pre-release) versions of the application software to select users, experts, customers, and professional reviewers as a preview. In exchange for the early preview, users try it out and give feedback on the experience. Often little or no guidance is given for the review process beyond just "tell us what you think is good and bad and what needs fixing, what additional features would you like to see, etc."

An alpha version of a product is an earlier, less polished version, usually with a smaller and more trusted "audience." Beta is as close to the final product as they can make it and is sent out to a larger community. Most companies develop a beta trial mailing list of a community of early adopters and expert users, mostly known to be friendly to the company and its products and helpful in their comments.

Alpha and beta testing are easy and inexpensive ways to get feedback. But you do not get the kind of detailed UX problem data observed during usage and associated closely with user actions and their consequences in the context of specific interaction design features—the kind of data essential for isolating specific UX problems within the formative evaluation process.

Alpha and beta testing are very much individualized to a given development organization and environment. Full descriptions of how to do alpha and beta testing are beyond our scope. Like alpha and beta testing, user field survey information is retrospective and, while it can be good for getting at user satisfaction, it does not capture the details of use within the usage experience. Anything is better than nothing, but let us hope this is not the only formative evaluation used within the product lifecycle in a given organization.

13.9.2 Remote UX Evaluation

Remote UX evaluation methods (Dray & Siegel, 2004; Hartson & Castillo, 1998) are good for evaluating systems after they have been deployed in the field. Methods include:

- simulating lab-based UX testing using the Internet as a long extension cord to the user (e.g., UserVue by TechSmith)
- online surveys for getting after-the-fact feedback
- software instrumentation of click stream and usage event information
- software plug-ins to capture user self-reporting of UX issues

The Hartson and Castillo (1998) approach uses self-reporting of UX problems by users as the problems occur during their normal usage, allowing you to get at the perishable details of the usage experience, especially in real-life daily work usage. As always, the best feedback for design improvement is feedback deriving from Carter's (2007) "inquiry within experience," or formative data given concurrent with usage rather than retrospective recollection. A full description of how to do remote UX testing is highly dependent on the type of technology used to mediate the evaluation, and therefore not possible to describe in detail here.

13.9.3 Local UX Evaluation

Local UX evaluation is UX evaluation using a local prototype. A local prototype is very limited in both depth and breadth, restricted to a single interaction design issue involving particular isolated interaction details, such as the appearance of an icon, wording of a message, or behavior of an individual function. If your design team cannot agree on the details of a single feature, such as a particular dialogue box, you can mockup local prototypes of the alternatives and take them to users to compare in local UX evaluation.

Local Prototype

A local prototype represents the small area where horizontal and vertical slices intersect. A local prototype, with depth and breadth both limited, is used to evaluate design alternatives for a particular isolated interaction detail.

13.9.4 Automatic UX Evaluation

Lab-based and UX inspection methods are labor-intensive and, therefore, limited in scope (small number of users exercising small portions of large systems). But large and complex systems with large numbers of users offer the potential for a vast volume of usage data. Think of "observing" a hundred thousand users using Microsoft Word. Automatic methods have been devised to take advantage of this boundless pool of data, collecting and analyzing usage data without need for UX specialists to deal with each individual action.

The result is a massive amount of data about keystrokes, click-streams, and pause/idle times. But all data are at the low level of user actions, without any information about tasks, user intentions, cognitive processes, etc. There are no direct indications of when the user is having a UX problem somewhere in the midst of that torrent of user action data. Basing redesign on click counts and low-level user navigation within a large software application could well lead to low-level optimization of a system with a bad high-level design. A full description of how to do automatic usability evaluation is beyond our scope.

13.10 MORE ABOUT "DISCOUNT" UX ENGINEERING METHODS

13.10.1 Nielsen and Molich's Original Heuristics

The first set of heuristics that Nielsen and Molich developed for usability inspection (Molich & Nielsen, 1990; Nielsen & Molich, 1990) were 10 "general principles" for interaction design. They called them heuristics because they are not strict design guidelines. Table 13-3 lists these original heuristics from Nielsen's *Usability Engineering* book (Nielsen, 1993, Chapter 5).

13.10.2 "Discount" Formative UX Evaluation Methods

Although the concepts have been challenged, mainly by academics, as inferior and scientifically unsound, we use the term "discount method" in a positive sense. UX evaluation is the center of the iterative process and, despite its highly varied effectiveness, somehow in practice it still works. Here we wholeheartedly affirm the value of discount UX methods among your UX engineering tools!

What is a "discount" evaluation method?

Because UX inspection techniques are less costly, they have been called "discount" evaluation techniques (Nielsen, 1989). Although the term was intended to reflect the advantage of lower costs, it soon was used pejoratively to connote inferior bargain-basement goods (Cockton & Woolrych, 2002;

The 10 Original Nielsen and Molich Usablity Inspection Heuristics

- Simple and natural dialogue
  - Good graphic design and use of color
  - Screen layout by gestalt rules of human perception
  - Less is more; avoid extraneous information
- Speak the users' language
  - User-centered terminology, not system or technology centered
  - Use words with standard meanings
  - Vocabulary and meaning from work domain
  - Use mappings and metaphors to support learning
- Minimize user memory load
  - Clear labeling
- Consistency
  - Help avoid errors, especially by novices
- Feedback
  - Make it clear when an error has occurred
  - Show user progress
- Clearly marked exits
  - Provide escape from all dialogue boxes
- Shortcuts
  - Help expert users without penalizing novices
- Good error messages
  - Clear language, not obscure codes
  - Be precise rather than vague or general
  - Be constructive to help solve problem
  - Be polite and not intimidating
- Prevent errors
  - Many potential error situations can be avoided in design
  - Select from lists, where possible, instead of requiring user to type in
  - Avoid modes
- Help and documentation
  - When users want to read the manual, they are usually desperate
  - Be specific with online help

Table 13-3

Original Nielsen and Molich heuristics

Gray & Salzman, 1998) because of the reduced effectiveness and susceptibility to errors in identifying UX problems.

Inspection methods have been criticized as "damaged merchandise" (Gray & Salzman, 1998) or "discount goods" (Cockton & Woolrych, 2002); however we feel that, as in most things, the value of these methods depends on the context of their use. Although the controversy could be viewed by those outside of HCI research as academic fun and games, it could be important to you because it is about very practical aspects of your choices of UX evaluation methods and bounds in their use.

Do "discount" methods work?

It depends on what you mean by "work." Much of the literature by researchers studying the effectiveness of UX evaluation methods decries the shortcomings of inspection methods when measured by a science-oriented yardstick.

Studies have established that even with a large number of evaluators, some evaluations reveal only a percentage of the existing problems. We know that there is a broad variability of results across methods and across people using the same method. Different evaluators even report very different problems when observing the same evaluation session. Different UX teams interpret the same evaluation report in different ways.

However, in an engineering context, "working" means being effective and being cost-effective, and in this context discount UX engineering methods have a well-documented record of success. From a practical perspective, it is difficult to avoid the conclusion that using these methods is still better than not doing anything about evaluating UX.

Yes, you might miss many real user experience problems, but you will get some good ones, too. That is the trade-off you must be willing to accept if you use "discount" methods. You might even get some false positives, things that look like problems but really are not. It is hoped that you can sort those out. In any case, the idea is that you will be able to achieve a good engineering result much faster and with far less cost than a full empirical treatment that some authors demand.

Finally, although lab-based evaluation is often held up as the "gold standard" or yardstick against which other evaluation methods are compared, lab testing is not perfect, either, and does not escape criticism for limitations in effectiveness (Molich et al., 1998, 1999; Newman, 1998; Spool & Schroeder, 2001). The lab-based approach to UX testing suffers from many of the same kinds of flaws as do discount and other inspection methods.

Pros and cons as engineering tools

Of course, with any discount approach, there are trade-offs. The upside is that, in the hands of an experienced evaluator, inspection methods can be very effective—you can get a lot of UX problems dealt with and out of the way at a low cost. Another advantage is that UX inspection methods can be very fast, more quickly responsive than lab testing, for example, to fast iteration. Under the right conditions, you can do a UX inspection and its analysis, fix the major problems, and update the prototype design in a day!

The major downsides are that because inspection methods do not employ real users, they can be error-prone, can tend to find a higher proportion of lower severity problems, and can suffer from validity problems. This means they will yield some false positives (UX issues that turn out not to be real problems) and will miss some UX problems because of false negatives. Having to deal with low-severity problems and false positives can be distracting to UX practitioners and can be wasteful of resources.

Another potential drawback is that the UX experts doing the inspection may not know the subject-matter domain or the system in depth. This can lead to a less effective inspection but can be offset somewhat by including a subject-matter expert on the inspection team.

Evaluating UX evaluation methods

Some of the value of current methods for assessing and improving UX in interactive software systems is somewhat offset by a general lack of understanding of the capabilities and limitations of each. Practitioners need to know which methods are more effective and in what ways and for what purposes. Thus emerged the need to evaluate and compare usability evaluation methods. The literature has a number of limited studies and commentaries on the effectiveness of usability evaluation methods, each report with its own different goals, results, and inferences.

However, there are no standard criteria for usability evaluation method comparison from study to study. And researchers planning full formal summative studies of competing methods in a real-world commercial development project environment are faced with virtually prohibitive difficulty and expense. It is hard enough to develop a system once, let alone redeveloping it over and over with multiple different approaches.

So we have a few imperfect but still enlightening studies to go by, mostly studies emerging as a by-product or afterthought attached to some other primary effort. In sum, usability evaluation methods have not been evaluated and compared reliably.

In the literature, usability inspection methods are often compared with lab-based testing, but we do not see inspection as a one-or-the-other alternative or a substitute for lab-based testing. Each method is one of the available UX engineering tools, each appropriate under its own conditions.

Andrew Sears made some of the most important early contributions about usability metrics (e.g., thoroughness, validity, and reliability) in usability evaluation methods (Sears, 1997; Sears & Hess, 1999). Hartson, Andre, and Williges (2003) introduced usability evaluation method comparison criteria and extended the measures of Sears to include effectiveness, an overall metric taking into account both thoroughness and validity. Their weightings between thoroughness and validity have the potential to enhance the possibilities for usability evaluation method performance measures in comparison studies.

Hartson, Andre, and Williges (2003) include a modest review of 18 comparative usability evaluation method studies.

Gray and Salzman (1998) spoke to the weaknesses of most usability evaluation method comparison studies conducted to that date. Their critical review of usability evaluation method studies concluded that flaws in experimental design and execution "call into serious question what we thought we knew regarding the efficacy of various usability evaluation methods." Using specific critiques of well-known usability evaluation method studies to illustrate, they argued the case that experimental validity (of various kinds) and other shortcomings of statistical analyses posed a danger in using the "conclusions" to recommend usability evaluation methods to practitioners.

To say that this paper was controversial is an understatement. Perhaps it was in part the somewhat cynical title ("Damaged Merchandise") or the overly severe indictment of the research arm of HCI, but the comments, rebuttals, and rejoinders that followed added more than a little fun and excitement into the discipline.

Also, we have noticed a trend since this paper to transfer the blame from the studies of discount usability evaluation methods to the methods themselves, a subtle attempt to paint the methods with the same "damaged merchandise" brush. The CHI'95 panel called "Discount or Disservice?" (Gray et al., 1995) is an example. In Gray and Salzman (1998), the term "damaged merchandise" was, at least ostensibly, aimed at flawed studies comparing usability evaluation methods. But many have taken the term to refer to the usability evaluation methods themselves and this panel title does nothing to disabuse us of this semantic sleight of hand.

More recently, in a comprehensive meta study of usability methods and practice, Hornbaek (2006) looked at 180 (!) studies of usability evaluation methods. Hornbaek proposed more meaningful usability measures, both objective and subjective, and contributed a useful in-depth discussion of what it means to measure usability, an elusive but fundamental concept in this context.

Finally, one of the practical problems with evaluation methods and their evaluation is the question of "Now that you have found the usability problems, what is next?" John and Marks (1997) consider downstream (after usability data gathering) utility, the usefulness of usability evaluation method outputs (problem reports) in convincing team members of the need to fix a problem and the usefulness in helping to effect the fixes. Only a few others also consider this issue, including Medlock et al. (2005), Gunn (1995), and Sawyer, Flanders, and Wixon (1996).

The Comparative Usability Evaluation (CUE) series

In a series of usability evaluation method evaluation studies that became known as the Comparative Usability Evaluation series (seven studies that we know of as of this writing), a number of usability evaluation methods were tested under a variety of conditions and a major observation emerged under the name of the evaluator effect (Hertzum & Jacobsen, 2003), which essentially states that the variation among results from different evaluators using the same method on the same target application can be so large as to call into question the effectiveness of the methods. These studies have been called by some the studies that discredit usability engineering, but we think they just bring some important issues about reality to light.

In CUE-1 (Molich et al., 1998), four professional usability labs performed usability tests of a Windows calendar management application. Of the 141 usability problems reported overall, 90% were reported by only one lab and only one problem was reported by as many as four labs.

In CUE-2 (Molich et al., 2004), nine organizations evaluated a Website, focusing on a prescribed task set. Seventy-five percent of the 310 overall problems were reported by just one team, while only 2 problems were reported by as many as six groups.

CUE-3 (Hertzum, Jacobsen, & Molich, 2002) again evaluated a Website using a specific task set. This time the experimenters began with 11 individuals. The subject evaluators then met in four groups to combine their individual results. Following group discussions, the individuals "felt that they were largely in agreement," despite only a 9% overlap in reported problems between any two evaluators. This perception of agreement in the face of data apparently to the contrary seemed to be based on the feeling that the different problem reports were actually about similar underlying problems but coming at them from different directions.

In a secondary part of CUE-4, the authors concluded that a large proportion of recommendations given following a usability evaluation were neither useful nor usable for making design changes to improve product usability (Molich, Jeffries, & Dumas, 2007). The authors concluded that designers have difficulty acting on most problem descriptions because problem reports are often poorly written, unconvincing, and ineffective at guiding a design solution. To make it worse, in many cases the entire outcome rides on the report itself as there is no opportunity to explain the problems or argue the case afterward.

As of this writing, the latest in the CUE series was CUE-9 (Molich, 2011).

13.10.3 Yet Somehow Things Work

Press on

So what is all the fuss in the literature about damaged merchandise, discount methods, heuristic methods, and so on? Scientifically, there are valid issues with these methods. However, the evaluator effect applies to virtually all kinds of UX evaluation, including our venerable yardstick of performance, the lab-based formative evaluation. Formative evaluation, in general, just is not very reliable or repeatable.

There is no one evaluation method that will reveal all the UX problems. So what is a UX newbie to do? Give it up? No, this is engineering and we just have to get over it, be practical, and do our best—and sometimes it works really well.

While researchers continue to pursue and validate better methods, we make things work and we use tools and methods that are far less than perfect. We always seem to get a better design by evaluating and iterating and that is the goal. One application of our methods may not find all UX problems, but we usually get some good ones. If we fix those, maybe we will get the others the next time.

We will find the important ones in other ways—we are not doing the whole process with our eyes closed. In the meantime, experienced practitioners read about how these evaluation methods do not work and smile as they head off to the lab or to an inspection session.

Among the reasons we have to be optimistic in the long run about our UX evaluation methods are:

- Goals are engineering goals, not scientific goals
- Iteration helps close the gap
- Disagreement in the studies was subject to interpretation
- Evaluation methods can be backed up with UX expertise

Practical engineering goals

Approaching perfection is expensive. In engineering, the goal is to make it good enough. Wixon (2003) speaks up for the practitioner in the discussion of usability evaluation methods. From an applied perspective, he points out that a focus on validity and proper statistical analysis in these studies is not serving the needs of practitioners in finding the most suitable usability evaluation method and best practices for their work context in the business world.

Wixon (2003) would like to see more emphasis on usability evaluation method comparison criteria that take into account factors that determine their success in real product development organizations. As an example, the value of a method might be less about absolute numbers of problems detected and more about how well a usability evaluation method fits into the work style and development process of the organization. And to this we can only say amen.

Managing risk by mitigating evaluation errors

Cockton and Woolrych (2002) cast errors made with usability evaluation methods (discount inspection methods and "lite" lab-based usability testing methods) in terms of risks, "But are discount methods really too risky to justify the 'low' cost?" What kinds of risks are there? There is the risk of not fixing usability issues missed by the method and the risk of "fixing" false alarms.

To be sure, however, the risks associated with errors are real and are part of any engineering activity involving evaluation and iterative improvement. But we have to ask, how serious are the risks? Rarely can an error of these types make or break the success of the system. As Cockton and Woolrych (2002, pp. 17–18) point out, "errors . . . may be more costly in some contexts than others."

Where human lives are at risk, we are compelled to spend more resources to be more thorough in all our process activities and will surely not allow an evaluation error to weaken the design in the end. In most applications, though, each error simply means that we missed an opportunity to improve usability in one detail of the design.

Managing the risk of false negatives with iteration

Many of the comparisons of usability inspection methods point out the susceptibility of these methods to making errors in identifying usability problems, with disparaging conclusions. However, these conclusions are usually made in the context of science, where evaluation errors can count heavily against the method. In balance, others (Manning, 2002) question the working assumptions of such problem validity arguments when examined in the light of real-world development projects.

One kind of problem identification error, a false negative—failure to detect a real usability problem—can lead to missing out on needed fixes. The risk here, of course, is not greater than it would be if no evaluation is done. So every problem you do find is one for the good. What, then, are the alternatives? Discount methods are being used presumably because of budget constraints, so the more expensive lab-based testing is not going to be the answer.

One important factor that some studies of evaluation methods neglect is iteration. To temper the consequences of missing some problems the first time around, you always have other iterations and other evaluation methods that might well catch them by the end of the day. If we look at the results over a few iterations instead of each attempt in isolation, we are likely to see net occurrences of false negatives reduced greatly.

If we find a set of bona fide problems and fix them, we remove them from contention in the next cycle of evaluation, which helps us focus on the remaining problems. If we combine different results (i.e., different problems uncovered) from different evaluators or different iterations, the overall process can still converge.

Managing the risk of false positives with UX expertise

Another kind of problem identification error is a false positive—identifying something as a problem when it is not. The risk associated with this kind of error, that of trying to fix a problem that is not real, could exact a penalty. For example, false positives in problem identification can lead to unneeded and possibly damaging "fixes." But, as we said, this risk occurs with any kind of evaluation method.

The important point to remember here is that UX inspection is only an engineering tool. You, the practitioner, must maintain your engineering judgment and not let evaluation results be interpreted as the final word. You are still in charge.

Also, as many point out, this is just the initial finding of candidate problems. To abate the effects of false positives, think of the method as an engineering tool not giving you absolute indicators of problems but *suggesting possible problems*, possibilities that you, the expert practitioner, must still investigate, analyze, and decide upon. Then, if there are still false positives, you can blame yourself and not the inspection method. In the discount methods controversy, we lay a lot of responsibility on the methods for finding problems without considering that the UX evaluation methods are backed up by UX specialists.

One important way that a UX specialist can augment the limited power of a UX evaluation method is by learning from problems that are found and keeping alert for similar issues elsewhere in the design. An interaction design is a web of features and relationships. If you detect one instance of a UX problem in a particular design feature, you are likely to encounter similar problems in similar situations elsewhere as you go about the fixes and redesign.

Suppose there are 10 instances of a UX problem of a certain general type in your application, but our UX evaluation method finds only 1. There is still a good chance that analysis and redesign for that problem will lead a dedicated and observant UX specialist eventually to find and fix some other similar or related problems, giving you a UX evaluation method/practitioner team with a higher net problem detection rate.

Look at the bright side of studies

In CUE-3 (Hertzum, Jacobsen, & Molich, 2002), the dissimilarity among results across individual evaluators was not viewed as disagreements by the evaluators but as different expressions of the same underlying problems. Although statistically the evaluators had a relatively small overlap in problems reported, after a group discussion the evaluators all *felt* they "were largely in agreement." The evaluators perceived their disparate observations as multiple sources of evidence in support of the same issues, not as disagreements.

We have also experienced this in our consulting work when different problem reports at first seemed not comparable, but further discussion revealed that they were saying different things about essentially the same underlying problems, and we felt that even if we had not detected this in the analysis stage, the different views would have converged in the process of fixing the problems.

This seems to say that the evaluation methods were not as bad at problem detection as data initially implied. However, it also seems to shift the spotlight to difficulties in how we analyze and report problems in those methods. There is a large variation in the diagnoses and expressions used to describe problems.

Finally, in situations where thoroughness is low, low reliability across evaluators can actually be an asset. As long as each evaluator is not finding most or all of the problems, differences in detection across evaluators mean that, by adding more evaluators, you can find more problems in their combined reports through a diversity in detection abilities.

In sum, although criticized as false economy in some HCI literature, especially the academic literature, these so-called "discount" methods are practiced heavily and successfully in the field.

Rigorous Empirical Evaluation: Preparation

14

Be prepared; that's the Boy Scouts' marching song. . . . Don't be nervous, don't be flustered, don't be scared. . . . Be prepared!

– Tom Lehrer

Objectives

After reading this chapter, you will:
1. Know how to plan for rigorous empirical UX evaluation in the lab and in the field
2. Be able to select people for team roles
3. Know how to select effective tasks for empirical UX evaluation
4. Be prepared to select an evaluation method and various data collection techniques, including critical incident identification, think-aloud techniques, co-discovery, and questionnaires
5. Have the working knowledge to select, recruit, and prepare for participants
6. Know how to perform pilot testing before evaluation
7. Understand the concepts and issues relating to determining the right number of participants for a given evaluation situation

14.1 INTRODUCTION

14.1.1 You Are Here

We begin each process chapter with a "you are here" picture of the chapter topic in the context of the overall Wheel lifecycle template; see Figure 14-1. This chapter, about preparing for evaluation, begins a series of chapters about rigorous empirical UX evaluation.

This chapter begins a series of four about rigorous empirical UX evaluation methods, of which lab-based testing is the archetype example. Some of what is in these chapters applies to either lab-based or in-the-field empirical evaluation,

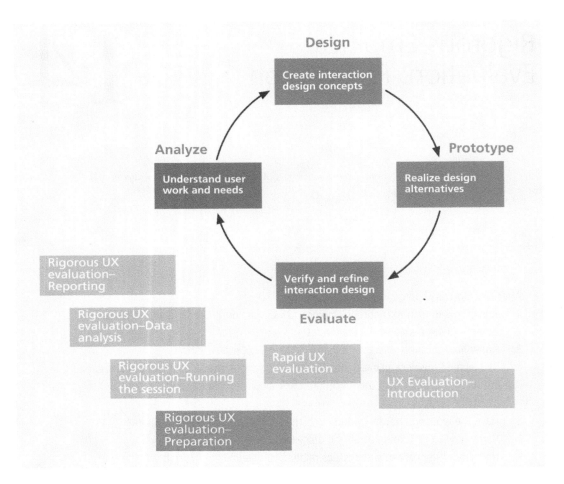

Figure 14-1

You are here, at preparing for evaluation, within the evaluation activity in the context of the overall Wheel lifecycle template.

but parts are specific to just lab based. Field-based rigorous empirical UX evaluation is essentially the same as lab based except the work is done on location in the field instead of in a lab.

Although we do include quantitative UX data collection and analysis, this is emphasized less than it used to be in previous usability engineering books because of less focus in practice on quantitative user performance measures and more emphasis on evaluation to reveal UX problems to be fixed.

14.2 PLAN FOR RIGOROUS EMPIRICAL UX EVALUATION

Planning your empirical UX evaluation means making cost-effective decisions and trade-offs. As Dray and Siegel (1999) warn, "Beware of expediency as a basis for decision making." In other words, do not let small short-term savings undercut your larger investment in evaluation and in the whole process lifecycle.

14.2.1 A Rigorous UX Evaluation Plan

The purpose of your plan for rigorous UX evaluation, whether lab based or in the field, is to describe evaluation goals, methods, activities, conditions, constraints, and expectations. Especially if the plan will be read by people outside your immediate project group, you might want an upfront "boilerplate" introduction with some topics like these, described very concisely:

- Goals and purpose of this UX evaluation
- Overview of plan
- Overview of product or parts of product being evaluated (for people outside the group)
- Goals of the product user interface (i.e., what will make for a successful user experience)
- Description of the intended user population
- Overview of approach to informed consent
- Overview of how this evaluation fits into the overall iterative UX process lifecycle
- Overview of the UX evaluation process in general (e.g., preparation, data collection, analysis, reporting, iteration)
- General evaluation methods and activities planned for this session
- Estimated schedule
- Responsible personnel

The body of the plan can include topics such as:

- Description of resources and constraints (e.g., time needed/available, state of prototype, lab facilities and equipment)
- Pilot testing plan
- Approach to evaluation, choices of data collection techniques
- Mechanics of the evaluation (e.g., materials used, informed consent, location of testing, UX goals and metrics involved, tasks to be explored, including applicable benchmark tasks)
- All instruments to be used (e.g., benchmark task descriptions, questionnaires)
- Approaches to data analysis
- Specifics of your approach to evaluate emotional impact and, if appropriate, phenomenological aspects of interaction

14.2.2 Goals for Rigorous UX Evaluation Session

One of the first things to do in an evaluation plan is to set, prioritize, and document your evaluation goals. Identify the most important design issues and user tasks to investigate. Decide which parts of the system or functionality you simply will not have time to look at.

Your evaluation goals, against which you should weigh all your evaluation choices and activities, can include:

- Application scope (parts of the system to be covered by this evaluation)
- Types of data to collect (see Chapter 12)
- UX goals, targets, and metrics, if any, to be addressed
- Matching this evaluation to the current stage of product design evolution

14.3 TEAM ROLES FOR RIGOROUS EVALUATION

Select your team members for evaluation activities. Encourage your whole project team to participate in at least some evaluation. The greater the extent that the whole team is involved from the start, in both the planning and the execution of the studies, the better chance you have at addressing everyone's concerns. Broad participation begets buy-in and ownership, necessary for your results to be taken as a serious mandate to fix problems.

However, your evaluation team will practically be limited to practitioners with active roles, perhaps plus a few observers from the rest of your project team or organization. So, everyone on your evaluation team is an "evaluator," but you also need to establish who will play more specific roles, including the facilitator, the prototype "executor," and all observers and data collectors. Whether your prototype is low or high fidelity, you will need to select appropriate team roles for conducting evaluation.

14.3.1 Facilitator

Participant

"Participant" is the term we use for the subject or outside person who helps the team design and evaluate interaction, usually by performing tasks and giving feedback.

Select your facilitator, the leader of the evaluation team. The facilitator is the orchestrator, the one who makes sure it all works right. The facilitator has the primary responsibility for planning and executing the testing sessions, and the final responsibility to make sure the laboratory is set up properly. Because the facilitator will be the principal contact for participants during a session and responsible for putting the participant at ease, you should select someone with good "people skills."

14.3.2 Prototype Executor

If you are using a low-fidelity (e.g., paper) prototype, you need to select a prototype executor, a person to "execute" the prototype as though it were being run on a computer. The person in this role *is* the computer.

The prototype executor must have a thorough technical knowledge of how the design works. So that the prototype executor responds only to participant actions, he or she must have a steady Vulcan sense of logic. The executor must also have the discipline to maintain a poker face and not speak a single word throughout the entire session.

14.3.3 Quantitative Data Collectors

If you intend to collect quantitative data, you will need quantitative data collectors. Depending on your UX metrics and quantitative data collection instruments, people in these roles may be walking around with stopwatches and counters (mechanical, electronic, or paper and pencil). Whatever quantitative data are called for by the UX metrics, these people must be ready to take and record those data. Quantitative data collectors must be attentive and not let data slip by without notice. They must have the ability to focus and not let their minds wander during a session. If you can afford it, it is best to let someone specialize in only taking quantitative data. Other duties and distractions often lead to forgetting to turn on or off timers or forgetting to count errors.

14.3.4 Qualitative Data Collectors

Although facilitators are usually experienced in data collection, they often do not have time to take data or they need help in gathering all qualitative data. When things are happening fast, the need for facilitation can trump data taking for the facilitator.

Select one or more others as data collectors and recorders. No evaluation team member should ever be idle during a session. Thoroughness will improve with more people doing the job. Everyone should be ready to collect qualitative data, especially critical incident data; the more data collectors, the better.

14.3.5 Supporting Actors

Sometimes you need someone to interact with the participant as part of the task setting or to manage the props needed in the evaluation. For example, for task realism you may need someone to call the participant on a telephone in the participant room or, if your user participant is an "agent" of some kind, you may need a "client" to walk in with a specific need involving an agent task using the system. Select team members to play supporting roles and handle props.

Critical Incident

A critical incident is a UX evaluation event that occurs during user task performance or other user interaction, observed by the facilitator or other observers or sometimes expressed by the user participant, that indicates a possible UX problem. Critical incident identification is arguably the single most important source of qualitative data.

14.4 PREPARE AN EFFECTIVE RANGE OF TASKS

If evaluation is to be task based, including lab-based testing and task-driven UX inspection methods, select appropriate tasks to support evaluation. Select different kinds of tasks for different evaluation purposes.

14.4.1 Benchmark Tasks to Generate Quantitative Measures

If you plan to use UX goals and targets to drive your UX evaluation, everyone in an evaluator role should have already participated with other members of the project team in identifying benchmark tasks and UX target attributes and metrics (Chapter 10). These attributes and metrics must be ready and waiting as a comparison point with actual results to be observed in the informal summative component of the evaluation sessions with participants.

Be sure that descriptions of all benchmark tasks associated with your UX targets and metrics are in final form, printed off, and ready to use by participants to generate data to be measured. Benchmark tasks portray representative, frequent, and critical tasks that apply to the key work role and user class represented by each participant (Chapter 10). Make sure each task description says only *what* to do, with no hints about *how* to do it. Also, do not use any language that telegraphs any part of the design (e.g., names of user interface objects or user actions, or words from labels or menus).

14.4.2 Unmeasured Tasks

Like benchmark tasks, additional unmeasured tasks, used especially in early cycles of evaluation, should be ones that users are expected to perform often. Unmeasured tasks are tasks for which participant performance will not be measured quantitatively but which will be used to add breadth to qualitative evaluation. Evaluators can use these representative tasks to address aspects of the design not covered in some way by the benchmark tasks.

In early stages, you might employ only unmeasured tasks, the sole goal of which is to observe critical incidents and identify initial UX problems to root out, to fix at least the most obvious and most severe problems before any measured user performance data can be very useful.

Just as for benchmark tasks created for testing UX attributes, you should write up representative unmeasured task descriptions, which should be just as specific as the benchmark task descriptions, and give them to the participant to perform in the evaluation sessions.

14.4.3 Exploratory Free Use

In addition to strictly specified benchmark and unmeasured tasks, the
evaluator may also find it useful to observe the participant in informal *free use*
of the interface, a free-play period without the constraints of predefined
tasks. This does not necessarily mean that they are even doing tasks, just
exploring.

Be prepared to ask your participants to explore and experiment with the
interaction design, beyond task performance. To engage a participant in free
use, the evaluator might simply say "play around with the interface for awhile,
doing anything you would like to, and talk aloud while you are playing." Free use
is valuable for revealing participant expectations and system behavior in
situations not anticipated by designers, often situations that can break a poor
design.

14.4.4 User-Defined Tasks

Sometimes tasks that users come up with will address unexpected aspects of your
design (Cordes, 2001). You can include user-defined tasks by giving your
participants a system description in advance of the evaluation sessions and ask
them to write down some tasks they think are appropriate to try or you can wait
until the session is under way and ask each participant extemporaneously to
come up with tasks to try.

If you want a more uniform task set over your participants but still wish to
include user-defined tasks, you can ask a different set of potential users to come
up with a number of candidate task descriptions before starting any evaluation
session. This is a good application for a focus group. You can vet, edit, and merge
these into a set of user-defined tasks to be given to each participant as part
of each evaluation session.

14.5 SELECT AND ADAPT EVALUATION METHOD AND DATA COLLECTION TECHNIQUES

14.5.1 Select Evaluation Method and Data Collection Techniques

Using the descriptions of the evaluation methods and data collection techniques
in Chapter 12, including the descriptions of the kinds of evaluation each is used
for, select your evaluation method and data collection techniques to fit your
evaluation plan and goals and the particular evaluation needs of your system or
product.

For example, at a high level, you should choose first between rigorous or rapid evaluation methods (see Chapter 12). If you choose rigorous, you might choose between a lab-based or in-the-field method. If you choose rapid methods, your next choice should be from among the many such evaluation methods given in Chapter 13.

Your approach to choosing evaluation methods and techniques should be goal driven. For example, when you wish to evaluate usefulness—the coverage, completeness, and appropriateness of functionality and the coverage, completeness, and appropriateness of its support in the user interface—consider doing it:

- Objectively, by cross-checks of functionality implied by your hierarchical task inventory, design scenarios, conceptual design, and task intention descriptions.
- Subjectively, by user questionnaires (Chapter 12).
- Longitudinally, by following up with real users in the field after a product or system is released. Use downstream questionnaires directed at usefulness issues to guiding functional design thinking for subsequent versions.

Your choices of specific data collection techniques should also be goal driven. If you are using participants, as you will in rigorous evaluation, you should strongly consider using the critical incident identification, think-aloud, and co-discovery techniques (Chapter 12). If you are doing a task-driven expert UX inspection (Chapter 13), you can collect data about your own critical incidents.

Questionnaires (Chapter 12) are a good choice if you want to supplement your objective UX evaluation data with subjective data directly from the user. Questionnaires are simple to use, for both analyst and participant, and can be used with or without a lab. Questionnaires can yield quantitative data as well as qualitative user opinions.

For example, a questionnaire can have numerical choices that participants must choose from to provide quantitative data or it can have open-ended questions to elicit qualitative free-form feedback. Questionnaires are good for evaluating specific predefined aspects of the user experience, including perceived usability and usefulness.

If you want to collect data to evaluate emotional impact, questionnaires are probably the least expensive choice and the easiest to administer. More advanced data collection techniques for evaluating emotional impact include biometrics and other ways to identify or measure physiological responses in users (Chapter 12).

If you choose to use a questionnaire in your evaluation, your next step is to use the information on questionnaires in Chapter 12 to decide which questionnaire to use. For example, you might choose our old standby, the Questionnaire for User Interface Satisfaction (QUIS), for subjective evaluation of, and user satisfaction about, traditional user performance and usability issues in screen-based interaction designs; the System Usability Scale (SUS) for a versatile and broadly applicable general purpose subject user experience evaluation instrument; or the Usefulness, Satisfaction, and Ease of Use (USE) questionnaire for a general-purpose subjective user experience evaluation instrument.

Part of choosing a questionnaire will involve deciding the timing of administration, for example, after each task or at the end of each session.

14.5.2 Adapt Your Choice of Evaluation Method and Data Collection Techniques

For UX evaluation, as perhaps for most UX work, our motto echoes that old military imperative: Improvise, adapt, and overcome! Be flexible and customize your methods and techniques, creating variations to fit your evaluation goals and needs. This includes adapting any method by leaving out steps, adding new steps, and changing the details of a step.

14.6 SELECT PARTICIPANTS

The selection and recruitment of participants are about finding representative users outside your team and often outside your project organization to help with evaluation. This section is mainly focused on participants for lab-based UX evaluation, but also applies to other situations where participants are needed, such as some non-lab-based methods for evaluating emotional impact and phenomenological aspects.

In formal summative evaluation, this part of the process is referred to as "sampling," but that term is not appropriate here because what we are doing has nothing to do with the implied statistical relationships and constraints.

14.6.1 Establish Need and Budget for Recruiting User Participants Upfront

Finding and recruiting evaluation participants might be part of the process where you are tempted to cut corners and save a little on the budget or might be something you think to do at the last minute.

In participant recruiting, to protect the larger investment already made in the UX lifecycle process and in setting up formative evaluation so far, you need to secure a reasonable amount of resources, both budget money and schedule time to recruit and remunerate the full range and number of evaluation participants you will need. If you do this kind of evaluation infrequently, you can engage the services of a UX evaluation consulting group or a professional recruiter to do your participant recruiting.

14.6.2 Determine the Right Participants

Look for participants who are "representative users," that is, participants who match your target work activity role's user class descriptions and who are knowledgeable of the general target system domain. If you have multiple work roles and corresponding multiple user classes, you must recruit participants representing *each* category. Prepare a short written demographic survey to administer to participants to confirm that each one meets the requirements of your intended work activity role's user class characteristics.

Participants must also match the user class attributes in any UX targets they will help evaluate. For example, if initial usage is specified, you need participants unfamiliar with your design. So, for example, even though a user may be a perfect match to a given key work role's user class characteristics, if the UX target involved specifies "initial performance" as the UX attribute and this participant has already seen and used the interaction design, maybe in a previous iteration, this person is not the right participant for this part of the evaluation.

"Expert" participants

Recruit an expert user, someone who knows the system domain and knows your particular system, if you have a session calling for experienced usage. Expert users are good at generating qualitative data. These expert users will understand the tasks and can tell you what they do not like about the design. But you cannot necessarily depend on them to tell you how to make the design better.

Recruit a UX expert if you need a participant with broad UX knowledge and who can speak to design flaws in terms of design guidelines. As participants, these experts may not know the system domain as well and the tasks might not make as much sense to them, but they can analyze user experience, find subtle problems (e.g., small inconsistencies, poor use of color, confusing navigation), and offer suggestions for solutions.

Consider recruiting a so-called double expert, a UX expert who also knows your system very well, perhaps the most valuable kind of participant. But the question of what constitutes being an expert of value to your evaluation is not always clear-cut. Also, the distinction between expert and novice user is not a simple dichotomy. Not all experts make good evaluation participants and not all novices will perform poorly. And being an expert is relative: an expert in one thing can very well be a novice at something else. And even the same person can be an expert at one thing today and less of an expert in a month due to lack of practice and retroactive interference (intervening activities of another type).

14.6.3 Determine the Right Number of Participants

The question of how many participants you need is entirely dependent on the kind of evaluation you are doing and the conditions under which you are doing it. There are some rules of thumb, such as the famous "three to five participants is enough" maxim, which is quoted so often out of context as to be almost meaningless. However, real answers are more difficult. See the end of this chapter for further discussion about the "three to five users" rule and its limitations.

The good news is that your experience and intuition will be good touchstones for knowing when you have gotten the most of an iteration of UX evaluation and when to move on. One telltale sign is the lack of many new critical incidents or UX problems being discovered with additional participants.

You have to decide for yourself every time you do UX testing—how many participants you can or want to afford. Sometimes it is just about achieving your UX targets, regardless of how many participants and iterations it takes. More often it is about getting in, getting some insight, and getting out.

14.7 RECRUIT PARTICIPANTS

Now the question arises as to where to find participants. Inform your customer early on about how your evaluation process will proceed so you will have the best chance of getting representative users from the customer organization at appropriate times.

14.7.1 Recruiting Methods and Screening

Here are some hints for successful participant recruiting.

- Try to get the people around you (co-workers, colleagues elsewhere in your organization, spouses, children, and so on) to volunteer their time to act as participants, but be sure their characteristics fit your key work role and the corresponding user class needs.

- Newspaper ads and emailings can work to recruit participants, but these methods are usually inefficient.
- If the average person off the street fits your participant profile (e.g., for a consumer software application), hand out leaflets in shopping malls and parking lots or post notices in grocery stores or in other public places (e.g., libraries).
- Use announcements at meetings of user groups and professional organizations if the cross section of the groups matches your user class needs.
- Recruit students at universities, community colleges, or even K–12, if appropriate.
- Consider temporary employment agencies as another source for finding participants.

A possible pitfall with temporary employment agencies is that they usually know nothing about UX evaluation, nor do they understand why it is so important to choose appropriate people as participants. The agency goal, after all, is to keep their pool of temporary workers employed, so screen their candidates with your user classes.

14.7.2 Participant Recruiting Database

No matter how you get contact information for your potential participants (advertising campaign, references from marketing, previously used participants), if you are going to be doing evaluation often, you should maintain a participant recruiting database. Because all the participants you have used in the past should be in this database, you can draw on the good ones for repeat performances.

You can also sometimes use your own customer base or your customer's contact lists as a participant recruiting source. Perhaps your marketing department has its own contact database.

14.7.3 Incentives and Remuneration

Generally, you should not ask your participants to work for free, so you will usually have to advertise some kind of remuneration. Try to determine the going rate for evaluation participants in your local area.

You will usually pay a modest hourly fee (e.g., about a dollar above minimum wage for an off-the-street volunteer). Expert participants cost more, depending on your specialized requirements. Do not try to get by too cheaply; you might get what you pay for.

Instead of or in addition to money, you can offer various kinds of premium gifts, such as coffee mugs with your company logo, gift certificates for local restaurants and shops, T-shirts proclaiming they survived your UX tests, free pizza, or even chocolate chip cookies! Sometimes just having a chance to learn about a new product before it is released or to help shape the design of some new technology is motivation enough.

14.7.4 Difficult-to-Find User Participants

Be creative in arranging for hard-to-find participant types. Sometimes, the customer—for whatever reasons—simply will not let the developer organization have access to representative users. The Navy, for example, can be rightfully hesitant about calling in its ships and shipboard personnel from the high seas to evaluate a system being developed to go on board.

Specialized roles (such as an ER physician) have time constraints that make if difficult, or impossible, to schedule them in advance. Sometimes you can have an "on call" agreement through which they call you if they have some free time and you do your best to work them in.

Sometimes when you cannot get a representative user, you can find a user representative, someone who is not exactly in the same role but who knows the role from some other angle. A domain expert is not necessarily the same as a user, but might serve as a participant, especially in an early evaluation cycle. We once were looking for a particular kind of agent of an organization who worked with the public, but had to settle, at least at the beginning, for supervisors of those agents.

14.7.5 Recruiting for Co-Discovery

Consider recruiting pairs of participants specifically for co-discovery evaluation. Your goal is to find people who will work well together during evaluation and, as a practical matter, who are available at the same time. We have found it best not to use two people who are close friends or who work together on a daily basis; such close relationships can lead to too much wise-cracking and acting out.

In extreme cases, you might find two participants who are friends or work together who exemplify a kind of "married couple" phenomenon. They finish each other's sentences and much of their communication is implicit because they think alike. This is likely to yield less useful think-aloud data for you.

Look for people whose skills, work styles, and personality traits complement each other. Sometimes this is a good place to give them the Myers–Briggs test (Myers et al., 1998) for collaborative personality types.

14.7.6 Manage Participants as Any Other Valuable Resource

Once you have gone through the trouble and expense to recruit participants, do not let the process fail because a participant forgot to show up. Devise a mechanism to manage participant contact to keep in touch, remind in advance of appointments, and to follow up, if useful, afterward.

You need a standard procedure, and fool-proof way to remind you to follow it, for calling your participants in advance to remind them of their appointment, just as they do in doctor's offices. No-show participants cost money in unused lab facilities, frustration in evaluators, wasted time in rescheduling, and delays in the evaluation schedule.

14.7.7 Select Participants for Subsequent Iterations

A question that commonly arises is whether you should use the same participants for more than one cycle of formative evaluation. Of course you would not use a repeat participant for tasks addressing an "initial use" UX attribute.

But sometimes reusing a participant (maybe one out of three to five) can make sense. This way, you can get a reaction to design changes from the previous cycle, in addition to a new set of data on the modified design from the two new participants. Calling on a previously used participant tells them you value their help and gives them a kind of empowerment, a feeling that they are helping to make a difference in your design.

14.8 PREPARE FOR PARTICIPANTS

14.8.1 Lab and Equipment

If you are planning lab-based evaluation, the most obvious aspect of preparation is to have the lab available and configured for your needs. If you plan to use specialized equipment, such as for physiological measurement, you also need to have that set up and an expert scheduled to operate it.

If you plan to collect quantitative UX data, prepare by having the right kind of timers on hand, from simple stopwatches to instrumented software for automatically extracting timing data. You can also get high-precision timing data from video recordings of the session (Vermeeren et al., 2002).

Using video to compute timing originated with the British data collection system called DRUM (Macleod & Rengger, 1993). DRUM was the tool support for the larger usability evaluation methodology called MUSiC (Macleod et al., 1997). Today, most software available to control and analyze digital video streams (e.g., TechSmith's Morae) can do this routinely. As part of your post-session processing, you just tag the start and end of task performance in the video stream and the elapsed time is computed directly.

A Modern UX Lab at Bloomberg LP

Bloomberg LP, a leader in financial informatics, unveiled a modern UX evaluation lab in 2011. We describe some of the main features of the lab in this sidebar.

The lab has two areas—a participant room and an observation room—separated by a one-way mirror. Each has an independent entrance. The participant room has a multi-monitor workstation on which Bloomberg's desktop applications are evaluated. The following photos depict a formative evaluation session in progress at this station.

On the other side of this participant room, another station is designed for evaluations with paper prototypes or mobile devices. In the following photo we show a formative evaluation session using paper prototypes where the facilitator (left) is responding to the actions of the participant (center) as the note taker (right) observes.

In the photos that follow, we show the same station being used to evaluate a mobile prototype (left). The photo on the right shows a close-up of the mobile device holder with a mounted camera. This setup allows the participant to hold and move the mobile device as she interacts while allowing a full capture of the user interface and her actions using the mounted camera.

The following photos are views of the observation room. This room is kept dark to prevent people in the participant room from seeing through. The lab is set up to pipe up to five selections of the seven video sources and four screen capture sources from the participant room to the large screens seen at the top in the observation room.

In the photo on the left you can see the participant room showing through the one-way mirror. In this photo we see stakeholders observing and tagging the video stream of the ongoing evaluation at four different stations.

In the photo on the right, you can see a view of the evaluation using the mobile prototype. Note on the left-hand screen above a close-up view of the evaluation from the overhead camera. The feed from the camera mounted on the mobile device holder is not shown in this photo.

This UX lab has been instrumental in defining the interaction designs of Bloomberg's flagship desktop and mobile applications. Special thanks to Shawn Edwards, the CTO; Pam Snook; and Vera Newhouse at Bloomberg L.P. for providing us these lab photos.

14.8.2 Session Parameters

Evaluators must determine protocol and procedures for conducting the testing—exactly what will happen and for how long during an evaluation session with a participant.

Task and session lengths

The typical length of time of evaluation session for one participant is anywhere from 30 minutes to 4 hours. However, most of the time you should plan on an average session length of 2 hours or less.

However, some real-world UX evaluation sessions can become a day-long experience for a participant. The idea is to get as much as possible from each user without burning him or her out.

If you require sessions longer than a couple of hours, it will be more difficult for participants. In such cases, you should:

- Prepare participants for possible fatigue in long sessions by warning them in advance.
- Mitigate fatigue by scheduling breaks between tasks, where participants can get up and walk around, leave the participant room, get some coffee or other refreshment, and even run screaming back home.
- Have some granola bars and/or fruit available in case hunger becomes an issue.
- Always have water, and possibly other beverages, on hand to assuage thirst from the hard work you are putting them through.

Number of full lifecycle iterations

Just as a loose rule of thumb from our experience, the typical number of full UX engineering cycle iterations per version or release is about three, but resource constraints often limit it to fewer iterations. In many projects you can expect only one iteration. Of course, any iterations are better than none.

14.8.3 Informed Consent

As practitioners collecting empirical data involving human subjects, we have certain legal and ethical responsibilities. There are studies, of course, in which harm could come to a human participant, but the kinds of data collection performed during formative evaluation of an interaction design are virtually never of this kind.

Nonetheless, we have our professional obligations, which center on the informed consent form, a document to establish explicitly the rights of your participants and which also serves as legal protection for you and your organization. Therefore, you should always have all participants, anyone from who you collect data of any kind, sign an informed consent form regardless of whether data are collected in the lab, in the field, or anywhere else.

Informed consent permission application

Your preparation for informed consent begins with an application to your institutional review board (IRB), an official group within your organization responsible for the legal and ethical aspects of informed consent (see later). The evaluator or project manager should prepare an IRB application that typically will include:

- summary of the evaluation plan
- statement of complete evaluation protocol
- statement of exactly how human subjects will be involved
- your written subject/participant instructions
- a copy of your informed consent form
- any other standard IRB forms for your organization

Because most UX evaluation does not put participants at risk, the applications are usually approved without question. The details of the approval process vary by organization, but it can take up to weeks and can require changes in the documents. The approval process is based on a review of the ethical and legal issues, not the quality of the proposed evaluation plan.

Informed consent form

The informed consent form, an important part of your IRB application and an important part of your lab-based UX evaluation, is a requirement; it is not optional. The informed consent form is to be read and signed by each participant and states that the participant is volunteering to participate in your evaluation, that you are taking data that the participant helped generate, and that the participant gives permission to use data—usually with the provision that the participant's name or identity will not be associated with data, that the participant understands the evaluation is in no way harmful, and that the participant may discontinue the session at any time. The consent form may also include non-disclosure requirements.

This form must spell out participant rights and what you expect the participants to do, even if there is overlap with the general instructions sheet. The form they sign must be self-standing and must tell the whole story.

Be sure that your informed consent form contains:

- a statement that the participant can withdraw anytime, for any reason, or for no reason at all
- a statement of any foreseeable risks or discomforts
- a statement of any benefits (e.g., educational benefit or just the satisfaction of helping make a good design) or compensation to participants (if there is payment, state exactly how much; if not, say so explicitly)
- a statement of confidentiality of data (that neither the name of the participant nor any other kind of identification will be associated with data after it has been collected)
- all project/evaluator contact information
- a statement about any kind of recording (e.g., video, audio, photographic, or holodeck) involving the participant you plan to make and how you intend to use it, who will view it (and not), and by what date it will be erased or otherwise destroyed
- a statement that, if you want to use a video clip (for example) from the recording for any other purpose, you will get their additional approval in writing
- clear writing in understandable language

An example of a simple informed consent form is shown in Figure 14-2.

Informed consent may or may not also be required in the case where your participants are also organization employees. In any case you should have two copies of the consent form ready for reading and signing by participants when they arrive. One copy is for the participant to keep.

14.8.4 Other Paperwork
General instructions

In conjunction with developing evaluation procedures, you, as the evaluator, should write *introductory instructional remarks* that will be read uniformly by each participant at the beginning of the session. All participants thereby start with the same level of knowledge about the system and the tasks they are to perform. This uniform instruction for each participant will help ensure consistency across the test sessions.

These introductory instructions should explain briefly the purpose of the evaluation, tell a little bit about the system the participant will be using, describe what the participant will be expected to do, and the procedure to be followed by the participant. For example, instructions might state that a participant will be asked to perform some benchmark tasks that will be given by the evaluator, will be allowed to use the system freely for awhile, then will be

Informed Consent for Participant of Development Project

<Name of your development organization> <Date or version number of form>

Title of Project: *<Project title>*

Project team member(s) directly involved: *<Team member names>*

Project manager: *<Project manager name>*

I. THE PURPOSE OF YOUR PARTICIPATION IN THIS PROJECT

As part of the *<project title>* project, you are invited to participate in evaluating and improving various designs of *<name of system or product>*, *<description of system or product>*.

II. PROCEDURES

You will be asked to perform a set of tasks using the *<name of system or product>*. These tasks consist of *<description of range of tasks>*. Your role in these tests is to help us evaluate the designs. We are not evaluating you or your performance in any way. As you perform various tasks with the system, your actions and comments will be noted and you will be asked to describe verbally your learning process. You may be asked questions during and after the evaluation, in order to clarify our understanding of your evaluation. You may also be asked to fill out a questionnaire relating to your usage of the system.

The evaluation session will last no more than four hours, with the typical session being about two hours. The tasks are not very tiring, but you are welcome to take rest breaks as needed. If you prefer, the session may be divided into two shorter sessions.

III. RISKS

There are no known risks to the participants of this study.

IV. BENEFITS OF THIS PROJECT

Your participation in this project will provide information that may be used to improve our designs for *<name of system or product>*. No guarantee of further benefits has been made to encourage you to participate. (Change this, if a benefit such as payment or a gift is offered.) You are requested to refrain from discussing the evaluation with other people who might be in the candidate pool from which other participants might be drawn.

V. EXTENT OF ANONYMITY AND CONFIDENTIALITY

The results of this study will be kept strictly confidential. Your written consent is required for the researchers to release any data identified with you as an individual to anyone other than personnel working on the project. The information you provide will have your name removed and only a subject number will identify you during analyses and any written reports of the research.

The experiment may be videotaped. If it is taped, the tapes will be stored securely, viewed only by the experimenters and erased after 3 months. If the experimenters wish to use a portion of your videotape for any other purpose, they will get your written permission before using it. Your signature on this form does not give them permission to show your videotape to anyone else.

VI. COMPENSATION

Your participation is voluntary and unpaid. (Change this, if a benefit such as payment or a gift is offered.)

VII. FREEDOM TO WITHDRAW

You are free to withdraw from this study at any time for any reason.

VIII. APPROVAL OF RESEARCH

This research has been approved, as required, by the Institutional Review Board *<or the name of your review committee>* for projects involving human subjects at *<your organization>*.

IX. PARTICIPANT RESPONSIBILITIES AND PERMISSION

I voluntarily agree to participate in this study, and I know of no reason I cannot participate. I have read and understand the informed consent and conditions of this project. I have had all my questions answered. I hereby acknowledge the above and give my voluntary consent for participation in this project. If I participate, I may withdraw at any time without penalty. I agree to abide by the rules of this project

_____   _____

Signature   Date

_____   _____

Name (please print)   Contact: phone or address or email

Figure 14-2

Sample informed consent form for participants.

given some more benchmark tasks, and finally will be asked to complete an exit questionnaire.

In your general instructions to participants, make it clear that the purpose of the session is to evaluate the system, not to evaluate them. You should say explicitly *"You are helping us evaluate the system—we are not evaluating you!"* Some participants may be fearful that if somehow their performance is not up to "expectations," participation in this kind of test session could reflect poorly on them or even be used in their employment performance evaluations (if, for example, they work for the same organization that is designing the interface they are helping evaluate). They should be reassured that this is not the case. This is where it is important for you to reiterate your guarantee of confidentiality with respect to individual information and anonymity of data.

The instructions may inform participants that you want them to think aloud while working or, for example, may indicate that they can ask the evaluator questions at any time. The expected length of time for the evaluation session, if known (the evaluator should have some idea of how long a session will take after performing pilot testing), should also be included. Finally, you should always say, clearly and explicitly, that the participant is free to leave at any time.

Print out and copy the general instructions so that you can give one to each participant.

Non-disclosure Agreements (NDAs)

Sometimes an NDA is required by the developer or customer organizations to protect the intellectual property contained in the design. If you have an NDA, print out copies for reading, signing, and sharing with the participant.

Questionnaires and surveys

If your evaluation plan includes administration of one or more participant questionnaires, make sure that you have a good supply available. It is best to keep blank questionnaires in the control room or away from where a newly arriving participant could read them in advance.

Data collection forms

Make up a simple data collection form in advance. Your data collection form(s) should contain fields suitable for all types of quantitative data you collect and, probably separate, data collection forms for recording critical incidents and UX problems observed during the sessions. The latter should include spaces for the kind of supplementary data you like to keep, including associated task, effect on user (e.g., minor or task-blocking), guidelines involved, potential cause of problem in design, relevant designer knowledge (e.g., how it was supposed to work), etc. Keep your data collection forms simple and easy to use on the fly. Consider a spreadsheet form on a laptop.

14.8.5 Training Materials

Use training materials for participants only if you anticipate that a user's manual, quick reference cards, or any sort of training material will be available to and needed by users of the final system. If you do use training materials in evaluation, make the use of these materials explicit in the task descriptions.

If extensive participant training is required, say for an experienced participant role, it should have been administered in advance of evaluation. In general, training the user how to use a system during the evaluation session must be avoided unless you are evaluating the training. If the materials are used more as reference materials than training materials, participants might be given time to read any training material at the beginning of the session or might be given the material and told they can refer to it, reading as necessary to find information as needed during tasks. The number of times participants refer to the training material, and the amount of assistance they are able to obtain from the material, for example, can also be important data about overall UX of the system.

14.8.6 Planning Room Usage

As part of the evaluation plan for each major set of evaluation sessions, you need to document the configurations of rooms, equipment connections, and evaluator roles plus the people in these roles. Post diagrams of room and equipment setups so you do not have to figure this out at the last minute, when participants are due to arrive.

14.8.7 Ecological Validity in Your Simulated Work Context

Ecological Validity

Ecological validity refers to the realism with which a design of evaluation setup matches the user's real work context. It is about how accurately the design or evaluation reflects the relevant characteristics of the ecology of interaction, i.e., its context in the world or its environment.

Thomas and Kellogg (1989) were among the first to warn us of the need for realistic contextual conditions in usability testing. If an element of work or usage context could not be addressed in the usability lab, they advised us to leave the lab and seek other ways to assess these ecological concerns. The challenge is to ensure that usability evaluation conditions reflect real-world usage conditions well enough to evoke the corresponding kinds of user performance and behavior. Your response to this challenge is especially important if you are addressing issues beyond the usual UX concepts to the full user experience and the out-of-the-box experience.

How do you know what you need for ecological validity? Usage or design scenarios are a good source of information about props and roles needed for tasks. Does your service agent user talk with a person through a hole in a glass panel or across a desk sitting down? Do they talk with patients, clients, or customers on the telephone? How does holding a telephone affect simultaneous computer task performance? Have your props and task aids ready at hand when the sessions begin.

One interesting "far-out" example of a prop for ecological validity is the "third age suit" developed at Loughborough University and used by architects, automobile designers, and others whose users include older people. The suit is like an exoskeleton of Velcro and stiff material, limiting mobility and simulating stiffness, osteoarthritis, and other confining and restricting conditions. New designs can be evaluated with this prop to appreciate their usability by older populations.

The early A330 Airbus—An example of the need for ecological validity in testing

We experienced a real-world example of a product that could have benefited enormously from better ecological validity in its testing. We traveled in an A330 Airbus airplane when that model first came out; our plane was 1 week old. (Advice: for many reasons, do not be the first to travel in a new airplane design.) We were told that a human-centered approach was taken in the A330 Airbus design, including UX testing of buttons, layout, and so on of the passenger controls for the entertainment system. Apparently, though, they did not do enough in situ testing. Each passenger had a personal viewing screen for movies and other entertainment, considered an advantage over the screens hanging from the ceiling. The controls for each seat were more or less like a TV remote control, only tethered with a "pull-out" cord. When not in use, the remote control snapped into a recessed space on the seat arm rest. Cool, eh?

The LCD screen had nice color and brightness but a low acceptable viewing angle. Get far off the axis (away from perpendicular to the screen) and you lose all brightness and, just before it disappears altogether, you see the picture as a color negative image. But the screen is right in front of you, so no problem, right? Right, until in a real flight the person in front of you tilts back the seat. Then we could barely see it. We could tell it was affecting others, too, because we could see many people leaning their heads down into an awkward position just to see the screen. After a period of fatigue, many people gave up, turned it off, and leaned back for comfort. If the display screen was used in UX testing, and we have to assume it was, the question of tilting the seat never entered the discussion, probably because the screen was propped up on a stand in front of each participant in the UX lab. Designers and evaluators just did not think about passengers in front of screen users tilting back their seats. Testing in a more realistic setting, better emulating the ecological conditions of real flight, would have revealed this major flaw.

It does not end there. Once the movie got going, most people stowed the remote control away in the arm rest. But, of course, what do you also rest on an arm rest? Your arm. And in so doing, it was easy to bump a button on the control and make some change in the "programming." The design of this clever feature almost always made the movie disappear at a crucial point in the plot. And because we were syncing our movie viewing, the other one of us had to pause the movie while the first one had to go back through far too many button pushes to get the movie back and fast-forwarded to the current place.

It still does not end here. After the movie was over (or for some viewers, after they gave up) and we wanted to sleep, a bump of the arm on the remote caused the screen to light up brightly, instantly waking us to the wonderful world of entertainment. The flight attendant in just 1 week with this design had already come up with a creative workaround. She showed us how to pull the remote out on its cord and dangle it down out of the way of the arm rest. Soon, and this is the UX-gospel truth, almost everyone in the plane had a dangling remote control swinging gracefully in the aisle like so many synchronized reeds in the breeze as the plane moved about on its course. All very reminiscent of a wonderful Gary Larson cartoon showing a passenger sitting in flight. Among the entertainment controls on his arm rest is one switch, labeled "Wings stay on" and "Wings fall off." The caption reads, "Fumbling for his recline button, Ted unwittingly instigates a disaster."

The Social Security Administration (SSA) Model District Office (MDO)—An extreme and successful example

In the mid-1990s we worked extensively with the SSA in Baltimore, mainly in UX lifecycle training. A system we worked with there is used by a public service agent who serves clients, people who walk in off the street or call on the phone. The agent is the user, but the clients are essential to usage ecology; client needs provide the impetus for the user to act, the need for a system task. For evaluation then, they need people to act as clients, perhaps using scripts that detail the services needed, which then drive the computer-based tasks of the agent. And they need telephones and/or "offices" into which clients can come for service.

We worked with a small group pioneering the introduction of usability engineering techniques into an "old school," waterfall-oriented, mainframe software development environment. Large Social Security systems were migrating slowly from mainframes (in Baltimore) plus terminals (by the thousands over the country) to client–server applications, some starting to run on PCs, and they wanted UX to be a high priority. Sean Wheeler was the group spark plug and UX champion, strongly supported by Annette Bryce and Pat Stoos.

What impressed us the most about this organization was their Model District Office. A decade earlier, as part of a large Claims Modernization Project, a program of system design and training to "revolutionize the way that SSA serves the public," they had built a complete and detailed model of a Social Security Administration district office from middle America right in the middle of SSA headquarters building in Baltimore. The MDO, with its carpeting, office furniture, and computer terminals, right down to the office lamps and pictures on the wall, was indistinguishable from a typical agency office in a typical town. They brought in real SSA employees from field offices from all over the United States to sit in the MDO to pilot and test new systems and procedures.

When SSA was ready to focus on UX, the MDO provided a perfect evaluation environment; simply put, it was an extreme and successful example of leveraging ecological validity for application development and testing, as well as for user training. In the end, the group created a UX success story upstream against the inertia and enormous weight of the rest of the organization and ended up winning a federal award for the quality of their design!

As a testament to their seriousness about ecological validity and UX, the SSA was spending about $1 million a year to bring employees in to stay and work at the MDO, sometimes for a few months at a time. Their cost justification calculations proved the activity was saving many times more.

14.8.8 The UX Evaluation Session Work Package

To summarize, as you do the evaluation preparation and planning described in this chapter, you need to gather your evaluation session work package, all the materials you will need in the evaluation session. Bring this evaluation session work package to each evaluation session.

Examples of package contents include:

- The evaluation configuration plan, including diagrams of rooms, equipment, and people in evaluation roles
- General instruction sheets
- Informed consent forms, with participant names and date entered

- Any non-disclosure agreements
- All questionnaires and surveys, including any demographic survey
- All printed benchmark task descriptions, one task per sheet of paper
- All printed unmeasured task descriptions (these can be listed several to a page)
- For each evaluator, a print out (or laptop version) of the UX targets associated with the day's sessions
- All data collection forms, on paper or on laptops
- Any props needed to support tasks
- Any training materials to be used as part of the evaluation
- Any compensation to be given out (e.g., money, gift cards, T-shirts, coffee mugs, used cars)
- Any special instructions to watch out for particular parts of the design, evaluation scripts, things to do before each participant session (e.g., to reset browser caches so that no auto complete entries from previous participant's session interferes with the current session), etc.

Why should benchmark tasks be printed just one per sheet of paper? What about the trees? We want our participants to focus on just the task at hand. If you give them descriptions of additional tasks, they will read them prematurely and distract themselves by thinking about those, too. It is just human nature. You need to control their mental focus.

Also, focusing on the participant, it is possible that not all participants will complete all tasks. There is no need for anyone to see that they have not accomplished them all. If they see only one at a time, they will never know and never feel bad.

Exercise

See Exercise 14-1, Formative UX Evaluation Preparation for Your System

14.9 DO FINAL PILOT TESTING: FIX YOUR WOBBLY WHEELS

If your UX evaluation plan involves using a prototype, low or high fidelity, make sure it is robust before you do anything more to prepare for your UX evaluation, regardless of whether your evaluation is lab based. If the evaluation team has not yet performed thorough pilot testing of the product or prototype, now is the time to give it a final shakedown. Exercise the prototype thoroughly. Pilot testing is essential to remove any major weaknesses in the prototype and any "show stopper" problems.

You need to be confident that the prototype will not "blow up" unceremoniously the first time it is brought into the proximity of real user participants. It is embarrassing to have to apologize and dismiss a participant because the hardware or software wheels came off during an evaluation session. And, because good representative participants may be hard to find, you do not want to add to your time and expense by "burning" user participants unnecessarily.

While pilot testing of the prototype may be obvious to prepare for lab-based testing, it is similarly important prior to critical reviews and UX inspections by outside human–computer interaction (HCI) experts. These experts do not work for free, and you will not want things going amiss during a session, causing delays while a hefty hourly fee is being paid for expert advice.

In addition to shaking down your prototype, think of your pilot testing as a dress rehearsal to be sure of your lab equipment, benchmark tasks, procedures, and personnel roles:

- Make sure all necessary equipment is available, installed, and working properly, whether it be in the laboratory or in the field.
- Run through the evaluation tasks completely at least once using the intended hardware and software (i.e., the interface prototype) by someone other than the person(s) who created the task descriptions.
- Make sure the prototype supports all the necessary user actions.
- Make sure the participant instructions and benchmark task descriptions are worded clearly and unambiguously.
- Make sure all session materials, such as any instruction sheets, the informed consent, and so on, are sufficient.
- Make sure that the metrics the benchmark tasks are intended to produce are practically measurable. Counting the number of tasks completed in either 5 seconds or 5 hours, for example, is not reasonable.
- Be sure that everyone on the evaluation team understands his or her role.
- Be sure that all the roles work together in the fast-paced events associated with user interaction.

14.10 MORE ABOUT DETERMINING THE RIGHT NUMBER OF PARTICIPANTS

One of your activities in preparing for formative evaluation is finding appropriate users for the evaluation sessions. In formal summative evaluation, this part of the process is referred to as "sampling," but that term is not appropriate here because what we are doing has nothing to do with the implied statistical relationships and constraints.

14.10.1 How Many Are Needed? A Difficult Question

How many participants are enough? This is one of those issues that some novice UX practitioners take so seriously and yet it is a question to which there is no definitive answer. Indeed, there cannot be one answer. It depends so much on the specific context and parameters of your individual situation that you have to answer this question for yourself each time you do formative evaluation.

There are studies that lead UX gurus to proclaim various rules of thumb, such as "three to five users are enough to find 80% of your UX problems," but when you see how many different assumptions are used to arrive at those "rules" and how few of those assumptions are valid within your project, you realize that this is one place in the process where it is most important for you to use your own head and not follow vague generalizations.

And, of course, cost is often a limiting factor. Sometimes you just get one or two participants in each of one or two iterations and you have to be satisfied with that because it is all you can afford. The good news is that you can do a lot with only a few good participants. There is no statistical requirement for large numbers of "subjects" as there is for formal summative evaluation; rather, the goal is to focus on extracting as much information as possible from every participant.

14.10.2 Rules of Thumb Abound

There are bona fide studies that predict the optimum number of participants needed for UX testing under various conditions. Most "rules of thumb" are based empirically but, because they are quoted and applied so broadly without regard to the constraints and conditions under which the results were obtained, these rules have become among the most folklorish of folklore out there.

Nielsen and Molich (1990) had an early paper about the number of users/participants needed to find enough UX problems and found that 80% of their known UX problems could be detected with four to five participants, and the most severe problems were usually found with the first few participants. Virzi (1990, 1992) more or less confirmed Nielsen and Molich's study.

Nielsen and Landauer (1993) found that detection of problems as a function of the number of participants is well modeled as a Poisson process, supporting the ability to use early results to estimate the number problems left to be found and the number of additional participants needed to find a certain percentage.

Depending on the circumstances, though, some say that even five participants is no way near enough (Hudson, 2001; Spool & Schroeder, 2001), especially for complex applications or large Websites. In practice, each of these numbers has proven to be right for some set of conditions, but the question is whether they will work for you in your evaluation.

14.10.3 An Analytic Basis for the Three to Five Users Rule
The underlying probability function

In Figure 14-3 you can see graphs, related to the binomial probability distribution, of cumulative percentages of problems likely to be found for a given number of participants used and at various detection rates, adapted from Lewis (1994).

Y-axis values in these curves are for "discovery likelihood," expressed as a cumulative percentage of problems likely to be found, as a function of the number of participants or evaluators used. These curves are based on the probability formula:

discovery likelihood (cumulative percentage of problems likely to be found = $1-(1-p)^n$, where n is the number of participants used (X-axis values) and p is what we call the "detection rate" of a certain category of participants.

As an example, this formula tells us that a sample size of five participant evaluators (n) with an individual detection rate (p) of at least 0.30 is sufficient to find approximately 80% of the UX problems in a system.

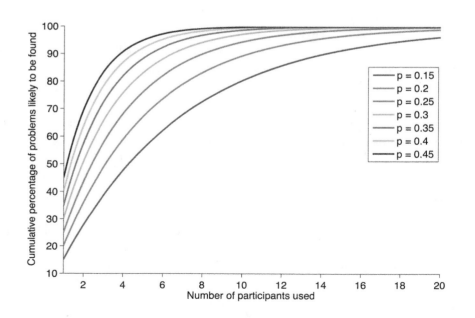

Figure 14-3

Graphs of cumulative percentages of problems likely to be found for a given number of participants used and at various detection rates [adapted from Lewis (1994)].

The old balls-in-an-urn analogy

Let us think of an interaction design containing flaws that cause UX problems as analogous to the old probability setting of an urn containing various colored balls. Among an unknown number of balls of all colors, suppose there are a number of red balls, each representing a different UX problem.

Suppose now that a participant or evaluator reaches in and grabs a big handful of balls from the urn. This is analogous to an evaluation session using a single expert evaluator, if it is a UX inspection evaluation, or a single participant, if it is a lab-based empirical session. The number of red balls in that handful is the number of UX problems identified in the session.

In a UX inspection, it is the expert evaluator, or inspector, who finds the UX problems. In an empirical UX test, participants are a catalyst for UX problem detection—not necessarily detecting problems themselves but encountering critical incidents while performing tasks, enabling evaluators to identify the corresponding UX problems. Because the effect is essentially the same, for simplicity in this discussion we will use the term "participant" for both the inspector and the testing participant and "find problems" for whatever way the problems are found in a session.

Participant detection rates

The detection rate, p, of an individual participant is the percentage of existing problems that this participant can find in one session. This corresponds to the number of red balls a participant gets in one handful of balls. This is a function of the individual participant. For example, in the case of the balls in the urn, it might be related to the size of the participant's hand. In the UX domain, it is perhaps related to the participant's evaluation skills.

In any case, in this analysis, if a participant has a detection rate of $p = 0.20$, it means that this participant will find 20% of the UX problems existing in the design. The number of participants with that same individual detection rate who, in turn, reach into the urn is the value on the X axis. The curve shown with a green line is for a detection rate of $p = 0.20$. The other curves are for different detection rates, from $p = 0.15$ up to $p = 0.45$.

Most of the time we do not even know the detections rates of our participants. To calculate the detection rate for a participant, we would have to know how many total UX problems exist in a design. But that is just what we are trying to find out with evaluation. You could, we guess, run a testing session with the participant against a design with a certain number of known flaws. But that would tell you that participant's detection rate for that day, in that context, and for that system. Unfortunately, a given participant's detection rate is not constant.

Cumulative percentage of problems to be found

The Y axis represents values of the cumulative percentage of problems to be found. Let us look at this first for just one participant. The curve for $p = 0.20$, for example, has a Y axis value of 20%, for $n = 1$ (where the curve intersects the Y axis). This is consistent with our expectation that one participant with $p = 0.20$ will find 20% of the problems, or get 20% of the red balls, in the first session.

Now what about the "cumulative" aspect? What happens when the second participant reaches into the urn depends on whether you replaced the balls from the first participant. This analysis is for the case where each participant returns all the balls to the urn after each "session"; that is, none of the UX problems are fixed between participants.

After the first participant has found some problems, there are fewer *new* problems left to find by the second participant. If you look at the results with the two participants independently, they each help you find a somewhat different 20% of the problems, but there is likely to be overlap, which reduces the cumulative effect (the union of the sets of problems) of the two.

This is what we see in the curves of Figure 14-3 as the percentage of problems likely to be found drops off with each new participant (moving to the right on the X axis) because the marginal number of new problems found is decreasing. That accounts for the leveling off of the curves until, at some high number of participants, essentially no new problems are being found and the curve is asymptotically flat.

Marginal added detection and cost–benefit

One thing we do notice in the curves of Figure 14-3 is that, despite the drop-off of effective detection rates, as you continue to add more participants you will continue to uncover more problems. At least for a while. Eventually, high detection rates coupled with high numbers of participants will yield results that asymptotically approach about 100% in the upper right-hand part of the figure and virtually no new problems will be found with subsequent participants.

But what happens along the way? Each new participant helps you find fewer new problems, but because the cost to run each participant is about the same, with each successive participant the process becomes less efficient (fewer new problems found for the same cost).

As a pretty good approximation of the cost to run a UX testing session with n participants, you have a fixed cost to set up the session plus a variable cost (or cost per participant) $= a + bn$. The benefit of running a UX testing session with n participants is the discovery likelihood. So the cost benefit is the ratio benefit/cost, each as a function of n, or benefit/cost $= (1- (1 - p^n) / (a + bn)$.

If you graph this function (with some specific values of a and b) against $n = 1$, $2, \ldots$, you will see a curve that climbs for the first few values of n and then starts dropping off. The values of n around the peak of cost–benefit are the optimum (from a cost–benefit perspective) number of participants to use. The range of n for which the peak occurs depends on parameters a, b, and p of your setup; your smileage can vary.

Nielsen and Landauer (1993) showed that real data for both UX inspections and lab-based testing with participants did match this mathematical cost–benefit model. Their results showed that, for their parameters, the peak occurred for values of n around 3 to 5. Thus, the "three to five users" rule of thumb.

Assumptions do not always apply in the real world

This three-to-five users rule, with its tidy mathematical underpinning, can and does apply to many situations similar to the conditions Nielsen and Landauer (1993) used, and we believe their analysis brings insight into the discussion. However, we know there are many cases where it just does not apply.

For starters, all of this analysis, including the analogy with the balls-in-an-urn setting, depends on two assumptions:

- Each participant has a constant detection rate, p
- Each UX problem is equally likely to be found in testing

If UX problems were balls in an urn, our lives would be simpler. But neither of these assumptions is true and the UX life is not simple.

Assumptions about detection rates. Each curve in Figure 14-3 is for a fixed detection rate and the cost–benefit calculation given earlier was based on a fixed detection rate, p. But the "evaluator effect" tells us not only will different evaluators find different problems, but it tells us that even the detection rate can vary widely over participants (Hertzum & Jacobsen, 2003).

In fact, a given individual does not even have a fixed "individual detection rate"; it can be influenced from day to day or even from moment to moment by how rested the participant is, blood caffeine and ethanol levels, attitude, the system, how the evaluators conduct the evaluation, what tasks are used, the evaluator's skills, and so on.

Also, what does it *really* mean for a testing participant to have a detection rate of $p = 0.20$? How long does it take in a session for that participant to achieve that 20% discovery? How many tasks? What kinds of tasks? What if that participant continues to perform more tasks? Will no more critical incidents be encountered after 20% detection is achieved?

Assumptions about problem detectability. The curves in Figure 14-3 are also based on an assumption that all problems are equally detectable (like all red balls in the urn are equally likely to be drawn out). But, of course, we know that some problems are almost obvious on the surface and other problems can be orders of magnitude more difficult to ferret out. So detectability, or likelihood of being found, can vary dramatically across various UX problems.

Task selection. One reason for the overlap in problems detected from one participant to another, causing the cumulative detection likelihood to fall off with additional participants, as it does in Figure 14-3, is the use of prescribed tasks. Participants performing essentially the same sets of tasks are looking in the same places for problems and are, therefore, more likely to uncover many of the same problems.

However, if you employ user-directed tasks (Spool & Schroeder, 2001), participants will be looking in different places and the overlap of problems found could be much less. This keeps the benefit part of the curves growing linearly for more participants, causing your optimum number of participants to be larger.

Application system effects. Another factor that can torpedo the three-to-five users rule is the application system being evaluated. Some systems are very much larger than others. For example, an enormous Website or a large and complex word processor will harbor many more possibilities for UX problems than, say, a simple inter-office scheduling system. If each participant can explore only a small portion of such an application, the overlap of problems among participants may be insignificant. In such cases the cost–benefit function will peak with many more participants than three to five.

You have to settle for a sensible approach with a practical outcome

Okay, so what is the answer? What is the best number of participants to use in testing? Our friend Jim Foley's answer to any HCI question was never more appropriate than it is here: It depends! It takes as many participants as it takes for your situation, your application, your design, your resources, and your goals.

You have to decide for yourself every time you do UX testing—how many participants can you afford. You cannot compute and graph all the curves we have been talking about because you will never know how many UX problems exist in the design so you will never know what percentage of the existing problems you have found. You do not have to use those curves, anyway, to have a pretty good intuitive feeling for whether you are still detecting useful new problems with each new participant. Look at the results from each participant and each iteration and ask if those results were worth it and whether it is worth investing a little more. Based on how much time and money you can afford and how easily you can recruit participants, use your UX practitioner thinking skills and ask yourself, do you feel lucky? Huh? Do you think there are more reasonably significant UX problems still out there that you can still find and fix and thereby improve the product? Then go ahead; make the UX practitioner's day—iterate.

Rigorous Empirical Evaluation: Running the Session

15

Objectives

After reading this chapter, you will:

1. Know the preliminaries and protocol issues in dealing with rigorous UX evaluation participants
2. Be prepared to generate and collect objective and subjective quantitative UX evaluation data
3. Know how to generate and collect qualitative UX data by critical incident identification, think-aloud techniques, and post-session interviews and probing
4. Be able to use special techniques for gathering emotional impact and phenomenological data
5. Know the mechanics of wrapping up a session

15.1 INTRODUCTION

15.1.1 You Are Here

We begin each process chapter with a "you are here" picture of the chapter topic in the context of the overall Wheel lifecycle template; see Figure 15-1. This chapter is about running a lab-based evaluation, a step of rigorous UX evaluation.

15.2 PRELIMINARIES WITH PARTICIPANTS

15.2.1 Introduce Yourself and the Lab: Be Sure Participants Know What to Expect

In this chapter, our story opens with the arrival of participants at your UX lab. If you have a separate reception room in your UX facility, this is where you meet your participants before getting down to business with evaluation. Greet and welcome each participant and thank him or her for helping. Bring them in and show them around.

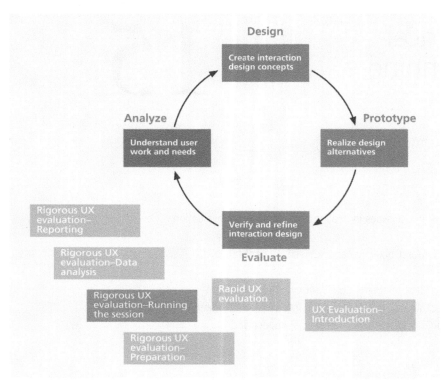

Figure 15-1

You are here, at running the session, within the evaluation activity in the context of the overall Wheel lifecycle template.

Introduce them to the setup and show them the lab. If you have one-way glass, explain it and how it will be used and show them the other side— what happens "behind the curtain." Openly declare any video recording you will do (which should have been explained in the consent form, too). Make participants feel that they are partners in their role.

Tell your participants all about the design being evaluated and about the process in which they are participating. For example, you might say "We have early screen designs for our product in the form of a low-fidelity prototype of a new system for . . . ." Tell them how they can help and what you want them to do.

Do your best to relieve anxiety and satisfy curiosity. Be sure that your participants have all their questions about the process answered before you proceed into evaluation. Make it very clear that they are helping you evaluate and are not evaluating them in any way. For example, "You are here to evaluate a new design for . . .; you will be asked to try some tasks using the computer, to help us find places where the design is not supportive enough for you."

15.2.2 Paperwork

While still in the reception room or as soon as the user has entered the participant room:

- Have each participant read the general instructions and explain anything verbally, as needed.
- Have the participant read the institutional review board consent form (Chapter 14) and explain the consent form verbally as well.

- Have the participant sign the consent form (two copies); it must be signed "without duress." You keep one signed copy and give the participant the other signed copy. Your copy must be retained for at least 3 years (the period may vary by organization).
- Have the participant sign a non-disclosure form, if needed.
- Have the participant fill out any demographic survey you have prepared.

A short written demographic survey can be used to confirm that each participant does, indeed, meet the requirements of your intended work activity role and corresponding user class characteristics.

15.2.3 The Session Begins

Give the participants a few minutes to familiarize themselves with the system unless walk up and use is a goal. If you are using benchmark tasks, after the preliminaries and when you both are ready to start, have the participant read the first benchmark or other task description and ask if there are any questions. If you are taking timing data, do not include the benchmark task reading time as part of the task.

Once the evaluation session is under way, interesting things can start happening quickly. Data you need to collect may start arriving in a flood. It can be overwhelming, but, by being prepared, you can make it easy and fun, especially if you know what kinds of data to collect. We will look at the possible kinds of data and the methods for generating and collecting them. But first, we need to get some protocol issues out of the way.

15.3 PROTOCOL ISSUES

Session protocol is about the mechanical details of session setup and your relationship with participants and how you handle them throughout each session.

15.3.1 Attitude toward UX Problems and toward Participants

Before you actually do evaluation, it is easy to agree that this UX testing is a positive thing and we are all working together to improve the design. However, once you start hearing about problems participants are having with the design, it can trigger unhelpful reactions in your ego, instincts, and pride. Proceed in your testing with a positive attitude and it will pay off.

15.3.2 Cultivating a Partnership with Participants

Take the time to build rapport with your participants. More important to the success of your UX evaluation sessions than facilities and equipment is the rapport you establish with participants, as partners in helping you evaluate and improve the product design. Once in the participant room, the facilitator should take a little time to "socialize" with the participant. If you have taken the participant on a "tour" of your facilities, that will have been a good start.

If you are using co-discovery techniques (Chapter 12), allow some time for co-discovery partners to get to know each other and do a little bonding, perhaps while you are setting things up. Starting the session as total strangers can make them feel awkward and can interfere with their performance.

15.3.3 Interaction with Participant during the Session

So far, you have done the necessary preparation for your evaluation, including preparation of benchmark task descriptions, procedures, and consent forms, as well as participant preparation. It is finally time to get an evaluation session underway. The facilitator helps ensure that the session runs smoothly and efficiently.

It is generally the job of the facilitator to listen and not talk. But at key junctures you might elicit important data, if it does not interfere with task timing or if you are focusing on qualitative data. You can ask brief questions, such as "What are you trying to do?" "What did you expect to happen when you clicked on the such-and-such icon?" "What made you think that approach would work?"

If you are focusing on qualitative data, the evaluator may also ask leading questions, such as "How would you like to perform that task?" "What would make that icon easier to recognize?" If you are using the "think-aloud" technique for qualitative data gathering, encourage the participant by prompting occasionally: "Remember to tell us what you are thinking as you go."

Do not "blow off" problems perceived by the participant as just, for example, an anomaly in the prototype. If you think that an issue pointed out as a UX problem by a participant is actually not a genuine issue, write it down as a problem for the moment, anyway. Otherwise you will discourage them from mentioning problems that might not be as real as they seem.

If participants show signs of stress or fatigue, give them a break. Let them leave the participant room, walk around, and/or have some refreshments. Do not be too up-tight about the session schedule. It is almost impossible to set a time schedule for tasks and steps for the participant in a session. It is better to present a list of objectives and let the participant know where you both are, as a team, in working toward those goals. To the extent possible, let the participant decide when to take breaks and when to stop for lunch.

15.3.4 To Help the Participant or Not to Help the Participant?

Give hints if necessary, but direct help almost always works against the goals of the session. Sometimes when participants are not making progress, they can benefit from a hint to get them back on track so that their session again becomes useful. You want to see whether the *participant* can determine how to perform the task. You should not give them information about how to complete a task. So, if participants ask for help, how can you let them know you are there for them without doing some coaching? Often the best way is to lead them to answer their own questions.

For example, do not answer questions such as "is this right?" directly, but by asking your own questions, directing them to think it through for themselves. With experience, evaluators become very creative at being appropriately evasive while still helping a participant out of a problem without adversely affecting data collected. Sometimes it helps to tell the participant upfront that you will decline to answer design-related questions to see how the participant interacts with the system. Make note of those questions and answer them at the end of the session.

15.3.5 Keeping Your Participant at Ease

Remind yourself and your whole team that you should never, never laugh at anything during a UX evaluation session. You may be in the control room and think you have a sound-proof setup but laughter has a way of piercing the glass. Because participants cannot see people behind the glass, it is easy for participants to assume that someone is laughing at them.

If participants become visibly flustered, frustrated, "zoned out," or blame themselves continually for problems in task performance, they may be suffering from stress and you should intervene. Take a short break and reassure and calm them. Remind them that "you are evaluating the design; we are not evaluating you." If participants become so discouraged that they want to quit the entire session, there is little you can or should do but thank them, pay them, and let them go.

15.3.6 Protocols for Evaluating with Low-Fidelity Prototypes

Have your paper prototype laid out and ready to go. Well before starting a session using a paper prototype, the team should prepare for using the prototype by assembling all the parts and pieces of the prototype. To prevent the easel (Chapter 11) from moving during the action, consider taping it to the

Figure 15-2

Typical setup at the end of a table for evaluation with a paper prototype.

working table between the participant, the facilitator, and the executor, as shown in Figure 15-2.

"Boot up" the prototype by putting the initial "screen" on the easel, having each moving part ready at hand and convenient to find and grab to enter it into the action. Make sure that any changes made to data and prototype internal states by previous participants are reset to original values for the current participant.

Before each participant enters, the "executor" should arrange everything necessary for running the prototype, including stacks of prototype parts and other equipment (e.g., marking pens, extra paper or plastic, tape).

Have the whole evaluation team ready to assume their roles and be ready to carry them out in the session.

- Evaluation *facilitator*, to keep the session moving, to interact with participants, and to take notes on critical incidents (pick a person who has leadership abilities and "people" skills).
- Prototype *executor*, to move transparencies and provide "computer" responses to user actions (pick a person who knows the design well and is good at the cold and consistent logic of "playing" computer).
- User performance *timer*, to time participants performing tasks and/or count errors (to collect quantitative data)—the timer person may want to practice with a stopwatch a bit before getting into a real session.
- Critical incident note takers (for spotting and recording critical incidents and UX problems).

Review your own in-session protocol. Some of the "rules" we suggest include:

- Team members *must not coach* participants as they perform tasks.
- The executor *must not anticipate user actions* and especially must not give the correct computer response for a wrong user action! The person playing computer must respond only to what the user actually does!
- The person playing computer may not speak, make gestures, etc.
- You may not change the design on the fly, unless that is a declared part of your process.

Figure 15-3 shows another view of a participant with a paper prototype.

15.4 GENERATING AND COLLECTING QUANTITATIVE UX DATA

If your evaluation plan calls for taking quantitative data, participants perform prescribed benchmark tasks during a session and evaluators take numeric data. For example, an evaluator may measure the time it takes the participant to perform a task, count the number of errors a participant makes while performing a task, count the number of tasks a participant can perform within a given time period, and so on, depending on the measures established in your UX targets.

Figure 15-3
Participant pondering a paper prototype during formative evaluation.

15.4.1 Objective Quantitative Data

The main idea is to use participant performance of benchmark tasks as a source of objective (observed) quantitative UX data.

Timing task performance

By far the simplest way to measure time on task is by using a stopwatch manually. It is really the only sensible way for low-fidelity, especially paper, prototypes. Timing with a stopwatch is also acceptable for software prototypes and is still the de facto standard way, sufficing for all situations except those demanding the most precision. If timing manually, you usually start the timer when the participant has finished reading the benchmark task description, has no questions, and you say "please start."

Try not to use very short benchmark tasks. It can be difficult to get accurate timings with a stopwatch on very short tasks. Something in the order of 5 minutes or more is easy to time.

If precise timing measurements are required, it is possible to embed software timers to instrument the software internally. These routines keep time stamps denoting when execution of the application software enters and exits key software modules. Software timers also free up one data collector for other jobs, such as observing critical incidents, but they do require more post-session work to compile timing data.

Counting user errors

The key to counting errors correctly is in knowing what constitutes an error. Not everything that goes wrong, not even everything a user does wrong, during task performance should be counted as a user error. So what are we looking for? A user error is usually considered to have occurred when the participant takes *any action that does not lead to progress in performing the desired task*. The main idea is to catch the times that a participant takes a "wrong turn" along the expected path of task performance, especially including cases where the design was inadequate to direct the interaction properly.

Wrong turns include choosing an incorrect item from a menu or selecting the wrong button, choices that do not lead to progress in performing the desired task. Other examples include selecting the wrong menu, button, or icon when the user thought it was the right one, double-clicking when a single click is needed, and vice versa.

If a participant takes a wrong turn but is able to back up and recover, an error has still occurred. In addition, it is important to note the circumstances under which the participant attempted to back up and whether the participant was successful in figuring out what was wrong. These occasions can provide qualitative data on user error recovery strategies that you might not be able to get in any other way.

The simplest way to count user errors during task performance is to use a manual event counter such as a handheld "clicker" for counting people coming through a gate for an event. Manual counters are perfect for low-fidelity, especially paper, prototypes. For software prototypes and operational software applications, if you use video to capture the interactions, you can tag the video stream with error points and the video analysis software can tally the count easily.

What generally does not count as a user error?

Typically, we do not count accessing online help or other documentation as an error. As a practical matter, we also want to exclude any random act of curiosity or exploration that might be interjected by the user (e.g., "I know this is not right, but I am curious what will happen if I click this"). Also a different successful path "invented" by the user is not really an error, but still could be noted as an important observation.

And we do not usually include "oops" errors, what Norman (1990, p. 105) calls "slips." These are errors that users make by accident when, in fact, they know better. For example, the user knows the right button to click but clicks the wrong one, perhaps through a slip of the hand, a brain burp, or being too hasty.

However, we do note an oops error and watch for it again. If it recurs, it may not be random and you should look for a way the design might have caused it. Finally, we do not usually include typing errors, unless their cause could somehow be traced to a problem in the design or unless the application is about typing.

15.4.2 Subjective Quantitative Data: Administering Questionnaires

If you are using questionnaires, the data collection activity is when you administer them. Have the participant fill out the questionnaires you have chosen per the timing you have decided, such as after a task or at the end of a session.

15.5 GENERATING AND COLLECTING QUALITATIVE UX DATA

In Chapter 12 we discussed how the goal of qualitative data collection is to identify usability problems and their causes within the design. In lab-based testing with participants, this goal is achieved primarily through observation and recording of critical incidents, often with the help of the think-aloud technique.

15.5.1 Collecting Critical Incident Information

The way that you collect and tag critical incident data as you go will have much to say about the accuracy and efficiency of your subsequent data analysis. Get your detailed critical incident and UX problem information recorded as clearly, precisely, and completely as you can in real time during data collection.

Do not count on going back and reviewing video recordings to get the essence of the problems. In the raw data stream, there are huge amounts of "noise," data not relevant to UX analysis. Important events, such as critical incident occurrences, are embedded in and obscured by irrelevant data. The wheat is still within the chaff.

Finding critical incidents within this event stream by viewing the video is laborious and time-consuming, which is one important reason for using direct (real-time) critical incident observation by an evaluator as a primary data collection technique. Do as much filtering as possible at the moment of data capture.

As events unfold, it is the job of the skilled evaluator to capture as much information about each critical incident as possible, as they happen in real time.

Critical Incident

A critical incident is a UX evaluation event that occurs during user task performance or other user interaction, observed by the facilitator or other observers or sometimes expressed by the user participant, that indicates a possible UX problem. Critical incident identification is arguably the single most important source of qualitative data.

Think-Aloud Technique

The think aloud technique is a qualitative data collection technique in which user participants verbally externalize their thoughts about their interaction experience, including their motives, rationale, and perceptions of UX problems. By this method, participants give the evaluator access to an understanding of their thinking about the task and the interaction design.

In early stages or when you do not have any software tool support, you can just take notes on the critical incidents that you spot.

In Chapter 16 we discuss UX problem instance records. It is helpful to use that as a template to support completeness in collecting critical incident data.

15.5.2 Critical Incident Data Collection Mechanisms

Video recording for critical incident data collection. In some labs, video recording is used routinely to capture all user and screen actions and facilitator and participant comments. Once you get into video recording, it is probably best to use a software support tool to control the video equipment for recording, review, and later analysis and for tagging the video with evaluator comments.

If you use video recording, the minimal video to capture is the real-time sequencing of screen action, showing both user inputs and system reactions and displays. Software support tools such as Morae™ or OVO™ can capture full-resolution video stream of screen action automatically. This is adequate for a large portion of the UX evaluation sessions we do. However, if participant physical actions, gestures, and/or facial expressions are important, as they might well be to evaluate emotional impact, digital video streams from cameras can be added and most capture software will synchronize all the video inputs automatically.

For some purposes, you can use one video camera aimed at the participant's hands to see details of physical actions and gestures and another at the participant's face to see expressions and, if useful, you can even have a third camera to capture a wide-angle overview of evaluator, participant, the computer, or other device being evaluated—the full context of the user experience.

Critical incident markers: Filtering raw data. Each critical incident marker created by the evaluator points to a particular place in the raw video stream, tagging the wheat as it still resides within the chaff. This real-time tagging enables evaluators to ignore the chaff in any further analysis, boosting the efficiency of the data analysis process enormously.

Tagging critical incidents is somewhat analogous to a similar kind of data tagging in crime scene data collection and analysis: little flags or tags are arranged in proximity to items that are identified as evidence so that the crime scene analysts can focus on the important items easily. Each "start" and "stop" tag (Figure 15-4) denotes a video clip, which constitutes filtered raw data representing a critical incident.

Critical incident comments: Interpretive data. In addition to marking critical incidents, evaluators sometimes want to make comments explaining critical incidents. The comments are linked to the corresponding video clips so that analysts subsequently can view the related clips as they read the comments.

The comments are an interpretive "coating" on filtered raw data. Figure 15-4 illustrates the video stream tagged with critical incident markers and associated evaluator comments.

Working without a net: Not recording raw data. It is more efficient if you do not have to use video recording. Although video recording of interaction even with paper prototypes can be appropriate and useful, evaluators certainly do not always record video of the interaction events, especially for evaluations of early prototypes where the fast pace of iterative design changes calls for lightweight data collection and analysis.

Operating without the safety net of a video recording results in immediate loss of raw data. Evaluators depend solely on the comments, and the analysis process begins with just the interpretive accounts of data, but this if often fully adequate and appropriate for early versions of a design or when rapid methods are required for all versions.

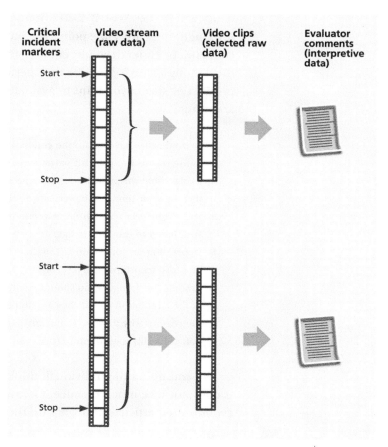

Figure 15-4

Overview of raw data filtering by tagging critical incidents and adding interpretive comments.

Manual note taking for critical incident data collection. Manual note taking is the most basic mechanism and is still a useful and efficient approach in many UX labs. Evaluators take comprehensive, real-time raw critical incident notes with a laptop or with pencil and paper. When thoughts come faster than they can write, they might make audio notes on a handheld digital voice recorder—anything to capture raw data while it is still fresh.

Even if you are also making audio or video recordings, you should take notes as though you are not. It is a mistake to rely on your video recordings as a primary method of raw data capture. It is just not practical to go back and get your raw critical incident notes by reviewing the entire video. The video, however, can be a good backup, something you can look at for missing data, to resolve a question, or to clear up a misunderstanding.

15.5.3 Think-Aloud Data Collection

Although there are some points to watch for, in its simplest form this technique could not be easier. It simply entails having participants think out loud and share their thoughts verbally while they perform tasks or otherwise interact with a product or system you want to evaluate. Within the UX evaluation method you are using:

- At the beginning, explain the concept of thinking aloud and explain that you want to use this technique with participants.
- Explain that this means you will expect them to talk while they work and think, sharing their thoughts by verbalizing them to you.
- You might start with a little "exercise" to get warmed up and to get participants acclimated to thinking aloud.
- Depending on your main UX evaluation method, you may capture think-aloud data by audio recording, video recording, and/or written or typed notes.
- Among the thoughts you should encourage participants to express are descriptions of their intentions, what they are doing or are trying to do, and their motivations, the reasons why they are doing any particular actions.
- You especially want them to speak out when they get confused, frustrated, or blocked.

Depending on the individual, thinking aloud usually comes quite naturally; it does not take much practice. Occasionally you might have to encourage or remind the participant to keep up the flow of thinking aloud.

15.6 GENERATING AND COLLECTING EMOTIONAL IMPACT DATA

Collecting emotional impact data depends on observing and measuring indicators of emotional response through verbal communication, facial expressions, body language, behaviors, and physiological changes.

15.6.1 Applying Self-Reporting Verbal Techniques for Collecting Emotional Impact Data

Applying the think-aloud technique to evaluate emotional impact

We have already talked about using the think-aloud technique for capturing the participant's view of interaction, critical incidents, and UX problems. The think-aloud technique is also excellent for obtaining a window into the mind of the user with respect to emotional feelings as they occur.

Depending on the nature of the interaction, emotional impact indicators may be infrequent in the flow of task performance user actions, and you may see them mainly as a by-product of your hunt for usability problem indicators. So, when you do encounter an emotional impact indicator during observation in task performance, you certainly should make a note of it. You can also make emotional impact factors the primary focus during the think-aloud technique.

■ When you explain the concept of thinking aloud, be sure participants understand that you want to use this technique to explore emotional feelings resulting from interaction and usage.

■ Explain that this means you will expect them to share their emotions and feelings while they work and think by talking about them to you.

■ As you did when you used the think-aloud technique to capture qualitative UX data, you may wish to begin with a little "exercise" to be sure participants are on the same page about the technique.

■ As before, you can capture think-aloud data by audio recording, video recording, and/or written or typed notes.

■ Also as before, you may have to remind participants occasionally to keep the thinking aloud flowing.

During the flow of interaction:

■ You can direct participants to focus their thinking aloud on comments about joy of use, aesthetics, fun, and so on.

■ You should observe and note the more obvious manifestations of emotional impact, such as expressions like "I love this" and "this is really cool" and "wow" expressions, annoyances, or irritation.

■ You also need to watch out for the more subtle expressions that can provide insights into the user experience, such as a slight intake of breath.

■ As a practitioner, you also must be sensitive to detecting when emotional impact goes flat, when there is no real joy of use. Ask participants about it, causes, and about how it can be improved.

Finally, a caution about cultural dependency. Most emotions themselves are pretty much the same across cultures, and non-verbal expressions of emotion, such as facial expressions and gestures, are fairly universal. But cultural and social factors can govern an individual's willingness to communicate about emotions. Different cultures may also have different vocabularies and different perspectives on the meaning of emotions and the appropriateness of sharing and revealing them to others.

Applying questionnaires to evaluate emotional impact

Based on your project context and the type of application, use the discussion of questionnaires in Chapter 12 to select and apply a questionnaire to evaluate emotional impact.

15.6.2 Applying Direct Non-Verbal Techniques for Collecting Emotional Impact Data

Using non-verbal techniques for collecting emotional impact usually means deploying probes and instrumentation; see Chapter 12 for a discussion of physiological measurements.

15.7 GENERATING AND COLLECTING PHENOMENOLOGICAL EVALUATION DATA

Get ready for a study of emotional impact situated in the real activities of users over time, if possible from the earliest thinking about the product to adoption into their lifestyles. You will need to choose your data collection techniques to compensate for not being able to be with your participants all the time, which means including self-reporting.

We encourage you to improvise a self-reporting technique yourself, but you should definitely consider a diary-based technique, in which each participant maintains a "diary," documenting problems, experiences, and phenomenological occurrences within long-term usage. Diaries can be kept via paper and pencil notes, online reports, cell-phone messages, or voice recorders.

For a diary-based technique to be effective, participants must be primed in advance:

- Give your users a list of the kinds of things to report.
- Give them some practice exercises in identifying relevant situations and reporting on them.
- Get them to internalize the need to post a report whenever they confront a usage problem, use a new feature, or encounter anything interesting or fun within usage.

To encourage participants to use voice-mail for reporting, consider paying them a per-call monetary compensation (in addition to whatever payment you give them for participating in the study). In the Palen and Salzman study, they found that a per-call payment encouraged participants to make calls. There is a possibility that this incentive might bias participants into making some unnecessary calls, but that did not seem to happen in this study.

To perhaps get more representative data, you might choose to trigger reporting to control the timing (Chapter 12, under data collection technique for phenomenological aspects), rather than letting your participant perform reporting at when it is convenient or times when things are going well with the product. For example, you can give your participant a dedicated pager (Buchenau & Suri, 2000) to signal randomly timed "events" at which times the participant is asked to report on their usage and context.

Another way you could choose to sample phenomenological usage is by periodic questionnaires over time. You can use a series of such questionnaires to elicit understanding of changes in usage over those time periods.

You can also choose to do direct observation and interviews in simulated real usage situations (Chapter 12, under data collection technique for phenomenological aspects). You will need to create conditions to encourage episodes of phenomenological activity to occur during these observational periods.

As an example of using this technique, Petersen, Madsen, and Kjaer (2002) conducted a longitudinal study of the use of a TV and video recorder by two families in their own homes. During the time of usage, periodic interviews were scheduled in the analysts' office, except in cases where users had difficulty in getting there and, then, the interviews were conducted in the users' homes.

During the interviews, the evaluators posed numerous usage scenarios and had the participants do their best to enact the usage while giving their feedback, especially about emotional impact. All interviews were videotaped. The idea is to set up conditions so that you can capture the essence of real usage and reflect real usage in a tractable time frame.

Here are some tips for success:

- Establish the interview schedule to take into account learning through usage by implementing a sequence of sessions longitudinally over time.
- As in contextual inquiry, it is necessary to observe user activities rather than just to ask about them. As we know, the way people talk about what they do is often not the same as what they actually do.
- Be cautious and discreet with videotaping in more private settings, such as the participant's home, usually found in this kind of usage context.

As you collect data, you will be looking for indicators of all the different ways your users involve the product in their lives, the high points of joy in use, how the basic mode of usage changes, evolves, or emerges over time, and especially how usage is adapted to emerge as new and unusual kinds of usage. As said in Chapter 12, you want to be able to tell stories of usage and good emotional impact over time.

15.8 WRAPPING UP AN EVALUATION SESSION

Returning to the more traditional lab-based or similar evaluation methods, we now need to do several things to wrap up an evaluation session.

15.8.1 Post-Session Probing Via Interviews and Questionnaires

Immediately after the sessions, but while your participant is still present, is the best opportunity to ask probing questions to clear up any confusion you have about critical incidents or UX problems. Conduct post-session interviews and administrator questionnaires to capture user thoughts and feelings while they are fresh.

Clarify ambiguities about the nature of any problems. Be sure you understand the *real* problems and their causes. Interact with your participant as a doctor does in diagnosing a patient. If you wait until the participant is gone, you lose the opportunity to ask further questions to disambiguate the diagnoses and causes.

Facilitators often start with some kind of standard *structured interview*, asking a series of preplanned questions aimed at probing the participant's thoughts about the product and the user experience. A typical post-session interview might include, for example, the following general questions. "What did you like best about the interface?" "What did you like least?" "How would you change so-and-so?" An interesting question to ask is "What are the three most important pieces of information that you must know to make the best use of this interface?"

For example, in one design, some of the results of a database query were presented graphically to the user as a data plot, the data points of which were displayed as small circles. Because most users did not at first realize that they could get more information about a particular data point if they clicked on the corresponding circle, one very important piece of information users needed to know about the design was that they should treat a circle as an icon and that they could manipulate it accordingly.

It can be even more effective to follow up with unstructured opportunistic questioning. Find out why certain things happened. Be sure to ask about any critical incidents that you are not sure about or potential UX problems for which you do not yet completely understand the causes.

15.8.2 Reset for the Next Participant

After running an evaluation session with one participant, you should clean up everything to be ready for the next participant. This means removing any effects from the previous session that might affect the participant or task performance in the next session. Often you will have to do this kind of cleanup even between tasks for the same participant.

If you are using a paper prototype, you still must reset internal states and data back to initial conditions needed by the first task using the prototype. For example, if previous participants made changes to the prototype, such as filling in information on a paper or plastic form, provide a fresh clean form. If the user made changes to a "database," recorded anywhere that will be visible to the next participant, these have to be reset for a fresh participant.

For Web-based evaluation, clear out the browser history and browser cache, delete temporary files, remove any saved passwords, and so on. For a software prototype, save and backup any data you want to keep. Then reset the prototype state and remove any artifacts introduced in the previous session.

Delete any temporary files or other saved settings. Reset any user-created content on the prototype, such as any saved appointments, contacts, or files. Reset any other tools, such as Web-based surveys or questionnaires, to make sure one participant's answers are not visible to the next one.

Finally, give the participant(s) their pay, gifts, and/or premiums, thank them, and send them on their way.

> *Exercise*
>
> See Exercise 15-1, UX Evaluation Data Collection for Your System

15.9 THE HUMAINE PROJECT

The European community project HUMAINE (Human-Machine Interaction Network on Emotions) issued a technical report detailing a taxonomy of affective measurement techniques (Westerman, Gardner, & Sutherland, 2006). They point out that there is a history of physiological and psychophysiological measurement in human factors practice since the late 1970s to detect, for example, stress due to operator overload, and an even longer history of this kind of measurement in psychological research.

In the HUMAINE report, the authors discuss the role of medicine in physiological measurement, including electroencephalograms and event-related potential, measured with electroencephalography, a technique that detects and measures electrical activity of the brain through the skull and scalp. Event-related potentials can be roughly correlated to cognitive functions involving memory and attention and changes in mental state.

As the authors say, these physiological measurements have the advantage over self-reporting methods in that they can monitor continuously, require no conscious user actions, and do not interrupt task performance or usage activity. To be meaningful, however, such physiological measurements have to be associated with time stamps on a video of user activity.

A major disadvantage, ruling the approach out for most routine UX evaluation, is the requirement for attached sensors. New, less intrusive instrumentation is being developed. For example, Kapoor, Picard, and Ivanov (2004) report being able to detect changes in user posture, for example, due to fidgeting, with pressure sensors attached to a chair.

Rigorous Empirical Evaluation: Analysis

16

If it ain't broke, it probably doesn't have enough features.

– Anonymous

Objectives

After reading this chapter, you will:

1. Be able to analyze informal summative (quantitative) usability data, compare results with usability targets, and decide whether you can stop iterating
2. Have the working knowledge to analyze formative (qualitative) critical incident and UX problem data
3. Know how to perform cost-importance analysis to prioritize UX problems to fix
4. Be able to maintain and manage UX problem data
5. Know how to connect back to the UX process lifecycle

16.1 INTRODUCTION

16.1.1 You Are Here

We begin each process chapter with a "you are here" picture of the chapter topic in the context of the overall Wheel lifecycle template; see Figure 16-1. This chapter is about analyzing data collected during evaluation.

The focus of research and practice has slowly been shifting away from methods for usability data collection and comparisons of those data collection methods to issues about how best to use data generated or collected by these methods (Howarth, Andre, & Hartson, 2007). So, now that we have data, what's next?

Figure 16-1

You are here; at data analysis, within the evaluation activity in the context of the overall Wheel lifecycle template.

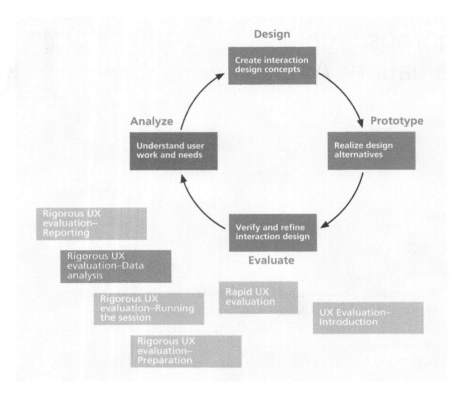

16.2 INFORMAL SUMMATIVE (QUANTITATIVE) DATA ANALYSIS

As we have said, the quantitative data analysis for informal summative evaluation associated with formative evaluation does not include inferential statistical analyses, such as analyses of variance (ANOVAs), *t* tests, or *F* tests. Rather, they use simple "descriptive" statistics (such as mean and standard deviation) to make an engineering determination as to whether the interaction design has met the UX target levels. If the design has not yet met those targets, qualitative analysis will indicate how to modify the design to improve the UX ratings and help converge toward those goals in subsequent cycles of formative evaluation.

Iteration can seem to some like a process going around in circles, which can be scary to managers. As we will see later, your informal summative analysis, coupled with your UX targets and metrics, is a control mechanism to help managers and other project roles know whether the iterative process is converging toward a usable interaction design and when to stop iterating.

16.2.1 Lining up Your Quantitative Ducks

The first step in analyzing quantitative data is to compute simple descriptive statistics (e.g., averages) for timing, error counts, questionnaire ratings, and so on, as stated in the UX targets. Be careful about computing only mean values, though, because the mean is not resistant to outliers and, therefore, can be a misleading indicator. Because we are not doing formal quantitative analysis, the small number of participants typical in formative evaluation can lead to a mean value that meets a reasonable UX target and you can still have serious UX problems.

It may help to include standard deviation values, for example, to indicate something about the rough level of confidence you should have in data. For example, if three participants are all very close in performance times for a particular task, the numbers should give you pretty good confidence, and the average is more meaningful. If there is a big spread, the average is not very meaningful and you should find out why there is such a variance (e.g., one user spent a huge amount of time in an error situation). Sometimes it can mean that you should try to run a few more participants.

After you compute summary statistics of quantitative data, you add them to the "Observed Results" column at the end of the UX target table. As an example, partial results from a hypothetical evaluation of the Ticket Kiosk System are shown in Table 16-1 using some of the UX targets established in Table 10-10.

Table 16-1

Example of partial informal quantitative testing results for the Ticket Kiosk System

Work Role: User Class	UX Goal	UX Measure	Measuring Instrument	UX Metric	Baseline Level	Target Level	Observed Results	Meet Target?
Ticket buyer: Casual new user, for occasional personal use	Walk-up ease of use	Initial user performance	BT1: Buy special event ticket	Average time on task	3 min as measured at the kiosk	2.5 min	3.5 min	No
Ticket buyer: Casual new user, for occasional personal use	Walk-up ease of use for new user	Initial user performance	BT2: Buy movie ticket	Average number of errors	<1	<1	2	No
Ticket buyer: Casual new user, for occasional personal use	Initial customer satisfaction	First impression	Questions Q1–Q10 in questionnaire XYZ	Average rating across users and across questions	7.5/10	8/10	7.5	No

Next, by directly comparing the observed results with the specified UX goals, you can tell immediately which UX targets have been met, and which have not, during this cycle of formative evaluation. It is useful to add, as we have done in Table 16-1, yet one more column to the right-hand end of the UX target table, for "Did you meet UX target?" Entries can be Yes, No, or Almost.

In looking at the example observed results in Table 16-1, you can see that our example users did not meet any of the UX target levels. This is not unusual for an early evaluation of a still-evolving design. Again, we stress that this was only informal summative analysis—it cannot be used *anywhere* for claims and cannot be used for any kind of reporting outside the UX group or, at most, the project team. It is *only* for managing the iterative UX engineering process internally. If you want results from which you can make claims or that you can make public, you need to do (and pay for) a formal summative evaluation.

Not All Errors Are Created Equal

Andrew Sears, Professor and Dean, B. Thomas Golisano
College of Computing and Information Sciences, Rochester Institute of Technology

As we design and evaluate user interfaces, we must decide what metrics will be used to assess the efficacy of our design. Perhaps the most common choices are the speed–error–satisfaction triad that we see used not only in usability studies but also in more formal evaluations such as those that appear in scholarly journals and conference proceedings. After all, a fast system that leads to many errors is not particularly useful, and even a fast and error-free system is not useful if nobody will use it (unless you are dealing with one of those less common situations where users do not have a choice).

If we accept that each of these aspects of usability should be considered in some form and define how each will be assessed, we can begin to evaluate how well a system performs along each dimension, we can introduce changes and evaluate the impact of these changes, and we can fine-tune our designs. There are many techniques that help usability engineers identify problems, including approaches that result in problems being classified in one way or another in an effort to help prioritize the process of addressing the resulting collection of problems. Prioritization is important because there may not be time to fix every problem given the time pressures often experienced as new products are developed. Prioritization is even more important when one considers the variable nature of the "problems" that can be identified when using different evaluation techniques.

While the severity of a problem may be considered when deciding which problems to fix, the focus is typically on eliminating errors. However, through our research with several error-prone technologies, it has become clear that focusing exclusively on eliminating errors may lead to less than optimal outcomes. These technologies, including speech and gesture recognition, can produce unpredictable errors that can result in dramatically different consequences for the user of the system. It was in this context that we began to rethink the need to eliminate errors. This shift in focus was motivated, in part, by the fact that *we could not necessarily eliminate all errors but we noticed that there were opportunities to change what happened when errors did occur*. It was also motivated by the observation that people are really quite good at processing input where some details are missing or inaccurate. Perhaps the simplest example would be when you are participating in a conversation, but the person you are talking to mumbles or background noise masks a few words. Often, it is possible to fill in the gaps and reconstruct what was missed originally.

Two specific examples may be useful in seeing how these ideas can be applied when designing or redesigning information technologies. The first example considers what happens when an individual is interacting with a speech-based system. At times, the speech recognition engine will misinterpret what was said. When using speech to navigate within a text document, such errors can result in a variety of consequences, including ignoring what was said, moving the cursor to the wrong location, or even inserting extra text. Recovering from each of these consequences involves a different set of actions, which require different amounts of work. By recognizing that an error has occurred, and using this information to change the consequences that an individual must overcome, we can improve the usability of a system even without eliminating the error. At times, *a slightly higher error rate may be desirable if this allows the severity of the consequences to be reduced sufficiently*. This example is explored in more depth by Feng and Sears (2009). This article discusses the issue of designing for error-prone technologies and the importance of considering not only the number of errors users encounter but the severity of the consequences associated with those errors.

A second example looks at the issue of taking notes using mobile technologies. The process of entering text on mobile devices is notorious for being slow and error prone. If someone tries to record a brief note while correcting all errors, the process tends to be sufficiently slow to discourage many individuals. At the same time, people tend to be quite good at dealing with many different types of errors. Because these brief notes tend to be used to remind the user of important details, having an error-free note may not be that important as long as the erroneous note is sufficient to remind the user of the information, event, or activity that inspired them originally to record the note. Our studies found that a note-taking mechanism that did not allow users to review and correct their notes could allow users to recall important details just as effectively as error-free notes while significantly reducing the time they spent recording the note. Dai et al. (2009) explore this example in more detail, showing how users can overcome errors.

Errors are inevitable, but not all errors result in the same consequences for the user. Some errors introduce significant burdens, creating problems that the user must then fix before they can continue with their original task. Other errors may be irritating, requiring users to repeat their actions, but do not introduce new problems. Still other errors may be annoying but may not prevent the user from accomplishing his or her task. Understanding how an error affects the user and when there are opportunities to reduce the consequences of errors (sometimes this can involve increasing the number of errors but still results in an overall improvement in the usability of the system) can allow for more effective systems to be designed even when errors cannot be prevented.

References

Dai, L., Sears, A., & Goldman, R. (2009). Shifting the focus from accuracy to recallability: A study of informal note-taking on mobile information technologies. *ACM Transactions on Computer-Human Interaction, 16*(1), 46 Pages.

Feng, J., & Sears, A. (2009). Beyond errors: Measuring reliability for error-prone interaction devices. *Behaviour and Information Technology, 29*(2), 149–163.

16.2.2 The Big Decision: Can We Stop Iterating?

Now it is time for a major project management decision: Should you continue to iterate? This decision should be a team affair and made at a global level, not just considering quantitative data. Here are some questions to consider:

- Did you simultaneously meet all your target-level goals?
- What is your general team feeling about the conceptual design, the overall interaction design, the metaphor, and the user experiences they have observed?

If you can answer these questions positively, you can accept the design as is and stop iterating. Resource limitations also can force you to stop iterating and get on with pushing this version out in the hope of fixing known flaws in the next version. If and when you do decide to stop iterating, do not throw your *qualitative* data away, though; you paid to get it, so keep this round of problem data for next time.

If your UX targets were not met—the most likely situation after the first cycle(s) of testing—and resources permit (e.g., you are not out of time or money), you need to iterate. This means analyzing the UX problems and finding a way to solve them in order of their cost and effect on the user experience.

Convergence toward a quality user experience

Following our recurring theme of using your own thinking and experience in addition to following a process, we point out that this is a good place to use your intuition. As you iterate, you should keep an eye on the quantitative results over multiple iterations: Is your design at least moving in the right direction?

It is always possible for UX levels to get worse with any round of design changes. If you are not converging toward improvement, why not? Are UX problem fixes uncovering problems that existed but could not be seen before or are UX problem fixes causing new problems?

16.3 ANALYSIS OF SUBJECTIVE QUESTIONNAIRE DATA

Depending on which questionnaire you used, apply the appropriate calculations for the final scores (Chapter 12).

16.4 FORMATIVE (QUALITATIVE) DATA ANALYSIS

Our friend Whitney Quesenbery gave us this nutshell digest of her approach to usability problem analysis, which she in turn adapted from someone else:

> The team usually includes all the stakeholders, not just UX folks, and we rarely have much time. First, we agree on what we saw. No interpretation, just observation. This gets us all on the same page. Then we brainstorm until we agree on "what it means." Then we brainstorm design solutions.

16.4.1 Introduction

Formative analysis of qualitative data is the bread and butter of UX evaluation. The goal of formative data analysis is to identify UX problems and causes (design flaws) so that they can be fixed, thereby improving product user experience. The process of determining how to convert collected data into scheduled design and implementation solutions is essentially one of negotiation in which, at various times, all members of the project team are involved. In the first part of qualitative analysis you should have all your qualitative data represented as a set of UX problem instances so that you can proceed with diagnosis and problem solutions.

Did not find many UX problems? Better look again at your data collection process. We seldom, if ever, see an interaction design for which UX testing does not reveal lots of UX problems. Absence of evidence is not evidence of absence.

Figure 16-2 illustrates the steps of qualitative data analysis: consolidating large sets of raw critical incident comments into UX problem instances, merging UX problem instances into UX problem records, and grouping of UX problem records so that we can fix related problems together.

For practical purposes we have to separate our material into chapters. In practice, early analysis—especially for qualitative data—overlaps with the data collection process. Because evaluator comments are interpretive, we have

Problem Instance (UX)

A UX problem instance is a single occurrence of an encounter with a given problem by a given user, inspector, or participant. When more than one participant experiences what is essentially the same problem, the encounters are counted as different instances so they are not reported as different problems.

Critical Incident

A critical incident is a UX evaluation event that occurs during user task performance or other user interaction, observed by the facilitator or other observers or sometimes expressed by the user participant, that indicates a possible UX problem. Critical incident identification is arguably the single most important source of qualitative data.

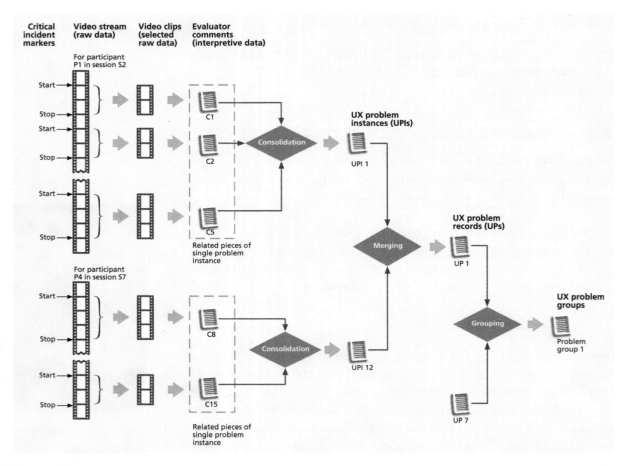

Figure 16-2

Consolidating, merging, and grouping of UX problem data.

already begun to overlap analysis of qualitative data with their capture. The earlier you think about UX problems and their causes, the better chance you have at getting all the information you will need for problem diagnosis. In this chapter, we move from this overlap with data collection into the whole story of qualitative data analysis.

16.4.2 Get an Early Jump on Problem Analysis
Keep a participant around to help with early analysis
In a typical way of doing things, data collection is "completed," the participant is dismissed, and the team does high fives and cracks open the bubbly before turning its attention to data analysis. But this Dilbertian HFTAWR (high-frivolity-to-actual-work ratio) approach puts the problem analyst at a disadvantage when

the need inevitably arises to ask the participant questions and resolve ambiguities. The analyst can sometimes ask the facilitator or others who collected data, but often at significant communication effort.

Neither the facilitator nor the analyst now has access to the participant. Too often the problem analyst can only try to interpret and reconstruct missing UX data. The resulting completeness and accuracy become highly dependent on the knowledge and experience of the problem analyst.

We suggest bringing in the problem analyst as early as possible, especially if the analyst is not on the data collection team. And, to the extent it is practical, start analyzing qualitative data while a participant is still present to fill in missing data, clarify ambiguous issues, and answer questions.

Early UX problem data records

If data collectors used software support tools, the critical incident notes may already be in rudimentary problem records, possibly with links to tagged video sequences. With even minimal support from some kind of database tool, evaluators can get a leg up on the process yet to come by entering their critical incident descriptions directly into data records rather than, say, just a word processor or spreadsheet. The earlier you can get your raw critical incident notes packaged as data records, the more expedient the transition to subsequent data analysis.

Clean up your raw data before your memory fades

However you get data, you still have mostly raw qualitative data at this point. Many of the critical incident notes are likely to be terse observational comments that will be difficult to integrate in subsequent analysis, particularly if the person performing UX problem analysis is not the same person who observed the incidents and recorded the comments.

Therefore, it is essential for data collectors to clean up the raw data as soon after data collection as time and evaluator skills permit to capture as complete a record of each critical incident as possible while perishable detailed data are still fresh. In this transition from data collection to data analysis, experienced data collectors will anticipate the need for certain kinds of content later in problem analysis.

Clarify and amplify your emotional impact data

UX problems involving emotional impact are, by nature, usually broader in scope and less about details than usability problems. Therefore, for UX problems about emotional impact, it is important to get at the underlying essence of the observations while the explanatory context is still fresh. Otherwise, in our experience, you may end up with a vague problem description of some symptoms too nebulous to use.

16.4.3 Sources of Raw Qualitative Data

We are talking primarily about data from lab-based UX testing here, but critical incident data can come from other sources such as expert UX inspections. It is our job to sort through these, often unstructured, data and extract the essential critical incident and UX problem information. Regardless of the source of the raw data, much of the data analysis we do in this chapter is essentially the same.

Some sources are less detailed and some are more synoptic, for example, evaluator problem notes from a session without video recording tend to be more summarized, or summary problem descriptions can come from a UX inspection, in which there are no real critical incidents as there are no real users.

For these less detailed data, inputs to data analysis are often in the form of narratives about perceived UX-related situations and you might have to work a bit harder to extract the essence. These reports often roll up more than one problem in one description and you need to unpack individual UX issues into UX problem instances, as discussed next.

16.4.4 Isolate Individual Critical Incident Descriptions

On occasion, participants can experience more than one distinct UX problem at the same time and a single critical incident comment can refer to all of these problems. The first step in the sequence for refining raw data into UX problem reports is to scan the raw critical incident notes, looking for such notes about more than one UX problem, and separate them into multiple critical incident notes, each about a single UX problem.

Here is an example from one of our UX evaluation sessions for a companion Website for the Ticket Kiosk. The participant was in the middle of a benchmark task that required her to order three tickets to a Three Tenors concert. As she proceeded through the task, at one point she could not locate the button (which was below the "fold") to complete the transaction.

When she finally scrolled down and saw the button, the button label said "Submit." At this point she remarked "I am not sure if clicking on this button will let me review my order or just send it in immediately." This is an example of a critical incident that indicates more than one UX problem: the button is located where it is not immediately visible and the label is not clear enough to help the user make a confident decision.

16.4.5 Consolidating Raw Critical Incident Notes into UX Problem Instances

The UX problem instance concept

Howarth et al. (Howarth, Andre, & Hartson, 2007; Howarth, Smith-Jackson, & Hartson, 2009) introduced the concept of UX problem instances to serve as a bridge between raw critical incident descriptions and UX problem records. A UX problem instance is a single occurrence of a particular problem experienced by a single participant.

The same UX problem may be encountered and recorded in multiple instances—occurring in the same or different sessions, observed by the same or different evaluators, experienced by the same or different participants, within the context of the same or of a different task. These are not each separate problems, but several instances of the same problem.

Critical incidents vs. UX problem instances

We have been using the term "critical incident" for some time and now we are introducing the idea of a UX problem instance. These two concepts are very similar and, if used loosely, can be thought of as referring to more or less the same thing. The difference rests on a bit of a nuance: A critical incident is an observable *event* (that happens over time) made up of user actions and system reactions, possibly accompanied by evaluator notes or comments, that *indicates* a UX problem instance.

Critical incident data are raw data and just a record of what happened and are not yet interpreted in terms of a problem or cause and, therefore, not in a form used easily in the analysis that follows. The UX problem instance is a more "processed" or more abstract (in the sense of capturing the essence) notion that we do use in the analysis.

Gathering up parts of data for a critical incident

Raw data for a single critical incident can appear in parts in the video/data stream interspersed with unrelated material. These data representing parts of a critical incident may not necessarily be contiguous in a real-time stream because the participant, for example, may be multitasking or interrupting the train of thought.

To build a corresponding UX problem instance, we need to consolidate all data (e.g., raw notes, video and audio sequences) about each critical incident. The second column from the left in Figure 16-2 shows sets of clips related to the same critical incident being extracted from the video stream. This step pulls out all the pieces of one single critical incident that then indicates (makes up) the UX problem instance.

This extraction of related parts of a single critical incident description will be fairly straightforward. Raw data related to a given critical incident instance, if not contiguous in the stream of events, will usually be in close proximity.

Example: Consolidating Critical Incident Parts of a Single UX Problem Instance

These abstract ideas are best conveyed by a simple example, one we borrow from Howarth, Andre, and Hartson (2007), based on real raw data taken from a UX evaluation of a photo management application. Using this application, users can manage photographs, already on a PC or received via email, into albums contained on their computers.

For this example, our user is trying to upload a picture to put in an album. The transcript of raw data (video stream plus evaluator comments) goes something like what you see in Figure 16-3.

Figure 16-3

Example "transcript" of raw data stream showing multiple critical incident notes pertaining to a single UX problem instance.

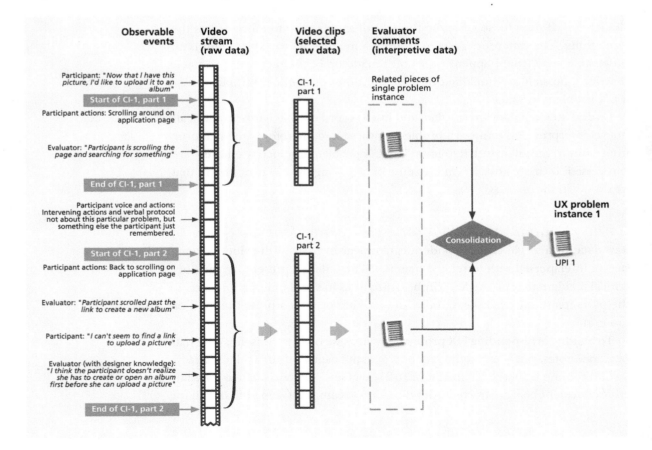

In consolidating the raw critical incident notes (and associated video and audio clips) relating to this one UX problem instance, the practitioner would include both parts of the transcript (the two parts next to the curly braces, for CI-1, part 1 and CI-1, part 2) but would not include the intervening words and actions of the participant not related to this UX problem instance.

Putting it into a UX problem instance

This is a good time for a reality check on the real value of this critical incident to your iterative process. Using good UX engineering judgment, the practitioner keeps only ones that represent "real" UX instances.

As you put the critical incident pieces into one UX problem instance, you abstract out details of the data (the he-said/she-said details) and convert the wording of observed interaction event(s) and think-aloud comments into the wording of an interpretation as a problem/cause.

16.4.6 A Photo Album Example

Using the Howarth et al. (2007) example of a photo album management application, consider the task of uploading a photo from email and importing it into the album application.

16.4.7 UX Problem Instances

UX problem instance content

To begin with, in whatever scheme you use for maintaining UX data, each UX problem instance should be linked back to its constituent critical incident data parts, including evaluator comments and video clips, in order to retain full details of the UX problem instance origins, if needed for future reference.

The next thing to do is to give the problem a name so people can refer to this problem in discussions. Next we want to include enough information to make the UX problem instance as useful as possible for data analysis. Much has been said in the literature about what information to include in a UX problem record, but common sense can guide you. You need enough information to accomplish the main goals:

- understand each problem
- glean insight into its causes and possible solutions
- be conscious of relationships among similar problems

You will support these goals by problem records fields containing the following kinds of information.

Problem statement: A summary statement of the problem as an effect or outcome experienced by the user, but not as a suggested solution. You want to keep your options flexible when you do get to considering solutions.

User goals and task information: This information provides problem context to know what the user was trying to do when the problem was encountered. In the photo album example, the user has photos on a computer and had the goal of uploading another picture from email to put in an album contained in the photo management application.

Immediate intention: One of the most important pieces of information to include is the user's immediate intention (at a very detailed level) exactly when the problem was encountered, for example, the user was trying to see a button label in a small font or the user was trying to understand the wording of a label.

More detailed problem description: Here is where you record details that can harbor clues about the nature of the problem, including a description of user actions and system reactions, the interaction events that occurred.

Designer knowledge (interpretation and explanation of events): Another very important piece of information is an "outside the user" explanation of what might have happened in this problem encounter. This is usually based on what we call "designer knowledge." If the participant was proceeding on an incorrect assumption about the design or a misunderstanding of how the design works, the correct interpretation (the designer knowledge) can shed a lot of light on what the participant should have done and maybe how the design could be changed to lead to that outcome.

Designer knowledge is a kind of meta comment because it is not based on observed actions. It is based on knowledge about the design possessed by the evaluator, but not the participant, of why the system did not work the way the user expected and how it does work in this situation. We set up the evaluator team to ensure that someone with the requisite designer knowledge will be present during the evaluation session to include that information in the UX problem instance content that we now need in this transition to data analysis. Here is an example of designer knowledge, in this case about a critical incident that occurred in evaluation of the photo album application, as shown near the bottom left-hand side of Figure 16-3: "I think the participant doesn't realize she has to create or open an album first before she can upload a picture."

Causes and potential solutions: Although you may not know the problem causes or potential solutions at first, there should be a place in the problem record to record this diagnostic information eventually.

UX problem instance project context

In addition to the problem parameters and interaction event context, it can be useful to maintain links from a problem instance to its project context. Project context is a rather voluminous and largely uninteresting (at least during the session) body of data that gives a setting for UX data within administrative and project-oriented parameters.

While completely out of the way during data collection and not used for most of the usual analysis process, these project context data can be important for keeping track of when and by whom problem data were generated and collected and to which version or iteration of the design data apply. This information is linked and cross-linked so that, if you need to, you can find out which evaluators were conducting the session in which a given critical incident occurred and on what date, and using which participant (participant id, if not the name). Project context data can include (Howarth, Andre, & Hartson, 2007):

- organization (e.g., company, department)
- project (e.g., product or system, project management, dates, budget, personnel)
- version (e.g., design/product release, version number, iteration number)
- evaluation session (e.g., date, participants, evaluators, associated UX target table)
- task run (e.g., which task, associated UX targets)

16.4.8 Merge Congruent UX Problem Instances into UX Problem Records

We use the term *congruent* to refer to multiple UX problem instances that represent the same underlying UX problem (not just similar problems or problems in the same category).

Find and merge multiple UX problem instances representing the same problem

In general, the evaluator or analyst cannot be expected to know about or remember previous instances of the same problem, so new critical incident descriptions (and new UX problem instances accordingly) are created each time an instance is encountered. Now you should look through your problem instances and find sets that are congruent.

How do you know if two problem descriptions are about the same underlying problem? Capra (2006, p. 41) suggests one way using a practical solution-based criterion: "Two problems, A and B, were considered the same [congruent] if fixing problem A also fixes problem B and fixing problem B also fixes problem A." Capra's approach is based on criteria used in the analysis of UX reports collected in CUE-4 (Molich & Dumas, 2008). The symmetric aspect of this criterion rules out a case where one problem is a subset of the other.

As an example from our Ticket Kiosk System evaluation, one UX problem instance states that the participant was confused about the button labeled "Submit" and did not know that this button should be clicked to move on in the transaction to pay for the tickets. Another (congruent) UX problem instance account of the same problem (encountered by a different participant) said that the participant complained about the wording of the button label "Submit," saying it did not help understand where one would go if one clicked on that button.

Create UX problem records

In the merging of congruent UX problem instances, the analyst creates one single UX problem record for that problem. This merging combines the descriptions of multiple instances to produce a single complete and representative UX problem description.

The resulting problem description will usually be slightly more general by virtue of filtering out irrelevant differences among instances while embracing their common defining problem characteristics. In practice, merging is done by taking the best words and ideas of each instance description to synthesize an amalgam of the essential characteristics.

As an example of merging UX problem instances in the photo album application example, we see UX problem instances UPI-1 and UPI-12 in the middle of Figure 16-2, both about trying to find the upload link to upload pictures before having created an album into which to upload. The problem in UPI-1 is stated as: "The participant does not seem to understand that she must first create an album."

The problem in UPI-12 says "User can't find link to upload pictures because the target album has not yet been created." Two users in different UX evaluation sessions encountered the same problem, reported in slightly different ways. When you merge the two descriptions, factoring out the differences, you get a slightly more general statement of the problem, seasoned with a pinch of designer knowledge, in the resulting UX problem record, UP-1: "Participants don't understand that the system model requires them to create an album before pictures can be uploaded and stored in it."

In your system for maintaining UX data (e.g., problem database), each UX problem record should be linked back to its constituent instances in order to retain full details of where merged data came from. The number of UX problem instances merged to form a given UX problem is useful information about the frequency of occurrence of that problem, which could contribute to the weight of importance to fix in the cost-importance ratings (coming up soon later).

If an instance has a particularly valuable associated video clip (linked to the instance via the video stream tag), the UX problem record should also contain a link to that video clip, as the visual documentation of an example occurrence of the problem. Some UX problems will be represented by just one UX problem instance, in which case it will just be "promoted" into a UX problem record.

Thence, UX problem instances will be used only for occasional reference and the UX problem records will be the basis for all further analysis.

16.4.9 Group Records of Related UX Problems for Fixing Together

UX problems can be related in many different ways that call for you to consider fixing them at the same time.

- Problems may be in physical or logical proximity (e.g., may involve objects or actions within the same dialogue box).
- Problems may involve objects or actions used in the same task.
- Problems may be in the same category of issues or design features but scattered throughout the user interaction design.
- Problems may have consistency issues that require similar treatments.
- Observed problem instances are indirect symptoms of common, more deeply rooted, UX problems. A telling indicator of such a deeply rooted problem is complexity and difficulty in its analysis.

By some means of association, for example, using an affinity diagram, group together the related records for problems that should be fixed together, as done with UP-1 and UP- 7 at the right-hand side of Figure 16-2. The idea is to create a common solution that might be more general than required for a single problem, but which will be the most efficient and consistent for the whole group.

Example: Grouping Related Problems for the Ticket Kiosk System

Consider the following UX problems, adapted with permission, from a student team in one of our classes from an evaluation of the Ticket Kiosk System:

Problem 9: The participant expected a graphic of seat layout and missed seeing the button for that at first; kept missing "View Seats" button.

Problem 13: For "Selected Seats," there is no way to distinguish balcony from floor seats because they both use the same numbering scheme and the shape/layout used was not clear enough to help users disambiguate.

Problem 20: In "View Seats" view, the participant was not able to figure out which of the individual seats were already sold because the color choices were confusing.

Problem 25: The participant did not understand that blue seat sections are clickable to get detailed view of available seats. She commented that there was not enough information about which seats are available.

Problem 26: Color-coding scheme used to distinguish availability of seats was problematic. On detailed seat view, purple was not noticeable as a color due to bad contrast. Also, the text labels were not readable because of contrast.

Suggested individual solutions were:

Problem 9 Solution: Create an icon or graphic to supplement "View Seats" option. Also show this in the previous screen where the user selects the number of seats.

Problem 13 Solution: Distinguish balcony seats and floor seats with a different numbering scheme and use better visual treatment to show these two as different.

Problem 20 Solution: Use different icons and colors to make the distinction between sold and available seats clearer. Also add a legend to indicate what those icons/colors mean.

Problem 25 Solution: Make the blue seat clickable with enhanced physical affordances, and when one is clicked, display detailed seat information, such as location, price, and so on.

Problem 26 Solution: Change the colors; find a better combination that can distinguish the availability clearly. Consider using different fills instead of just colors. Probably should have thicker font for labels (maybe bold would do it).

These problems may be indicative of a much broader design problem: a lack of effective visual design elements in seat selection part of the workflow. We can group and label all these problems into the problem group:

Group 1: Visual designs for seat selection workflow.

With a group solution of:

> Group 1 Solution: Comprehensively revise all visual design elements for seat selection workflow. Update style guide accordingly.

Higher level common issues within groups

When UX problem data include a number of critical incidents or problems that are quite similar, you will group these instances together because they are closely related. Then you usually look for common issues among the problems in the group.

But sometimes the real problem is not explicit in the commonality within the group, but the problems only represent symptoms of a higher level problem. You might have to deduce that this higher level problem is the real underlying cause of these common critical incidents.

For example, in one application we evaluated, users were having trouble understanding several different quirky and application-specific labels. We first tried changing the label wordings, but eventually we realized that the reason they did not "get" these labels was that they did not understand an important aspect of the conceptual design. Changing the labels without improving their understanding of the model did not solve the problem.

16.4.10 Analyze Each Problem
Terminology

To begin with, there is some simple terminology that we should use consistently. Technically, *UX problems* are not in the interaction design per se, but are usage difficulties faced by users. That is, users experience UX problems such as the inability to complete a task. Further, UX problems are caused by flaws in the interaction design. *Symptoms* are observable manifestations of problems (e.g., user agitation, expressed frustration, or anger).

Thus, the things we actually seek to fix are design flaws, the *causes* of UX problems. Some (but not all) problems can be observed; but causes have to be deduced with diagnosis. Solutions are the treatments (redesign changes) to fix the flaws. Further downstream evaluation is needed to confirm a "cure."

Sometimes we say "the poor design of this dialogue box is a UX problem" but, of course, that is a short-hand way of saying that the poor design can cause users to experience problems. It is okay to have this kind of informal difference in terminology, we do resort to it ourselves, as long as we all understand the real meaning behind the words.

Table 16-2 lists the terminology we use and its analog in the medical domain.

General Concept	Medical	Usability/User Experience
Problems	Illness or physical problems experienced by patient	UX problems experienced by user (e.g., inability to complete task)
Symptoms	Symptoms (e.g., difficulty in walking, shortness of breath)	Symptoms (e.g., frustration, anger)
Diagnosis (causes of symptoms)	Identify the disease that cause the symptoms (e.g., obesity)	Identify interaction design flaws that cause the UX problems
Causes of causes	Identify the cause(s) of the disease (e.g., poor lifestyle choices)	Determine causes of interaction design flaws (e.g., poor UX process choices)
Treatment	Medicine, dietary counseling, surgery to cure disease	Redesign fixes/changes to interaction design
Cure confirmation	Later observation and testing	Later evaluation

16.4.11 UX Problem Data Management

As time goes by and you proceed further into the UX process lifecycle, the full life story of each UX problem grows, entailing slow expansion of data in the UX problem record. Each UX problem record will eventually contain information about the problem: diagnosis by problem type and subtype, interaction design flaws as problem causes, cost/importance data estimating severity, management decisions to fix (or not) the problem, costs, implementation efforts, and downstream effectiveness.

Most authors mention UX problems or problem reports but do not hint at the fact that a complete problem record can be a large and complex information object. Maintaining a complete record of this unit of UX data is surely one place where some kind of tool support, such as a database management system, is warranted. As an example of how your UX problem record structure and content can grow, here are some of the kinds of information that can eventually be attached to it. These are possibilities we have encountered; pick the ones that suit you:

Problem name

Problem description

Task context

Effects on users (symptoms)

Links to video clip(s)

Associated designer knowledge

Problem diagnosis (problem type and subtype and causes within the design)

Links to constituent UX problem instances

Links for relationships to other UX problems (e.g., in groups to be fixed together)

Links to project context

    Project name

    Version/release number

    Project personnel

    Link to evaluation session

        Evaluation session date, location, etc.

        Session type (e.g., lab-based testing, UX inspection, remote evaluation)

        Links to evaluators

        Links to participants

    Cost-importance attributes for this iteration (next section)

        Candidate solutions

        Estimated cost to fix

        Importance to fix

        Priority ratio

        Priority ranking

        Resolution

    Treatment history

        Solution used

        Dates, personnel involved in redesign, implementation

        Actual cost to fix

        Results (e.g., based on retesting)

For more about representation schemes for UX problem data, see Lavery and Cockton (1997).

16.4.12 Abridged Qualitative Data Analysis

As an abridged approach formative (qualitative) data analysis:

- Just take notes about UX problems in real time during the session.
- Immediately after session, make UX problem records from the notes.

As an alternative, if you have the necessary simple tools for creating UX problem records:

- Create UX problem records as you encounter each UX problem during the session.
- Immediately after the session, expand and fill in missing information in the records.
- Analyze each problem, focusing on the real essence of the problem and noting causes (design flaws) and possible solutions.

16.5 COST-IMPORTANCE ANALYSIS: PRIORITIZING PROBLEMS TO FIX

It would be great to fix all UX problems known after each iteration of evaluation. However, because we are taking an engineering approach, we have to temper our enthusiasm for perfection with an eye toward cost-effectiveness.

So, now that we are done, at least for the moment, with individual problem analysis, we look at some aggregate problem analysis to assess priorities about what problems to fix and in what order. We call this cost-importance analysis because it is based on calculating trade-offs between the cost to fix a problem and the importance of getting it fixed. Cost-importance analysis applies to any UX problem list regardless of what evaluation method or data collection technique was used.

Although these simple calculations can be done manually, this analysis lends itself nicely to the use of spreadsheets. The basic form we will use is the cost-importance table shown in Table 16-3.

16.5.1 Problem

Starting with the left-most column in Table 16-3, we enter a concise description of the problem. Analysts needing to review further details can consult the problem data record and even the associated video clip. We will use some sample UX problems for the Ticket Kiosk System in a running example to illustrate how we fill out the entries in the cost-importance table.

In our first example problem the user had decided on an event to buy tickets for and had established the parameters (date, venue, seats, price, etc.) but did not realize that it was then necessary to click on the "Submit" button to finish up the event-related choices and move to the screen for making payment. So we enter a brief description of this problem in the first column of Table 16-4.

Table 16-3

Basic form of the cost-importance table

Problem	Imp.	Solution	Cost	Prio. Ratio	Prio. Rank	Cuml. Cost	Resolution

Problem	Imp.	Solution	Cost	Prio. Ratio	Prio. Rank	Cuml. Cost	Resolution
User confused by the button label "Submit" to proceed to payment part of the purchasing transaction							

Table 16-4

Problem description entered into cost-importance table

16.5.2 Importance to Fix

The next column, labeled "Imp" in the table, is for an estimate of the importance to fix the problem, independent of cost. While importance includes severity or criticality of the problem, most commonly used by other authors, this parameter can also include other considerations. The idea is to capture the effect of a problem on user performance, user experience, and overall system integrity and consistency. Importance can also include intangibles such as management and marketing "feelings" and consideration of the cost of not fixing the problem (e.g., in terms of lower user satisfaction), as well as "impact analysis" (next section).

Because an importance rating is just an estimate, we use a simple scale for the values:

- Importance = M: Must fix, regardless
- Importance = 5: The most important problems to fix after the "Must fix" category
  - If the interaction feature involved is mission critical
  - If the UX problem has a major impact on task performance or user satisfaction (e.g., user cannot complete key task or can do so only with great difficulty)
  - If the UX problem is expected to occur frequently or could cause costly errors
- Importance = 3: Moderate impact problems
  - If the user can complete the task, but with difficulty (e.g., it caused confusion and required extra effort)
  - If the problem was a source of moderate dissatisfaction
- Importance = 1: Low impact problems
  - If problem did not impact task performance or dissatisfaction much (e.g., mild user confusion or irritation or a cosmetic problem), but is still worth listing

This fairly coarse gradation of values has proven to work for us; you can customize it to suit your project needs. We also need some flexibility to assign intermediate values, so we allow for importance rating adjustment factors, the primary one of which is estimated frequency of occurrence. If this problem is expected to occur very often, you might adjust your importance rating upward by one value.

Conversely, if it is not expected to occur very often, you could downgrade your rating by one or more values. As Karat, Campbell, and Fiegel (1992) relate frequency of occurrence to problem severity classification, they ask: Over all the affected user classes, how often will the user encounter this problem?

Applying this to our importance rating, we might start with a problem preventing a task from being completed, to which we would initially assign Importance = 5. But because we expect this UX problem to arise only rarely and it does not affect critical tasks, we might downgrade its importance to 4 or even 3. However, a problem with moderately significant impact might start out rated as a 3 but, because it occurs frequently, we might upgrade it to a 4.

For example, consider the Ticket Kiosk System problem about users being confused by the button label "Submit" to proceed to payment in the ticket-purchasing transaction. We rate this fairly high in importance because it is part of the basic workflow of ticket buying; users will perform this step often, and most participants were puzzled or misled by this button label.

However, it was not shown to be a show-stopper, so we initially assign it an importance of 3. But because it will be encountered by almost every user in almost every transaction, we "promoted" it to a 4, as shown in Table 16-5.

Learnability can also be an importance adjustment factor. Some problems have most of their impact on the first encounter. After that, users learn quickly to overcome (work around) the problem so it does not have much effect in subsequent usage. That could call for an importance rating reduction.

16.5.3 Solutions

The next column in the cost-importance table is for one or more candidate solutions to the problems. Solving a UX problem is redesign, a kind of design, so you should use the same approach and resources as we did for the original design, including consulting your contextual data. Other resources and activities that might help include design principles and guidelines, brainstorming, study of other similar designs, and solutions suggested by users

Table 16-5

Estimate of importance to fix entered into cost-importance table

Problem	Imp.	Solution	Cost	Prio. Ratio	Prio. Rank	Cuml. Cost	Resolution
User confused by the button label "Submit" to conclude ticket purchasing transaction	4						

and experts. It is almost never a good idea to think of more training or better documentation as a UX problem solution.

Solutions for the photo album problem example

Let us look at some solutions for a problem in the example concerning the photo album application introduced earlier in this chapter. Users experienced a problem when trying to upload photos into an album. They did not understand that they had to create an album first. This misunderstanding about the workflow model built into the application now requires us to design an alternative.

It appears that the original designer was thinking in terms of a planning model by which the user anticipates the need for an album in advance of putting pictures into it. But our users were apparently thinking of the task in linear time, assuming (probably without thinking about it) that the application would either provide an album when it was needed or let them create one. A usage-centered design to match the user's cognitive flow could start by offering an active upload link.

If the user clicks on it when there is no open album, the interaction could present an opportunity for just-in-time creation of the necessary album as part of the task flow of uploading of a picture. This can be accomplished by either asking if the user wants to open an existing album or creating a new one.

Taking a different design direction, the interaction can allow users to upload pictures onto a "work table" without the need for pictures to necessarily be in an album. This design provides more interaction flexibility and potential for better user experience. This design also allows users to place single photos in multiple albums, something that users cannot do easily in their current work domain (without making multiple copies of a photo).

Ticket Kiosk System example

Coming back to the confusing button label in the Ticket Kiosk System, one obvious and inexpensive solution is to change the label wording to better represent where the interaction will go if the user clicks on that button. Maybe "Proceed to payment" would make more sense to most users.

We wrote a concise description of our proposed fix in the Solution column in Table 16-6.

	Problem	Imp.	Solution	Cost	Prio. Ratio	Prio. Rank	Cuml. Cost	Resolution
Table 16-6 *Potential problem solution entered into cost-importance table*	User confused by the button label "Submit" to conclude ticket purchasing transaction	4	Change the label wording to "Proceed to Payment"					

16.5.4 Cost to Fix

Making accurate estimates of the cost to fix a given UX problem takes practice; it is an acquired engineering skill. But it is nothing new; it is part of our job to make cost estimates in all kinds of engineering and budget situations. Costs for our analysis are stated in terms of resources (e.g., time, money) needed, which almost always translates to person-hours required.

Because this is an inexact process, we usually round up fractional values just to keep it simple. When you make your cost estimates, do not make the mistake of including only the cost to implement the change; you must include the cost of redesign, including design thinking and discussion and, sometimes, even some experimentation. You might need help from your software developers to estimate implementation costs.

Because it is very easy to change label wordings in our Ticket Kiosk System, we have entered a value of just one person-hour into the Cost column in Table 16-7.

Cost values for problem groups

Table 16-8 shows an example of including a problem group in the cost-importance table.

Note that the cost for the group is higher than that of either individual problem but lower than their sum.

	Problem	Imp.	Solution	Cost	Prio. Ratio	Prio. Rank	Cuml. Cost	Resolution
Table 16-7 *Estimate of cost to fix entered into cost-importance table*	User confused by the button label "Submit" to conclude ticket purchasing transaction	4	Change the label wording to "Proceed to Payment"	1				

Table 16-8

Cost entries for problem groups entered into cost-importance table

Problem Group	Problem	Imp.	Solution	Group Solution	Single Costs	Group Cost
Transaction flow for purchasing tickets	7. The user wanted to enter or choose date and venue first and then click "Purchase Tickets," but the interaction design required them to click on "Purchase Tickets" before entering specific ticket information.	3	Change to allow actions in either order and label it so	Establish a comprehensive and more flexible model of transaction flow and add labeling to explain it.	3	5
	17. The "Purchase Tickets" button took user to screen to select tickets and commit to them, but then users did not realize they had to continue on to the another screen to pay for them.		Provide better labeling for this flow		3	

Calibration feedback from down the road: Comparing actual with predicted costs

To learn more about making cost estimates and to calibrate your engineering ability to estimate costs to fix problems, we recommend that you add a column to your cost-importance table for actual cost. After you have done the redesign and implementation for your solutions, you should record the actual cost of each and compare with your predicted estimates. It can tell you how you are doing and how you can improve your estimates.

16.5.5 Priority Ratio

The next column in the cost-importance table, the priority ratio, is a metric we use to establish priorities for fixing problems. We want a metric that will reward high importance but penalize high costs. A simple ratio of importance to cost fits this bill. Intuitively, a high importance will boost up the priority but a high cost will bring it down. Because the units of cost and importance will usually yield a fractional value for the priority ratio, we scale it up to the integer range by multiplying it by an arbitrary factor, say, 1000.

If the importance rating is "M" (for "must fix regardless"), the priority ratio is also "M." For all numerical values of importance, the priority ratio becomes:

$$\text{Priority ratio} = (\text{importance}/\text{cost})^* 1000$$

Example: Priority Ratios for Ticket Kiosk System Problems

For our first Ticket Kiosk System problem, the priority ratio is $(4/1) \times 1000 = 4000$, which we have entered into the cost-importance table in Table 16-9.

In the next part of this example, shown in Table 16-10, we have added several more Ticket Kiosk System UX problems to fill out the table a bit more realistically.

Note that although fixing the lack of a search function (the sixth row in Table 16-10) has a high importance, its high cost is keeping the priority ratio low. This is one problem to consider for an Importance = M rating in the future. At the other end of things, the last problem (about the Back button to the Welcome screen) is only Importance = 2, but the low cost boosts the priority ratio quite high. Fixing this will not cost much and will get it out of the way.

16.5.6 Priority Rankings

So far, the whole cost-importance analysis process has involved only some engineering estimates and some simple calculations, probably in a spreadsheet. Now it gets even easier. You have only to sort the cost-importance table by priority ratios to get the final priority rankings.

First, move all problems with a priority ratio value of "M" to the top of the table. These are the problems you must fix, regardless of cost. Then sort the rest of the table in descending order by priority ratio. This puts high importance, low cost problems at the top of the priority list, as shown at **A** in the upper left-hand quadrant of Figure 16-4. These are the problems to fix first, the fixes that will give the biggest bang for the buck.

Being the realist (our nice word for cynic) that you are, you are quick to point out that, in the real world, things do not line up with high importance and low cost together in the same sentence. You pay for what you get. But, in fact, we do find a lot of problems of this kind in early iterations.

Table 16-9

Priority ratio calculation entered into cost-importance table

Problem	Imp.	Solution	Cost	Prio. Ratio	Prio. Rank	Cuml. Cost	Resolution
User confused by the button label "Submit" to conclude ticket purchasing transaction	4	Change the label wording to "Proceed to Payment"	1	4000			

Table 16-10

Priority ratios for more Ticket Kiosk System problems

Problem	Imp.	Solution	Cost	Prio. Ratio	Prio. Rank	Cuml. Cost	Resolution
User confused by the button label "Submit" to conclude ticket purchasing transaction	4	Change the label wording to "Proceed to Payment"	1	4000			
Did not recognize the "counter" as being for the number of tickets. As a result, user failed to even think about how many tickets he needed.	M	Move quantity information and label it	2	M			
Unsure of current date and what date he was purchasing tickets for	5	Add current date field and label all dates precisely	2	2500			
Users were concerned about their work being left for others to see	5	Add a timeout feature that clears the screens	3	1667			
User confused about "Theatre" on the "Choose a domain" screen. Thought it meant choosing a physical theater (as a venue) rather than the category of theatre arts.	3	Improve the wording to "Theatre Arts"	1	3000			
Ability to find events hampered by lack of a search capability	4	Design and implement a search function	40	100			
Did not recognize what geographical area theater information was being displayed for	4	Redesign graphical representation to show search radius	12	333			
Did not like having a "Back" button on second screen since first screen was only a "Welcome"	2	Remove it	1	2000			
Transaction flow for purchasing tickets (group problem; see Table 16-8)	3	Establish a comprehensive and more flexible model of transaction flow and add labeling to explain it	5	600			

A good example is a badly worded button label. It can completely confuse users but usually costs almost nothing to fix. Sometimes low-importance, low-cost problems float up near the top of the priority list. You will eventually want to deal with these. Because they do not cost much, it is usually a good idea to just fix them and get them out of the way.

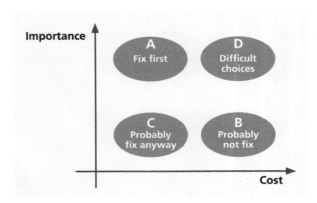

Figure 16-4

The relationship of importance and cost in prioritizing which problems to fix first.

The UX problems that sort to the bottom of the priority list are costly to fix with little gain in doing so. You will probably not bother to fix these problems, as shown at **B** in the lower right-hand quadrant of Figure 16-4.

Quadrants **A** and **B** sort out nicely in the priority rankings. Quadrants **C** and **D**, however, may require more thought. Quadrant **C** represents problems for which fixes are low in cost and low in importance. You will usually just go ahead and fix them to get them off your plate. The most difficult choices appear in quadrant **D** because, although they are of high importance to fix, they are also the most expensive to fix.

No formula will help; you need good engineering judgment. Maybe it is time to request more resources so these important problems can be fixed. That is usually worth it in the long run.

The cost-importance table for the Ticket Kiosk System, sorted by priority ratio, is shown in Table 16-11.

16.5.7 Cumulative Cost

The next step is simple. In the column labeled "Cuml. Cost" of the cost-importance table sorted by priority ratio, for each problem enter an amount that is the cost of fixing that problem plus the cost of fixing all the problems above it in the table. See how we have done this for our example Ticket Kiosk System cost-importance table in Table 16-11.

16.5.8 The Line of Affordability

Using your budget, your team leader or project manager should determine your "resource limit," in person-hours, that you can allocate to making design changes for the current cycle of iteration. For example, suppose that for the Ticket Kiosk System we have only a fairly small amount of time available in the schedule, about 16 person hours.

Draw the "line of affordability," a horizontal line in the cost-importance table just above the line in the table where the cumulative cost value first exceeds your resource limit. For the Ticket Kiosk System, the line of affordability appears just above the row in Table 16-11 where the cumulative cost hits 27.

Table 16-11

The Ticket Kiosk System cost-importance table, sorted by priority ratio, with cumulative cost values entered, and the "line of affordability" showing the cutoff for this round of problem fixing

Problem	Imp.	Solution	Cost	Prio. Ratio	Prio. Rank	Cuml. Cost	Resolution
Did not recognize the "counter" as being for the number of tickets. As a result, user failed to even think about how many tickets he needed.	M	Move quantity information and label it	2	M	1	2	
User confused by the button label "Submit" to conclude ticket purchasing transaction	4	Change the label wording to "Proceed to Payment"	1	4000	2	3	
User confused about "Theatre" on the "Choose a domain" screen. Thought it meant choosing a physical theater (as a venue) rather than the category of theatre arts.	3	Improve the wording to "Theatre Arts"	1	3000	3	4	
Unsure of current date and what date he was purchasing tickets for	5	Add current date field and label all dates precisely	2	2500	4	6	
Did not like having a "Back" button on second screen since first screen was only a "Welcome"	2	Remove it	1	2000	5	7	
Users were concerned about their work being left for others to see	5	Add a timeout feature that clears the screens	3	1667	6	10	
Transaction flow for purchasing tickets (group problem; see Table 16-8)	3	Establish a comprehensive and more flexible model of transaction flow and add labeling to explain it.	5	600	7	15	
Line of affordability (16 person-hours—2 work days)							
Did not recognize what geographical area theater information was being displayed for	4	Redesign graphical representation to show search radius	12	333	8	27	
Ability to find events hampered by lack of a search capability	4	Design and implement a search function	40	100	9	67	

Just for giggles, it might be fun to graph all your problems (no, not all *your* problems; we mean all your cost-importance table entries) in a cost-importance space like that of Figure 16-4. Sometimes this kind of graphical representation can give insight into your process, especially if your problems tend to appear in clusters. Your line of affordability will be a vertical line that cuts the cost axis at the amount you can afford to spend on fixing all problems this iteration.

16.5.9 Drawing Conclusions: A Resolution for Each Problem

It's time for the payoff of your cost-importance analysis. It's time for a resolution—a decision—about how each problem will be addressed.

First, you have to deal with your "Must fix" problems, the show-stoppers. If you have enough resources, that is if all the "Must fix" problems are above the line of affordability, fix them all. If not, you already have a headache. Someone, such as the project manager, has to earn his or her pay today by making a difficult decision.

The extreme cost of a "Must fix" problem could make it infeasible to fix in the current version. Exceptions will surely result in cost overruns, but might have to be dictated by corporate policy, management, marketing, etc. It is an important time to be true to your principles and to everything you have done in the process so far. Do not throw it away now because of some perceived limit on how much you are willing to put into fixing problems that you have just spent good money to find.

Sometimes you have resources to fix the "Must fix" problems, but no resources left for dealing with the other problems. Fortunately, in our example we have enough resources to fix a few more problems. Depending on their relative proximity to the line of affordability, you have to decide among these choices as a resolution for all the other problems:

- fix now
- fix, time permitting
- remand to "wait-and-see list"
- table until next version
- postpone indefinitely; probably never get to fix

In the final column of the cost-importance table, write in your resolution for each problem, as we have done for the Ticket Kiosk System in Table 16-12.

Finally, look at your table; see what is left below the line of affordability. Is it what you would expect? Can you live with not making fixes below that line? Again, this is a crossroads moment. You will find that in reality that low-

Table 16-12

Problem resolutions for Ticket Kiosk System

Problem	Imp.	Solutions	Cost	Prio. Ratio	Prio. Rank	Cuml. Cost	Resolution
Did not recognize the "counter" as being for the number of tickets. As a result, user failed to even think about how many tickets he needed.	M	Move quantity information and label it	2	M	1	2	Fix in this version
User confused by the button label "Submit" to conclude ticket purchasing transaction	4	Change the label wording to "Proceed to Payment"	1	4000	2	3	Fix in this version
User confused about "Theatre" on the "Choose a domain" screen. Thought it meant choosing a physical theater (as a venue) rather than the category of theatre arts.	3	Improve the wording to "Theatre Arts"	1	3000	3	4	Fix in this version
Unsure of current date and what date he was purchasing tickets for	5	Add current date field and label all dates precisely	2	2500	4	6	Fix in this version
Did not like having a "Back" button on second screen since first screen was only a "Welcome"	2	Remove it	1	2000	5	7	Fix in this version
Users were concerned about their work being left for others to see	5	Add a timeout feature that clears the screens	3	1667	6	10	Fix in this version
Transaction flow for purchasing tickets (group problem; see Table 16-8)	3	Establish a comprehensive and more flexible model of transaction flow and add labeling to explain it	5	600	7	15	Fix in this version
Line of affordability (16 person-hours—2 work days)							
Ability to find events hampered by lack of a search capability	4	Design and implement a search function	40	100	9	67	Wait until next version, or after that

importance/high-cost problems are rarely addressed; there simply will not be time or other resources. That is okay, as our engineering approach is aiming for cost-effectiveness, not perfection. You might even have to face the fact that some important problems cannot be fixed because they are simply too costly.

However, in the end, do not just let numbers dictate your actions; think about it. Do not let a tight production schedule or budget force release of something that could embarrass your organization. Quality is remembered long after schedules are forgotten.

16.5.10 Special Cases

Tie-breakers

Sometimes you will get ties for priority rankings, entries for problems with equal priority for fixing. If they do not occur near the line of affordability, it is not necessary to do anything about them. In the rare case that they straddle the line of affordability, you can break the tie by almost any practical means, for example, your team members may have a personal preference.

In cases of more demanding target systems (e.g., an air traffic control system), where the importance of avoiding problems, especially dangerous user errors, is a bigger concern than cost, you might break priority ties by adjusting the priorities via weighting importance higher than cost in the priority ratio formula.

Cost-importance analysis involving multiple problem solutions

Sometimes you can think of more than one solution for a problem. It is possible that, after a bit more thought, one solution will emerge as best. If, however, after careful consideration you still have multiple possibilities for a problem solution, you can keep all solutions in the running and in the analysis until you see something that helps you decide.

If all solutions have the same cost to fix, then you and your team will just have to make an engineering decision. This might be the time to implement all of them and retest, using local prototyping (Chapter 11) to evaluate alternative design solutions for just this one feature.

Usually, though, solutions are distinguished by cost and/or effectiveness. Maybe one is less expensive but some other one is more desirable or more effective; in other words, you have a cost–benefit trade-off. You will need to resolve such cost–benefit problems separately before entering the chosen solution and its cost into the cost-importance table.

Problem groups straddling the line of affordability

If you have a group of related problems right at the line of affordability, the engineering answer is to do the best you can before you run out of resources. Break the group back apart and do as many pieces as possible. Give the rest of the group a higher importance in the next iteration.

Priorities for emotional impact problems

Priorities for fixing emotional impact problems can be difficult to assess. They are often very important because they can represent problems with product or system image and reputation in the market. They can also represent high costs to fix because they often require a broader view of redesign, not just focusing on one detail of the design as you might for a usability problem.

Also, emotional impact problems are often not just redesign problems but might require more understanding of the users and work or play context, which means going all the way back in the process to contextual inquiry and contextual analysis and a new approach to the conceptual design. Because of business and marketing imperatives, you may have to move some emotional impact problems into the "Must fix" category and do what is necessary to produce an awesome user experience.

16.5.11 Abridged Cost-Importance Analysis

As an abridged version of the cost-importance analysis process:

- Put the problem list in a spreadsheet or similar document.
- Project it onto a screen in a room with pertinent team members to decide priorities for fixing the problems.
- Have a discussion about which problems to fix first based on a group feeling about the relative importance and cost to fix each problem, without assigning numeric values.
- Do a kind of group-driven "bubble sort" of problems in which problems to fix first will float toward the top of the list and problems you probably cannot fix, at least in this iteration, will sink toward the bottom of the list.
- When you are satisfied with the relative ordering of problem priorities, start fixing problems from the top of the list downward and stop when you run out of time or money.

16.6 FEEDBACK TO PROCESS

Now that you have been through an iteration of the UX process lifecycle, it is time to reflect not just on the design itself, but also on how well your process worked. If you have any suspicions after doing the testing that the quantitative criteria were not quite right, you might ask if your UX targets worked well.

For example, if all target levels were met or exceeded on the very first round of evaluation, it will almost certainly be the case that your UX targets were too lenient. Even in later iterations, if all UX targets are met but observations during evaluation sessions indicate that participants were frustrated and performed tasks poorly, your intuition will probably tell you that the design is nevertheless not acceptable in terms of its quality of user experience. Then, obviously, the UX team should revisit and adjust the UX targets or add more considerations to your criteria for evaluation success.

Next, ask yourself whether the benchmark tasks supported the evaluation process in the most effective way. Should they have been simpler or more complex, narrower or broader? Should any benchmark task description be reworded for clarification or to give less information about how to do a task?

Finally, assess how well the overall process worked for the team. You will never be in a better position to sit down, discuss it, and document possible improvements for the next time.

16.7 LESSONS FROM THE FIELD

16.7.1 Onion-Layers Effect

There are many reasons to make more than one iteration of the design–test–redesign part of the UX lifecycle. The main reason, of course, is to continue to uncover and fix UX problems until you meet your UX target values. Another reason is to be sure that your "fixes" have not caused new problems. The fixes are, after all, new and untested designs.

Also, in fixing a problem, you can uncover other UX problems lurking in the dark and inky shadows of the first problem. One problem can be obscured by another, preventing participants and evaluators from seeing the second problem, until the top layer of the onion[1] is peeled off by solving that "outer" problem.

16.7.2 UX Problem Data as Feedback to Process Improvement

In our analysis we are also always on the lookout for *causes of causes*. It sometimes pays off to look at your UX process to find causes of the design flaws that cause UX problems, places in your process where, if you could have done something differently, you might have avoided a particular kind of design flaw. If you suffer from an overabundance of a particular kind of UX problem and can determine how your process is letting them into the designs,

---

[1] Thanks to Wolmet Barendregt for the onion-layer analogy.

maybe you can head off that kind of problem in future designs by fixing that part of the process.

For example, if you are finding a large number of UX problems involving confusing button or icon labels or menu choices, maybe you can address these in advance by providing a place in your design process where you look extra carefully at the precise use of words, semantics, and meanings of words. You might even consider hiring a professional writer to join the UX team. We ran into a case like this once.

For expediency, one project team had been letting their software programmers write error messages as they encountered the need for them in the code. This situation was a legacy from the days when programmers routinely did most of the user interface. As you can imagine, these error messages were not the most effective. We helped them incorporate a more structured approach to error message composition, involving UX practitioners, without unduly disrupting the rest of their process.

Similarly, large numbers of problems involving physical user actions are indicators of design problems that could be addressed by hiring an expert in ergonomics, human factors engineering, and physical device design. Finally, large numbers of problems involving visual aspects of design, such as color, shape, positioning, or gray shading, might indicate the need for hiring a graphic designer or layout artist.

Exercise

See Exercise 16-1, UX Data Analysis for Your System

Evaluation Reporting

17

Objectives

After reading this chapter, you will:

1. Know how to report informal summative evaluation results
2. Be ready to report qualitative formative evaluation results, including the influence of audience and goals on content, format and vocabulary, and tone
3. Understand influences on problem report effectiveness

17.1 INTRODUCTION

17.1.1 You Are Here

We begin each process chapter with a "you are here" picture of the chapter topic in the context of the overall Wheel lifecycle template; see Figure 17-1. Having gotten through UX evaluation preparation, data collection, and analysis, we conclude the evaluation chapters with this one: reporting your formative UX evaluation results. The reporting described in this chapter is largely aimed at rigorous empirical methods, but much applies as well to rapid methods.

17.1.2 Importance of Quality Communication and Reporting

Evaluation reports often occur as communication across discontinuities of time, location, and people. Redesign activities are often separated from UX evaluation by delays in time that can cause information loss due to human memory limitations. This is further aggravated if the people doing the redesign are not the same ones who conducted the evaluation.

Finally, evaluation and redesign can occur at different physical locations, rendering all information not well communicated to be unrecoverable. UX evaluation reports with inadequate contextual information or incomplete UX problem descriptions will be too vague for designers who were not present for the UX testing.

Figure 17-1

You are here; at reporting, within the evaluation activity in the context of the overall Wheel lifecycle template.

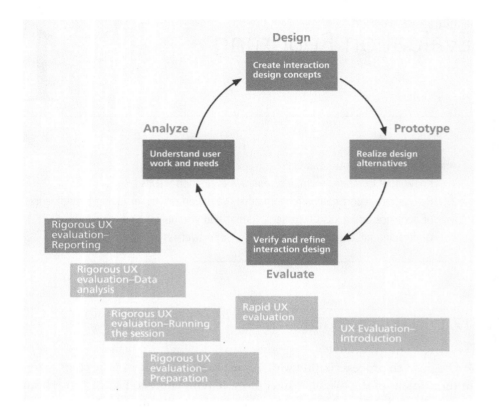

To the project team, the report for an evaluation within an iteration is a redesign proposal. Hornbæk and Frøkjær (2005) show the need for usability evaluation reports that summarize and convey usability information, not just lists of problem descriptions by themselves.

All the effort and cost you invested thus far in UX evaluation can be wasted at the last minute if you do not follow up now to:

- inform the team and project management about the UX problems in the current design
- persuade them of the need to invest even more in fixing those problems.

17.1.3 Participant Anonymity

We remind you, before we get into the details, that regardless of the kind of evaluation or reporting you are doing, you must preserve participant anonymity. You should have promised this on your informed consent form, and you have an ethical, and perhaps a legal, obligation to protect it religiously thereafter. The necessity for preserving participant anonymity extends especially to evaluation reporting.

There is simply no need for anyone in your reporting audience to know the identity of any participant. This means not including any names in the report and not showing faces in video clips. This latter requirement can be met with some simple video blurring.

Participant anonymity does not mean that you, as the evaluator or facilitator, do not know the names of participants. Somewhere along the line someone must have recruited and signed up and possibly even paid the participants. You should keep participant identification information in just one place—on a sheet of paper or in a database mapping the names to identification codes. Codes, never names, are used everywhere else in the evaluation process—on data collection forms, during data analysis, and in all reports.

17.2 REPORTING INFORMAL SUMMATIVE RESULTS

Formative evaluation, by definition, has a qualitative formative component and an optional informal summative component (Chapter 12). There are still no standards for reporting informal summative results in connection with formative evaluation (more about this in the next section).

Because product design is not research but engineering, we are not concerned with getting at scientific "truth"; ours is a more practical and less exact business. Our evaluation drives our engineering judgment, which is also based on hunches and intuition that are, in turn, based on skill and experience.

As we said in Chapter 12, the audience for your informal summative evaluation results should be *strictly* limited to your own project group. They are to be used *only* as an engineering tool within the project.

17.2.1 What if You Are Required to Produce a Formative Evaluation Report for Consumption Beyond the Team?

The meaning of "internal use" can vary some, but it usually means restricted to the project group (e.g., designers, evaluators, implementers, project manager) and definitely not for public dissemination. Formative evaluation reports must remain within a group who all understand the limitations on how data can be used. At times that could also include higher level managers and others in the larger organization.

But sometimes you do not have a choice; you can be ordered to produce a formative evaluation report for broader dissemination. Suppose the marketing people want to make claims about levels of user experience reached via your engineering process. Our first line of advice is to follow our principle and simply not let specific informal summative evaluation results out of the project group. Once the results are out of your hands, you lose control of what is done with them, and you could be made to share the blame for their misuse.

Your next response should be to inform. Explain the limited nature of data and the professional and ethical issues in misrepresenting the power to make claims from data. If, at the end of the day, you still have to issue a formative evaluation report, we recommend you bend over backward in labeling the report with caveats and qualifications that make it clear to all readers that the informal summative UX results are intended to be used only as a project management tool and should not be used in public claims.

17.2.2 What if You Need a Report to Convince the Team to Fix the Problems?

What good is doing the UX evaluation if no one is convinced the problems you found are "real" and, as a result, the design does not get changed? It may be part of the job of UX engineers to convince others in the project team to take action about poor UX, as revealed by UX evaluation. This part of the role is especially important in large organizations where people who collect data are not necessarily the same people, or even people who have a close working relationship with, those who make the decisions about design changes.

It is not uncommon for project teams to request a UX testing report to see for themselves what the UX situation is and how badly the recommended changes are needed. This could just be part of the normal way your organization works or, depending on the working relationship among project team members, this situation could be indicative of a management or organizational problem rather than a technical one.

The need for the rest of your team, including management, to be convinced of the need to fix UX problems that you have identified in your UX engineering process could be considered a kind of litmus test for a lack of teamwork and trust within your organization. If everyone is working together as a team, no one should have to convince the others of the value of their efforts on the project; they all just do what the process calls for.

We do not live in a perfect world, however, and the people requesting your UX report may have some power over you. For example, your manager or the software engineers might stand between you and the changes to the software. If they require a report that "proves" the need for design changes, you must make it clear that what they are asking for is not your report but a report of a summative study. Of course, they will have to pay for someone to perform that study, which could go a long way in heading off such requests the next time.

Sometimes the other project team members know how the UX people work and trust them. For them, if the UX practitioner says a certain design change is needed, they go with it, but still might want an explanation to help them understand the need and help cement their buy in. In this case, it is not a problem to share the report, as these are your team members.

17.3 REPORTING QUALITATIVE FORMATIVE RESULTS

All UX practitioners should be able to write clear and effective reports about problems found but, in their "CUE-4" studies, Dumas, Molich, and Jeffries (2004) found that many cannot. They observed a large variation in reporting over several teams of usability specialists and that most reports were inadequate by their standards. It is hoped that this chapter will help you communicate clearly and effectively via the planning and construction of your UX evaluation reports.

If you use rapid evaluation methods for data collection, it is especially important to communicate effectively about the analysis and results because this kind of data can otherwise be dismissed easily "as unreliable or inadequate to inform design decisions" (Nayak, Mrazek, & Smith, 1995). Even in lab-based testing, though, the primary type of data from formative evaluation is qualitative, and raw qualitative data must be skillfully distilled and interpreted to avoid the impression of being "soft" and subjective.

17.3.1 Common Industry Format (CIF) for Reporting Formal Summative UX Evaluation Results

In October 1997, the U.S. National Institute of Standards and Technology (NIST) started an effort to "increase the visibility of software usability." NIST was to be a facilitator in bringing together software vendors and consumer organizations, with the stated goal to develop and evaluate a common usability reporting format for sharing usability data with consumer organizations. The idea was to make software product usability visible to customers and consumers through (theretofore nonexistent) standard, comparable, methods of reporting measured usability through "the Common Industry Format (CIF) for reporting usability results".

The pressure to bring products to market rapidly had affected usability adversely, as it still now does. The idea was to force software suppliers to face the fact that their customers were concerned about usability and, if usability could be made visible to consumers, it would become a competitive market factor with software that is measurably more usable winning out. In the face of the many possible ways to report summative usability evaluation results, a common reporting format would add consistency and comparability.

Oriented toward off-the-shelf software products and Websites, the CIF provides a kind of "Consumer Reports" support for software buyers, affording a way to compare usability of competitive software products (Quesenbery, 2005, p. 452).

It is clear from the goals that this standard pertained to formal summative evaluation and not formative evaluation, although at the time it was still too early for that limitation or even the distinction to be articulated.

The CIF standard calls out requirements for reports to include:

- A description of the product
- Goals of the testing
- A description of the number and types of participants
- Tasks used in evaluation
- The experimental design of the test (very important for formal summative studies because of the need for eliminating any biases and to ensure the results do not suffer from external, internal, and other validity concerns)
- Evaluation methods used
- Usability measures and data collection methods employed
- Numerical results, including graphical methods of presentation

The American National Standards Institute (ANSI) approved this standard for summative reporting as ANSI-NCITS 354-2001 in December 2001 and it became an international standard, ISO/IEC 25062: Software Engineering—Software Product Quality Requirements and Evaluation (SQuaRE), in May 2005.

17.3.2 Common Industry Format (CIF) for Reporting Qualitative Formative Results

Following this initial effort on a Common Industry Format for reporting formal summative evaluation results, the group, under the direction of Mary Theofanos, Whitney Quesenbery, and others, organized two workshops in 2005 (Theofanos et al., 2005), these aimed at a CIF for formative reports (Quesenbery, 2005; Theofanos & Quesenbery, 2005).

In this work they recognized that because most evaluations conducted by usability practitioners are formative, there was a need for an extension of the original CIF project to identify best practices for reporting formative results.

They concluded that requirements for content, format, presentation style, and level of detail depended heavily on the audience, the business context, and the evaluation techniques used.

While their working definition of "formative testing" was based on having representative users, here we use the slightly broader term "formative evaluation" to include usability inspections and other methods for collecting formative usability and user experience data, not necessarily requiring representative users.

17.4 FORMATIVE REPORTING CONTENT

In this section we cover the different types of reporting content that could go into a formative evaluation report. In later sections we discuss which of these content types are suitable to different audiences.

17.4.1 Individual Problem Reporting Content

Many researchers and practitioners have suggested various content items that might prove useful for problem diagnosis and redesign. The idea is to provide all the essential facts a designer will need to understand and fix the problem. Of course, at this point, the evaluators would have had to collect sufficient data to be able to provide all this information. The basic information needed includes:

- the problem description
- a best judgment of the causes of the problem in the design
- an estimate of its severity or impact
- suggested solutions

In the first of these items, be sure to describe each problem as a problem, not as a solution. Because the problems were experienced by users doing tasks, describe them in that context—users and tasks and the effects of the problems on users. This means saying, for example, "users could not figure out what to do next because they did not notice the buttons" instead of "we need flashing red buttons."

The second item, the engineering judgment of the causes of the problem in the interaction design, is an essential part of the diagnosis of a UX problem and perhaps the most important part of the report. Because the flaw in the design is what needs to be fixed, you should connect it with the appropriate design guidelines and/or heuristic violations, as much as possible in terms of interaction issues and human–computer interaction principles.

Next is an estimate of severity or importance in terms of the impact on users. To be convincing, this must be well reasoned. Finally, to help designers act to fix the problems, recommend one or more possible design solutions, along with cost estimates and tradeoffs for each, especially if a solution has a downside. To justify the fixes, make compelling arguments for improved design and positive impact on users.

There are many other kinds of information that can be useful in a UX problem report content, including an indication of how many times each UX problem was encountered, by each user and by all users, to help convey its importance.

17.4.2 Include Video Clips Where Appropriate

Show video clips of users, made anonymous, encountering critical incidents if you are giving an oral report or include links in a written report. Use the visual power of video to share the highlights of your evaluation process, including some examples of UX problem encounters.

17.4.3 Pay Special Attention to Reporting on Emotional Impact Problems

Special discussion should be directed to reporting emotional impact problems, as those problems can be the most important for product improvement and marketing advantage, but these problems and their solutions can also be the most elusive. Emotional impact problems should be flagged as a somewhat different kind of problem with different kinds of recommendations for solutions.

Provide a holistic summary of the overall emotional impact on participants. Report specific positive and negative highlights with examples from particular episodes or incidents. If possible, try to inspire by comparing with products and systems having high emotional impact ratings.

17.4.4 Including Cost-Importance Data

Usually, cost-importance analysis is considered part of the nitty-gritty engineering details that would be beyond the interest or understanding of those outside the UX team and its process. However, cost-importance analysis, especially the prioritization process, can be of great interest to those who have to fix the problems and those who have to pay for it.

Importance ratings and supporting rationale can be helpful in convincing designers to fix at least the most urgent problems. The cost-importance table, such as Table 16-12, plus any discussion supporting the choice of table entries will tell the story.

17.5 FORMATIVE REPORTING AUDIENCE, NEEDS, GOALS, AND CONTEXT OF USE

As Theofanos and Quesenbery (2005) say, choices about content, format, vocabulary, and tone are all about the relationship between the author and the audience. Nayak et al. (1995) discuss some of the difficulties of conveying UX information, such as explaining observation-based data and understanding the needs of the target audience. Because the needs, goals, and context of use for a given evaluation report are dependent on the audience, this section is organized on the various kinds of audiences.

The 2005 UPA Workshop Report on formative evaluation reporting (Theofanos et al., 2005) stresses different reporting requirements for different business contexts and audiences and different combinations thereof. Their view of reporting goals includes the following:

- Documenting the process: The author is usually part of the team, and the goal is to document team process and decision making. The scope of the "team" is left undefined and could be just the evaluation team or the whole project team, or perhaps even the development organization as a whole.
- Feeding the process: This is the primary context in our perspective, an integral part of feedback for iterative redesign. The goal is to inform the team about evaluation results, problems, and suggested solutions. In this report the author is considered to be related to the team but not necessarily a member of the team. However, it would seem that the person most suited as the author would usually be a UX practitioner who is part of the evaluator team and, if UX practitioners are considered part of the project team, a member of that team, too.
- Informing and persuading: The audience depends on working relationships within the organization. It could be the evaluator team informing and persuading the designers and developers (i.e., software implementers) or it could be the whole project team (or part thereof) informing and persuading management, marketing, and/or the customer or client.

17.5.1 Introducing UX Engineering to Your Audience

Because your goal is to persuade your audience of the need to invest time and cost into taking action to fix problems discovered, you must include your audience in the process and reasoning that led from raw data to conclusions so that your recommendations do not appear to be pulled out of the air. To include them in your process, you must explain the process.

Therefore, sometimes the main purpose of an evaluation report is to introduce the concepts of UX and UX engineering to an audience (your project team, management, marketing, etc.) not yet aware. This kind of audience requires a different kind of report from all the others. It is more like an evaluation report contained within a more general presentation. First you have to establish your credentials and credibility and gain their engagement.

The goals for reporting to this kind of audience include (more or less in this order):

- Engender awareness and appreciation
- Teach concepts
- Sell buy-in
- Present results

Start on the first goal by building rapport and empathy. You are all on the same side. Help them feel "safe"; you would never try to sell them on something that was not good for them and the organization. You want to get them to appreciate the need for usability and a good user experience to appreciate the value of these things to them and their organization. This is basically a motivation for UX based on a business case (Chapter 24).

The next goal of your presentation is teaching. The idea is to explain terminology and concepts. You want to educate them about what UX is and how the UX engineering process works to improve UX. Explain that evaluation is not everything in the process but is a key part. Help them understand how to view evaluation results. It is not negative stuff, it is not criticism, and, above all, it is not a personal thing. It is positive, good stuff, and is a team thing; it is an opportunity and a means to improve.

The third goal is about persuasion and selling of the concept. You want to get their buy-in to the idea of doing UX. You want them to want to include a UX component in their overall development process (and budgets and schedules).

Finally, if you have done your job with the other goals, they should be receptive—no, eager—to hear about the results of your latest evaluation and to talk about how they can make the necessary design changes and iterate to improve the current design.

17.5.2 Reporting to Inform Your Project Team

The primary audience for a report of UX problem details is your own project team—the designers and implementers who will fix the problems. Unless your project team is very small and everyone was present for evaluation data collection and analysis, you will always need to share your evaluation results with your team.

However, you do not always have to do "formal" reporting. The key goal is to convey results and product implications clearly and meaningfully to your workmates, informing them about UX flaws in the design and/or informally measured shortcomings in user performance with the purpose of understanding what needs to be done to improve the design in the next iteration.

For the interaction designers and UX practitioners, UX problems can be presented as they are related to specific parts of the interaction dialogues (e.g., a particular dialogue box). For the software engineers, you might organize your UX problems by software module, as that is the way they think.

Suppose you know the people on the team; you, the evaluator, know the designers and/or developers. As a UX practitioner, you may even *be* the designer or you work very closely with the designer(s) and you also know the developers. You decide and make the design changes and then persuade the developers to implement them. In this case your report can be short and to the point, with little need for embellishments or blandishments.

Sometimes, especially in large development organizations, the people who write the evaluation reports are sending them to a development team they do not know. They may not even have a chance to meet with the designers to present the results personally or to explain points or answer questions. This case is a bit more demanding of your reporting—needing a complete and standalone document. It calls for a bit more politeness or formality, more completeness, and definitely more selling of the changes *and* their implementation.

Dumas, Molich, and Jeffries (2004) point out the case of a UX consultant, where there is often no opportunity to explain comments or negotiate recommendations after the report is delivered.

Start with a "boilerplate" summary of the basics, including evaluation goals, methods, and UX targets and benchmark tasks used. Screen shots and video clips illustrating actual problem encounters are always good for selling your points about problems.

Your audience will expect you to prioritize your redesign recommendations, and cost-importance analysis (Chapter 16) is a good way to do this. Assuming that your team has technical savvy, use tables to summarize your findings; do not make them plow through a lot of text for the essence. If your development schedule is short and things are already moving fast, keep the report and your problem list short.

17.5.3 Reporting to Inform and/or Influence Your Management

The team's key goal for reporting to this audience is to influence and convince them that this is part of the process and that the process is working. You want them to understand that although you now have a version of a prototype or product, we are not done yet and we all need to iterate.

Reports to management have to be short and sweet. Be concise and get to the point. Start with an executive summary. You usually should also very briefly explain the process, the evaluation goals, the methods, and the UX targets and benchmark tasks used. Because this can be counted as at least a partly "internal" audience, you can share high-level aspects of informal quantitative testing (e.g., user performance and satisfaction scores), but just trends observed, not numbers and no "claims," and remember not to call it a "study."

Focus on UX problems that can be fixed within the number of people hours allocated in the budget but paint a complete picture of your findings. A cost-importance analysis that prioritizes UX problems based on a ratio of estimated cost to perceived importance (Chapter 16) may be a key element in demonstrating how you chose the problems to be fixed. This analysis can also highlight other problems currently out of reach but that could be fixed with more resources.

Define your priorities and relate them directly to business goals. This is easier if you used UX targets driven by UX goals (Chapter 10), based on business and product goals. You need an "explicit connection between the business or test goals and the results" (Theofanos & Quesenbery, 2005; Theofanos et al., 2005). Screen shots and video clips, made anonymous, illustrating actual problem encounters might be useful in engaging them in the whole evaluation scene.

17.5.4 Reporting to Your Customer or Client

As with most audiences, it is best to not start by hitting them square on with what is wrong with the system. This audience needs first to understand the whole concept of engineering for UX and the methods you use and how they help improve the product. They also have to be in favor of using this process before you tell them the process has revealed that their baby is ugly, but can be fixed. So, if they are unfamiliar with the UX process, a first goal may be to educate them about it so that they will understand the rest of what you have to report.

Another common goal is to impress them that you know what you are doing, you are earning your keep, and that the project is going well.

If you want to include UX problems, go easy on the doses of bad news. Clients and customers will not want to hear that there is a whole list of problems with the design of their system. This undermines confidence and makes them nervous. For clients, UX problems are best described with scenarios that show stories of how design flaws affected users and how your UX engineering process finds and fixes those problems. Here is where screen shots and very short before-and-after video clips (made anonymous with proper video blurring or with written permission of participants) can be effective.

17.5.5 Formative Evaluation Reporting Format and Vocabulary

Consistency in reporting UX problems is important for all audiences. Evaluation reports are, above all, a means of communication, and understanding is hampered by wildly varying vocabulary, differences among diagnoses and descriptions of the same kinds of problems, the language and style of expression in UX problem descriptions, and level of description contained (e.g., describing surface observables versus the use of abstraction to get at the nature of the underlying problem). Standards for reporting formative results, such as the CIF for formative results (discussed earlier in this chapter), help control broad variation in content, structure, and quality of UX problem reports.

To convey the essence of a problem and its potential solutions it can take several sentences or even a paragraph or more. As a more readable alternative to putting all that text in a table (e.g., a cost-importance table), you can put identification numbers in the problem-and-solution columns and write out the descriptive text in paragraph form. For example, you might put a "1" in the problem column of your table and maybe "1a" and "1b" to represent two possible solutions in that column. Then, in the accompanying text, you might have:

> Problem 1: Help system was difficult to use.
> Solution 1a: Use hypertext for the help screens, including a table of contents for general help.
> Solution 1b: Use context-sensitive help. For example, when users are in the HotList dialogue box and click on the Help button, they are taken to the HotList help screen instead of the help table of contents or the general help screen.

Jargon

As UX practitioners we, like most others in technical disciplines, have our own jargon—about UX. But, as UX practitioners, we must also know that our UX problem reports are like "error messages" to designers and that guidelines for error message design apply to our reports as well. And one of those guidelines about messages is to avoid jargon.

So, while we might not put jargon in our interaction designs, we might well be tempted to use our own technical language in our reports about UX. Yes, our audience is supposed to include UX professionals as interaction designers but you cannot be sure how much they share your specialized vocabulary. Spell things out in plain natural language.

Precision and specificity

You are communicating with others to accomplish an outcome that you have in mind. To get the audience to share the vision of that outcome or to even understand what outcome you want, you need to communicate effectively; perhaps the first rule for effective communication is to be precise and specific. It takes more effort to write effective reports.

Sloppy terminology, vague directions, and lazy hand-waving are likely to be met with indifference, and the designers and other practitioners are less likely to understand the problems and solutions we propose in the report. This kind of effect of a problem report on our audience usually results in their being unconvinced that there is a real problem.

So instead of saying a dialogue box message text is hard to understand and recommending that someone write it more clearly, you should, in fact, make your own best effort at rewording to clarify the text and say why your version is better. The criterion for effectiveness is whether the designer who receives your problem report will be able to make better design choices (Dumas, Molich, & Jeffries, 2004).

17.5.6 Formative Reporting Tone

The British are too polite to be honest, but the Dutch are too honest to be polite.

–Candid Dutch saying

All your audiences deserve respect in evaluation reports. Start with customers and clients, for example; most UX practitioners appreciate the need to temper their reports with a modicum of restraint. But even your own team should be addressed with courtesy.

Respect feelings: Bridle your acrimony

Do not attack; do not demean; do not insult. Your goal is to get designers to act on the reports and fix the problems. Their anger and resentment, while possibly offering a measure of joy to the occasional twisted evaluator, will not serve your professional goals. A UX problem report is a dish best served cold.

As Dumas, Molich, and Jeffries put it: "express your annoyance tactfully." It is true that typos, spelling errors, or grammatical boo-boos are very avoidable. They tend to agitate evaluators, but you must be professional and resist impassioned attacks. Avoid comments that use the terms unconscionable, unprofessional, incompetent, no excuse for this, this is nonsense, this is lazy, this is sloppy, or these designers clearly do not care about our users.

Some evaluators believe that being too polite might get in the way or be perceived as a little condescending and that being blunt helps convey the message; "someone obviously needs strong words to make them see how far off base they are. Being 'diplomatic' and euphemistic about the problems just leads to our reports being discounted and ignored." But please understand that a UX report is not a forum for practitioners with axes to grind. Many designers say they are insulted by emotional rants and that "being blunt is not helpful; it is simply rude" (Dumas, Molich, & Jeffries, 2004).

The bottom line is: be likeable. Likeability breeds persuasiveness (Wilson, 2007) and projects a collaborative atmosphere rather than an adversarial one.

Accentuate the positive and avoid blaming

Most practitioners do realize that they should start with good things to say about the system being evaluated. However, even when encouraged to be positive, some practitioners in studies (Dumas, Molich, & Jeffries, 2004) proved to be reticent in this regard. This may be because their usual audience is the project team, who just wants to know what the problems are so that they can start fixing them. The evaluators may believe that the designers are strictly technical people who would not involve their feelings in their work.

However, even if the report is mainly critical, it is best to start with *something* positive. Include information about places where participants did not have problems, where they were successful in task completion, and where users expressed great satisfaction or joy of use. Videos clips of good things happening can start things off with very positive feelings. The rest is, then: "We are on a roll: How can we make it even better?"

Work hard to present reports about design flaws as opportunities for design improvement, not as a criticism. A good way to do this is to remind them that the goal of formative evaluation is to find problems so that you can fix them. Therefore, a report containing information about problems found is an indication of success in the process. Congratulations, team; your process is working!

17.5.7 Formative Reporting over Time

Do not delay or postpone evaluation reporting. Get the report out as early as possible. Once the job is done, people who need the results need them immediately. News about problems received later than necessary may not be well received and might have to be "tabled" until the next version. It is especially important to keep your project team in the loop: give them a preliminary report; do not make them wait for the final report a month later.

Keep them updated continuously. The full written report should be sent out within a few days or weeks, not months, and there should be no surprises by this time.

The UPA Workshop Report (Theofanos et al., 2005) clearly established that most UX professionals deliver more than one evaluation report over time. Starting immediately after testing, reports lean toward raw, undigested data, notes, and observations. Later reports tend to be more formal, with analysis applied to smooth out raw data and findings. Later, archival reports may be a way of saving all the original recordings, logs, and notes in case the evaluation must be repeated in the future.

17.5.8 Problem Report Effectiveness: The Need to Convince and Get Action with Formative Results

Wilson (2007) poses the question this way: "How do I get the product team (or the "developers") to listen to my recommendations about how to make the product better?" If it involves software implementers or others who may not have been part of the evaluation effort or who care more about programming effort than usability or user experience, your report may need to do some selling.

Without being manipulative, you can offer positive benefits to the project team and management that will buy good will and, quid pro quo, get your UX role taken seriously. Wilson (2007) tells about a usability team report that included a section on "Good Things About Product X." It was so well appreciated by sales and marketing that they gave "bootleg" copies to their customers. In turn, marketing gave the UX team new and extended access to customers.

Law (2006) conducted a study on the factors that influenced designers in deciding which problems to fix. She defines downstream utility as "the effectiveness with which the resolution to a UX problem is implemented," determined analytically in terms of the impact of fixing or not fixing the UX problems. The developer effect is the "developers' bias toward fixing UX problem with particular characteristics." To Law, the persuasive power of usability test results to induce fixes and the effectiveness of the fixes depend on factors such as:

- problem severity: more severe problems are more salient and carry more weight with designers
- problem frequency: more frequently occurring problems are more likely to be perceived as "real"
- perceived relevance of problems: designers disagreeing with usability practitioners on the relevance (similar to "realness") of problems did not fix problems that practitioners recommended be fixed

Elaborateness of usability problem descriptions and redesign proposals turned out to *not* be a factor in influencing designers, suggesting diminishing returns for increased verbosity in usability problem descriptions. Similarly (and possibly counter intuitively), an estimated effort to fix a problem did not seem to be an influence.

Hornbæk and Frøkjær (2005) interviewed designers regarding the utility of redesign proposals in evaluation reports. An essential conclusion was that designers do not want to see just problem descriptions without redesign proposals. Even if they did not take the direction recommended in a redesign proposal, the proposal usually gave them new ideas about how to attack even well-known problems.

Finally, beware of the passive-aggressive reception of your report. In our consulting we have seen designers agree with evaluation reports mainly because their managers had established evaluation and iteration as required parts of the lifecycle process. They agree to make a few changes and to consider the rest. But in these cases it was not a buy-in but a sop to make the UX people go away. No convincing was possible and no door was left open to try.

In the final analysis and depending on the size and makeup of your team, the need to convince designers to make the changes you recommend becomes about cultivating trust. If UX practitioners deliver high-quality UX problem reports, with supporting data, it builds trust with the designers. As the working relationship develops and trust grows, there is less need for convincing.

Sometimes project groups work together for one project and then team up with others for the next project, not working together long enough to develop a real trusting relationship. The less rapport and empathy among team members, the more need for high-quality evaluation reports presented in a consistent format and, possibly, supported with data.

If the trust level is high within your audience, you can keep your evaluation reports simple and focus on results and recommendations rather than persuasion.

17.5.9 Reporting on Large Amounts of Qualitative Data

If you are reporting on a large amount of formative evaluation, about a large number of UX problems, you need to be well organized. If you ramble and jump around among different kinds of problems without an integrated perspective, it will be like a hodgepodge to your audience and you will lose them, along with their support for making changes based on your evaluation.

One possible approach is to use a highly abridged version of the affinity diagram technique (Chapter 4). We showed how to use an affinity diagram to organize work activity data, and you can use the same technique here to organize

Affinity Diagram

An affinity diagram is a hierarchical technique for organizing and grouping the issues and insights across large quantities of qualitative data and showing it in a visual display, usually posted on one or more walls of a room.

Exercise

See Exercise 17-1, Formative Evaluation Reporting for Your System

all your UX problem data for reporting. Post notes about each problem at the detailed level and group them according to commonalities, for example, with respect to task structure, organization of functionality, or other system structure.

17.5.10 Your Personal Presence in Formative Reporting

Do not just write up a report and send it out, hoping that will do the job. If possible, you should be there to make a presentation when you deliver the report. The difference your personal presence at the time of reporting can make in reaching your goals, especially in influencing and convincing, is inestimable. Nothing beats face-to-face communication to set the desired tone and expectations. There is no substitute for being there to answer questions and head off costly misunderstandings. If the audience is distributed geographically, this is a good time to use videoconferencing or at least a teleconference.

Wrapping up UX Evaluation

18

After reading this chapter, you will:
1. Understand goal-directed UX evaluation
2. Know how to select suitable UX evaluation methods
3. Understand how to be practical in your approach to UX evaluation, knowing when to be flexible about processes

---

18.1 GOAL-DIRECTED UX EVALUATION

The bottom line for developing the evaluation plan is to be flexible and do what it takes to make it work. We have given you the basics; it is up to you to come up with the variations. Adapt, evolve, transform, invent, and combine methods (Dray & Siegel, 1999). For example, supplement your lab-based test with an analytical method (e.g., your own UX inspection).

18.1.1 No Such Thing as the "Best UX Evaluation Method"

When you seek a UX evaluation method for your project, it usually is not about which method is "better," but which one helps you meet your goals in a particular evaluation situation. No existing evaluation method can serve every purpose and each has its own strengths and weaknesses. You need to know your goals going in and tailor your evaluation methods to suit.

And goals can vary a lot. In the very early design stages you will likely have a goal of getting the right design, looking at usefulness and a good match to high-level workflow needs, which requires one kind of evaluation. When you get to later stages of refining a design and mainly want feedback about how to improve UX, you need an entirely different kind of evaluation approach.

So much has been written about which UX evaluation method is better, often criticizing methods that do not meet various presumed standards. Too often these debates continue in absolute terms, when the truth is: It depends! We believe it is not about which method is "better," but which one helps you meet your goals in a particular evaluation situation.

In fact, each aspect of the overall evaluation process depends on your evaluation goals, including design of evaluation sessions (e.g., focus, procedures), types of data to be collected, techniques for data analysis, approaches to reporting results, and (of course) cost. Tom Hewett was talking about evaluation goals way back in the 1980s (Hewett, 1986).

18.2 CHOOSE YOUR UX EVALUATION METHODS

This is an overview of some UX evaluation methods and data collection techniques and how to choose them. Other methods and techniques are available, but most of them will be variations on the themes we present here.

Here we use the term "evaluation method" to refer to a choice of process and the term "technique" as a skill-based activity, usually within a method. For example, lab-based testing is an evaluation method, and critical incident identification is a data collection technique that can be used to collect qualitative data within the lab-based method. One of the earliest decisions you have to make about your approach to UX evaluation in any given stage of any given project is the basic choice of UX evaluation method.

18.2.1 Goals Tied to Resources

Sometimes you just cannot afford a fully rigorous UX evaluation method. Sometimes paying less is necessary; it is a rapid or "discount" method or nothing. Some criticism of discount methods is based on whether they are as effective as more expensive methods, whether they find UX problems as well as other methods such as lab-based UX testing. This misses the point: you choose rapid or "discount" evaluation methods because they are faster and less expensive! They are not generally as effective as rigorous methods, but often they are good enough within an engineering context.

Some criticism is even aimed at whether "discount" methods provide statistically significant results. How can that be an issue when there is no intention for that kind of result? A more appropriate target for critical review of "discount" methods would be about how much you get for how much you pay. Different methods meet different goals. If statistical significance is a goal, only formal summative evaluation will do, and you have to pay for it.

18.2.2 UX Evaluation Methods and Techniques by Stage of Progress

In Table 18-1 we show some simple stages of design representations such as storyboards and prototypes and representative formative evaluation approaches appropriate to those stages.

Design walkthroughs and other design reviews are rapid and flexible methods that employ informal demonstrations of design concepts or early versions of designs to obtain initial reactions before many design details exist. Usually at this point in a project, you have only scenarios, storyboards, screen sketches, or, at most, a low-fidelity (non-interactive) prototype.

So you have to do the "driving"; it is too early for anyone else in a user role to engage in real interaction. Walkthroughs are an important way to get early feedback from the rest of the design team, customers, and potential users. Even early lab-based tests can include walkthroughs (Bias, 1991). Also, sometimes the term is used to refer to a more comprehensive team evaluation, more like a team-based UX inspection.

By the time you have constructed a low-fidelity prototype, a paper prototype, for example, UX inspection methods and lightweight quasi-empirical testing are appropriate. Inspection methods are, in practice, perhaps the most used and most useful UX evaluation methods for this stage.

Sometimes evaluators overlook the value of critical review or UX inspection by a UX expert. Unlike most participants in lab-based testing, an expert will be broadly knowledgeable in the area of interaction design guidelines and will have

Stage of Design Representation	Formative Evaluation Approach
Design scenarios (Chapter 6), storyboards (Chapter 8), and detailed design (Chapter 9)	Design walkthroughs (Chapter 13) Local evaluation (Chapter 13)
Low-fidelity prototypes (Chapter 11)	UX inspection (Chapter 13) Quasi-empirical UX testing (Chapter 13)
High-fidelity prototypes (Chapter 11)	RITE (Chapter 13)
Programmed prototype (Chapter 11) or operational product	Rigorous (e.g., lab-based) UX testing (Chapters 12 and 14 through 17) RITE (Chapter 13) Alpha, beta testing (Chapter 13)
Post-deployment	User surveys/questionnaires (Chapter 12) Remote UX evaluation (Chapter 13) Automatic evaluation (Chapter 13)

Table 18-1

Appropriateness of various formative UX evaluation approaches to each stage of progress within the project

extensive experience in evaluating a wide variety of interaction styles. The most popular UX inspection method (Chapter 13) is the heuristic evaluation (HE) method.

High-fidelity prototypes, including programmed prototypes and operational products, are very complete design representations that merit complete or rigorous evaluation, as by lab-based testing. The RITE method is a good choice here, too, because it is an empirical method that uses participants but is rapid. Alpha and beta testing with selected users and/or customers are appropriate evaluation methods for pre-release versions of the near-final product.

Finally, you can continue to evaluate a system or product even after deployment in the field via remote surveys and/or questionnaires and remote UX evaluation, a method that has the advantage of operating within the context of real-world usage.

18.2.3 Synthesize Your Own Hybrid Method

As you gain experience, you will synthesize hybrid approaches as you go, adapting, transforming, and combining methods to suit each unique situation. For example, in a recent UX session we observed some phenomena we thought might be indicative of a UX problem but which did not lead to critical incidents occurring with users in the lab. So after the UX lab session, we added our own analytic component to investigate these issues further.

In this particular example, the system was strongly organized and presented to the user by function. Users found it awkward to map the functions into task sequences; they had to bounce all over the interface to access parts that were closely related in task flow. It took some intense team analysis to get a handle on this and to come up with some specialized local prototypes to test further just this one issue and evaluate some alternative design solutions.

This is not the kind of UX problem that will just pop out of a critical incident with a user in the lab as does, for example, a label wording commented on by a user. Rather, it is a deeper UX problem that might have caused users some discomfort, but they may have been unable to articulate the cause. Sometimes a problem requires the attention of an expert evaluator or interaction designer who can apply the necessary abstractions. If we had not been willing to do some additional analysis, not part of the original plan, we might have missed this important opportunity to improve the quality of user experience in our design.

18.3 FOCUS ON THE ESSENTIALS

18.3.1 Evaluate Design Concepts before Details

When practitioners do UX testing, they often think first of low-level UX, the usability about details of button placement and label wording, and most lab-based usability evaluation ends up being aimed at this level. As we said in earlier chapters, however, the fit of the design to support work practice is fundamental. Find out how they do the work and design a system to support it. What is the point of using low-level usability evaluation to hone the details of what is basically a poor, or at least the wrong, design while blocking your ability to see broader and more useful design ideas?

Our friend and colleague Whitney Quesenbery (2009) has said:

> If there is a single looming problem in UX these days, it is that usability analysts too often get caught up in enumerating detailed observations, and spend a good deal less time than they should in thinking carefully about the underlying patterns and causes of the problems. This turns UX into a sort of QA checklist, rather than letting us usability analysts be the analysis partners we should be to the designers. Some of this, of course, is a legacy of having UX evaluation done too late, some is because there is often so much to do in fixing "obvious" problems, but some is because we have not taken seriously our role in supplying insights into human behavior.

In early stages when the concepts are young, formative evaluation should focus on high-level concepts, such as support of the work with the right work roles, workflows, the right general form of presenting the design to the user, mission-critical design features (e.g., potential "hanging chads" in the design), and safety-related features.

18.3.2 User Experience In Situ vs. User Reflections

The more directly the evaluation is related to actual usage, the more precise its indicators of UX problems will be. It is difficult to beat empirical evaluation with a "think-aloud technique" for accessing immediate and precise UX data when evaluating the design of an artifact in the context of usage experience.

Indirect and subjective evaluation such as obtained by a post-performance questionnaire can be less expensive and, if focused carefully on the important issues, can be effective. Alpha and beta testing (Chapter 13) are even less direct to the usage experience, severely limiting their effectiveness as formative evaluation methods.

At least when it comes to detailed formative evaluation, Carter (2007) nicely reminds us to think in terms of "inquiry within experience," evaluating the design of an artifact in the context of usage experience. To Carter, a survey or questionnaire is an abstraction that removes us from the user and the usage events, sacrificing a close connection to user experience in real time while the design is being used.

User surveys or questionnaires, even when administered immediately at the end of a UX testing session, are retrospective. A questionnaire produces only subjective data and, as Elgin (1995) states, "Subjective feedback is generally harder to interpret than objective feedback in a known setting...." More importantly, survey or questionnaire data cannot be the immediate and precise data about task performance that are essential for capturing the perishable details necessary to formative UX evaluation.

For evaluating design details, it is about getting into the user's head with "thinking-aloud" techniques. But the further the time of UX data capture from the time of occurrence, the more abstraction and need for retrospective recall, thereby the more loss of details. We looked at techniques for capturing indicators of UX problems and for capturing indicators of success with UX as observed directly within the real-time occurrence of usage experience (Chapter 12).

18.3.3 Evaluating Emotional Impact and Phenomenological Aspects

Do not just focus on usability or usefulness in your evaluations. Remember that one of your most important evaluation goals can be to give emotional impact and phenomenological aspects attention, too. Specific evaluation methods for emotional impact were detailed in Chapter 12.

18.4 PARTING THOUGHTS: BE FLEXIBLE AND AVOID DOGMA DURING UX EVALUATION

18.4.1 Keep the Flexibility to Change Your Mind

Your organization is paying for evaluation, and it is your responsibility to get the most out of it. The key is flexibility, especially the flexibility to abandon some goals in favor of others in conflict situations. Your evaluation goals can be predetermined, but you can also come up with new or different goals as a result of what happens during evaluation.

As an illustration of staying flexible within goal-directed UX evaluation, consider an evaluation session in which you are doing the typical kind of UX evaluation and something goes wrong for the user. If you stop and ask the user questions about what went wrong and why, you will lose out on gathering quantitative performance data, one of your goals. However, because that data now will not be very useful, and understanding UX problems and their causes is your most important goal, you should stop and talk.

In most formative evaluation cases, when there is a conflict between capturing quantitative (e.g., task timing) and qualitative data (e.g., usability problem identification), qualitative data should take precedence. This is because when user performance breaks down, performance data are no longer useful, but the incident now becomes an opportunity to find the reason for the breakdown.

As part of your pre-evaluation preparation, you should prioritize your goals to prepare for conflicting goal situations. As Carter (2007) says, you should retain the freedom for interruption and intervention (even when the original goal was to collect quantitative data).

18.4.2 Do Not Let UX Evaluation Dogma Supplant Experience and Expertise

Give people a process they can follow and sometimes they hang on to it until it becomes a religion. We encourage you, instead, to do your own critical thinking. You still have to use your head and not just follow a "process." Be ready to adapt and change directions and techniques. Be ready to abandon empirical testing for thoughtful expert analytic evaluation if the situation so demands.

According to Greenberg and Buxton (2008), "evaluation can be ineffective and even harmful if naively done 'by rule' rather than 'by thought.'" Instead of following a plan unquestioningly, you must make choices as you go that will help you reach your most important goals. It is *your* job to think about and judge what is happening and where things are going within the project. Sauro (2004, p. 31) warns against "one-size-fits-all usability pronouncements" mimed and unencumbered by the thought process.

The dogma of our usual doctrine of usability testing reveres objective observation of users doing tasks. But sometimes we can evaluate a design subjectively, applying our own personal knowledge and expertise as a UX professional. As Greenberg and Buxton (2008, p. 114) put it, "Our factual methods do not respect the subjective: they do not provide room for the experience of the advocate, much less their arguments or reflections or intuitions about a design."

Greenberg and Buxton quote a wonderful passage from the literature of architecture about the "experienced designer-as-assessor." The quote (from Snodgrass and Coyne, 2006, p. 123) defends design evaluation by an architect designer, illustrating the fact that just because the person is a designer does not rule them out as an evaluator.

In fact, the designer has acquired a rich understanding of architectural design principles, processes, and evaluation criteria. They make the case that just because an evaluation is done subjectively by an expert, it does not mean that the results will be wild and uncontrolled. The work of expert assessors is built on a common foundation of knowledge, fundamentals, and conventions. The striking similarity to our situation should not be surprising—it is all about design.

18.5 CONNECTING BACK TO THE LIFECYCLE

Congratulations! You have just completed one complete iteration through the Wheel interaction design and evaluation lifecycle template. This ends the process part of the book. You have only to implement your chosen design solutions and realize the benefits of improved usability and user experience, connecting back to the UX lifecycle, cycling back through design and prototyping and evaluation again.

When you connect each UX problem back to the lifecycle for fixing and iteration, where do you connect? You have to use your engineering judgment about what each problem needs in order to get fixed.

For most simple UX problems, much of the work for fixing the problems has been done when you worked out design solutions for each of the observed problems. However, a UX problem that seems to involve a lack of understanding of work practice and/or requirements may need to connect back to contextual inquiry and contextual analysis rather than just going back to design.

UX Methods for Agile Development

19

Objectives

After reading this chapter, you will:

1. Understand the basic characteristics of agile SE methods
2. Recognize the drawbacks of agile SE methods from the UX perspective
3. Know what is needed to integrate UX into an agile environment
4. Understand a synthesized approach to integrating UX into an agile environment
5. Appreciate the need for a dove-tailed staggering of process steps for UX to fit into the overall development process

19.1 INTRODUCTION

Just as our use of the term UX is convenient shorthand for the entire broad concept of designing for user experience, we use the term "SE" to refer to the entire broad concept that embraces the terms software engineering, software, software development, and the software engineering domain. This chapter is about an important way those two domains can come together in an efficient project development environment.

We believe that the rigorous UX process (Chapters 3 through 12 and 14 through 17) is the most effective path to ensuring a quality user experience with systems with complex work domains and complex interaction. However, because the fully rigorous UX process is also the most expensive and time-consuming, it cannot always be applied. Nor is it always appropriate, for example, for systems and products at the other end of the system complexity space in Figure 2-7.

Less-than-perfect development environments, short schedules, and limited budgets demand effective ways to adapt UX process methods to the turmoil and pressure of the real professional world. Anxious customers, especially for systems with simple domains such as commercial products, may demand early deliverables, including previews of prototypes about which they can give

Domain-Complex Systems

Domain-complex systems are systems with a high degree of intricacy and technical content in the corresponding field of work. Often, characterized by convoluted and elaborate mechanisms for how parts of the system work and communicate, they usually have complicated workflow containing multiple dependencies and communication channels. Examples include an air traffic control system and a system for analyzing seismic data for oil exploration.

feedback. In such cases practitioners can use abridged versions of the fully rigorous lifecycle process, skipping some process activities altogether and using rapid techniques for others.

Alternatively, the software development side might require an agile development environment. Agile SE approaches, now well known and popularly used, are incremental, iterative, and test-driven means of delivering pieces of useful working software to customers frequently, for example, every two weeks. However, agile SE approaches do not account for UX. Because traditional UX processes do not fit well within a project environment using agile SE methods, the UX side must find ways to adjust their methods to fit SE constraints.

Therefore, the entire system development team needs an overall approach that includes UX while retaining the basics of the SE approach. In this chapter we present a variation of our UX process methods that will integrate well with existing agile SE processes by accounting for the constraints imposed by those agile SE processes.

We begin by describing the essence of the agile SE approach and then identify what is needed on the UX side so that the two processes fit together. Finally, we describe an approach that brings the UX lifecycle process and agile SE together, retaining the essentials of each but requiring some adjustments on both sides.

19.2 BASICS OF AGILE SE METHODS

Much of this section is based on Beck (2000), one of the most authoritative sources of information on agile SE development methods as embodied in the approach called eXtreme Programming (XP).[1] We have taken words from Beck and other authors and tried to blend them into a summary of the practice. Accurate representations are credited to these authors while errors in representation are our fault.

19.2.1 Characteristics of Agile SE Methods

Agile SE development methods begin coding very early. Agile SE has a shorter, almost nonexistent, requirements engineering phase and far less documentation than that of traditional software engineering. As typified in XP, agile SE code implementation occurs in small increments and iterations.

Small releases are delivered to the customer after each short iteration, or development cycle. In most cases, these small releases, although limited in

---

[1]There are other "brands" of approaches to agile SE methods beyond XP, including Scrum (Rising & Janoff, 2000), but for convenience we focus on XP.

functionality, are intended to be working versions of the whole system, which run by themselves. Nonetheless, each release is supposed to deliver some useful capability for the customer.

In simplest terms, agile SE development methods "describe the problem simply in terms of small, distinct pieces, then implement these pieces in successive iterations" (Constantine, 2002, p. 3). Each piece is tested until it works and is then integrated into the rest. Next the whole is tested in what Constantine calls "regression testing" until it all works. As a result, the next iteration always starts with something that works.

To clarify the concept of agile software methods, a group met at a workshop in Snowbird, Utah in February 2001 and worked out an "agile manifesto" (Beck, 2000). From their stated principles behind this manifesto, goals for agile software development emerged:

- Satisfy the customer by giving them early and continuous deliverables that produce valuable and working software.
- Recognize that changing requirements are the norm in any software development effort.
- Understand that time and budget constraints must be managed.

Practitioners of agile SE methods value (Beck, 2000):

- Individuals and interactions over processes and tools
- Working software over comprehensive documentation
- Customer collaboration over contract negotiation
- Responding to change over following a plan

The agile software development methods are further characterized by the need for communication, especially continuous communication with the customer. Informal communication is strongly preferred over formal. Close communication is emphasized to the point that they have an onsite customer as part of the team, giving feedback continuously.

A main principle of agile SE methods is to avoid Big Design UpFront (BDUF). This means the approach generally eschews upfront ethnographic and field studies and extensive requirements engineering. The idea is to get code written as soon as possible and resolve problems by reacting to customer feedback later.

And because change is happening everywhere, SE practitioners verify that they are writing the code correctly by the practice of pair programming. Code is written by two programmers working together and sharing one computer and one screen, that is, always having a colleague watching over the programmer's shoulder.

Of course, pair programming is not new with agile methods. Even outside agile SE methods and before they existed, pair programming was a proven technique with a solid track record (Constantine, 2002). Another way they verify the code being written is via regular and continuous testing against an inventory of test cases.

19.2.2 Lifecycle Aspects

If this process were to be represented by a lifecycle diagram, it would not be a waterfall or even an iteration of stages, but a set of overlapping micro-development activities. In the waterfall approach, developers finish entire requirements analysis before starting design and the entire design before starting implementation.

But in agile approaches developers do just enough—a micro-level of each activity—to support one small feature request; see Figure 19-1, which illustrates XP as an example agile method. In the middle of these extremes are approaches where these activities are performed in larger scope units. In these middle-of-the-road approaches, lifecycle activities are applied at the level of overall system components or subsystems. In contrast, in agile methods it is applied at the level of features in those components.

For example, building an e-commerce Website in the waterfall approach would require listing all requirements that must be supported in the Website before starting a top-down design. In an agile approach, the same Website would be built as a series of smaller features, such as a shopping cart or check out module.

Figure 19-1

Comparison of scope of development activities across methodologies, taken with permission from Beck (1999, Figure 1).

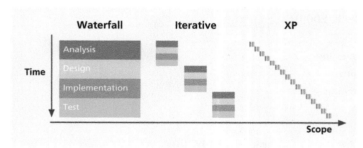

19.2.3 Planning in Agile SE Methods

In our discussion of how an agile SE method works, we are roughly following XP as a guide. As shown in Figure 19-2, each iteration consists of two parts: planning and a sprint to implement and test the code for one release.

Figure 19-2

Abstraction of an agile SE release iteration.

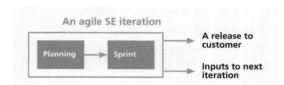

Customer stories

The planning part of each iteration in Figure 19-2 yields a set of customer-written stories, prioritized by cost to implement. A customer story, a key concept in the process, has a role a bit like that of a use case, a scenario, or a requirement. A customer story, written on a story (index) card, is a description of a customer-requested feature. It is a narrative about how the system is supposed to solve a problem, representing a chunk of functionality that is coherent in some way to the customer.

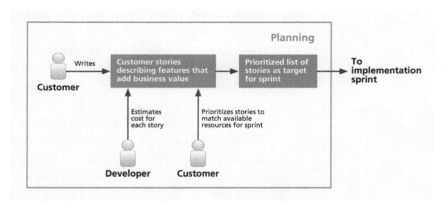

Figure 19-3
Customer stories as the basis of planning.

Story-based planning

Expanding the "planning" box of Figure 19-2, we get the details of how customer stories are used in planning, as shown in Figure 19-3.

As shown in Figure 19-3, developers start the planning process by sitting down with onsite customer representatives. They ask customer representatives to think about the most useful chunks of functionality that can add business or enterprise value. The customer writes stories about the need for these pieces of functionality. This is the primary way that the developers understand users and their needs, indirectly through the customer representatives.

Developers assess the stories and estimate the effort required to implement (program) a solution for each, writing the estimate on the story card. Typically, in XP, each story gets a 1-, 2-, or 3-week estimate in "ideal development time."

The customer sorts and prioritizes the story cards by choosing a small set for which the cost estimates are within a predetermined budget and which represent features they want to include in a "release." Prioritization might result in lists of stories or requirements labeled as "do first," "desired—do, if time," and "deferred—consider next time." Developers break down the stories into development tasks, each written on a task (for the developers to do) card.

The output of the planning box, which goes to the upcoming implementation sprint, is a set of customer-written stories, prioritized by cost to implement.

Controlling scope

Customer stories are the local currency in what Beck (2000, p. 54) calls the "planning game" through which the customer and the developers negotiate the scope of each release. At the beginning there is a time and effort "budget" of the person-hours or level of effort available for implementing all the stories, usually per release.

As the customer prioritizes story cards, the total of the work estimates is kept and, when it reaches the budget limit, the developers' "dance card" is full. Later, if the customer wants to "cut in" with another story, they have to decide which existing customer story with an equal or greater value must be removed to make room for the new one. So no one, not even the boss, can just add more features.

This approach gives the customer control of which stories will be implemented but affords developers a tool to battle scope or feature creep. Developer estimates of effort could be way off, probably in most cases underestimating the effort necessary, but at least it lets them draw a line. With experience, developers get pretty good at this estimation given a particular technology platform and application domain.

19.2.4 Sprints in Agile SE Methods

Expanding the "sprint" box of Figure 19-2, as shown in Figure 19-4, each agile SE sprint consists of activities that are described in the following sections.

Acceptance test creation

The customer writes the functional acceptance tests. There is no process for this, so it can be kind of fuzzy, but it does put the customer in control of acceptance of the eventual code. With experience, customers get good at this.

Unit code test creation

The team divides the work by assigning customer stories to code for that sprint. A programmer picks a customer story card and finds a programming partner. Before any coding, the pair together writes unit tests that can verify that functionality is present in the code that is yet to be written as an implementation.

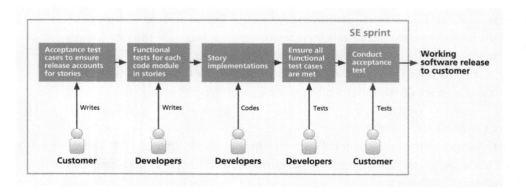

Figure 19-4

An agile SE sprint.

Implementation coding

The programming pairs work together to write the code for modules that support the functionality of the customer story. As they work, the partners do on-the-fly design (the agile SE literature says almost nothing about design).

The programmers do not worry about the higher level architecture; the system architecture supposedly evolves with each new slice of functionality that is added to the overall system. The programming pair integrates this code into the latest version.

Code testing

Next, the programming pair runs the unit code tests designed for the modules just implemented. In addition, they run all code tests again on all modules coded so far until all tests are passed. By testing the new functionality with not only tests written for this functionality, but with all tests written for previous pieces of functionality, SE developers make sure that the realization of this functionality in code is correct and that it does not break any of the previously implemented modules. This allows developers to make code modifications based on changing requirements, while ensuring that all parts of the code continue to function properly.

Acceptance testing and deployment

Developers submit this potentially shippable product functionality to the customer for acceptance review. Upon acceptance, the team deploys this small iterative "release" to the customer.

19.3 DRAWBACKS OF AGILE SE METHODS FROM THE UX PERSPECTIVE

From the SE perspective, much about agile SE methods is, of course, positive. These methods make SE practitioners feel productive and in control because they, and not some overarching design, drive the process. These methods are less expensive, faster, and lighter weight, with early deliverables. The pair-programming aspect also seems to produce high-reliability code with fewer bugs. Nonetheless, agile SE methods are programming methods, developed by programmers for programmers, and they pose some drawbacks from the UX perspective.

Agile SE methods, being driven predominantly by coders, are optimized for code, judged by quality of code, and have a strong bias toward code concerns. There is no definition or consideration of usability or user experience (Constantine, 2002). Users, user activities, and the user interface are not part of the mix; the user interface becomes whatever the code hackers produce by chance and then must be "fixed" based on customer feedback.

In addition, there is no upfront analysis to glean general concepts of the system and associated work practice. The one customer representative on the team is not required even to be a real user and cannot represent all viewpoints, needs and requirements, usage issues, or usage context. There may be no real user data at all upfront, and coding will end up being "based only on assumptions about user needs" (Memmel, Gundelsweiler, & Reiterer, 2007, p. 169). There is no identification of user tasks and no process for identifying tasks.

Beyer, Holtzblatt, and Baker (2004) echo this criticism of using a customer representative as the only application domain expert. As they point out, under their "Axiom 2: Make the user the expert," many customer representatives are not also users and, therefore, cannot necessarily speak for the work practice of others. Instead, they recommend devoting an iteration of contextual analysis with real users to requirements definition. They say they have done quick contextual design with five to eight users through early design solutions in one to two weeks.

Beyond these specific drawbacks, the agile SE method has no room for ideation in design. And it can be difficult to scale up the process to work on very large systems. The number of customer stories becomes large without bounds. Similarly, it is difficult to scale up to larger development groups; the time and effort to communicate closely with everyone eventually become prohibitive and close coordination is lost.

19.4 WHAT IS NEEDED ON THE UX SIDE

In some ways, the UX process lifecycle is a good candidate to fit with agile software methods because it is already iterative. But there is a big difference. The traditional UX lifecycle is built on having a complete understanding of users and their needs long before a single line of software code is ever written. In this section we discuss the considerations necessary to adjust UX methods to adapt to agile SE approaches (Memmel, Gundelsweiler, & Reiterer, 2007).

To work in the UX domain, an agile method must retain some early analysis activities devoted to understanding user work activities and work context and gleaning general concepts of the system. At the same time, to be compatible with the agile SE side of development, UX methods must:

- be lightweight
- emphasize team collaboration and require co-location
- include effective customer and user representatives
- adjust UX design and evaluation to be compatible with SE sprint-based incremental releases by switching focus from top-down holistic design to bottom-up features design
- include ways to control scope

Thoughts on Integrating UX into Agile Projects

Dr. Deborah J. Mayhew, Consultant, Deborah J. Mayhew & Associates[1]
CEO, The Online User eXperience Institute[2]

I have been working in software development since 1975 and have watched a number of formal, commercial software engineering methodologies (including one of the first in the industry) emerge, evolve, and be abandoned for the next new idea. The latest one is agile, which has been around for almost 10 years now. When it first emerged I had been working in the UX field for about 20 years. I had written my book *The Usability Engineering Lifecycle* (1999b, Morgan Kaufmann Publishers), which describes a top-down, iterative approach to software user interface design set in the context of the prevalent development methodologies at that time: object-oriented software engineering and iterative development. The Usability Engineering Lifecycle (UEL) fit in quite nicely with those software engineering methodologies.

Then the agile methodology began to get popular. Initially, I learned about this new development methodology by working with a client who was building project management software tools to support agile project managers. I was trying to help this client design a usable interface to their software tools, and they were developing their tools using the agile methodology, so I had to try to adapt my approach to usability engineering into that methodology.

I struggled with this because it seemed to me that there was an inherent conflict: the agile methodology focuses on very small modules of functionality and code at a time, doing requirements analysis, design and development start to finish on each one, often with different development teams assigned to different modules being developed on overlapping timelines.

In contrast, the successful design of a user interface requires a top-down approach because all the functionality must be presented through a consistent overall architecture. A piecemeal approach to interface design, in which many different developers design separate modules of code, had always been a big stumbling block to good user

---

[1]http://drdeb.vineyard.net
[2]http://www.ouxinstitute.com

interface design in the past, and it seemed that the agile methodology would perpetuate that problem even while solving others.

So, I was skeptical that good usability engineering practices could be applied successfully in an agile development environment.

I have only recently had another opportunity to work with a development team following some version of the agile methodology and have evolved with them what I think is a successful approach to overcoming the potential conflicts between agile and the UEL approach to designing for an optimal user experience.

My client had already adapted the agile methodology in a way consistent with Nielsen's findings about best practices for integrating usability engineering into agile development projects (Jakob Nielsen's Alertbox, November 4, 2009, http://www.useit.com/alertbox/agile-user-experience.html). In Nielsen's words, the key things are to

> Separate design and development, and have the user interface team progress one step ahead of the implementation team ...

and to

> Maintain a coherent vision of the user interface architecture. Create the initial vision during a 'sprint zero' period—before any implementation has started—and maintain it through annual (or semi-annual) design vision sprints ...

I believe that these approaches are necessary but not sufficient. They do not solve the problem of separate agile teams creating different modules of code, with no one overseeing the user interface *across the whole system*. Each team can do visioning up front, and design before development in a "sprint zero" phase, but that does not ensure consistency in the user interface *across code modules developed by different teams*.

My client had embarked on a very large, multiyear project. They were breaking down what in the end would be one very large functionally rich system into small chunks of functionality and assigning these chunks to different agile teams, each with their own assigned user interface designers. These teams were working mostly independently on overlapping project schedules. They had an approach similar to Nielsen's ideas of a planning phase at the beginning of each project for high-level design, and a "sprint zero" in which detailed user interface design could start and stay a step ahead of coding. There was, however, only haphazard communication and coordination across teams regarding user interface design.

To be a little more concrete, an analogous project to the one I actually worked on would be the development of a system to support the customer support representatives of a credit card company. The functional chunks cast as separate projects in this analogy would be individual user tasks, such as processing requests for monthly payments, balance transfers from other credit cards, adding new credit cards to an account holder's account, closing out an account, contesting a fraudulent charge, and the like. A single customer service representative might be handling all these types of tasks, but different agile teams were designing and developing them.

When I got involved with my client's overall effort, separate projects were at many different stages in their agile processes, some still in the early planning and designing stages, others well along in their sprint process. My role was to provide feedback on design ideas generated by the project interaction designers on the projects, some of which were in early planning, some in sprint zero, and some halfway or more through their sprints.

I started performing heuristic evaluations for individual agile teams, one at a time. As I proceeded from project to project, I naturally started seeing two things: inconsistencies in interface design across projects and less than optimal designs within projects. In response to these observations, I started doing two things.

First, with each heuristic evaluation, I documented some sample redesign ideas in wireframe form to better communicate the issues I was identifying. As I went from one project to the next, I consistently applied the same redesign approaches when I encountered analogous design situations. So, for example, the first time I discovered a need for a widget to expand and contract details, I would document a particular design for that purpose. Then when I encountered the same need on another project, I would be sure to recommend the exact same design to address that need.

Second, I started capturing in list form those design situations that were coming up repetitively across pages and projects (the need to expand and contract information details would be an example of something in that list). This list became the foundation of what would eventually become a set of user interface design standards for the whole system. Those standards might not exactly reflect my design suggestions, but at least everything that a standard could be designed for would be identified and documented in one place.

Sometimes I would design for a situation when I first encountered it, apply it in later situations, and then even later come across the same situation on a new page or project in which my design solution just did not work well. In those cases, I would revisit the consistent design I had generated to date, redesign it, and then reapply the new standard to all analogous situations encountered across all projects I had evaluated to date, as well as going forward.

In this way, a common set of standards was continuously developed and evolved as each new agile project launched and proceeded. Rework was required when the need for a different standard was discovered on new but analogous functionality, but at least there was a single mind (mine) overseeing all the related agile projects so that opportunities for consistency were discovered and ultimately attended to. This just does not happen when different designers are responsible for different modules of functionality and no one is keeping track of the big picture.

I think proceeding in this way to design the overall user interface of a system that is divided up into many agile projects is analogous to designing the system architecture in this methodology. Modules of code designed and developed by separate and relatively independent teams have a similar risk of ending up being a mish mash of inefficient and hard to maintain code. Someone needs to oversee the evolution of the final system architecture, and rework may be required to go back and recode modules that did not adhere to the final system architecture model when they were developed initially. If we are willing to do the rework, this is a reasonable way to address both system architecture and user interface architecture in a methodology that certainly has other benefits but carries the risk of resulting in systems with no underlying models that support both technical and human needs.

19.4.1 The UX Component Must Be Lightweight

According to Memmel, Gundelsweiler, and Reiterer (2007), many of the rigorous UX processes out there, such as Mayhew (1999b), Rogers, Sharp, and Preece (2011), and the full Wheel process described in this book, are considered as heavyweight processes, too cumbersome for the unstoppable trend of shorter time-to-market and shorter development lifecycles. As a result, developers are turning to lighter-weight development processes.

However, the term "lightweight process" can be thought of as a euphemism for "cutting corners." As Constantine (2001) puts it, "shortcutting a proven process means omitting or short-changing some productive activities, and the piper will be paid, if not now, then later."

Sometimes, however, we have no choice. The project parameters demand fast turnaround and the rigorous process simply will not do. Therefore, we seek something in the middle ground, a lighter-weight process that, although compromising quality somewhat, can still meet schedule demands and allow us to deliver a system or product with value for the customer.

Traveling light means communicating rather than documenting. In general, heavyweight SE processes require detailed, up-to-date-documentation and models, whereas lightweight SE processes rely on index cards and hand-drawn abstract models. The artifacts maintained should be few, simple, and valuable (Beck, 2000, p. 42).

19.4.2 The UX Component Requires Collaboration and Co-Location with the SE Team

Traditional UX practice often implied handing off a refined interaction design as a formal hi-fi prototype or a complete wireframe deck. We did our contextual inquiry and analysis independently of their requirements gathering. Now this "fire-walling" of the UX and SE teams will not work. We must work together with the same customer representatives and users.

Our deliverables will now be less formal and somewhat incomplete because the details will be handled on a social channel, meaning we will communicate directly, person to person. Each team, UX and SE, must have access and visibility into the other team's progress, challenges, and bottlenecks so that they can plan to maintain synchronization.

To achieve this intimate communication, the entire project team has to be co-located. You all have to work in the same room, a working arena plus walls for whiteboards, posters, and diagrams. Everyone has to be continuously present *as part of the team*—readily available and knowledgeable.

You cannot rely on just email or a call on the phone. When you need to talk with someone else on the team, that person must be sitting with you as you work. This imperative for co-location in the agile approach can be a show-stopper. If, for any reason, your organization cannot afford to keep the entire project team in one location, it will preclude the agile approach.

19.4.3 Effective Customer and User Representatives Are Essential

An important SE requirement is continuous access to one or more co-located customer representatives, but on the UX side we will also need access to real users. Many "methods" call for including customers and users. So when you say that you need a customer representative in your project, others in your organization and in the customer organization may not understand how seriously this role is taken in agile methods and how integral it is to project success. Unless you have articulated criteria for the customer representative role, you are likely to get someone who happens to be available regardless of their real connection to the system.

Your customer and user representatives must truly represent the organization paying for development and must care about the project as a real stakeholder in the outcome. These representatives must have a good knowledge of all work roles, corresponding user classes, workflows, and the work domain. And perhaps the most important requirement is that these representatives must have the authority to make decisions about project scope and enough knowledge about what the organization really needs.

19.4.4 A Paradigm Shift: Depth-First, Vertical Slicing

Almost everything in both the process and the deliverables depends on whether the project approach is breadth first or depth first. Acceptance of the outcome will depend on how well the customer understands these choices and agrees to the approach you choose; it is up to you to set expectations accordingly.

The traditional UX process is breadth first, looking at the whole system broadly from the beginning—methodically and systematically building horizontal slices and integrating and growing them vertically. The resulting product is an integrated system design built top-down or inside-out in "horizontal" layers. This approach involves building a whole elephant from the inside out, laying down a skeleton, adding inner organs, fleshing it out with muscles to hold it all together, and wrapping it up with a skin.

However, as we said before, this approach works against early deliverables to the customer. There is often nothing to show customers early on. There just is not anything that even looks like an elephant until halfway or even later through the project.

In traditional development methods, associated deliverables will begin with documentation of development work products and descriptions of design-informing models, such as personas, user classes, or task descriptions. Development does not get to design-representing deliverables such as screen sketches, storyboards, and low-fidelity prototypes until later in the process.

So the customer has to be patient, but "patient" does not describe most customers we have met so far. Nor can you blame them; they do not want to be paying the bills for a long time without seeing any results.

Alternatively, and in almost complete contrast, agile methods are depth first, taking a narrow product scope but starting with more depth, building vertical slices and integrating and growing them horizontally. This is the approach you need when you have limited resources and have short-term demand for design-related deliverables, such as a prototype. The narrow product scope means addressing only a few selected features supporting related user work activities and system functions, but developing them in some depth.

This is like building an elephant by gluing together deep, but narrow, vertical slices. It might be for only a slim section of the backbone, maybe a part of a kidney or a slice of the liver, and a little bit of skin. But you are not going to see anything of the face, the feet, or the tail, for example. In other words, the customer might see some screen sketches and a low-fidelity prototype a lot earlier but they will be limited to a narrow set of features. This agile approach has a benefit in today's development market in that you can get at least something as a running deliverable much faster.

As more and more vertical slices become available, you put them together to construct the whole system. If slices here and there do not quite line up in this integration step, you must adjust them to fit. As you add each new slice, adjust the new slice and/or the rest of the elephant, as needed.

19.4.5 Controlling Scope Is a Necessity

Earlier in this chapter, we explained that agile SE customer stories are the basis for planning, through which the customer and the developers negotiate the scope of each release. At the beginning there is a time and effort "budget" of only so many person-hours or only a certain level of effort available for implementing all the stories.

Exactly the same approach to controlling scope works when UX and SE are integrated, still using the cost to implement the software as the criterion for setting scope boundaries. However, UX plays an involved role in negotiating with customers based on early conceptual design and user experience needs. More about this soon.

19.5 PROBLEMS TO ANTICIPATE

In a special-interest-group workshop at CHI 2009 (Miller & Sy, 2009), a group of UX practitioners met to share their experiences in trying to incorporate a user-centered design approach into the agile SE process. Among the difficulties experienced by these practitioners in their own environments were:

- sprints too short; not enough time for customer contact, design, and evaluation
- inadequate opportunities for user feedback and the user feedback they did get was ignored
- customer representative weak, not committed, and lack of co-location
- no shared vision of broader conceptual design because focus is on details in a bottom-up approach
- there is a risk of piecemeal results

Regarding the last bullet, building a system a little piece at a time is not without risks. Nielsen (2008) claims that agile methods can end up being a terrible way to do usability engineering. His reasons centered mostly on the fact that taking one piece at a time tended to destroy the whole picture of user experience. If requirements come in piecemeal, it is harder to see the big picture or the conceptual design. He claims that a piecemeal process hinders consistency and is a barrier to an integrated design, leading to a fragmented user experience.

Beyer, Holtzblatt, and Baker (2004) also believe that it is difficult to design small chunks of the interaction design without first knowing the basic interaction design architecture—how the system is structured to support user tasks and how the system functions are organized. In contextual design, interaction architecture is established with storyboards and what they call the "user environment design," which they say is just what you need for effective user stories.

In the end, it is up to skilled and experienced UX practitioners to keep the big picture in mind and do as much as possible along the way to maintain coherence in the overall design.

19.6 A SYNTHESIZED APPROACH TO INTEGRATING UX

Because traditional agile SE methods do not consider the user interface, usability, and user experience, there is a need to incorporate some of the user-centered design techniques of UX into the overall system development process. Most of the related literature is about either adjusting "discount" UX or user-centered design methods to somehow keep pace with existing agile SE methods or trying to do just selected parts of user-centered design processes in the presence of an essentially inflexible agile SE method.

While it is possible that XP, for example, and some abbreviated user-centered design techniques can coexist and work together, in these add-on approaches the two parts are not really combined (McInerney & Maurer, 2005; Patton, 2002, 2008). This creates a coping scenario for the UX side, as UX practitioners attempt to live with the constraints while trying to ply their own processes within an overall development environment driven solely by the agile SE method.

The traditional user-centered design process, even rapid or abridged versions, and the agile SE process are a fundamental mismatch and will always have difficulty fitting together within a project. This means that we need to synthesize an approach to allow the UX process in an integrated agile environment without compromising on essential UX needs, the topic of this section.

Here we especially acknowledge the influence of Constantine and Lockwood (2003), Beyer, Holtzblatt, and Baker (2004), Meads (2010), and Lynn Miller (2010). What we have synthesized here is also built on our experience with traditional UX methods and our broad experience in industry consulting and practice that required quicker and less costly design methods and where customers often demanded early deliverables.

19.6.1 Integrating UX into Planning

Figure 19-5 shows a scheme for integrating the UX role into the planning box of Figure 19-2.

Add some small upfront analysis (SUFA)

If we simply try to include the UX role as an add-on to the agile SE process, the entire operation would still proceed without benefit of any upfront analysis or contact with multiple people in the customer organization and with multiple users in all the key work roles. As a result, there would be no initial knowledge of requirements, users, work practice, tasks, or other

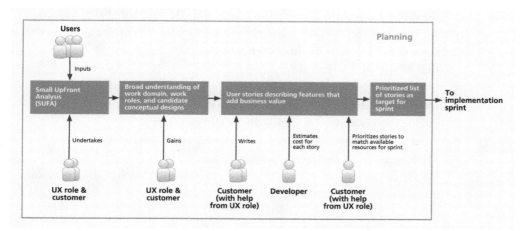

Figure 19-5
Integrating the UX role into
planning.

design-informing models. This would be crippling for any kind of UX lifecycle process.

Any serious proposal for integrating UX into planning must include an initial abbreviated form of contextual inquiry and contextual analysis, something that we call "Small UpFront Analysis" (SUFA), in the left-most box of Figure 19-5. The UX role works with the customer to perform some limited contextual inquiry and analysis (Chapters 3 and 4).

In addition, the UX person also assists the customer in other responsibilities, such as writing and prioritizing stories. These stories are now called users stories rather than customer stories because their substance came from users in the upfront analysis.

Although this begins to change the basic agile pattern, it gives the UX team more traction in bringing UX into the overall process. Interest in enhancing this kind of additional upfront analysis is gaining ground. There is some initial agreement (Beyer, Holtzblatt, & Baker, 2004; Constantine & Lockwood, 1999) on the necessity for talking with multiple customer representatives and real users to help understand the overall system and design needs.

Some (Constantine & Lockwood, 1999; Memmel, Gundelsweiler, & Reiterer, 2007) add that a measure of user and/or task modeling would be a very useful supplement in that same spirit. There is obviously a resulting loss of agility but, without these additions, the whole approach might not work for UX.

Beyer and Holtzblatt's "original" approach to upfront analysis and design is called contextual design (Beyer & Holtzblatt, 1998) and has a head start toward agile methods because it is already customer centered. They took another step toward agility with the follow-up book (Holtzblatt, Wendell, & Wood, 2005) and developed that into a true agile method in Beyer, Holtzblatt, and Baker (2004). Much of this section is based on their explication of the agile version of rapid contextual design in this latter reference.

Goals of the SUFA include:

- understand the users' work and its context
- identify key work roles, work activities, and user tasks
- model workflow and activities in the existing enterprise and system
- forge an initial high-level conceptual design
- identify selected user stories that reflect user needs in the context of their work practice

Because of the "S" in SUFA, the contextual inquiry and analysis involved must be very limited, but even the most abbreviated contextual studies can yield a great deal of understanding about the work roles and the flow model as well as some initial task modeling. By adding this SUFA we can build a good overview of the system as a framework for talking about the little pieces we will be developing in the agile method.

A broad understanding of scope and purpose of the project (second box from the left in Figure 19-5) will allow us to plan the design and implementation of a series of sprints around the tasks and functionality associated with different work roles. This SUFA has to be focused carefully so that it can occur in a very short cycle—maybe even in one week!

Even though the UX person is trained to do a SUFA and could do it alone, the customer should help with SUFA, as shown at the lower left in Figure 19-5, to be in a better position to later write user stories (next section).

User interviews and observation. Your customer will help you identify users to interview. Create a flow model on the fly and in collaboration with the customer representative. Identify all key work roles in this diagram. Annotate it with all important tasks and activities that can be deduced from the user stories.

Agile contextual inquiry can be as brief or as lengthy as desired or afforded. We suggest interviewing and observing the work practice of at least one or two people in each key work role. There is no recording and no transcript of interviews. The UX practitioners write notes by hand directly on index cards—a Constantine hallmark. Use small size, $3'' \times 5''$, index cards to discourage verbosity in the notes.

Aim toward effective user stories. We are looking for user stories to drive our small pieces of interaction design and prototyping. But what kind of user stories do we seek? Stories about work activities, roles, and tasks can still be a good way for designers to start. However, as Meads (2010) says, users are not interested in tasks per se, but are more interested in features. Following his advice, *we focus on features,* which are used to carry out related user work activities and tasks within a work context.

UX role helps customer write user stories

In the third box from the left in Figure 19-5, the UX person helps the customer write user stories. Because both roles participated in the SUFA, user story writing will be easier, faster, and more representative of real user needs. The UX role influences the customer toward creating stories based on workflows observed in the agile contextual inquiry part of SUFA.

UX role helps customer prioritize user stories

By helping the customer representative prioritize the user stories, the UX person can keep an eye on the overarching vision of user experience and a cohesive conceptual design, thereby steering the result toward an effective set of stories for an iteration.

19.6.2 Integrating UX into Sprints

In Figure 19-6 we show UX counterpart activities occurring during an agile SE sprint (Figure 19-4).

While the SE people are doing a sprint, the UX person and customer perform their own version of a sprint, which is shown in Figure 19-6. They begin by picking a story and, with the conceptual design in mind, start ideation and sketching of an interaction design to support the functionality of the user story.

The design is cast in a narrow vertical prototype for just this feature for evaluation. Often time permits only a low-fidelity (e.g., paper) prototype. If there is time the design partners make a set of wireframes to describe the

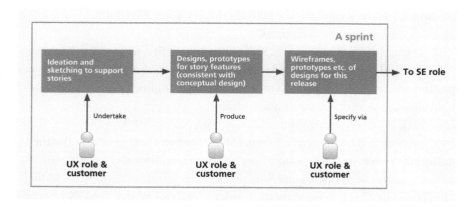

Figure 19-6

UX counterpart of an agile SE sprint.

interaction design. This feature prototype is integrated into their growing overall user interface prototype.

If there is time, the UX design partners do some user experience evaluation on this one part of the design and iterate the design accordingly. If there is even more time (unlikely in an agile environment), in the spirit of agile SE methods, the UX design partners can run this collection of all evaluations again on the whole integrated prototype to ensure that the addition of this design feature did not break the usability of any previous features.

UX practitioners submit this user interface prototype to the customer for acceptance review. Finally, the team "deploys" this small iterative interaction design "release" by sending it on to agile SE developers for coding as part of their next sprint.

19.6.3 Synchronizing the Two Agile Workflows

We have described agile SE planning and agile SE sprints, plus UX integration into planning and UX integration into sprints earlier in this chapter. But we have not yet talked about how the UX and SE teams work together and synchronize the workflow in their respective parts of the agile process.

Dove-tailed work activities

Miller (2010) proposed a "staggered" approach to parallel track agile development that featured a "criss-cross" interplay between UX activities and SE activities across multiple cycles of agile development. As Patton (2008) put in his blog, the overall approach is characterized as "work ahead, follow behind."

As Patton says, UX people on agile teams "become masters of development time travel, nimbly moving back and forth through past, present, and future development work."

Based roughly on Miller's idea, we show a scheme in Figure 19-7 for how UX people and SE people can synchronize their work via a dovetail alternation of activities across progressive iterations.

In the original agile SE approach, SE people started first with sprint 1, taking a set of stories and building a release. That worked when the only thing that was happening was implementation. Now that we are bringing in UX design and evaluation into the mix, we need a few changes.

First, the UX people need some lead time in their sprint 0, in Figure 19-7, to get the interaction designs ready for the SE people in their sprint 1. During this ramping-up sprint 0, SE people can focus on building the software infrastructure and services required to support the whole system, what Miller calls building the "high-development, low-UI features." When the UX people are done with designs for release 1, they hand them off to SE people for

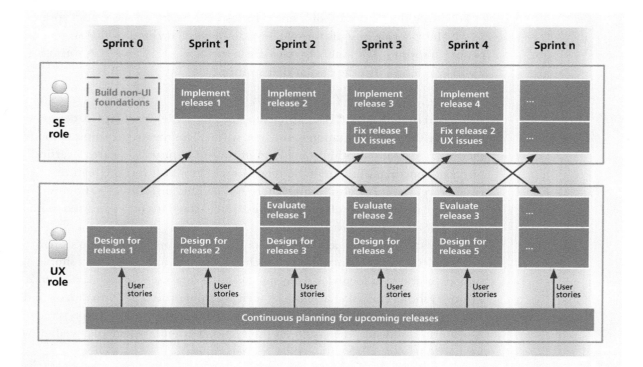

Figure 19-7

*Alternating UX and SE
workflow in an agile
process.*

implementation in sprint 1, which includes implementation of both functional stories and interaction design components for that cycle.

Previously, the team had something to release right after sprint 1, but now it takes two sprint cycles, sprint 0 and sprint 1, to get the first release out. This is just a start-up artifact and is not a problem for subsequent releases.

Not all UX design challenges are equal; sometimes there is not enough time to address UX design adequately in a given sprint. Then that design will have to evolve over the design and evaluation activities of more than one sprint. Also, sometimes in interaction design, we want to try out two variations because we are not sure, so that will have to take place over multiple sprints.

Because of the staggering or dovetailing of activities, people on each part of the team are typically working on multiple things at a time. For example, right after handing off the designs for release 1 to the SE people, the UX people start on designs for release 2 and continue doing this until the end of sprint 1 (while the SE people are coding release 1). In any given sprint, say, sprint n, the UX people are performing inquiry and planning for sprint $n + 2$, while doing interaction design (and prototyping) for sprint $n + 1$, and evaluation of the interaction design for sprint $n - 1$.

Following the "lifecycle" of a single release, release n, we see that in sprint $n - 1$, the UX role designs for release n, to be implemented by the SE people in sprint n. UX evaluates release n in sprint $n + 1$. SE fixes it in sprint $n + 2$ and re-releases it at the end of that sprint.

Prototyping and UX evaluation

At the end of each sprint, UX people must be able to deliver their UX design to SE people for implementation in the next sprint. This means they must embody their design solution within some kind of prototype, usually a narrow vertical prototype encompassing multiple related user stories for just the feature (user story) they are considering. There will be time only for a low-fidelity prototype; these days wireframes are the de facto standard for prototypes in this kind of development environment.

Perhaps an even more agile form of low-fidelity prototype is a design scenario, maybe in the form of storyboards, which can be used as an early and simple vehicle to draw out feedback from the customer and users. Kane (2003, pp. 2, Figure 1) shows how a scenario can be seen as a mini-prototype, both narrow and shallow, at the intersection between a vertical and a horizontal prototype. A scenario can distill "the system to the minimal essential elements needed for useful feedback" (Nielsen, 1994 Nielsen, 1994a).

The traditional UX process, of course, calls for extensive UX evaluation of the prototype. However, there will almost never be time to evaluate the prototype in this same sprint, but you will be able to evaluate this UX design in the next sprint.

Prototype integration

UX is all about holistic designs, and you cannot ensure that your emerging design is on track to provide such a holistic user experience unless you have a representation of the overall design and not just little pieces. Therefore, after each new feature is manifest as a prototype (e.g., wireframe), it is integrated into the growing overall user interface prototype, covering all the user stories so far and the broader UX vision. The small feature prototype drives coding but the integrated prototype helps everyone with a coherent view of the overall emerging interaction design.

The value of early delivery

As Memmel, Gundelsweiler, and Reiterer (2007) say, you have the potential to deliver design visions to customers before you even have completed requirements analysis. In contrast, with the traditional rigorous UX process, this is an amazingly early deliverable and amazingly early involvement of the customer.

Feedback for the first feature can go far beyond just that one feature and its usage. This is the first opportunity for the team to get *any* real feedback. A lot of additional things will come out of that, not specific to that feature. For example, you will get feedback on how the process is working. You will get feedback on the overall style of your design. You will hear other questions and issues that customers are thinking about that you would not have access to until much later in the fully rigorous process. Your customers may even reprioritize the story cards based on this interaction. This early feedback fits well with the agile principle of abundant communication.

Exactly what is "delivery" in an agile environment?

A stated goal of agile SE methods is to release a product every few weeks. Why would anyone want to do that? Why would customers and users put up with it? Well, if you are talking only about functional software and not the user interface, customers will love it. They get to see very early manifestations of a working system, however severely the functionality may be limited. Also, agile SE developers can actually release their small iterations of functional code even to end users, as changes in the internal code are not visible to customers or users.

However, multiple releases of the user interface, each with a changing design, are not a good thing for users, who cannot be expected to track the continuous changes. They invest in learning a user interface; so a constant flow of even small changes, even if they are improvements, will not be acceptable.

This is always a risk with an agile approach, so it is up to the UX person to mitigate these transitions by making each release an addition to the capabilities but not completely new. Users should be able to do more, but not necessarily change how they do things that are already delivered.

Continuous delivery

Delivery to customers and users is continuous but in pieces. At the end of any given sprint, call it sprint n, the customer sees a UX prototype of the upcoming release and in the next sprint, sprint $n + 1$, they see the full functional implementation of that prototype. In sprint $n + 2$, they see UX evaluation findings for that same prototype and, in sprint $n + 3$, they see the final redesign. Each of these points in time is an opportunity for the customer to give feedback on the interaction design.

Planning across iterations

Figure 19-7 shows planning in a single box at the bottom, extending across all the sprint cycles. That is to convey the idea that planning does not occur in discrete little boxes over time at just the right spot in the flow. Planning is more of an "umbrella" activity, distributed over time and is cumulative in that the process builds up a "knowledge base" founded on agile contextual inquiry with users. The planning process does not start over for the planning of each cycle.

Instead the same knowledge base is consulted, updated, and massaged, working with the original SUFA results and anything added to supplement those results. Because an overview and conceptual design are evolving in the process, this kind of UX planning brings some top-down benefits to an otherwise exclusively bottom-up process.

Communication during synchronization

This kind of interwoven development process brings with it the risk of falling apart if anything goes wrong. This intensifies the need for constant communication so that everyone remains aware of what everyone else is doing, what progress is being made by others, and what problems are being encountered.

Agile processes can be more fragile than their heavyweight counterparts. Because each part depends on the others in a tightly orchestrated overall activity, if something goes wrong in one place, there is no time to react to surprises and the whole thing can collapse like a house of cards.

Including emotional impact

How can you take emotional impact into account within an agile approach? It is more difficult to think about emotional impact within an agile approach because you do not have good ways to connect to the overall user experience for the system. You will have limited time to create a conceptual design that fosters a strong positive emotional response. You will have to manage and do as much as you can by including emotional impact as part of the small upfront analysis, in design ideation, and in evaluation.

Style guides

Maintaining a style guide throughout the UX part of an agile development process is perhaps even more important than it is in the fully rigorous process (Constantine & Lockwood, 2003). An agile style guide with the minimal design templates, motifs for visual elements, and design "patterns" (e.g., a standard design for a dialogue box) supports reuse, saves the time of reinventing common design elements, and helps ensure design consistency of look and feel across features. Your style guide can also document "best practices" as you gain experience in this agile approach.

Affordances Demystified

20

Objectives

After reading this chapter, you will:

1. Have acquired a clear understanding of the concept of affordances
2. Know and understand differences among the types of affordances in UX design
3. Know how to apply the different types of affordances together in UX design
4. Be able to identify false affordances and know how to avoid them in UX design
5. Recognize user-created affordances and their implications to design

To begin with, we gratefully acknowledge the kind permission of Taylor & Francis, Ltd. to use a paper published in *Behaviour & Information Technology* (Hartson, 2003) as the primary source of material for this chapter. This chapter is a prerequisite for the next two chapters, on the User Action Framework and design guidelines, but we hope that you find it an interesting topic on its own.

20.1 WHAT ARE AFFORDANCES?

Although a crucially important and powerful concept, the notion of "affordance," as pointed out by Norman (1999), has suffered misunderstanding and misuse (or perhaps uninformed use) by researchers and practitioners alike and in our literature. In this section we define the general concept of affordances as used in human–computer interaction (HCI) design and give more specific definitions for each of four kinds of affordance.

20.1.1 The Concept of Affordance

The relevant part of what the dictionary says about "to afford" is that it means to offer, yield, provide, give, or furnish. For example, a study window in a house may afford a fine view of the outdoors; the window helps one see that nice view. In HCI design, where we focus on helping the user, an affordance is something that *helps a user do something*. In interaction design, affordances are characteristics of user interface objects and interaction design features that help users perform tasks.

20.1.2 Definitions of the Different Kinds of Affordance

In an effort to clarify the concept of affordance and how it is used in interaction design, we have defined (Hartson, 2003) four types of affordances, each of which plays a different role in supporting users during interaction, each reflecting user processes and the kinds of actions users make in task performance. Those kinds of affordances are as follows:

- Cognitive affordances help users with their cognitive actions: thinking, deciding, learning, remembering, and knowing about things.
- Physical affordances help users with their physical actions: clicking, touching, pointing, gesturing, and moving things.
- Sensory affordances help users with their sensory actions: seeing, hearing, and feeling (and tasting and smelling) things.
- Functional affordances help users do real work (and play) and get things done, to use the system to do work.

In analysis and design, each type of affordance must be identified for what it is and considered on its own terms. Each type of affordance uses different mechanisms, corresponds to different kinds of user actions, and has different requirements for design and different implications in evaluation and problem diagnosis.

As an example to get you started, consider a button available for clicking somewhere on a user interface. Sensory affordance helps you sense (in this case, see) it. Sensory affordance can be supported in design by, for example, the color or location of the button. Cognitive affordance helps you understand the button by comprehending what the button is used for, via the meaning of its label. Physical affordance helps you click on this button, so its design support could include the size of the button or its distance from other buttons.

20.2 A LITTLE BACKGROUND

Who "invented" the concept of affordances? Of course we all know it was Donald Norman. Well, not quite. While Norman did introduce the concept to HCI, the concept itself goes back at least as far as James J. Gibson (1977, 1979), and probably further.

Gibson is a perceptual psychologist who took an "ecological" approach to perception, meaning he studied the relationship between a living being and its environment, in particular what the environment offers or affords the animal.

Gibson's affordances are the properties and objects of the environment as reckoned relative to the animal, and "the 'values' and 'meanings' of things in the environment [that] can be directly perceived" (Gibson, 1977) by the animal. In this book, human users of computer systems are the animals (are not they, though?).

Norman (1999) begins his *interactions* article by referring to Gibson's definitions of "afford" and "affordance," as well as to discussions he and Gibson have had about these concepts. Paraphrasing Gibson (1979, p. 127) within an HCI design context, affordance (as an attribute of an interaction design feature) is what that feature *offers* the user, what it *provides* or *furnishes*.

Here Gibson is talking about physical properties. Gibson gives an example of how a horizontal, flat, and rigid surface affords support for an animal for standing or walking. In his ecological view, affordance is reckoned with respect to the animal/user, which is part of the affordance relationship.

Thus, as Norman (1999) points out, Gibson sees an affordance as a physical relationship between an actor (e.g., user) and physical artifacts in the world reflecting possible actions on those artifacts. Such an affordance does not have to be visible, known, or even desirable.

Since Norman brought the term affordance into common usage in the HCI domain with his book *The Design of Everyday Things* (Norman, 1990), the term has appeared many times in the literature. However, terminology surrounding the concept of affordance in the literature has been used with more enthusiasm than knowledge, and we are left with some confusion.

Beyond Gibson and Norman, Gaver (1991) and McGrenere and Ho (2000) have influenced our thinking about affordances. Gaver (1991) sees affordances in design as a way of focusing on strengths and weaknesses of technologies with respect to the possibilities they offer to people who use them.

He extends the concepts by showing how complex actions can be described in terms of groups of affordances, sequential in time and/or nested in space, showing how affordances can be revealed over time, with successive user actions, for example, in the multiple actions of a hierarchical drop-down menu. Gaver (1991) defined his own terms somewhat differently from those of Norman or Gibson. That McGrenere and Ho (2000) also needed to calibrate their terminology against Gaver's further demonstrates the difficulty of discussing these concepts without access to a richer, more consistent vocabulary.

In most of the related literature, design of cognitive affordances (whatever they are called in a given paper) is acknowledged to be about design for the cognitive part of usability, ease of use in the form of learnability for new and intermittent users (who need the most help in knowing how to do something).

All authors who write about affordances give their own definitions of the concept, but there is scant mention of physical affordance design.

Sensory affordance is neglected even more in the literature. Most other authors include sensory affordance only implicitly and/or lumped in with cognitive affordance rather than featuring it as a separate explicit concept. Thus, when these authors talk about perceiving affordances, including Gaver's (1991) and McGrenere and Ho's (2000) phrase "perceptibility of an affordance," they are referring (in our terms) to a combination of sensing (e.g., seeing) and understanding physical affordances through sensory affordances and cognitive affordances.

Gaver refers to this same mix of affordances when he says "People perceive the environment directly in terms of its potential for action." As we explain in the next section, our use of the term "sense" has a markedly narrower orientation toward discerning via sensory inputs such as seeing and hearing.

20.3 FOUR KINDS OF AFFORDANCES IN UX DESIGN

20.3.1 Cognitive Affordance

Cognitive affordance is a design feature that helps, aids, supports, facilitates, or enables thinking, learning, understanding, and knowing about something. Cognitive affordances play starring roles in interaction design, especially for less experienced users who need help with understanding and learning.

Because of this role, cognitive affordances are among the most significant usage-centered design features in present-day interactive systems, screen based or otherwise. They are the key to answering Norman's question (1999, p. 39) on behalf of the user: "How do you know what to do?"

As a simple example, the symbol of an icon that clearly conveys its meaning could be a cognitive affordance enabling users to understand the icon in terms of the functionality behind it and the consequences of clicking on it. Another cognitive affordance might be in the form of a clear and concise button label.

Cognitive affordance is usually associated with the semantics or meaning of user interface artifacts. In this regard, cognitive affordance is used as feed forward. It is help with *a priori* knowledge, that is, knowledge about the associated functionality before selecting an object such as a button, icon, or menu choice. In short, a button label helps you in knowing about what functionality will be invoked if you click on that button.

Communication of meaning via cognitive affordance often depends on shared conventions. The symbols themselves may have no inherent meaning, but a shared convention about the meaning allows the symbol to convey that meaning.

Another use of cognitive affordance is in feedback—helping a user know what happened after a button click, for example, and execution of the corresponding system functionality. Feedback helps users in knowing whether the course of interaction has been successful so far.

20.3.2 Physical Affordance

Physical affordance is a design feature that helps, aids, supports, facilitates, or enables doing something physically. Adequate size and easy-to-access location could be physical affordance features of an interface button design enabling users to click easily on the button.

Because physical affordance has to do with physical objects, we treat active interface objects on the screen, for example, as real physical objects, as they can be on the receiving end of real physical actions (such as clicking or dragging) by users. Physical affordance is associated with the "operability" characteristics of such user interface artifacts. As many in the literature have pointed out, it is clear that a button on a screen cannot really be pressed, which is why we try to use the terminology "clicking on buttons."

Physical affordances play a starring role in interaction design for experienced or power users who have less need for elaborate cognitive affordances but whose task performance depends largely on the speed of physical actions. Design issues for physical affordances are about physical characteristics of a device or interface that afford physical manipulation. Such design issues include Fitts' law (Fitts, 1954; MacKenzie, 1992), physical disabilities and limitations, and physical characteristics of interaction devices and interaction techniques.

20.3.3 Sensory Affordance

Sensory affordance is a design feature that helps, aids, supports, facilitates, or enables user in sensing (e.g., seeing, hearing, feeling) something. Sensory affordance is associated with the "sense-ability" characteristics of user interface artifacts, especially when it is used to help the user sense (e.g., see) cognitive affordances and physical affordances. Design issues for sensory affordances include noticeability, discernibility, legibility (in the case of text), and audibility (in the case of sound) of features or devices associated with visual, auditory, haptic/tactile, or other sensations.

While cognitive affordance and physical affordance are stars of interaction design, sensory affordance plays a critical supporting role. As an example, the legibility of button label text is supported by an adequate size font and appropriate color contrast between text and background. In short, sensory affordance can be thought of as an attribute that affords cognitive affordance and physical affordance; users must be able to sense cognitive affordances and physical affordances in order for them to aid the user's cognitive and physical actions.

Why do we call it "sensory affordance" and not "perceptual affordance?" In the general context of psychology, the concepts of sensing and perception are intertwined. To avoid this association, we use the term "sensing" instead of "perception" because it excludes the component of cognition usually associated with perception (Hochberg, 1964). This allows us to separate the concepts of sensory and cognitive affordance into mostly non-overlapping meanings.

While overlapping and borderline cases are interesting to psychologists, HCI designers need to separate the concepts because design issues for user sensory actions are almost entirely orthogonal to design issues for cognitive actions. As an illustration, consider text legibility, which at a low level is about identifying shapes in displayed text as letters in the alphabet, but not about the meanings of these letters as grouped into words and sentences.

But text legibility can be an area where user perception, sensing, and cognition overlap. To make out text that is just barely or almost barely discernible, users can augment or mediate sensing with cognition, using inference and the context of words in a message to identify parts of the text that cannot be recognized by pure sensing alone. Context can make some candidate letters more likely than others. Users can recognize words in their own language more easily than words in another language or as groups of nonsense letter combinations.

In HCI, however, we seek to avoid marginal design and ensure that designs work for wide-ranging user characteristics. Therefore, we require effective design solutions for both kinds (sensory and cognitive) of affordances, each considered separately, in terms of its own characteristics. Simply put, a label in a user interface that cannot be fully discerned by the relevant user population, without reliance on cognitive augmentation, is a failed HCI design.

Thus, we wish to define sensing at a level of abstraction that eliminates these cases of borderline user performance so that HCI designers can achieve legibility, for example, beyond question for the target user community. In other words, we desire an understanding of affordance that will guide the HCI designer to attack a text legibility problem by adjusting the font size, for example, not by adjusting the wording to make it easier to deduce text displayed in a tiny font.

In our broadest view, a user's sensory experience can include gestalt, even aesthetic, aspects of object appearance and perceptual organization

(Arnheim, 1954; Koffka, 1935), such as figure–ground relationships, and might sometimes include some judgment and lexical and syntactic interpretation in the broadest spatial or auditory sense (e.g., what is this thing I am seeing?), but does not get into semantic interpretation (e.g., what does it mean?). In the context of signal processing and communications theory, this kind of sensing would be about whether messages are received correctly, but not about whether they are understood.

20.3.4 Functional Affordance

Functional affordances connect physical user actions to invoke system, or back end, functionality. Functional affordances link usability or UX to usefulness and add purpose for physical affordance. They are about higher level user enablement in the work domain and add meaning and goal orientation to design discussions.

We bring Gibson's ecological view into contextualized HCI design by including a purpose in the definition of each physical affordance, namely associated functional affordance. Putting the user and purpose of the affordance into the picture harmonizes nicely with our interaction- and user-oriented view in which *an affordance helps or aids the user in doing something.*

Yes, a user can click on an empty or inactive part of the screen, but that kind of clicking is without reference to a purpose and without the requirement or expectation that any useful reaction by the system will come of it. In the context of HCI design, a user clicks to accomplish a goal, to achieve a purpose (e.g., clicking on a user interface object, or artifact, to select it for manipulation or clicking on a button labeled "Sort" to invoke a sorting operation).

McGrenere and Ho (2000) also refer to the concept of application usefulness, something they call "affordances in software," which are at the root of supporting a connection between the dual concepts of usability and usefulness (Landauer, 1995). In an external view it is easy to see a system function as an affordance because it helps the user do something in the work domain.

This again demonstrates the need for a richer vocabulary, and conceptual framework, to take the discussion of affordances beyond user interfaces to the larger context of overall system design. We use the term *functional affordance* to denote this kind of higher level user enablement in the work domain.

20.3.5 Summary of Affordance Types

Table 20-1 contains a summary of these affordance types and their roles in interaction design.

Table 20-1

Summary of affordance types

Affordance Type	Description	Example
Cognitive affordance	Design feature that helps users in knowing something	A button label that helps users know what will happen if they click on it
Physical affordance	Design feature that helps users in doing a physical action in the interface	A button that is large enough so that users can click on it accurately
Sensory affordance	Design feature that helps users sense something (especially cognitive affordances and physical affordances)	A label font size large enough to be discerned
Functional affordance	Design feature that helps users accomplish work (i.e., usefulness of a system function)	The internal system ability to sort a series of numbers (invoked by users clicking on the Sort button)

20.4 AFFORDANCES IN INTERACTION DESIGN

20.4.1 Communication and Cultural Conventions

An important function of cognitive affordance is communication, agreement about meaning via words or symbols. Communication is exactly what makes precise wording effective as a cognitive affordance: something to help the user in knowing, for example, what to click on. We see symbols, constraints, and shared conventions as essential underlying mechanisms that make cognitive affordances work, as Norman (1999) says, as "powerful tools for the designer."

In the tradition of *The Design of Everyday Things* (Norman, 1990), we illustrate with a simple and ubiquitous non-computer device, a device for opening doors. The hardware store carries both round doorknobs and lever-type door handles. The visual design of both kinds conveys a cognitive affordance, helping users think or know about usage through the implied message their appearance gives to users: "This is what you use to open the door." The doorknob and lever handle each suggests, in its own way, the grasping and rotating required for operation.

But that message is understood only because of shared cultural conventions. There is nothing intrinsic in the appearance of a doorknob that necessarily conveys this information. On another planet, it could seem mysterious and confusing, but for us a doorknob is an excellent cognitive affordance because almost all users do share the same easily recognized cultural convention.

This "on another planet" idea led to an interesting exercise in a class of graduate students on how cultural conventions influence our perception of affordances. We handed out identical empty Coke bottles to several groups and asked them to look at the bottles, to hold and handle them, and to think about what kinds of uses the inherent affordances evoke. We wanted them to get down to Gibson's ecological level.

Students responded with the usual answers about affordances evinced by sight and touch. Visually, a Coke bottle has obvious affordances as a vessel to hold water, it can hold flowers, or it can serve as a rough volume measuring device. The heft and sturdiness sensed when held in one's hand indicate affordances to serve as a paperweight, a plumb bob on a string, or even an oddly shaped rolling pin.

Then we asked them if they had seen the movie called *The Gods Must Be Crazy*. Although this cool movie was apparently before the time of most of them, some eyebrows were raised in an "ah ha" moment. In this movie, an empty coke bottle falls out of the sky from a passing airplane and is found by a family of Bushmen in the deep Kalahari. The Kalahari Bushmen, who have never seen a bottle before, can rely on only its inherent characteristics as clues to physical affordances leading to possible uses. The perceived affordances were not influenced by cultural conventions or practice.

The Bushmen used it for a variety of tasks—to transport water, to pound soft roots and other vegetation, as an entertainment device when they figured out how to use it as a whistle, and eventually as a weapon to attack one another.

That these affordances became so apparent to the Bushmen, but might not be obvious to most people from an industrialized part of the world, indicates the impact of social experience and cultural conventions to influence, and even prejudice, one's perception of an object's affordances.

20.4.2 Cognitive Affordance as "Information in the World"

Norman characterizes a view of cognitive affordance that we share (Norman, 1999, p. 39): "When you first see something you have never seen before, how do you know what to do? The answer, I decided, was that the required information was in the world: the appearance of the device could provide the critical clues required for its proper operation." This view of cognitive affordance as information in the world to aid understanding is fundamental and resonates with the ecological view of Gibson. The attribute that communicates the use of an object is an integral part of the object. This definitely works for, say, a label on a user interface button.

20.4.3 Affordance Roles—An Alliance in Design

In most interaction designs, the four types of affordance work together, connected in the design context of a user's work environment. To accomplish work goals, the user must sense, understand, and use affordances within an interaction design.

Each kind of affordance plays a different role in the design of different attributes of the same artifact, including design of appearance, content, and manipulation characteristics to match users' needs, respectively, in the sensory, cognitive, and physical actions they make as they progress through the cycle of actions during task performance.

As Gaver (1991, p. 81) says, thinking of affordances in terms of design roles "allows us to consider affordances as properties that can be designed and analysed in their own terms." Additionally, even though the four affordance roles must be considered together in an integrated view of artifact design, these words from Gaver speak to the need to distinguish individually identifiable affordance roles.

Coming back to the example about devices for opening doors, the simplest is a round doorknob. Its brass color might be a factor in noticing or finding it as you approach the door. The familiar location and shape of a doorknob convey cognitive affordance via the implied message that it is what you use to open the door. A doorknob also affords physical grasping and rotating for door operation. Some designs, such as a lever, are considered to give better physical affordance than that of a round knob because the lever is easier to use with slippery hands or by an elbow when the hands are full. The push bar on double doors is another example of a physical affordance helpful to door users with full hands.

Sometimes the physical affordance to help a user open a door is provided by the door itself; people can open some swinging doors by just pushing on the door. In such cases, designers often help users by installing, for example, a brass plate to show that one should push and where to push. Even though this plate might help avoid handprints on the door, it is a cognitive affordance and not a real physical affordance because it adds nothing to the door itself to help the user in the physical part of the pushing action. Sometimes the word "push" is engraved in the plate to augment the clarity of meaning as a cognitive affordance.

Similarly, sometimes the user of a swinging door must open it by pulling. The door itself does not usually offer sufficient physical affordance for the pulling action so a pull handle is added. A pull handle offers both cognitive and physical affordance, providing a physical means for pulling as well as a visual indication that pulling is required.

As an example of how the concepts might guide HCI designers, suppose the need arises in an interaction design for a button to give the user access to a certain application feature or functionality. The designer would do well to begin by asking if the intended functionality, the functional affordance, is appropriate and useful to the user. Further interaction design questions are moot until this is resolved positively.

The designer is then guided to support cognitive affordance in the button design, to advertise the purpose of the button by ensuring, for example, that its meaning (in terms of a task-oriented view of its underlying functionality) is clearly, unambiguously, and completely expressed in the label wording, to help the user know when it is appropriate to click on the button while performing a task. Then, the designer is asked to consider sensory affordance in support of cognitive affordance in the button design, requiring an appropriate label font size and color contrast, for example, to help the user discern the label text to read it.

The designer is next led to consider how physical affordance is to be supported in the button design. For example, the designer should ensure that the button is large enough to click on it easily to accomplish a step in a task. Designers should try to locate the button near other artifacts used in the same and related tasks to minimize mouse movement between task actions. But also designers should locate each button far enough away from other, non-related, user interface objects to avoid clicking on them erroneously.

Finally, the designer is guided to consider sensory affordance in support of physical affordance in the button design by ensuring that the user notices the button so that it can be clicked. For example, the button must be a color, size, and shape that make it noticeable and must be located in the screen layout so that it is near enough to the user's focus of attention. If the artifact is a feedback message, it also requires attention to sensory affordance (e.g., to notice the feedback), cognitive affordance (e.g., to understand what the message says about a system outcome), and physical affordance (e.g., to click on a button to dismiss the message box).

In sum, the concept of affordance does not offer a complete prescriptive approach to interaction design but does suggest the value of considering all four affordance roles together in the design of an interaction artifact by asking (not necessarily always in this order):

- Is the functionality to which this interaction or artifact gives access useful in achieving user goals through task performance (functional affordance, or purpose of physical affordance)?
- Does the design include clear, understandable cues about how to use the artifact (cognitive affordance) or about system outcomes if the artifact is a feedback message?
- Can users easily sense visual (or other) cues about artifact operation (sensory affordance in support of cognitive affordance)?
- Is the artifact easy to manipulate by all users in the target user classes (physical affordance)?
- Can users easily sense the artifact for manipulation (sensory affordance in support of physical affordance)?

Considering one affordance role but ignoring another is likely to result in a flawed design. For example, if the wording for a feedback message is carefully crafted to be clear, complete, and helpful (good cognitive affordance), but users do not notice the message because it is displayed out of the users' focus of attention (poor sensory affordance) or users cannot read it because the font is too small, the net design is ineffective. A powerful drag-and-drop mechanism may offer good physical and functional affordance for opening files, but lack of a sufficient cognitive affordance to show how it works could mean that most users will not use it.

Another example of a way that cognitive affordance and physical affordance work together in interaction design can also be seen in the context of designing constraints for error avoidance. "Graying out" menu items or button labels to show that inappropriate choices are unavailable at a given point within a task is a simple, but effective, error avoidance design technique.

This kind of cognitive affordance presents a logical constraint to the user, showing visually that this choice can be eliminated from possibilities being considered at this point. In that sense, the grayed-out label is a cognitive affordance on its own, quite different from the cognitive affordance offered by the label when it is not grayed out.

If cognitive and physical affordances are connected in the design, a grayed-out button or menu choice also indicates a physical constraint in that the physical and functional affordance usually offered by the menu item or button to access corresponding functionality is disabled so that a persistent user who clicks on the grayed-out choice anyway cannot cause harm.

Because these two aspects of graying-out work together so well, many people think of them as a single concept, but the connection of these dual aspects is important.

20.5 FALSE COGNITIVE AFFORDANCES MISINFORM AND MISLEAD

Because of the power of cognitive affordances to influence users, misuse of cognitive affordances in design can be a force *against* usability and user experience. When cognitive affordances do not telegraph physical affordances, it is not helpful.

Worse yet, when cognitive affordances falsely telegraph physical affordances, it is worse than not helping; it leads users directly to errors. Gibson calls this "misinformation in affordances"; for example, as conveyed by a glass door that appears to be an opening but does not afford passage. Draper and Barton (1993) call these "affordance bugs."

Sometimes a door has both a push plate and a pull handle as cognitive affordances in its design. The user sees this combination of cognitive affordances as an indication that either pushing or pulling can operate this as a swinging door. When the door is installed or constrained so that it can swing in only one direction, however, the push plate and pull handle introduce conflicting information or misinformation in the cognitive affordances that interfere with the design as a connection to physical affordances.

We know of a door with a push plate and a pull handle that was installed or latched so that it could only be pushed. A "push" sign had been added, perhaps to counter the false cognitive affordance of the pull handle. The label, however, was not always enough to overcome the power of the pull handle as a cognitive affordance; we observed some people still grab the handle and attempt to pull the door open.

Figure 20-1 contains a photograph of a door sign in a local store that is confusing because of the conflicts among its cognitive affordances.

This sign is on the inside of the door. The explanation from a clerk in the store was that it really means to enter only from the outside and not to go through the door from the inside. One can only nod and sigh. They

Figure 20-1

A door with a confusing sign containing conflicting cognitive affordances.

were probably reusing an available design object, the "Do Not Enter" sign, instead of tailoring a sign more specific to the usage situation. The resulting mashup was nonsense.

Another example of a false cognitive affordance showed up in a letter received recently from an insurance company. There was a form at the bottom to fill out and return, with this line appearing just above the form, as seen in Figure 20-2.

-------------------- Do not detach --------------------

Figure 20-2

False cognitive affordances in a form letter that looks like an affordance to cut.

Because that dashed line looked so much like the usual "Cut on this line to detach" cognitive affordance, one might easily detach the form before realizing that the customer information above would be lost. A better design might simply omit this warning because, without it, the typical user would not even think of ripping the paper.

Examples of false cognitive affordances in user interfaces abound. A common example is seen in Web page links that look like buttons, but do not behave like buttons. The gray background of the links in the top menu bar of a digital library Website,

| Simple Search | Advanced Search | Browse | Register | Help |

Figure 20-3

False cognitive affordances in a menu bar with links that look like buttons.

Figure 20-3, makes them seem like buttons. A user might click on the background, assuming it is part of a button, and not get any result. Because the "button" is actually just a hyperlink, it requires clicking exactly on the text.

Below-the-fold issues on Web pages can be compounded by having a horizontal line on a page that happens to fall at the bottom of a screen. Users see the line, a false affordance, and assume falsely that it is the bottom of the page and so do not scroll, missing possibly vital information below.

Sometimes a false cognitive affordance arises from deliberate abuse of a shared convention to deceive the user. Some designers of pop-up advertisements "booby trap" the "X" box in the upper right-hand corner of the pop-up window, making it a link to launch one or more new pop-ups when users click on the "X", trapping users into seeing more pop-up ads when their intention clearly was to close the window.

Figure 20-4

Radio switch with mixed affordances.

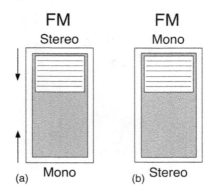

As another example, consider a radio with the slider switch, sketched in Figure 20-4a, for selecting between stereo and monaural FM reception. The names for the switch positions (Stereo, Mono) are a good match to the user's model, but the arrows showing which way to slide the switch are unnecessary and introduce confusion when combined with the labels.

The design has mixed cognitive affordances: the names of the modes at the top and bottom of the switch are such a strong cognitive affordance for the user that they conflict with the arrows.

The arrows in Figure 20-4a call for moving the switch up to get monaural reception and down to get stereo. At first glance, however, it looks as though the up position is for stereo (toward the "stereo" label) and down is for monaural, but the arrows make the meaning exactly the opposite. The names alone, as shown in Figure 20-4b, are the more normal and natural way to label the switch.

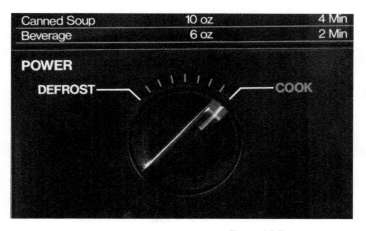

As another example, Figure 20-5 is a photo of part of the front of an old microwave. The dial marks between the settings for "Defrost" and "Cook" seem to indicate a range of possible settings but, in fact, it is a binary choice: either "Defrost" or "Cook" but nothing in between. The designer could not resist the temptation to fill in the space between these choices with misleading "design details" that are false affordances.

Figure 20-5
Useless dial marks between power settings on a microwave.

As a further example, in Figure 20-6, we see a sign that has made the rounds on the Internet, mainly because it is so funny. It is an example of a cognitive affordance that is misleading.

20.6 USER-CREATED AFFORDANCES AS A WAKE-UP CALL TO DESIGNERS

If a device in the everyday world does not suit the user, we will frequently see the user modify the apparatus, briefly and unknowingly switching to the role of designer. We have all seen the little cognitive or physical affordances added to devices by users—Post-it™ notes added to a computer monitor or keyboard or a better grip taped to the handle of something. These trails of user-created artifacts blazed in the wake of spontaneous formative evaluation in the process of day-to-day usage are like wake-up messages, telling designers what the users think they missed in the design.

Figure 20-6
Misdirection in a cognitive affordance.

A most common example of trails (literally) of user-made artifacts is seen in the paths worn by people as they walk. Sidewalk designers usually like to make the sidewalk patterns regular, symmetric, and rectilinear. However, the most efficient paths for people getting from one place to the other are often less tidy but more direct. Wear patterns in the grass show where people need or want to walk and, thus, where the sidewalks should have been located. The rare and creative sidewalk designer will wait until seeing the worn paths, employing the user-made artifacts as clues to drive the design.

Sometimes the affordances are already there but they are not effective. As Gaver says, when affordances suggest actions different from the way something is designed, errors are common and signs are necessary. The signs are artifacts, added because the designs themselves did not carry sufficient cognitive affordance.

We have all seen the cobbled design modifications to everyday things, such as an explanation written on, an important feature highlighted with a circle or a bright color, a feature (e.g., instructions) moved to a location where it is more likely to be seen. Users add words or pictures to mechanisms to explain how to operate them, enhancing cognitive affordance.

Neither do physical affordances escape these design lessons from users. You see added padding to prevent bruised knuckles. A farmer has a larger handle welded onto a tractor implement, enhancing physical affordance of the factory-made handle and its inadequate leverage. User-created artifacts also extend to sensory affordances.

For example, a homeowner replaces the street number sign on her house with a larger one, making it easier to see. Such user-made artifacts are a variation on the "user-derived interfaces" theme of Good et al. (1984), through which designers, after observing users perform tasks in their own way, modified interaction designs so that the design would have worked for those users.

Example:

In Figure 20-7, a photo of a glass door in a convenience store, we show an example of a user-added cognitive affordance. The glass and stainless steel

Figure 20-7

Glass door with a user-added cognitive affordance (arrow) indicating proper operation.

design is elegant: the perfectly symmetric layout and virtually unnoticeable hinges contribute to the uncluttered aesthetic appearance, but these same attributes work against cognitive affordance for its operation.

The storeowner noticed many people unsure about which side of the stainless steel bar to push or pull to open the door, often trying the wrong side first. To help his customers with what should have been an easy task in the first place, he glued a bright yellow cardboard arrow to the glass, pointing out the correct place to operate the door.

Example:

The icons shown in Figure 20-8 are for lightness and darkness settings on a home office copier/printer, icons with ambiguous meanings. The icon for lighter copies showed more white but the white can be interpreted as part of the copy and it seems more dense than the icon for darker copies so the user had to add his own label, as you can see in the figure.

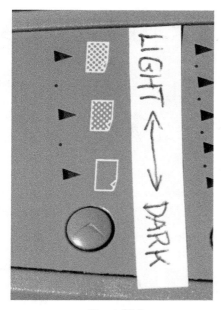

Figure 20-8

A user-created cognitive affordance explaining copier darkness settings.

These trails of often inelegant but usually effective artifacts added by frustrated users leave a record of affordance improvements that designers should consider for all their users. Perhaps if designers of the everyday things that Norman (1990) discusses had included usability testing in the field, they would have found these problems before the products went to market.

In the software world, most applications have only very limited capabilities for users to set their preferences. Would not it be much nicer for software users if they could modify interaction designs as easily as applying a little duct tape, a Post-it, or extra paint here and there?

In Figure 20-9 we show how a car owner created an artifact to replace an inadequate physical affordance—a built-in drink holder that was too small and too flimsy for today's super-sized drinks.

Figure 20-9

A user-made automobile cup-holder artifact, used with permission from Roundel *magazine, BMW Car Club of America, Inc. (Howarth, 2002).*

During one trip, the user improvised with a shoe, resulting in this interesting example of a user-installed artifact.

As an example, consider a desktop printer used occasionally to print a letter on a single sheet of letterhead stationery. Inserting the stationery on top of the existing plain paper supply in the printer does this rather easily. The only problem is that it is not easy to determine the correct orientation of the sheet to be inserted because:

Figure 20-10

A user-created cognitive affordance to help users know how to insert blank letterhead stationery.

- there is no clear mental model of how the sheet travels through in the interior mechanism of the printer
- printers can vary in this configuration
- the design of the printer itself gives no cognitive affordance for loading a single sheet of letterhead

Thus, the user attached his own white adhesive label, shown in Figure 20-10, that says "Stationery: upside down, face up," adding yet another user-created artifact attesting to inadequate design. As Norman (1990, p. 9) says, "When simple things need pictures, labels, or instructions, the design has failed."

As you know, the world is full of examples of user-created cognitive affordances, attesting to the need for better design for everyone. As another example here, in Figure 20-11 we show a road sign at a country road corner in Maine.

We were looking for the campground and the sign confirmed that we were close, but we were not sure which way to turn to get there. Then we saw the arrow that someone else had added on the post to the left of the sign, which helped us complete our task. It was also an indication that we were not the first to encounter this UX problem.

Figure 20-11

A user-created cognitive affordance added to a roadside sign; see arrow on post to left of the sign.

20.7 EMOTIONAL AFFORDANCES

Because of the importance of emotional impact as part of the user experience, we see the possibility of a new type of affordance—an emotional affordance. We suggest the value of considering emotional affordances in interaction design,

affordances that help lead users to a positive emotional response. This means features or design elements that make an emotional connection with the user. These will include design features that connect to our subconscious and intuitive appreciation of fun, aesthetics, and challenges to growth.

This new kind of affordance plays well into the original Gibson ecological view of affordances that are about the relationship between a living being and its environment. This is just what we are talking about with respect to emotional impact, especially phenomenological aspects. Gibson's affordances are about values and meanings that can be perceived directly in the environment.

Apple products are bristling with emotional affordances, and it is an operational concept in the automobile design world. The mobile world is trying to leverage emotional affordances to attract customers. Let us work together to make this a new kind of affordance in full standing with the others.

Emotional Impact

Emotional impact is the affective component of user experience that influences user feelings. Emotional impact includes such effects as pleasure, fun, joy of use, aesthetics, desirability, pleasure, novelty, originality, sensations, coolness, engagement, novelty, and appeal and can involve deeper emotional factors such as self-expression, self-identity, a feeling of contribution to the world, and pride of ownership.

The Interaction Cycle and the User Action Framework

21

Objectives

After reading this chapter, you will:

1. Understand Norman's stages-of-action model of interaction
2. Understand the gulf of execution and the gulf of evaluation and their importance in interaction design
3. Understand the basic concepts of the Interaction Cycle and the User Action Framework (UAF)
4. Know the stages of user actions within the Interaction Cycle
5. Appreciate the role of affordances within the UAF
6. Appreciate the practical value of the UAF

21.1 INTRODUCTION

21.1.1 Interaction Cycle and User Action Framework (UAF)

The Interaction Cycle is our adaptation of Norman's "stages-of-action" model (Norman, 1986) that characterizes sequences of user actions typically occurring in interaction between a human user and almost any kind of machine. The User Action Framework (Andre et al., 2001) is a structured knowledge base containing information about UX design, concepts, and issues.

Within each part of the UAF, the knowledge base is organized by immediate user intentions involving sensory, cognitive, or physical actions. Below that level the organization follows principles and guidelines and becomes more detailed and more particularized to specific design situations as one goes deeper into the structure.

To clarify the distinction, the Interaction Cycle is a representation of user interaction sequences and the User Action Framework is a knowledge base of interaction design concepts, the top level of which is organized as the stages of the Interaction Cycle.

21.1.2 Need for a Theory-Based Conceptual Framework

As Gray and Salzman (1998, p. 241) have noted, "To the naïve observer it might seem obvious that the field of HCI would have a set of common categories with which to discuss one of its most basic concepts: Usability. We do not. Instead we have a hodgepodge collection of *do-it-yourself* categories and various collections of *rules-of-thumb*."

As Gray and Salzman (1998) continue, "Developing a common categorization scheme, preferably one grounded in theory, would allow us to compare types of usability problems across different types of software and interfaces." We believe that the Interaction Cycle and User Action Framework help meet this need. They are an attempt to provide UX practitioners with a way to frame design issues and UX problem data within the structure of how designs support user actions and intentions.

As Lohse et al. (1994) state, "Classification lies at the heart of every scientific field. Classifications structure domains of systematic inquiry and provide concepts for developing theories to identify anomalies and to predict future research needs." The UAF is such a classification structure for UX design concepts, issues, and principles, designed to:

- Give structure to the large number of interaction design principles, issues, and concepts
- Offer a more standardized vocabulary for UX practitioners in discussing interaction design situations and UX problems
- Provide the basis for more thorough and accurate UX problem analysis and diagnosis
- Foster precision and completeness of UX problem reports based on essential distinguishing characteristics

Although we include a few examples of design and UX problem issues to illustrate aspects and categories of the UAF in this chapter, the bulk of such examples appear with the design guidelines (Chapter 22), organized on the UAF structure.

21.2 THE INTERACTION CYCLE

21.2.1 Norman's Stages-of-Action Model of Interaction

Norman's stages-of-action model, illustrated in Figure 21-1, shows a generic view of a typical sequence of user actions as a user interacts with almost any kind of machine.

The stages of action naturally divide into three major kinds of user activity. On the execution (Figure 21-1, left) side, the user typically begins at the top of the figure by establishing a goal, decomposing goals into tasks and intentions, and mapping intentions to action sequence specifications. The user manipulates system controls by executing the physical actions (Figure 21-1, bottom left), which cause internal system state changes (outcomes) in the world (the system) at the bottom of the figure.

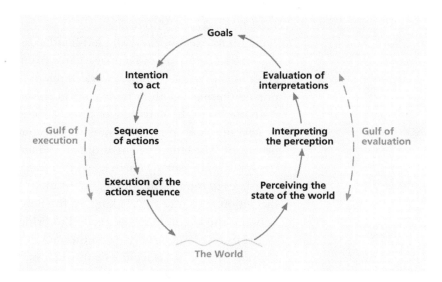

Figure 21-1
Norman's (1990) stages-of-action model, adapted with permission.

On the evaluation (Figure 21-1, right) side, users perceive, interpret, and evaluate the outcomes with respect to goals and intentions through perceiving the system state by sensing feedback from the system (state changes in "the world" or the system). Interaction success is evaluated by comparing outcomes with the original goals. The interaction is successful if the actions in the cycle so far have brought the user closer to the goals.

Norman's model, along with the structure of the analytic evaluation method called the cognitive walkthrough (Lewis et al., 1990), had an essential influence on our Interaction Cycle. Both ask questions about whether the user can determine what to do with the system to achieve a goal in the work domain, how to do it in terms of user actions, how easily the user can perform the required physical actions, and (to a lesser extent in the cognitive walkthrough method) how well the user can tell whether the actions were successful in moving toward task completion.

21.2.2 Gulfs between User and System

Originally conceived by Hutchins, Hollan, and Norman (1986), the gulfs of execution and evaluation were described further by Norman (1986). The two gulfs represent places where interaction can be most difficult for users and where designers need to pay special attention to designing to help users. In the gulf of execution, users need help in knowing what actions to make on what objects. In the gulf of evaluation, users need help in knowing whether their actions had the expected outcomes.

The gulf of execution

The gulf of execution, on the left-hand side of the stages-of-action model in Figure 21-1, is a kind of language gap—from user to system. The user thinks of goals in the language of the work domain. In order to act upon the system to pursue these goals, their intentions in the work domain language must be translated into the language of physical actions and the physical system.

As a simple example, consider a user composing a letter with a word processor. The letter is a work domain element, and the word processor is part of the system. The work domain goal of "creating a permanent record of the letter" translates to the system domain intention of "saving the file," which translates to the action sequence of "clicking on the Save icon." A mapping or translation between the two domains is needed to bridge the gulf.

Let us revisit the example of a thermostat on a furnace from Chapter 8. Suppose that a user is feeling chilly while sitting at home. The user formulates a simple goal, expressed in the language of the work domain (in this case the daily living domain), "to feel warmer." To meet this goal, something must happen in the physical system domain. The ignition function and air blower, for example, of the furnace must be activated. To achieve this outcome in the physical domain, the user must translate the work domain goal into an action sequence in the physical (system) domain, namely to set the thermostat to the desired temperature.

The gulf of execution lies between the user knowing the effect that is desired and what to do to the system to make it happen. In this example, there is a cognitive disconnect for the user in that the physical variables to be controlled (burning fuel and blowing air) are not the ones the user cares about (being warm). The gulf of execution can be bridged from either direction—from the user and/or from the system. Bridging from the user's side means teaching the user about what has to happen in the system to achieve goals in the work domain. Bridging from the system's side means building in help to support the user by hiding the need for translation, keeping the problem couched in work domain language. The thermostat does a little of each—its operation depends on a shared knowledge of how thermostats work but it also shows a way to set the temperature visually.

To avoid having to train all users, the interaction designer can take responsibility to bridge the gulf of execution from the system's side by an effective conceptual design to help the user form a correct mental model. Failure of the interaction design to bridge the gulf of execution will be evidenced in observations of hesitation or task blockage *before* a user action because the user does not know what action to take or cannot predict the consequences of taking an action.

In the thermostat example the gap is not very large, but this next example is a definitive illustration of the language differences between the work domain and the physical system. This example is about a toaster that we observed at a hotel brunch buffet. Users put bread on the input side of a conveyor belt going into the toaster system. Inside were overhead heating coils and the bread came out the other end as toast.

The machine had a single control, a knob labeled Speed with additional labels for Faster (clockwise rotation of the knob) and Slower (counterclockwise rotation). A slower moving belt makes darker toast because the bread is under the heating coils longer; faster movement means lighter toast. Even though this concept is simple, there was a distinct language gulf and it led to a bit of confusion and discussion on the part of users we observed. The concept of speed somehow just did not match their mental model of toast making. We even heard one person ask "Why do we have a knob to control toaster speed? Why would anyone want to wait to make toast slowly when they could get it faster?" The knob had been labeled with the language of the system's physical control domain.

Indeed, the knob did make the belt move faster or slower. But the user does not really care about the physics of the system domain; the user is living in the work domain of making toast. In that domain, the system control terms translate to "lighter" and "darker." These terms would have made a much more effective design for knob labels by helping bridge the gulf of execution from the system toward the user.

The gulf of evaluation

The gulf of evaluation, on the right side of the stages-of-action model in Figure 21-1, is the same kind of language gap, only in the other direction. The ability of users to assess outcomes of their actions depends on how well the interaction design supports their comprehension of the system state through their understanding of system feedback.

System state is a function of internal system variables, and it is the job of the interaction designer who creates the display of system feedback to bridge the gulf by translating a description of system state into the language of the user's work domain so that outcomes can be compared with the goals and intentions to assess the success of the interaction.

Failure of the interaction design to bridge the gulf of evaluation will be evidenced in observations of hesitation or task blockage *after* a user action because the user does not understand feedback and does not fully know what happened as a result of the action.

21.2.3 From Norman's Model to Our Interaction Cycle

We adapted and extended Norman's theory of action model of Figure 21-1 into what we call the *Interaction Cycle*, which is also a model of user actions that occur in typical sequences of interaction between a human user and a machine.

Partitioning the model

Because the early part of Norman's execution side was about planning of goals and intentions, we call it the *planning* part of the cycle. Planning includes formulating goal and task hierarchies, as well as decomposition and identification of specific intentions.

Planning is followed by formulation of the specific actions (on the system) to carry out each intention, a cognitive action we call *translation*. Because of the special importance to the interaction designer of describing action and the special importance to the user of knowing these actions, we made translation a separate part of the Interaction Cycle.

Norman's "execution of the action sequence" component maps directly into what we call the *physical actions* part of the Interaction Cycle. Because Norman's evaluation side is where users assess the outcome of each physical action based on system feedback, we call it the *assessment* part.

Adding outcomes and system response

Finally, we added the concepts of *outcomes* and a system response, resulting in the mapping to the Interaction Cycle as shown in Figure 21-2. Outcomes is represented as a "floating" sector between physical actions and assessment in the Interaction Cycle because the Interaction Cycle is about user interaction and what happens in outcomes is entirely internal to the system and not part of what the user sees or does. The system response, which includes all system feedback and which occurs at the beginning of and as an input to the assessment part, tells users about the outcomes.

The resulting Interaction Cycle

We abstracted Norman's stages into the basic kinds of user activities within our Interaction Cycle, as shown in Figure 21-2.

The importance of translation to the Interaction Cycle and its significance in design for a high-quality user experience is, in fact, so great that we made the relative sizes of the "wedges" of the Interaction Cycle parts represent the weight of this importance visually.

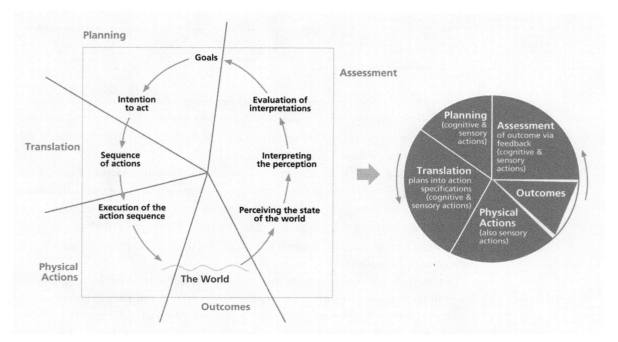

Figure 21-2

Transition from Norman's model to our Interaction Cycle.

Example: Creating a Business Report as a Task within the Interaction Cycle

Let us say that the task of creating a quarterly report to management on the financial status of a company breaks down into these basic steps:

- Calculate monthly profits for last quarter
- Write summary, including graphs, to show company performance
- Create table of contents
- Print the report

In this kind of task decomposition it is common that some steps are more or less granular than others, meaning that some steps will decompose into more sub-steps and more details than others. As an example, Step 1 might decompose into these sub-steps:

- Open spreadsheet program
- Call accounting department and ask for numbers for each month

- Create column headers in spreadsheet for expenses and revenues in each product category
- Compute profits

The first step here, to open a spreadsheet program, might correspond to a simple pass through the Interaction Cycle. The second step is a non-system task that interrupts the workflow temporarily. The third and fourth steps could take several passes through the Interaction Cycle.

Let us look at the "Print report" task step within the Interaction Cycle. The first intention for this task is the "getting started intention"; the user intends to invoke the print function, taking the task from the work domain into the computer domain. In this particular case, the user does not do further planning at this point, expecting the feedback from acting on this intention to lead to the next natural intention.

To translate this first intention into an action specification in the language of the actions and objects within the computer interface, the user draws on experiential knowledge and/or the cognitive affordances (Chapter 20) provided by display of the Print choice in the File menu to create the action specification to select "Print...". A more experienced user might translate the intention subconsciously or automatically to the short-cut actions of typing "Ctrl-P" or clicking on the Print icon.

The user then carries out this action specification by doing the corresponding physical action, the actual clicking on the Print menu choice. The system accepts the menu choice, changes state internally (the outcomes of the action), and displays the Print dialogue box as feedback. The user sees the feedback and uses it for assessment of the outcome so far. Because the dialogue box makes sense to the user at this point in the interaction, the outcome is considered to be favorable, that is, leading to accomplishment of the user's intention and indicating successful planning and action so far.

21.2.4 Cooperative User-System Task Performance within the Interaction Cycle

Primary tasks

Primary tasks are tasks that have direct work-related goals. The task in the previous example of creating a business report is a primary task. Primary tasks can be user initiated or initiated by the environment, the system, or other users. Primary tasks usually represent simple, linear paths through the Interaction Cycle.

User-initiated tasks. The usual linear path of user-system turn taking going counterclockwise around the Interaction Cycle represents a user-initiated task because it starts with user planning and translation.

Tasks initiated by environment, system, or other users. When a user task is initiated by events that occur outside that user's Interaction Cycle, the user actions become reactive. The user's cycle of interaction begins at the outcomes part, followed by the user sensing the subsequent system response in a feedback output display and thereafter reacting to it.

Path variations in the Interaction Cycle

For all but the simplest tasks, interaction can take alternative, possibly nonlinear, paths. Although user-initiated tasks usually begin with some kind of planning, Norman (1986) emphasizes that interaction does not necessarily follow a simple cycle of actions. Some activities will appear out of order or be omitted or repeated. In addition, the user's interaction process can flow around the Interaction Cycle at almost any level of task/action granularity.

Multiuser tasks. When the Interaction Cycles of two or more users interleave in a cooperative work environment, one user will enter inputs through physical actions (Figure 21-3) and another user will assess (sense, interpret, and evaluate)

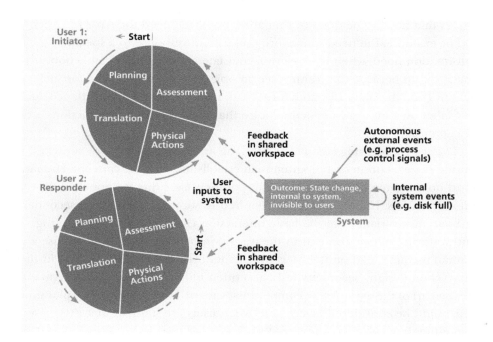

Figure 21-3

Multiuser interaction, system events, and asynchronous external events within multiple Interaction Cycles.

the system response, as viewed in a shared workspace, revealing system outcomes due to the first user's actions. For the user who initiated the exchange, the cycle begins with planning, but for the other users, interaction begins by sensing the system response and goes through assessment of what happened before it becomes that second user's turn for planning for the next round of interaction.

Secondary tasks, intention shifts, and stacking

Secondary tasks and intention shifts. Kaur, Maiden, and Sutcliffe (1999), who based an inspection method primarily for virtual environment applications on Norman's stages of action, recognized the need to interrupt primary work-oriented tasks with secondary tasks to accommodate intention shifts, exploration, information seeking, and error handling. Kaur, Maiden, and Sutcliffe (1999) created different and separate kinds of Interaction Cycles for these cases, but from our perspective, these cases are just variations in flow through the same Interaction Cycle.

Secondary tasks are "overhead" tasks in that the goals are less directly related to the work domain and usually oriented more toward dealing with the computer as an artifact, such as error recovery or learning about the interface. Secondary tasks often stem from changes of plans or intention shifts that arise during task performance; something happens that reminds the user of other things that need to be done or that arise out of the need for error recovery.

For example, the need to explore can arise in response to a specific information need, when users cannot translate an intention to an action specification because they cannot see an object that is appropriate for such an action. Then they have to search for such an object or cognitive affordance, such as a label on a button or a menu choice that matches the desired action (Chapter 20).

Stacking and restoring task context. Stacking and restoring of work context during the execution of a program is an established software concept. Humans must do the same during the execution of their tasks due to spontaneous intention shifts. Interaction Cycles required to support primary and secondary tasks are just variations of the basic Interaction Cycle. However, the storing and restoring of task contexts in the transition between such tasks impose a human memory load on the user, which could require explicit support in the interaction design. Secondary tasks also often require considerable judgment on the part of the user when it comes to assessment. For example, an exploration task might be considered "successful" when users are satisfied that they have had enough or get tired and give it up.

Example of stacking due to intention shift. To use the previous example of creating a business report to illustrate stacking due to a spontaneous intention shift, suppose the user has finished the task step "Print the report" and is ready to move on. However, upon looking at the printed report, the user does not like the way it turned out and decides to reformat the report. The user has to take some time to go learn more about how to format it better. The printing task is stacked temporarily while the user takes up the information-seeking task.

Such a change of plan causes an interruption in the task flow and normal task planning, requiring the user mentally to "stack" the current goal, task, and/or intention while tending to the interrupting task, as shown in Figure 21-4. As the primary task is suspended in mid-cycle, the user starts a new Interaction Cycle at planning for the secondary task. Eventually the user can unstack each goal and task successively and return to the main task.

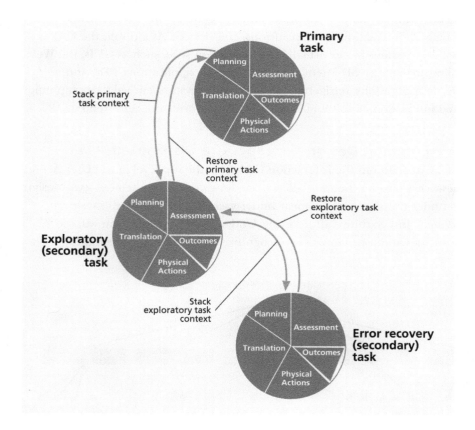

Figure 21-4

Stacking and returning to Interaction Cycle task context instances.

21.3 THE USER ACTION FRAMEWORK—ADDING A STRUCTURED KNOWLEDGE BASE TO THE INTERACTION CYCLE

21.3.1 From the Interaction Cycle to the User Action Framework

As shown in Figure 21-5, we use stages of the Interaction Cycle as the high-level organizing scheme of the UAF. The UAF is a hierarchically structured, interaction style-independent and platform-independent, knowledge base of UX principles, issues, and concepts. The UAF is focused on interaction designs and how they support and affect the user during interaction for task performance as the user makes cognitive, physical, or sensory actions in each part of the Interaction Cycle.

21.3.2 Interaction Style and Device Independent

The Interaction Cycle was an ideal starting point for the UAF because it is a model of sequences of sensory, cognitive, and physical actions users make when interacting with any kind of machine, and it is general enough to include potentially all interaction styles, platforms, and devices. As a result, the UAF is applicable or extensible to virtually any interaction style, such as GUIs, the Web, virtual environments, 3D interaction, collaborative applications, PDA and cellphone applications, refrigerators, ATMs, cars, elevators, embedded computing, situated interaction, and interaction styles on platforms not yet invented.

21.3.3 Common Design Concepts Are Distributed

Figure 21-5

Basic kinds of user actions in the Interaction Cycle as the top-level UAF structure.

The stage of action in the Interaction Cycle is at the top level of the User Action Framework. Consider the translation stage, for example. At the next level, design issues under translation will appear under various attributes such as sensory affordances and cognitive affordances. Under sensory actions, you will see various issues about presentation of cognitive affordances for translation, such

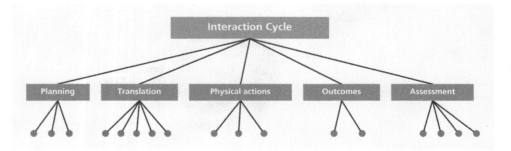

as visibility, noticeability, and legibility. Under cognitive actions you will see issues about cognitive affordances, such as clarity of meaning and precise wording.

Eventually, at lower levels, you will see that common UX design issues such as consistency, simplicity, the user's language, and concise and clear use of language are distributed with lots of overlap and sharing throughout the structure where they are applied to each of the various kinds of interaction situations. For example, an issue such as clarity of expression (precise use of language) can show up in its own way in planning, translation, and assessment. This allows the designer, or evaluator, to focus on how the concepts apply specifically in helping the user at each stage of the Interaction Cycle, for example, how precise use of wording applies to either the label of a button used to exit a dialogue box or the wording of an error message.

21.3.4 Completeness

We have tried to make the UAF as complete as possible. As more and more real-world UX data were fitted into the UAF, the structure grew with new categories and subcategories, representing an increasingly broader scope of UX and interaction design concepts. The UAF converged and stabilized over its several years of development so that, as we continue to analyze new UX problems and their causes, additions of new concepts to the UAF are becoming more and more rare.

However, absolute completeness is neither feasible nor necessary. We expect there will always be occasional additions, and the UAF is designed explicitly for long-term extensibility and maintainability. In fact, the UAF structure is "self extensible" in the sense that, if a new category is necessary, a search of the UAF structure for that category will identify where it *should* be located.

21.4 INTERACTION CYCLE AND USER ACTION FRAMEWORK CONTENT CATEGORIES

Here we give just an overview of top-level UAF categories, the content for each is stated abstractly in terms of UX design concepts and issues. In practice, these concepts can be used in several ways, including as a learning tool (students learn the concept), a design guideline (an imperative statement), in analytic evaluation (as a question about whether a particular part of a design supports the concept), and as a diagnostic tool (as a question about whether a UX problem in question is a violation of a concept).

Each concept at the top decomposes further into a hierarchy of successively detailed descriptions of interaction design concepts and issues in the over 300 nodes of the full UAF. As an example of the hierarchical structure, consider this breakdown of some translation topics:

Translation
    Presentation of a cognitive affordance to support translation
        Legibility, visibility, noticeability of the cognitive affordance
           Fonts, color, layout
              Font color, color contrast with background

21.4.1 Planning (Design Helping User Know What to Do)

Planning is the part of the Interaction Cycle containing all cognitive actions by users to determine "what to do?" or "what can I do?" using the system to achieve work domain goals. Although many variations occur, a typical sequence of planning activities involves these steps, not always this clear cut, to establish a hierarchy of plan entities:

- Identify *work needs* in the subject matter domain (e.g., communicate with someone in writing)
- Establish *goals* in the work domain to meet these work needs (e.g., produce a business letter)
- Divide goals into *tasks* performed on the computer to achieve the goals (e.g., type content, format the page)
- Spawn *intentions* to perform the steps of each task (e.g., set the left margin)

After each traversal of the Interaction Cycle, the user typically returns to planning and establishes a new goal, intention, and/or task.

Planning concepts

Interaction design support for user planning is concerned with how well the design helps users understand the overall computer application relative to the perspective of work context, the work domain, and environmental requirements and constraints in order to determine in general how to use the system to solve problems and get work done. Planning support has to do with the system model, conceptual design, and metaphors, the user's awareness of system features and capabilities (what the user *can* do with the system), and the user's knowledge of possible system modalities. Planning is about user strategies for approaching the system to get work done.

Planning content in the UAF

UAF content under planning is about how an interaction design helps users plan goals and tasks and understand how to use the system. This part of the UAF contains interaction design issues about supporting users in planning the use of the system to accomplish work in the application domain. These concepts are addressed in specific child nodes about the following topics:

User model and high-level understanding of system. Pertains to issues about supporting user acquisition of a high-level understanding of the system concept as manifest in the interaction design. Elucidates issues about how well the interaction design matches users' conception of system and user beliefs and expectations, bringing different parts of the system together as a cohesive whole.

Goal decomposition. Pertains to issues about supporting user decomposition of tasks to accomplish higher-level work domain goals. This category includes issues about accommodating human memory limitations in interaction designs to help users deal with complex goals and tasks, avoid stacking and interruption, and achieve task and subtask closure as soon as possible. This category also includes issues about supporting user's conception of task organization, accounting for goal, task, and intention shifts, and providing user ability to represent high-level goals effectively.

Task/step structuring and sequencing, workflow. Pertains to issues about supporting user's ability to structure tasks within planning by establishing sequences of tasks and/or steps to accomplish goals, including getting started on tasks. This category includes issues about appropriateness of task flow and workflow in the design for the target work domain.

User work context, environment. Pertains to issues about supporting user's knowledge (for planning) of problem domain context, and constraints in work environment, including environmental factors, such as noise, lighting, interference, and distraction. This category addresses issues about how non-system tasks such as interacting with other people or systems relate to planning task performance in the design.

User knowledge of system state, modalities, and especially active modes. Pertains to supporting user knowledge of system state, modalities, and active modes.

Supporting learning at the planning level through use and exploration. Pertains to supporting user's learning about system conceptual design through exploratory and regular use. This category addresses issues about learnability of conceptual design rationale through consistency and explanations in design, and about what the system can help the user do in the work domain.

21.4.2 Translation (Design Helping User Know How to Do Something)

Translation concerns the lowest level of task preparation. Translation includes anything that has to do with deciding how you can or should make an action on an object, including the user thinking about which action to take or on what object to take it, or what might be best action to take next within a task.

Translation is the part of the Interaction Cycle that contains all cognitive actions by users to determine *how* to carry out the intentions that arise in planning. Translation results in what Norman (1986) calls an "action specification," a description of a physical action on an interface object, such as "click and drag the document file icon," using the computer to carry out an intention.

Translation concepts

Planning and translation can both seem like some kind of planning, as they both occur before physical actions, but have a distinctive difference. Planning is higher level goal formation, and translation is a lower level decision about which action to make on which object.

Here is a simple example about driving a car. Planning for a trip in the car involves thinking about traveling to get somewhere, involving questions such as "where are you going," "by what route," and do we need to stop and get gas and/or groceries first?" So planning is in the work domain, which is travel, not operating the car.

In contrast, translation takes the user into the system, machine, or physical world domain and is about formulating actions to operate the gas pedal, brake, and steering wheel to accomplish the tasks that will help you reach your planning, or travel, goals. Because steps such as "turn on headlight switch," "push horn button," and "push brake pedal" are actions on objects, they are the stuff of translation.

Over the bulk of interaction that occurs in the real world, translation is arguably the single-most important step because it is about how you do things. Translation is perhaps the most challenging part of the cycle for both users and designers. From our own experience over the years, we guess that the largest bulk of UX problems observed in UX testing, 75% or more, falls into this category.

This experience is also reflected by that of Cuomo and Bowen (1992), who also classified UX problems per Norman's theory of action and found the majority of problems in the action specification stage (translation). Clearly, translation deserves special attention in a UX and interaction design context.

Translation content in the UAF

UAF content under translation is about how an interaction design helps users know what actions to take to carry out a given intention. This part of the UAF contains interaction design issues about the effectiveness of sensory and cognitive affordances, such as labels, used to support user needs to determine (know) how to do a task step in terms of what actions to make on which UI objects and how. These concepts are addressed in specific child nodes about the following topics:

Existence of a cognitive affordance to show how to do something. Pertains to issues about ensuring existence of needed cognitive affordances in support of user cognitive actions to determine how to do something (e.g., task step) in terms of what action to make on what UI object and how. This category includes cases of necessary but missing cognitive affordances, but also cases of unnecessary or undesirable but existing cognitive affordances.

Presentation (of a cognitive affordance). Pertains to issues about effective presentation or appearance in support of user sensing of cognitive affordances. This category includes issues involving legibility, noticeability, timing of presentation, layout and spatial grouping, complexity, and consistency of presentation, as well as presentation medium (e.g., audio, when needed) and graphical aspects of presentation. An example issue might be about presenting the text of a button label in the correct font size and color so that it can be read/sensed.

Content, meaning (of a cognitive affordance). Pertains to issues about user understanding and comprehension of cognitive affordance content and meaning in support of user ability to determine what action(s) to make and on what object(s) for a task step. This category includes issues involving clarity, precision, predictability of the effects of a user action, error avoidance, and effectiveness of content expression. As an example, precise wording in labels helps user predict consequences of selection. Clarity of meaning helps users avoid errors.

Task structure, interaction control, preferences and efficiency. Pertains to issues about logical structure and flow of task and task steps in support of user needs within task performance. This category includes issues about alternative ways to do tasks, shortcuts, direct interaction, and task thread continuity (supporting the most likely next step). This category also includes issues involving task structure simplicity, efficiency, locus of user control, human memory limitations, and accommodating different user classes.

Support of user learning about what actions to make on which UI objects and how through regular and exploratory use. Pertains to issues about supporting user learning at the action-object level through consistency and explanations in the design.

21.4.3 Physical Actions (Design Helping User Do the Actions)

After users decide which actions to take, the physical actions part of the Interaction Cycle is *where users do the actions*. This part includes all user inputs acting on devices and user interface objects to manipulate the system, including typing, clicking, dragging, touching, gestures, and navigational actions, such as walking in virtual environments. The physical actions part of the Interaction Cycle *includes no cognitive actions*; thus, this part is not about thinking about the actions or determining which actions to do.

Physical actions—concepts

This part of the Interaction Cycle has two components: (2) sensing the objects in order to manipulate them and (2) manipulation. In order to manipulate an object in the user interface, the user must be able to sense, for example, see, hear, or feel, the object, which can depend on the usual sensory affordance issues as object size, color, contrast, location, and timing of its display.

Physical actions are especially important for analysis of performance by expert users who have, to some extent, "automated" planning and translation associated with a task and for whom physical actions have become the limiting factor in task performance.

Physical affordance design factors include design of input/output devices (e.g., touchscreen design or keyboard layout), haptic devices, interaction styles and techniques, direct manipulation issues, gestural body movements, physical fatigue, and such physical human factors issues as manual dexterity, hand–eye coordination, layout, interaction using two hands and feet, and physical disabilities.

Fitts' law. The practical implications of Fitts' law (Fitts, 1954; Fitts & Peterson, 1964) are important in the physical actions part of the Interaction Cycle. Users vary considerably in their natural manual dexterity, but all users are governed by Fitts' law with respect to certain kinds of physical movement during interaction, especially cursor movement for object selection and dragging and dropping objects.

Fitts' law is an empirically based mathematical formula governing movement from an initial position to a target at a terminal position. The time to make the movement is proportional to the $\log_2$ of the distance and inversely proportional to $\log_2$ of the width or cross-section of the target normal to the direction of the motion.

First applied in HCI, to the new concept of a mouse cursor control device by Card, English, and Burr (1978), it has since been the topic of many HCI studies and publications. Among the most well known of these developments are those of McKenzie (1992).

Fitts' law has been modified and adapted to many other interaction situations, including among many, two-dimensional tasks (MacKenzie & Buxton, 1992), pointing and dragging (Gillan et al., 1990) trajectory-based tasks (Accot & Zhai, 1997), and moving interaction from visual to auditory and tactile designs (Friedlander, Schlueter, & Mantei, 1998).

When Fitts' law is applied in a bounded work area, such as a computer screen, boundary conditions impose exceptions. If the edge of the screen is the "target," for example, movement can be extremely fast because it is constrained to stop when you get to the edge without any overshoot.

Other software modifications of cursor and object behavior to exceed the user performance predicted by this law include cursor movement accelerators and the "snap to default" cursor feature. Such features put the cursor where the user is most likely to need it, for example, the default button within a dialogue box. Another attempt to beat Fitts' law predictions is based on selection using area cursors (Kabbash & Buxton, 1995), a technique in which the active pointing part of the cursor is two dimensional, making selection more like hitting with a "fly swatter" than with a precise pointer.

One interesting software innovation for outdoing Fitts' limitations is called "snap-dragging" (Bier, 1990; Bier & Stone, 1986), which, in addition to many other enhanced graphics-drawing capabilities, imbues potential target objects with a kind of magnetic power to draw in an approaching cursor, "snapping" the cursor home into the target.

Another attempt to beat Fitts' law is to ease the object selection task with user interface objects that expand in size as the cursor comes into proximity (McGuffin & Balakrishnan, 2005). This approach allows conservation of screen space with small initial object sizes, but increased user performance with larger object sizes for selection.

Another "invention" that addresses the Fitts' law trade-off of speed versus accuracy of cursor movement for menu selection is the pie menu (Callahan et al., 1988). Menu choices are represented by slices or wedges in a pie configuration. The cursor movement from one selection to another can be tailored continuously by users to match their own sense of their personal manual dexterity. Near the outer portions of the pie, at large radii, movement to the next choice is slower but more accurate because the area of each choice is larger.

Movement near the center of the pie is much faster between choices but, because they are much closer together, selection errors are more likely.

Several design guidelines relate Fitts' law to manual dexterity in interaction design in Chapter 22.

Haptics and physicality. Haptics is about the sense of touch and the physical contact between user and machine through interaction devices. In addition to the usual mouse as cursor control, there are many other devices, each with its own haptic issues about how best to support natural interaction, including joysticks, touchscreens, touchpads, eye tracking, voice, trackballs, data gloves, body suits, head-mounted displays, and gestural interaction.

Physicality is about real physical interaction with real devices such as physical knobs and levers. It is about issues such as using real physical tuning and volume control knobs on a radio as opposed to electronic push buttons for the same control functions.

Norman (2007b) called that feeling of grabbing and turning a real knob "physicality." He claims, and we agree, that with real physical knobs, you get more of a feeling of *direct* control of physical outcomes.

Several design guidelines in Chapter 22 relate haptics to physicality in interaction design.

Physical actions content in the UAF

UAF content under physical actions is about how an interaction design helps users actually make actions on objects (e.g., typing, clicking, and dragging in a GUI, scrolling on a Web page, speaking with a voice interface, walking in a virtual environment, hand movements in gestural interaction, gazing with eyes). This part of the UAF contains design issues pertaining to the support of users in doing physical actions. These concepts are addressed in specific child nodes about the following topics:

Existence of necessary physical affordances in user interface. Pertains to issues about providing physical affordances (e.g., UI objects to act upon) in support of users doing physical actions to access all features and functionality provided by the system.

Sensing UI objects for and during manipulation. This category includes the support of user sensory (visual, auditory, tactile, etc.) needs in regard to sensing UI objects for and during manipulation (e.g., user ability to notice and locate physical affordance UI objects to manipulate).

Manipulating UI objects, making physical actions. A primary concern in this UAF category is the support of user physical needs at the time of actually making physical actions, especially making physical actions efficient for expert users.

This category includes how each UI object is manipulated and how manipulable UI objects operate.

Making UI object manipulation physically easy involves controls, UI object layout, interaction complexity, input/output devices, interaction styles and techniques. Finally, this is the category in which you consider Fitts' law issues having to do with the proximity of objects involved in task sequence actions.

21.4.4 Outcomes (Internal, Invisible Effect/Result within System)

Physical user actions are seen by the system as inputs and usually trigger a system function that can lead to system state changes that we call *outcomes* of the interaction. The outcomes part of the Interaction Cycle represents the system's turn to do something that usually involves computation by the non-user-interface software or, as it is sometimes called, core functionality. One possible outcome is a *failure* to achieve an expected or desired state change, as in the case of a user error.

Outcomes—concepts

A user action is not always required to produce a system response. The system can also autonomously produce an outcome, possibly in response to an internal event such as a disk getting full; an event in the environment sensed by the system such as a process control alarm; or the physical actions of other users in a shared work environment.

The system functions that produce outcomes are purely internal to the system and do not involve the user. Consequently, outcomes are technically not part of the user's Interaction Cycle, and the only UX issues associated with outcomes might be about usefulness or functional affordance of the non-user-interface system functionality.

Because internal system state changes are not directly visible to the user, outcomes must be revealed to the user via system feedback or a display of results, to be evaluated by the user in the assessment part of the Interaction Cycle.

Outcomes content in the UAF

UAF content under outcomes is about the effectiveness of the internal (non-user-interface) system functionality behind the user interface. None of the issues in this UAF category are directly related to the interaction design. However, the lack of necessary functionality can have a negative affect on the user experience because of insufficient usefulness. This part of the UAF contains issues about existence, completeness, correctness, suitability of needed backend functional affordances. These concepts are addressed in specific child nodes about the following topics:

Existence of needed functionality or feature (functional affordance). Pertains to issues about supporting users through existence of needed non-user-interface functionality. This category includes cases of missing, but needed, features and usefulness of the system to users.

Existence of needed or unwanted automation. Pertains to supporting user needs by providing needed automation, but not including unwanted automation that can cause loss of user control.

Computational error. This is about software bugs within non-user-interface functionality of the application system.

Results unexpected. This category is about avoiding surprises to users, for example through unexpected automation or other results that fail to match user expectations.

Quality of functionality. Though a necessary function or feature may exist, there may still be issues about how well it works to satisfy user needs.

21.4.5 Assessment (Design Helping User Know if Interaction Was Successful)

The assessment part of the Interaction Cycle corresponds to Norman's (1986) evaluation side of interaction. A user in assessment performs sensory and cognitive actions needed to sense and understand system feedback and displays of results as a means to comprehend internal system changes or outcomes due to a previous physical action.

The user's objective in assessment is to determine whether the outcomes of all that previous planning, translation, and physical actions were favorable, meaning desirable or effective to the user. In particular, an outcome is favorable if it helps the user approach or achieve the current intention, task, and/or goal; that is, if the plan and action "worked."

Assessment concepts

The assessment part parallels much of the translation part, only focusing on system feedback. Assessment has to do with the existence of feedback, presentation of feedback, and content or meaning of feedback. Assessment is about whether users can know when an error occurred, and whether a user can sense a feedback message and understand its content.

Assessment content in the UAF

This part of the UAF contains issues about how well feedback in system responses and displays of results within an interaction design help users know if the interaction is working so far. Being successful in the previous planning, translation, and physical actions means that the course of interaction has moved the user toward the interaction goals. These concepts are addressed in specific child nodes about the following topics:

Existence of feedback or indication of state or mode. Pertains to issues about supporting user ability to assess action outcomes by ensuring existence of feedback (or mode or state indicator) when it is necessary or desired and nonexistence of feedback when it is unwanted.

Presentation (of feedback). Pertains to issues about effective presentation or appearance, including sensory issues and timing of presentation, in support of user sensing of feedback.

Content, meaning (of feedback). Pertains to issues about understanding and comprehension of feedback (e.g., error message) content and meaning in support of user ability to assess action outcomes. This category of the UAF includes issues about clarity, precision, and predictability. The effectiveness of feedback content expression is affected by precise use of language, word choice, clarity due to layout and spatial grouping, user centeredness, and consistency.

21.5 ROLE OF AFFORDANCES WITHIN THE UAF

Each kind of affordance has a close relationship to parts of the Interaction Cycle. During interaction, users perform sensory, cognitive, and physical actions and require affordances to help with each kind of action, as shown abstractly in Figure 21-6. For example, in planning, if the user is looking at buttons and menus while trying to determine what can be done with the system, then the sensory and cognitive affordances of those user interface objects are used in support of planning.

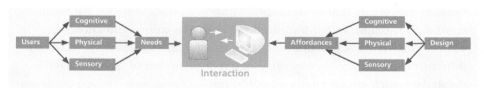

Figure 21-6
Affordances connect users with design.

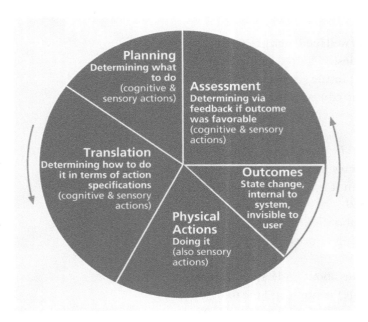

Figure 21-7

*Interaction cycle of the UAF
indicating affordance-
related user actions.*

Similarly, in translation, if a user needs to understand the purpose of a user interface object and the consequences of user actions on the object, then the sensory and cognitive affordances of that object support that translation. Perhaps the most obvious is the support physical affordances give to physical actions but, of course, sensory affordances also help; you cannot click on a button if you cannot see it.

Finally, the sensory and cognitive affordances of feedback objects (e.g., a feedback message) support users in assessment of system outcomes occurring in response to previous physical actions as inputs.

In Figure 21-7, we have added indications of the relevant affordances to each part of the Interaction Cycle.

21.6 PRACTICAL VALUE OF UAF

21.6.1 Advantage of Vocabulary to Think About and Communicate Design Issues

One of the most important advantages to labeling and structuring interaction design issues within the UAF is that it codifies a vocabulary for consistency across UX problem descriptions. Over the years this structured vocabulary has helped us and our students in being precise about how we talk about UX problems, especially in including descriptions of specific causes of the problems in those discussions.

As an analogy, the field of mechanical engineering has been around for much longer than our discipline. Mechanical engineers have a rich and precise working vocabulary that fosters mutual understanding of issues, for example, crankshaft rotation. In contrast, because of the variations and ambiguities in UX terminology, UX practitioners often end up talking about two different things or even talking at cross purposes. A structured and "standardized" vocabulary, such as can be found within the UAF, can help reduce confusion and promote agreement in discussions of the issues.

21.6.2 Advantage of Organized and Structured Usability Data

As early as 1994, a workshop at the annual CHI conference addressed the topic of what to do after usability data are collected (Nayak, Mrazek, & Smith, 1995). Researchers and practitioners took up questions about how usability data should be gathered, analyzed, and reported. Qualitative usability data are observational, requiring interpretation. Without practical tools to structure the problems, issues, and concepts, however, researchers and practitioners were concerned about the reliability and adequacy of this analysis and interpretation. They wanted effective ways to get from raw observational data to accurate and meaningful conclusions about specific flaws in interaction design features. The workshop participants were also seeking ways to organize and structure usability data in ways to visualize patterns and relationships.

We believe that the UAF is one effective approach to getting from raw observational data to accurate and meaningful conclusions about specific flaws in interaction design features. The UAF offers ways to organize and structure usability data in ways to visualize patterns and relationships.

21.6.3 Advantage of Richness in Usability Problem Analysis Schemes

Gray and Salzman (1998) cited the need for a theory-based usability problem categorization scheme for comparison of usability evaluation method performance, but they also warn of classification systems that have too few categories. As an example, the Nielsen and Molich (1990) heuristics were derived by projecting a larger set of usability guidelines down to a small set.

Although Nielsen developed heuristics to guide usability inspection, not classification, inspectors finding problems corresponding to a given heuristic find it convenient to classify them by that heuristic. However, as John and Mashyna (1997) point out in a discussion of usability tokens and types (usability problem instances and usability problem types), doing so is tantamount to projecting a large number of usability problem categories down to a small number of equivalence classes.

The result is that information distinguishing the cases is lost and measures for usability evaluation method classification agreement are inflated artificially because problems that would have been in different categories are now in the same super-category. The UAF overcomes this drawback by breaking down classifications into a very large number of detailed categories, not lumping together usability problems that have only passing similarities.

21.6.4 Advantage of Usability Data Reuse

Koenemann-Belliveau et al. (1994) made a case for leveraging usability evaluation effort beyond fixing individual problems in one user interface to building a knowledge base about usability problems, their causes, and their solutions. They state: "We should also investigate the potential for more efficiently *leveraging* the work we do in empirical formative evaluation—ways to 'save' something from our efforts for application in subsequent evaluation work" (Koenemann-Belliveau et al., 1994, p. 250).

Further, they make a case for getting more from the rich results of formative evaluation, both to improve the UX lifecycle process and to extend the science of HCI. Such a database of knowledge base of reusable usability problems data requires a storage and retrieval structure that will allow association of usability problem situations that are the "same" in some essential underlying way. The UAF, through the basic structure of the Interaction Cycle, provides just this kind of organization.

We will make use of the UAF structure to organize interaction design guidelines in Chapter 22.

UX Design Guidelines

22

To err is human; forgive by design.

– Anonymous

Objectives

After reading this chapter, you will:

1. Appreciate the difficulties in using and interpreting UX design guidelines
2. Understand the role of human memory limitations in guidelines
3. Understand and apply some of the basic UX design guidelines with respect to user actions for each stage of the Interaction Cycle

---

22.1 INTRODUCTION

22.1.1 Scope and Universality

There are, of course, many books and articles on design guidelines for graphical user interfaces (GUIs) and other user interfaces and their widgets—how to create and employ windows, buttons, pull-down menus, pop-up menus, cascading menus, icons, dialogue boxes, check boxes, radio buttons, options menus, forms, and so on. But we want you to think about interaction design and design guidelines much more broadly than that, even well beyond Web pages and mobile devices.

You will find that this chapter takes a broader approach, transcending design just for computer interfaces and particular platforms, media, or devices. There is a world of designs out there and, as Don Norman (1990) says, seeing the guidelines applied to the design of everyday things helps us understand the application of guidelines to interaction by humans with almost any kind of device or system.

> ### Design (UX) Guidelines
>
> A UX, or interaction, design guideline is a statement suggesting recommendations and considerations to inform the design of a specific aspect or component of interaction in a certain context. Some design guidelines come from study data, but most come from principles, maxims, and experience.

User Interfaces for Handheld Devices

Brad A. Myers
Carnegie Mellon University

The term "handheld devices" includes mobile phones (in particular, "smartphones," which have more elaborate functions and user interfaces), as well as personal digital assistants, pagers, calculators, and specialized devices such as handheld scanners and data entry devices. Portable devices that are larger than the size of a hand, such as tablets such as the Apple iPad, are generally *not* considered to be *handheld* devices.

How do interfaces designed for handheld devices differ from conventional user interfaces? The first point to emphasize is that all of the processes and techniques described in this book, from contextual inquiries through iterative prototyping through user testing, all apply to handheld user interfaces, just as for any other user interface, so the process and techniques are not different. The key difference with handheld devices is the *context of use*. By definition, handheld devices are used while being held in one hand, which means that generally at most one other hand is available to perform input. Furthermore, handheld devices are mostly used *on the go*, which means that the user is busy doing other tasks (such as walking, talking on the phone, or taking an inventory at a store) at the same time as using the handheld. Another key difference is that handhelds have *much smaller screens* than conventional computers or tablets. Thus, information designs and even interaction techniques designed for conventional computers may not work on handhelds. For example, multicolumn Web pages are very difficult to read on handhelds, and a pop-up menu with more than 10 items cannot be used easily. Finally, because handheld devices are often controlled with a finger, as there typically is not a mouse pointer, target areas must be sufficiently large so that users can select what they want accurately. Some handhelds require the use of a *stylus* (a pen-like tool for pointing to or writing on the screen) instead of (or in addition to) a finger, which means that smaller items can be selected. However, stylus-based interfaces for handhelds are becoming less common.

The implications of these differences on the design of handheld user interfaces include the following.[1]:

- Optimize interactions for immediate use. User interfaces on handheld devices must make the most common actions available immediately. Users expect to be able to pull the device out of their pocket and perform a task quickly with minimal interactions and minimal waiting. For example, because the most common task for a calendar while on the go is to look up the next appointment, the user interface should default to showing what is on the calendar for the current time. The user interface must allow the user to exit immediately as well, as users can be interrupted at any time, for example, by the phone ringing. Designers of the original Palm handheld made the important observation that the most important tasks should be performed with one click, even at the cost of consistency, so on the Palm, creating a new event at a particular time just requires tapping on the calendar screen, compared to deleting an event (which is relatively rare), requires multiple taps and dialog boxes.[2]

---

[1]These recommendations are adapted from the following books, which are excellent guides for handheld designers: Weiss, S. (2002). *Handheld Usability*. West Sussex, England: John Wiley & Sons, Ltd.; and Bergman, E. (Ed.)(2000). *Information Appliances and Beyond*. San Francisco: Morgan Kaufmann Publishers.

[2]Bergman, E., & Haitani, R. (2000). Designing the Palmpilot: A conversation with Rob Haitani. In E. Bergman (Ed.), *Information Appliances and Beyond*. San Francisco: Morgan Kaufmann, pp. 82–102.

- **Minimize textual input.** Even more than minimizing input in general, text entry continues to be difficult with small devices, so requiring more than a word or two to be typed is problematic, and applications should be resilient to typing errors.
- **Concise output.** The information to be displayed must be optimized for the small displays of these devices. Designs for desktops will typically need to be redesigned to make more efficient use of the screen space. For example, avoid blank lines.
- **Conform to platform conventions.** Because interfaces must look like other applications on that particular handheld, iPhone user interfaces must look like other iPhone applications. If a user interface must run on different handhelds, it will probably need to be redesigned substantially. For example, the Android user interface conventions are quite different from the iPhone's. Even within a platform there might be variations. For example, an Android phone can have a variety of physical buttons and form factors, which a user interface must use correctly.
- **Allow disconnected and poorly connected use.** Although networks continue to improve, an application should not assume it will always be well connected. Devices can go out of range, even in the middle of a transaction, and the user interface must respond appropriately. It is never acceptable for the handheld to refuse to respond to the user even if the network disappears. Users expect to be able to perform tasks even when the network is turned off, such as on an airplane.

Because handheld devices will be the dominant way that most people in the world access computation, designing effective user interfaces for these devices will likely be a significant part of a designer's activities.

The principles and guidelines in this chapter are universal; you will see in this chapter that the same issues apply to ATMs, elevator controls, and even highway signage. We, too, have a strong flavor of *The Design of Everyday Things* (Norman, 1990) in our guidelines and examples. We agree with Jokela (2004) that usability and a quality user experience are also essential in everyday consumer products.

We hope you will forgive us for excluding guidelines about internationalization or accessibility (as we advised in the Preface section, *What We Do Not Cover*). The book, and especially this chapter, is already large and we cannot cover everything.

Usability Principles for New Frontiers in the Virtual Environment User Experience

Theresa (Teri) A. O'Connell
President, Humans & Computers, Inc.

As the Starship Enterprise pushed ever deeper into space, Star Trek's Captain Picard encountered the challenge of making new laws for new cultures in new environments. Usability and human factors engineers face the same challenge today in defining usability principles for virtual environments (VEs). We can learn a lot from Captain Picard's experience. Like him, we adapt the traditional to the new, sometimes even deriving novel, untried usability principles from the old.

Some VEs, for example, training environments and advanced visual analytic tools, have a single purpose. Game worlds can have serious or entertainment purposes. Other VEs are multifunctional. Second Life can be a home-away-from home, classroom-away-from-campus, office-beyond-the-workplace, or exotic-vacation-sans-travel-time. Whatever their purpose, all VEs have one thing in common. The user experience when playing, working, learning, relaxing, or collaborating in a VE differs from that of traditional computing. So, designing a VE for a good user experience requires new ways of thinking about usability principles.

It turns out that many usability principles that apply when you are playing the role of a healer, hobnobbing with virtual buddies, or slaying monsters are the same as those that apply when you are surfing the Internet or writing a paper. We just have to apply them a bit differently in VEs. The resulting principles for design and testing are not mutually exclusive—they interact to create a successful and satisfying user experience. We can see how this works by taking a quick look at some usability principles from the perspective of the VE user experience for gamers and visual analysts.

Give users a sense of control over their experiences is a great grandparent of all usability principles. This prerequisite for user satisfaction is traditionally applied by providing obvious, consistently located, and easy-to-use controls. It applies directly to VE design in strategies, such as right clicking for immediate access to avatar controls, for example, teleportation in case of griefer attacks.

But, sometimes, collaboration requires ceding control, at least temporarily. This happens to players of massive multiplayer online role-playing games (MMORPG) and analysts manipulating huge complex visual analytic data sets when their success depends on collaboration. Adapting the user control usability principle, we *give users control over their own interactions, but cede control to serve VE goals*, in this case, to allow collaboration. For example, online game dashboard adaptability gives gamers autonomy over what is theirs. But an inability to steal the microphone while another player talks prevents interruptions, serving the goal of courteous collaboration. During testing, we measure collaboration success by comparing game scores of teams that must take turns sending voice communications to collaborate and teams that do not.

Engage the user is the e-commerce mantra. Its *sticky* goal is to keep shoppers onsite and buying. In games, the usability principle is *engagement trumps everything else*. Engagement is a primary purpose of VE design for many reasons. Engagement increases enjoyment and enhances learning. It draws gamers into gameplay, e.g., for example, by providing an enjoyable simple quest for novices and then progressing them to higher challenge levels.

Engagement enriches the user experience. But engagement intersects with another classic usability principle, *prevent visual overload*, for example, by streamlining backgrounds or minimizing animations. VEs can be visually dense. We engage gamers and inform analysts with lots of interesting things to look at, but we risk distraction and visual overload.

In first-person shooter games such as Left 4 Dead, the element of surprise is integral to engagement. In adventure games, while distracting, a dense, engaging background harbors surprise. In such a case, distraction is okay. The new principle becomes *control visual overload, making sure that visually rich displays engage the user but do not impede VE goals*.

Instead of minimizing animation, we turn animation into a tool to attract attention and engage, for example, with surprise attacks by nonplaying characters. In visual analytic tools, we sometimes interrupt workflow with an eye-catching animation when important new information becomes available. During testing, we measure impact on satisfaction by comparing survey responses from players or analysts who experience interruption and those who do not. We survey players and analysts to learn how engaging they consider different aspects of the user experience, for example, building game scores or answering a question in an analytical VE.

Visual density also leads to a usability principle that requires the VE to *assist analysis by helping analysts identify important data quickly*, for example, suspicious entities. To test, we measure success by logging and counting interactions with this data, for example, the number of times analysts manipulate isolated data points into clusters or social networks to investigate entity connections. Testing against ground truth, we count the number of known connections analysts identified. We use eye tracking to create heat maps showing analysts' gaze paths and fixations. If their eyes continuously scan the environment, but never rest on salient new data, we know it is likely that the background is too dense and impedes analysis.

When we design and test the VE for a high-quality user experience, just like Captain Picard, we are going to encounter unimagined challenges. One of our strategies will be to update traditional usability principles. This means that every design or testing team facing the challenges of producing a VE that leads to a high-quality user experience needs a person who has a strong background in fields such as the human factors behind usability principles.

22.1.2 Background

We cannot talk about interaction design guidelines without giving a profound acknowledgement to what is perhaps the mother (and father) of all guidelines publications, the book of 944 design guidelines for text-based user interfaces of bygone days that Smith and Mosier of Mitre Corporation developed for the U.S. Air Force (Mosier & Smith, 1986; Smith & Mosier, 1986).

We were already working in human–computer interaction (HCI) and read it with great interest when it came out. Almost a decade later, an electronic version became available (Iannella, 1995). Other early guidelines collections include Engel and Granda (1975), Brown (1988), and Boff and Lincoln (1988).

Interaction design guidelines appropriate to the technology of the day appeared throughout the history of HCI, including "the design of idiot-proof interactive programs" (Wasserman, 1973); ground rules for a "well-behaved" system (Kennedy, 1974); design guidelines for interactive systems (Pew & Rollins, 1975); usability maxims (Lund, 1997b); and eight golden rules of interface design (Shneiderman, 1998). Every practitioner has a favorite set of design guidelines or maxims.

Eventually, of course, the attention of design guidelines followed the transition to graphical user interfaces (Nielsen, 1990; Nielsen et al., 1992).

As GUIs evolved, many of the guidelines became platform specific, such as style guides for Microsoft Windows and Apple. Each has its own set of detailed requirements for compliance with the respective product lines.

As an example from the 1990s, an interactive product from Apple called Making it Macintosh (Alben, Faris, & Saddler, 1994; Apple Computer Inc, 1993) used computer animations to highlight the Macintosh user interface design principles, primarily to preserve the Macintosh look and feel. Many of the early style guides, such as OSF Motif (Open Software Foundation, 1990) and IBM's Common User Access (Berry, 1988), came built into software tools for enforcing that particular style.

The principles behind the guidelines came mainly from human psychology. Our friend Tom Hewitt (1999) was probably the most steadfast HCI voice for understanding psychology as a foundation for UX design principles and guidelines. These principles first evolved into design guidelines in human factors engineering.

Some UX design guidelines, especially those coming from human factors, are supported with empirical data. Most guidelines, however, have earned their authority from a strong grounding in the practice and shared experience of the UX community—experience in design and evaluation, experience in analyzing and solving UX problems.

Based on the National Cancer Institute's Research-Based Web Design and Usability Guidelines project begun in March 2000, the U.S. Department of Health and Human Services has published a book containing an extensive set of interaction design guidelines and associated reference material (U.S. Department of Health and Human Services, 2006). Each guideline has undergone extensive internal and external review with respect to tracking down its sources, estimating its relative importance in application, and determining the "strength of evidence," for example, strong research support vs. weak research support, supporting the guideline.

As is the case in most domains, design guidelines finally opened the way for standards (Abernethy, 1993; Billingsley, 1993; L. Brown, 1993; Quesenbery, 2005; Strijland, 1993).

22.1.3 Some of Our Examples Are Intentionally Old

We have been collecting examples of good and bad interaction and other kinds of design for decades. This means that some of these examples are old. Some of these systems no longer exist. Certainly some of the problems have been fixed over time, but they are still good examples and their age shows how as a community we have advanced and improved our designs. Many new users may think the interfaces to modern commercial software applications have always been as they are. Read on.

22.2 USING AND INTERPRETING DESIGN GUIDELINES

Are most design guidelines not obvious? When we teach these design guidelines, we usually get nods of agreement upon our statement of each guideline. There is very little controversy about the interaction design guidelines stated absolutely, out of context. Each general guideline is obvious; it just makes sense. How else would you do it?

However, when it comes to applying those same guidelines in specific usability design and evaluation situations, there is bewilderment. People are often unsure about which guidelines apply or how to apply, tailor, or interpret them in a specific design situation (Potosnak, 1988). We do not even agree on the meaning of some guidelines. As Lynn Truss (2003) says in the context of English grammar, that even considering people who are rabidly in favor of using the rules of grammar, it is impossible to get them all to agree on the rules and their interpretation and to pull in the same direction.

Bastien and Scapin (1995, p. 106) quote a study by de Souza and Bevan (1990): de Souza and Bevan "found that designers made errors, that they had difficulties with 91% of the guidelines, and that integrating detailed design guidelines with their existing experience was difficult for them."

There is something about UX design guidelines in almost every HCI book, often specific to user interface widgets and devices. You will not see guidelines here of the type: "Menus should not contain more than X items." That is because such guidelines are meaningless without interpretation within a design and usage context. In the presence of sweeping statements about what is right or wrong in UX design, we can only think of our long-time friend Jim Foley who said "The only correct answer to any UX design question is: It depends."

We believe much of the difficulty stems from the broad generality, vagueness, and even contradiction within most sets of design guidelines. One of the guidelines near the top of almost any list is "be consistent," an all-time favorite UX platitude. But what does it mean? Consistency at what level; what kind of consistency? Consistency of layout or semantic descriptors such as labels or system support for workflow?

There are many different kinds of consistency with many different meanings in many different contexts. Although we use the same words in discussions about applying the consistency guideline, we are often arguing about different things. That guideline is just too broad and requires too much interpretation for the average practitioner to fit it easily to a particular instance.

Another such overly general maxim is "keep it simple," certainly a shoo-in to the UX design guidelines hall of fame. But, again, what is simplicity? Minimize the things users can do? It depends on the kind of users, the complexity of their work domain, their skills and expertise.

To address this vagueness and difficulty in interpretation at high levels, we have organized the guidelines in a particular way. Rather than organize the guidelines by the obvious keywords such as consistency, simplicity, and the language of the user, we have tried to associate each guideline with a specific interaction design situation by using the structure of the Interaction Cycle and the User Action Framework (UAF) to organize the guidelines. This allows specific guidelines to be linked to user actions for planning, making physical actions, or assessing feedback and user actions for sensing objects and other interaction artifacts, understanding cognitive content, or physically manipulating those objects.

Finally, we warn you, as we have done often, to use your head and not follow guidelines blindly. While design guidelines and custom style guides are useful in supporting UX design, remember that there is no substitute for a competent and experienced practitioner. Beware of the headless chicken guy unencumbered by the thought process: "Do not worry, I have the style guide." Then you *should* worry, especially if the guide turns out to be a programming guide for user interface widgets.

22.3 HUMAN MEMORY LIMITATIONS

Because some of the guidelines and much of practical user performance depend on the concepts of human working memory, we interject a short discussion of the same here, before we get into the guidelines themselves. We treat human memory here because:

- it applies to most of the Interaction Cycle parts, and
- it is one of the few areas of psychology that has solid empirical data supporting knowledge that is directly usable in UX design.

Our discussion of human memory here is by no means complete or authoritative. Seek a good psychology book for that. We present a potpourri of concepts that should help your understanding in applying the design guidelines related to human memory limitations.

22.3.1 Sensory Memory

Sensory memory is of very brief duration. For example, the duration of visual memory ranges from a small fraction of a second to maybe 2 seconds and is strictly about the visual pattern observed, not anything about identifying what was seen or what it means. It is raw sensory data that allow direct comparisons with temporally nearby stimuli, such as might occur in detecting voice inflection. Sensory persistence is the phenomenon of storage of the stimulus in the sensory organ, not the brain.

For example, visual persistence allows us to integrate the fast-moving sequences of individual image frames in movies or television, making them appear as a smooth integrated motion picture. There are probably not many UX design issues involving sensory memory.

22.3.2 Short-Term or Working Memory

Short-term memory, which we usually call working memory, is the type we are primarily concerned with in HCI and has a duration of about 30 seconds, a duration that can be extended by repetition or rehearsal. Other intervening activities, sometimes called "proactive interference," will cause the contents of working memory to fade even faster.

Working memory is a buffer storage that carries information of immediate use in performing tasks. Most of this information is called "throw-away data" because its usefulness is short term and it is undesirable to keep it longer. In his famous paper, George Miller (1956) showed experimentally that under certain conditions, the typical capacity of human short-term memory is about seven plus or minus two items; often it is less.

22.3.3 Chunking

The items in short-term memory are often encodings that Simon (1974) has labeled "chunks." A chunk is a basic human memory unit containing one piece of data that is recognizable as a single gestalt. That means for spoken expressions, for example, a chunk is a word, not a phoneme, and in written expressions a chunk is a word or even a single sentence, not a letter.

Random strings of letters can be divided into groups, which are remembered more easily. If the group is pronounceable, it is even easier to remember, even if it has no meaning. Duration trades off with capacity; all else being equal, the more chunks involved, the less time they can be retained in short-term memory.

Example: Phone numbers designed to be remembered

Not counting the area code, a phone number has seven digits, not a coincidence that this exactly meets the Miller estimate of working memory capacity. If you look up a number in the phone book, you are loading your working memory with seven chunks. You should be able to retain the number if you use it within the next 30 seconds or so.

With a little rehearsal and without any intervening interruption of your attention, you can stretch this duration out to 2 minutes or longer. A telephone number is a classic example of working memory usage in daily life. If you get distracted between memory loading and usage, you may have to look the number up again, a scenario we all have experienced. If the prefix (the first three digits) is familiar, it is treated as a single chunk, making the task easier.

Sometimes items can be grouped or recoded into patterns that reduce the number of chunks. When grouping and recoding is involved, storage can trade off with processing, just as it does in computers. For example, think about keeping this pattern in your working memory:

001010110111000

On the surface, this is a string of 15 digits, beyond the working memory capacity of most people. But a clever user might notice that this is a binary number and the digits can be grouped into threes:

001 010 110 111 000

and converted easily to octal digits: 12670. With a modicum of processing we have grouped and recoded the original 15 chunks into a more manageable 5.

The following is a trick case, but it is illustrative of the principle in an extreme setting. Ostensibly this sequence of letters contains 18 items:

NTH EDO GSA WTH ECA TRU

Because there is no obvious way to group or encode them into chunks, the 18 items, as shown, represent 18 chunks. If each three-letter group spelled a word, there would be 6 chunks. If you know the trick to this example and imagine the initial "N" being moved to the right-hand end, you get not only six words, but a sentence, which amounts to one large chunk:

THE DOG SAW THE CAT RUN

22.3.4 Stacking

One of the ways user working memory limitations are affected by task performance is when task context stacking is required. This occurs when another situation arises in the middle of task performance. Before the user can continue with the original task, its context (a memory of where the user was in the task) must be put on a "stack" in the user's memory.

This same thing happens to the context of execution of a software program when an interrupt must be processed before proceeding: the program execution context is stacked in a last-in-first-out (LIFO) data structure. Later, when the system returns to the original program, its context is "popped" from the stack and execution continues. It is pretty much the same for a human user whose primary task is interrupted. Only the stack is implemented in human working memory.

This means that user memory stacks are small in capacity and short in duration. People have leaky stacks; after enough time and interruptions, they forget what they were doing. When people get to "pop" a task context from their stacks, they get "closure," a feeling of cognitive relief due to the lifting of the cognitive load of having to retain information in their working memories. One way to help users in this regard is to design large, complex tasks as a series of smaller operations rather than one large hierarchically structured task involving significant stacking. This lets them come up for air periodically.

22.3.5 Cognitive Load

Cognitive load is the load on working memory at a specific point in time (G. Cooper, 1998; Sweller, 1988, 1994). Cognitive load theory (Sweller, 1988, 1994) has been aimed primarily at improvement in teaching and learning through attention to the role and limitations of working memory but, of course, also applies directly to human–computer interaction. While working with the computer, users are often in danger of having their working memory overloaded. Users can get lost easily in cascading menus with lots of choices at each level or tasks that lead through large numbers of Web pages.

If you could chart the load on working memory as a function of time through the performance of a task, you would be looking at variations in the cognitive load across the task steps. Whenever memory load reaches zero, you have "task closure." By organizing tasks into smaller operations instead of one large hierarchical structure you will reduce the average user cognitive load over time and achieve task closure more often.

22.3.6 Long-Term Memory

Information stored in short-term memory can be transferred to long-term memory by "learning," which may involve the hard work of rehearsal and repetition. Transfer to long-term memory relies heavily on organization and structure of information already in the brain. Items transfer more easily if associations exist with items already in long-term memory.

The capacity of long-term memory is almost unlimited—a lifetime of experiences. The duration of long-term memory is also almost unlimited but retrieval is not always guaranteed. Learning, forgetting, and remembering are all associated with long-term memory. Sometimes items can be classified in more than one way. Maybe one item of a certain type goes in one place and another item of the same type goes elsewhere. As new items and new types of items come in, you revise the classification system to accommodate. Retrieval depends on being able to reconstruct structural encoding.

When we forget, items become inaccessible, but probably not lost. Sometimes forgotten or repressed information can be recalled. Electric brain stimulation can trigger reconstructions of visual and auditory memories of past events. Hypnosis can help recall vivid experiences of years ago. Some evidence indicates that hypnosis increases willingness to recall rather than ability to recall.

22.3.7 Memory Considerations and Shortcuts in Command versus GUI Selection Interaction Styles

Recognition vs. recall

Because we know that computers are better at memory and humans are better at pattern recognition, we design interaction to play to each other's strengths. One way to relieve human memory requirements in interaction design is by leveraging the human ability for recognition.

You hear people say, in many contexts, "I cannot remember exactly, but I will recognize it when I see it." That is the basis for the guideline to use recognition over recall. In essence, it means letting the user choose from a list of possibilities rather than having to come up with the choice entirely from memory.

Recognition over recall does work better for initial or intermittent use where learning and remembering are the operational factors, but what happens to people who do learn? They migrate from novice to experienced userhood. In UAF terms, they begin to remember how to make translations of frequent intentions into actions. They focus less on cognitive actions to know what to do and more on the physical actions of doing it. The cognitive affordances to help new users make these translations can now begin to become barriers to performance of the physical actions.

Moving the cursor and clicking to select items from lists of possibilities become more effortful than just typing short memorized commands. When more experienced users do recall the commands they need by virtue of their frequent usage, they find command typing a (legal) performance enhancer over the less efficient and, eventually, more boring and irritating physical actions required by those once-helpful GUI affordances.

Even command users get some memory help through command completion mechanisms, the "hum a few bars of it" approach. The user has to remember only the first few characters and the system provides possibilities for the whole command.

Shortcuts

When expert users get stuck with a GUI designed for translation affordances, it is time for shortcuts to come to the rescue. In GUIs, these shortcuts are physical affordances, mainly "hot key" equivalents of menu, icon, and button command choices, such as Ctrl-S for the Save command.

The addition of an indication of the shortcut version to the pull-down menu choice, for example, Ctrl+S added to the Save choice in the File menu, is a simple and subtle but remarkably effective design feature to remind all users of the menu about the corresponding shortcuts. All users can migrate seamlessly between using the shortcuts on the menus to learn and remember the commands and bypassing the menus to use the shortcuts directly. This is true "as-needed" support of memory limitations in design.

22.3.8 Muscle Memory

Muscle memory is a little bit like sensory memory in that it is mostly stored locally, in the muscles in this case, and not the brain. Muscle memory is important for repetitive physical actions; it is about getting in a "rhythm." Thus, muscle memory is an essential aspect of learned skills of athletes. In HCI, it is important in physical actions such as typing.

Example: Muscling light switches

In this country at least, we use an arbitrary convention that moving an electrical switch up means "on" and down means "off." Over a lifetime of usage, we develop muscle memory because of this convention and hit the switch in an upward direction as we enter the room without pausing.

However, if you have lights on a three-way switch, "on" and "off" cannot be assigned consistently to any given direction of the switch. It depends on the state of the whole set of switches. So, often you might find yourself hitting a light switch in an upward direction without thinking as you sweep past. If it is a three-way switch, sometimes the light fails to turn on because the switch was already up with the lights off. No amount of practice or trying to remember can overcome this conflict between muscle memory and this device.

22.4 SELECTED UX DESIGN GUIDELINES AND EXAMPLES

The selected UX design guidelines in this section are generally organized by the UAF structure. We illustrate many of the guidelines and principles with examples that we have gathered over the years, including many design examples from everyday things, such as hair dryers, automobiles, road signage, public doorways, and so on, which demonstrate the universality of the principles and concepts. Those examples that are directly about computer interaction are mostly platform independent except, of course, screen shots that are specific to a particular system.

To review the structure of the Interaction Cycle from the previous chapter, we show the simplest view of this cycle in Figure 22-1.

In sum, parts of the Interaction Cycle are:

Figure 22-1

Simplest view of the Interaction Cycle.

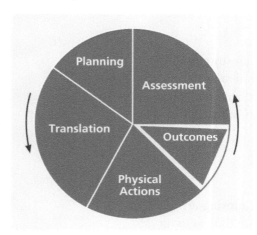

- planning: how the interaction design supports users in determining what to do
- translation: how the interaction design supports users in determining how to do actions on objects
- physical actions: how the interaction design supports users in doing those actions
- outcomes: how the non-interaction functionality of the system helps users achieve their work goals
- assessment of outcomes: how the interaction design supports users in determining whether the interaction is turning out right

We will have sample UX design guidelines for each of these plus an overall category.

22.5 PLANNING

In Figure 22-2 we highlight the planning part of the Interaction Cycle. Support for user planning is often the missing color in the user interface rainbow.

Planning guidelines are to support users as they plan how they will use the system to accomplish work in the application domain, including cognitive user actions to determine what tasks or steps to do. It is also about helping users understand what tasks they can do with the system and how well it supports learning about the system for planning. If users cannot determine how to organize several related tasks in the work domain because the system does not help them understand exactly how it can help do these kinds of tasks, the design needs improvement in planning support.

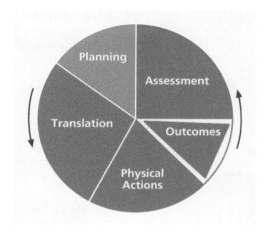

Figure 22-2
The planning part of the Interaction Cycle.

22.5.1 Clear System Task Model for User

Support the user's ability to acquire an overall understanding of the system at a high level, including the system model, design concept, and metaphors. (NB: the special green font used in the next line denotes such a guideline.)

Help users plan goals, tasks by providing a clear model of how users should view system in terms of tasks

Support users' high-level understanding of the whole system with a clear conceptual design, not just how to use one feature.

Help users with system model, metaphors, work context

Support users' overall understanding of the system, design concept, and any metaphors used with a clear conceptual design. Metaphors, such as the analogy of using a typewriter in a word processor design, are ways that existing user knowledge of previous designs and phenomena can be leveraged to ease learning and using of new designs.

Design to match user's conception of high-level task organization

Support user task decomposition by matching the design to users' concept of task decomposition and organization.

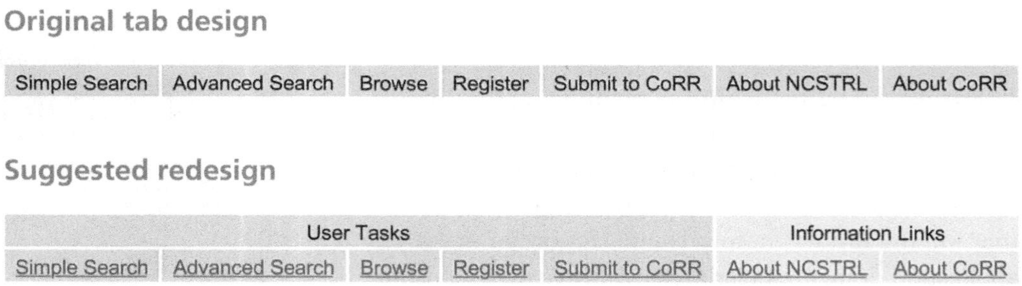

Original tab design

| Simple Search | Advanced Search | Browse | Register | Submit to CoRR | About NCSTRL | About CoRR |

Suggested redesign

User Tasks					Information Links	
Simple Search	Advanced Search	Browse	Register	Submit to CoRR	About NCSTRL	About CoRR

Figure 22-3

Tab reorganization to match task structure.

Example: Get organized

Tabs at the top of every page of a particular digital library Website are not well organized by task. They are ordered so that information-seeking tasks are mixed with other kinds of tasks, as shown in the top of Figure 22-3. Part of the new tab bar in our suggested new design is shown in the bottom of Figure 22-3.

Help users understand what system features exist and how they can be used in their work context

Support user awareness of specific system features capabilities and understanding of how they can use those features to solve work domain problems in different work situations. Support user ability to attain awareness of specific system feature or capability.

Example: Mastering the Master Document feature

Consider the case of the Master Document feature in Microsoft Word™. For convenience and to keep file sizes manageable, users of Microsoft Word™ can maintain each part of a document in a separate file. At the end of the day they can combine those individual files to achieve the effect of a single document for global editing and printing.

However, this ability to treat several chapters in different files as a single document is almost impossible to figure out. The system does not help the user determine what can be done with it or how it might help with this task.

Help users decompose tasks logically

Support user task decomposition, logically breaking long, complex tasks into smaller, simpler pieces.

Make clear all possibilities for what users can do at every point

Help users understand how to get started and what to do next.

Keep users aware of system state for planning next task

Maintain and clearly display system state indicators when next actions are state dependent.

Keep the task context visible to minimize memory load

To help users compare outcomes with goals, maintain and clearly display user request along with results.

Example: Library search by author

In the search mode within a library information system, users can find themselves deep down many levels and screens into the task where card catalog information is being displayed. By the time they dig into the information structure that deeply, there is a chance users may have forgotten their exact original search intentions. Somewhere on the screen, it would be helpful to have a reminder of the task context, such as "You are *searching by author* for: Stephen King."

22.5.2 Planning for Efficient Task Paths
Help users plan the most efficient ways to complete their tasks

Example: The helpful printing command

This is an example of good design, rather than a design problem, and it is from Borland's 3-D Home Architect™. Using this house-design program, when a user tries to print a large house plan, it results in an informative message in a dialogue box that says: Current printer settings require 9 pages at this scale. Switching to Landscape mode allows the plan to be drawn with 6 pages. Click on Cancel if you wish to abort printing. This tip can be most helpful, saving the time and paper involved in printing it wrong the first time, making the change, and printing again.

Strictly as an aside here, this message still falls short of the mark. First, the term "abort" has unnecessary violent overtones. Plus, the design could provide a button to change to landscape mode directly, without forcing the user to find out how to make that switch.

22.5.3 Progress Indicators
Keep users aware of task progress, what has been done and what is left to do

Support user planning with task progress indicators to help users manage task sequencing and keep track of what parts of the task are done and what parts are left to do. During long tasks with multiple and possibly repetitive steps, users can lose track of where they are in the task. For these situations, task progress indicators or progress maps can be used to help users with planning based on knowing where they are in the task.

Example: Turbo-Tax keeps you on track

Filling out income tax forms is a good example of a lengthy multiple-step task. The designers of Turbo-Tax™ by Intuit, with a "wizard-like" step-at-a-time prompter, went to great lengths to help users understand where they are in the overall task, showing the user's progress through the steps while summarizing the net effect of the user's work at each point.

22.5.4 Avoiding Transaction Completion Slips
A transaction completion slip is a kind of error in which the user omits or forgets a final action, often a crucial action for consummating the task. Here we provide an associated guideline and some examples.

Provide cognitive affordances at the end of critical tasks to remind users to complete the transaction

Example: Hey, do not forget your tickets

A transaction completion slip can occur in the Ticket Kiosk System when the user gets a feeling of closure at the end of the interaction for the transaction and fails to take the tickets just purchased. In this case, special attention is needed to provide a good cognitive affordance in the interaction design to remind the user of the final step in the task plan and help prevent this kind of slip: "Please take your tickets" (or your bank card or your receipt).

Example: Another forgotten email attachment

As another example, we cannot count the number of times we have sent or received email for which an attachment was intended but forgotten. Recent versions of Google's Gmail have a simple solution. If any variation of the word "attach" appears in an email but

it is sent without an attachment, the system asks if the sender intended to attach something, as you can see in Figure 22-4. Similarly, if the email author says something such as "I am copying . . .", and there is no address in the Copy field, the system could ask about that, too.

Figure 22-4
Gmail reminder to attach a file.

An example of the same thing, this time using a plugin[3] for the Mac Mail program, is shown in Figure 22-5.

Example: Oops, you did not finish your transaction

On one banking site, when users transfer money from their savings accounts to their checking accounts, they often think the transaction is complete when it is actually not. This is because, at the bottom right-hand corner of the last page in this transaction workflow, just below the "fold" on the screen, there is a small button labeled Confirm that is often completely missed.

Users close the window and go about their business of paying bills, unaware that they are possibly heading toward an overdraft. At least they should have gotten a pop-up message reminding them to click the Confirm button before letting them logout of the Website.

Later, when one of the users called the bank to complain, they politely declined his suggestion that they should pay the overdraft fee because of their liability due to poor usability. We suspect they must have gotten other such complaints, however, because the flaw was fixed in the next version.

Figure 22-5
Mac reminder to attach a file.

Example: Microwave is anxious to help

As a final example of avoiding transaction completion slips, we cite a microwave oven. Because it takes time to defrost or cook the food, users often start it and do something

---

[3]http://eaganj.free.fr/code/mail-plugin/

else while waiting. Then, depending on the level of hunger, it is possible to forget to take out the food when it is done.

So microwave designers usually include a reminder. At completion, the microwave usually beeps to signal the end of its part of the task. However, a user who has left the room or is otherwise occupied when it beeps may still not be mindful of the food waiting in the microwave. As a result, some oven designs have an additional aspect to the feature for avoiding this classic slip. The beep repeats periodically until the door is opened to retrieve the food.

The design for one particular microwave, however, took this too far. It did not wait long enough for the follow-up beep. Sometimes a user would be on the way to remove the food and it would beep. Some users found this so irritating that they would hurry to rescue the food before that "reminder" beep. To them, this machine seemed to be "impatient" and "bossy" to the point that it had been controlling the users by making them hurry.

22.6 TRANSLATION

Translation guidelines are to support users in sensory and cognitive actions needed to determine how to do a task step in terms of what actions to make on which objects and how. Translation, along with assessment, is one of the places in the Interaction Cycle where cognitive affordances play the major role.

Many of the principles and guidelines apply to more than one part of the Interaction Cycle and, therefore, to more than one section of this chapter. For example, "Use consistent wording" is a guideline that applies to several the parts of the Interaction Cycle—planning, translation, and assessment. Rather than repeat, we will put them in the most pertinent location and hope that our readers recognize the broader applicability.

Translation issues include:

- existence (of cognitive affordance)
- presentation (of cognitive affordance)
- content and meaning (of cognitive affordance)
- task structure

22.6.1 Existence of Cognitive Affordance

Figure 22-6 highlights the "existence of cognitive affordance" part within the breakdown of the translation part of the Interaction Cycle.

If interaction designers do not provide needed cognitive affordances, such as labels and other cues, users will lack the support they need for learning and knowing what actions to make on what objects in order to carry out their task intentions. The existence of cognitive affordances is necessary to:

- show which user interface object to manipulate
- show how to manipulate an object
- help users get started in a task
- guide data entry in formatted fields
- indicate active defaults to suggest choices and values
- indicate system states, modes, and parameters
- remind about steps the user might forget
- avoid inappropriate choices
- support error recovery
- help answer questions from the system
- deal with idioms that require rote learning

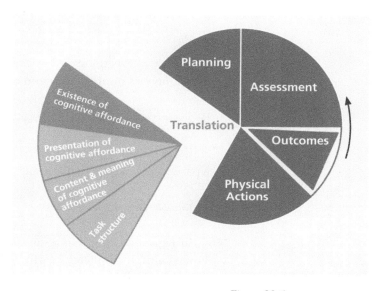

Figure 22-6
Existence of a cognitive affordance within translation.

Provide effective cognitive affordances that help users get access to system functionality

Support users' cognitive needs to determine how to do something by ensuring the existence of an appropriate cognitive affordance. Not giving feed-forward cognitive affordances, cues such as labels, data field formats, and icons, is what Cooper (2004, p. 140) calls "uninformed consent"; the user must proceed without understanding the consequences.

Help users know/learn what actions are needed to carry out intentions

It is possible to build in effective cognitive affordances that help novice users and do not get in the way of experienced users.

Help users know how to do something at action/object level

Users get their operational knowledge from experience, training, *and cognitive affordances in the design.* It is our job to provide this latter source of user knowledge.

Help users predict outcome of actions

Users need feed-forward in cognitive affordances that explains the consequences of physical actions, such as clicking on a button.

Help users determine what to do to get started

Users need support in understanding what actions to take for the first step of a particular task, the "getting started" step, often the most difficult part of a task.

Example: Helpful PowerPoint

In Figure 22-7 there is a start-up screen of an early version of Microsoft PowerPoint. In applications where there is a wide variety of things a user can do, it is difficult to know what to do to get started when faced with a blank screen. The addition of one simple cognitive and physical affordance combination, Click to add first slide, provides an easy way for an uncertain user to get started in creating a presentation.

Similarly, in Figure 22-8 we show other such helpful cues to continue, once a new slide is begun.

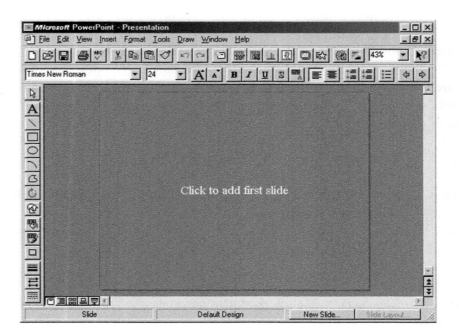

Figure 22-7

Help in getting started in PowerPoint (screen image courtesy of Tobias Frans-Jan Theebe).

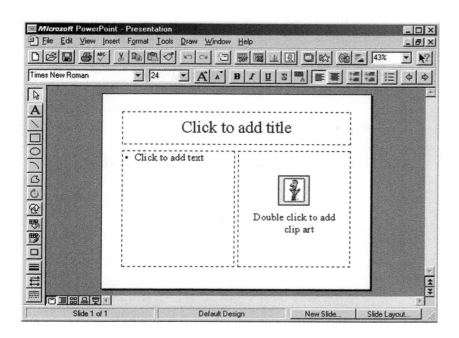

Figure 22-8
More help in getting started (screen image courtesy of Tobias Frans-Jan Theebe).

Provide a cognitive affordance for a step the user might forget

Support user needs with cognitive affordances as prompts, reminders, cues, or warnings for a particular needed action that might get forgotten.

22.6.2 Presentation of Cognitive Affordance
In Figure 22-9, we highlight the "presentation of cognitive affordance" portion of the translation part of the Interaction Cycle.

Presentation of cognitive affordances is about how cognitive affordances *appear* to users, not how they convey meaning. Users must be able to sense, for example, see or hear, a cognitive affordance before it can be useful to them.

Figure 22-9
Presentation of cognitive affordances within translation.

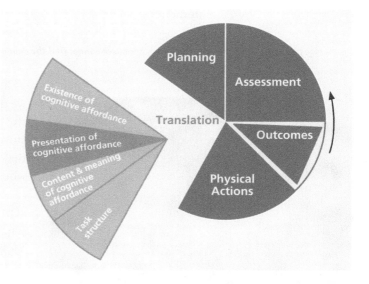

Support user with effective sensory affordances in presentation of cognitive affordances

Support user sensory needs in seeing and hearing cognitive affordances by effective presentation or appearance. This category is about issues such as legibility, noticeability, timing of presentation, layout, spatial grouping, complexity, consistency, and presentation medium, for example, audio, when needed. Sensory affordance issues also include text legibility and content contained in the appearance of a graphical feature, such as an icon, but only about whether the icon can be seen or discerned easily. For an audio medium, the volume and sound quality are presentation characteristics.

Cognitive affordance visibility

Obviously a cognitive affordance cannot be an effective cue if it cannot be seen or heard when it is needed. Our first guideline in this category is conveyed by the sign in Figure 22-10, if only we could be sure what it means.

Make cognitive affordances visible

If a cognitive affordance is invisible, it could be because it is not (yet) displayed or because it is occluded by another object. A user aware of the existence of the cognitive affordance can often take some actions to summon an invisible cognitive affordance into view. It is the designer's job to be sure each cognitive affordance is visible, or easily made visible, when it is needed in the interaction.

Figure 22-10
Good advice anytime.

Example: Store user cannot find the deodorant

This example is about a user (shopper) whom we think would rate himself at least a little above the novice level in shopping at his local grocery store. But recently, on a trip to get some deodorant, he was forced to reconsider his rating when his quick-in-and-quick-out plan was totally foiled. First, the store had been completely remodeled so he could not rely on his memory of past organization. However, because he was looking for only one item, he was optimistic.

He made a fast pass down the center aisle, looking at the overhead signs in each side aisle for anything related to deodorant, but nothing matched his search goal. There were also some sub-aisles in a different configuration along the front of the store. He scanned those aisles unsuccessfully. Although the rubber on his shopping cart tires was burning, he felt his fast-shopping plan slipping away so he did what no guy wants to do, he asked for directions.

Figure 22-11
Aesthetic panel blocks visibility of sign as cognitive affordance.

The clerk said, "Oh, it is right over there," pointing to one of the upfront aisles that he had just scanned. "But I do not see any sign for deodorant," he whined, silently blaming himself, the user, for the inability to see a sign that must have been somewhere right there in front on him. "Oh, yeah, there is a sign," she replied (condescendingly, he thought), "you just have to get up real close and look right behind that panel on the top of the end shelf." Figure 22-11 shows what that panel looked like to someone scanning these upfront aisles.

In Figure 22-12 you can see the "deodorant" sign revealed if you "just get up real close and look right behind that panel on the top of the end shelf."

The nice aesthetic end panels added much to the beauty of the shopping experience, but were put in a location that exactly blocked the "deodorant" sign and others, rendering that important cognitive affordance invisible from most perspectives in the store.

When our now-humbled shopper reminded the store clerk that this design violated the guideline for visibility for presentation of cognitive affordances, he was encouraged that he had reached her interaction design sensibilities when he overheard her hushed retort, "Whatever!". He left thinking, "that went well."

Figure 22-12
The sign is visible if you look carefully.

Cognitive affordance noticeability
Make cognitive affordances noticeable

When a needed cognitive affordance exists and is visible, the next consideration is its noticeability or likelihood of being noticed or sensed. Just putting a cognitive affordance on the screen is not enough, especially if the user does not necessarily know it exists or is not necessarily looking for it. These design issues

are largely about supporting awareness. Relevant cognitive affordances should come to users' attention without users seeking it. The primary design factor in this regard is location, putting the cognitive affordance within the users' focus of attention. It is also about contrast, size, and layout complexity and their effect on separation of the cognitive affordance from the background and from the clutter of other user interface objects.

Example: Status lines often do not work

Message lines, status lines, and title lines at the top or bottom of the screen are notoriously unnoticeable. Each user typically has a narrow focus of attention, usually near where the cursor is located. A pop-up message next to the cursor will be far more noticeable than a message in a line at the bottom of the screen.

Example: Where the heck is the log-in?

For some reason, many Websites have very small and inconspicuous log-in boxes, often mixed in with many objects most users do not even notice in the far top border of the page. Users have to waste time in searching visually over the whole page to find the way to log in.

Cognitive affordance legibility
Make text legible, readable

Text legibility is about being discernable, not about the words being understandable. Text presentation issues include the way the text of a button label is presented so it can be read or sensed, including such appearance or sensory characteristics as font type, font size, font and background color, bolding, or italics of the text, but it is not about the content or meaning of the words in the text. The meaning is the same regardless of the font or color.

Cognitive affordance presentation complexity
Control cognitive affordance presentation complexity with effective layout, organization, and grouping

Support user needs to locate and be aware of cognitive affordances by controlling layout complexity of user interface objects. Screen clutter can obscure needed cognitive affordances such as icons, prompt messages, state indicators, dialogue box components, or menus and make it difficult for users to find them.

Cognitive affordance presentation timing

Support user needs to notice cognitive affordance with appropriate timing of appearance or display of cognitive affordances. Do not present a cognitive affordance too early or too late or with inadequate persistence; that is, avoid "flashing."

Present cognitive affordance in time for it to help the user before the associated action

Sometimes getting cognitive affordance presentation timing right means presenting at exactly the point in a task and under exactly the conditions when the cognitive affordance is needed.

Example: Just-in-time towel dispenser message

Figures 22-13 and 22-14 are photographs of a paper towel dispenser in a public bathroom. They illustrate an example of a good design that involves just-in-time visibility of presentation of a cognitive affordance.

In Figure 22-13, the next available towel is visible and the cognitive affordance in the sketch on the cover of the dispenser clearly says "Pull the towel down with both hands."

In Figure 22-14 you can see how designers covered the case where the next towel failed to drop down so users cannot grab it. Now a different user action is needed to get a towel, so a different cognitive affordance is required.

Designers provided this new cognitive affordance, telling the user to Push the lever to get the next towel started down into position. When a towel was already in place, this second cognitive affordance was not needed and was not visible, being obscured by the towel, but it does become visible just when it is needed.

Example: Special pasting

When a user wishes to paste something from one Word document to another, there can be a

Figure 22-13

The primary cognitive affordance for taking a paper towel.

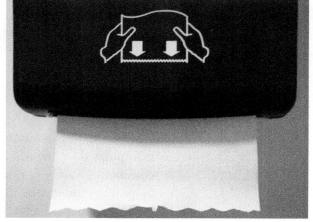

Figure 22-14

The backup cognitive affordance to help start a new paper towel.

question about formatting. Will the item retain its formatting, such as text or paragraph style, from the original document or will it adopt the formatting from the place of insertion in the new document? And how can the choice be controlled by the user? When you want more control of a paste operation, you might choose Paste Special ... from the Edit menu.

But the choices in the Paste Special dialogue box say nothing about controlling formatting. Rather, the choices can seem too technical or system centered, for example, Microsoft Office Word Document Object or Unformatted Unicode Text, without an explanation of the resulting effect in the document. While these choices might be precise about the action and its results to some users, they are cryptic even to most regular users.

In recent versions of Word, a small cognitive affordance, a tiny clipboard icon with a pop-up label Paste Options appears, but it appears *after* the paste operation. Many users do not notice this little object, mainly because by the time it appeared, they have experienced closure on the paste operation and have already moved on mentally to the next task. If they do not like the resulting formatting, then changing it manually becomes their next task.

Even if users do notice the little object, it is possible they might confuse it with something to do with undoing the action or something similar because Word uses that same object for in-context undo. However, if a user does notice this icon and does take the time to click on it, that user will be rewarded with a pull-down menu of useful options, such as Keep Source Formatting, Match Destination Formatting, Keep Text Only, plus a choice to see a full selection of other formatting styles.

Just what users need! But it is made available too late; the chance to see this menu comes *after* the user action to which it applied. If choices on this after-the-fact menu were available on the Paste Special menu, it would be perfect for users.

Cognitive affordance presentation consistency

When a cognitive affordance is located within a user interface object that is also manipulated by physical actions, such as a label within a button, maintaining a consistent location of that object on the screen helps users find it quickly and helps them use muscle memory for fast clicking. Hansen (1971) used the term "display inertia" in reference to one of his top-level principles, optimize operations, to describe this business of minimizing display changes in response to user inputs, including displaying a given user interface object in the same place each time it is shown.

Give similar cognitive affordances consistent appearance in presentation

Example: Archive button jumps around

When users of an older version of Gmail were viewing the list of messages in the Inbox, the Archive button was at the far left at the top of the message pane, set off by the blue border, as shown in Figure 22-15.

But on the screen for reading a message, Gmail had the Archive button as the second object from the left at the top. In the place where the Archive button was earlier, there was now a Back to Inbox link, as seen in Figure 22-16. Using a link instead of a button in this position is a slight inconsistency, probably without much effect on users. But users feel a larger effect from the inconsistent placement of the Archive button.

Selected messages can be archived from either view of the email by clicking on the Archive button. Further, when archiving messages from the Inbox list view, the user sometimes goes to the message-reading view to be sure. So a user doing

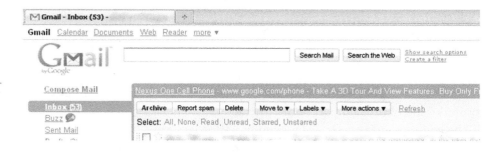

Figure 22-15

The Archive button in the Inbox view of an older version of Gmail.

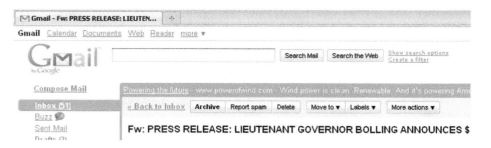

Figure 22-16

The Archive button in a different place in the message reading view.

Figure 22-17

The Archive button in the Inbox view of a later version of Gmail.

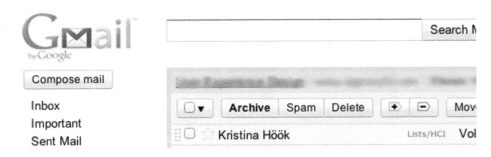

an archiving task could be going back and forth between the Inbox listing of Figure 22-15 and message viewing of Figure 22-16.

For this activity, the location of the Archive button is never certain. The user loses momentum and performance speed by having to look for the Archive button each time before clicking on it. Even though it moves only a short distance between the two views, it is enough to slow down users significantly because they cannot run the cursor up to the same spot every time to do multiple archive actions quickly. The lack of display inertia works against an efficient sensory action of finding the button and it works against muscle memory in making the physical action of moving the cursor up to click.

It seems that Google people have fixed this problem in subsequent versions, as attested to by the same kinds of screens in Figures 22-17 and 22-18.

22.6.3 Content and Meaning of Cognitive Affordance

> *Just what part of quantum theory do you not understand?*
>
> – Anonymous

Figure 22-19 highlights the "content and meaning of cognitive affordance" portion of the translation part of the Interaction Cycle.

Figure 22-18

The Archive button in the same place in the new message reading view.

The content and meaning of a cognitive affordance are the knowledge that must be conveyed to users to be effective in helping them as affordances to think, learn, and know what they need to make correct actions. The cognitive affordance design concepts that support understanding of content and meaning include clarity, distinguishability from other cognitive affordances, consistency, layout and grouping to control complexity, usage centeredness, and techniques for avoiding errors.

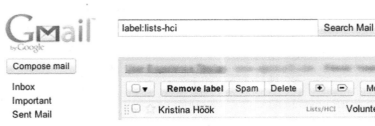

Help user determine actions with effective
content/meaning in cognitive affordances

Support user ability to determine what
action(s) to make and on what object(s)
for a task step through understanding
and comprehension of cognitive
affordance content and meaning: what it
says, verbally or graphically.

Clarity of cognitive affordances
Design cognitive affordances for clarity

Use precise wording, carefully chosen
vocabulary, or meaningful graphics to
create correct, complete, and sufficient
expressions of content and meaning of
cognitive affordances.

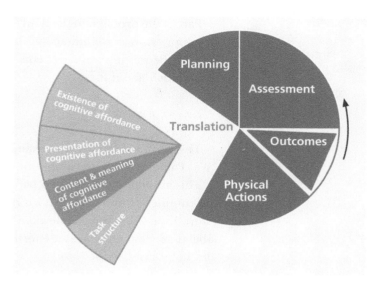

Figure 22-19
Content/meaning within
translation.

Precise wording

Support user understanding of cognitive affordance content by precise
expression of meaning through precise word choices. Clarity is especially
important for short, command-like text, such as is found in button labels, menu
choices, and verbal prompts. For example, the button label to dismiss a dialogue
box could say Return to . . . , where appropriate, instead of just OK.

Use precise wording in labels, menu titles, menu choices, icons, data fields

The imperative for clear and precise wording of button labels, menu choices,
messages, and other text may seem obvious, at least in the abstract. However,
experienced practitioners know that designers often do not take the time to
choose their words carefully.

In our own evaluation experience, this guideline is among the most violated
in real-world practice. Others have shared this experience, including Johnson
(2000). Because of the overwhelming importance of precise wording in
interaction designs and the apparent unmindful approach to wording by many
designers in practice, we consider this to be one of the most important
guidelines in the whole book.

Part of the problem in the field is that wording is often considered a relatively unimportant part of interaction design and is assigned to developers and software people not trained to construct precise wording and not even trained to think much about it.

Example: Wet paint!

This is one of our favorite examples of precise wording, probably overdone: "Wet Paint. This is a warning, not an instruction."

This guideline represents a part of interaction design where a great improvement can be accrued for only a small investment of extra time and effort. Even a few minutes devoted to getting just the right wording for a button label used frequently has an enormous potential payoff. Here are some related and helpful sub-guidelines:

Use a verb and noun and even an adjective in labels where appropriate
Avoid vague, ambiguous terms
Be as specific to the interaction situation as possible; avoid one-size-fits-all messages
Clearly represent work domain concepts

Example: Then, how can we use the door?

As an example of matching the message to the reality of the work domain, signs such as "Keep this door closed at all times" probably should read something more like "Close this door immediately after use."

Use dynamically changing labels when toggling

When using the same control object, such as a Play/Pause button on an mp3 music player, to control the toggling of a system state, change the object label to show that it is consistently a control to get to the next state. Otherwise the current system state can be unclear and there can be confusion over whether the label represents an action the user can make or feedback about the current system state.

Example: Reusing a button label

In Figure 22-20 we show an early prototype of a personal document retrieval system. The underlying model for deleting a document involves two steps: marking the document for deletion and later deleting all marked documents permanently. The small check box at the lower right is labeled: Marked for Deletion.

The designer's idea was that users would check that box to signify the intention to delete the record. Thereafter, until a permanent purge of marked records, seeing a check in this box signifies that this record is, indeed, marked for deletion. The problem comes before the user checks the box.

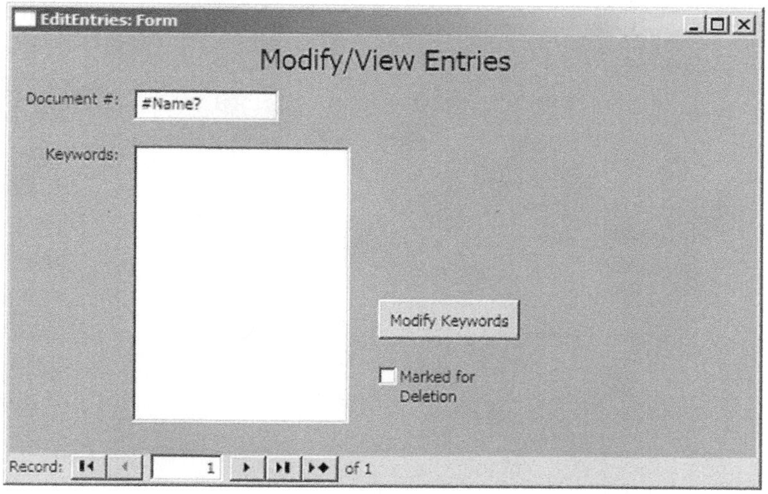

The user wants to delete the record (or at least mark it for deletion), but this label seems to be a statement of system state rather than a cognitive affordance for an action, implying that it is already marked for deletion. However, because the check box is not checked, it is not entirely clear. Our suggestion was to re-label the box in the unchecked state to read: Check to mark for deletion, making it a true cognitive affordance for action in this state. After checking, Marked for Deletion works fine.

Figure 22-20
The Marked for Deletion check box in a document retrieval screen (screen image courtesy of Raphael Summers).

Data value formats. Support user needs to know how to enter data, such as in a form field, with a cognitive affordance or cue to help with format and kinds of values that are acceptable.

Provide cognitive affordances to indicate formatting within data fields

Data entry is a user work activity where the formatting of data values is an issue. Entry in the "wrong" format, meaning a format the user thinks is right but the system designers did not anticipate, can lead to errors that the user must spend time to resolve or, worse yet, have undetected data errors. It is relatively easy for designers to indicate expected data formats, with cognitive affordances associated with the field labels, with sample data values, or both.

Example: How should I enter the date?

In Figure 22-21 we show a dialogue box that appears in an application that is, despite the cryptic title Task Series, for scheduling events. In the Duration

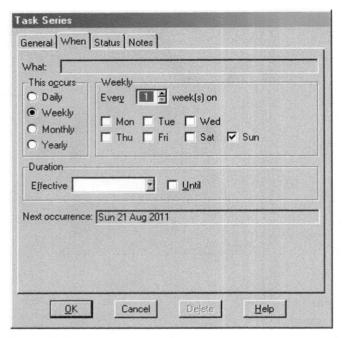

Figure 22-21

Missing cognitive affordance about Effective Date data field format (screen image courtesy of Tobias Frans-Jan Theebe).

section, the Effective Date field does not indicate the expected format for data values. Although many systems are capable of accepting date values in almost any format, new or intermittent users may not know if this application is that smart. It would have been easy for the designer to save users from hesitation and uncertainty by suggesting a format here.

Constrain the formats of data values to avoid data entry errors

Sometimes rather than just show the format, it is more effective to constrain values so that they are acceptable as inputs.

An easy way to constrain the formatting of a date value, for example, is to use drop-down lists, specialized to hold values appropriate for the month, day, and year parts of the date field. Another approach that many users like is a "date picker," a calendar that pops up when the user clicks on the date field. A date can be entered into the field only by way of selection from this calendar.

A calendar with one month of dates at a time is perhaps the most practical. Side arrows allow the user to navigate to earlier or later months or years. Clicking on a date within the month on the calendar causes that date to be picked for the value to be used. By using a date-picker, you are constraining both the data entry method and the format the user must employ, effectively eliminating errors due to either allowing inappropriate values or formatting ambiguity.

Provide clearly marked exits

Support user ability to exit dialogue sequences confidently by using clearly labeled exits. Include destination information to help users predict where the action will go upon leaving the current dialogue sequence. For example, in a dialogue box you might use Return to XYZ after saving instead of OK and Return to XYZ without saving instead of Cancel.

To qualify this example, we have to say that the terms OK and Cancel are so well accepted and so thoroughly part of our current shared conventions that, even though the example shows potentially better wordings, the conventions now carry the same meaning at least to experienced users.

Provide clear "do it" mechanism

Some kinds of choice-making objects, such as drop-down or pop-up menus, commit to the choice as soon as the user indicates the choice; others require a separate "commit to this choice" action. This inconsistency can be unsettling for some users who are unsure about whether their choices have "taken." Becker (2004) argues for a consistent use of a "Go" action, such as a click, to commit to choices, for example, choices made in a dialogue box or drop-down menu. And we caution to make its usage clear to avoid task completion slips where users think they have completed making the menu choice, for example, and move on without committing to it with the Go button.

Be predictable; help users predict outcome of actions with feed-forward information in cognitive affordances. Predictability helps both learning and error avoidance

Distinguishability of choices in cognitive affordances
Make choices distinguishable

Support user ability to differentiate two or more possible choices or actions by distinguishable expressions of meaning in their cognitive affordances. If two similar cognitive affordances lead to different outcomes, careful design is needed so users can avoid errors by distinguishing the cases.

Often distinguishability is the key to correct user choices by the process of elimination; if you provide enough information to rule out the cases not wanted, users will be able to make the correct choice. Focus on differences of meaning in the wording of names and labels. Make larger differences graphically in similar icons.

Example: Tragic airplane crash

This is an unfortunate, but true, story that evinces the reality that human lives can be lost due to simple confusion over labeling of controls. This is a very serious usability case involving the dramatic and tragic October 31, 1999 EgyptAir Flight 990 airliner crash (Acohido, 1999) possibly as a result of poor usability in design. According to the news account, the pilot may have been confused by two sets of switches that were similar in appearance, labeled very similarly, as Cut out and Cut off, and located relatively close to each other in the Boeing 767 cockpit design.

Exacerbating the situation, both switches are used infrequently, only under unusual flight conditions. This latter point is important because it means that the pilots would not have been experienced in using either one. Knowing pilots receive extensive training, designers assumed their users are experts. But because these particular controls are rarely used, most pilots are novices in their use, implying the need for more effective cognitive affordances than usual.

One conjecture is that one of the flight crew attempted to pull the plane out of an unexpected dive by setting the Cut out switches connected to the stabilizer trim but instead accidentally set the Cut off switches, shutting off fuel to both engines. The black box flight recorder did confirm that the plane did go into a sudden dive and that a pilot did flip the fuel system cutoff switches soon thereafter.

There seem to be two critical design issues, the first of which is the distinguishability of the labeling, especially under conditions of stress and infrequent use. To us, not knowledgeable in piloting large planes, the two labels seem so similar as to be virtually synonymous.

Making the labels more complete would have made their much more distinguishable. In particular, adding a noun to the verb of the labels would have made a huge difference: Cut out trim versus Cut off fuel. Putting the all-important noun first might be an even better distinguisher: Fuel off and Trim out. Just this simple UX improvement might have averted the disaster.

The second design issue is the apparent physical proximity of the two controls, inviting the physical slip of grabbing the wrong one, despite knowing the difference. Surely stabilizer trim and fuel functions are completely unrelated. Regrouping by related functions—locating the Fuel off switch with other fuel-related functions and the Trim out switch with other stabilizer-related controls—might have helped the pilots distinguish them, preventing the catastrophic error.

Finally, we have to assume that safety, absolute error avoidance in this situation, would have to be a top priority UX goal for this design. To meet this goal, the Fuel off switch could have been further protected from accidental operation by adding a mechanical feature that requires an additional conscious action by the pilot to operate this seldom-used but dangerous control. One possibility is a physical cover over the switch that has to be lifted before the switch can be flipped, a safety feature used in the design of missile launch switches, for example.

Consistency of cognitive affordances

Consistency is one of those concepts that everyone thinks they understand but almost no one can define.

Be consistent with cognitive affordances
Use consistent wording in labels for menus, buttons, icons, fields

Being consistent in wording has two sides: using the same terms for the same things and using different terms for different things. The next three guidelines and examples are about using the same terms for the same things.

Use similar names for similar kinds of things
Do not use multiple synonyms for the same thing

Example: Continue or retry?

This example comes from the very old days of floppy disks, but could apply to external hard disks of today as well. It is a great example of using two different words for the same thing in the short space of the one little message dialogue box in Figure 22-22.

If, upon learning that the current disk is full, the user inserts a new disk and intends to continue copying files, for example, what should she click, Retry or Cancel? Hopefully she can find the right choice by the process of elimination, as Cancel will almost certainly terminate the operation. But Retry carries the connotation of starting over. Why not match the goal of continuing with a button labeled Continue?

Use the same term in a reference to an object as the name or label of the object

If a cognitive affordance suggests an action on a specific object, such as "Click on Add Record," the name or label on that object must be the same, in this case also Add Record.

Example: Press what?

From more modern days and a Website for Virginia Tech employees, Figure 22-23 is another clear example of how easy it is for this kind of design flaw to slip by designers, a type of flaw that is usually found by expert UX inspection.

Figure 22-22

Inconsistent wording: Continue or Retry? (screen image courtesy of Tobias Frans-Jan Theebe).

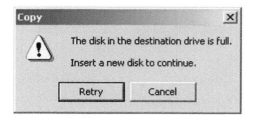

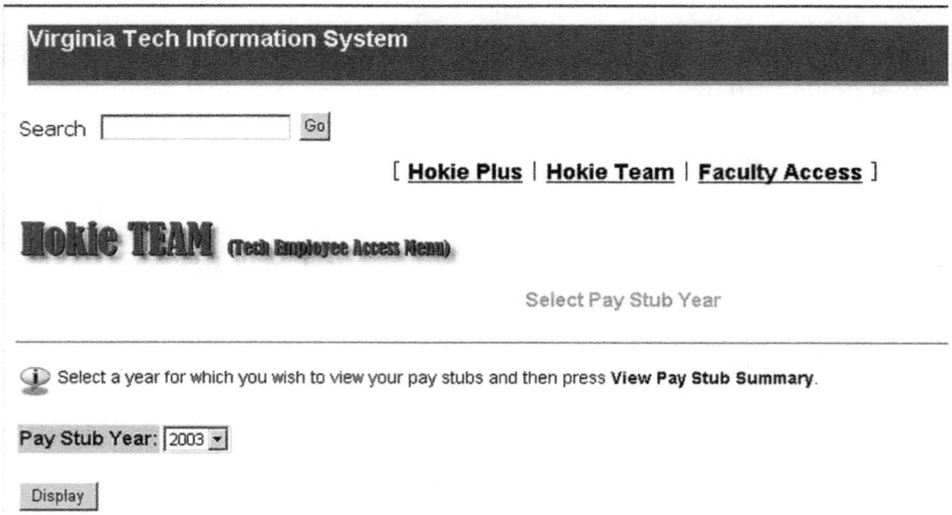

Figure 22-23

Cannot click on "View Pay Stub Summary."

Virginia Tech Information System

Search [   ] [Go]

[**Hokie Plus** | **Hokie Team** | **Faculty Access**]

Hokie TEAM (Tech Employee Access Menu)

Select Pay Stub Year

ⓘ Select a year for which you wish to view your pay stubs and then press **View Pay Stub Summary**.

Pay Stub Year: [2003 ▾]

[Display]

This is another example of inconsistency of wording. The cognitive affordance in the line above the Pay Stub Year selection menu says press View Pay Stub Summary, but the label on the button to be pressed says Display. Maybe this big a difference in what is supposed to be the same is due to having different people working on different parts of the design. In any case we noticed that in a subsequent version, someone had found and fixed the problem, as seen in Figure 22-24.

In passing, we note an additional UX problem with each of these screens, the cognitive affordance Select Pay Stub year in the top half of the frame is redundant with Select a year for which you wish to view your pay stubs in the bottom section. We would recommend keeping the second one, as it is more informative and is grouped with the pull-down menu for year selection.

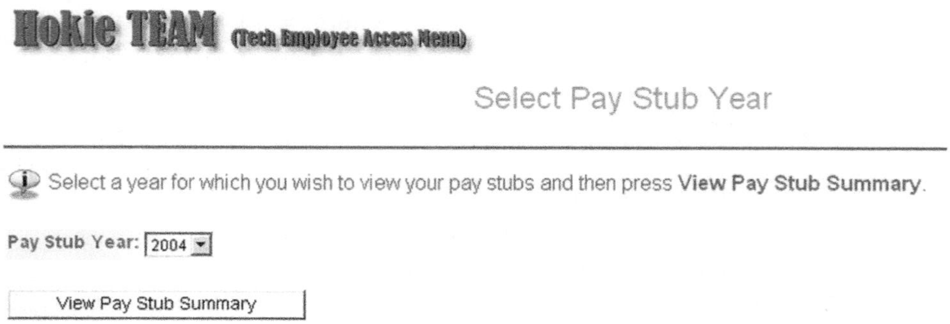

Hokie TEAM (Tech Employee Access Menu)

Select Pay Stub Year

ⓘ Select a year for which you wish to view your pay stubs and then press **View Pay Stub Summary**.

Figure 22-24

Problem fixed with new button label.

Pay Stub Year: [2004 ▾]

[View Pay Stub Summary]

The first Select Pay Stub year looks like some kind of title but is really kind of an orphan. The distance between this cognitive affordance and the user interface object to which it applies, plus the solid line, makes for a strong separation between two design elements that should be closely associated. Because it is unnecessary and separate from the year menu, it could be confusing. For all the years we were available as an HCI and UX resource, we were never asked to help with the design or evaluation of any software by the university. That is undoubtedly typical.

Use different terms for different things, especially when the difference is subtle

This is the flip side of the guideline that says to use the same terms for the same things. As we will see in the following example, terms such as Add can mean several different but closely related things. If you, the interaction designer, do not distinguish the differences with appropriately precise terminology, it can lead to confusion for the user.

Example: The user thought files were already "Added"

When using Nero Express to burn CDs and DVDs for data transfer and backup, users put in a blank disc and choose the Create a Data Disc option and see the window shown in Figure 22-25.

In the middle of this window is an empty space that looks like a file directory. Most users will figure out that this is for the list of the files and folders they want to put on the disc. At the top, where it will be seen only if the user looks around, it gives the cue: "Add data to your disc." In the normal task path, there is really only one action that makes sense, which is clicking on the Add button at the top on the right-hand side.

This is taken by the user to be the way you add files and folders to this list. When users click on

Figure 22-25
First Nero Add button.

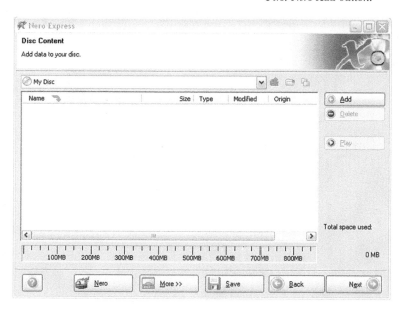

Add, they get the next window, shown in Figure 22-26, overlapping the initial window.

This window also shows a directory space in the middle for browsing the files and folders and selecting those to be added to the list for the disc. The way that one commits the selected files to go on the list for the disc is to click on the Add button in this window. Here the term Add really means to add the selected files to the disc list. In the first window, however, the term Add really meant proceed to file selection for the disc list, which is related but slightly different. Yes, the difference is subtle but it is our job to be precise in wording.

Be consistent in the way that similar choices or parameter settings are made

If a certain set of related parameters are all selected or set with one method, such as check boxes or radio buttons, then all parameters related to that set should be selected or set the same way.

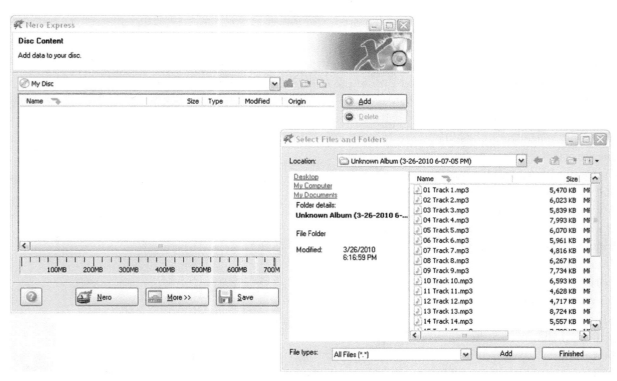

Figure 22-26

Another window and another Add button.

Example: The Find dialogue box in Microsoft Word

Setting and clearing search parameters for the Find function are done with check boxes on the lower left-hand side (Figure 22-27) and with pull-down menus at the bottom of the dialogue box for font, paragraph, and other format attributes and special characteristics. We have observed many users having trouble turning off the format attributes, which is because the "command" for that is different than all the others.

It is accomplished by clicking on the No Formatting button on the right-hand side at the bottom; see Figure 22-27. Many users simply do not see that because nothing else uses a button to set or reset a parameter so they are not looking for a button.

The following example is an instance of the same kind of inconsistency, not using the same kind of selection method for related parameters, only this example is from the world of food ordering.

Example: Circle your selections

In Figure 22-28 you see an order slip for a sandwich at Au Bon Pain. Under Create Your Own Sandwich it says Please circle all selections but the very next choice is between two check boxes for selecting the sandwich size. It is a minor thing that probably does not impact user performance but, to a UX stickler, it stands out as an inconsistency in the design.

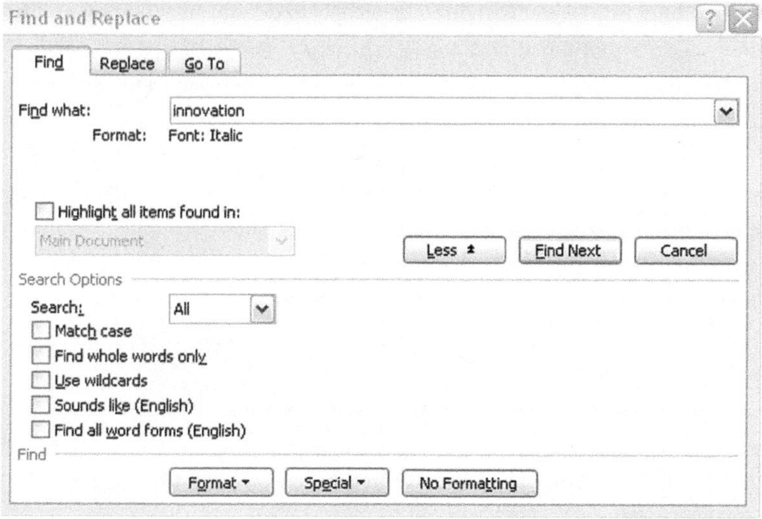

Figure 22-27

Format with a menu but No Formatting with a button.

au bon pain

Name _____   ☐ **Here**   ☐ **To Go**

CREATE YOUR OWN SANDWICH

| ☐ **whole** | Please circle all selections
(includes one meat, bread, spreads, and toppings) | ☐ **half** |

MEAT select one; 1.75 each additional	Tuna	Smoked Ham	Roast Beef	Smoked Turkey	Grilled Chicken (not available as a 1/2 sandwich)
BREAD	Baguette Multi-Grain Baguette Sliced Country White	Sliced Multi-Grain Sliced Tomato Herb Lahvash	Croissant Soft Roll Bagel _____ (indicate choice of bagel)		
ADD-ONS .79 each	Swiss Cheddar	Fresh Mozzarella Bacon			
SPREADS	Mayo	Herb Mayo	Dijon Mustard	Honey Dijon	Chili Dijon
TOPPINGS	Tomato	Romaine Lettuce	Red Onion	Cucumber	

Figure 22-28

"Circle all selections," but size choice is by check boxes.

We wrap up this section on consistency of cognitive affordances with the following example about how many problems with consistency in terminology we found in an evaluation of one Web-based application.

Example: Consistency problems

In this example we consider only problems relating to wording consistency from a lab-based UX evaluation of an academic Web application for classroom support. We suspect this pervasiveness of inconsistency was due to having different people doing the design in different places and not having a project-wide custom style guide or not using one to document working terminology choices.

In any case, when the design contains different terms for the same thing, it can confuse the user, especially the new user who is trying to conquer the system vocabulary. Here are some examples of our UX problem descriptions, "sanitized" to protect the guilty.

- The terms "revise" and "edit" were used interchangeably to denote an action to modify an information object within the application. For example, Revise is used as an action option for a selected object in the Worksite Setup page of My Workspace, whereas Edit is used inside the Site Info page of a given worksite.

- The terms "worksite" and "site" are used interchangeably for the same meaning. For example, many of the options in the menu bar of My Workspace use the term "worksite," whereas the Membership page uses "site," as in My Current Sites.

- The terms "add" and "new" are used interchangeably, referring to the same concept. Under the Manage Groups option, there is a link for adding a group, called New. Most everywhere else, such as for adding an event to a schedule, the link for creating a new information object is labeled Add.

- The way that lists are used to present information is inconsistent:
  - In some lists, such as the list on the Worksite Setup page, check boxes are on the left-hand side, but for most other lists, such as the list on the Group List page, check boxes are on the right.

■ To edit some lists, the user must select a list item check box and then choose the Revise option in a menu bar (of links) at the top of the page and separated from the list. In other lists, each item has its own Revise link. For yet other lists there is a collection of links, one for each of the multiple ways the user can edit an item.

Controlling complexity of cognitive affordance content and meaning

Decompose complex instructions into simpler parts

Cognitive affordances do not afford anything if they are too complex to understand or follow. Try decomposing long and complicated instructions into smaller, more meaningful, and more easily digested parts.

Example: Say what?

The cognitive affordance of Figure 22-29 contains instructions that can bewilder even the most attentive user, especially someone in a wheelchair who needs to get out of there fast.

Use layout and grouping of cognitive affordances to control content and meaning complexity

Use appropriate layout and grouping by function of cognitive affordances to control content and meaning complexity

Support user cognitive affordance content understanding through layout and spatial grouping to show relationships of task and function.

Group together objects and design elements associated with related tasks and functions

Functions, user interface objects, and controls related to a given task or function should be grouped together spatially. The indication of relationship is strengthened by a graphical demarcation, such as a box around the group.

Figure 22-29

Good luck in evacuating quickly.

Label the group with words that reflect the common functionality of the relationship. Grouping and labeling related data fields are especially important for data entry.

Do not group together objects and design elements that are not associated with related tasks and functions

This guideline, the converse of the previous one, seems to be observed more often in the breach in real-world designs.

Example: Here are your options

The Options dialogue box in Figure 22-30, from an older version of Microsoft Word, illustrates a case where some controls are grouped incorrectly with some parameter settings.

The metaphor in this design is that of a deck of tabbed index cards. The user has clicked on the General tab, which took the user to this General "card" where the user made a change in the options listed. While in the business of setting options, the user then wishes to go to another tab for more settings. The user hesitates, concerned that moving to another tab without "saving" the settings in the current tab might cause them to be lost.

Figure 22-30

OK and Cancel controls on individual tab "card" (screen image courtesy of Tobias Frans-Jan Theebe).

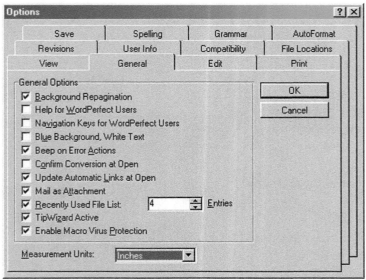

So this user clicks on the OK to get closure for this tabbed card before moving on. To his surprise, the entire dialogue box disappears and he must start over by selecting Options from the Tools menu at the top of the screen.

The surprise and extra work to recover were the price of the use of layout and grouping as an incorrect indication of the scope or range covered by the OK and Cancel buttons. Designers have made the buttons actually apply to the entire Options dialogue box, but they put the buttons on the currently open tabbed card, making them appear to apply just to the card or, in this case, just to the General category of options.

The Options dialogue box from a different version of Microsoft PowerPoint in Figure 22-31 is a better design that places all the tabbed cards on a larger background and the OK and Cancel controls are on this background, showing clearly that the controls are grouped with the whole dialogue box and not with individual tabbed cards.

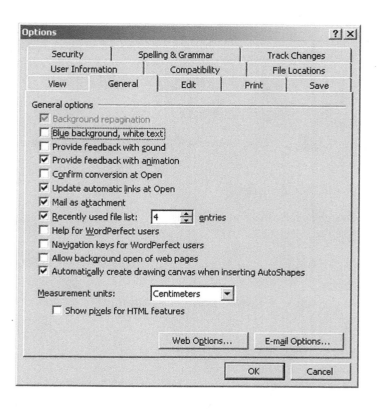

Example: Where to put the Search button?

Some parameters associated with a search function in a digital library are shown in Figure 22-32. In the original design, shown at the top of Figure 22-32, the Search button is located right next to the OR radio-button choice at the bottom. Perhaps it is associated with the Combine fields with feature? No, it actually was intended to be associated with the entire search box, as shown in the "Suggested redesign" at the bottom of Figure 22-32.

Figure 22-31

OK and Cancel controls on background underneath all the tab "cards" (screen image courtesy of Tobias Frans-Jan Theebe).

Example: Are we going to Eindhoven or Catalonia?

Here is a non-computer (sort of) example from the airlines. While waiting in Milan one day to board a flight to Eindhoven, passengers saw the display shown in Figure 22-33. As the display suggests, the Eindhoven flight followed a flight to Catalonia (in Spain) from the same gate.

As the flight to Catalonia began boarding, confusion started brewing in the boarding area. Many people were unsure about which flight was boarding, as both flights were displayed on the board. The main source of trouble was due to the way parts of the text were grouped in the flight announcements on the overhead board. The state information Embarco (meaning departing) was closer to the Eindhoven listing than to that of Catalonia, as shown in

Original design

Search specific bibliographic fields

Author	
Title	
Abstract	
	Combine fields with ◉ AND ○ OR [**Search**]

Suggested redesign

Search specific bibliographic fields

Author	
Title	
Abstract	

Combine fields with ◉ AND ○ OR

[**Search**]

Figure 22-32

(Top) Uncertain association with Search; (bottom) problem fixed with better layout and grouping.

Figure 22-33. So Embarco seemed to be grouped with and applied to the Eindhoven flight.

Confusion was compounded by the fact that it was 9:30 AM; the Catalonia flight was boarding late enough so that boarding could have been mistaken for the one to Eindhoven. Further conspiring against the waiting passengers was the fact that there were no oral announcements of the boardings, although there was a public address system. Many Eindhoven passengers were getting into the Catalonia boarding line. You could see them turning Eindhoven passengers away but still there was no announcement to clear up the problem.

Sometime later, the flight state information Embarco changed to Chiuso (meaning closed), as seen in Figure 22-34.

Many of the remaining Eindhoven passengers immediately became agitated, seeing the Chiuso and thinking that the Eindhoven flight was closed before they had a chance to board. In the end, everything was fine but the poor layout of the display on the flight announcement board caused stress among passengers and extra work for the airline gate attendants. Given that this situation can occur many times a day, involving many people every day, the cost of this poor UX must have been very high, even though the airline workers seemed to be oblivious as they contemplated their cappuccino breaks.

Figure 22-33

A sketch of the airline departure board in Milan.

Example: Hot wash, anyone?

In another simple example, in Figure 22-35 we depict a row of push-button controls once seen on a clothes washing machine.

The choices of Hot wash/cold rinse, Warm wash/cold rinse, and Cold wash/cold rinse all represent similar semantics (wash and rinse temperatures settings) and, therefore, should be grouped together. They are also expressed in similar syntax and words so it is consistent labeling. However, because all three choices include a cold rinse, why not just say that with a separate label and not include it in all the choices?

The real problem, though, is that the fourth button, labeled Start represents completely different functionality and should not be grouped with the other push buttons. Why do you think the designers made such an obvious mistake in grouping by related functionality? We think it is because one single switch assembly is less expensive to buy and install than two separate assemblies. Here, cost won over usability.

Example: There goes the flight attendant, again

On an airplane flight once, we noticed a design flaw in the layout of the overhead controls for a pair of passengers in a two-seat configuration, a flaw that created problems for flight attendants and passengers. This control panel had push-button switches at the left and right for turning the left and right reading lights on and off.

The problem is that the flight attendant call switch was located just between the two light controls. It looked nice and symmetric, but its close proximity to the light controls made it a frequent target of unintended operation. On this flight we saw flight attendants moving through the cabin frequently, resetting call buttons for numerous passengers.

In this design, switches for two related functions were separated by an unrelated one; the grouping of controls within the layout was not by function. Another reason calling for even further physical separation of the two kinds of switches is that light switches are used frequently while the call switch is not.

Likely user choices and useful defaults

Sometimes it is possible to anticipate menu and button choices, choices of data values, and choices of task paths that users will most likely want or need to take. By providing direct access to those choices and, in some cases making them the defaults, we can help make the task more efficient for users.

Support user choices with likely and useful defaults

Many user tasks require data entry into data fields in dialogue box and screens. Data entry is often a tedious and

Figure 22-34
Oh, no, Chiuso.

Figure 22-35
Clothes washing machine controls with one little inconsistency.

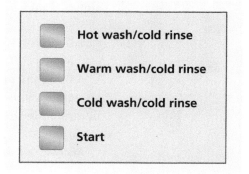

repetitive chore, and we should do everything we can to alleviate some of the dreary labor of this task by providing the most likely or most useful data values as defaults.

Example: What is the date?

Many forms call for the current date in one of the fields. Using today's date as the default value for that field should be a no-brainer.

Example: Tragic choice of defaults

Here is a serious example of a case where the choice of default values resulted in dire consequences. This story was relayed by a participant in one of our UX short courses at a military installation. We cannot vouch for its verity but, even if it is apocryphal, it makes the point well.

A front-line spotter for missile strikes has a GPS on which he can calculate the exact location of an enemy facility on a map overlay. The GPS unit also serves as a radio through which he can send the enemy location back to the missile firing emplacement, which will send a missile strike with deadly accuracy.

He entered the coordinates of the enemy just before sending the message, but unfortunately the GPS battery died before he could send the message. Because time was of the essence, he replaced the battery quickly and hit Send. The missile was fired and it hit and killed the spotter instead of the enemy.

When the old battery was removed, the system did not retain the enemy coordinates and, when the new battery was installed, the system entered its own current GPS location as default values for the coordinates. It was easy to pick off the local GPS coordinates of where the spotter was standing.

In isolation of other important considerations, it was a bit like putting in today's date as the default for a date; it is conveniently available. But in this case, the result of that convenience was death by friendly fire. With a moment's thought, no one could imagine making the spotter's coordinates the default for aiming a missile. The problem was fixed immediately!

Provide the most likely or most useful default selections

Among the most common violations of this guideline is the failure to select an item for a user when there is only one item from which to select, as illustrated in the next example.

Example: Only one item to select from

Here is a special case of applying this guideline where there is only one item from which to select. In this case it was one item in a dialogue box list. When this user opened a directory in this dialogue box showing only one item, the Select button was grayed out because the user is required to select something from the list before the Select button becomes active. However, because there was only one item, the user assumed that the item would be selected by default.

When he clicked the grayed-out Select button, however, nothing happened. The user did not realize that even though there is only one item in the list, the design requires selecting it before proceeding to click on the Select button. If no item is chosen, then the Select button does not give an error message nor does it prompt the user; it just sits there waiting for the user to do the "right thing." The difficulty could have been avoided by displaying the list of one item with that item already selected and highlighted, thus providing a useful default selection and allowing the Select button to be active from the start.

Offer most useful default cursor position

It is a small thing in a design, but it can be so nice to have the cursor just where you need it when you arrive at a dialogue box or window in which you have to work. As a designer, you can save users the work and irritation of extra physical actions, such as an extra mouse click before typing, by providing appropriate default cursor location, for example, in a data field or text box, or within the user interface object where the user is most likely to work next.

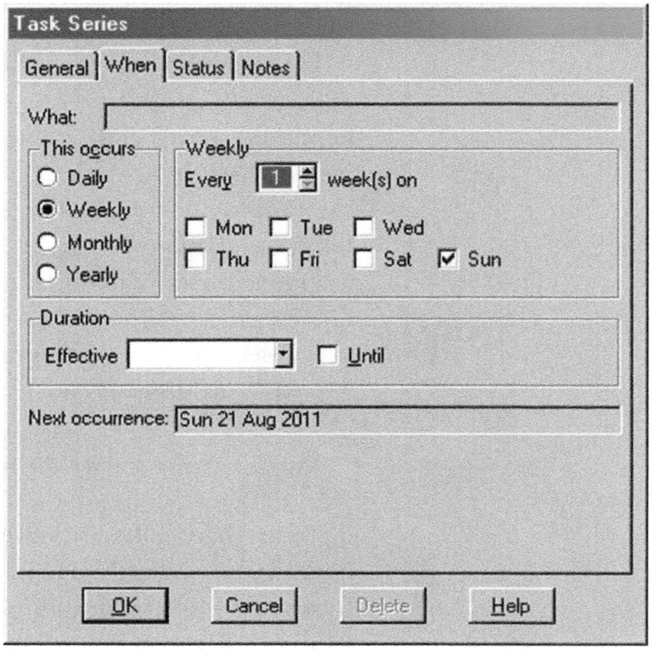

Figure 22-36
Placement of default working location could be better (screen image courtesy of Tobias Frans-Jan Theebe).

Example: Please set the cursor for me

Figure 22-36 contains a dialogue box for planning events in a calendar system. Designers chose to highlight the frequency of occurrences of the event in terms of the number of weeks, in the Weekly section. This might be a little helpful to users who will type a value into the "increment box" of this data field, but users are just as likely to use the up and down arrows of the increment box to set Values, in which case the default highlighting does not help. Further evaluation will be necessary to confirm this, but it is possible that putting the default cursor in the Effective Date field at the bottom might be more useful.

Supporting human memory limitations in cognitive affordances

Earlier we elaborated on the concept of human memory limitations in human–computer interaction. This section is the first of several in which we get to put this knowledge to work in specific interaction design situations.

Relieve human short-term memory loads by maintaining task context visibly or audibly for the user

Provide reminders to users of what they are doing and where they are within the task flow. Post important parts of the task context, parameters the user must keep track of within the task, so that the user does not have to commit them to memory.

Support human memory limits with recognition over recall

For cases where choices, alternatives, or possible data entry values are known, designing to use recognition over recall means allowing the user to select an item from among choices rather than having to specify the choice strictly from memory. Selection among presented choices also makes for more precise communication about choices and data values, helping avoid errors from wording variations and typos.

One of the most important applications of this guideline is in the naming of files for an operation such as opening a file. This guideline says that we should allow users to select the desired file name from a directory listing rather than requiring the user to remember and type in the file name.

Example: What do you want, the part number?

To begin with, the cognitive affordance shown in Figure 22-37 describing the desired user action is too vague and open-ended to get any kind of specific input from a user. What if the user does not know the exact model number and what kind of description is needed? This illustrates a case where it would be better to use a set of hierarchical menus to narrow down the category of the product in mind and then offer a list in a pull-down menu to identify the exact item.

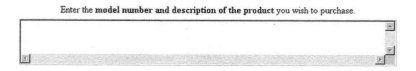

Enter the **model number and description of the product** you wish to purchase.

Figure 22-37

What do you want, the part number?

Example: Help with Save As

In Figure 22-38 we show a very early Save As dialogue box in a Microsoft Office application. At the top is the name of the current folder and the user can navigate to any other folder in the usual way. But it does not show the names of files in the current folder.

This design precedes modern versions that show a list of existing files in this current folder, as shown in Figure 22-39.

This list supports memory by showing the names of other, possibly similar, files in the folder. If the user is employing any kind of implicit file-naming convention, it will be evident, by example, in this list.

For example, if this folder is for letters to the IRS and files are named by date, such as "letter to IRS, 3-30-2010," the list serves as an effective reminder of this naming convention. Further, if the user is saving another letter to the IRS here, dated 4-2-2010, that can be done by clicking on the 3-30-2010 letter and getting that name in the File name: text box and, with a few keystrokes, editing it to be the new name.

Avoid requirement to retype or copy from one place to another

In some applications, moving from one subtask to another requires users to remember key data or other related information and bring it to the second subtask themselves. For example, suppose a user selects an item of some kind during a task and then wishes to go to a different part of the application and apply another function to which that item is an input. We have experienced applications that required us to remember the item ourselves and re-enter it as we arrived at the new functionality.

Be suspicious of usage situations that require users to write something down in order to use it somewhere else in the application; this is a sign of an opportunity to support human memory better in

Figure 22-38

Early Save As dialogue box with no listing of files in current folder (screen image courtesy of Tobias Frans-Jan Theebe).

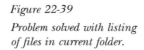

Figure 22-39

Problem solved with listing of files in current folder.

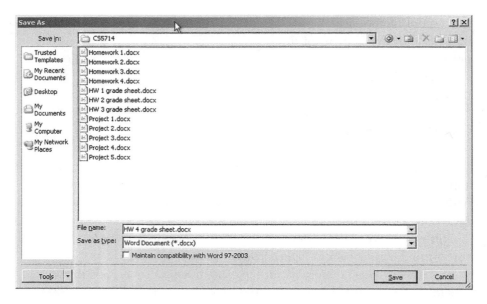

the design. As an example, consider a user of a Calendar Management System who needs to reschedule an appointment. If the design forces the user to delete the old one and add the new one, the user has to remember details and re-enter them. Such a design does not follow this guideline.

Support special human memory needs in audio interaction design

Voice menus, such as telephone menus, are more difficult to remember because there is no visual reminder of the choices as there is in a screen display. Therefore, we have to organize and state menu choices in a way to reduce human memory load.

For example, we can give the most likely or most frequently used choices first because the deeper the user goes into the list, the more previous choices there are to remember. As each new choice is articulated, the user must compare it with each of the previous choices to determine the most appropriate one. If the desired item comes early, the user gets cognitive closure and does not need to remember the rest of the items.

Cognitive directness in cognitive affordances

Cognitive directness is about avoiding mental transformations for the user. It is about what Norman (1990, p. 23) calls "natural mapping." A good example from the world of physical actions is a lever that goes up and down on a console but is used to steer something to the left or the right. Each time it is used, the user must rethink the connection, "Let us see; lever up means steer to the left."

A classic example of cognitive directness, or the lack thereof, in product design is in the arrangement of knobs that control the burners of a cook top. If the spatial layout of the knobs is a spatial map to the burner configuration, it is easy to see which knob controls which burner. Seems easy, but many designs over the years have violated this simple idea and users have frequently had to reconstruct their own cognitive mapping.

Avoid cognitive indirectness

Support user cognitive affordance content understanding by presenting choices and information in cognitively direct expressions rather than in some kind of encoding that requires the user to make a mental translation. The objective of this guideline is to help the user avoid an extra step of translation, resulting in less cognitive effort and fewer errors.

Example: Rotating a graphical object

For a user to rotate a two-dimensional graphical object, there are two directions: clockwise and counterclockwise. While "Rotate Left" and "Rotate Right" are not technically correct, they might be better understood by many than "Rotate CW" and "Rotate CCW." A better solution might be to show small graphical icons, circles with an arc arrow over the top pointing in clockwise and counterclockwise directions.

Example: Up and down in Dreamweaver

Macromedia Dreamweaver™ is an application used to set up simple Web pages. It is easy to use in many ways, but the version we discuss here contains an interesting and definitive example of cognitive indirectness in its design. In the right-hand side pane of the site files window in Figure 22-40 are local files as they reside on the user's PC.

The left-hand side pane of Figure 22-40 shows a list of essentially the same files as they reside on the remote machine, the Website server. As users interact with Dreamweaver to edit and test Web pages locally on their PCs, they upload them periodically to the server to make them part of the operational Website. Dreamweaver has a convenient built-in "ftp" function to

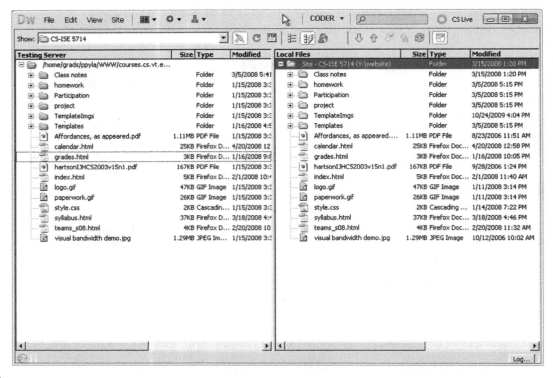

Figure 22-40

Dreamweaver up and down arrows for up- and downloading.

implement this file transfer. Uploading is accomplished by clicking on the up-arrow icon just above the Local site label and downloading uses the down arrow.

The problem comes in when users, weary from editing Web pages, click on the wrong arrow. The download arrow can bring the remote copy of the just-edited file into the PC. Because the ftp function replaces files with the same name as new ones arriving without asking for confirmation, this feature is dangerous and can be costly. Click on the wrong icon and you can lose a lot of work.

"Uploading" and "downloading" are system-centered, not usage-centered, terms and have arbitrary meaning about the direction of data flow, at least to the average non-systems person. The up- and down-arrow icons do nothing to mitigate this poor mapping of meaning. Because the sets of files are on the left-hand side and right-hand side, not up and down, often users must stop and think about whether they want to transfer data left or right on the screen and then translate it into "up" or "down." The icons for transfer of data should reflect this directly; a left arrow and a right arrow would do nicely. Furthermore, given that the "upload" action is the more frequent operation, making the corresponding arrow (left in this example) larger provides a better cognitive (and physical affordance in terms of click target size) affordance.

Example: The surprise action of a car heater control

In Figure 22-41 you can see a photo of the heater control in a car. It looks extremely simple; just turn the knob.

However, to a new user the interaction here could be surprising. The control looks as though you grab the knob and the whole thing turns, including the numbers on its face. However, in actuality, only the outside rim turns, moving the indicator across the numbers, as seen in the sequence of Figure 22-42.

Figure 22-41
How does this car heater fan control work?

Figure 22-42
Now you can see that the outer rim is what turns (photos courtesy of Mara Guimarães Da Silva).

So, if the user's mental model of the device is that rotating the knob clockwise slows down the heater fan, he or she is in for a surprise. The clockwise rotation moves the indicator to higher numbers, thus speeding up the heater fan. It can take users a long time to get used to having to make that kind of a cognitive transformation.

Complete information in cognitive affordances

Support the user's understanding of cognitive affordances by providing complete and sufficient expression of meaning, to disambiguate, make more precise, and clarify. For each label, menu choice, and so on the designer should ask "Is there enough information and are there enough words used to distinguish cases?"

Be complete in your design of cognitive affordances; include enough information for users to determine correct action

The expression of a cognitive affordance should be complete enough to allow users to predict the consequences of actions on the corresponding object.

Prevent loss of productivity due to hesitation, pondering

Completeness helps the user distinguish alternatives without having to stop and contemplate the differences. Complete expressions of cognitive affordance meaning help avoid errors and lost productivity due to error recovery.

Use enough words for unambiguous labels

Some people think button labels, menu choices, and verbal prompts should be terse; no one wants to read a paragraph on a button label. However, reasonably long labels are not necessarily bad and adding words can add precision. Often a verb plus a noun are needed to tell the whole story. For example, for the label on a button controlling a step in a task to add a record in an application, consider using Add Record instead of just Add.

As another example of completeness in labeling, for the label on a knob controlling the speed of a machine, rather than Adjust or Speed, consider using Adjust Speed or maybe even Clockwise to increase speed, which includes information about how to make the adjustment.

Add supplementary information, if necessary

If you cannot reasonably get all the necessary information in the label of a button or tab or link, for example, consider using a fly-over pop up to supplement the label with more information.

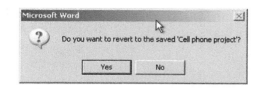

Figure 22-43
What are the consequences of "reverting?"

Give enough information for users to make confident decisions

Example: What do you mean "revert?"

In Figure 22-43 is a message from Microsoft Word that has given us pause more than once. We think we know what button we should click but we are not entirely confident and it seems as though it could have a significant effect on our file.

Example: Quick, what do you want to do?

Figure 22-44 contains a message dialogue box from Microsoft Outlook that can strike fear into the heart of a user. It just does not give enough information about the consequences of either choice presented. If the user exits anyway, does it still send the outstanding messages or do they get lost? To make matters worse, there is undue pressure that the system will take control and exit if the user cannot decide in the next 8 seconds.

Give enough alternatives for user needs

Few things are as frustrating to users as a dialogue box or other user interface object presenting choices that do not include the one alternative the users really needs. No matter what the user does next, it will not turn out well.

Figure 22-44
Urgent but unclear question.

Usage centeredness in cognitive affordances
Employ usage-centered wording, the language of the user and the work context, in cognitive affordances

We find that many of our students do not understand what it means to be user centered or usage centered in interaction design. Mainly

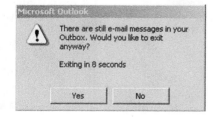

it means to use the vocabulary and concepts of the user's work context rather than the vocabulary and context of the system. This difference between the language of the user's work domain and the language of the system is the essence of "translation" in the translation part of the Interaction Cycle.

As designers, we have to help users make that translation so they do not have to encode or convert their work domain vocabulary into the corresponding concepts in the system domain. The story of the toaster in Chapter 21 is a good example of a design that fails to help the user with this translation from task or work domain language to system control language. The conveyor belt speed control is labeled with system language, "Faster" and "Slower" instead of being labeled in terms of the work domain of toast making, "Lighter" and "Darker."

Avoiding errors with cognitive affordances

The Japanese have a term, "poka-yoke," that means error proofing. It refers to a manufacturing technique to prevent parts of products from being made, assembled, or used incorrectly. Most physical safety interlocks are examples. For instance, interlocks in most automatic transmissions enforce a bit of safety by not allowing the driver to remove the key until the transmission is in park and not allowing shifting out of park unless the brake is depressed.

Find ways to anticipate and avoid user errors in your design

Anticipating user errors in the workflow, of course, stems back to contextual inquiry and contextual analysis, and concern for avoiding errors continues throughout requirements, design, and UX evaluation.

Figure 22-45
It is hard to tell which is the shampoo.

Example: Here is soap in your eyes

Consider the context of a shower in which there are two bottles, one for shampoo and one for conditioner, examples of which you can see in Figure 22-45. But the problem is that one cannot see them well enough to know which is which. The important distinguishing labels, for shampoo and for conditioner, are "hidden" within a lot of other text and are in such a small font as to be illegible without focused attention, especially with soap in the eyes.

So users sometimes add their own (user-created) affordances by, in this case, adding labels on the tops of the bottles to tell them apart in the shower, as shown in Figure 22-46.

You can see, in Figure 22-47, an example of a kind of shampoo bottle design that would have avoided the problem in the first place.

In this clever design, the shampoo, the first one you need, is right-side up and the labeling on the conditioner bottle, the next one you need, is printed so that you stand the bottle "upside down."

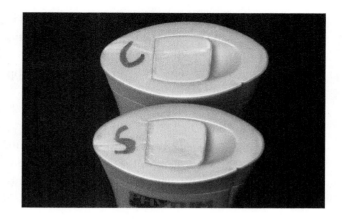

Figure 22-46
Good: some user-created cognitive affordances added.

Help users avoid inappropriate and erroneous choices

This guideline has three parts: one to disable the choices, the second to show the user that they are disabled, and the third to explain why they are disabled.

Disable buttons, menu choices to make inappropriate choices unavailable

Help users avoid errors within the task flow by disabling choices in buttons, menus, and icons that are inappropriate at a given point in the interaction.

Gray out to make inappropriate choices appear unavailable

Figure 22-47
Better: a design to distinguish the bottles.

As a corollary to the previous guideline, support user awareness of unavailable choices by making cognitive affordances for those choices *appear* unavailable, in addition to *being* unavailable. This is done by making some adjustment to the presentation of the corresponding cognitive affordance.

One way is to remove the presentation of that cognitive affordance, but this leads to an inconsistent overall display and leaves the user wondering where that

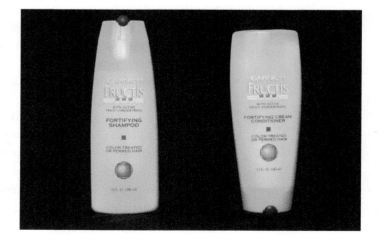

cognitive affordance went. The conventional approach is to "gray out" the cognitive affordance in question, which is universally taken to mean the function denoted by the cognitive affordance still exists as part of the system but is currently unavailable or inappropriate.

But help users understand why a choice is unavailable

If a system operation or function is not available or not appropriate, it is usually because the conditions for its use are not met. One of the most frustrating things for users, however, is to have a button or menu choice grayed out but no indication about *why* the corresponding function is unavailable. What can you do to get this button un-grayed? How can you determine the requirements for making the function available?

We suggest an approach that would be a break with traditional GUI object behavior but that could help avoid that source of user frustration. Clicking on a grayed-out object could yield a pop up with this crucial explanation of why it is grayed out and what you must do to create the conditions to activate the function of that user interface object.

Example: When am I supposed to click the button?

In a document retrieval system, one of the user tasks is adding new keywords to existing documents, documents already entered into the system. Associated with this task is a text box for typing in a new keyword and a button labeled Add Keyword. The user was not sure whether to click on the Add Keyword button first to initiate that task or to type the new keyword and then click on Add Keyword to "put it away."

A user tried the former and nothing happened, no observable action and no feedback, so the user deduced that the proper sequence was to first type the keyword and then click the button. No harm done except a little confusion and lost time. However, the same glitch is likely to happen again with other users and with this user at a later time.

The solution is to gray out the Add Keyword button to show when it does not apply, making it obvious that it is not active until a keyword is entered. Per our suggestion earlier, we could add an informative pop-up message that appears when someone clicks on the grayed-out button to the effect that the user must first type something into the new keyword text box before this button becomes active and allows the user to commit to adding that keyword.

Cognitive affordances for error recovery

Provide a clear way to undo and reverse actions

As much as possible, provide ways for users to back out of error situations by "undo" actions. Although they are more difficult to implement, multiple levels of undo and selective undo among steps are more powerful for the user.

Offer constructive help for error recovery

Users learn about errors through error messages as feedback, which is considered in the assessment part of the Interaction Cycle. Feedback occurs as part of the system response (Chapter 21). A system response designed to support error recovery will usually supplement the feedback with feed-forward, a cognitive affordance here in the translation part of the Interaction Cycle to help users know what actions or task steps to take for error recovery.

Cognitive affordances for modes

Modes are states where actions have different meanings than the same actions in different states. The simplest example is a hypothetical email system. When in the mode of managing email files and directories, the command Ctrl-S means Save. However, when you are in the mode of composing an email message, Ctrl-S means Send. This design, which we have seen in the "old days," is an invitation to errors. Many a message has been sent prematurely out of the habit of doing a Ctrl-S periodically out of habit to be sure everything is saved.

The problem with most modes in interaction design is the abrupt change of the meanings of user actions. It is often difficult for users to shift focus between modes and, when they forget to shift as they cross modal boundaries, the outcomes can be confusing and even damaging. It is a kind of bait and switch; you just get your users comfortable in doing something one way and then change the meaning of the actions they are using.

Modes within interaction designs can also work strongly against experienced users, who move fast and habitually without thinking much about their actions. In a kind of "UX karate," they get leaning one way in one mode and then their own usage momentum gets used against them in the other mode.

Avoid confusing modalities

If it is possible to avoid modes altogether, the best advice is to do so.

Example: Do not be in a bad mode

Think about digital watches. Enough said.

Distinguish modes clearly

If modes become necessary in your interaction design, the next-best advice is to be sure that users are aware of each mode and avoid confusion across modes.

Use "good modes" where they help natural interaction without confusion

Not all modes are bad. The use of modes in design can represent a case for interpreting design guidelines, not just applying them blindly. The guideline to avoid modes is often good advice because modes tend to create confusion. But modes can also be used in designs in ways that are helpful and not at all confusing.

Example: Are you in a good mode?

An example of a good mode needed in a design comes from audio equalizer controls on the stereo in a particular car. As with most radio equalizers, there are choices of fixed equalizer settings, often called "presets," including audio styles such as voice, jazz, rock, classical, new age, and so on.

However, because there is no indication in the radio display of the current equalizer setting, you have to guess or have faith. If you push the Equalizer button to check the current setting, it actually changes the setting and then you have to toggle back through all the values to recover the original setting. This is a non-modal design because the Equalizer button means the same thing every time you push it. It is consistent; every button push yields the same result: toggling the setting.

It would be better to have a slightly moded design so that it starts in a "display mode," which means an initial button push causes it to display the current setting without changing the setting so that you can check the equalizer setting without disturbing the setting itself. If you do wish to change the setting, you push the same Equalizer button again within a certain short time period to change it to the "setting mode" in which button pushes will toggle the setting. Most such buttons behave in this good moded way, except in this particular car.

22.6.4 Task Structure

In Figure 22-48 we highlight the "task structure" portion of the translation part of the Interaction Cycle.

Support of task structure in this part of the Interaction Cycle means supporting user needs with the logical flow of tasks and task steps, including human memory support in the task structure; task design simplicity, flexibility, and efficiency; maintain the locus of control with the user within a task; and offer natural direct manipulation interaction.

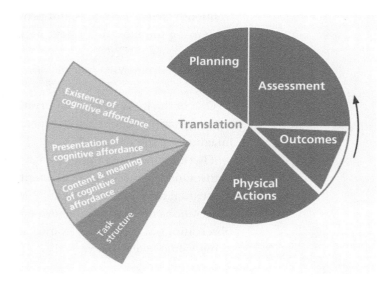

Figure 22-48
The task structure part of translation.

*Human working memory
loads in task structure*
Support human memory limitations in the design of task structure

The most important way to support human memory limitations within the design of task structure is to provide task closure as soon and as often as possible; avoid interruption and stacking of subtasks. This means "chunking" tasks into small sequences with closure after each part.

While it may seem tidy from the computer science point of view to use a "preorder" traversal of the hierarchical task structure, it can overload the user's working memory, requiring stacking of context each time the user goes to a deeper level and "popping" the stack, or remembering the stacked context, each time the user emerges up a level in the structure.

Interruption and stacking occur when the user must consider other tasks before completing the current one. Having to juggle several "balls" in the air, several tasks in a partial state of completion, adds an often unnecessary load to human memory.

Design task structure for flexibility and efficiency
Support user with effective task structure and interaction control

Support user needs for flexibility within the logical task flow by providing alternative ways to do tasks. Meet user needs for efficiency with shortcuts for frequently performed tasks and provide support for task thread continuity, supporting the most likely next step.

Provide alternative ways to perform tasks

One of the most striking observations during task-based UX evaluation is the amazing variety of ways users approach task structure. Users take paths never imagined by the designers.

There are two ways designers can become attuned to this diversity of task paths. One is through careful attention to multiple ways of doing things in contextual inquiry and contextual analysis and the other is to leverage observations of such user behavior in UX evaluation. Do not just discount observations of users gone "astray" as "incorrect" task performance; try to learn about valuable alternative paths.

Provide shortcuts

No one wants to have to make too many mouse clicks or other user actions to complete a task, especially in complex task sequences (Wright, Lickorish, & Milroy, 1994). For efficiency within frequently performed tasks, experienced users especially need shortcuts, such as "hot key" (or "accelerator key") alternatives for other more complicated action combinations, such as selecting choices from pull-down menus.

Keyboard alternatives are particularly useful in tasks that otherwise require keyboard actions such as form filling or word processing; staying within the keyboard for these "commands" avoids having the physical "switching" actions required for moving between the keyboard and mouse, for example, two physically different devices.

Grouping for task efficiency
Provide logical grouping in layout of objects
Group together objects and functions related by task or user work activity

Under the topic of layout and grouping to control content and meaning complexity, we grouped related things to make their meanings clear. Here we advocate grouping objects and other things related to the same task or user work activity as a means of conveniently having the needed components for a task at hand. This kind of grouping can be accomplished spatially with screen or other device layout or it can be manifest sequentially, as in a sequence of menu choices.

As Norman (2006) illustrates, in a taxonomic "hardware store" organization, hammers of all different kinds are all hanging together and all different kinds of nails are organized in bins somewhere else. But a carpenter organizes his or her tools so that the hammer and nails are in proximity because the two are used together in work activities.

But avoid grouping of objects and functions if they need to be dealt with separately

Grouping user interface objects such as buttons, menus, value settings, and so on creates the impression that the group comprises a single focus for user action. If more is needed for that task goal, each requiring separate actions, do not group the objects tightly together but make clear the separate objectives and the requirement for separate actions.

Example: Oops, I forgot to do the rest of it

A dialogue box from a paper prototype of a Ticket Kiosk System is shown in Figure 22-49.

It contains two objectives and two corresponding objects for value settings by the user—proximity of the starting time of a movie and the distance of the movie theater from the kiosk. Most of the participants who used this dialogue box as part of a ticket-buying task made the first setting and clicked on Continue, not noticing the second component. The solution that worked was to separate the two value-setting operations into two dialogue boxes, forcing a separation of the focus and linearizing the two actions.

Figure 22-49
An overloaded dialogue box in a paper prototype.

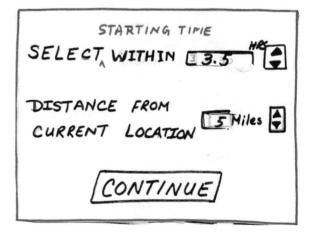

Task thread continuity: Anticipating the most likely next step or task path
Support task thread continuity by anticipating the most likely next task, step, or action

Task thread continuity is a design goal relating to task flow in which the user can pursue a task thread of possibly many steps without an interruption or "discontinuity." It is accomplished in design by anticipating most likely and other possible next steps at any point in the task flow and providing, at hand, the necessary cognitive, physical, and functional affordances to continue the thread.

The likely next steps to support can include tasks or steps the user may wish to take but which are not necessarily part of what designers envisioned as the "main" task thread. Therefore, these various task directions might not be identified by pure task analysis, but are steps that a practitioner or designer might see in contextual inquiry while watching users perform the tasks in a real work activity context. Effective observation in UX evaluation also can reveal diversions, branching, and alternative task paths that users associate with the main thread.

Attention to task thread continuity is especially important when designing the contents of context menus, right-click menus associated with objects or steps in tasks. It is also important when designing message dialogue boxes that offer branching in the task path, which is when users need at hand other possibilities associated with the current task.

Example: If you tell them what they should do, help them get there

Probably the most defining example of task thread continuity is seen in a message dialogue box that describes a problematic system state and suggests one or more possible courses of action as a remedy. But then the user is frustrated by a lack of any help in getting to these suggested new task paths.

Task thread continuity is easily supported by adding buttons that offer a direct way to follow each of the suggested actions. Suppose a dialogue box message tells a user that the page margins are too wide to fit on a printed page and suggests resetting page margins so that the document can be printed. It is enormously helpful if this guideline is followed by including a button that will take the user directly to the page setup screen.

Example: Seeing the query with the results

Designers of information retrieval systems sometimes see the task sequence of formulating a query, submitting it, and getting the results as closure on the task structure, and it often is. So, in some designs, the query screen is replaced with the results screen. However, for many users, this is not the end of the task thread.

Once the results are displayed, the next step is to assess the success of the retrieval. If the query is complex or much has happened since the query was submitted, the user will need to review the original query to determine whether the results were what was expected. The next step may be to modify the query and try again. So this often simple linear task can have a thread with larger scope. The design should support these likely alternative task paths.

Example: May we help you spend more money?

Designers of successful online shopping sites such as Amazon.com have figured out how to make it convenient for shoppers by providing for likely next steps (seeing and then buying) in their shopping tasks. They support convenience in ordering with the ubiquitous Buy it now or Add to cart buttons. They also support product research. If a potential customer shows interest in a product, the site quickly displays other products and accessories that go with it or alternative similar products that other customers have bought.

Example: What if I want to save it in a new folder?

In early Microsoft Office applications the Save As dialogue box did not contain the icon for creating a new folder (the next to the right-hand icon at the top of the dialogue box in Figure 22-50). Eventually, designers realized that as part of the "Save As" task, users had to think about where to put the file and, as part of that planning for organizing their file structures, they often needed to create new folders to modify or expand the current file structure.

Early users had to back out of the "Save As" task and go to Windows Explorer, navigate to the proper context, create the folder, and then return to the Office application and do the "Save As" all over again. By including the ability to create a new folder within the Save As dialogue box, this likely next step was accommodated directly.

In some cases, the most likely next step is so likely that task thread continuity is supported by adding a slight amount of automation and doing the step for the user. The following example is one such case.

Example: Resetting over and over

For frequent users of Word, the Outline view helps organize material within a document. You can use the Outline view to move quickly from where you are

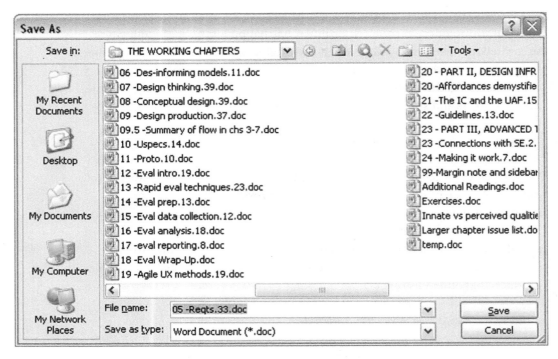

Figure 22-50

Addition of an icon to create a new file in the Save As dialogue box.

in the document to another specific location. In the Outline view, you get a choice of the number of levels of outline to be shown. It is common for users to want to keep this Outline view level setting at a high level, affording a view of the whole outline. So, for many users, the most likely-used setting would be that high setting. Many users rarely even choose anything else.

Regardless of any user's level preferences, if a user goes to the Outline view it is because he or she wants to see and use the outline. But the default level setting in Word's Outline view is the only setting that really is not an outline. The default Word Outline view, Show all levels, is a useless mash-up of outline parts and non-outline text. As a default this setting is the least useful for anyone.

Every time users launch a Word document, they face that annoying Outline view setting. Even once you have shown your preference by setting the level, the system inevitably strays away from that setting during editing, forcing you to reset it frequently. Frequent users of Word will have made this setting thousands of times over the years. Why cannot Word help users by saving the settings they use so consistently and have set so often?

Designers might argue that they cannot assume they know what level a user needs so they follow the guideline to "give the user control." But why design a default that guarantees the user will have to change it instead of something that might be useful to at least some users some of the time? Why not detect the highest level present in the document and use that as a default? After all, the user did request to see the outline.

Example: Why make me choose from just one thing?

Earlier we described an example in which the user had to select an item from a dialogue box list of choices, even though there was only one item in the list. Our point there was that preselecting the item for the user made for a useful default.

The same idea applies here: When there is only one choice, the designer can support user efficiency through task thread continuity by assuming the most likely next action to be selecting that only choice and making the selection in advance for the user. An example of this comes from Microsoft Outlook.

When an Outlook user selects Rules and Alerts from the Tools menu and clicks on the Run Rules Now button, the Run Rules Now dialogue box appears. In cases where there is only one rule, it is highlighted in the display, making it *look* selected. However, be careful, that rule is not selected; the highlighting is a false affordance.

Look closely and you see that the checkbox to its left is unchecked and *that* is the indication of what is selected. The result is the Run Now button is grayed out, causing some users to pause in confusion about why the rule cannot now be run. Most such users figure it out eventually, but lose time and patience in the confusion. This UX glitch can be avoided by preselecting this only choice as the default.

Not undoing user work
Make the most of user's work
Do not make the user redo any work.
Do not require users to reenter data

Do you not hate it when you fill out part of a form and go away to get more information or to attend temporarily to something else and, when you come back, you return to an empty form? This usually comes from lazy programming because it takes some buffering to retain your partial information. Do not do this disservice to your users.

Retain user state information

It helps users keep track of state information, such as user preferences, that they set in the course of usage. It is exasperating to have to reset preferences and other state settings that do not persist across different work sessions.

Example: Hey, remember what I was doing?

It would help users a lot if Windows could be a little bit more helpful in keeping track of the focus of their work, especially keeping track of where they have been working within the directory structure. Too often, you have to reestablish your work context by searching through the whole file directory in a dialogue box to, say, open a file.

Then, later, if you wish to do a Save As with the file, you may have to search that whole file directory again from the top to place the new file near the original one. We are not asking for built-in artificial intelligence, but it would seem that if you are working on a file in a certain part of the directory structure and want to do a Save As, it is very likely that the file is related to the original and, therefore, needs to be saved close to it in the file structure.

Keeping users in control
Avoid the *feeling* of loss of control

Sometimes, although users are still actually in control, interaction dialogue can make users feel as though the computer is taking control. Although designers may not give a second thought to language such as "You need to answer your email," these words can project a bossy attitude to users. Something such as "You have new email" or "New email is ready for reading" conveys the same meaning but does so in a way that helps users feel that they are not being commanded to do something; they can respond whenever they find it convenient.

Avoid real loss of control

More bothersome to users and more detrimental to productivity is a real loss of user control. You, the designer, may think you know what is best for the user, but you will do best to avoid the temptation of being high handed in matters of control within interaction. Few kinds of user experience give rise to anger in users than a loss of control. It does not make them behave the way you think they should; it only forces them to take extra effort to work around your design.

One of the most maddening examples of loss of user control we have experienced comes from EndNote™, an otherwise powerful and effective bibliographic support application for word processing. When EndNote is used as a plug-in to Microsoft Word, it can be scanning your document invisibly for actions to take with regard to your bibliographic citations.

If an action is deemed necessary, for example, to format an in-line citation, EndNote often arbitrarily takes control away from a user doing editing and moves the cursor to the location where the action is needed, often many pages away from the focus of attention of the user and usually without any indication of what happened. At that point, users are probably not interested in thinking about bibliographic citations but are more concerned with their task at hand, such as editing. All of a sudden control is jerked away and the working context disappears. It takes extra cognitive energy and extra physical actions to get back to where the user was working. The worst part is that it can happen repeatedly, each time with an increasingly negative emotional user reaction.

Direct manipulation and natural interaction control

From the earliest computer usage, users have given "commands" to computers to get them to perform functions. Invoking a computer function "by command" is an indirect way to get something done by asking the computer to do it for you. In many kinds of applications there is a more direct way—essentially to do it yourself through direct manipulation (Shneiderman, 1983; Hutchins, Hollan, & Norman, 1986).

The introduction of direct manipulation, the essence of GUIs, as an interaction technique (Shneiderman, 1983) has been one of the most important in terms of designing interaction to be natural for human users. Instead of syntactic commands, operations are invoked by user actions manipulating user interface objects.

For example, instead of typing "del my_file.doc," one might delete the file by clicking on and dragging the file icon to the "trashcan" object. Unlike the case in command-driven interaction, direct manipulation features continuous representation, usually visual, of interaction objects. As Shneiderman, who gets credit for identifying and characterizing direct manipulation as an interaction style, puts it, a key characteristic is "rapid incremental reversible operations whose impact on the object of interest is immediately visible" (Shneiderman, 1982, p. 251; 1983).

Users can perform tasks easily by pointing to visual representations of familiar objects. They can see results immediately and visually, for example, a file going into a folder. The direct manipulation interaction style is easy to learn and encourages exploration. Direct manipulation goes hand in hand with metaphors, like a stack of cards for addresses. Users apply direct manipulation actions to the objects of the metaphor, for example, moving cards within a stack. And, of course, the visual thinking and actions of direct manipulation apply beyond metaphors to manipulating objects in three dimensions as in virtual and augmented reality applications.

One way that the notion of direct manipulation enters into the design of physical products such as radios and television sets is by way of the concept of *physicality*. If controls for these physical devices, such as volume and tuning controls, are implemented with real knobs, users can operate them by physically grasping and turning them. This is literally a kind of direct manipulation.

Physicality

Physicality is about real physical interaction with real devices like physical knobs and levers.

Give direct manipulation support

Example: Please add an appointment for me

Take adding an appointment to a computer-based calendar as an example. We illustrate the command-driven approach with the following task sequence. The user navigates to the desired day within the calendar and clicks on the time slot to select it. Then clicking the Add appointment button brings up a dialogue box in which the user types the text in one or more fields describing the appointment.

Then clicking on OK or Save appointment dismisses the dialogue box, essentially asking the computer to store the appointment. In the direct manipulation paradigm, the calendar looks and feels much like a paper calendar. The user types the appointment information directly into the time slot on the calendar, just as one might write on a paper calendar with a pencil. There is no need to ask for the appointment to be saved; anything you "write" in the calendar stays there, just as it does on a paper calendar.

Always provide a way for the user to "bail out" of an ongoing operation

Do not trap a user in an interaction. Always allow a way for users to escape if they decide not to proceed after getting part way into a task sequence.

The usual way to design for this guideline is to include a Cancel, usually as a dialogue box button.

22.7 PHYSICAL ACTIONS

Physical actions guidelines support users in doing physical actions, including typing, clicking, dragging in a GUI, scrolling on a Web page, speaking with a voice interface, walking in a virtual environment, moving one's hands in gestural interaction, and gazing with eyes. This is the one part of the user's Interaction Cycle where there is essentially no cognitive component; the user already knows what to do and how to do it.

Issues here are limited to how well the design supports the physical actions of doing it, acting upon user interface objects to access all features and functionality within the system. The two primary areas of design considerations are how well the design supports users in sensing the object(s) to be manipulated and how well the design supports users in doing the physical manipulation. As a simple example, it is about seeing a button and clicking on it.

Figure 22-51

Sensing the user interface (UI) object, within physical actions.

Physical actions are the one place in the Interaction Cycle where physical affordances are relevant, where you will find issues about Fitts' law, manual dexterity, physical disabilities, awkwardness, and physical fatigue.

22.7.1 Sensing Objects of Physical Actions

In Figure 22-51 we highlight the "sensing user interface object" part within the breakdown of the physical actions part of the Interaction Cycle.

Sensing objects to manipulate

The "sensing user interface object" portion of the physical actions part is about designing to support user sensory, for example, visual, auditory, or tactile, needs in locating the appropriate physical affordance quickly in order to manipulate it. Sensing for physical actions is about presentation of physical affordances, and the associated design

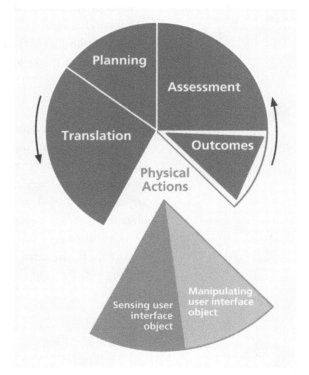

issues are similar to those of the presentation of cognitive affordances in other parts of the Interaction Cycle, including visibility, noticeability, findability, distinguishability, discernability, sensory disabilities, and presentation medium.

Support users making physical actions with effective sensory affordances for **sensing** physical affordances

Make objects to be manipulated visible, discernable, legible, noticeable, and distinguishable. When possible, locate the focus of attention, the cursor, for example, near the objects to be manipulated.

Example: Black on black

One of us has a stereo with a CD player with controls, such as for play and stop, that are black buttons embossed with black icons. This black-on-black motif is cool looking but has a negative impact on usability. You can see the raised embossing of the icons in good light, but sometimes you like to hear your music in a low-light ambiance, a condition that makes it very difficult to see the icons.

Most people know that you should push the play button when you want to play a CD, but in low light it is difficult to tell where that button is on the plain black front of the CD player. This is definitely a case of the sensory design not supporting the ability to locate the object of an intended physical action.

Sensing objects during manipulation

Not only is it important to be able to sense objects statically to initiate physical actions but users need to be able to sense the cursor and the physical affordance object dynamically to keep track of them during manipulation. As an example, in dragging a graphical object, the user's dynamic sensory needs are supported by showing an outline of the graphical object, aiding its placement in a drawing application.

As another very simple example, if the cursor is the same color as the background, the cursor can disappear into the background while moving it, making it difficult to judge how far to move the mouse back to get it visible again.

22.7.2 Help User in Doing Physical Actions

In Figure 22-52 we highlight the "manipulating user interface object" part within the breakdown of the physical actions part of the Interaction Cycle.

This part of the Interaction Cycle is about supporting user physical needs at the time of making physical actions; it is about making user interface object manipulation physically easy. It is especially about designing to make physical actions efficient for expert users.

Support user with effective physical affordances for manipulating objects, help in doing actions

Issues relevant to supporting physical actions include awkwardness and physical disabilities, manual dexterity and Fitts' law, plus haptics and physicality.

Awkwardness and physical disabilities

One of the easiest aspects of designing for physical actions is avoiding awkwardness. It is also one of the easiest areas in which to find existing problems in UX evaluation.

Avoid physical awkwardness

Issues of physical awkwardness are often about time and energy expended in physical motions. The classic example of this issue is a user having to alternate constantly among multiple input devices such as between a keyboard and a mouse or between either device and a touchscreen.

This device switching involves constant "homing" actions that require time-consuming and effortful distraction of cognitive focus and visual attention. Keyboard combinations requiring multiple fingers on multiple keys can also be awkward user actions that hinder smooth and fast interaction.

Accommodate physical disabilities

Not all human users have the same physical abilities—range of motion, fine motor control, vision, or hearing. Some users are innately limited; some have disabilities due to accidents. Although in-depth coverage of accessibility issues is beyond our scope, accommodation of user disabilities is an extremely important

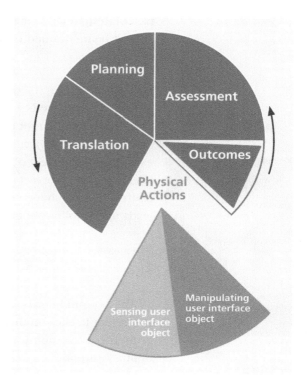

Figure 22-52

Manipulating the user interface (UI) object within physical actions.

Haptics

Haptics is about the sense of touch and the physical contact between user and machine through interaction devices.

part of designing for the physical actions part of the Interaction Cycle and must at least be mentioned here.

Manual dexterity and Fitts' law

Design issues related to Fitts' law are about movement distances, mutual object proximities, and target object size. Performance is reckoned in terms of both time and errors. In a strict interpretation, an error would be clicking anywhere except on the correct object. A more practical interpretation would limit errors to clicking on incorrect objects that are nearby the correct object; this is the kind of error that can have a more negative effect on the interaction. This discussion leads to the following guidelines.

Design layout to support manual dexterity and Fitts' law
Support targeted cursor movement by making selectable objects large enough

The bottom line about sizes cursor movement targets is simple: small objects are harder to click on than large ones. Give your interaction objects enough size, both in cross section for accuracy in the cursor movement direction and in the depth to support accurate termination of movement within the target object.

Group clickable objects related by task flow close together

Avoid fatigue, and slow movement times. Large movement distances require more time and can lead to more targeting errors. Short distances between related objects will result in shorter movement times and fewer errors.

But not too close, and do not include unrelated objects in the grouping

Avoid erroneous selection that can be caused by close proximity of target objects to non-target objects.

Example: Oops, I missed the icon

A software drawing application has a very large number of functions, most of which are accessible via small icons in a very crowded tool bar. Each function can also be invoked by another way (e.g., a menu choice), and our observations tell us that users mainly use the tool bar icons for familiar and frequently used functions.

Fitts' Law

Fitts' Law is an empirically-based mathematical formula governing straight linear movement from an initial position to a target at a terminal location. The time to make the movement is proportional to the log2 of the distance and inversely proportional to log2 of the width of the target in the direction of the motion.

As a result, they do not usually have trouble figuring out which icon to click on. If it is not a familiar function, they do not use the icons. The problem is about what happens when they do use the tool icons because there are so many icons, they are small, and they are crowded together. This, combined with the fast actions of experienced users, leads to clicking on the wrong icon more often than users would like.

Constraining physical actions to avoid physical overshoot errors
Design physical movement to avoid physical overshoot

Just as in the case of cursor movement, other kinds of physical actions can be at risk for overshoot, extending the movement beyond what was intended. This concept is best illustrated by the hair dryer switch example that follows.

Example: Blow dry, anyone?

Suppose you are using the hair dryer, let us say, on the low setting. To move the hair dryer switch takes a certain threshold pressure to overcome initial resistance. Once in motion, however, unless the user is adept at reducing this pressure instantly, the switch can move beyond the intended setting.

A strong detent at each switch position can help prevent the movement from going too far, but it is still easy to push the switch too far, as the photo of a hair dryer switch in Figure 22-53 illustrates. Starting in the Low position and pushing the switch toward Off, the switch configuration makes it easy to move accidentally beyond Off over to the High setting.

Figure 22-53

A hair dryer control switch inviting physical overshoot.

This is *physical overshoot* and is easy to prevent with a switch design that goes directly from High to Low and then to Off in a logical progression. Having the Off position at one end of the physical movement is a kind of physical constraint or boundary condition that allows you to push the switch to Off firmly and quickly without demanding a careful touch or causing worry of overshooting.

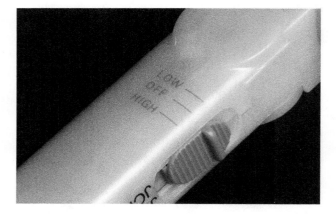

The rocker switch design in Figure 22-54 is a bit better with respect to physical overshoot because it is easier to control the position of a rocker switch as it is being moved. Still, a design

Figure 22-54
A little better design.

with Off at one end of the movement would be a more certain design for preventing physical overshoot. It is probably easier to manufacture a switch with the neutral Off position in the middle.

Example: Downshifting on the fly

The automatic transmission shifter of a pickup truck shown in the lower part of Figure 22-55 is an example of a design where physical overshoot is common. You can see the shift control configuration of the truck with the common linear progression of gears from low to high. Most of the time this is adequate design, but when you are coming down a long hill, you might want to downshift to maintain the speed limit without wearing out the brakes.

However, because the shifting movement is linear, when you pull that lever down from D, it is too easy to overshoot third gear and end up in second. The result of this error becomes immediately obvious from the screaming of the engine at high RPM.

This downshifting overshoot is remedied by the gear shifting pattern of a Toyota Sienna van, shown in Figure 22-56. The gear labeled 4-D is fourth, or high, gear that includes an automatic overdrive for highway travel.

When you shift down to third gear, the movement is constrained physically by a "template" overlaying the shifting lever and overshoot is prevented. It is very unlikely that a user will accidentally shift into second gear because that

Figure 22-55
Typical automatic transmission shifting pattern.

requires a conscious extra action of moving the lever to the right and then further down.

Finally, Figure 22-57 shows the gear-shifting pattern for a Winnebago View, which is a very small RV built on a Mercedes-Benz Sprinter chassis and drive train. It has a "tilt shift," which means that when the transmission is in drive, you can access lower gears successively by tilting the shift lever to the left and you can shift back up to higher gears by shifting the lever to the right. This is probably the easiest to use and safest of all options in terms of the risk of downshifting overshoot.

Haptics and physicality

Haptics is about the sense of touch and physical grasping, and physicality is about real physical interaction using real physical devices, such as real knobs and levels, instead of "virtual" interaction via "soft" devices.

Include physicality in your design when the alternatives are not as satisfying to the user

Example: Beamer without knobs

The BMW iDrive idea seemed so good on paper. It was simplicity in itself. No panels cluttered with knobs and buttons. How cool and forward looking. Designers realized that drivers could do *anything* via a set of menus. But drivers soon realized that the controls for everything were buried in a maze of hierarchical menus. No longer could you reach out and tweak the heater fan speed without looking. Fortunately, knobs are now coming back in BMWs.

Example: Roger's new microwave

Here is an email from our friend, Roger Ehrich, from back in 2002, only slightly edited:

> Hey Rex, since our microwave was about 25 years old, we worried about radiation leakage, so we reluctantly got a new one. The old one had a knob that you twisted to set the time, and a START button that, unlike in Windows, actually started the thing.
>
> The new one had a digital interface and Marion and I spent over 10 minutes trying to get it to even turn on, but we got nothing but an error message. I feel you should never get an error message from an appliance! Eventually we got it to turn on. The sequence was not complicated, but it will not tolerate any variation in user behavior. The problem is that the design is modal, some buttons being multi-functional and sequential. A casual user like me will forget and get it wrong again. Better for me to take my popcorn over to a neighbor who remembers what to do. Anyway, here's to the good old days and the timer knob.
>
> –Regards, Roger

Figure 22-56

Shifting pattern in Toyota Sienna van, helping prevent physical overshoot.

Figure 22-57

Shifting pattern in Mercedes-Benz Sprinter, even better at helping prevent physical overshoot.

Figure 22-58

Car radio with digital up and down buttons instead of a tuning knob.

Figure 22-59

Great physicality in the radio volume control and heater control knobs.

Example: Car radio needs knobs

Figure 22-58 shows a photo of radio controls in a car.

There is no knob for tuning; tuning is done by pushing the up and down arrows on the left-hand side. At least there is a real volume control knob but it is small with almost no depth, making it a poor physical affordance for grasping, even with slender fingertips.

As you try to get a better grip, it is easy to push it inwardly unintentionally, causing the knob and what it controls to become modal, going away from being volume control and becoming a knob to control equalizer settings. To get back to the knob being a volume control, you have to wait until the equalizer mode times out or you must toggle through all the equalizer settings back out to the volume control mode—all, of course, without taking your eyes off the road.

In contrast, Figure 22-59 is a photo of the radio and heater controls of a pickup truck.

Still no tuning knob; too bad. But the large and easily grasped outside ring of the volume control knob is a joy to use and it is not doubled up with any other mode. Also note the heater control knobs below the radio. Again, the physicality of grabbing and adjusting these knobs gives great pleasure on a cold winter morning.

22.8 OUTCOMES

In Figure 22-60 we highlight the outcomes part of the Interaction Cycle.

The outcomes part of the Interaction Cycle is about supporting users through complete and correct "backend" functionality. There are no issues about interaction design in outcomes. The relation to UX is through usefulness and functional affordances. Beyond this connection to UX, outcomes are computations and state changes that are internal to the system, invisible to users,

Because the outcomes part is technically not part of the user's interaction, it is represented in Figure 22-59 as an isolated segment of the Interaction Cycle. Once the results of computation or the outcomes of a user request are displayed to the user, the issues all shift to the assessment part of the Interaction Cycle. Interaction designers must make the effect of outcomes visible via system feedback. So, while issues about whether the results are appropriate or correct do relate to the internal functionality and, therefore, do come under outcomes, any issues about what users see or think about the outcomes after the system computation come under the assessment part of the Interaction Cycle.

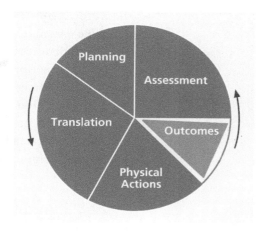

Figure 22-60

The outcomes part of the Interaction Cycle.

22.8.1 System Functionality

The outcomes part of the Interaction Cycle is mainly about non-user-interface system functionality, which includes all issues about software bugs on the software engineering side and issues about completeness and correctness of the backend functional software.

Check your functionality for missing features
Do not let your functionality grow into a Jack-of-all-trades, but master of none

Figure 22-61

The Wenger Giant Swiss Army Knife, the most multi-bladed knife on the planet, and for an MSRP of only $1400.

If you try to do too many things in the functionality of your system, you may end up not doing anything well. Norman has warned us against general-purpose machines intended to do many different functions. He suggests, rather, "information appliances" (Norman, 1998), each intended for more specialized functions.

As an extreme, perhaps even ludicrous, but real-world example, consider the Wenger Giant Swiss Army Knife,[4] shown in Figure 22-61.

If you find yourself in need of a chuckle, see the Amazon reviews of this knife[5] (where it sells for a mere $900).

Check your functionality for non-user-interface software bugs

---

[4]http://www.wengerna.com/giant-knife-16999
[5]http://www.amazon.com/Wenger-16999-Giant-Swiss-Knife/dp/B001DZTJRQ

22.8.2 System Response Time

If the system response time is slow and users have to cool their heels for several billion nanoseconds, it can impact their perceived usage experience. Computer hardware performance, networking, and communications are usually to blame, leaving nothing you can do in the interaction design to help.

In discussion with networking and communications people, you might find a way to break up transactions in a different way to distribute the computational load over time a little. If the problem is intolerable for your users, the entire systems architecture team will have to talk about it.

22.8.3 Automation Issues

Automation, in the sense we are using the term here, means moving functions and control from the user to the internal system functionality. This can result in not letting users do something the designers think they should not do or something that the designers did not think about at all. In many such cases, however, users will encounter exceptions where they really need to do it.

As an analogy, think of a word processor that will not let you save a document if it has anything marked as a spelling or grammatical error. The rationale is easy: "The user will not want to save a document that contains errors. They will want to get it right before they save it away." You know the story, and cases almost always arise in which such a rationale proves to be wrong. Because automation and user control can be tricky, we phrase the next guideline about this kind of automation guardedly.

Avoid loss of user control from too much automation

The following examples show very small-scale cases of automation, taking control from the user. Small though they may be, they can still be frustrating to users who encounter them.

Example: Does the IRS know about this?

The problem in this example no longer exists in Windows Explorer, but an early version of Windows Explorer would not let you name a new folder with all uppercase letters. In particular, suppose you needed a folder for tax documents and tried to name it "IRS." With that version of Windows, after you pressed Enter, the name would be changed to "Irs."

So, in slight confusion, you try again but no deal. This had to be a deliberate "feature," probably made by a software person to protect users from what appeared to be a typographic error, but that ended up being a high-handed grasping of user control.

Example: The John Hancock problem

Figure 22-62 shows part of a letter being composed in an early version of Microsoft Word and exhibiting another example of automation that takes away user control.

Let us just say that a user named H. John Hancock was observed typing a business letter, intending to sign it at the end as:

H. John Hancock
Sr. Vice President

Instead he got:

H. John Hancock
I.

Mr. Hancock was confused about the "I" so he backed up and typed the name again but, when he pressed Enter again, he got the same result. At first he did not know what was happening, why the "I" appeared, or how to finish the letter without getting the "I" there. At least for a few moments, the task was blocked and Mr. Hancock was frustrated.

Being a somewhat experienced user of Word, his composition of text going back to some famous early American documents, he eventually determined that the cause of the problem was that the Automatic Numbered List option was turned on as a kind of mode. At least for this occasion and this user,

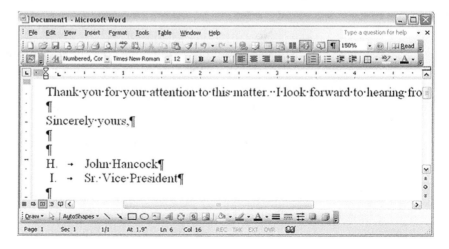

Figure 22-62
The H. John Hancock problem.

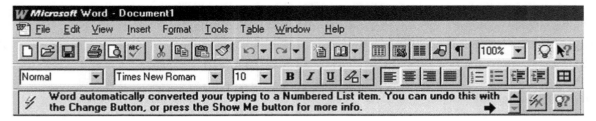

Figure 22-63

If only Mr. Hancock had seen this (screen image courtesy of Tobias Frans-Jan Theebe).

the Automatic numbered list option imposed too much automation and not enough user control.

That the user had difficulty understanding what was happening is due to the fact that, for this user, there was no indication of the Automatic numbered list mode. In fact, however, the system did provide quite a helpful feedback message in response to the automated action it had taken, via the "status" message of Figure 22-63, displayed at the top of the window.

However, Mr. Hancock did not notice this feedback message because it violated the assessment guideline to "Locate feedback within the user's focus of attention, perhaps in a pop-up dialogue box but not in a message or status line at the top or bottom of the screen."

Help the user by automating where there is an obvious need

This section is about automation issues, but not all about avoiding automation. In some cases, automation can be helpful. The following example is about one such case.

Example: Sorry, off route; you lose!

No matter how good your GPS system is, as a human driver you can still make mistakes and drive off course, deviating from the route planned by the system. The Garmin GPS units are very good at helping the driver recover and get back on route. It recalculates the route from the current position immediately and automatically, without missing a beat. Recovery is so smooth and easy that it hardly seems like an error.

Before this kind of GPS, in the early days of GPS map systems for travel navigation, there was another system developed by Microsoft, called Streets and Trips. It used a GPS receiver antenna plugged into a USB port in a laptop. The unit had one extremely bad trait. When the driver got off track, the screen displayed the error message, Off Route! in a large bright red font.

Somehow you just had to know that you had to press one of the F, or function, keys to request recalculation of the route in order to recover. When you are busy contending with traffic and road signs, that is the time you would gladly have the system take control and share more of the responsibility, but you did not get that help. To be fair, this option probably was available in one of the preference settings or other menu choices, but the default behavior was not very usable and this option was not discovered very easily.

Designers of the Microsoft system may have decided to follow the design guideline to "keep the locus of control with the user." While user control is often the best thing, there are times when it is critical for the system to take charge and do what is needed. The work context of this UX problem includes:

- The user is busy with other tasks that cannot be automated.
- It is dangerous to distract the user/driver with additional workload.
- Getting off track can be stressful, detracting further from the focus.
- Having to intervene and tell the system to recalculate the route interferes with the user's most important task, that of driving.

Another way to interpret these twin guidelines about automation is to keep the user in control at higher task levels, where the user has done the initial planning and is driving to get somewhere. But take control from the user when the need is obvious and the user is busy.

This interpretation of the two guidelines means that, on one hand, the system does not insist on staying on this route regardless of driver actions, but quietly allows the driver to make impromptu detours. This interpretation also means that, on the other hand, the system should be expected to continue to recalculate the route to help the driver eventually reach his or her destination.

22.9 ASSESSMENT

Assessment guidelines are to support users in understanding information displays of results of outcomes and other feedback about outcomes such as error indications. Assessment, along with translation, is one of the places in the Interaction Cycle where cognitive affordances play a primary role.

22.9.1 System Response

A system response can contain:

- feedback, information about course of interaction so far
- information display, results of outcome computation
- feed-forward, information about what to do next.

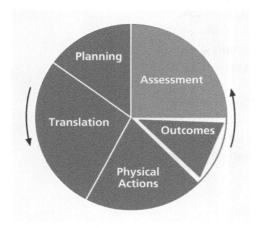

As an example, consider this message: "The value you entered for your name was not accepted by the system. Please try again using only alphabetic characters."

- The first sentence, "The value you entered for your name was not accepted by the system," is feedback about a slight problem in the course of interaction and is an input to the assessment part of the Interaction Cycle.
- The second sentence, "Please try again using only alphabetic characters," is feed-forward, a cognitive affordance as input to the translation part of the next iteration within the Interaction Cycle.

Figure 22-64

The assessment part of the Interaction Cycle.

22.9.2 Assessment of System Feedback

Figure 22-64 highlights the assessment part of the Interaction Cycle.

Feedback about errors and interaction problems is essential in supporting users in understanding the course of their interactions. Feedback is the only way users will know if an error has occurred and why. There is a strong parallel between assessment issues about cognitive affordances as feedback and translation issues about cognitive affordances as feed-forward, including existence of feedback when it is needed, sensing feedback through effective presentation, and understanding feedback through effective representation of content and meaning.

Figure 22-65

Existence of feedback, within assessment.

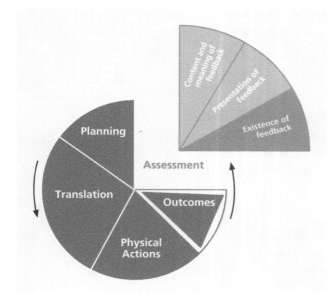

22.9.3 Existence of Feedback

In Figure 22-65 we highlight the "existence of feedback" portion of the assessment part of the Interaction Cycle.

The "existence of feedback" portion of the assessment part of the Interaction Cycle is about providing necessary feedback to support users' need to know whether the course of interaction is proceeding toward meeting their planning goals.

Provide feedback for all user actions

For most systems and applications, the existence of feedback is essential for users; feedback keeps users on track. One notable exception is the Unix operating system, in which no news is always good news. No feedback in Unix means no errors. For expert users, this tacit positive feedback is efficient and keeps out of the way of high-powered interaction. For most users of most other systems, however, no news is just no news.

Provide progress feedback on long operations

For a system operation requiring significant processing time, it is essential to inform the user when the system is still computing. Keep users aware of function or operation progress with some kind of feedback as a progress report, such as a percent-done indicator.

Example: Database system not helpful about progress in Pack operation

Consider the case of a user of a dbase-family database application who had been deleting lots of records in a large database. He knew that, in dbase applications, "deleted" records are really only marked for deletion and can still be undeleted until a Pack operation is performed, permanently removing all records marked for deletion.

At some point, he did the Pack operation, but it did not seem to work. After waiting what seemed like a long time (about 10 seconds), he pushed the Escape key to get back control of the computer and things just got more confusing about the state of the system.

It turns out that the Pack operation was working, but there was no indication to the user of its progress. By pushing the Escape key while the system was still performing the Pack function, the user may have left things in an indeterminate state. If the system had let him know it was, in fact, still doing the requested Pack operation, he would have waited for it to complete.

Request confirmation as a kind of intervening feedback

To prevent costly errors, it is wise to solicit user confirmation before proceeding with potentially destructive actions.

But do not overuse and annoy

When the upcoming action is reversible or not potentially destructive, the annoyance of having to deal with a confirmation may outweigh any possible protection for the user.

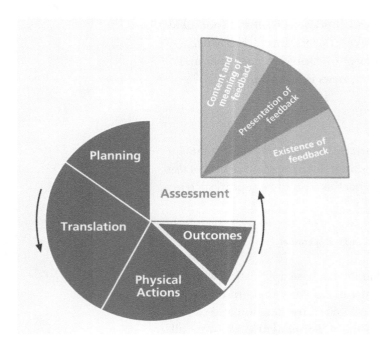

22.9.4 Presentation of Feedback

Figure 22-66 highlights the "presentation of feedback" portion of the assessment part of the Interaction Cycle.

This portion of the assessment part of the Interaction Cycle is about supporting user sensing, such as seeing, hearing, or feeling, of feedback with effective design of feedback presentation and appearance. Presentation of feedback is about how feedback *appears* to users, not how it conveys meaning. Users must be able to sense (e.g., see or hear) feedback before it can be useful to them in usage.

Figure 22-66

Presentation of feedback, within assessment.

Support user with effective sensory affordances in **presentation** of feedback

Feedback visibility

Obviously feedback cannot be effective if it cannot be seen or heard when it is needed.

Make feedback visible

It is the designer's job to be sure each instance of feedback is visible when it is needed in the interaction.

Feedback noticeability

Make feedback noticeable

When needed feedback exists and is visible, the next consideration is its noticeability or likelihood of being noticed or sensed. Just putting feedback on the screen is not enough, especially if the user does not necessarily know it exists or is not necessarily looking for it.

These design issues are largely about supporting awareness. Relevant feedback should come to users' attention without users seeking it. The primary design factor in this regard is location, putting feedback within the users' focus of attention. It is also about contrast, size, and layout complexity and their effect on separation of feedback from the background and from the clutter of other user interface objects.

Locate feedback within the user's focus of attention

A pop-up dialogue box that appears directly within the user's focus of attention in the middle of the screen is much more noticeable than a message or status line at the top or bottom of the screen.

Make feedback large enough to notice

Feedback legibility
Make text legible, readable

Text legibility is about being discernable, not about its content being understandable. Font size, font type, color, and contrast are the primary relevant design factors.

Feedback presentation complexity
Control feedback presentation complexity with effective layout, organization, and grouping

Support user needs to locate and be aware of feedback by controlling layout complexity of user interface objects. Screen clutter can obscure needed feedback and make it difficult for users to find.

Feedback timing
Support user needs to notice feedback with appropriate timing of appearance or display of feedback. Present feedback promptly and with adequate persistence, that is, avoid "flashing."

Help users detect error situations early

Example: Do not let them get into too much trouble

A local software company asked us to inspect one of their software tools. In this tool, users are restricted to certain subsets of functionality based on privileges, which in turn are based on various key work roles. A UX problem with a large impact on users arose when users were not aware of which parts of the functionality they were allowed to use.

As the result of a designer assumption that each user would know their privilege-based limitations, users were allowed to navigate deeply into the structure of tasks that they were not supposed to be performing. They could carry out all the steps of the corresponding transactions but when they tried to "commit" the transaction at the end, they were told they did not have the privileges to do that task and were blocked and their time and effort were wasted. It would have been easy in the design to help users realize much earlier that they were on a path to an error, thereby saving user productivity.

Feedback presentation consistency

Maintain a consistent appearance across similar kinds of feedback
Maintain a consistent location of feedback presentation on the screen to help users notice it quickly

Feedback presentation medium

Consider appropriate alternatives for presenting feedback.

Figure 22-67

Content/meaning of feedback, within assessment.

Use the most effective feedback presentation medium
Consider audio as alternative channel

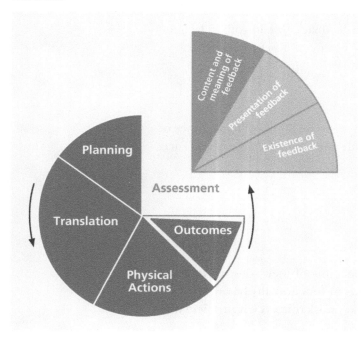

Audio can be more effective than visual media to get users' attention in cases of a heavy task load or heavy sensory work load. Audio is also an excellent alternative for vision-impaired users.

22.9.5 Content and Meaning of Feedback

In Figure 22-67 we highlight the "content and meaning of feedback" portion of the assessment part of the Interaction Cycle.

The content and meaning of feedback represent the knowledge that must be conveyed to users to be effective in helping them understand action outcomes and interaction progress.

This understanding is conveyed through effective content and meaning in feedback, which is dependent on clarity, completeness, proper tone, usage centeredness, and consistency of feedback content.

Help users understand outcomes with effective content/meaning in feedback

Support user ability to determine the outcomes of their actions through understanding and comprehension of feedback content and meaning.

Clarity of feedback
Design feedback for clarity

Use precise wording and carefully chosen vocabulary to compose correct, complete, and sufficient expressions of content and meaning of feedback.

Support clear understanding of outcome (system state change) so users can assess effect of actions
Give clear indication of error conditions

Example: Unavailable?

Figure 22-68 contains an error message that occurred during a Save As file operation in an early version of Microsoft Word. This is a classic example that has generated considerable discussion among our students. The UX problems and design issues extend well beyond just the content of the error message.

In this Save As operation the user was attempting to save a file of unformatted data, calling it "data w/o format" for short. The resulting error message is confusing because it is about a folder not being accessible because of things like unavailable volumes or password protection. This seems about as unclear and unrelated to the task as it could be.

In fact, the only way to understand this message is to understand something more fundamental about the Save As dialogue box. The design of the File Name: text field is *overloaded*. The usual input entered here is a file name, which is by default associated with the folder name in the Save in: field at the top.

Figure 22-68
A confusing and seemingly irrelevant error message.

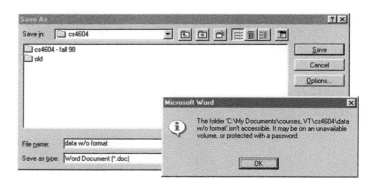

But some designer must have said "That is fine for all the GUI wusses, but what about our legions of former DOS users, our heroic power users who want to enter the full command-style directory path name for the file?" So the design was overloaded to accept full path names of files as well, but no clue was added to the labeling to reveal this option. Because path names contain the slash (/) as a dedicated delimiter, a slash within a file name cannot be parsed unambiguously so it is not allowed.

In our class discussions of this example, it usually takes students a long time to realize that the design solution is to unload the overloading by the simple addition of a third text field at the bottom for Full file directory path name:. Slashes in file names still cannot be allowed because any file name can also appear in a path name, but at least now, when a slash does appear in a file name in the File Name: field, a simple message, "Slash is not allowed in file names," can be used to give a clear indication of the real error.

The most recent version of Word, as of this writing, half-way solves the problem by adding to the original error message: "or the file name contains a \ or /".

Precise wording

Support user understanding of feedback content by precise expression of meaning through precise word choices. Do not allow wording of feedback to be treated as an unimportant part of interaction design.

Completeness of feedback

Support user understanding of feedback by providing complete information through sufficient expression of meaning, to disambiguate, make more precise, and clarify. For each feedback message, the designer should ask "Is there enough information?" "Are there enough words used to distinguish cases?"

Be complete in your design of feedback; include enough information for users to fully understand outcomes and be either confident that their command worked or certain about why it did not

The expression of a cognitive affordance should be complete enough to allow users to fully understand the outcomes of their actions and the status of their course of interaction.

Prevent loss of productivity due to hesitation, pondering

Having to ponder over the meaning of feedback can lead to lost productivity. Help your users move on to the next step quickly, even if it is error recovery.

Add supplementary information, if necessary

Short feedback is not necessarily the most effective. If necessary, add additional information to make sure that your feedback information is complete and sufficient.

Give enough information for users to make confident decisions about the status of their course of interaction
Help users understand what the real error is
Give enough information about the possibilities or alternatives so users can make an informed response to a confirmation request

Example: Quick, what to do?

In Figure 22-69 is an exit message from the Microsoft Outlook email system that we used previously (Figure 22-44) as an example about completeness of cognitive affordances and giving enough information for users to make confident decisions. This message is displayed when a user tries to exit the Outlook email system before all queued messages are sent. We also use it as an example here in the assessment section, even though technically the part of the system response that is at issue here is the lack of a cognitive affordance as feed-forward.

When users first encountered this message, they were often unsure about how to respond because it did not inform them of the consequences of either choice. What are the consequences of "exiting anyway?" One would hope that the system could go ahead and send the messages, regardless, but why then did it give this message? So maybe the user will lose those messages. What made it worse was the fact that control would be snatched away in 8 seconds, and counting. How imperious!

Most users we tested with took the right one, it seems, by making what they thought to be the conservative choice, not exiting yet. Figure 22-70 is an updated version of this same message, only this time it gives a bit more information about the repercussions of exiting prematurely, but it still does not say if exiting will cause messages to be lost or just queued for later.

Figure 22-69
Not enough information in this feedback, or feed-forward, message.

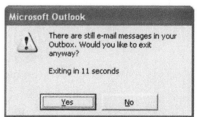

Figure 22-70
This is better, but still could be more helpful.

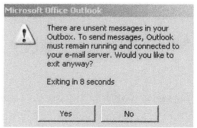

Figure 22-71

Useless message shows poor designer attitude.

Tone of feedback expression

When writing the content of a feedback message, it can be tempting to castigate the user for making a "stupid" mistake. As a professional interaction designer you must separate yourself from those feelings and put yourselves in the shoes of the user. You cannot know the conditions under which your error messages are received, but the occurrence of errors could well mean that the user is already in a stressful situation so do not be guilty of adding to the user's distress with a caustic, sarcastic, or scornful tone.

Design feedback wording, especially error messages, for positive psychological impact
Make the system take blame for errors
Be positive, to encourage
Provide helpful, informative error messages, not "cute" unhelpful messages

Example: Say what?

The almost certainly apocryphal message in Figure 22-71 is an extreme example of an unhelpful message.

Usage centeredness of feedback

Employ usage-centered wording, the language of the user and the work context, in displays, messages, and other feedback

We mentioned that user centeredness is a design concept that often seems unclear to students and some practitioners. Because it is mainly about using the vocabulary and concepts of the user's work context rather than the technical vocabulary and context of the system, we should probably call it "work-context-centered" design. This section is about how usage centeredness applies to feedback in the assessment part of the Interaction Cycle.

Figure 22-72

Gobbledygook email message.

Mail Server Query

Results for hartson.cs.vt.edu

send: invalid spawn id (6) while executing "send "1$pid\r"" (file "./genpid_query.pass" line 31)

In Figure 22-72 we see a real email system feedback message received by one of us many years ago, clearly system centered, if anything, and not user or work context centered. Systems people will argue correctly that the technical information in this message is valuable to them in tracing the source of the problem.

That is not the issue here; rather it is a question of the message audience. This message is sent to users, not the systems people, and it is clearly an unacceptable message to users. Designers must seek ways to get the right message to the right audience. One solution is to give a non-technical explanation here and add a button that says "Click here for a technical description of the problem for your systems representative." Then put this jargon in the next message box.

This message in the next example is similar in some ways, but is more interesting in other ways.

Example: Out of paper, again?

As an in-class exercise, we used to display the computer message in Figure 22-73 and ask the students to comment on it.

Some students, usually ones who were not engineering majors, would react negatively from the start. After a lot of the usual comments pro and con, we would ask the class whether they thought it was usage centered. This usually caused some confusion and much disagreement. Then we ask a very specific question: Do you think this message is really about an *error*? In truth, the correct answer to this depends on your viewpoint, a reply we *never* got from a student.

The system-centered answer is yes; technically an "error condition" arose in the operating system error-handling component when it got an interrupt from the printer, flagging a situation in which there is a need for action to fix a problem. The process used inside the operating system is carried out by what the software systems people call an error-handling routine. This answer is correct but not absolute.

From a user-, usage-, or work-context-centered view, it is definitely and 100% *not an error*. If you use the printer enough, it will run out of paper and you will have to replace the supply. So running out of paper is part of the normal workflow, a natural occurrence that signals a point where the human has a responsibility within the overall collaborative human-system task flow. From this perspective, we told our students we had to conclude that this was not an acceptable message to send to a user; it was not usage centered.

We decided that this exercise was a definitive litmus test for determining whether students could think user

Figure 22-73

Classic system-centered "error" message.

centrically. Some of our undergraduate CS students never got it. They stubbornly stuck to their judgment that there was an error and that it was perfectly appropriate to send this message to a user to get attention to attending the error.

Each semester we told them that it was okay that they did not "get it"; that they could still live productive lives, just not in any UX development role. Not everyone is cut out to take on a UX role in a project.

Just to finish up the analysis of this message:

■ Why is the message box titled Printers Folder? Does this refer to some system aspect that should be opaque to the user?

■ The printer is out of paper. Add paper. Is the need to add paper when the printer is out of paper not obvious enough? If so, the Add paper imperative is redundant and even condescending.

■ To continue printing, click retry. Why "click retry" if the objective is to continue printing? Why not Click continue printing and label the Retry button as Continue Printing?

■ Windows will automatically retry after 5 seconds. First, it should be Windows will periodically try to continue printing. Beyond that, this may seem to be a useless and maybe intrusive "feature" but it could be helpful if the printer is remote—the user would not have to go back and forth to click on the button here and to see if the printer is printing. Beyond that, the 5 seconds does seem a bit arbitrary and probably too short a time to get new paper loaded, but this is not harmful.

Consistency of feedback
Be consistent with feedback

In the context of feedback, the requirement for consistency is essentially the same as it was for the expression of cognitive affordances: choose one term for each concept and use it throughout the application.

Label outcome or destination screen or object consistently with starting point and action

This guideline is a special case of consistency that applies to a situation where a button or menu selection leads the user to a new screen or dialogue box, a common occurrence in interaction flow. This guideline requires that the name of the destination given in the departure button label or menu choice be the same as its name when you arrive at the new screen or dialogue box. The next example is typical of a common violation of this guideline.

Example: Am I in the right place?

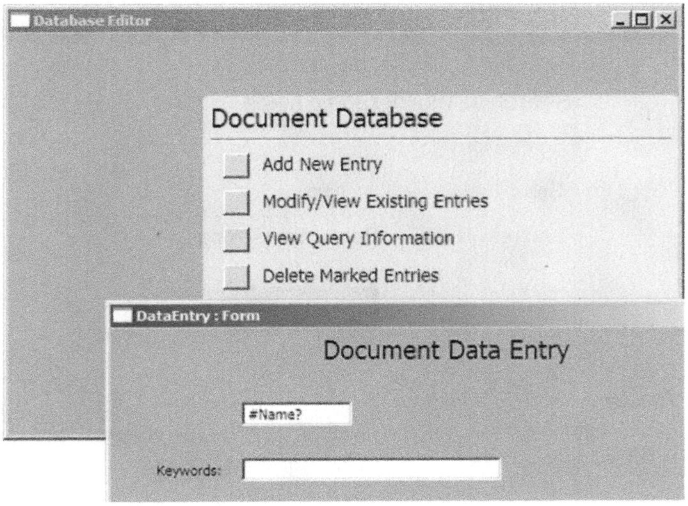

In Figure 22-74 we see an overlay of two partial windows within a personal document system. In the bottom layer is a menu listing some possible operations within this document system. When you click on Add New Entry, you go to the window in the top layer, but the title of that window is not Add New Entry, it is Document Data Entry. To a user, this *could* mean the same thing, but the words used at the point of departure were Add New Entry.

Finding different words, Document Data Entry, at the destination can be confusing and can raise doubts about the success of the user action. The explanation given us by the designer was that the destination window in the top layer is a destination shared by both the Add New Entry menu choice and the Modify/View Existing Entries menu choice. Because state variables are passed in the transition, the corresponding functionality is applied correctly, but the same window was used to do the processing.

Therefore, the designer had picked a name that sort of represented both menu choices. Our opinion was that the destination window name ended up representing neither choice well and it takes only a little more effort to use two separate windows.

Figure 22-74

Arrival label does not match departure label (screen image courtesy of Raphael Summers).

Example: Title of destination does not match Simple Search Tab label

In this example, consider the Simple Search tab, displayed at the top of most screens in this digital library application and shown in Figure 22-75.

That tab leads to a screen that is labeled Search all bibliographic fields, as shown in Figure 22-76.

We had to conclude that the departure label on the Simple Search tab and the destination label, Search all bibliographic fields, do not match well enough because we observed users showing surprise upon arrival and not being sure about whether they had arrived at the right place. We suggested a slight change in the wording of the destination label for the Simple Search function to include the same name, Simple

Figure 22-75

The Simple Search tab at the top of a digital library application screen.

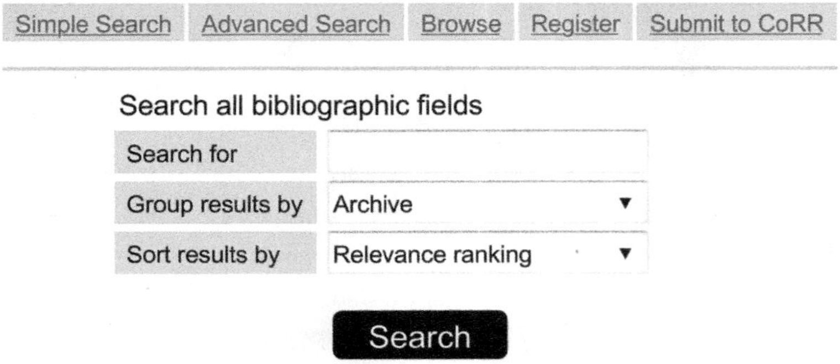

| Simple Search | Advanced Search | Browse | Register | Submit to CoRR |

Search all bibliographic fields

Search for	
Group results by	Archive ▾
Sort results by	Relevance ranking ▾

Search

Figure 22-76

However, it leads to Search all bibliographic fields, not a match.

Search, used in the tab and not sacrifice the additional information in the destination label, Search all bibliographic fields, as shown in Figure 22-77.

User control over feedback detail
Organize feedback for ease of understanding

When a significant volume of feedback detail is available, it is best not to overwhelm the user by giving all the information at once. Rather, give the most important information, establishing the nature of the situation, upfront and provide controls affording the user a way to ask for more details, as needed.

Provide user control over amount and detail of feedback
Give only most important information at first; more on demand

22.9.6 Assessment of Information Displays
Information organization for presentation
Organize information displays for ease of understanding

Figure 22-77

Problem fixed by adding Simple Search: to the destination label.

There are entire books available on the topics of information visualization and information display design, among which the work of Tufte (1983, 1990, 1997) is perhaps the most well known. We do not attempt to duplicate that material here, but rather reference the interested reader to pursue these topics in detail from those sources. We can, however, offer a few simple guidelines to help with the routine presentation of information in your displays of results.

| Simple Search | Advanced Search | Browse | Register | Submit to CoRR |

Simple search: Search all bibliographic fields

Search for	
Group results by	Archive ▾
Sort results by	Relevance ranking ▾

Search

Eliminate unnecessary words
Group related information
Control density of displays; use white space to set off

Columns are easier to read than wide rows

This guideline is the reason that newspapers are printed in columns.

Use abstraction per Shneiderman's "mantra": Overview first; zoom and filter; details on demand

Ben Shneiderman has a "mantra" for controlling complexity in information display design (Shneiderman & Plaisant, 2005, p. 583):

- overview first
- zoom and filter
- details on demand

Example: The great train mystery

Train passengers in Europe will notice entering passengers competing for seats that face the direction of travel. At first, it might seem that this is simply about what people were used to in cars and busses. But some people we interviewed had stronger feelings about it, saying they really were uncomfortable traveling backward and could not enjoy the scenery nearly as much that way.

Believing people in both seats see the same things out the window, we wondered if it really mattered, so we did a little psychological experiment and compared our own user experiences from both sides. We began to think about the view in the train window as an information display.

In terms of bandwidth, though, it did not seem to matter; the total amount of viewable information was the same. All passengers see the same things and they see each thing for the same amount of time. Then we recalled Ben Shneiderman's rules for controlling complexity in information display design (see earlier discussion).

Applying this guideline to the view from a train window, we realized that a passenger traveling forward is moving *toward* what is in the view. This traveler sees the overview in the distance first, selects aspects of interest, and, as the trains goes by, zooms in on those aspects for details.

In contrast, a passenger traveling backward sees the close-up details first, which then zoom out and fade into an overview in the distance. But this close-up view is not very useful because it arrives too soon without a point of focus. By the time the passenger identifies something of interest, the chance to zoom in on it has passed; it is already getting further away. The result can be an unsatisfying user experience.

Visual bandwidth for information display

One of the factors that limit the ability of users to perceive and process displayed information is visual bandwidth of the display medium. If we are talking about the usual computer display, we must use a display monitor with a very small space for all our information presentation. This is tiny in comparison to, say, a newspaper.

When folded open, a newspaper has many times the area, and many times the capacity to display information, of the average computer screen. And a reader/user can scan or browse a newspaper much more rapidly. Reading devices such as Amazon's Kindle™ and Apple's iPad™ are pretty good for reading and thumbing through whole book pages, but lack the visual bandwidth afforded for "fanning" through pages for perusal or scanning provided by a real paper book.

Designs that speed up scrolling and paging do help but it is difficult to beat the browsing bandwidth of paper. A reader can put a finger in one page of a newspaper, scan the major stories on another page, and flash back effortlessly to the "book-marked" page for detailed reading.

Figure 22-78

Limited horizontal visual bandwidth.

Example: Visual bandwidth

In our UX classes we used to have an in-class demonstration to illustrate this concept. We started with sheets of paper covered with printed text. Then we gave students a set of cardboard pieces the same size as the paper but each with a smaller cutout through which they must read the text.

One had a narrow vertical cutout that the reader must scan, or scroll, horizontally across the page. Another had a low horizontal cutout that the reader must scan vertically up and down the page. A third one had a small square in the middle that limited visual bandwidth in both vertical and horizontal directions and required the user to scroll in both directions.

You can achieve the same effect on a computer screen by resizing the window and adjusting the width and height accordingly. For example, in Figure 22-78, you can see limited horizontal visual bandwidth, requiring excessive horizontal scrolling to read. In Figure 22-79, you can see limited vertical visual bandwidth, requiring excessive

vertical scrolling to read. And in Figure 22-80, you can see limited horizontal and vertical visual bandwidth, requiring excessive scrolling in both directions. It was easy for students to conclude that any visual bandwidth limitation, plus the necessary scrolling, was a palpable barrier to the task of reading information displays.

Figure 22-79

Limited vertical visual bandwidth.

22.10 OVERALL

This section concludes the litany of guidelines with a set of guidelines that apply globally and generally to an overall interaction design rather than being associated with a specific part of the Interaction Cycle.

22.10.1 Overall Simplicity

As Norman (2007a) points out, most people think of simplicity in terms of a product that has all the features but operates with a single button. His point is that people genuinely want features and only say they want simplicity. At least for consumer appliances, it is all about marketing and marketing people know that features sell. And more features imply more controls.

Norman (2007a) says that even if a product design automates some features well enough so that fewer controls are necessary, people are willing to pay more for machines with more controls. Users do not want to give up control. Also, more controls give the *appearance* of more power, more functionality, and more features.

Figure 22-80

Limited horizontal and vertical visual bandwidth.

But in the computer you use to get things done at work, complexity can be a barrier to productivity. The desire is for full functionality without sacrificing UX.

Do not try to achieve the appearance of simplicity by just reducing usefulness

A well-known Web-search service provider seeking improved ease of use "simplified" their search page. Unfortunately, they did it without a real understanding of what simplicity means. They just reduced their functionality but did nothing to improve the usability of the remaining functionality. The result was a less useful search function and the user is still left to figure out how to use it.

Organize complex systems to make the most frequent operations simple

Some systems cannot be entirely simple, but you can still design to keep some of the most frequently used operations or tasks as simple as possible.

Example: Oh, no, they changed the phone system!

Years ago our university began using a special digital phone system. It had, and still has, an enormous amount of functionality. Everyone in the university was asked to attend a one-day workshop on how to use the new phone system. Most employees rebelled and refused to attend a workshop to learn how to use a telephone—something they had been using all their lives.

They were issued a 50-page user's guide entitled "Excerpts from the PhoneMail System User Guide." Fifty pages and still an excerpt; who is going to read that? The answer is that almost everyone had to read at least parts of it because the designer's approach was to make all functions equally difficult to do. The 10% of the functionality that people had to use every day was just as mysterious as the other 90% that most people would never need. Decades later, people still do not like that phone system, but they were captive users.

22.10.2 Overall Consistency

Historically, "be consistent" is one of the earliest interaction design guidelines ever and probably the most often quoted. Things that work the same way in one place as they do in another just make logical sense.

But when HCI researchers have looked closely at the concept of consistency in interaction design over the years, many have concluded that it is often difficult to pin it down in specific designs. Grudin (1989) shows that the concept is difficult to define (p. 1164) and hard to identify in a design, concluding that it is an issue without much real substance. The transfer effects that support ease of learning can conflict with ease of use (p. 1166). And blind adherence without interpretation within usage context to the rule can lead to foolish or undesirable consistency, as shown in the next example.

Be consistent by doing similar things in similar ways

Example: And what country shall we send it to?

Suppose that the menu choices in all pull-down menus in an application are ordered alphabetically for fast searching. But one pull-down menu is in a form in which the user enters a mailing address. One of the fields in the form is for "country" and the pull-down list contains dozens of entries. Because the majority of customers for this Website are expected to live in the United States, ease of use will be better in a design with "United States" at the top of the pull-down list instead of near the bottom of an alphabetical list, even though that is inconsistent with all the other pull-down menus in the application.

Use consistent layout/location for objects across screens
Maintain custom style guides to support consistency

Structural consistency

We think Reisner (1977) helped clarify the concept of consistency, in the context of database query languages, when she coined the term "structural consistency." In referring to the use of query languages, structural consistency simply required similar syntax (wording or user actions) to denote similar or related semantics. So, in our context, the expression of cognitive affordances for two similar functions should also be similar.

However, in some situations, consistency can work against distinguishability. For example, if a design contains two different kinds of delete functions, one of which is used routinely to delete objects within an application, but the other is dangerous because it applies to files and folders at a higher level, the need to distinguish these delete functions for safety may override this guideline for making them similar.

Use structurally similar names and labels for objects and functions that are structurally similar

Example: Next and previous

A simple example is seen in the common Next and Previous buttons that might appear, for example, for navigation among pictures in an online photo gallery. Although these two buttons are opposite in meaning, they both are a similar *kind* of thing; they are symmetric and structurally similar navigation controls. Therefore, they should be labeled in a similar way. For example, Go forward and Previous picture are not as symmetric and not as similar from a linguistic perspective.

Consistency is not absolute

Many design situations have more than one consistency issue and sometimes they trade-off against each other. We have a good example to illustrate.

Example: May I mix you a screwdriver?

Consider the case of multi-blade screwdrivers that are handy for dealing with different sizes and types of screws. In particular, they each have both flat-blade and Phillips-blade driver bits and each of these types comes in both small and large sizes.

Figure 22-81 illustrates two of these so-called "4-in-1" screwdrivers. As part of a discussion of consistency, we bring screwdrivers like these to class for an in-class exercise with students. We begin by showing the class the screwdrivers and explain how the bits are interchangeable to get the needed combination of blade type and size.

Next we pick a volunteer to hold and study one of these tools and then speak to the class about consistency issues in its design. They pull it apart, as shown in Figure 22-82.

Figure 22-81

Multipurpose screwdrivers.

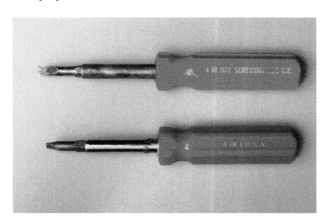

The conclusion always is that it is a consistent design. We have another volunteer study the other screwdriver, always reaching the same conclusion. Then we show the class that there are differences between the two designs, which become apparent when you compare the bits at the ends of each tool, as shown in Figure 22-83.

One tool is consistent by blade type, having both flat blades, large and small, on one insertable piece and both Phillips blades on the other piece. The other tool is consistent by size, having both large blades on one insertable piece and both small blades on the other piece.

We now ask them if they still think each design is consistent and they do. They are each consistent; they each have intra-product consistency. Neither is more consistent than the other, but each is consistent in a different way and are not consistent with each other.

Consistency in design is supposed to aid predictability but, because there is more than one way to be consistent in this example, you still lack inter-product consistency and you do not necessarily get predictability. Such is one difficulty of interpreting and applying this seemingly simple design guideline.

Figure 22-82
Revealing the inner parts of the two screwdrivers.

Consistency can work against innovation

Final caveat: While a style guide works in favor of consistency and reuse, remember that is also can be a barrier to inventiveness and innovation (Kantrovich, 2004). Being the same all the time is not necessarily cool! When the need arises to break with consistency for the sake of innovation, throw off the constraints and barriers and dive through the wormhole to the creative side.

22.10.3 Humor

Avoid poor attempts at humor

Poor attempts at humor usually do not work. It is easy to do humor badly and it can easily be misinterpreted by users. You may be sitting in your office feeling good and want to write a cute error message, but users receiving it may be tired and stressed and the last thing they need is the irritation of a bad joke.

Figure 22-83
The two sets of screwdriver bits.

22.10.4 Anthropomorphism

Simply put, anthropomorphism is the attribution of human characteristics to non-human objects. We do it every day; it is a form of humor. You say "my car is sick today" or "my computer does not like me" and everyone understands what you mean. In interaction design, however, the context is usually about getting work done and

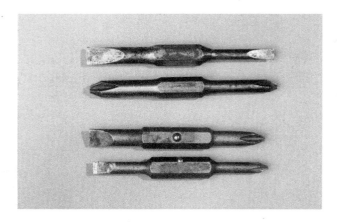

anthropomorphism can be less appreciated, especially if the user is already having difficulties.

Avoiding anthropomorphism
Avoid the use of anthropomorphism in interaction designs

Shneiderman and Plaisant (2005, pp. 80, 484) say that a model of computers that leads one to believe they can think, know, or understand in ways that humans do is erroneous and dishonest. When the deception is revealed, it undermines trust.

Avoid using first-person speech in system dialogue

"Sorry, but I cannot find the file you need" is less honest and no more informative than something such as "File not found" or "File does not exist." If attribution must be given to what it is that cannot find your file, you can reduce anthropomorphism by using the third person, referring to the software, as in "Windows is unable to find the application that created this file." This guideline urges us to especially eschew chatty and over-friendly use of first-person cuteness, as we see in the next example.

Example: Who is there?

Figure 22-84 contains a message from a database system after a search request had been submitted. Ignoring other obvious UX problems with this dialogue box and message, most users find this kind of use of first person as dishonest, demeaning, and unnecessary.

Avoid condescending offers to help

Just when you think all hope is lost, then along comes Clippy or Bob, your personal office assistant or helpful agent. How intrusive and ingratiating! Most users dislike this kind of pandering and insinuating into your affairs, offering blandishments of hope when real help is preferred.

People expect other humans to be able to solve problems better than a machine. If your interaction dialogue portrays the machine as a human, users will expect more. When you cannot deliver, however, it is overpromising. The example that follows is ridiculous and cute but it also makes our point.

Figure 22-84

Message tries to make computer seem like a person.

Example: Come on, Clippy, you can do better

Clearly the pop-up "help" in Figure 22-85 is not a real example, but this kind of pop-up in general can be intrusive. In real usage situations, most users expect better.

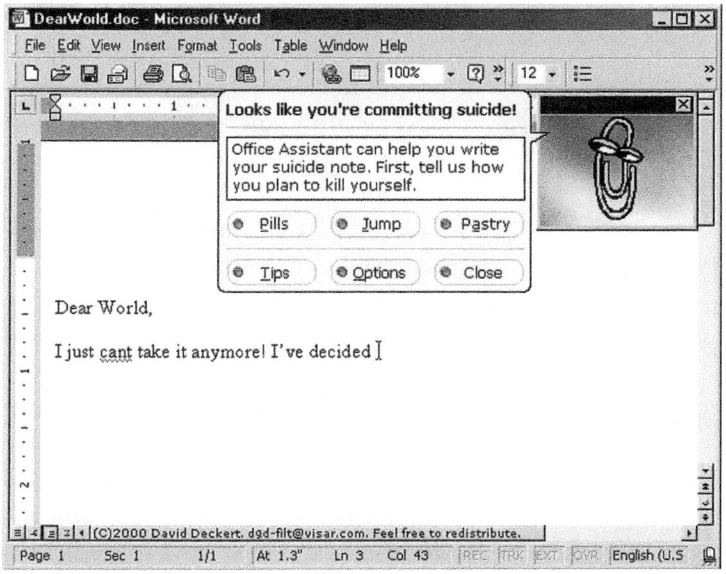

The case in favor of anthropomorphism

On the affirmative side, Murano (2006) shows that, in some contexts, anthropomorphic feedback can be more effective than the equivalent non-anthropomorphic feedback. He also makes the case for why users sometimes prefer anthropomorphic feedback, based on subconscious social behavior of humans toward computers.

Figure 22-85
Only too glad to help.

In his first study, Murano (2006) explored user reactions to language-learning software with speech input and output using speech recognition. Users were given anthropomorphic feedback in the form of dynamically loaded and software-activated video clips of a real language tutor giving feedback.

In this kind of software usage situation, where the objectives and interaction are very similar to what would be expected from a human language tutor, "the statistical results suggested the anthropomorphic feedback to be more effective. Users were able to self-correct their pronunciation errors more effectively with the anthropomorphic feedback. Furthermore it was clear that users preferred the anthropomorphic feedback." The positive results are not surprising because this kind of application naturally uses human–computer interaction that is very close to natural human-to-human interaction.

In a second study, Murano (2006) looked at Unix for a rank beginner, again employing speech input and output with speech recognition and again employing anthropomorphic video clips of real humans as feedback. He found anthropomorphic feedback to be more effective and more desired by users than other feedback.

However, we cannot see natural language interaction with Unix as a viable long-term alternative. Unix is complex and difficult to learn, not intended for beginners. Anyone intending to use Unix for more than just an experiment will perforce not remain a beginner for long. Any expert Unix user we have ever seen would surely find speech interaction less convenient and less precise than the lightning-fast typed commands usually associated with UNIX usage. If the interaction in this study was not anthropomorphic per se, speech input and output can convey the feeling of being the "equivalent" of anthropomorphic.

In his third study, Murano (2006) determined that, for direction-finding tasks, a map plus some guiding text was more effective than anthropomorphic feedback using video clips of a human giving directions verbally, with user preferences about evenly divided. The bottom line for Murano is that some application domains are more suited for anthropomorphic interaction than others.

Well-known studies by Reeves and Nass (1996) attempted to answer the question why anthropomorphic interaction might be better for some users in some kinds of applications. They concluded that people naturally tend to interact with a computer the same social way we interact with people, especially in cases where feedback is given as natural language speech (Nass, Steuer, & Tauber, 1994). People treat computers in a social manner if the output of computers treats them in a social manner.

While a social manner of interaction did seem to be effective and desired by users of tasks that have a human-to-human counterpart, including tasks such as natural language learning and tutoring in a teacher–student kind of interaction, it is unlikely that a mutually social style and anthropomorphic interaction would have a place in the thousands of other kinds of tasks that make up a large portion of real computer usage—installing driver software, creating a text document, updating a data spreadsheet,

The bottom line for us is that users may think they would prefer anthropomorphic user-computer dialogue because it is somehow friendlier or maybe they would prefer to interact with another human rather than having to interact with a computer. But the fact remains: a computer is not human. So eventually expectations will not be met. Especially for the use of computers to get things done in business and work environments, we expect users to tire quickly of anthropomorphic feedback, particularly if it soon becomes boring by a lack of variety over time.

22.10.5 Tone and Psychological Impact

Use a tone in dialogue that support a positive psychological impact

Avoid violent, negative, demeaning terms

Avoid use of psychologically threatening terms, such as "illegal," "invalid," and "abort"

Avoid use of the term "hit"; instead use "press" or "click"

22.10.6 Use of Sound and Color

The use of color in displays is a topic that fills volumes of publications for research and practice. Read more about it in some of these references (Nowell, Schulman, & Hix, 2002; Rice, 1991a, 1991b). The use of color in interaction design, or any kind of design, is a complex topic, well beyond the scope of this book.

Avoid irritation with annoying sound and color in displays

Bright colors, blinking graphics, and harsh audio not only are annoying but can have a negative effect on user productivity and the user experience over the long-term.

Use color conservatively

Do not count on color to convey much information in your designs. It is good advice to render your design in black and white first so that you know it works without reliance on color. That will rule out usability problems some users may have with color perception due to different forms of color blindness, for example.

At the end of the day, color decisions are often out of the hands of interaction designers, anyway, being constrained by corporate or organizational standards and branding concerns.

Use pastels, not bright colors

Bright colors seem attractive at first, but soon lead to distraction, visual fatigue, and distaste.

Be aware of color conventions (e.g., avoid red, except for urgency)

Again, color conventions are beyond our scope. They are complicated and differ with international cultural conventions. One clear-cut convention in our Western culture is about the use of red. Beyond very limited use for emergency or urgent situations, red, especially blinking red, is alarming as well as irritating and distracting.

We heard a story at the Social Security Administration that they had an early design in which any required field in a form would blink in red if the user tried to save the form or go to the next form before filling in these fields. Later someone

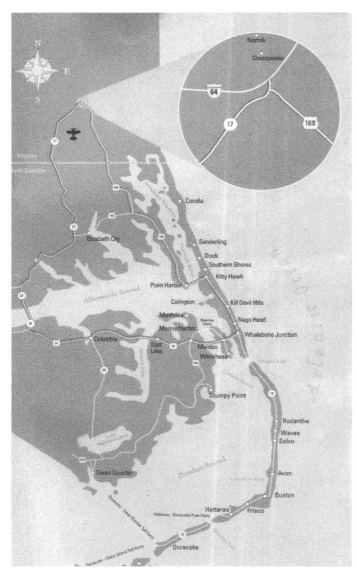

Figure 22-86

Map of Outer Banks, but which is water and which is land?

on the team read that blinking red can bring out latent epilepsy in some people and it got changed.

Example: Help, am I at sea?

Figure 22-86 is a map of the Outer Banks in North Carolina. We have never been able to use this map easily because it violates deeply established color conventions used in maps. Blue is almost always used to denote water in maps, while gray, brown, green, or something similar is used for land. In this map, however, blue, even a deep blue, is used to represent land and because there is about as much land as sea in this map, users experience a cognitive disconnect that confuses and makes it difficult to get oriented.

Watch out for focusing problem with red and blue

Chromostereopsis is the phenomenon humans face when viewing an image containing significant amounts of pure red and pure blue. Because red and blue are at opposite ends of the visual light spectrum and occur at different frequencies, they focus at slightly different depths within the eye and can appear to be at different distances from the eye. Adjacent red and blue in an image can cause the muscles used to focus the eye to oscillate, moving back and forth between the two colors, eventually leading to blurriness and fatigue.

Example: Roses are red; violets are blue

In Figure 22-87 we placed adjacent patches of blue and red. If the color reproduction in the book is good, some readers may experience chromostereopsis while viewing this figure.

22.10.7 Gratuitous Graphics

Jon Meads, our friend who runs Usability Architects, Inc., wants us to understand the difference between graphic design and usability (Meads, 1999):

> As usability consultants, we're often asked by potential clients to bring in a portfolio of "screens" that we've designed. But we don't have any, because we don't design "screens"; we design interaction, the intended behavior by which people will use a product or a Website.

Figure 22-87
Chromostereopsis: humans focus at different depths in the eye for red and blue.

He points out that graphic design is good for attracting attention, getting a user to stop at your Website, but it takes good UX to get them to stay at your Website. He says that Web pages that dazzle can also distract and turn off users who just want to get something done. It is a question of balance of look and feel, and behavior.

Avoid fancy or cute design without a real purpose

> *To impress, all you need is a trebuchet and a piano.*
>
> – Chris Stevens, Northern Exposure

A fancy appearance to a software application or Website can be an asset, but while bling-bling makes for nice jewelry, the "flash and trash" approach to interaction design can detract from usability. As Jon Meads puts it, "Usability is not graphic design."

Aaron Marcus (2002) agrees, warning us that in the rush to provide aesthetics, fun, and pleasure in the UX, we may overdo it and move toward a commercialization of UX that will, in fact, dehumanize the user experience.

22.10.8 Text Legibility

It is obvious that text cannot convey the intended content if it is illegible.

Make presentation of text legible
Make font size large enough for all users
Use good contrast with background

■ Use both color and intensity to provide contrast.

Use mixed case for extensive text
Avoid too many different fonts, sizes
Use legible fonts

- Try Ariel, sans serif Verdana, or Georgia for online reading.

Use color other than blue for text

- It is difficult for the human retina to focus on pure blue for reading.

Accommodate sensory disabilities and limitations

- Support visually challenged, color blind users.

22.10.9 User Preferences
Allow user settings, preference options to control presentational parameters

Afford users control of sound levels, blinking, color, and so on. Vision-impaired users, especially, need preference settings or options to adjust the text size in application displays and possibly to hear an alternative audio version of the text.

22.10.10 Accommodation of User Differences
As we have said, a treatise on accessibility is outside our scope and is treated well in the literature. Nonetheless, all interaction designers should be aware of the requirement to accommodate users with special needs.

Accommodate different levels of expertise/experience with preferences

Most of us have seen this sign in our offices or on a bumper sticker: Lead, follow, or get out of the way. In interaction design, we might modify that slightly to: Lead, follow, *and* get out of the way.

- Lead novice users with adequate cognitive affordances
- Follow intermittent or intermediate users with lots of feedback to keep them on track
- Get out of the way of expert users; keep cognitive affordances from interfering with their physical actions

Constantine (1994b) has made the case to design for intermediate users, which he calls the most neglected user segment. He claims that there are more intermediate users than beginners or experts.

Don't let affordances for new users be performance barriers to experienced users

Although cognitive affordances provide essential scaffolding for inexperienced users, expert users interested in pure productivity need effective physical affordances and few cognitive affordances.

22.10.11 Helpful Help
Be helpful with Help

Do not send your users to Help in a handbasket. For those who share our warped sense of humor, we quote from the manual for Dirk Gently's (Adams, 1990, p. 101) electronic *I Ching* calculator as an example of perhaps not so helpful help. As the protagonist consults the calculator for help to a burning personal question,

> The little book of instructions suggested that he should simply concentrate "soulfully" on the question which was "besieging" him, write it down, ponder on it, enjoy the silence, and then once he had achieved inner harmony and tranquility he should push the red button. There wasn't a red button, but there was a blue button marked 'Red' and this Dirk took to be the one.

Entertaining, yes; helpful, no. Note that it also makes reference at the end to an amusing little problem with cognitive affordance consistency.

22.11 CONCLUSIONS

Be cautious using guidelines.
Use careful thought and interpretation when using guidelines.
In application, guidelines can conflict and overlap.
Guidelines do not guarantee usability.
Using guidelines does NOT eliminate need for usability testing.
Design by guidelines, not by politics or personal opinion.

Connections with Software Engineering

23

Oh, East is East and West is West, and never the twain shall meet,
Till Earth and Sky stand presently at God's great Judgment Seat;
But there is neither East nor West, Border, nor Breed, nor Birth,
When two strong men stand face to face, tho' they come from the ends of the earth!

–Rudyard Kipling

Objectives

After reading this chapter, you will:
1. Understand the similarities and differences between software engineering (SE) and UX lifecycles
2. Appreciate how the locus of influence among the major roles can affect the direction of product development
3. Know how communication, coordination, and other factors form the foundation for success in SE–UX connections
4. Understand the challenges of connecting SE and UX
5. Know about possible solutions to connecting SE and UX successfully

23.1 INTRODUCTION

In Chapter 2 we showed how software systems with interactive components have two distinct logical parts: the functional core and the user interface. Although the separation of code into two clearly identifiable components is not always possible, the two parts are conceptually distinct and each must be developed on its own terms with its own roles within the project team (Pyla et al., 2003, 2005, 2007). Figure 23-1 is an abstraction of this separation and resulting connections.

The user-interface part, the focus of this book, often accounts for half or more of the total lines of code in the overall system (Myers & Rosson, 1992). It begins

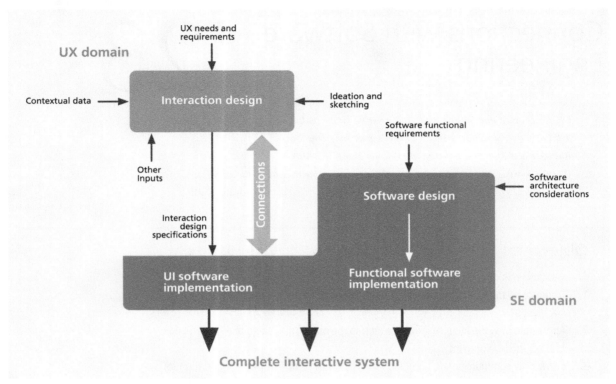

Figure 23-1

An abstract representation of the separation of, and communication between, the two components of system development.

with contextual inquiry, takes shape in design, gets refined in evaluation, and is ultimately implemented in user-interface software.

Therefore, a practical objective of UX practitioners is to provide interaction design specifications, as we discussed in Chapter 9, which can be used by software engineers to build the user interface component of a system.

The functional part of a software system, sometimes called the functional core, is manifest as non-user-interface software. The design and development of this functional core requires specialized software engineering knowledge, training, and experience in topics such as algorithms, data structures, software architectures, calling structures, and database management. The goal of SE is to create efficient and reliable software systems containing the specified functionality, as well as integrating and implementing user-interface software.

To achieve the UX and SE goals for an interactive system, that is, to create an efficient and reliable system with required functionality and a quality user experience, effective development processes are required for both UX and SE lifecycles. The Wheel UX lifecycle template in this book is a time-tested process for ensuring a quality user experience.

The SE development lifecycle, with its significantly longer history and tradition than that of UX, comes in many flavors. On one end of this spectrum is the rigid Waterfall Model (Royce, 1970): a sequence of stages for concept definition, requirements engineering, design (preliminary and detailed design), design review, implementation, integration and testing (I&T), and deployment. On the other end of this spectrum are the agile methods (Chapter 19), a test-driven incremental approach where delivering periodic releases of software modules that add business value to the customer is the focus of the process.

23.1.1 Similarities between Lifecycles

At a high level, UX and SE share the same objectives of understanding the customer's and users' wants and needs, translating these needs into system requirements, designing a system to satisfy these requirements, and testing to help ensure their realization in the final product. At the process level, both lifecycles have similar stages, such as identifying needs, designing, and evaluating, even though these stages entail different philosophies and practices, as discussed in the next section.

23.1.2 Differences between Lifecycles

As often mentioned in this book, UX practitioners iterate early and frequently with design scenarios, screen sketches, paper prototypes, and low-fidelity, roughly coded software prototypes before much, if any, software is committed to the user interface. Often this frequent and early iteration is done on a small scale and scope, primarily as a means to evaluate a part of an interaction design in the context of a small number of user tasks.

UX roles evaluate interaction designs in a number of ways, including early design walkthroughs, rapid evaluation techniques, and lab-based techniques. The primary goal is to find UX problems or flaws in the interaction design so that the design can be improved iteratively.

Even though there is iteration in traditional SE development lifecycles, more so in agile approaches than in the Waterfall approach, the iteration is still on a larger scale (coarser granularity) and scope. In the Waterfall approach, iteration takes place at the granularity of lifecycle stages, such as requirements or design. In agile approaches, while there is iteration at the code-module level, it is still coarser than most kinds of UX iteration because it includes both software code and interaction design.

Another difference between these two lifecycles has to do with terminology. Even though certain terms appear in both lifecycles, they often mean different things.

For example, scenarios in SE (called "use cases" in the object-oriented design paradigm) are used to "identify a thread of usage for the system to be constructed (and) provide a description of how the system will be used" (Pressman, 2009). Whereas in UX, a design usage scenario is "a narrative or story that describes the activities of one or more persons, including information about goals, expectations, actions, and reactions (of persons)" (Rosson & Carroll, 2002).

Overall, software engineers concentrate on the system whereas usability engineers concentrate on the users.

23.2 LOCUS OF INFLUENCE IN AN ORGANIZATION

In our experience we have seen three major roles in an organization that have a significant influence on the direction of a product development: business role, design or "creative" role, and software or development role. Each role brings a unique skillset, perspective, or bias to a project effort.

The business role is concerned with the subject matter of that work domain. For example, if you are building a software application for helping civil engineers construct bridges, your "business" stakeholders will include structural engineers and other people who know the mechanics of construction and engineering. Sometimes marketing also plays a key role in formulating the product direction under this business role umbrella.

Gross generalizations notwithstanding, in our experience we found that people in business roles usually care about feature coverage. They tend to think of a product's quality in terms of what it can do, how comprehensively it accounts for the business needs, how its features stack against the competition, and all the nuances with which a particular business need is addressed.

The software or development role shares some of the business role's tendency to think of a product's quality in terms of features or "use-cases" supported. Perhaps an even stronger tendency of this role is to think of quality in terms of code reliability, maintainability of code modules, speed of execution, and other software performance attributes. The underlying sentiment is that optimizing the functional core of a system is more important than all other concerns.

The UX or design role, however, tends to prioritize user needs and experience over all other factors. This often trades off with feature counts because simplicity and ease of use correlate inversely with abundance of options and features on a user interface. For these roles, quality manifests itself in terms of usability, user satisfaction, usefulness, and emotional impact.

This locus-of-influence perspective is somewhat orthogonal to general project management concerns such as cost and resource allocation; each role tends to prioritize different aspects of the overall project effort given cost and resource constraints. As a thought experiment, if you were to think of a measure of the amount of influence or authority a given role has in an organization and average it across all the people who play that role in an organization, you will get what we call the locus-of-influence factor. The higher the value of this factor for a given role, the greater the influence on the product direction.

The locus-of-influence factors for the three roles color the personality of an organization that builds interactive systems. It becomes the DNA that permeates all aspects of the culture, including the everyday operations and priorities of that organization. When you hear people say "Google has an engineering culture," they are probably referring to a heavy weighting of this factor toward SE. Similarly, when people call Apple a design company, they are referring to a high value for UX or design role there.

As an extension to this thought experiment, now assume you are somehow able to assess quantitatively the amount of influence each role exerts on the overall product direction, what we call the locus of influence for each role. Suppose we are also able to combine those measures in a reasonable way to get what we call the locus of influence in an organization. This abstract measure represents an aggregate of the underlying forces, biases, aspirations, and direction that propel a product through the development lifecycle.

This locus of influence for a company is usually a by-product of the company's history, leadership, culture, expertise of roles, and the perception of value of each role's expertise. So what happens to the project effort when you manipulate the locus of influence for each role? We discuss some generalizations for each of the interesting cases.

23.2.1 Scenario 1: SE as Primary Product Architects

In an organization with a predominantly high engineering or programming locus of influence, the project is biased toward code and technology concerns. The SE role, perhaps working with business, elicits requirements from customers and envisions the product design. These requirements tend to have a functional flavor rather than a user-centered one. The SE role translates the gathered requirements into functional design, which then gets implemented in code.

The emphasis of quality is on code and other software engineering concerns such as cohesion and coupling. Because an SE role's job performance is judged in light of these concerns, it is natural that they work toward building the best functional core they can.

The interaction design concerns are not a big priority in such an organization, and people in the SE role probably do not have much training or expertise in designing for user experience. We know of many companies where, even today, SE roles create the interaction designs for the system. Even if there are specialist UX roles in this scenario, they are often brought in near the end of the lifecycle for "fixing" the experience and "making things pretty." The UX role is a "priest in a parachute," brought in at the end to bless the product by suggesting some quick, and mostly cosmetic, changes because it is too late to change anything major.

UX roles in this kind of a culture are constrained by SE decisions and state of progress. Because SE roles ultimately implement the interaction designs, there is no "cultural" force to ensure that the designs by the UX roles are adopted.

Any change proposed by the UX role can require a difficult and often protracted negotiation between SE and UX roles. The UX role is required to "prove" that their suggestions are better and legitimate. This scenario can be more extreme in organizations with legacy software infrastructure.

We know of organizations where SE roles are valued higher than any other role, even to the extent of limiting career advancement options to other roles. We have seen frustrated colleagues leave organizations because their contributions were not considered an important part of the overall project effort.

In summary, the scenario of having SE roles as primary product architects suffers from an implicit conflict of interest due to the fact that something that is easy to use is almost always not easy to implement. Cooper (2004) succinctly sums up this scenario via the title of his popular book: *The Inmates Are Running the Asylum.*

23.2.2 Scenario 2: UX as Primary Product Architects

In an organization with a predominantly high design or user experience locus of influence, the project is biased toward users, usage, usability, and emotional impact. The UX role conducts contextual inquiry, analyzes and models the work practice, envisions an interaction design, and provides an experience for the user. This emphasis on usage-in-context ensures grounding in user concerns, goals, and aspirations, which in turn leads to a system with better usability.

As an aside, why is this scenario likely to produce a system that fosters a better user experience? Why will the outcome be any different when essentially the process is similar to that in scenario 1 where SE roles conduct requirements engineering activities with users and customers? Is not this essentially a similar activity conducted by different roles? Are UX roles better than SE roles when it comes to requirements? No. This is not about who is better. It is about each role's innate tendencies, allegiances, foci, and training.

UX roles are naturally interested in users because they design for usage. SE roles are interested in system functionality because they implement that functionality. UX role instincts tend to be about workflows, barriers, and breakdowns in work practice, social aspects of work, and emotional impact of a system. SE role instincts tend to be about algorithms and data structures, separation of concerns among data and presentation layers, class hierarchies, and code reuse. UX roles, starting with their human–computer interaction (HCI) 101 classes, are trained in concepts such as contextual and task analysis. SE roles, starting with their SE 101 classes, are trained in requirements engineering via use-case modeling and functional decomposition.

Therefore, it is no surprise that, all other things being equal, a UX role will produce a more user-centered and user experience-oriented analysis of the work domain and what is needed in the envisioned system. Conversely, the SE role will produce a more system-centered and functionality-oriented analysis of the work domain and how it can be supported by the system.

Getting back to the scenario, the UX role, after analyzing the work practice, designs the envisioned interaction and hands it off to the SE role for implementation. In an organization like this, the designers have a free reign and usually tend to produce interaction designs that push the envelope with respect to innovation and complexity. This model puts pressure on the SE role to implement these sometimes blue-sky designs. This can become a coping scenario for SE if the technology of the target platform does not support what is needed in the UX designs or the SE role does not have the required skills or training to translate the UX designs into code.

There are two possible outcomes in this scenario: (1) the SE role works toward updating the underlying technology to support the new interaction design needs or (2) the SE role resorts to "hacking" the available infrastructure to implement the designs. Obviously the former is more advisable but requires significant effort—an unlikely option for systems with a considerable legacy code base. The latter delivers the envisioned user experience but results in a system with brittle code and maintenance challenges.

Another issue with this scenario has to do with the communication of constraints. The UX role does not know which aspects of its interaction designs are feasible and which are expensive or impossible to implement. This is because being easy to envision in a prototyping platform may not translate easily into being easy to implement in the actual target platform.

Emphasis on interaction in the prototype almost always leads to stubbing of computational functionality. The temptation is to stub the difficult parts of the computational design without first understanding their design requirements. Later, development of the stubbed functions can reveal basic problems that affect the system at many levels above the stub in question. The result is upheaval rather than a smooth progression toward an implementation.

In summary, the scenario of having UX roles as primary product architects tends to push the envelope when it comes to design, with SE playing a "support" role for the overall vision.

23.2.3 Scenario 3: SE and UX as Collaborators

It is not our intention in the previous two scenarios to take sides. We believe that both the SE team and the UX team are essential and complementary. This complementarity is the perspective of our third scenario, which occurs within organizations where the three factors of influence are about even. In an environment of collaboration between SE and UX roles—the two roles work as equal partners together and with the business role. Working together, they undertake early analysis activities. The UX roles conduct contextual inquiry and analysis while briefing the SE role periodically on findings and the emerging needs for the product. In other words, an UX role's concerns and analyses for the user interface imply requirements for the SE role, because they have to implement the UI software component of the system. The two roles may also collaborate during this phase and conduct these activities together.

As the UX role undertakes ideation, sketching, and other early design activities, they keep the SE role updated. They ensure feasibility of their explorations and address potential constraints early on. The UX role prototypes the interaction and the SE role designs the backend. The UX role iteratively refines the interaction design via evaluation, while keeping the SE role informed of any surprises or findings with functional implications. The UX role delivers the final prototypes or other models as specification of the interaction design that the SE role implements along with the backend functionality.

This kind of an organizational environment plays to the strengths and expertise of the different roles. When there are discussions, debates, or disagreements, all opinions are heard and the final decision is left to the role responsible for that area. For example, final interaction design decisions are left to the UX role and final technology decisions to SE roles.

The implicit requirement for this scenario to work is intimate communication and coordination between SE and UX roles. We discuss this further later.

Once this kind of synchronization is established, we have known such organizations to be very productive with high throughput. These organizations tend to produce quality products—the best user experience within the technology constraints—even if they tend to be more evolutionary than revolutionary in terms of innovation.

In summary, the scenario of having UX and SE roles collaboratively driving a product direction tends to result in productive work environments, which generally produce optimal design solutions given technology constraints. However, there is no overt push to break out of existing constraints and innovate beyond normal progression of the product evolution.

23.3 WHICH SCENARIO IS RIGHT FOR YOU?

This is an important question and, like most things in HCI, the answer is "it depends." It depends on the nature of the product under development, available resources, company culture, expertise of people, and competition in that product area.

In our experience, we found scenario 1, where SE roles lead the product strategy, almost never advisable where a quality user experience is a goal. Interaction design concerns must take precedence if user experience is a product differentiator in the market.

Scenario 2, where UX roles lead the product strategy, is good for interactive systems trying to push the envelope, break into a market, or displace an existing market leader. This approach allows designers to flex their wings and create an interaction design that is unencumbered by constraints. Often such "pie in the sky" ideas require major changes on the SE side.

Scenario 3 is practical and probably appropriate for most situations. Separation of concerns—each role concentrating on their domains while being mindful of the other role's constraints—provides a work environment where things get done quickly without endless debates and arguments. Because neither side pushes the other beyond "normal" expectations, the end product tends to be functional with a good user experience, but rarely a paradigm shifter.

23.4 FOUNDATIONS FOR SUCCESS IN SE–UX DEVELOPMENT

23.4.1 Communication

Although SE and UX roles can successfully do much of their work independently and in parallel, because of the tight coupling between the backend and the user interface, a successful project requires that the two roles communicate so that each knows generally what the other is doing and how that might affect its own activities and work products.

The two roles cannot collaborate without communication, and the longer they work without knowing about the other's progress and insights, the more their work is likely to diverge, and the harder it becomes to bring the two lifecycle products together at the end. Communication is important between SE and UX roles to have activity awareness about how the other group's design is progressing, what process activity they are currently performing, what features are being focused on, what insights and concerns they have for the project, what directions they are taking, and so on.

Especially during the early requirements and design activities, each group needs to be "light on its feet" and able to inform and respond to events and activities occurring in the counterpart lifecycle. However, in many organizations, such necessary communication does not take place because the two lifecycles operate independently; that is, there is no structured development framework to facilitate communication between these two lifecycles, leaving cross-domain (especially) communication dependent on individual whim or chance.

Based on our experience, ad hoc communication processes have proven to be inadequate and often result in nasty surprises that are revealed only at the end when serious communication finally does occur. This usually happens too late in the overall process.

There is a need for a role or a system to ensure that the necessary information is being communicated to all relevant parties in the system development effort. Usually, that role is a "project manager" who keeps track of the overall status of each role, work products, and bottlenecks or constraints. For larger organizations with more complex projects, there is a need for communication systems to automate and help the project manager manage some of these responsibilities.

23.4.2 Coordination

When the two lifecycle concepts are applied in isolation, the resulting lack of understanding between the two roles, combined with an urgency to get their own work done, often leads to working without collaboration and coordination. This often results in not getting the UX needs of the system represented in the software design.

Without coordination, the two roles duplicate their efforts in UX and SE activities when they could be working together. For example, both SE and UX roles conduct separate field visits and client interviews for systems analysis and requirements gathering during the early stages of the project. Without collaboration, each project group reports its results in documentation not usually seen by people in the other lifecycle. Each uses those results to drive only their part of the system design and finally merge at the implementation stage. However, because these specifications were created without coordination and communication, when they are now considered together in detail, developers typically discover that the two design parts do not fit with one another because of large differences and incompatibilities.

Moreover, this lack of coordinated activities presents the appearance of a disjointed development team to the client. It is likely to cause confusion in the clients: "why are we being asked similar questions by two different groups from the same development team?"

Coordination will help in team building, communication, and in each lifecycle role recognizing the value, and problems, of the other, in addition to early agreement on goals and requirements. In addition, working together on early lifecycle activities is a chance for each role to learn about the value, objectives, and problems of the other.

23.4.3 Synchronization

Eventually the two lifecycle roles must synchronize the work products for implementation and testing. However, waiting until one absolutely must synchronize creates problems. Synchronization of the design work products of the two lifecycle roles is usually put off until the implementation and testing phases near the end of the development effort, which creates big surprises that are often too costly to address.

For example, it is not uncommon to find UX roles being brought into the project late in the development process, even after the SE implementation stage (scenario 1 above). They are asked to test and/or "fix" the usability of an already implemented system, and then, of course, many changes proposed by the UX roles that require significant modifications must be ignored due to budget and time constraints. Those few changes that actually do get included require a significant investment in terms of time and effort because they must be retrofitted (Boehm, 1981).

Therefore, it is better to have many synchronization points, earlier and throughout the two project lifecycles. These timely synchronization points would allow earlier, more frequent, and less costly "calibration" to keep both design parts on track for a more harmonious final synchronization with fewer harmful surprises.

The idea is for each role to have timely readiness of work products when the other project role needs them. This prevents situations where one project role must wait for the other one to complete a particular work product. However, the more each team works without communication and collaboration, the less likely they will be able to schedule their project activities to arrive simultaneously at common checkpoints.

23.4.4 Dependency and Constraint Enforcement

Because each part of an interactive system must operate with the other, many system requirements have both SE and UX components. If an SE component or feature is first to be considered, the SE role should inform the UX role that an interaction design counterpart is needed, and vice versa.

When the two roles gather requirements separately and without communication, it is easy to capture requirements that are conflicting, incompatible, or one-sided. Even if there is some ad hoc form of communication between the two groups, it is inevitable that some parts of the requirements or design will be forgotten or will "fall through the cracks."

The lack of understanding of the constraints and dependencies between the two lifecycles' timelines and work products often create serious problems, such as inconsistencies in the work products of the SE and UX design. As an example, software engineers perform a detailed functional analysis from the requirements of the system to be built. Interaction designers perform a hierarchical task analysis, with usage scenarios to guide design for each task, based on their requirements. These requirements and designs are maintained separately and not necessarily shared. However, each view of the requirements and design has elements that reflect constraints or dependencies in elements of the counterpart view.

For example, each task in the task analysis on the UX side implies the need for corresponding functions in the SE specifications. Similarly, each function in the software design may reflect the need for access to this functionality through one or more user tasks in the user interface. Without the knowledge of such dependencies, when tasks are missing in the user interface or functions are missing in the software because of changes on either lifecycle, the respective sets of designs have a high probability of becoming inconsistent.

In our experience, we often encounter situations that illustrate the fact that design choices made in one lifecycle constrain the design options in the other. For example, we see situations where user interfaces to software systems were designed from a functional point of view and the code was factored to minimize duplication on the backend core. The resulting systems had user interfaces that did not have proper interaction cues to help the user in a smooth task transition. Instead, a task-oriented approach would have supported users with screen transitions specific to each task, even though this would have resulted in a possibly "less efficient" composition for the backend.

Another case in our experience was about integrating a group of individually designed Web-based systems through a single portal. Each of these systems was designed for separate tasks and functionalities. These systems were integrated on the basis of functionality and not on the way the tasks would flow in the new system. The users of this new system had to go through awkward screen transitions when their tasks referenced functions from the different existing systems.

Constraints, dependencies, and relationships exist not only among activities and work products that cross over between the two lifecycles, but they also exist within each of the lifecycles. For example, on the UX side, a key task identified in task analysis should be considered and matched later for a design scenario and a benchmark task.

"We Cannot Change THAT!": Usability and Software Architecture

Len Bass, NICTA, Sydney, Australia
Bonnie E. John, IBM T. J. Watson Research Center and Carnegie Mellon University

Usability analyses or user test data are in; the development team is poised to respond. The software had been modularized carefully so that modifications to the user interfaces (UI) would be fast and easy. When the usability problems are presented, someone around the table exclaims, "Oh, no, we cannot change THAT!"

The requested modification or feature reaches too far into the architecture of the system to allow economically viable and timely changes to be made. Even when the functionality is right, even when the UI is separated from that functionality, architectural decisions made early in development have precluded the implementation of a usable system. Members of the design team are frustrated and disappointed that despite their best efforts, despite following current best practice, they must ship a product that is far less usable than they know it could be.

This scenario need not be played out if important usability concerns are considered during the earliest design decisions of a system, that is, during design of the software architecture. Software architecture refers to the internal structure of the software—what pieces are going to make up the system and how they will interact. The relationships between architectural decisions and software quality attributes such as performance, availability, security, and modifiability are relatively well understood and taught routinely in software architecture courses. However, the prevailing wisdom in the last 25 years has been that usability had no architectural role except through modifiability; design the UI to be modified easily and usability will be realized through iterative design, analysis, and testing. Software engineers developed "separation patterns" or generalized architecture designs that separated the user interface into components that could change independently from the core application functionality.

The Model–View–Controller (MVC) pattern, http://en.wikipedia.org/wiki/Model–view–controller, is an example of one of these. Separation of the user interface has been quite effective and is used commonly in practice, but it has problems: (1) there are many aspects of usability that require architectural support other than separation and (2) the later changes are made to the system, the more expensive they are to achieve. Forcing usability to be achieved through modification means that time and budget pressures are likely to cut off iterations on the user interface and result in a system that is not as usable as possible.

Consider, for example, giving the user the ability to cancel a long-running command. In order for the user to cancel a command, the system must first recognize that the particular operation will indeed be long enough that the user might want to cancel (as opposed to waiting for it to complete and then undo). Second, the system must display a dialogue box giving the user the ability to cancel. Third, the system must recognize when the user selects the "cancel" button regardless of what else it is doing and respond quickly (or the user will keep hitting the cancel button). Next, the system must terminate the active operation and, finally, the system must restore the system to its state prior to the issuance of that command (having stored all the necessary information prior to the invocation of the command), informing the user if it fails to restore any of the state.

In order for cancel to be supported, aspects of the MVC must all cooperate in a systematic fashion. Early software architecture design will determine how difficult it is to implement this coordination. Difficulty translates into time and cost, which, in turn, reduce the likelihood that the cancel command will be implemented.

Cancel is one of two dozen or so usability operations that we have identified as having a significant impact on the usability of a system. These *architecturally significant usability scenarios* include undo, aggregating data, and allowing the user to personalize their view. For a more complete list of these operations, see Bass and John (2003).

After identifying the architecturally significant usability scenarios important for the end users of a system, the developers—software engineers—must know how to design the architecture and implement the command and all of the subtleties involved in delivering a usable product. For the most part, this information is not taught in standard computer science courses today. Consequently, most software developers will learn this only through painful experience. To help this situation, we have developed *usability-supporting architectural patterns* embodied in a checklist describing responsibilities of the software that architecture designers and developers should consider when implementing these operations (Adams et al., 2005; Golden, 2010). However, only some usability scenarios have been embodied in responsibility checklists and knowledge of the existence of these checklists among practicing developers is very limited.

Organizations that have used these materials, however, have found them valuable. NASA used our usability-supporting architectural patterns in the design of the Mars Exploration Rover Board (MERBoard), a wall-sized collaborative workspace intended to facilitate shoulder-to-shoulder collaboration by MER science teams. During a redesign of the MERBoard software architecture, 17 architecturally significant usability scenarios were identified as essential for MERBoard and a majority of the architecture's components were modified in response to the issues raised by the usability-supporting architectural patterns (Adams et al., 2005). ABB considered usability-supporting architectural patterns in the design of a new product line architecture, finding 14 issues with their initial design and crediting this process with a 17:1 return on investment of their architect's time—1-day's work by two people saved 5 weeks of work later (Stoll et al., 2009). For more information, see the Usability and Software Architecture Website at http://www.cs.cmu.edu/~bej/usa/index.html.

References

Adams, R. J., Bass, L., & John, B. E. (2005). Applying general usability scenarios to the design of the software architecture of a collaborative workspace. In A. Seffah, J. Gulliksen & M. Desmarais (Eds.), *Human-Centered Software Engineering: Frameworks for HCI/HCD and Software Engineering Integration*. Kluwer Academic Publishers.

Bass, L., & John, B. E. (2003). Linking usability to software architecture patterns through general scenarios. *Journal of Systems and Software, 66*(3), 187–197.

Golden, E. (2010). *Early-Stage Software Design for Usability*. Ph.D. dissertation in Human-Computer Interaction: Human-Computer Interaction Institute, School of Computer Science, Carnegie Mellon University.

Stoll, P., Bass, L., Golden, E., & John, B. E. (2009). Supporting usability in product line architectures. In *Proceedings of the 13th International Software Product Line Conference*, San Francisco, CA August 24–28, 2009.

23.4.5 Anticipating Change within the Overall Project Effort

In the development of interactive systems, each phase and each iteration have a potential for change. In fact, at least the early part of the UX process is intended to change the design iteratively. This change can manifest itself during the requirements phase (growing and evolving understanding of the emerging system by project team members and users), design stage (evaluation identifies that the interaction metaphor was not easily understood by users), and so on. Such changes often affect both lifecycles because of the various dependencies that exist between and within the two processes.

Therefore, change can be visualized conceptually as a design perturbation that has a ripple effect on all stages in which previous work has been done. For example, during the UX evaluation, the UX role may recognize the need for a new task to be supported by the system. This new task requires updating the previously generated hierarchical task inventory (HTI) document and generation of new usage scenarios to reflect the new addition (along with the rationale).

On the SE side, this change to the HTI generates the need to change the functional decomposition (for example, by adding new functions to the functional core to support this task on the user interface). These new functions, in turn, mandate a change to the design, schedules, and, in some cases, even the architecture of the entire system.

Thus, one of the most important requirements for system development is to identify the possible implications and effects of each kind of change and to account for them in the design accordingly.

One particular kind of dependency between lifecycle parts represents a kind of "feed forward," giving insight to future lifecycle activities. For example, during the early design stages in the UX lifecycle, usage scenarios provide insights as to how the layout and design of the user interface might look like. In other words, for project activities that are connected to one another (in this case, the initial screen design is dependent on or connected to the usage scenarios), there is a possibility that the designers can forecast or derive insights from a particular design activity.

Sometimes the feed-forward is in the form of a note: "when you get to screen design, do not forget to consider such and such." Therefore, when the project team member encounters such premonitions or ideas about potential effects on later stages (on the screen design in this example), there is a need to document them when the process is still in the initial stages (usage scenario phase). When the team member reaches the initial screen design stage, previously documented insights are then readily available to aid the screen design activity.

Figure 23-2

User interaction design as input to UI software design.

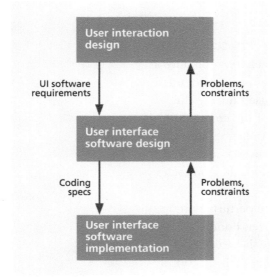

23.5 THE CHALLENGE OF CONNECTING SE AND UX

23.5.1 User Interaction Design, Software, and Implementation

In Figure 23-2 we show software design and implementation for just UI software (middle and bottom boxes). While this separation of UI software from non-user-interface (functional core) software is an acceptable abstraction, it is actually an oversimplification.

The current state of the art in software engineering embodies a well-developed lifecycle concept and well-developed process for producing requirements and design specifications for the whole software system. But they do not have a process for developing UI software separately from the functional (non-UI) software.

Furthermore, there are currently no major software development lifecycle concepts that adequately support including the UX lifecycle as a serious part of the overall system development process. Most software engineering textbooks (Pressman, 2009; Sommerville, 2006) just mention the UI design without saying anything about how it happens. Most software engineering courses in colleges and universities describe a software development lifecycle without any reference to the UI. Students are taught about the different stages of developing interactive software and, as they finish the implementation stages in the lifecycle, the UI somehow appears automagically. Important questions about how the UI is designed, by whom, and how the two corresponding SE and UX lifecycles are connected are barely mentioned (Pyla et al., 2004).

So, in practice, most software requirements specifications include little about the interaction design. If they do get input from UX people, they include use cases and screen sketches as part of their requirements, or they might sketch these up themselves, but that is about the extent of it. However, in reality there is a need for UX people to produce interaction design specifications and for SE people to make a connection with them in their lifecycle. And this is best done in the long run within a broader, connected lifecycle model embracing both lifecycle processes and facilitating communication across and within both development domains.

23.5.2 The Promise of Agile Development

In Chapter 19, we attempted such an integrated model in an agile development context. Even though traditional agile methods (such as XP) do not explicitly mention UX processes, we believe that the underlying philosophy of these methodologies to be flexible, ready for change, and evaluation-centered has the potential to bridge the gap between SE and UX if they are extended to include UI components and techniques. As we mentioned in Chapter 19, this requires compromises and adjustments on both sides to respect the core tenets of each lifecycle.

23.5.3 The Pipedream of Completely Separate Lifecycles

Although we have separated out the UX lifecycle for discussion in most of this book for the convenience of not having to worry too much about the SE counterpart, we realize that because the two worlds of development cannot exist in isolation, we do try to face our connection to the SE world in this chapter.

23.5.4 How about Lifecycles in Series?

Consider the make-believe scenario, very similar to the one discussed earlier, in which timing means nothing and SE people sit around waiting for a complete and final interaction design to be ready. Then a series connection of the two lifecycles, as shown in Figure 23-3, might work.

The UX people work until they achieved a stable interaction design and have decided (by whatever criterion) to stop iterating. Then they hand off that finished version of the interaction design and agree that it will not be changed by further iteration in this version of the system.

The output of the UX lifecycle used as input to the SE lifecycle is labeled "interaction design specifications as UI software requirements inputs" to emphasize that the interaction design specifications are not yet software

Figure 23-3

UX and SE lifecycles in series.

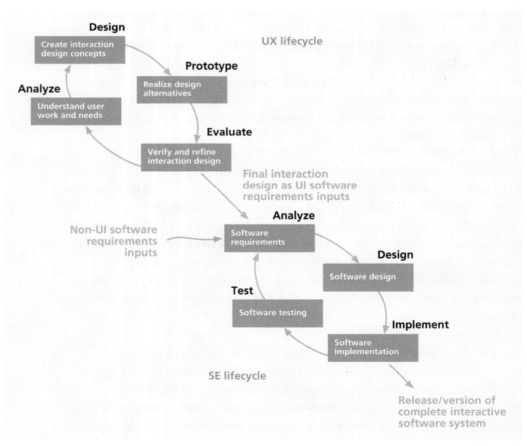

requirements but inputs to requirements because only SE people can make software requirements and those requirements are for the entire system. We, the HCI folks, provide the inputs to only part of that requirements process.

There are, of course, at least two things very wrong about the assumptions behind this series connection of lifecycles. First, and most obvious, the timing just will not work. The absolute lack of parallelism leads to terrible inefficiencies, wasted time, and an unduly long overall product lifecycle.

Once the project is started, the SE people could and would, in fact, work in parallel on compiling their own software requirements, deferring interaction design requirements in anticipation of those to come from the UX people. However, if they must wait until the UX people have gotten through their entire iterative lifecycle, they will not get the interaction design specifications to use in specifying UI software requirements until far into the project schedule.

The second fatal flaw of the series lifecycle connection is that the SE side cannot accommodate UI changes that inevitably will occur after the interaction design "handoff." There is never a time this early in the overall process when the UX people can declare their interaction design as "done." UX people are constantly iterating and, even after the last usability testing session, design changes continue to occur for many reasons, for example, platform constraints do not allow certain UI features.

23.5.5 Can We Make an Iterative Version of the Serial Connection?

To get information about the evolving interaction design to SE people earlier and to accommodate changes due to iteration, perhaps we can change the configuration in Figure 23-3 slightly so that each iteration of the interaction design, instead of just the final interaction design, also goes through the software lifecycle; see Figure 23-4.

While this would help alleviate the timing problem by keeping SE people informed much earlier of what is going on in the UX cycle, it could be confusing and frustrating to have the UX requirements inputs changing so often. Each UX iteration feeds an SE iteration, but the existing SE lifecycle concepts are not equipped for iteration this finely grained; they cannot afford to keep starting over with changing requirements.

23.5.6 It Needs to Be More Collaborative and Parallel

So variations of a series lifecycle connection are fraught with practical challenges. We need parallelism between these two lifecycles. As shown in Figure 23-5, there is a need for something in-between to anchor this parallelism.

Figure 23-4

Iterating a serial connection.

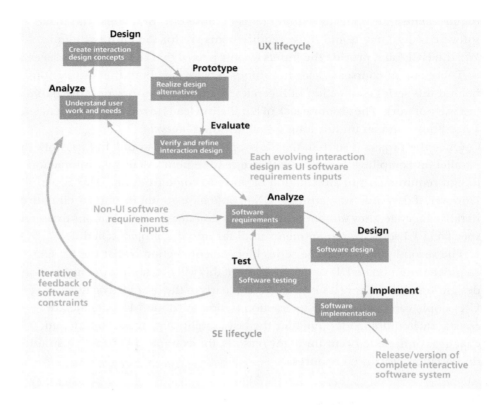

Figure 23-5

Need for connections between the two lifecycles.

As we mentioned earlier, however, this parallel configuration has the strongest need for collaboration and coordination, represented by the connecting box with the question mark in Figure 23-5. Without such communication parallel lifecycles cannot work. However, traditional SE and UX lifecycles do not have mechanisms for that kind of communication. So in the interest of a realistic UX/SE development collaboration without undue

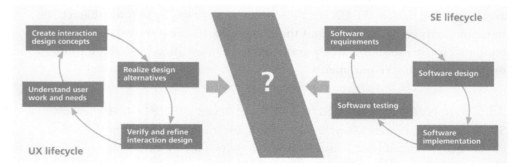

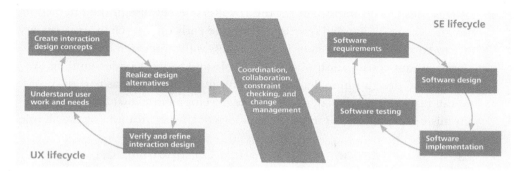

Figure 23-6
More parallel connections
between the two lifecycles.

timing constraints, we propose some kind of parallel lifecycle connection, with a communication layer in-between, such as that of Figure 23-6.

Conceptually, the two lifecycles are used to develop two views of the same overall system. Therefore, the different activities within these two lifecycles have deep relationships among them. Consequently, it is important that the two development roles communicate after each major activity to ensure that they share the insights from their counterpart lifecycle and to maintain situational awareness about their progress.

The box in the middle of Figure 23-6 is a mechanism for communication, collaboration, constraint checking, and change management discussed earlier. This communication mechanism allows (or forces) the two development domains to keep each other informed about activities, work products, and (especially) design changes. Each stage of each lifecycle engages in work product flow and communication potentially with each stage of the other lifecycle but the connection is not one to one between the corresponding stages.

Because SE people face many changes to their own requirements, change is certainly not a foreign concept to them, either. It is all about how you handle change. In an ideal world, SE people can just plug in the new interaction design, change the requirements that are affected, and move forward. In the practical world, they need situational awareness from constant feedback from UX people to prepare SE people to answer two important questions: Can our current design accommodate the existing UX inputs? Second, based on the trajectory of UX design evolution, can we foresee any major problems?

Having the two lifecycles parallel has the advantage that it retains the two lifecycles as independent, thereby protecting their individual and inherent interests, foci, emphases, and philosophies. It also ensures that the influence and the expertise of each lifecycle are felt throughout the entire process, not just during the early parts of development.

This is especially important for the UX lifecycle because, if the interaction design were to be handed over to the SE role early on, any changes necessary due to constraints arising later in the process will be decided by the SE role alone without consultation with the UX role and without understanding of the original design rationale. Moreover, having the UX role as part of the overall team during the later parts of the development allows for catching any misrepresentations or misinterpretations of UI specifications by the SE role.

23.5.7 Risk Management through Communication, Collaboration, Constraint Checking, and Change Management

Taking a risk management perspective, the box in the middle of Figure 23-6 allows each lifecycle to say to the other "show me your risks" so that they can anticipate the impact on their own risks and allocate resources accordingly. Identifying and understanding risks are legitimate arguments for getting project resources as an investment in reducing overall project risks.

If a challenge is encountered in a stage of one lifecycle, it can create a large overall risk for parallel but non-communicating lifecycles because of a lack of timely awareness of the problem in the other lifecycle. Such risks are minimal in a series configuration, but that is unrealistic for other reasons. For example, a problem that stretches the timeline on the UX side can eventually skew the timeline on the SE side.

In Figure 23-6, the risk can be better contained because early awareness affords a more agile response in addressing it. In cases where the UX design is not compatible with the SE implementation constraints, Figure 23-3 represents a very high risk because neither group is aware of the incompatibility until late in the game. Figure 23-4 represents only a medium risk because the feedback loop can help developers catch major problems. Figure 23-6, however, will minimize risk by fostering earlier communication throughout the two lifecycles; risks are more distributed.

23.6 THE RIPPLE MODEL TO CONNECT SE AND UX

To connect the SE and UX lifecycles, we developed "Ripple" (so named because of the ripple effect of a thread of communication), a communication-fostering framework (Pyla, 2009).

The Ripple model, shown in Figure 23-7, describes the specific environment, tool support, entities, and various components involved in a particular interactive system development project. The Ripple model is expressed at a level

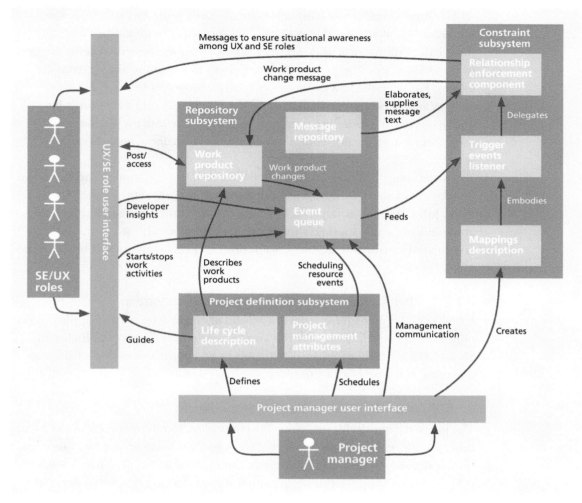

Figure 23-7
The Ripple model.

of detail that is useful for developers to adopt and employ manually for a particular project context or as a framework on which to design an automated software system to manage the communication required between the two lifecycles.

As an example, a software implementation of the Ripple model would work as follows (using quotes to set off state-change indicators that could be used as communication triggers): A person in a UX role, John Doe, logs into the system, "starts" working on task analysis by selecting that activity in Ripple, which "creates" a hierarchical task inventory (HTI) document, which will be stored in a work product repository.

The Ripple implementation automatically detects the fact that John Doe started task analysis, and the work product repository automatically detects the creation of this new work product. Upon creation, these two events are sent to the event queue component directing them to be sent to the appropriate parties. For example, if a dependency relationship exists between UX's task analysis and SE's functional analysis: "every task in UX role's HTI must have one or more corresponding functions to support the task on the backend," the system automatically sends a message to the functional analysis work activity in SE.

This message will be waiting when the SE role logs in through the developer interface and starts to work on the functional analysis activity. Similarly, when John Doe sends the insight about the need for a new task, the system automatically sends messages to all other developers who work on task-related activities (e.g., usage scenarios) and this message will be delivered immediately.

23.6.1 The Ripple Project Definition Subsystem

Using a project manager interface, a project manager accesses the Ripple project definition subsystem to specify the component parts of a project, including SE and UX lifecycle types, work activities to be conducted as part of the two lifecycles, roles, and work products.

23.6.2 The Ripple Constraint Subsystem

The job of the constraint subsystem is to represent, monitor, and enforce various dependency relationships among different entities between the two lifecycles during development. Through these constraints, different time-based events in the development space can trigger other events that need to be performed to maintain stability in the design.

Using the Ripple *Mappings Description Component*, the project manager can declare the different relationships that exist among various entities within the development space. For example, consider the relationship between the SE role's functional decomposition work product and the UX role's hierarchical task list work product: a mapping element must be declared so that a change to one of these work products requires at least a consideration of change to the other.

A project manager can declare a mapping between these two work activities to be dependent on the source work activity (e.g., HTI, by UX role), a trigger event that perturbs the design space (e.g., new task description added to HTI by UX role), a related work activity elsewhere in the design space (e.g., functional analysis by SE role), or the type of relationship (e.g., every task in UX role's HTI must have one or more corresponding functions to support the task on the backend).

The *Trigger Event Listener* is a software agent that monitors the event queue for trigger events to enforce a relationship. For each event arriving at the event queue, the trigger event listener checks the mappings description to identify the corresponding relationship and delegates the enforcement of that relationship to the *Relationship Enforcement Component* by passing to it the event and its corresponding relationship. For example, in the case of the UX role creating a new task in the HTI, the module upon verifying the existence of a relationship, wherein the SE role is required to update their functional decomposition work product, informs the relationship enforcement component to notify the SE role about this change.

23.6.3 The Ripple Repository Subsystem

Various work products of the combined design process are stored as a shared design representation in a single repository called the *Work Product Repository* with each of the SE and UX roles having two separate views to this dataset. Developers are required to post new work products created at the end of each work activity here, creating "posting" trigger events.

The Ripple implementation of this repository has mechanisms to detect any queue events as and when time-based events for work products, such as *work product created* or *is being modified*, occur. Once detected, these events are sent to the event queue to be acted upon by the trigger event listener.

23.7 CONCLUSIONS

23.7.1 You Need a True Separate Role for Interaction Design

Although we have seen remarkable exceptions where software engineering people are also very good at interaction design, we generally stand by our conclusion that the UX process generally should not be done by a software engineering person. We need a true separate role for *interaction designer*.

In past years, this role has blossomed into a major career niche, going under many appellations, including user experience specialist, usability engineer, UX practitioner, UX designer, and information architect. While people entered this field from human factors, psychology, computer science, or engineering, now there are academic programs tailored specifically to train people to meet the demand for these skills.

People in all roles in both domains must work together and share in the design and development not just of the user interface, but of the whole interactive system. While these roles correspond to distinguishable activities, they are mutually dependent aspects of the same whole effort. These roles represent essential ingredients in the development process, and trade-offs concerning any one of them must be considered with regard to its impact on the other roles. Ever since we started working in this field, we have believed that *cooperating and complementary roles, coming from both software and UX domains, are essential to the design of high-quality user interfaces.* The roles require a lot of communication during interaction design and development as they work across the software, interaction, and work domain boundaries within a team of closely coordinated peers.

23.7.2 Sometimes Team Members Need to Wear Multiple Hats

Small organizations or resource-constrained teams sometimes force a situation where both interaction design and software design are, in fact, done by the same *person*, but that person must be aware of taking on both roles, roles that differ in about every way, requiring different skills, approaches, methods, and mind-sets. So, one individual person can take on two or more roles, a person wearing multiple hats. As anyone who has had multiple roles living in one head under the hats will tell you, the key is in maintaining the role distinction, keeping the roles separated, and being aware of which activity one is doing at any given time.

Failure to keep the roles separate will subject the hat wearer to a fundamental conflict of interest between the two roles. What is best for users is almost always not easiest for programmers. When push comes to shove, it is far too easy to resolve this conflict of interest in favor of easier programming, at the cost of the user experience. We have seen it far too often and far too blatantly. Cooper (2004, p. 16) puts it well:

> The process of programming subverts the process of making easy-to-use products for the simple reason that the goals of the programmer and the goals of the user are dramatically different. The programmer wants the construction process to be smooth and easy. The user wants the interaction with the program to be smooth and easy. These two objectives almost never result in the same program. In the computer industry today, the programmers are given the responsibility for creating interaction that makes the user happy, but in the unrelenting grip of this conflict of interest, they simply cannot do so.

So, wearing multiple hats requires the wearer to be faithful to the needs and goals of each hat. While you are reading this book, you should be wearing your interaction designer hat.

23.7.3 Interaction Design Needs Specialized Expertise and Training

Significant training and educational prerequisites for the software engineer's role are obvious, but how hard can it be to make an interaction design? Do you really need a whole different role just to do interaction design? It definitely does not take a rocket scientist.[1] Is not it just common sense, something most anyone on the development team can do if they put their minds to it? If it were just common sense, we would have to wonder why good sense is not more common in the designs we use.

It is especially easy for software people to think that they can do interaction design with the best of them. Talk with many programmers about user interfaces and you will hear about widgets, interaction styles, callbacks, and everything you will need to build a user interface. You may sense a feeling of confidence—a feeling that helpful style guides and new interface software programming tools have catapulted this programmer into a real user interface expert.

Anyone, in fact, *can* produce *some* user interaction design. However, just because a programmer has an interface software toolkit does not mean that he or she can design a highly usable interaction design, and it does not mean that they necessarily know a good user interaction design when they see one. In our experience, we have actually encountered junior software folks smiling broadly as they wave the standards or guidelines manual and proclaim that not only can they now create the interaction design, but there "will not be any need for UX testing if I just follow the guidelines."

As we now know, there is a significant prerequisite for the interaction designer's role, too, including psychology, human factors, industrial design, systems engineering, and everything in this book! But computer science and software engineering are not among those prerequisites. Sure, design guidelines are important, but what is less well understood is the absolute necessity for a good UX lifecycle process, including lifecycle concepts, and process activities and techniques. Additionally, there is the song we played in the Preface: a requisite mind-set for truly appreciating the plight of the user.

---

[1]What is the big deal about comparing everyone to a rocket scientist? You really have to know only one thing to be a rocket scientist: rocket science.

23.7.4 Success Criteria for Developing Interactive Systems

Although we have talked much about processes, the bottom line is that the success of an interactive system development project is, at its base, all about the people. If team members in each role have respect for the other roles, and each team member has the requisite capabilities to carry out the assigned roles, the project will find a way to succeed.

Experienced developers already appreciate the importance of communication but, in the fog of battle, people get busy and people get consumed with their own responsibilities. So, the project needs to be infused with reminders to maintain communication about activities and progress, especially about problems and changes.

Finally, because resources are always limited, the team must act in ways to take utmost advantage of what resources they have. Among the issues this translates into are the staggering of the two corresponding lifecycles so that one does not constrain the productivity of the others and constantly ensuring situational awareness of overall process and the design.

Making It Work in the Real World

24

Objectives

After reading this chapter, you will:

1. Understand what it takes to put the UX process to work as a practitioner in the field
2. Know how to be a smart UX practitioner
3. Know how to participate in UX professionalism
4. Understand the impact and limitations of cost-justifying a UX process
5. Appreciate the business and politics of UX within your organization

24.1 PUTTING IT TO WORK AS A NEW PRACTITIONER

Here is a little advice on getting started in applying the UX process within your organization. Some readers will already be engaged in the UX process and can ignore the points that no longer apply.

24.1.1 Professional Preparation

Find someone with whom you can apprentice

If possible, as you are getting started, find an established UX practitioner, in your organization or elsewhere, with whom you can work to "learn the trade." Just following an expert around for a while can give you a great deal of confidence to try some of the UX process activities on your own.

It is especially important for you to sit in on design sessions and observe UX evaluation sessions. In a small company, it may be hard to find a knowledgeable person with whom you can apprentice; you may be the resident expert! In most large companies, however, you should be able to find someone suitable.

Get training for project team members

Get appropriate training on these new techniques for members of the project team, especially those who are being given responsibility for the UX process. Even those who are not involved directly in the UX lifecycle process can benefit from some formal training because these ideas may be dramatically different from those they encounter in their own domain. Having all members of the team with a common baseline of knowledge in these techniques is helpful in making it all work.

Get consulting help when needed, especially during start-up

By having an expert around while you try these activities the first time or two, you will learn a great deal more about how to do them and how not to do them and you will gain skills and confidence that will allow you to continue with subsequent activities yourself. There are two sources of consultants that you can tap.

If your organization is large enough, there are probably already people somewhere in it whom you can bring in to help you get started. If not, if you are breaking entirely new ground in your organization by trying these ideas or if your organization is fairly small, then you may want an outside consultant to help you get started. While this may sound like an expensive proposition, remember what Red Adair, the famous Texas oil-well firefighter, said when someone confronted him about his costs for putting out oil-well fires: "If you think the experts are expensive, wait until you bring in the amateurs!"

Start a regularly scheduled brown-bag UX lunch bunch

Within your project, your organization, or your community start a regular get-together for people with a mutual interest in UX design. This kind of a support group can have many purposes, from serving as a critique group for emerging interaction designs; to getting advice on some particular process activity; to sharing experiences with the process; or to being an educational forum for presenting and sharing relevant topics, showing videotapes of interest, and so on.

Perhaps most importantly, a special interest group for UX raises awareness of the UX process activities that are happening. Publicize it widely, on electronic bulletin boards and any other communication medium you have available. Begin by meeting once a month, and then meet more often if interest and attendance warrant it. Instead, perhaps, subgroups with interest in some specific topic(s) may want to meet more often. Many places that have tried this idea have been amazed at how quickly their group has grown and how popular and effective it can be.

Start a small internal newsletter and/or electronic bulletin board specifically related to UX activities in your organization

A nice spin-off to the brown-bag lunch idea is a small newsletter to serve as another forum for exchanging ideas. This newsletter can be published electronically. In it, you can talk about actual evaluation sessions, suggest readings from new articles and books, give conference reports, and relate success stories—essentially the same kinds of things that you discuss during the brown-bag lunch groups.

An internal electronic bulletin board or a blog is also an excellent medium for exchanging information, asking questions, posting answers, making suggestions, and so on. This kind of communication will increase the visibility of human–computer interaction (HCI) and UX greatly in your organization.

Attend conferences related to human–computer interaction and UX

The Usability Professionals Association (UPA)[1] has an annual conference that appeals to practitioners in the field. Sponsored by SIGCHI, a special interest group of the Association for Computing Machinery, the Conference on Human Factors in Computing Systems[2] (known as the CHI, pronounced like the Greek letter χ) is the largest annual conference on HCI. CHI has a decidedly research flavor but features many activities and attractions oriented toward practitioners, too. CHI has a variety of activities, including the standard fare of paper presentations, panels, and poster sessions. It also has special-interest group meetings; impromptu birds-of-a-feather sessions; book exhibits; demonstrations of tools and other applications by both research and commercial groups; and exhibits of unusual, often futuristic, user interface technology.

For the new or aspiring UX practitioner, we especially recommend the UPA conferences and their Body of Knowledge project.[3] The mission is to create "a living reference that represents the collective knowledge of the usability profession and provides an authoritative source of reference and define the scope of the profession."

In addition, the annual User Interface Software and Technology Symposium (UIST)[4] is a smaller, single-track forum for exchanging state-of-the-art ideas and results, more on the software side of things. The Human Factors and

---

[1]http://www.upassoc.org/

[2]http://www.sigchi.org/conferences

[3]http://www.upassoc.org/upa_projects/body_of_knowledge/bok.html

[4]www.acm.org/uist/

Ergonomics Society[5] also has conferences with many sessions dedicated to user interface issues. HCI International,[6] Interact,[7] CSCW,[8] DIS,[9] and other conferences also abound.

We also recommend the Interaction Design Association (IxDA), a global network dedicated to serving the professional practice of interaction design and the professional needs of an international community of practitioners, teachers, and students of interaction design. The "IxDA network provides an on-line forum for the discussion of interaction design issues and provides other opportunities and platforms for people who are passionate about Interaction Design to gather and advance the discipline."[10]

Prepare a UX portfolio

Also, if you are looking at the job market, it is time to compile a portfolio of your existing UX work. Many companies interviewing for new UX professionals are asking for this now. Highlight the process you followed, the prototypes you created, the redesigns you made, and so on. Your portfolio must tell a story of each design project you undertook: the users affected, the challenges faced, and the innovation provided. Make it visual with design sketches, screen images, and other design artifacts, with appropriate annotations. Include surprises and unique insights. Use it as a conversational prop when you are presenting in person, for example, at a job interview.

24.1.2 Administrative Preparation

Get a commitment from management to try these new techniques

You cannot operate in a vacuum. In most organizations you need permission to try new things. Share what you know about UX and get your management committed to trying it. First, lay out your UX process plan, at least roughly. Then, have a one-on-one meeting with one or more key upper-level managers and convince them to let you try your plan.

If you are prepared and keep the plan pretty simple, chances are very good that you will get the support you want. Ask this manager to call a meeting to discuss the plan with the project team. Let the manager run the meeting, as if it is

---

[5]hfes.org/

[6]http://www.hci-international.org/

[7]http://interact2011.org/

[8]http://www.cscw2012.org/

[9]http://www.dis2012.org/

[10]http://www.ixda.org/

all the manager's idea. If this does not work, you run the meeting, but have the manager there to support you.

Establish UX leadership

Get at least one person on the project team who can be the UX leader. Maybe this person is you! If it is not possible, for whatever reason, to get a full-time person, start with a part-time person. Find a way with management to give that person primary responsibility for design, evaluation, and iterative refinement of the interaction design.

Also give that person the authority to carry out the responsibilities of the job. Later, as the importance of this role becomes more recognized and appreciated within your organization, you can add other people to your emerging UX team.

Get a commitment from project team members to try these new ideas

Those members of the team who are not responsible for developing the interaction design should be made aware of what those who are responsible for it will be doing and why. Get at least some level of commitment from these non-user-interface people for the ideas you will be trying out so that they will know what to expect.

Generate a failure story and then a success story, no matter how small

Often, when managers and team members are asked "What will it take for you to get approval to begin trying some of these new ideas?" they respond, "Failure!" To convince people that these ideas will work, start by showing them failure when the right process is *not* used for developing the user interaction design. Set up some version of a system that needs a lot of UX improvement.

In your UX lab, make a 5-minute video of a user having a really terrible time trying to use the interface. Using the techniques presented in this book, revise the interaction design, or at least the worst part of it. Then make another 5-minute video of a user, the same one if it is feasible. Use the revised design to perform the same tasks as in the first video. Presumably, of course, the user will love—or at least like and be able to use—the revised design.

Show the two video clips to managers and explain to them the process that got you from the first version to the second one. If your video clips are different enough, they will make the point for you dramatically. What managers will usually want to know after such a presentation is "Why did not we start using this

UX process before now?" This success story, demonstrating the effectiveness of the process in action, can do more to help sell these ideas than almost anything else you can do.

24.1.3 Technical Preparation

Start a blog about your UX activities

It will be a valuable and illuminating experience to maintain a record or journal, as you go, of how you applied various techniques in the UX process and how well they worked. Maintain it as an online blog and others can participate. You will also impress your teammates with the ability to recall what you all decided earlier and it might help keep the team from going in circles and reinventing process ideas.

Get some practice doing contextual inquiry and analysis

On your next project, follow some of the steps of contextual inquiry and analysis and go out and interview and observe customers and users in the application domain. You will be surprised how easy and effective it soon becomes.

Personalize and actualize a process

Throughout this book we have encouraged you to personalize the process, taking from our process what works, what you can afford, and what meets your goals for a project. Now is the time to codify and document those process and technique selections and actualize them—put them into action.

Marc Rettig (1992), whose HCI and UX writing has resonated with us over the years, gave this advice back in the 1990s to software programmers who found themselves in a position where they had to do interaction design: Get a process. He offers this "catchy truism," "good management means doing the right things, and doing them right." Doing the right things is about having a process. Guidance in doing them right is given in the techniques in the process-oriented chapters, the techniques that support the lifecycle process.

Set up a UX lab

Find an enclosed (or enclosable) corner, a broom closet, a vacant office, some space somewhere, and make it your official UX lab. This single activity, along with getting a UX practitioner on the project team, can have a huge impact on attitude toward these new ideas.

Put a big, bold sign on the door. People will wonder what is going on in there and will start asking questions about what a UX lab is and what it is to be used for. This will begin raising awareness about the increasing importance of UX in your project and organization—good PR! Get in the minimal equipment recommended and then—starting small—use it to do some formative evaluations of your evolving user interaction designs.

24.1.4 Give It a Try
Start small

There is a lot of material in this book. The best way to get it under your belt in real projects is to start small and work up to the whole process. Choose an interaction design project that is small enough so that you will not be overwhelmed from the beginning as you apply these new techniques.

If you are required to work on a large project, choose some reasonable portion of it to focus on initially. Select, for example, a smallish subsystem of your large project or a few of its most important functions and features. The project (or part of the project) you choose should be one that has some visibility, but that is not extremely high risk.

As Nielsen (1994c) said, "Anything is better than nothing." People often fear that they will not be successful the first time they try these techniques. These techniques are so effective that you almost cannot lose. Any data you collect from even a short session with a single user is invaluable input that you can use to make improvements in the interaction design. Do not be afraid to try these techniques; you will become comfortable with them quickly.

Prototype and evaluate only a core part of the interaction design the first few times you attempt to do formative evaluation

> **Formative Evaluation**
>
> Formative evaluation is a primarily diagnostic approach to UX evaluation with emphasis on collecting qualitative data to identify and fix UX problems and their causes in the design.

If you try to encompass too much of the interaction design in the initial prototype, you will probably spend too much time developing it, and you could become overwhelmed if you attempt to evaluate all parts of it. For your first few prototypes and subsequent formative evaluation cycles, incorporate a core set of functions, those functions without which a user cannot perform useful work with the system being developed.

Keeping the prototype small will allow you to keep the formative evaluation process manageable until you become more knowledgeable and confident with it. Later prototypes can, and of course should, include much more of the system functionality.

Do some observations of users with a prototype of the interaction design

If you cannot get management to agree to let you try all these ideas at once, then at a minimum get them to let you either go off-site or bring in one or two participants, whichever is most appropriate for your situation, for a short period of time—2 hours, half a day, a day—to evaluate your interaction designs. Informally observe people using the system and give management a short report on your observations. Include in your report the major problems identified and the expected impact of making changes to the interaction design based on your observations.

Have developers and managers watch at least one participant from an evaluation session

Often, developers, even after training, and managers, even after realizing the need for UX, are still reluctant to believe in the UX lifecycle process. One of the best ways to convince both developers and managers, for example, that evaluation with users is critical to ensuring a quality user experience is to have them observe some participants.

Once you get your UX lab set up, this is easy to do. Schedule a specific time for them to come to the lab and watch at least one participant during an evaluation session. If you have a video hookup or a one-way mirror with which they can observe from a different room than where the participant is working, that is best for the participant. If developers or managers simply will not come and watch a participant live during an evaluation session, show them a few short, carefully selected video clips of some sessions. This will go a long way toward convincing skeptics about the value of these techniques.

24.2 BE A SMART UX PRACTITIONER

As you gain experience, you will learn "tricks of the trade" that will make you more valuable as a UX practitioner on each project. We have said many times in this book not to apply the process blindly but with judgment. Find the most economical level of commitment to the process and be flexible in its application.

In a 1993 workshop (Atwood, 1994), researchers and practitioners pooled their experience to compile a list of tricks of the trade. The results are still relevant today.

- Better be fast and mostly right than slow and perfect. This follows our engineering advice to make it good enough, but not perfect. Engineering means "satisficing" (Simon, 1956).
- Chase what gives the most bang for the buck. UX practice is a cost–benefit balancing act. When you get good at this, you have increased your cost–benefit to your organization. When you can prove it to management, ask for a raise.
- Distinguish between customers and users.
- Serve as a catalyst/lighting rod. The UX practitioner has the advantage over many other jobs in the organization by being responsible for talking with customers, users, and developers.
- Push what works.
- Know when to turn it over to product development. Do not get "married" to your designs and prototypes; cut them loose—discard them if they are not working or let them graduate when they are ready.
- Know the development environment and the developer's concerns. Make sure your designs are well received. If you have been communicating all along, there should be no surprises at this point.
- Know the customer's and the users' concerns: the goal of contextual inquiry and contextual analysis.

We have a few of our own to add.

- Make yourself a best-practices list by choosing from options in this book.
- Make your paper prototypes work economically for you. Before you go to the lab for UX testing, use low-fidelity prototypes to be sure of the concepts, language use, nonexistence of showstoppers, and effective task flow. The UX lab is not a cost-effective place to discover the right verbs for button labels.
- Evaluate continuously, throughout the lifecycle.
- Early evaluation is to find UX problems, not performance measurements.
- Use goal-directed choices for process and techniques. It is not about which process or method is best but which works best under a given constraint in a given context.
- Get your software developers to agree on the process and what it means. For example, do not let them take your low-fidelity prototype too soon and start designing screens to match it exactly before you have iterated and worked out the details.

24.3 UX PROFESSIONALISM

Beyond the preparation for project work we recommend professional career preparation, including membership and participation in professional UX societies, conferences, and workshops. Find out which HCI and UX publications are most relevant to your interests and subscribe. Join the Usability Professionals' Association (UPA), the ACM Special Interest Group on CHI (SIGCHI)[11]—local and/or national—and/or any other professional organizations appropriate for your background and interests.

Get involved in a professional society and help steer it toward useful goals. Morris (2005) makes the case for stronger representation of HCI or UX as a profession to business. We have been looking inward to how getting organized within a professional group can help us all be better practitioners, which is good. But an effective professional organization succeeds by supporting business in areas related to the profession.

He cites the American Chemical Society, for example, as an organization that provides for chemists and their employers such services as employment registration and competitive analysis tools regarding salaries. Morris feels that we in HCI have not yet reached business with this kind of attention and are, therefore, often more or less invisible to management.

Stewart (2002), leader of System Concepts in the United Kingdom, gauges the HCI profession as finally becoming successful and tells us how to keep that from becoming a danger to us. He thinks that our growing acceptance as a profession will demand more from us as professionals, including improving our credentials and competence. He wants to see us more as a real profession and less as a black art and worries that otherwise acceptance of the importance of UX will unseat us because managers will see it as a function too important to leave to us.

24.4 COST-JUSTIFYING UX

One of the earliest articles stating concern over the cost of usability was by Mantei and Teorey (1988). Since then there have been many articles and a few books dedicated to the topic. Most notable is the Bias and Mayhew (1994) edited collection. The book starts by posing very important questions to which we need the answers when we propose doing usability or UX to our managers: How much usability or UX are we going to get and how much will it cost? How will we know we are getting it, and how much more money will it make for us on our products? It continues with a framework for answering these questions, a discussion of the business case for doing so, and offers some different approaches and case studies.

---

[11]http://www.sigchi.org/

The second edition (Bias & Mayhew, 2005) extends the ideas to the Web and is reviewed by Sutton (2007). Among the pioneers in cost–benefit and the business case analysis of usability engineering is Karat (1990a, 1990b, 1991, 1993).

24.4.1 Cost Cutting Is Not Always the Best Idea

Sometimes cutting costs can save otherwise wasted resources, but sometimes cost cutting directly reduces what you get in return. Cooper (2004, p. xxiii) is leery about an obsessive appetite for slashing costs at every turn: "unfortunately, most executives have an almost irresistible desire to reduce the time and money invested in programming. They see, incorrectly, the obsolete advantage in reducing costs."

Similarly, going with the lowest bidder is not always the best idea. For example, there is a story about the IRS buying a system from the *highest* bidder, but it gave them the highest payback in increased productivity.

24.4.2 Cost–Benefit and Business Case Analysis of UX

As Siegel (2003) points out, we can be very impatient about having to prove our value in a business case to our organization. We see the value of usability and UX as self-evident or we would not be working in the area. So, when business decision makers do not see it as clearly, we get frustrated.

Casting a broad net

Sometimes managers require cost–benefit analyses to be convinced of anything. In the case of UX, as in many cases, the customer, the person with authority to purchase an application or sign a development contract, is not always the final user. The distance between cost and benefit can be great. As it is often the case, UX usually has us paying the cost in one place and accruing the benefits in another place. Developers pay a cost to develop, customers pay a cost to own, and users pay a cost to use.

The concept of total cost of ownership (TCO) leads us to cast a broad net when looking for all the costs and benefits. As George Flanagan (1995) has told us, "the cost of end-user computing is greater than typically estimated and labor is the most significant component." He cited a survey of 500 business computer users in which usability was the characteristic identified most often with quality.

Weiss (2005) tells how the distance between usability development cost and benefit can be quite large in the telecom industry. Manufacturers bear the brunt of usability costs of producing mobile handsets, which they sell to carriers who retail them to their subscribers.

The fact that a manufacturer did, for example, usability testing is not an immediate selling point to carriers. The benefits of good quality in the phones and the penalties for bad design are felt by the end consumers. But, of course, the marketing impact can eventually trickle back up to the carriers and manufacturers so they must be concerned with usability and other quality factors to survive in the long run.

A rational argument about UX cost–benefit

Can we afford to include UX techniques in our system development process? Instead of the standard pat answer of "can we afford not to?," we think we can help shed some light on the question rather than the answer. Cost–benefit analyses have shown with dollar figures that usability or UX process costs are often quite low, especially in comparison to the benefits. But, to some, that is a counterintuitive finding because development costs always seem to be high.

"No-Risk" Usability Support

Randolph G. Bias, Ph.D., CHFP, Associate Professor, School of Information, The University of Texas at Austin[12], and Principal, The Usability Team[13]

One Wednesday when I was a full-time consultant our team received a call from a U.S. rental car company. Well, actually it was from the vendors who were responsible for designing the rental car company's Website. It seems they had a problem, they realized it was a usability problem, and could we run a usability study for them and make redesign recommendations? Sure, no problem. "By Friday?" Whoa. We were confident we could find representative users, business and leisure travelers, to serve as test participants. But we negotiated a delivery date of "this coming Monday" and got to work discussing their perceived problems, designing the usability study, and recruiting test participants.

We worked through the weekend, of course, and ended up grossing $14,000 for our 5-day gig, which ended with a deliverable of a usability test report complete with prioritized usability problems and recommended redesigns. The contracting team was pleased with the results and set about implementing some large subset of our recommendations.

In 1994, and again in 2005, Deborah Mayhew and I published edited volumes on *Cost-Justifying Usability*. I believe strongly that we usability professionals can help ensure our seat at the software development table so that we can

---

[12]http://www.ischool.utexas.edu/~rbias/website/
[13]www.theusabilityteam.com

maximally, positively influence the users' experience by attending to and comparing the tangible costs and benefits of our work. One of the challenges with such an approach is that there are just about always confounds—at the same time as usability improvements are made, there are also changes made to the marketing message, increases in the sales force, or any number of other changes, making it difficult to attribute with confidence any certain fraction of new benefits to the usability effort alone.

The joy of this exercise with the rental car Website team was that the *only* changes they instituted, in this revision, were those motivated by usability testing. A few weeks later I called them and asked if they had any data on improvements in user performance on their Website. The team was thrilled to report that from the first day of the new design they had realized a $200,000 per day bump in revenue, and that even if everyone who had failed to secure a reservation on the online site before the redesign had subsequently called the toll-free number to reserve a car, the company still was realizing a $50,000/day increase in revenue. Thus, the payback period for the usability investment, for this particular engagement, was "before lunch on the first day."

As someone who is convinced that the state of Web and other software design world is such that investments in professional, systematic usability engineering are just about always "worth it," this experience has led me and my current consulting partners (The Usability Team; www.theusabilityteam.com) to offer what we are calling "usability on spec" or "no-risk usability." We will work with you (Mr. or Ms. Web-or-Other-Software-Designer/Developer) to come up with a plan for some usability support, based on your site/product, your historical user data, the stage in your development process, and other variables. Then we will do the usability work for you, for free! But we will also negotiate some small percentage (say, 5%) of the measureable benefits realized after the usability improvements are implemented. [Note, in the example given earlier, using the conservative $50,000/day figure and assuming the same effect across a year, the company realized an $18 million benefit for their $14,000 investment, an approximately 1300:1 return on investment (ROI), and a 5% fee would have been over $900,000. Nothing ventured, nothing gained, eh.] While not every usability study will yield a four-figure ROI, and not every study will allow for such a crisp connection between usability costs and subsequent tangible benefits, we are eager to help all realize the importance and value of professional, systematic usability engineering of their customer-facing user interfaces.

However, usability or UX engineering, if done right, does not necessarily add greatly to overall development cost. The first reason is that most of the usability or UX costs are concentrated in early parts of the overall product lifecycle. Much of the UX engineering should be done *before* the system is implemented in software.

Out of the entire overall system development process, only a small cycle of analysis, design, prototyping, and evaluation represents the part associated with most UX engineering costs. Also, this mini-cycle is small and lightweight in comparison to other parts of the overall process, if it can be accomplished before a commitment to implementation in software.

Yes, this mini-cycle must necessarily be iterative, but it is only a small, lightweight part of the overall process. It is hoped that you can rearrange your project budget so that you do not use more resources for development overall, just different resources with a different distribution during the lifecycle.

Our second claim is that good usability saves on many other costs. As many of the writers on UX cost have said, "Pay me now or pay me more later." Poor usability is costly; good usability is all about saving costs. UX process costs are mostly one-time costs; operational costs can accrue for years. Downstream costs of poor usability can be substantial.

Usage costs, such as for lost user productivity, employee dissatisfaction, heavy user training, help desk operations, field support, or the cost of user errors, get more attention if those users are your employees. User errors are sources of costs that can keep cropping up over time if they cause other problems in your operation, such as database corruption.

Perhaps the cost of poor usability is the highest in the e-commerce world of the Web, where a bad design can mean lost revenue and losing a competitive edge in a fast-moving marketplace. The Internet is where you absolutely must avoid releasing something that will embarrass you and the organization, despite the pressure to development in "Internet time."

Costs of not having a good UX

According to a 2006 AP wire report (*The Roanoke Times*, 2006), a "Defense Department's computerized travel reservation system turned into a half-billion-dollar fiasco, so flawed that only 17 percent of the travelers are using it as intended, Senate investigators say." It was supposed to be the pentagon's private version of an Internet travel site, but it took a half-hour to book a simple itinerary that a regular travel agent could have booked in 5 minutes, and it was missing flight and hotel information and did not always provide the least expensive options.

In a similar story, Reuters UK Edition news service reported that a Taiwan stock trader in 2005 bought over $200 million (value in US$) worth of shares with one mis-stroke on her computer keyboard, causing a panic reaction on the market and an immediate loss to her company of $12 million.

The cost of poor usability also weighs in heavily at the help desk. According to Flanagan (1995) in a 90-day study of incoming calls to help desks for 24 different software products, over 60% of all calls were determined to be about usability issues and for 11 of the applications, over 90% of the calls were related to usability.

The cost of correcting a usability problem in a design depends on the stage of the project in which you catch the problem. Naturally, the earlier it is detected, the less it costs to fix. Early on, Mantei and Teorey (1988) stated that as problems are found later and later in the lifecycle, costs associated with fixing them increase in a geometric progression: a problem that costs $1 to fix in early analysis can cost $10 to fix in design, $100 to fix in a prototype, and $1000 to fix after deployment. On the other side of that coin, it has been estimated that for every $1 we spend on usability, we get from $2 to $10 in return from the market (Kreitzberg, 2000).

Is return on investment (ROI) the right place to look?

Most practitioners and management would agree that good usability and good UX are about good business, not about "being nice." So, if good usability makes for good business, what measures can be used to prove it? Certainly cost savings within the process are one way, maybe by comparing the "with and without usability" cases. For example, back in 1993, we heard of a NYNEX project in which the company saved $1 billion by prototyping and iteratively refining the interaction design for a voice-activated telephony system (Thomas, 1993). Such success stories are impressive, but rare. Beyond those, not everyone believes in the power of ROI calculations.

Daniel Rosenberg (2004), who oversaw UX at Oracle, says that ROI is a phantom not worth chasing. In his 20 plus years of experience, he has never been asked to produce an ROI analysis. He thinks that the kind of ROI analyses in the HCI literature do not fit the real world he lives in. Rather, he defines his professional goal as *adding value to products* through an improved UX. He is part of the commercial software industry that produces large and complex software suites for use in companies all over the world. It is a world in which a single sale of a system can bring in millions of dollars for a system that will be used by thousands of concurrent users.

At the other end of the scale are the small internal IT projects where, he says, the argument is usually made for usability ROI. Unfortunately, he said, "case study" stories based on little data get spread in the literature as "myths." The promise of better data is at least partially blocked by corporate legal departments who consider development cost data to be confidential. He points out correctly that the economics of software production are complex and contain too many confounding factors to do a convincing "before and after" or "with and without" comparison.

For example, increased revenue from a product that UX practitioners believe has been improved through usability testing might instead be due to changes in prices, size of the sales force, emphasis in a marketing campaign, and so on.

Instead, Rosenberg proposes that we consider more strategic indicators, indicators of longer term effects of product value for executives and upper management, a key example of which is the customer relationship. Customers of large commercial software systems can have an ownership or usage lifecycle of a decade, including in-the-field fixes and upgrades to new releases.

Over that time, total ownership costs can add up to much more than the original purchase price. Whereas ROI can be an internal fascination about how to save development costs, total cost of ownership (TCO) is an external measure of how well your product is working for your customers, a measure of the real value your product provides. He says that in business, saving money is tactical but making money is strategic.

Our friend Gitte Lindgaard (2004) balances Rosenberg's view by saying that, the absence of requests for ROI justification notwithstanding, "if we want our contribution to be taken seriously by other stakeholders, we absolutely must demonstrate the business value of HCI." We need to speak "clearly to business decision makers and target issues that are truly of concern to them." We must find the issues that will provide the most persuasive arguments and apply the most appropriate analysis techniques, and Lindgaard gives some compelling examples of doing just that.

Bloomer and Croft (1997) echo this sound advice, "start by finding the 'hot buttons' of the group," such as enhancing customer service, improving product quality, or reducing operational costs—and get data about problems in these areas. Even though most of us will never be asked to produce a usability justification analysis, we can and should seek actively to understand the broader business context of our work and find ways to take the initiative within that scope to define, address, and solve the organization's business problems.

Lund (1997a) looks at the problem of economic justification of usability and UX as more than just showing the difference between costs of usability and savings from usability in a project. That kind of data is going to be for a project that is in the past, but a company is interested in whether it is worth maintaining a permanent usability group in the future. What is the value of a UX group in the long-term, including projects that never get to market and, therefore, never generate revenue?

Lund takes a corporate bottom-line view in which the value of any activity or group in the company is assessed with respect to how it affects earnings. That translates directly into decreasing company costs and increasing product revenues, fundamental factors to which he says we must tie arguments for our existence. This includes helping the company identify new business opportunities emerging from technology and ideation that keep UX designers engaged in contributing to the business. In his company they keep track of the value of new product ideas generated by each department and the resulting revenues from those ideas maturing into marketed products.

Siegel (2003) gives us some advice on how to approach our own persuasive business case for UX. If you do use cost and savings figures, "show a conservative bias." Stretching the truth in your estimates can injure your credibility and can build false expectations. As Lindgaard also said, target your analysis to recognized company concerns. They will get the ear of management faster than new ideas from the "outside." It may be necessary to lay the groundwork for your arguments by establishing the right metrics for cost, for example, and taking enough data before making the justification case.

Do not promote your approach as a "new paradigm" that will "save the company." Suspicion that your proposal might be ideologically motivated can raise stiff resistance. Instead, bill it as an effective way to pursue established company goals and help the company do what it is already doing, such as understanding its users. If necessary, invoke the company mission statement, if it is appropriate.

One of Siegel's points encountered often in our consulting and industry practice is about "incrementalism." The usual approach to cost–benefit analysis is to look at the value of a product before and after applying usability testing, for example, to improve the design. However, this "incremental" approach ignores the "order-of-magnitude" improvements a very bad design can get from a complete re-analysis and redesign and not just usability testing.

A small example of cost savings

For a large distributed system, a very large government organization we worked with had about 75,000 active users at any point in time. On average, we showed, for one particular task, that the number of transactions per user in a day was about 20. This added up to a daily frequency for this one transaction of $75,000 \times 20 = 1,500,000$.

The user time per transaction ranged from 5 to 20 minutes. We determined that the average time saved per transaction, due to one specific improvement in usability, was about 30 seconds. At that time, the average fully loaded hourly rate for these agents/clerks was $25.00, so the average annual savings for just this one task and this one modest usability improvement, not counting other savings, such as for user training or help desk costs, were

= 75,000 users * 20 transactions/user-day * 0.5 minute/transaction * 230 days/year * $25/hour * 1 hour/60 minutes = $71,875,000.00.

For any reasonable usability engineering cost for this product, the payback is enormous. Managers will pay attention to this kind of cost analysis because they do similar analyses themselves for budgets. Also, you can remind them that long after schedules are forgotten, the user experience, good or bad, remains.

Mayhew (2010) offers a free downloadable cost-justification tool for these calculations.

Strategic planning for better UX in the future

The natural time for arguments in favor of adequate budget and schedules to allow for quality UX design is at the beginning of a project, even before a project begins. That is when such resources are allocated. However, that is also when everyone, especially managers, are enthusiastic (and most unrealistic) about getting it done fast. Although this is the opportune time to make a pitch for additional resources, this is also when everyone is excited about getting going on a big sprint. In any case, during a project is not a good time to argue for resources because that is when the allocations have already been done and everyone is obsessed with getting it done or getting a product out.

We offer an additional suggestion. Make your pitch for enough resources to make it better the first time (instead of having to fix it later) at the end of a project that did not go particularly well because there was not enough time to do it right. This is the time, even if only for a brief and forgettable moment before people move on, that everyone can see that it was not enough. Everyone can see ways that you could have done better. People will still have that feeling that, if only they had had more time, they could have made it much better. This is the time to point out in a non-emotional way that your team, and managers above the team, chronically do not allow enough time to get a design right the first time around.

24.5 UX WITHIN YOUR ORGANIZATION

24.5.1 Politics and Business of Selling UX

Your biggest challenge may be not technical, but possibly about selling the case to management (Trenner & Bawa, 1998). This selling requires workable techniques to convince managers that they should let you try these ideas out (Schaffer, 2004). The material presented in this book can form a basis for controllability, accountability, and quantitative methods that are so important, and rightfully so, to managers.

Most managers are familiar with software engineering principles and paradigms and probably even encourage or enforce their use. If you were around in the days when structured programming and software engineering were emerging as the accepted approaches to software development, you will remember that there was the inevitable opposition to it, largely because people claimed there was not time to do all those things in the development process.

Also, now, managers are going through a similar encounter with new methods and techniques, only this time it is for usability and UX (Mayhew, 2008). Now managers are hearing UX buzzwords, such as "user-centered design," "iterative refinement," or "rapid prototyping." And today we are hearing the same kind of resistance that the software engineering people heard decades ago. But already the arguments about why proper UX engineering cannot be done are bearing less and less weight as people realize that this leads to the situation where, as the saying goes, there is never time to do it right but always time to do it over.

However, many managers will need to understand this relatively new UX methodology. What they may not realize is that, by necessity, the UX lifecycle process is not linear but is highly and continually iterative. An iterative lifecycle can impact much of what managers have to deal with, including scheduling, control, organizational roles, territoriality, project management, communication, test facilities, and tools.

So, it is up to us—up to you—to help sell the new concepts, which could take you out of your comfort zone as a UX practitioner. You might want to just do your job and not have to hassle with trying to convince the rest of your organization of the value of UX. Do you believe in UX so fervently that you feel it should not need any selling?

Bloomer and Croft (1997) warn of trying to "evangelize rather than sell usability." If we try to spread our enthusiasm for how neat all this usability and UX stuff is, you may find it is not as interesting to management as you expected. It is not about beliefs; we have to demonstrate the benefits in business terms and demonstrate a connection of UX to achieving key business goals.

Selling the process

To the readers seeing much of this contextual inquiry and contextual analysis process for the first time, you might think it is just too much and can never get accepted in your organization. But, in fact, contextual inquiry has been finding acceptance in commercial software product and system development simply because it is effective and helps solve the problem of getting design requirements that represent real user needs in real work contexts. Yes, it is a big piece of process that was not there before, but you can start small, make some success stories, and sell its value to your organization.

Beyond the factors that trade off in making a wise choice of how much process to use, there always looms the prospect of criticism based merely on resistance to anything new, regardless of cost or benefit. Selling new or additional processes is always a challenge.

Selling UX as part of the business process

When you have difficulty in selling your vision of UX to management, maybe it is because you are still speaking the language of UX engineering. We all understand that language and are convinced of the value but that is preaching to the choir. And while we would love to see the whole organization revamped around a UX process, Rideout (1991) reminds us that it is unlikely your existing organizational structure will change to adapt to UX; "one of the most effective ways to bring UX engineering into an organization is to build it into existing processes."

Alton (2007) suggests that one way for the UX practitioner or UX leader to speak a language that business people understand is by making a connection to risk management. Worst-case analysis of risk means asking what is the worst thing that can happen, how likely is that to happen, what will it cost if it happens, and how much will it cost to keep it from happening, or at least to reduce the probability to an acceptable level?

In this light, usability and UX are more like business insurance, just like data security and backing up of files. For a new commercial Website, for example, one of the worst things that could happen is a failure that results in no one wanting to use your site. Your investment and future sales are in jeopardy. Let management decide how much that will cost the company.

Your job is to propose strategies based on UX engineering and user involvement to minimize the probability of this kind of failure and loss. The more the loss in the case of failure, the more you can afford to spend on UX. Alton shows how a user-involvement questionnaire can be applied to analyze exposure to risk based on the kinds of users and kinds of usage you expect.

Selling an investment in UX

Just selling ideas may not be enough. Depending on the nature of the projects in your organization and your emphases in design, you might need to convince management to invest in a UX evaluation lab and all its equipment or in an ideation studio. Design and ideation cannot happen at desks in offices or cubicles. A dedicated design studio space is a place to post sketches and drawings and display other artifacts, the visual and tactile context for ideation.

Legal and Intellectual Property Issues

Brad A. Myers, Carnegie Mellon University

User interfaces are subject to a variety of legal and intellectual property issues of which a commercial user interface developer (and especially, a manager) must be aware. Property is something that a person or company can own, and intellectual property (IP) is generally property that is nonphysical. Examples of the kinds of things that can be intellectual property include ideas, designs, expressions, names, formulas, lists, and so on. Intellectual property can be protected by various means, and the rules vary by country. In the United States, IP is enshrined in the U.S. Constitution, where Article 1, Section 8, Clause 8 provides that Congress shall have the power "To promote the Progress of Science and useful Arts, by securing for limited Times to Authors and Inventors the exclusive Right to their respective Writings and Discoveries."

Most people think of patents when they think of IP, but there are a variety of types.

- **Trade secrets** are intellectual property that a person or company keeps secret. People who are told the secret are generally required not to divulge it. For example, the formula used for Coca-Cola is a trade secret of the Coca Cola Company. Employees generally sign an agreement not to divulge a company's secrets, and others who are told are often required to sign a "nondisclosure agreement" in which they agree to keep the secret. Anyone can have a trade secret just by not telling others the information. However, trade secrets are rarely useful for protecting a user interface, as the user must be able to see the user interface to use it. However, the implementation of user interface algorithms is often a trade secret. An example would be the algorithm that predicts words from the user's typing using an onscreen keyboard.

- **Copyrights** are a legal mechanism that protects a particular expression of an idea. Copyrights are the primary way that literature, music, and artwork are protected. A copyright does not cover ideas and information, only the form or manner in which they are expressed. For example, one could not copyright the idea of dragging items to a trashcan icon to delete them, but one could copyright a particular drawing of a trashcan. Software code can be copyrighted, but this only protects the exact expression—implementing the same algorithm a different way would not be affected by a copyright. Copyrights are free and automatic—anyone can add a © symbol to any work to put the public on notice that the work is protected. Copyrights last for a certain amount a time, which varies based on various factors (e.g., in the United States, a copyright on a personally authored work such as a story lasts for the life of the author plus an additional 70 years. For a work made for hire, the copyright lasts for 95 years from the year of its first publication or 120 years from the year of its creation, whichever expires first. See http://www.copyright.gov/help/faq/faq-duration.html for full rules for the United States). After a copyright has expired, the work is generally available to the public for use. For example, the works of Mozart are no longer covered by copyright, but a particular performance of them (that particular expression) can still be copyrighted. If desired, user interface designers can copyright their particular user interface expressions (icons, background designs, window decorations, etc.) as well as their software code.

- **Trademarks** are a legal mechanism to protect a distinctive phrase or indicator that uniquely identifies a particular commercial product. The goal of trademarks is to avoid confusion in the consumer's mind. There are a variety of kinds of trademarks depending on what is being protected and how. Marks that denote trademarks include ® for registered trademark, ™ for trademark, SM for service mark, etc. Logos and names of companies and products will almost always be trademarks. Trademarks are issued by a government agency, such as the U.S. Patent and Trademark Office (USPTO), and are very expensive. Once issued, a trademark lasts for as long as the product or company is available commercially. If one uses a name that a company thinks is too similar to its trademark, then the company can sue to prevent that confusing name from being used.

■ **Patents** are a legal mechanism to protect an invention. They give the inventor a monopoly to use the invention for a period of time in exchange for revealing how the invention works. Patents were only ruled by the U.S. Supreme Court in 1981 to apply to software, and hence to user interfaces (before that, the rule was "for an idea to be patentable it must have first taken physical form"). Now, there are thousands of patents on user interface features and interaction techniques, with thousands more issued every year. A patent has a "specification" with its figures, which are the description of the invention, and the "claims," which describe what is actually protected by the patent. Patents must describe something new (that has never been described or seen in public before), useful for some purpose, nonobvious (it cannot only be an improvement that would be obvious to a regular person), and disclosed properly (so someone could reproduce the invention using the specification). Patents are issued by a government agency, such as the USPTO, and may cost about $20,000 to get. If one invents a new user interface, a patent can be written and filed, and then future users will have to license the patent to create an interface that works the same way. Conversely, if one creates a user interface that does what someone else's patent describes, then one can be sued in federal court for patent infringement.

Enlist a UX champion

Most of the many books and articles (Billingsley, 1995; Butler & Ehrlich, 1994) about getting UX to work within an organization advise recruiting a UX champion, for example. Look to senior management people who fund development projects; they will have the power to include UX as a key component of the development process. It is even better if you can find a senior executive who, perhaps through his or her own reading or conferences, already believes in the value of UX to the organization.

Sell UX as important to marketing

It might be possible to sell the business case for UX based on its ability to help with branding in the look and feel. No company has done this better than Apple Corporation and they are looked up to by many others for this connection of UX to branding on the marketing side.

Revise reward policies

It may seem obvious, but one way to help the UX culture flourish in your organization is to change the reward structure to favor product quality and the UX process. If people are rewarded on the basis of timelines and meeting delivery schedules, UX and other product quality factors will be eclipsed by these schedule-driven concerns. If people in your team roles are rebelling against changes in the development process, you may need an adjustment at the corporate level in the culture of how people are rewarded and focus more on how people follow the process.

Inertial resistance to change

Sometimes UX practitioners will run into resistance that comes from inertia or just plain opposition to change, especially in large, established organizations where software people and management are used to doing things the same way for years. Sometimes the resistance comes in the form of passive-aggressive behavior. They agree with you and say they will use the process, but they do not. Or they say, "We are already ready doing that process," when either they are not really doing it or they are not doing it correctly.

Anderson (2000) has tracked obstacles to adoption of processes for UX, including a lack of understanding of the process, fear of losing control, discomfort in moving from something familiar, competing ideologies, turf battles, and the feeling that UX is a marketing responsibility.

Alternatively, resistance to a UX process can stem from the impression that because the current way of development "is not broken," it does not need improving. If the design passes your UX testing, there is a tendency to think "the job is done and we should move on."

But beyond just performing benchmark tasks in time, UX practitioners must ask themselves constantly how to make it even better; can we make a better conceptual design? Even though we have ironed out the surface user performance questions, are there still deep UX issues?

Another way inertia shows up is in the lack of innovation in design. If your electronic forms on the Web are the same as the paper forms that preceded them because "that is the way we have always done it," it could be that you are just "paving the cow paths."

UX credibility

Selling any idea or technology to business management takes credibility, which first and foremost comes from delivering, from producing what is promised and more, and from doing it on time and within budget. That is what is required of everyone in a development environment, and UX practitioners are no exception.

Some established researchers and practitioners, such as Dennis Wixon and others, decry even the need to defend our credibility. "Why single out usability?" Why not ask software engineering to justify themselves. Well, we *are* the relatively new kid on the block and we have to earn organizational respect, just as the software engineering folks once did. Remember the state of structured programming back in the 1970s? Also, while you cannot build a software product without software engineering, you *can* build one without UX, as we well know.

Be a source of information about your profession. Be a resource of expertise and counsel others on their concerns about usability and UX. Give your own project team training in UX to ensure that they do not have gaps in their knowledge and skills.[14] Also, importantly, give yourself some visibility. No one in management will give much credibility to a process they know nothing about or a process that is essentially invisible within the organization.

You can boost your visibility within the organization via presentations within departmental meetings and periodically scheduled seminars and workshops, spreading the word until everyone is UX literate. Showcase a failure story and follow it with a genuine success story. Show before and after video presentations of lost, confused, bewildered, and frustrated users followed by happy and productive users due to design improvements. Seeing for themselves is one of the most effective ways to boost your credibility among people outside the UX team.

Be a UX evangelist and use "guerilla" tactics to insert UX into the corporate culture. For example, almost all companies have quality assurance people and activities. Visit the quality assurance people and convince them, over time, to incorporate usability and UX as part of their concept of quality. Having the support of a quality assurance group, long-established within the company, can only enhance your credibility.

24.5.2 Getting Away from the "Human Factors Pool" Model

In the early days, UX people were usually called human factors experts and, in many organizations, were kept corralled in a centralized "pool" of human factors consultants, often within a "service" arm of the organization lateral to the development groups, for example, in the quality assurance department or the documentation group.

Then they are split up and assigned to various business units doing development, much like orphans are farmed out to working families, with about as much clout in the new working environments. They are never really part of a development project and continue to report to their "home" departments while on loan to projects.

Once we had a couple of human factors people take us to lunch so they could unburden themselves about their plight. They came from a central human factors "pool" and were assigned to a project long after it had been designed and

---

[14]An example of a self-paced source for this kind of training is the Online User eXperience Institute (OUXI) at http://www.ouxinstitute.com/

parts had been implemented. Their job was to give feedback on the design but, of course, not too much feedback as it was impossible to make all but the most cosmetic changes by then.

They, however, had large issues with an enormous mismatch between the application organizational structure and the users' workflow. Several very closely related parts of a task were located in different screens in the design and the flow of the design was such that it was not easy to move among screens except by following the built-in logical "next screen" path. Clearly, the design would have a powerful negative impact on UX and user performance in the field, or at sea.

Although they protested vigorously about the huge design flaws, they were flatly ignored because they had no authority within the development project. It would be a long journey from this situation to where an organization has its own UX division reporting to the CEO and UX practitioners hold the power to enforce their design recommendations.

24.5.3 UX in the Organizational Structure

The question of UX ownership within an organization has been a popular discussion topic in articles and workshops. ACM *interactions* magazine covered it in a special section (Gabriel-Petit, 2005). Most of the articles began by saying that it was the wrong question to ask, that no one can "own" UX within an organization. Most of the authors got it right: no one "owns UX within the organization" or, better yet, everyone in the organization has a stake in "owning" the responsibility for UX.

Gabriel-Petit (2005, p. 17) said that the ownership of UX is best shared in a culture of collaboration and vision. Within that context a person with the most UX experience can function as a leader. Knemeyer (2005) says that business decision makers should own UX; it is the CEOs and administrators who set organizational goals and control budgets and even the HR people who hire the staff. The way to help shape UX in the organization is to influence thinking about it at these higher levels.

Aucella (1997) warns us that we should at least find *some* relatively permanent place for UX in the organizational scheme of things. Perhaps the UX approach was successful in one project but, when this project is over and team members disperse, UX can die off and not be pursued further if there is no "home" for UX in the organization. She recommends working toward buy-in within the project and beyond, before the end of the project.

Project meetings should include a focus on UX; try to develop a culture in which planning and budget negotiations include UX. Be sure you have at least one experienced UX practitioner to lead the effort and be sure to document the results prominently so that the "history" is preserved and not buried soon after the project is done.

If UX practitioners are loaned out to develop projects from a centralized "pool" of practitioners, a practitioner may serve on several development teams at once, moving from team to team at appropriate times in their respective development processes. This approach usually turns out to be undesirable because it tends to fragment the process, for the UX practitioners, and can stretch their usefulness too thin.

For example, one human factors engineer was assigned to rotate among 11 different projects with a total of 248 software engineers! This, of course, is an extreme case—so much so that this practitioner was relatively ineffective on any of the 11 projects. In addition to fragmentation, this on-loan-talent approach usually precludes participating in the feeling of team ownership of the product.

In the long run, the best day-to-day "home" for UX practitioners seems to be in carrying out UX roles as full-fledged members of project teams rather than being centralized in talent pools. Even if a central pool was dignified by making us our own department with corresponding standing within the overall organization, we would still have to function as outsiders with development projects.

It is much better to assign each UX practitioner to a specific permanent role within the organization. Project teams are already composed of different skills sets so why should the UX skill set be any different? Now we are all system developers, as it should be! You do not read articles anymore about who owns programming in a development organization; programmers work in development projects where they are needed, as part of a team.

Similarly, there are advantages to having UX practitioners co-located permanently with the rest of the project team and reporting administratively to the same managers. The risk of this arrangement, of course, is for the manager to not understand or appreciate the value of the UX practitioners, as that manager will be doing annual performance evaluations for raises and promotions. There is no longer any greater UX group in the organizational structure to protect the UX practitioners. That highlights the imperative to sell management on the value of UX.

In one successful instantiation of the team approach, the entire project team was located in close physical proximity with each other. The team consisted of one or more software engineers, user interaction designers, marketing people, graphic artists, human factors engineers, technical writers, and trainers. The usability lab was in the center of the physical space, with team members' offices located around the lab.

Some of the most interesting team interaction occurred when software engineers began attending usability evaluation sessions. At first, only one or two attended, but as the project progressed, there literally was standing room only in the control room of the lab. In fact, all team members were told when usability test sessions were scheduled, and many attended regularly. Everyone was anxious to see how users would respond to the newest cycle of changes to the interface.

Being able to position ourselves as part of the team this way is not a technical issue, but depends on management. As Don Norman once put it, "Bad products often arise because of poor organizational structure." The structure of a product often reflects the structure of the company that built it. Parts of a company that build the various parts of a product or system may not talk to each other; they may even compete with each other.

If your development organization is organized hierarchically, it may be easy to communicate up and down within the hierarchy, but it can be difficult to communicate across the structure. Before a cross-disciplinary team can make a decision within this infamous "stovepipe" organization, each question must travel up and down all the respective pipes.

Ferrara (2005) says that UX practitioners are responsible for the ultimate UX in products and will be held accountable for same. So, if they do not control the UX process, they must find ways to influence those who do, but should do so with respect and as a team effort. Hawdale (2005) weighs in, supporting the opinion that it is about leadership with vision.

The one who takes the lead and pursues a vision is the one others will look up to as the UX person. Tognazzini (2005) says that we must work harder to define ourselves as UX professionals and take control for design back from the engineers.

Until that happens we will fight against the odds, playing catch-up instead of having a fair chance at the head start we need to lead the project lifecycle rather than follow it. Strategic approaches to UX within an organization mean influencing people and integrating the profession and its practice into the organization. UX is an organizational effort, not just a technical one.

Also, strategic approaches are organization-wide approaches. When usability gets to a strategic level in a corporation, usability data are used in corporate-wide decision making, including product priorities. Rosenbaum, Rohn, and Humburg (2000) report on a series of CHI Conference workshops about strategic UX planning, about how usability or UX groups can make themselves "more effective and influential in how corporations develop products." Their findings are detailed but a few conclusions stand out.

For example, it seems reasonable that small UX groups in large organizations will perceive more difficulty in creating a broadly felt influence, but the survey showed that "organization size did not affect what organizational approaches and usability methods were rated most effective in achieving strategic usability." Apparently organization size also did not affect what factors were considered as obstacles to creating strategic impact. So we are all in the same boat, needing to build partnerships with marketing, engineering, and corporate management by educating about UX and selling its value.

As part of strategic thinking, Deborah J. Mayhew (1999a) asks how can UX practitioners position themselves as change agents? "Understanding what motivates organizations and causes them to change is key." To Mayhew, strategic establishment of usability or UX within a development organization occurs in three stages: promotion, implementation, and institutionalization. Promotion is selling, influencing others. Identify the obstacles to this kind of change in your organization and the right kind of motivation to overcome them.

Implementation means putting the process to work in real projects, which means getting the right people to manage and carry it out. To then institutionalize the process, you have to extrapolate your success and extend the influence of UX to be part of the development process at the organization level. The key is to be strategic in the implementation phase and plan for institutionalizing as you go. You have to get to know the people who document and enforce the organization process standards and help them integrate the UX process into their standard operating procedures.

24.5.4 Legacy Systems

A legacy system is a system with maintenance problems that date back possibly many years. Back in the 1990s, legacy systems were more of an issue than today. The question was what to do about large systems that had aged but were still working to provide important services (Schneidewind & Ebert, 1998)? The classic and most extreme cases of legacy systems were the old mainframe hardware and software systems with terminals being converted to systems of networked desktop computers.

Such cases are becoming mercifully rare. When these cases do occur, however, they have far-reaching implications and careful consideration must be focused on whether to continue maintaining the old system, redesign it, or retire it altogether in favor of a replacement.

The legacy problem still exists in different forms; existing systems get old and it is difficult to decide when to abandon system maintenance and opt for developing or buying a new system with new technology. It is a matter of risk management: When is the cost of old system shortcomings and constant maintenance, including instability in the face of incremental functionality changes, more than the cost of starting over?

Systems with better initial designs last longer. Almost always users want to keep the old system as long as possible, as that is what they are used to. However, they are often pleasantly surprised when they discover the improved UX in a well-designed new system.

Alternatively, realization of older functionality and user interfaces with new technology are often clumsy cut-and-paste reincarnations without good redesign to leverage the advantages, including UX advantages, of the new technology.

24.5.5 Transition to Production

We talked a bit about the transition from prototype design to the product. We cautioned not to hang onto it too long; let production developers do their thing. However, we do advise to keep an eye on it even after you let it go.

Beltram (2005) describes a particularly heart-breaking scenario in which the design was changed after the UX lifecycle was done, the interaction design had stabilized, and the unevaluated design was passed on for production development. After all the hard work of a long UX lifecycle, including presentations to management about the high level of UX achieved, the UX practitioner releases the design for production engineers to package it up for distribution.

However, a year later, the UX practitioner is faced with angry ranting customers and sees, for the first time, that many unbelievable changes have been made to her designs. Labels that had been painstakingly worded were changed for the worse, carefully placed navigation links were missing, and the user's workflow had been badly damaged. How could this possibly have happened?

In some organizations, especially those that develop software for domain-complex systems, there are some "extra, unacknowledged phases of design" that can occur in the process of getting the software ready for deployment; it is not always just building and shipping. Many things can happen after the UX cycle is over, including changes to address non-UX quality issues, changes in code to fix bugs, or some last-minute customization at the request of the customer—all done by people who did not work on the original project. As Beltram puts it, "That's a lot of cooks in the kitchen, all fussing with Nellie's original recipe."

Looking to the Future

Dennis Wixon, PhD, Startup Business Group, Microsoft Corporation

In looking over the last 30 years of growth of the computer industry, one obvious conclusion is that "the user has won." No product team or business would begin a new venture without considering seriously how they would achieve an excellent user experience. Given the vagaries of the development process, the final product may or may not provide that excellent experience. Certainly suboptimal (from a UX perspective) products are created with surprising regularity. However, I do not think anyone will ever hear statements such as "people like that do not deserve to be our customers." (Yes, I really heard that in one meeting many years ago.)

It would be tempting to say that such success was due to the creativity, hard work, and determination of a community of UX researchers, practitioners, designers, and academics, led and inspired by a few geniuses (e.g., Doug Englebart). Similarly, one could say that this progress was inevitable and driven by the inexorable economics of industry, that is, we had to broaden the market for technology beyond computer scientists, mathematicians, engineers, and hobbyists. To broaden that market we had to make computer technology approachable for novices, useful for workers, productive for businesses, and fun for gamers. We could also say that this progress was inevitable given the increase in performance and the reduction in price of technology, the growth of networking, and proliferation of form factors such as PCs, cellphones, game consoles, and tablets. These three factors (and numerous others) worked in synergy to drive the progress in user experience for the last 30 years.

Taking stock and even congratulating ourselves are no doubt in order. But as we do so, I would recommend that we turn our attention to the future. What are the challenges that we face over the next 30 years in creating quality user experience? The following are a few candidates; the reader is encouraged to add his/her own.

First, the growth of agile methods represents both a challenge and an opportunity. The speed and overall approach of agile software methods challenge both research and design methodologies. Some have argued that it is impossible to do good research or design in the context of an agile team. However, this argument ignores several important considerations. First, in many cases we do not have a choice. We need to embrace these approaches or be left behind. Second, many agile methods promise a partially working system as part of every sprint. Surely that promise offers opportunities for testing or review. Third, a number of methods for working with agile teams are described in this book. Certainly more will be created. The history of all the UX disciplines is adaptability, integration, and creativity. In summary, while I would not minimize the challenge, I would not ignore the opportunity.

Second, the proliferation of platforms represents another challenge. Again, this challenge also creates opportunity. The rapid growth of the cellphone market challenges designers to create great designs for tiny screens. It challenges research to understand usage for a wide variety of users in every imaginable context from a shopping mall to a rural farm. These challenges are compounded by a need to write software once and have it run on all platforms. However, there are also great opportunities. Logging technology enables us to understand aggregate usage in ways that were previously unimagined. The need to run on all platforms challenges teams to create flexible development environments. Advances in touch technology and voice recognition offer promise. We have already seen products with innovative and excellent user experience dominate the marketplace and inspire a variety of new products.

Third, the rise of analytics represents an opportunity and a challenge. Analytics provides an unprecedented window into user behavior. It is possible now to look at the behavior of entire populations of users and see how they use systems. At the same time, extracting valid conclusions can be challenging given the complexity of the environment in which usage occurs. One way to think of this is that our study of whole populations as they behave provides unprecedented ecological validity. However, this same environment is almost completely uncontrolled. Seeing a rise or fall in usage could be due to anything happening at that time. For example, if we observe a drop off in game play for a previously popular Internet game what do we conclude? We could conclude that the game has limited replayability or we might know that a new version of a widely popular competitor has just been launched and thus conclude that an external factor is causing the drop. Ironically, the most effective approach to the problem of so much data is more data and more diverse data. The more we know, the more measured and confident we can be in our conclusions.

Fourth, we do run the risk of retarding our future progress with some self-inflicted wounds. One example would be the current manufactured controversy between research and design. It is unproductive to say research can be dangerous. Any activity can be dangerous. Creative design is fraught with risk. Launching a product or service is risky and dangerous. Lack of activity can be dangerous too. Markets move on, and playing it safe can lead one to be not a player at all. We do not advance progress in user experience by creating rhetorical controversies between disciplines that need to work together. We do advance the field when we look at successful products and product failures and make an honest attempt to understand them and apply their lessons. For example, many years ago Petrosky wrote a book entitled *To Engineer Is Human* in which he conducted a brilliant analysis of engineering failures. This type of analysis does not lead to the intellectual cul-de-sac of suggesting we should not engineer new products. Instead it leads us to a deeper of understanding of how to avoid the mistakes of the past and make true progress.

Finally, I see a major challenge ahead. While UX has made significant headway in creating better products and contributing to business success, by and large, UX is still on the periphery in far too many businesses. By that I mean that user experience experts do not play as full a role in product decision making as other disciplines do. The contribution of UX to business success is unique, and UX needs to be an unfiltered voice in the product development process. There are many reasons for perpetuation of this "glass ceiling." Some of them are historical and cultural. But it is most important that UX professionals focus on those factors that they have some control over. They can focus on strategic work even if that means that detailed design and research may go undone. They can continue to innovate in methodology and design and integrate those methods with more traditional approaches. They can document their value and contribution to the success of products. They can shed some of the traditional values that have marginalized their work. One example is the belief that we need to have a complete design before we can collect data or offer an evaluation.

Overall, while there have been failures and setbacks, I see a past of accomplishment and a future of promise for UX.

24.6 PARTING WORDS

Congratulations! You made it through the book. May the UX force be with you.

References

ABC News Nightline, (1999). Deep Dive.

Abernethy, C. N. (1993). Expanding jurisdictions and other facets of human-machine interface IT standards. *StandardView, 1*(1), 9–21.

Accot, J., & Zhai, S. (1997). Beyond Fitts' law: Models for trajectory-based HCI tasks. In *Proceedings of the CHI Conference on Human Factors in Computing Systems* (pp. 295–302). Atlanta, GA.

Acohido, B. (1999, November 18). Did Similar Switches Confuse Pilots? Controls' Proximity Another Aspect of Crash Probe. *Seattle Times Investigative Reporter,* from http://community.seattletimes. nwsource.com/archive/?date=19991118&slug=2996058.

Adams, D. (1990). *The Long Dark Tea-Time of the Soul.* Pocket Books.

Alben, L., Faris, J., & Saddler, H. (1994). Making it Macintosh: Designing the message when the message is design. *interactions, 1*(1), 11–20.

Altom, T. (2007). Usability as risk management. *interactions, 14*(2), 16–17.

Anderson, R. I. (2000). Business: Making an e-business conceptualization and design process more "user"-centered. *interactions, 7*(4), 27–30.

Anderssona, B.-E., & Nilsson, S.-G. (1964). Studies in the reliability and validity of the critical incident technique. *Journal of Applied Psychology, 48*(6), 398–403.

Andre, T. S., Hartson, R., Belz, S. M., & McCreary, F. A. (2001). The user action framework: A reliable foundation for usability engineering support tools. *International Journal of Human-Computer Studies, 54*(1), 107–136.

Ann, E. (2009). What's design got to do with the world financial crisis? *interactions, 16*(3), 27–20.

Antle, A. N. (2009). Embodied child computer interaction: Why embodiment matters. *interactions, 16*(2), 27–30.

Apple Computer Inc, (1993). *Making It Macintosh: The Macintosh Human Interface Guidelines Companion.* Addison-Wesley.

Arnheim, R. (1954). *Art and Visual Perception: A Psychology of the Creative Eye.* University of California Press.

Atwood, M. E. (1994). Advances derived from real-world experiences: An INTERCHI '93 workshop report. *SIGCHI Bulletin, 26*(1), 22–24.

Aucella, A. F. (1997). Ensuring success with usability engineering. *interactions, 4*(3), 19–22.

August, J. H. (1991). *Joint Application Design: The Group Session Approach to System Design.* Yourdon Press.

Bailey, R. W. (1996). *Human Performance Engineering: Designing High Quality Professional User Interfaces for Computer Products, Applications, and Systems* (3rd ed.). Upper Saddle River, NJ: Prentice Hall.

Bangor, A., Kortum, P. T., & Miller, J. T. (2008). An empirical evaluation of the System Usability Scale. *International Journal of Human-Computer Interaction, 24*(6), 574–594.

Bannon, L. (2011). Reimagining HCI: Toward a more human-centered perspective. *interactions, 18*(4), 50–57.

Barnard, P. (1993). The contributions of applied cognitive psychology to the study of human-computer interaction. In R. M. Baecker, J. Grudin, B. Buxton & S. Greenberg (Eds.), *Readings in Human Computer Interaction: Toward the Year 2000* (pp. 640–658). San Francisco, CA: Morgan Kaufmann.

Baskinger, M., & Gross, M. (2010). Tangible interaction = Form + computing. *interactions*, *17*(1), 6–11.

Bastien, J. M. C., & Scapin, D. L. (1995). Evaluating a user interface with ergonomic criteria. *International Journal of Human-Computer Interaction*, *7*(2), 105–121.

Beale, R. (2007). Slanty design. *Communications of the ACM*, *50*(1), 21–24.

Beck, K. (1999). Embracing change with extreme programming. *IEEE Computer*, *32*(10), 70–77.

Beck, K. (2000). *Extreme Programming Explained: Embrace Change*. Addison-Wesley.

Becker, K. (2004). Log on, tune in, drop down: (and click "go" too!). *interactions*, *11*(5), 30–35.

Becker, S. A. (2005). E-government usability for older adults. *Communications of the ACM*, *48*(2), 102–104.

Beltram, D. (2005). Too many cooks. *interactions*, *12*(2), 66–67.

Bennett, J. L. (1984). Managing to meet usability requirements: Establishing and meeting software development goals. In J. Bennett, D. Case, J. Sandelin, & M. Smith (Eds.), *Visual Display Terminals* (pp. 161–184). Englewood Cliffs, NJ: Prentice-Hall.

Berger, N. (2006). The Excel story. *interactions*, *13*(1), 14–17.

Berry, R. E. (1988). Common user access: A consistent and usable human-computer interface for the SAA environments. *IBM Systems Journal*, *27*(3), 281–300.

Beyer, H., & Holtzblatt, K. (1998). *Contextual Design: Defining Customer-Centered Systems*. San Francisco, CA: Morgan-Kaufman.

Beyer, H., Holtzblatt, K., & Baker, L. (2004). An agile customer-centered method: Rapid contextual design. In *Extreme Programming and Agile Methods (LNCS 3134)* (pp. 50–59). Calgary, Canada: Springer Berlin/Heidelberg.

Bias, R. G. (1991). Walkthroughs: Efficient collaborative testing. *IEEE Software*, *8*(5), 94–95.

Bias, R. G., & Mayhew, D. J. (Eds.). (1994). *Cost-Justifying Usability*. Academic Press, Inc.

Bias, R. G., & Mayhew, D. J. (2005). *Cost-Justifying Usability: An Update for the Internet Age* (2nd ed.). San Francisco, CA: Morgan Kaufmann.

Bier, E. A. (1990). Snap-dragging in three dimensions. In *Proceedings of the Symposium on Interactive 3D Graphics* (pp. 193–204), Snowbird, UT.

Bier, E. A., & Stone, M. C. (1986). Snap-dragging. In *Proceedings of the Conference on Computer Graphics and Interactive Techniques* (pp. 233–240).

Billingsley, P. A. (1993). Reflections on ISO 9241: Software usability may be more than the sum of its parts. *StandardView*, *1*(1), 22–25.

Billingsley, P. A. (1995). Starting from scratch: Building a usability program at Union Pacific Railroad. *interactions*, *2*(4), 27–30.

Bittner, K., & Spence, I. (2003). *Use Case Modeling*. Addison-Wesley.

Bjerknes, G., Ehn, P., & Kyng, M. (Eds.), (1987). *Computers and Democracy: A Scandinavian Challenge*. Aldershot, UK: Avebury.

Bloomer, S., & Croft, R. (1997). Pitching usability to your organization. *interactions*, *4*(6), 18–26.

BMW AG. (2010). BMW automobiles. *http://www.bmw.com/com/en/insights/technology/joy/bmw_joy.html*. Last accessed 07/10/2011.

Bødker, S. (1989). A human activity approach to user interfaces. *Human-Computer Interaction*, *4*(3), 171–195.

Bødker, S. (1991). *Through the Interface: A Human Activity Approach to User Interface Design*. Hillsdale, NJ: Lawrence Erlbaum.

Bødker, S., & Buur, J. (2002). The design collaboratorium—A place for usability design. *ACM Transactions on Computer-Human Interaction*, *9*(2), 152–169.

Bødker, S., Ehn, P., Kammersgaard, J., Kyng, M., & Sundblad, Y. (1987). A utopian experience. In G. Bjerknes, P.Ehn & M.Kyng (Eds.), *Computers and Democracy—A Scandinavian Challenge* (pp. 251–278). Aldershot, UK: Avebury.

Boehm, B. W. (1981). *Software Engineering Economics*. Englewood Cliffs: Printice-Hall, Inc.

Boehm, B. W. (1988). A spiral model of software development and enhancement. *IEEE Computer, 21*(5), 61–72.

Boff, K. R., & Lincoln, J. E. (1988). *Engineering Data Compendium: Human Perception and Performance.* Dayton, OH: Wright-Patterson AFB, Harry G. Armstrong Aerospace Medical Research Laboratory.

Bolchini, D., Pulido, D., & Faiola, A. (2009). "Paper in screen" prototyping: An agile technique to anticipate the mobile experience. *interactions, 16*(4), 29–33.

Borchers, J. (2001). *A Pattern Approach to Interaction Design*. Wiley.

Borman, L., & Janda, A. (1986). The CHI conferences: A bibliographic history. *SIGCHI Bulletin, 17*(3), 51.

Borsci, S., Federici, S., & Lauriola, M. (2009). On the dimensionality of the System Usability Scale: A test of alternative measurement models. *Cognitive Process, 10*(3), 193–197.

Boucher, A., & Gaver, W. (2006). Developing the drift table. *interactions, 13*(1), 24–27.

Bradley, M. M., & Lang, P. J. (1994). Measuring emotion: The self-assessment manikin and the semantic differential. *Journal of Behavior Therapy and Experimental Psychiatry, 25*(1), 49–59.

Branscomb, L. M. (1981). The human side of computers. *IBM Systems Journal, 20*(2), 120–121.

Brassard, M. (1989). *The Memory Jogger Plus+*. Goal/QPC Inc.

Brooke, J. (1996). SUS: A quick and dirty usability scale. In P. W. Jordan, B. Thomas, B. A. Weerdmeester & I. L. McClleland (Eds.), *Usability Evaluation in Industry* (pp. 189–194). London, UK: Taylor & Francis.

Brown, C. M. (1988). *Human-Computer Interface Design Guidelines*. Norwood, NJ: Ablex Publishing.

Brown, L. (1993). Human-computer interaction and standardization. *StandardView, 1*(1), 3–8.

Brown, T. (2008, June). Design thinking. *Harvard Business Review*, 84–92.

Buchenau, M., & Suri, J. F. (2000). Experience prototyping. In: *Proceedings of the Conference on Designing Interactive Systems: Processes, Practices, Methods, and Techniques (DIS)* (pp. 424–433).

Butler, K. A. (1996). Usability engineering turns 10. *interactions, 3*(1), 58–75.

Butler, M. B., & Ehrlich, K. (1994). Usability engineering for Lotus 1-2-3 Release 4. In M. E. Wickland (Ed.), *Usability in Practice: How Companies Develop User-Friendly Products* (pp. 293–326). Boston, MA: Academic Press.

Buxton, W., & Sniderman, R. (1980). Iteration in the Design of the Human-Computer Interface. *Proceedings of the 13th Annual Meeting, Human Factors Association of Canada* (pp. 72–81).

Buxton, W., Lamb, M. R., Sherman, D., & Smith, K. C. (1983). Towards a Comprehensive User Interface Management System. *Computer Graphics, 17*(3), 35–42.

Buxton, B. (1986). There's more to interaction than meets the eye: Some issues in manual input. In A. D. Norman & S. W. Draper (Eds.), *User Centered System Design: New Perspectives on Human-Computer Interaction* (pp. 319–337). Hillsdale, NJ: Lawrence Erlbaum.

Buxton, B. (2007a). Sketching and Experience Design. In *Stanford University Human-Computer Interaction Seminar (CS 547)*. http://www.youtube.com/watch?v=xx1WveKV7aE. Last accessed 7/14/2011.

Buxton, B. (2007b). *Sketching User Experiences: Getting the Design Right and the Right Design*. San Francisco, CA: Morgan Kaufmann.

Callahan, J., Hopkins, D., Weiser, M., & Shneiderman, B. (1988). An empirical comparison of pie vs. linear menus. In: *Proceedings of the CHI Conference on Human Factors in Computing Systems* (pp. 95–100), Washington, DC.

Capra, M. G. (2006). *Usability Problem Description and the Evaluator Effect in Usability Testing.* Ph.D. Dissertation, Blacksburg: Virginia Tech.

Card, S. K., English, W. K., & Burr, B. J. (1978). Evaluation of mouse, rate-controlled isometric joystick, step keys, and text keys for text selection on a CRT. *Ergonomics, 21*(8), 601–613.

Card, S. K., Moran, T. P., & Newell, A. (1980). The keystroke-level model for user performance time with interactive systems. *Communications of the ACM, 23*(7), 396–410.

Card, S. K., Moran, T. P., & Newell, A. (1983). *The Psychology of Human-Computer Interaction.* Hillsdale, NJ: Lawrence Erlbaum.

Carey, T. T., & Mason, R. E. A. (1989). Information system prototyping: Techniques, tools, and methodologies. In *Software Risk Management* (pp. 349–359). Piscataway, NJ: IEEE Press.

Carmel, E., Whitaker, R. D., & George, J. F. (1993). PD and joint application design: A transatlantic comparison. *Communications of the ACM, 36*(6), 40–48.

Carroll, J. M. (1984). Minimalist design for active users. In: *Proceedings of the INTERACT Conference on Human-Computer Interaction* (pp. 39–44). Amsterdam.

Carroll, J. M. (1990). Infinite detail and emulation in an ontologically minimized HCI. In *Proceedings of the CHI Conference on Human Factors in Computing Systems* (pp. 321–328). Seattle, WA.

Carroll, J. M., Kellogg, W. A., & Rosson, M. B. (1991). The task-artifact cycle. In J. M. Carrol (Ed.), *Designing Interaction: Psychology at the Human-Computer Interface* (pp. 74–102). New York: Cambridge University Press.

Carroll, J. M., Mack, R. L., & Kellogg, W. A. (1988). Interface metaphors and user interface design. In M. Helander (Ed.), *Handbook of Human-Computer Interaction* (pp. 67–85). Holland: Elsevier Science.

Carroll, J. M., & Rosson, M. B. (1985). Usability specifications as a tool in iterative development. In H. R. Hartson (Ed.), *Advances in Human-Computer Interaction*Vol. 1(pp. 1–28). Norwood, NJ: Ablex.

Carroll, J. M., & Rosson, M. B. (1992). Getting around the task-artifact cycle: How to make claims and design by scenario. *ACM Transactions on Information Systems, 10*, 181–212.

Carroll, J. M., Singley, M. K., & Rosson, M. B. (1992). Integrating theory development with design evaluation. *Behaviour & Information Technology, 11*(5), 247–255.

Carroll, J. M., & Thomas, J. C. (1982). Metaphor and the cognitive representation of computing systems. *IEEE Transactions on Systems, Man and Cybernetics, 12*(2), 107–116.

Carroll, J. M., & Thomas, J. C. (1988). Fun. *SIGCHI Bulletin, 19*(3), 21–24.

Carter, P. (2007). Liberating usability testing. *interactions, 14*(2), 18–22.

Castillo, J. C., & Hartson, R. (2000). Critical incident data and their importance in remote usability evaluation. In *Proceedings of the Human Factors and Ergonomics Society Annual Meeting* (pp. 590–593).

Checkland, P., & Scholes, J. (1990). *Soft Systems Methodology in Action.* John Wiley.

Chin, J. P., Diehl, V. A., & Norman, K. L. (1988, May 15–19). Development of an instrument measuring user satisfaction of the human-computer interface. In *Proceedings of the CHI Conference on Human Factors in Computing Systems* (pp. 213–218). Washington, DC.

Chorianopoulos, K., & Spinellis, D. (2004). Affective usability evaluation for an interactive music television channel. *ACM Computers in Entertainment, 2*(3), 1–11.

Christensen, J. M., Topmiller, D. A., & Gill, R. T. (1988). Human factors definitions revisited. *Human Factors Society Bulletin, 31*(10), 7–8.

Churchill, E. F. (2009). Ps and Qs: On trusting your socks to find each other. *interactions, 16*(2), 32–36.

Clement, A., & Besselaar, P. V. D. (1993). A retrospective look at PD projects. *Communications of the ACM, 36*(6), 29–37.

Clubb, O. L. (2007). Human-to-computer-to-human interactions (HCHI) of the communications revolution. *interactions, 14*(2), 35–39.

Cobb, M. (1995). *Unfinished Voyages. A follow-up to The CHAOS Report.*

Cockton, G., & Woolrych, A. (2001). Understanding inspection methods: Lessons from an assessment of heuristic evaluation. In *Proceedings of the International Conference on Human-Computer Interaction (HCI International) and IHM 2001* (pp. 171–192).

Cockton, G., & Woolrych, A. (2002). Sale must end: Should discount methods be cleared off HCI's shelves? *interactions, 9*(5), 13–18.

Cockton, G., Lavery, D., & Woolrych, A. (2003). Changing analysts' tunes: The surprising impact of a new instrument for usability inspection method assessment. In *Proceedings of the International Conference on Human-Computer Interaction (HCI International)* (pp. 145–162).

Cockton, G., Woolrych, A., Hall, L., & Hindmarch, H. (2003). Changing analysts' tunes: The surprising impact of a new instrument for usability inspection method assessment? In P. Johnson & P. Palanque (Eds.), *People and Computers* (Vol. XVII). Springer-Verlag.

Constantine, L. L. (1994a). Essentially speaking. *Software Development, 2*(11), 95–96.

Constantine, L. L. (1994b). Interfaces for intermediates. *IEEE Software, 11*(4), 96–99.

Constantine, L. L. (1995). Essential modeling: Use cases for user interfaces. *interactions, 2*(2), 34–46.

Constantine, L. L. (2001). Cutting corners: Shortcuts in model-driven web development. *Beyond Chaos: ACM*, 177–184.

Constantine, L. L. (2002). Process agility and software usability: Toward lightweight usage-centered design. *Information Age, 8*(2).

Constantine, L. L., & Lockwood, L. A. D. (1999). *Software for Use: A Practical Guide to the Models and Methods of Usage-Centered Design.* Addison-Wesley Professional.

Constantine, L. L., & Lockwood, L. A. D. (2003). Card-based user and task modeling for agile usage-centered design. In *Proceedings of the CHI Conference on Human Factors in Computing Systems (Tutorial).*

Cooper, A. (2004). *The Inmates Are Running the Asylum: Why High Tech Products Drive Us Crazy and How to Restore the Sanity.* Indianapolis, IN: Sams–Pearson Education.

Cooper, A., Reimann, R., & Dubberly, H. (2003). *About Face 2.0: The Essentials of Interaction Design.* John Wiley.

Cooper, G. (1998). *Research into Cognitive Load Theory & Instructional Design at UNSW.* http://paedpsych. jku.at:4711/LEHRTEXTE/Cooper98.html. Last accessed 2/2/2011.

Costabile, M. F., Ardito, C., & Lanzilotti, R. (2010). Enjoying cultural heritage thanks to mobile technology. *interactions, 17*(3), 30–33.

Cox, D., & Greenberg, S. (2000). Supporting collaborative interpretation in distributed Groupware. In *Proceedings of the ACM Conference on Computer Supported Cooperative Work* (pp. 289–298). Philadelphia, PA.

Cross, K., Warmack, A., & Myers, B. A. (1999). *Lessons learned: Using Contextual Inquiry Analysis To Improve PDA Control of Presentations.* Unpublished report. Carnegie Mellon University.

Cuomo, D. L., & Bowen, C. D. (1992). Stages of user activity model as a basis for user-system interface evaluations. In *Proceedings of the Human Factors and Ergonomics Society Annual Meeting* (pp. 1254–1258).

Curtis, B., & Hefley, B. (1992). Defining a place for interface engineering. *IEEE Software, 9*(2), 84–86.

Curtis, P., Heiserman, T., Jobusch, D., Notess, M., & Webb, J. (1999). Customer-focused design data in a large, multi-site organization. In *Proceedings of the CHI Conference on Human Factors in Computing Systems* (pp. 608–615), Pittsburgh, PA.

Dagstuhl, S. (2010). Demarcating User eXperience Seminar. In *Dagstuhk Seminar.* http://www.dagstuhl.de/10373. Last accessed 08/16/2010.

Davis, F. D., Bagozzi, R. P., & Warshaw, P. R. (1992). Extrinsic and intrinsic motivation to use computers in the workplace. *Journal of Applied Psychology, 22*(14), 1111–1132.

del Galdo, E. M., Williges, R. C., Williges, B. H., & Wixon, D. R. (1986). An evaluation of critical incidents for software documentation design. In *Proceedings of the Human Factors and Ergonomics Society Annual Meeting* (pp. 19–23).

Desmet, P. (2003). Measuring emotions: Development and application of an instrument to measure emotional responses to products. In M. A. Blythe, A. F. Monk, K. Overbeeke & P. C. Wright (Eds.), *Funology: From Usability to Enjoyment* (pp. 111–123). Dordrecht, The Netherlands: Kluwer Academic.

Diaper, D. (1989). Task Analysis for Knowledge Descriptions (TAKD): The method and an example. In D. Diaper (Ed.), *Task Analysis for Human-Computer Interaction* (pp. 108–159). Chichester, England: Ellis Horwood.

Dick, W., & Carey, L. (1978). *The Systematic Design of Instruction.* Glenview, IL: Scott, Foresman.

Donohue, J. (1989). Fixing Fallingwater's flaws. *Architecture,* 99–101.

Dormann, C. (2003). Affective experiences in the home: Measuring emotion. In *Proceedings of the Conference on Home Oriented Informatics and Telematics, the Networked Home of the Future (HOIT)* Irvine, CA.

Dourish, P. (2001). *Where the Action Is: The Foundations of Embodied Interaction.* Cambridge, MA: MIT Press.

Draper, S. W., & Barton, S. B. (1993). Learning by exploration, and affordance bugs. In *Proceedings of the CHI Conference on Human Factors in Computing Systems (INTERCHI Adjunct)* (pp. 75–76), New York.

Dray, S., & Siegel, D. (2004). Remote possibilities? International usability testing at a distance. *interactions, 11*(2), 10–17.

Dray, S. M., & Siegel, D. A. (1999). Business: penny-wise, pound-wise: Making smart trade-offs in planning usability studies. *interactions, 6*(3), 25–30.

Dubberly, H., & Pangaro, P. (2009). What is conversation, and how can we design for it? *interactions, 16*(4), 22–28.

Dumas, J. S., Molich, R., & Jeffries, R. (2004). Describing usability problems: Are we sending the right message? *interactions, 11*(4), 24–29.

Dumas, J. S., & Redish, J. C. (1999). *A Practical Guide to Usability Testing* (Rev Sub ed.). Exeter, England: Intellect Ltd.

Dzida, W., Wiethoff, M., & Arnold, A. G. (1993). *ERGOGuide: The Quality Assurance Guide to Ergonomic Software: Joint internal technical report of GMD (Germany) and Delft University of Technology (The Netherlands).*

Ehn, P. (1988). *Work-Oriented Design of Computer Artifacts. Stockholm.* Sweden: Arbetslivcentrum.

Ehn, P. (1990). *Work-Oriented Design of Computer Artifacts* (2nd ed.). Hillsdale, NJ: Lawrence Erlbaum.

Ekman, P., & Friesen, W. (1975). *Unmasking the Face: A Guide to Recognizing Emotions from Facial Clues.* Englewood Cliffs, NJ: Prentice Hall.

Elgin, B. (1995). How can networked users provide their own usability feedback? Subjective usability feedback from the field over a network. *SIGCHI Bulletin, 27*(4), 43–44.

Engel, S. E., & Granda, R. E. (1975). *Guidelines for Man/Display Interfaces.* Report Number TR 00.2720. Poughkeepsie, NY: IBM.

Ferrara, J. C. (2005). Building positive team relationships for better usability. *interactions, 12*(3), 20–21.

Fitts, P. M. (1954). The information capacity of the human motor system in controlling the amplitude of movement. *Journal of Experimental Psychology, 47*(6), 381–391.

Fitts, P. M., & Jones, R. E. (1947). Psychological aspects of instrument display: Analysis of factors contributing to 460 "pilot error" experiences in operating aircraft controls. In H. W. Sinaiko (Ed.), *Reprinted in Selected Papers on Human Factors in the Design and Use of Control Systems (1961)* (pp. 332–358). New York: Dover.

Fitts, P. M., & Peterson, J. R. (1964). Information capacity of discrete motor responses. *Journal of Experimental Psychology, 67*(2), 103–112.

Flanagan, G. A. (1995). Usability management maturity, Tutorial, CHI '95. Unpublished CHI '95 Tutorial.

Flanagan, J. C. (1954). The critical incident technique. *Psychological Bulletin, 51*(4), 327–358.

Foley, J. D., & Van Dam, A. (1982). *Fundamentals of Interactive Computer Graphics.* Addison-Wesley Longman.

Foley, J. D., Van Dam, A., Feiner, S. K., & Hughes, J. F. (1990). *Computer Graphics: Principles and Practice* (2nd ed.). Addison-Wesley Longman Publishing Co., Inc.

Foley, J. D., & Wallace, V. L. (1974). The art of natural graphic man-machine conversation. *Proceedings of the IEEE, 62*(4), 462–471.

Forlizzi, J. (2005). Robotic products to assist the aging population. *interactions, 12*(2), 16–18.

Frank, B. (2006). The science of segmentation. *interactions, 13*(3), 12–13.

Friedlander, N., Schlueter, K., & Mantei, M. (1998). Bullseye! when Fitts' law doesn't fit. In *Proceedings of the CHI Conference on Human Factors in Computing Systems* (pp. 257–264), Los Angeles, California.

Frishberg, L. (2006). Presumptive design, or cutting the looking-glass cake. *interactions, 13*(1), 18–20.

Frishberg, N. (2006). Prototyping with junk. *interactions, 13*(1), 21–23.

Gabriel-Petit, P. (2005). Sharing ownership of UX (in Special Issue Whose profession is it anyway?). *interactions, 12*(3), 16–18.

Gannon, J. D. (1979). Human factors in software engineering. *IEEE Computer,* 6–60.

Gaver, W. W. (1991). Technology affordances. In *Proceedings of the CHI Conference on Human Factors in Computing Systems* (pp. 79–84), New Orleans, Louisiana.

Gellersen, H. (2005). Smart-Its: Computers for artifacts in the physical world. *Communications of the ACM, 48*(3), 66.

Genov, A. (2005). Iterative usability testing as continuous feedback: A control systems perspective. *Journal of Usability Studies, 1*(1), 18–27.

Gershman, A., & Fano, A. (2005). Examples of commercial applications of ubiquitous computing. *Communications of the ACM, 48*(3), 71.

Gibson, J. J. (1977). The theory of affordances. In R. Shaw & J. Bransford (Eds.), *Perceiving, Acting, and Knowing: Toward an Ecological Psychology* (pp. 67–82). Hillsdale, NJ: Lawrence Erlbaum.

Gibson, J. J. (1979). *The Ecological Approach to Visual Perception.* Houghton Mifflin.

Gilb, T. (1987). Design by objectives. *SIGSOFT Software Engineering Notes, 12*(2), 42–49.

Gillan, D. J., Holden, K., Adam, S., Rudisill, M., & Magee, L. (1990). How does Fitts' law fit pointing and dragging? In *Proceedings of the CHI Conference on Human Factors in Computing Systems* (pp. 227–234), Seattle, WA.

Go, K., & Carroll, J. M. (2004). The blind men and the elephant: Views of scenario-based system design. *interactions, 11*(6), 44–53.

Good, M., Spine, T., Whiteside, J. A., & George, P. (1986). User derived impact analysis as a tool for usability engineering. In *Proceedings of the CHI Conference on Human Factors in Computing Systems* (pp. 241–246), New York.

Good, M. D., Whiteside, J. A., Wixon, D. R., & Jones, S. J. (1984). Building a user-derived interface. *Communications of the ACM, 27*(10), 1032–1043.

Gould, J. D., Boies, S. J., Levy, S., Richards, J. T., & Schoonard, J. (1987). The 1984 Olympic Message System: A test of behavioral principles of system design. *Communications of the ACM, 30*(9), 758–769.

Gray, W. D., Atwood, M., Fisher, C., Nielsen, J., Carrol, J. M., & Long, J. (1995). Discount or disservice? Discount usability analysis–evaluation at a bargain price or simply damaged merchandise? In *Proceedings of the CHI Conference on Human Factors in Computing Systems (Panel Session)* (pp. 176–177), Denver, CO.

Gray, W. D., John, B. E., Stuart, R., Lawrence, D., & Atwood, M. E. (1990). GOMS meets the phone company: Analytic modeling applied to real-world problems. In *Proceedings of the INTERACT Conference on Human-Computer Interaction* (pp. 29–34).

Gray, W. D., & Salzman, M. C. (1998). Damaged merchandise? A review of experiments that compare usability evaluation methods. *Human-Computer Interaction, 13*(3), 203–261.

Greenbaum, J. M. & Kyng, M. (Eds.). (1991). *Design at Work: Cooperative Design of Computer Systems.* Lawrence Erlbaum.

Greenberg, S., & Buxton, B. (2008). Usability evaluation considered harmful (some of the time). In *Proceedings of the CHI Conference on Human Factors in Computing Systems* (pp. 111–120), Florence, Italy.

Grudin, J. (1989). The case against user interface consistency. *Communications of the ACM, 32*(10), 1164–1173.

Grudin, J. (2006). The GUI shock: Computer graphics and human-computer interaction. *interactions, 13*(2), 45–47, 55.

Gunn, C. (1995). An example of formal usability inspections at Hewlett-Packard Company. In: *Proceedings of the CHI Conference on Human Factors in Computing Systems (Conference Companion)* (pp. 103–104), Denver, CO.

Gutierrez, O. (1989). Prototyping techniques for different problem contexts. In *Proceedings of the CHI Conference on Human Factors in Computing Systems* (pp. 259–264).

Hackman, G., & Biers, D. (1992). Team usability testing: Are two heads better than one. In *Proceedings of the Human Factors and Ergonomics Society Annual Meeting* (pp. 1205–1209).

Hafner, K. (2007). Inside Apple stores, a certain aura enchants the faithful. *New York Times,* from http://www.nytimes.com/2007/12/27/business/27apple.html?ei=5124& en=6b1c27bc8cec74b5&ex=1356584400&partner=permalink&exprod=permalink& pagewanted=all.

Hallnös, L., & Redström, J. (2002). From use to presence: On the expressions and aesthetics of everyday computational things. *ACM Transactions on Computer-Human Interaction, 9*(2), 106–124.

Hammond, N., Gardiner, M. M., & Christie, B. (1987). The role of cognitive psychology in user-interface design. In M. M. Gardiner & B. Christie (Eds.), *Applying Cognitive Psychology to User-Interface Design* (pp. 13–52). Wiley.

Hamner, E., Lotter, M., Nourbakhsh, I., & Shelly, S. (2005). Case study: Up close and personal from Mars. *interactions, 12*(2), 30–36.

Hanson, W. (1971). User engineering principles for interactive systems. In *Proceedings of the Fall Joint Computer Conference* (pp. 523–532). Montvale, NJ.

Harrison, M., & Thimbleby, H. (Eds.). (1990). *Formal Methods in Human-Computer Interaction*. Cambridge University Press.

Hartson, H. R., & Hix, D. (1989). Toward empirically derived methodologies and tools for human-computer interface development. *International Journal of Man-Machine Studies, 31*, 477–494.

Hartson, R. (1998). Human-computer interaction: Interdisciplinary roots and trends. *Journal of Systems and Software, 43*, 103–118.

Hartson, R. (2003). Cognitive, physical, sensory, and functional affordances in interaction design. *Behaviour & Information Technology, 22*(5), 315–338.

Hartson, R., Andre, T. S., & Williges, R. C. (2003). Criteria for evaluating usability evaluation methods. *International Journal of Human-Computer Interaction, 15*(1), 145–181.

Hartson, R., & Castillo, J. C. (1998). Remote evaluation for post-deployment usability improvement. In *Proceedings of the Conference on Advanced Visual Interfaces (AVI)* (pp. 22–29), L'Aquila, Italy.

Hartson, R., & Smith, E. C. (1991). Rapid prototyping in human-computer interface development. *Interacting with Computers, 3*(1), 51–91.

Hassenzahl, M. (2001). The effect of perceived hedonic quality on product appealingness. *International Journal of Human-Computer Interaction, 13*(4), 48–499.

Hassenzahl, M., Beu, A., & Burmester, M. (2001). Engineering joy. *IEEE Software, 18*(1), 70–76.

Hassenzahl, M., Burmester, M., & Koller, F. (2003). AttrakDiff: Ein Fragebogen zur Messung wahrgenommener hedonischer und pragmatischer Qualität (AttrakDif: A questionnaire for the measurement of perceived hedonic and pragmatic quality). In *Proceedings of Mensch & Computer 2003: Interaktion in Bewegung* (pp. 187–196), Stuttgart.

Hassenzahl, M., Platz, A., Burmester, M., & Lehner, K. (2000). Hedonic and ergonomic quality aspects determine a software's appeal. In: *Proceedings of the CHI Conference on Human Factors in Computing Systems* (pp. 201–208), The Hague, The Netherlands.

Hassenzahl, M., & Roto, V. (2007). Being and doing: A perspective on user experience and its measurement. *Interfaces, 72*.

Hassenzahl, M., Schöbel, M., & Trautmann, T. (2008). How motivational orientation influences the evaluation and choice of hedonic and pragmatic interactive products: The role of regulatory focus. *Interacting with Computers, 20*, 473–479.

Hawdale, D. (2005). The vision of good user experience. *interactions, 12*(3), 22–23.

Heidegger, M. (1962). *Being and Time*. (J. Macquarrie & E. Robinson, Trans., 1st US ed.). New York: Harper & Row.

Helms, J. W., Arthur, J. D., Hix, D., & Hartson, H. R. (2006). A field study of the wheel: A usability engineering process model. *Journal of Systems and Software, 79*(6), 841–858.

Hertzum, M., & Jacobsen, N. E. (2003). The evaluator effect: A chilling fact about usability evaluation methods. *International Journal of Human-Computer Interaction, 15*(1), 183–204.

Hertzum, M., Jacobsen, N. E., & Molich, R. (2002). Usability inspections by groups of specialists: Perceived agreement in spite of disparate observations. In: *Proceedings of the CHI Conference on Human Factors in Computing Systems (Extended Abstracts)* (pp. 662–663), Minneapolis, MN.

Hewett, T. T. (1986). The role of iterative evaluation in designing systems for usability. In: *Proceedings of the Conference of the British Computer Society, Human Computer Interaction Specialist Group on People and Computers* (pp. 196–214), York, UK.

Hewett, T. T. (1999). Cognitive factors in design: Basic phenomena in human memory and problem solving. In *Proceedings of the CHI Conference on Human Factors in Computing Systems (Extended Abstracts)* (pp. 116–117).

Hinckley, K., Pausch, R., Goble, J. C., & Kassell, N. F. (1994). A survey of design issues in spatial input. In *Proceedings of the ACM Symposium on User Interface Software and Technology* (pp. 213–222). Marina del Rey, CA.

Hix, D., & Hartson, H. R. (1993). *Developing User Interfaces: Ensuring Usability Through Product & Process.* New York: John Wiley.

Hix, D., & Hartson, R. (1993). Formative evaluation: Ensuring usability in user interfaces. In L. Bass & P. Dewan (Eds.), *Trends in Software: User Interface Software* (pp. 1–30). New York: John Wiley & Sons.

Hix, D., & Schulman, R. S. (1991). Human-computer interface development tools: A methodology for their evaluation. *Communications of the ACM, 34*(3), 74–87.

Hochberg, J. (1964). *Perception.* Prentice-Hall.

Holtzblatt, K. (1999). Introduction to special section on contextual design. *interactions, 6*(1), 30–31.

Holtzblatt, K., Wendell, J. B., & Wood, S. (2005). *Rapid Contextual Design: A How-to Guide to Key Techniques for User-Centered Design.* San Francisco, CA: Morgan-Kaufman.

Hornbæk, K. (2006). Current practice in measuring usability: Challenges to usability studies and research. *International Journal of Human-Computer Studies, 64*(2), 79–102.

Hornbæk, K., & Frøkjær, E. (2005). Comparing usability problems and redesign proposals as input to practical systems development. In: *Proceedings of the CHI Conference on Human Factors in Computing Systems* (pp. 391–400), Portland, OR.

Howarth, D. (2002). Custom cupholder a shoe-in. In *Roundel* (p. 10). BMW Car Club publication.

Howarth, J., Andre, T. S., & Hartson, R. (2007). A structured process for transforming usability data into usability information. *Journal of Usability Studies, 3*(1), 7–23.

Howarth, J., Smith-Jackson, T., & Hartson, H. R. (2009). Supporting novice usability practitioners with usability engineering tools. *International Journal of Human-Computer Studies, 67*(6), 533–549.

Hudson, W. (2001). How many users does it take to change a Web site? *SIGCHI Bulletin,* 6.

Huh, J., Ackerman, M. S., Erickson, T., Harrison, S., & Sengers, P. (2007). Beyond usability: Taking social, situational, cultural, and other contextual factors into account. In *Proceedings of the CHI Conference on Human Factors in Computing Systems (Extended Abstracts)* (pp. 2113–2116). San Jose, CA.

Human Factor Research Group. (1990). SUMI Questionnaire. http://www.ucc.ie/hfrg/questionnaires/sumi/index.html. Last accessed 11/18/2010.

Human Factor Research Group (1996a). MUMMS Questionnaire. http://www.ucc.ie/hfrg/questionnaires/mumms/index.html.

Human Factor Research Group. (1996b). WAMMI Questionnaire. http://www.ucc.ie/hfrg/questionnaires/wammi/index.html. Last accessed 11/18/2010.

Husserl, E. (1962). *Ideas: General Introduction to Pure Phenomenology.* Collier Books.

Hutchins, E. L., Hollan, J. D., & Norman, D. A. (1986). Direct manipulation interfaces. In D. A. Norman & S. W. Draper (Eds.), *User Centered System Design: New Perspectives on Human-Computer Interaction* (pp. 87–125). Hillsdale, NJ: Lawrence Erlbaum.

Iannella, R. (1995). HyperSAM: A management tool for large user interface guideline sets. *SIGCHI Bulletin, 27*(2), 42–45.

Igbari, M., Schiffman, S. J., & Wieckowski, T. J. (1994). The respective roles of perceived usefulness and perceived fun in the acceptance of microcomputer technology. *Behaviour & Information Technology, 13*(6), 349–361.

Ishii, H., & Ullmer, B. (1997). Tangible bits: Towards seamless interfaces between people, bits and atoms. In *Proceedings of the CHI Conference on Human Factors in Computing Systems* (pp. 234–241). Atlanta, GA.

ISO 13407. (1999). *Human-centred design processes for interactive systems.* International Organization for Standardization.

ISO 9241-11. (1997). Ergonomic Requirements for Office Work with Visual Display Terminals (VDTs) Part 11: Guidance on Usability.

Jacob, R. J. K. (1993). Eye movement-based human-computer interaction techniques: Toward non-command interfaces. In R. Hartson & D. Hix (Eds.), *Advances in Human-Computer Interaction* (Vol. 4., pp. 151–190). Norwood, NJ: Ablex Publishing Corporation.

John, B. E., & Marks, S. J. (1997). Tracking the effectiveness of usability evaluation methods. *Behaviour & Information Technology, 16*(4), 188–202.

John, B. E., & Mashyna, M. M. (1997). Evaluating a multimedia authoring tool with cognitive walkthrough and think-aloud user studies. *Journal of the American Society for Information Science, 48*(11), 1004–1022.

Johnson, J. (2000). Textual bloopers: An excerpt from GUI bloopers. *interactions, 7*(5), 28–48.

Johnson, J., & Henderson, A. (2002). Conceptual models: Begin by designing what to design. *interactions, 9*(1), 25–32.

Jokela, T. (2004). When good things happen to bad products: Where are the benefits of usability in the consumer appliance market? *interactions, 11*(6), 28–35.

Jones, B. D., Winegarden, C. R., & Rogers, W. A. (2009). Supporting healthy aging with new technologies. *interactions, 16*(4), 48–51.

Jordan, P. W. (1996). Human factors in product use. *Applied Ergonomics, 29*, 25–33.

Judge, T. K., Pyla, P. S., McCrickard, S., & Harrison, S. (2008). Affinity diagramming in multiple display environments. In *Proceedings of CSCW 2008 Workshop on Beyond the Laboratory: Supporting Authentic Collaboration with Multiple Displays.* San Diego, CA.

Kabbash, P., & Buxton, W. A. S. (1995). The "prince" technique: Fitts' law and selection using area cursors. In *Proceedings of the CHI Conference on Human Factors in Computing Systems* (pp. 273–279), Denver, CO.

Kameas, A., & Mavrommati, I. (2005). Extrovert gadgets. *Communications of the ACM, 48*(3), 69.

Kane, D. (2003, June 25–28). Finding a place for discount usability engineering in agile development: Throwing down the gauntlet. In *Proceedings of the Agile Development Conference (ADC)* (pp. 40–46).

Kangas, E., & Kinnunen, T. (2005). Applying user-centered design to mobile application development. *Communications of the ACM, 48*(7), 55–59.

Kantrovich, L. (2004). To innovate or not to innovate. *interactions, 11*(1), 24–31.

Kapoor, A., Picard, R. W., & Ivanov, Y. (2004). Probabilistic combination of multiple modalities to detect interest. In *Proceedings of the International Conference on Pattern Recognition (ICPR)* (pp. 969–972).

Kapor, M. (1991). A software design manifesto. *Dr. Dobb's Journal, 16*(1), 62–67.

Kapor, M. (1996). A software design manifesto. In T. Winograd (Ed.), *Bringing Design to Software* (pp. 1–6). New York: ACM.

Karat, C.-M. (1990a). Cost-benefit analysis of iterative usability testing. In *Proceedings of the INTERACT Conference on Human-Computer Interaction* (pp. 351–356).

Karat, C.-M. (1990b). Cost-benefit analysis of usability engineering techniques. In *Proceedings of the Human Factors and Ergonomics Society Annual Meeting* (pp. 839–843).

Karat, C.-M. (1991). Cost-benefit and business case analysis of usability engineering, Tutorial, CHI '91. Unpublished CHI '91 Tutorial.

Karat, C.-M. (1993). Usability engineering in dollars and cents. *IEEE Software, 10*(3), 88–89.

Karat, C.-M., Campbell, R., & Fiegel, T. (1992, May 3–7). Comparison of empirical testing and walk-through methods in user interface evaluation. In *Proceedings of the CHI Conference on Human Factors in Computing Systems* (pp. 397–404). New York.

Karn, K. S., Perry, T. J., & Krolczyk, M. J. (1997). Testing for power usability: A CHI 97 workshop. *SIGCHI Bulletin, 29*(4).

Kaur, K., Maiden, N., & Sutcliffe, A. (1999). Interacting with virtual environments: An evaluation of a model of interaction. *Interacting with Computers, 11*(4), 403–426.

Kawakita, J. (1982). *The Original KJ Method*. Tokio: Kawakita Research Institute.

Kaye, J. J. (2004). Making scents: Aromatic output for HCI. *interactions, 11*(1), 48–61.

Kennedy, S. (1989). Using video in the BNR usability lab. *SIGCHI Bulletin, 21*(2), 92–95.

Kennedy, T. C. S. (1974). The design of interactive procedures for man-machine communication. *International Journal of Man-Machine Studies, 6*, 309–334.

Kensing, F., & Munk-Madsen, (1993). PD: Structure in the toolbox. *Communications of the ACM, 36* (6), 78–85.

Kieras, D. E. (1988). Towards a practical GOMS model methodology for user interface design. In M. Helander (Ed.), *Handbook of Human-Computer Interaction* (135–157). Elsevier Science.

Kieras, D. E., & Polson, P. G. (1985). An approach to the formal analysis of user complexity. *International Journal of Man-Machine Studies, 22*, 365–394.

Killam, H. W. (1991). Rogerian psychology and human-computer interaction. *Interacting with Computers, 3*(1), 119–128.

Kim, J., & Moon, J. Y. (1998). Designing towards emotional usability in customer interfaces—Trustworthiness of cyber-banking system interfaces. *Interacting with Computers, 10*(1), 1–29.

Kim, J. H., Gunn, D. V., Schuh, E., Phillips, B. C., Pagulayan, R. J., & Wixon, D. (2008). Tracking real-time user experience (TRUE): A comprehensive instrumentation for complex systems. In *Proceedings of CHI Conference on Human Factors in Computing Systems* (pp. 443–451). Florence, Italy.

Kirakowski, J., & Murphy, R. (2009). A comparison of current approaches to usability measurement. In *Proceedings of the UPA International Conference*. Portland, OR.

Knemeyer, D. (2005). Who owns UX? Not us!. *interactions, 12*(3), 18–20.

Koenemann-Belliveau, J., Carroll, J. M., Rosson, M. B., & Singley, M. K. (1994). Comparative usability evaluation: critical incidents and critical threads. In *Proceedings of the CHI Conference on Human Factors in Computing Systems* (pp. 245–251), Boston, MA.

Koffka, K. (1935). *Principles of Gestalt Psychology*. Harcourt, Brace.

Kreitzberg, C. B. (2000). Personal communication with Rex Hartson.

Kreitzberg, C. B. (2008). The LUCID framework: An introduction. http://www.leadersintheknow. biz/Portals/0/Publications/Lucid-Paper-v2.pdf. Last accessed 07/13/2011.

Kreitzburg, C. Technology and Chaos. http://www.digitalspaceart.com/projects/cogweb2002v2/ papers/charlie/charlie5.html. Last accessed 07/09/2011.

Kuniavsky, M. (2003). *Observing the User Experience: A Practitioner's Guide to User Research*. San Francisco, CA: Morgan Kaufmann.

Kwong, A. W., Healton, B., & Lancaster, R. (1998). State of siege: New thinking for the next decade of design. In *Proceedings of the IEEE Aerospace Conference* (pp. 85–93).

Kyng, M. (1994). Scandinavian design: Users in product development. In *Proceedings of the CHI Conference on Human Factors in Computing Systems* (pp. 3–9).

Lalis, S., Karypidis, A., & Savidis, A. (2005). Ad-hoc composition in wearable and mobile computing. *Communications of the ACM, 48*(3), 67–68.

Landauer, T. K. (1995). *The Trouble with Computers: Usefulness, Usability, and Productivity.* Cambridge, MA: MIT Press.

Landay, J. A., & Myers, B. A. (1995). Interactive sketching for the early stages of user interface design. In *Proceedings of the CHI Conference on Human Factors in Computing Systems* (pp. 43–50), Denver, CO.

Lathan, C., Brisben, A., & Safos, C. (2005). CosmoBot levels the playing field for disabled children. *interactions, 12*(2), 14–16.

Lavery, D., & Cockton, G. (1997). Representing predicted and actual usability problems. In *Proceedings of the International Workshop on Representations in Interactive Software Development* (pp. 97–108). London.

Lavie, T., & Tractinsky, N. (2004). Assessing dimensions of perceived visual aesthetics of web sites. *International Journal of Human-Computer Studies, 60*, 269–298.

Law, E. L.-C. (2006). Evaluating the downstream utility of user tests and examining the developer effect: A case study. *International Journal of Human-Computer Interaction, 21*(2), 147–172.

LeCompte, M. D., & Preissle, J. (1993). *Ethnography and Qualitative Design in Educational Research* (2nd ed.). San Diego: Academic Press.

Lederer, A. L., & Prasad, J. (1992). Nine management guidelines for better cost estimating. *Communications of the ACM, 35*(2), 51–59.

Lee, G. A., Kim, G. J., & Billinghurst, M (2005). Immersive authoring: What You eXperience Is What You Get (WYXIWYG). *Communications of the ACM, 48*(7), 76–81.

Lewis, C. (1982). *Using the 'thinking-aloud' method in cognitive interface design. Report Number Research Report RC 9265.* Yorktown Heights, NY: IBM T. T. Watson Research Center.

Lewis, C., Polson, P. G., Wharton, C., & Rieman, J. (1990). Testing a walkthrough methodology for theory-based design of walk-up-and-use interfaces. In *Proceedings of the CHI Conference on Human Factors in Computing Systems* (pp. 235–242), Seattle, WA.

Lewis, J. R. (1994). Sample sizes for usability studies: Additional considerations. *Journal of the Human Factors and Ergonomics Society, 36*, 368–378.

Lewis, J. R. (1995). IBM computer usability satisfaction questionnaires: Psychometric evaluation and instructions for use. *International Journal of Human-Computer Interaction, 7*, 57–78.

Lewis, J. R. (2002). Psychometric evaluation of the PSSUQ using data from five years of usability studies. *International Journal of Human-Computer Interaction, 14*, 463–488.

Lewis, J. R., & Sauro, J. (2009). The factor structure of the System Usability Scale. In *Proceedings of the International Conference on Human-Computer Interaction (HCI International).* San Diego, CA.

Likert, R. (1932). A technique for the measurement of attitudes. *Archives of Psychology, 140*, 55.

Lindgaard, G. (2004). Making the business our business: One path to value-added HCI. *interactions, 11*(3), 12–17.

Lindgaard, G., & Dudek, C. (2003). What is this evasive beast we call user satisfaction? *Interacting with Computers, 15*(3), 429–452.

Lindgaard, G., Fernandes, G. J., Dudek, C., & Brownet, J. (2006). Attention web designers: You have 50 milliseconds to make a good first impression!. *Behaviour & Information Technology, 25*(2), 115–126.

Logan, R. J. (1994). Behavioral and emotional usability: Thomson Consumer Electronics. In M. Wiklund (Ed.), *Usability in Practice* (pp. 59–82). San Diego, CA: Academic Press Professional.

Logan, R. J., Augaitis, S., & Renk, T. (1994). Design of simplified television remote controls: A case for behavioral and emotional usability. In *Proceedings of the Human Factors and Ergonomics Society Annual Meeting* (pp. 365–369). Santa Monica, CA.

Lohse, G. L., Biolsi, K., Walker, N., & Rueter, H. H. (1994). A classification of visual representations. *Communications of the ACM, 37*(12), 36–49.

Löwgren, J. (2004). Animated use sketches: As design representations. *interactions, 11*(6), 23–27.

Lund, A. M. (1997a). Another approach to justifying the cost of usability. *interactions, 4*(3), 48–56.

Lund, A. M. (1997b). Expert ratings of usability maxims. *Ergonomics in Design, 5*(3), 15–20.

Lund, A. M. (2001). Measuring usability with the USE questionnaire. *Usability & User Experience (the STC Usability SIG Newsletter), 8*(2).

Lund, A. M. (2004). Measuring Usability with the USE Questionnaire. http://www.stcsig.org/usabil ity/newsletter/0110_measuring_with_use.html. Last accessed 7/15/2011.

Macdonald, N. (2004). Can HCI shape the future of mass communications? *interactions, 11*(2), 44–47.

MacKenzie, I. S. (1992). Fitts' law as a research and design tool in human-computer interaction. *Human-Computer Interaction, 7*, 91–139.

MacKenzie, I. S. (1992). Fitts' law as a research and design tool in human-computer interaction. *Human-Computer Interaction, 7*, 91–139.

MacKenzie, I. S., & Buxton, W. (1992). Extending Fitts' law to two-dimensional tasks. In *Proceedings of the CHI Conference on Human Factors in Computing Systems* (pp. 219–226). Monterey, CA.

Macleod, M., Bowden, R., Bevan, N., & Curson, I. (1997). The MUSiC performance measurement method. *Behaviour & Information Technology, 16*(4), 279–293.

Macleod, M., & Rengger, R. (1993). The development of DRUM: A software tool for video-assisted usability evaluation. In *Proceedings of the International Conference on Human-Computer Interaction (HCI International)* (pp. 293–309).

Manning, H. (2002). Must the sale end? *interactions, 9*(6), 56, 55.

Mantei, M. M., & Teorey, T. J. (1988). Cost/benefit analysis for incorporating human factors in the software lifecycle. *Communications of the ACM, 31*(4), 428–439.

Marcus, A. (2002). The cult of cute: The challenge of user experience design. *interactions, 9*(6), 29–34.

Marcus, A. (2007). Happy birthday! CHI at 25. *interactions, 14*(2), 42–43.

Marcus, A., & Gasperini, J. (2006). Almost dead on arrival: A case study of non-user-centered design for a police emergency-response system. *interactions, 13*(5), 12–18.

Marine, L. (1994). Common ground. *The Newsletter of Usability Professionals, 4*, 2.

Markopoulos, P., Ruyter, B.d., Privender, S., & Breemen, A. V. (2005). Case study: Bringing social intelligence into home dialogue systems. *interactions, 12*(4), 37–44.

Mason, J. G. (1968, October). How to be of two minds. *Nation's Business*, 94–97.

May, L. J. (1998). Major causes of software project failures. *Crosstalk*, 9–12.

Mayhew, D. J. (1999). *The Usability Engineering Lifecycle: A Practitioner's Handbook for User Interface Design* (1st ed). San Francisco, CA: Morgan Kaufmann.

Mayhew, D. J. (1999a). Strategic development of the usability engineering function. *interactions, 6*(5), 27–33.

Mayhew, D. J. (1999b). *The Usability Engineering Lifecycle: A Practitioner's Handbook for User Interface Design*. San Francisco, CA: Morgan Kaufmann.

Mayhew, D. J. (2008). User experience design: The evolution of a multi-disciplinary approach. *Journal of Usability Studies, 3*(3), 99–102.

Mayhew, D. J. (2010). A spreadsheet-based tool for simple cost–benefit analyses of HSI contributions during software application development. In W. B. Rouse (Ed.), *The Economics of Human Systems Integration* (pp. 163–184). Hoboken, NJ: John Wiley & Sons.

McClelland, I., Taylor, B., & Hefley, B. (1996). CHI '96 workshop: User-centred design principles: How far have they been industrialized? *SIGCHI Bulletin, 28*(4), 23–25.

McCullough, M. (2004). *Digital Ground: Architecture, Pervasive Computing, and Environmental Knowing.* MIT Press.

McGrenere, J., & Ho, W. (2000). Affordances: Clarifying and evolving a concept. In *Proceedings of Graphics Interface* (pp. 179–186).

McGuffin, M. J., & Balakrishnan, R. (2005). Fitts' law and expanding targets: Experimental studies and designs for user interfaces. *ACM Transactions on Computer-Human Interaction, 12*(4), 388–422.

McInerney, P., & Maurer, F. (2005). UCD in agile projects: Dream team or odd couple? *interactions, 12*(6), 19–23.

Meads, J. (1999). Usability Is Not Graphic Design. http://stuff.ratjed.com/UsabilityIsNotGraphicDesign .htm. Last accessed 7/24/2011.

Meads, J. (2010). Personal communication with Rex Hartson.

Medlock, M. C., Wixon, D., McGee, M., & Welsh, D. (2005). The rapid iterative test and evaluation method: Better products in less time. In R. G. Bias & D. J. Mayhew (Eds.), *Cost Justifying Usability: An Update for an Internet Age* (pp. 489–517). San Francisco, CA: Morgan Kaufmann.

Medlock, M. C., Wixon, D., Terrano, M., Romero, R., & Fulton, B. (2002). Using the RITE method to improve products: A definition and a case study. In *Proceedings of the UPA International Conference.* Orlando, FL.

Meister, D. (1985). *Behavioral Analysis and Measurement Methods.* Wiley-Interscience.

Memmel, T., Gundelsweiler, F., & Reiterer, H. (2007). Agile human-centered software engineering. In *Proceedings of the British HCI Group Annual Conference on People and Computers,* (pp. 167–175) UK: University of Lancaster.

Miller, G. A. (1956). The magical number seven, plus or minus two: Some limits on our capacity for processing information. *Psychological Review, 63*(2), 81–97.

Miller, L. (2010). Case study of customer input for a successful product. http://www. agileproductdesign.com/useful_papers/miller_customer_input_in_agile_projects.pdf. Last accessed 7/23/2011.

Miller, L., & Sy, D. (2009, April 4–9). Agile User Experience SIG. In *Proceedings of the CHI Conference on Human Factors in Computing Systems* (pp. 2751–2754). Boston.

Miller, R. B. (1953). *A method for man-machine task analysis.* Report Number 53-137. Dayton, OH: Wright Air Development Center, Wright-Patterson Air Force Base.

Moggridge, B. (2007). *Designing Interactions.* MIT Press.

Molich, R. (2011). Comparative Usability Evaluation Reports. http://www.dialogdesign.dk/CUE-9. htm. Last accessed 07/15/2011.

Molich, R., Bevan, N., Butler, S., Curson, I., Kindlund, E., & Kirakowski, J. (1998, June). Comparative evaluation of usability tests. In *Proceedings of the UPA International Conference* (pp. 189–200). Washington, DC.

Molich, R., & Dumas, J. S. (2008). Comparative Usability Evaluation (CUE-4). *Behaviour & Information Technology, 27*(3), 263–282.

Molich, R., Ede, M. R., Kaasgaard, K., & Karyukin, B. (2004). Comparative usability evaluation. *Behaviour & Information Technology, 23*(1), 65–74.

Molich, R., Jeffries, R., & Dumas, J. S. (2007). Making usability recommendations useful and usable. *Journal of Usability Studies, 2*(4), 162–179.

Molich, R., & Nielsen, J. (1990). Improving a human-computer dialogue. *Communications of the ACM, 33*(3), 338–348.

Molich, R., Thomsen, A. D., Karyukina, B., Schmidt, L., Ede, M., van Oel, W., et al. (1999). Comparative evaluation of usability tests. In *Proceedings of the CHI Conference on Human Factors in Computing Systems (Extended Abstracts)* (pp. 83–84), Pittsburgh, PA.

Monk, A., & Howard, S. (1998). The rich picture: A tool for reasoning about work context. *interactions*, *5*(2), 21–30.

Moran, T. P. (1981a). The Command Language Grammar: A representation for the user interface of interactive computer systems. *International Journal of Man-Machine Studies, 15*(1), 3–50.

Moran, T. P. (1981b). Guest editor's introduction: An applied psychology of the user. *ACM Computing Surveys, 13*(1), 1–11.

Morris, J. S. (2005). Professional societies and business relevance. *interactions, 12*(3), 45–47.

Mosier, J. N., & Smith, S. L. (1986). Application of guidelines for designing user interface software. *Behaviour & Information Technology, 5*(1), 39–46.

Mowshowitz, A., & Turoff, M. (2005). Introduction to special issue: The digital society. *Communications of the ACM, 48*(10), 32–35.

Muller, M. J. (1991). PICTIVE: An exploration in participatory design. In *Proceedings of the CHI Conference on Human Factors in Computing Systems* (pp. 225–231). New Orleans, LA.

Muller, M. J. (1992). Retrospective on a year of participatory design using the PICTIVE technique. In *Proceedings of the CHI Conference on Human Factors in Computing Systems* (pp. 455–462), Monterey, CA.

Muller, M. J. (2003). Participatory design: The third space in HCI. In J. A. Jacko & A. Sears (Eds.), *The Human-Computer Interaction Handbook: Fundamentals, Evolving Technologies and Emerging Applications* (pp. 1051–1058). Lawrence Erlbaum.

Muller, M. J., & Kuhn, S. (1993). Participatory design. *Communications of the ACM, 36*(4), 24–28.

Muller, M. J., Matheson, L., Page, C., & Gallup, R. (1998). Participatory heuristic evaluation. *interactions, 5*(5), 13–18.

Muller, M. J., Wildman, D. M., & White, E. A. (1993). 'Equal opportunity' PD using PICTIVE. *Communications of the ACM, 36*(6), 64.

Mumford, E. (1981). Participative systems design: Structure and method. *Systems, Objectives, Solutions, 1*(1), 5–19.

Mundorf, N., Westin, S., & Dholakia, N. (1993). Effects of hedonic (emotional) components and user's gender on the acceptance of screen-based information services. *Behaviour & Information Technology, 12*, 293–303.

Murano, P. (2006). Why anthropomorphic user interface feedback can be effective and preferred by users. In C.-S. Chen, J. Filipe, I. Seruca & J. Cordeiro (Eds.), *Enterprise Information Systems* (Vol. 7, pp. 241–248). Dordrecht, The Netherlands: Springer.

Murphy, R. R. (2005). Humans, robots, rubble, and research. *interactions, 12*(2), 37–39.

Myers, B. A. (1989). User-interface tools: Introduction and survey. *IEEE Software, 6*(1), 15–23.

Myers, B. A. (1992). *State of the Art in User Interface Software Tools.* Carnegie Mellon University.

Myers, B. A. (1993). State of the art in user interface software tools. In R. Hartson & D. Hix (Eds.), *Advances in Human-Computer Interaction* (Vol. 4). Norwood, NJ: Ablex.

Myers, B. A. (1995). State of the art in user interface software tools. In R. M. Baecker, J. Grudin, W. A. S. Buxton & S. Greenberg (Eds.), *Readings in Human-Computer Interaction: Toward the Year 2000* (pp. 323–343). San Francisco: Morgan-Kaufmann Publishers, Inc.

Myers, B. A., Hudson, S. E., & Pausch, R. (2000). Past, present, and future of user interface software tools. *ACM Transactions on Computer-Human Interaction, 7*(1), 3–28.

Myers, B. A., & Rosson, M. B. (1992). Survey on user interface programming. In *Proceedings of the CHI Conference on Human Factors in Computing Systems* (pp. 195–202), Monterey, CA.

Myers, I. B., McCaulley, M. H., Quenk, N. L., & Hammer, A. L. (1998). *MBTI Manual (A Guide to the Development And Use of the Myers Briggs Type Indicator)* (3rd ed.). Consulting Psychologists Press.

Nardi, B. A. (1995). *Context and Consciousness: Activity Theory and Human Computer Interaction.* Cambridge, MA: MIT Press.

Nass, C., Steuer, J., & Tauber, E. R. (1994). Computers are social actors. In *Proceedings of the CHI Conference on Human Factors in Computing Systems* (pp. 72–78). Boston, MA.

Nayak, N. P., Mrazek, D., & Smith, D. R. (1995). Analyzing and communicating usability data: Now that you have the data what do you do? A CHI'94 workshop. *SIGCHI Bulletin, 27*(1), 22–30.

Newman, W. M. (1968). A system for interactive graphical programming. In *Proceedings of the Spring Joint Computer Conference* (pp. 47–54). Atlantic City, NJ.

Newman, W. M. (1998). On simulation, measurement, and piecewise usability evaluation. In G. M. Olson & T. P. Moran (Eds.), *Commentary 10 on "Damaged Merchandise," Human-Computer Interaction* (Vol. 13, Issue 3, pp. 316–323). Lawrence Erlbaum.

Nielsen, J. (1987). Using scenarios to develop user friendly videotex systems. In: *Proceedings of the NordDATA Joint Scandinavian Computer Conference* (pp. 133–138), Trondheim, Norway.

Nielsen, J. (1989). Usability engineering at a discount. In G. Salvendy & M. J. Smith (Eds.), *Designing and Using Human-Computer Interfaces and Knowledge-Based Systems* (pp. 394–401). Amsterdam: Elsevier Science.

Nielsen, J. (1990). Traditional dialogue design applied to modern user interfaces. *Communications of the ACM, 33*(10), 109–118.

Nielsen, J. (1992a). Finding usability problems through heuristic evaluation. In: *Proceedings of the CHI Conference on Human Factors in Computing Systems* (pp. 373–380), Monterey, CA.

Nielsen, J. (1992b). The usability engineering lifecycle. *IEEE Computer, 25*(3), 12–22.

Nielsen, J. (1993). *Usability Engineering.* Chestnut Hill, MA: Academic Press Professional.

Nielsen, J. (1994a). Enhancing the explanatory power of usability heuristics. In: *Proceedings of the CHI Conference on Human Factors in Computing Systems* (pp. 152–158), Boston, MA.

Nielsen, J. (1994b). Heuristic evaluation. In J. Nielsen & R. L. Mack (Eds.), *Usability Inspection Methods.* New York: John Wiley.

Nielsen, J. (1994c). Guerrilla HCI: Using discount usability engineering to penetrate the intimidation barrier. In R. G. Bias & D. J. Mayhew (Eds.), *Cost-Justifying Usability* (pp. 245–272). Orlando, FL: Academic Press.

Nielsen, J. (2008). Agile development projects and usability. http://www.useit.com/alertbox/agile-methods.html (useit.com Alertbox). Last accessed 07/23/2011.

Nielsen, J., Bush, R. M., Dayton, T., Mond, N. E., Muller, M. J., & Root, R. W. (1992). Teaching experienced developers to design graphical user interfaces. In: *Proceedings of the CHI Conference on Human Factors in Computing Systems* (pp. 557–564), Monterey, CA.

Nielsen, J., & Landauer, T. K. (1993). A mathematical model of the finding of usability problems. In *Proceedings of the INTERACT Conference on Human-Computer Interaction and CHI Conference on Human Factors in Computing Systems (INTERCHI)* (pp. 206–213), Amsterdam, The Netherlands.

Nielsen, J., & Molich, R. (1990). Heuristic evaluation of user interfaces. In *Proceedings of the CHI Conference on Human Factors in Computing Systems* (pp. 249–256), Seattle, WA.

Nieters, J. E., Ivaturi, S., & Ahmed, I. (2007). Making personas memorable. In: *Proceedings of the CHI Conference on Human Factors in Computing Systems (Extended Abstracts)* (pp. 1817–1824), San Jose, CA.

Nilsson, P., & Ottersten, I. (1998). Interaction design: Leaving the engineering perspective behind. In L. E. Wood (Ed.), *User Interface Design: Bridging the Gap from User Requirements to Design* (pp. 131–152).

Norman, D. A. (1986). Cognitive engineering. In D. A. Norman & S. W. Draper (Eds.), *User Centered System Design: New Perspectives on Human-Computer Interaction* (pp. 31–61). Hillsdale, NJ: Lawrence Erlbaum.

Norman, D. A. (1990). *The Design of Everyday Things.* New York: Basic Books.

Norman, D. A. (1998). *The Invisible Computer—Why Good Products Can Fail, the Personal Computer Is So Complex, and Information Appliances Are the Solution.* MIT Press.

Norman, D. A. (1999). Affordance, conventions, and design. *interactions, 6*(3), 38–43.

Norman, D. A. (2002). Emotion and design: Attractive things work better. *interactions, 9*(4), 36–42.

Norman, D. A. (2004). *Emotional Design: Why We Love (Or Hate) Everyday Things.* New York: Basic Books.

Norman, D. A. (2006). Logic versus usage: The case for activity-centered design. *interactions, 13*(6), 4563.

Norman, D. A. (2007a). Simplicity is highly overrated. *interactions, 14*(2), 40–41.

Norman, D. A. (2007b). The next UI breakthrough, part 2: Physicality. *interactions, 14*(4), 46–47.

Norman, D. A. (2008). Simplicity is not the answer. *interactions, 15*(5), 45–46.

Norman, D. A. (2009a). Designing the infrastructure. *interactions, 16*(4), 66–69.

Norman, D. A. (2009b). Systems thinking: A product is more than a product. *interactions, 16*(5), 52–54.

Nowell, L., Schulman, R., & Hix, D. (2002). Graphical encoding for information visualization: An empirical study. In *Proceedings of the IEEE Symposium on Information Visualization (INFOVIS).* (p. 43).

Olsen, D. R., Jr. (1983). Automatic generation of interactive systems. *Computer Graphics, 17*(1), 53–57.

O'Malley, C., Draper, S., & Riley, M. (1984, September 4–7). Constructive interaction: A method for studying human-computer-human interaction. In *Proceedings of the INTERACT Conference on Human-Computer Interaction* (pp. 269–274), London, UK.

Open Software Foundation, (1990). *OSF/Motif Style Guide: Revision 1.0.* Prentice-Hall, Inc.

Paradiso, J. A. (2005). Sensate media. *Communications of the ACM, 48*(3), 70.

Paradiso, J. A., Lifton, J., & Broxton, M. (2004). Sensate media—Multimodal electronic skins as dense sensor networks. *BT Technology Journal, 22*(4), 32–44.

Patton, J. (2002). Hitting the target: Adding interaction design to agile software development. In *Proceedings of OOPSLA 2002 Practitioners Reports* (pp. 1–7). Seattle, WA.

Patton, J. (2008, June 27). Twelve emerging best practices for adding UX work to Agile development. http://agileproductdesign.com/blog/emerging_best_agile_ux_practice.html. Last accessed 11/29/2010.

Paulk, M. C., Curtis, B., Chrissis, M. B., & Weber, C. (1993). *Capability Maturity Model for Software, Version 1.1.* Report Number CMU/SEI-93-TR-24. Pittsburgh, PA: Software Engineering Institute, Carnegie Mellon University.

Payne, S. J., & Green, T. R. G. (1986). Task-action grammars: A model of the mental representation of task languages. *Human-Computer Interaction, 2,* 93–133.

Payne, S. J., & Green, T. R. G. (1989). Task-action grammar: The model and its developments. In D. Diaper (Ed.), *Task Analysis for Human-Computer Interaction* (pp. 75–107). Chichester, England: Ellis Horwood.

Pering, C. (2002). Interaction design prototyping of communicator devices: Towards meeting the hardware-software challenge. *interactions, 9*(6), 36–46.

Petersen, M. G., Madsen, K. H., & Kjaer, A. (2002). The usability of everyday technology: Emerging and fading opportunities. *ACM Transactions on Computer-Human Interaction, 9*(2), 74–105.

Pew, R. N., & Rollins, A. M. (1975). *Dialog Specification Procedure* . Report Number 5129 (Rev. ed.). Cambridge, MA: Bolt, Beranek, and Newman.

Pogue, D. Appeal of iPad 2 is a matter of emotions. http://www.nytimes.com/2011/03/10/technology/personaltech/10pogue.html?_r=2&hpw. Last accessed 7/11/2011.

Potosnak, K. (1987). Where human factors fits in the design process. *IEEE Computer*, 90–92.

Potosnak, K. (1988). Getting the most out of design guidelines. *IEEE Software*, 5(1), 85–86.

Pressman, R. (2009). *Software Engineering: A Practitioner's Approach* (7th ed.). McGraw-Hill.

Pyla, P. S. (2009). *Connecting the Usability and Software Engineering Life Cycles: Using a Communication-Fostering Software Development Framework and Cross-Pollinated Computer Science Courses.* Saarbrücken, Germany: VDM Verlag.

Pyla, P. S., Hartson, H. R., Arthur, J. D., Smith-Jackson, T. L., Pérez-Quiñones, M. A., & Hix, D. (2007). Evaluating ripple: Experiences from a cross pollinated SE-UE study. In *Proceedings of CHI 2007 Workshop on Increasing the Impact of Usability Work in Software Development.*

Pyla, P. S., Pérez-Quiñones, M. A., Arthur, J. D., & Hartson, H. R. (2003). Towards a model-based framework for integrating usability and software engineering life cycles. In *Proceedings of Interact 2003 Workshop on Closing the Gaps: Software Engineering and Human Computer Interaction* (pp. 67–74).

Pyla, P. S., Pérez-Quiñones, M. A., Arthur, J. D., & Hartson, H. R. (2004). What we should teach, but don't: Proposal for a cross pollinated HCI-SE curriculum. In *Proceedings of Frontiers in Education (FIE) Conference* (S1H17–S1H22), Savannah, Georgia.

Pyla, P. S., Pérez-Quiñones, M. A., Arthur, J. D., & Hartson, H. R. (2005). Ripple: An event driven design representation framework for integrating usability and software engineering life cycles. In A. Seffah, J. Gulliksen & M. Desmarais (Eds.), *Human-Centered Software Engineering: Integrating Usability in the Software Development Lifecycle* (Vol. 8., pp. 245–265). Springer.

Quesenbery, W. (2005). Designing theatre, designing user experience. *interactions*, 12(2), 55–57.

Quesenbery, W. (2005). Usability standards: Connecting practice around the world. In *Proceedings of the IEEE International Professional Communication Conference (IPCC)* (pp. 451–457).

Quesenbery, W. (2009). Private communication with Rex Hartson.

Radoll, P. (2009). Reconstructing Australian aboriginal governance by systems design. *interactions*, 16(3), 46–49.

Reeves, B., & Nass, C. I. (1996). *The Media Equation: How People Treat Computers, Television, and New Media Like Real People and Places.* Stanford, CA: CSLI Publications.

Reisner, P. (1977). Use of psychological experimentation as an aid to development of a Query language. *IEEE Transactions on Software Engineering SE*, 3(3), 218–229.

Rettig, M. (1992). Interface design when you don't know how. *Communications of the ACM*, 35(1), 29–34.

Rettig, M. (1994). Prototyping for tiny fingers. *Communications of the ACM*, 37(4), 21–27.

Rhee, Y., & Lee, J. (2009). A model of mobile community: Designing user interfaces to support group interaction. *interactions*, 16(6), 46–51.

Rice, J. F. (1991a). Display color coding: 10 rules of thumb. *IEEE Software*, 8(1), 86.

Rice, J. F. (1991b). Ten rules for color coding. *Information Display*, 7(3), 12–14.

Rideout, T. (1991). Changing your methods from the inside. *IEEE Software*, 8(3), 99–100, 111.

Rising, L., & Janoff, N. S. (2000). The scrum software development process for small teams. *IEEE Software*, 17(4), 26–32.

Rogers, Y., Sharp, H., & Preece, J. (2011). *Interaction Design: Beyond Human-Computer Interaction* (3rd ed.). Wiley.

Rosenbaum, S., Rohn, J. A., & Humburg, J. (2000). A toolkit for strategic usability: Results from workshops, panels, and surveys. In: *Proceedings of the CHI Conference on Human Factors in Computing Systems* (pp. 337–344), The Hague, The Netherlands.

Rosenberg, D. (2004). The myths of usability ROI. *interactions, 11*(5), 22–29.

Rosson, M. B., & Carroll, J. M. (2002). *Usability Engineering: Scenario-Based Development of Human-Computer Interaction.* Morgan Kaufmann.

Royce, W. W. (1970, August 25–28). Managing the development of large scale software systems. In *Proceedings of IEEE Western Electronic Show and Convention (WESCON) Technical Papers* (pp. A/1 1–9). Los Angeles, CA. *(Reprinted in Proceedings of the Ninth International Conference on Software Engineering, Pittsburgh, ACM Press, 1989, pp. 328–338).*

Rudd, J., Stern, K., & Isensee, S. (1996). Low vs. high-fidelity prototyping debate. *interactions, 3*(1), 76–85.

Russell, D. M., Streitz, N. A., & Winograd, T. (2005). Building disappearing computers. *Communications of the ACM, 48*(3), 42–48.

Salter, C. (2009, June). 100 most creative people in business. *Fast Company*, 60.

Sauro, J. (2004). Premium usability: Getting the discount without paying the price. *interactions, 11*(4), 30–37.

Savio, N. (2010). Solving the world's problems through design. *interactions, 17*(3), 52–54.

Sawyer, P., Flanders, A., & Wixon, D. (1996). Making a difference—The impact of inspections. In *Proceedings of the CHI Conference on Human Factors in Computing Systems* (pp. 376–382). Vancouver, BC, Canada.

Schaffer, E. (2004). *Institutionalization of Usability: A Step-by-Step Guide.* Boston, MA: Addison-Wesley.

Schmandt, C. (2011). Private communication with Rex Hartson.

Schneidewind, N. F., & Ebert, C. (1998). Preserve or redesign legacy systems? *IEEE Software, 15*(4), 14–42.

Scholtz, J. (2005). Have robots, need interaction with humans!. *interactions, 12*(2), 12–14.

Schrepp, M., Held, T., & Laugwitz, B. (2006). The influence of hedonic quality on the attractiveness of user interfaces of business management software. *Interacting with Computers, 18*(5), 1055–1069.

Scriven, M. (1967). The methodology of evaluation. In R. Tyler, R. Gagne & M. Scriven (Eds.), *Perspectives of Curriculum Evaluation* (pp. 39–83). Chicago: Rand McNally.

Sears, A. (1997). Heuristic walkthroughs: Finding the problems without the noise. *International Journal of Human-Computer Interaction, 9*(3), 213–234.

Sears, A., & Hess, D. J. (1999). Cognitive walkthroughs: Understanding the effect of task-description detail on evaluator performance. *International Journal of Human-Computer Interaction, 11*(3), 185–200.

Sellen, A., Eardley, R., Izadi, S., & Harper, R. (2006). The whereabouts clock: Early testing of a situated awareness device. In *Proceedings of the CHI Conference on Human Factors in Computing Systems (Extended Abstracts).*

Sellers, M. (1994). Designing for demanding users. *interactions, 1*(3), 54–64.

Shattuck, L. W., & Woods, D. D. (1994). The critical incident technique: 40 years later. In *Proceedings of the Human Factors and Ergonomics Society Annual Meeting* (pp. 1080–1084).

Shih, Y.-H., & Liu, M. (2007). The importance of emotional usability. *Journal of Educational Technology Usability, 36*(2), 203–218.

Shneiderman, B. (1980). *Software Psychology: Human Factors in Computer and Information Systems.* Winthrop.

Shneiderman, B. (1982). The future of interactive systems and the emergence of direct manipulation. *Behavior and Information Technology, 1*(3), 237–256.

Shneiderman, B. (1983). Direct manipulation: A step beyond programming languages. *IEEE Computer, 16*(8), 57–69.

Shneiderman, B. (1998). *Designing the User Interface: Strategies for Effective Human-Computer Interaction* (3rd ed.). Menlo Park, CA: Addison Wesley.

Shneiderman, B., & Plaisant, C. (2005). *Designing the User Interface: Strategies for Effective Human-Computer Interaction* (4th ed.). Reading, MA: Addison-Wesley.

Sidner, C., & Lee, C. (2005). Robots as laboratory hosts. *interactions, 12*(2), 24–26.

Siegel, D. A. (2003). The business case for user-centered design: Increasing your power of persuasion. *interactions, 10*(3), 30–36.

Simon, H. A. (1956). Rational choice and the structure of the environment. *Psychological Review, 63*, 129–138.

Simon, H. A. (1974). How big is a chunk? *Science, 183*(4124), 482–488.

Slivka, E. (2009a, October 22). Apple Employee T-Shirt Unboxing Photos. In *MacRumors: Page 2.* http://www.macrumors.com/2009/10/22/apple-employee-t-shirt-unboxing-photos/. Last accessed 9/2/2010.

Slivka, E. (2009b, October 5). Apple Job Offer 'Unboxing' Pictures Posted. In *MacRumors: Page 2.* http://www.macrumors.com/2009/10/05/apple-job-offer-unboxing-pictures-posted/. Last accessed 09/02/2010.

Smith, D. C., Irby, C., Kimball, R., Verplank, B., & Harslem, E. (1989). Designing the Star user interface (1982). In *Perspectives on the Computer Revolution* (pp. 261–283). Ablex Publishing.

Smith, S. L., & Mosier, J. N. (1986). *Guidelines for Designing User Interface Software.* Report Number MTR-10090. Bedford, MA: Mitre Corp.

Snodgrass, A., & Coyne, R. (2006). *Interpretation in Architecture: Design as a Way of Thinking.* Routledge.

Sodan, A. C. (1998). Yin and yang in computer science. *Communications of the ACM, 41*(4), 103–114.

Sommerville, I. (2006). *Software Engineering* (8th ed.). Harlow, England: Addison Wesley.

Souza, F. D., & Bevan, N. (1990). The use of guidelines in menu interface design: Evaluation of a draft standard. In *Proceedings of the INTERACT Conference on Human-Computer Interaction* (pp. 435–440).

Spolsky, J. (2007, August 29). Even the Office 2007 box has a learning curve. http://www.joelonsoftware.com/items/2007/08/18.html. Last accessed 10/20/2010.

Spool, J., & Schroeder, W. (2001). Testing web sites: Five users is nowhere near enough. In *Proceedings of the CHI Conference on Human Factors in Computing Systems (Extended Abstracts)* (pp. 285–286), Seattle, WA.

Stake, R. (2004). *Standards-Based and Responsive Evaluation.* Sage Publications.

Stevens, W. P., Myers, G. J., & Constantine, L. L. (1974). Structured design. *IBM Systems Journal, 13*(2), 115–139.

Stewart, T. (2002). How to cope with success. *interactions, 9*(6), 17–21.

Strijland, P. (1993). Human interface standards: Can we do better? *StandardView, 1*(1), 26–30.

Sutherland, I. E. (1963). *Sketchpad: A Man-Machine Graphical Communication System.* Dissertation, Cambridge, MA: MIT.

Sutherland, I. E. (1964). *Sketchpad: A Man-Machine Graphical Communication System.* Cambridge, United Kingdom: University of Cambridge.

Sutton, S. (2007). Review of "Cost-Justifying Usability: An Update for the Internet Age (2nd ed.) by Randolph G. Bias and Deborah J. Mayhew, Editors." *interactions, 14*(5), 48–50.

Sweller, J. (1988). Cognitive load during problem solving: Effects on learning. *Cognitive Science, 12,* 257–285.

Sweller, J. (1994). Cognitive load theory, learning difficulty, and instructional design. *Learning and Instruction, 4*(4), 295–312.

Tatar, D., Harrison, S., & Sengers, P. (2007). The three paradigms of HCI. In *Proceedings of Alt.chi, CHI Conference on Human Factors in Computing Systems.* San Jose, CA.

Taylor, F. W. (1911). *The Principles of Scientific Management.* New York: Harper & Brothers.

The Open Group. Motif. http://www.opengroup.org/motif/. Last accessed 07/10/2011.

The Roanoke Times. (2006). Travel reservation system found to be costly flop. *The Roanoke Times,* (November 16).

The Standish Group. (1994). *The CHAOS Report.*

The Standish Group. (2001). *Extreme CHAOS.*

Theofanos, M., & Quesenbery, W. (2005). Towards the design of effective formative test reports. *Journal of Usability Studies, 1*(1), 27–45.

Theofanos, M., Quesenbery, W., Snyder, C., Dayton, D., & Lewis, J. (2005). Reporting on Formative Testing: A UPA 2005 Workshop Report. In *Proceedings of the UPA International Conference.* Montreal, Quebec.

Thibodeau, P. (2005, June 20). Large users hope for broader adoption of usability standard. *Computerworld.*

Thomas, J. C. (1993). Personal communication with Rex Hartson.

Thomas, J. C., & Kellogg, W. A. (1989). Minimizing ecological gaps in interface design. *IEEE Software, 6*(1), 78–86.

Thomas, P., & Macredie, R. D. (2002). Introduction to the new usability. *ACM Transactions on Computer-Human Interaction, 9*(2), 69–73.

Tognazzini, B. T. (2005). Why engineers own user experience design. *interactions, 12*(3), 32–34.

Tohidi, M., Buxton, W., Baecker, R. M., & Sellen, A. (2006). User sketches: A quick, inexpensive, and effective way to elicit more reflective user feedback. In *Proceedings of the Nordic Conference on Human-Computer Interaction* (pp. 105–114). Oslo, Norway.

Travis, A. T. (2009). Sketchy Wireframes: When you can't (or shouldn't) draw a straight line. http://boxesandarrows.com/view/sketchy-wireframes. Last accessed 7/14/2011.

Trenner, L., & Bawa, J. (1998). *The Politics of Usability: A Practical Guide to Designing Usable Systems in Industry.* Secaucus, NJ: Springer-Verlag New York, Inc.

Truss, L. (2003). *Eats, Shoots & Leaves: The Zero Tolerance Approach to Punctuation.* United Kingdom: Profile Books.

Tscheligi, M. (2005). Ambient intelligence: The next generation of user centeredness. *interactions, 12*(4).

Tufte, E. R. (1983). *The Visual Display of Quantitative Data.* Cheshire, CT: Graphics Press.

Tufte, E. R. (1990). *Envisioning Information.* Cheshire, CT: Graphics Press.

Tufte, E. R. (1997). *Visual Explanations: Images and Quantities, Evidence and Narrative.* Cheshire, CT: Graphics Press.

Tullis, T. S. (1990). High-fidelity prototyping throughout the design process. In *Proceedings of the Human Factors and Ergonomics Society Annual Meeting* (p. 266). Santa Monica, CA.

Tullis, T. S., & Albert, B. (2008). *Measuring the User Experience.* Burlington, MA: Morgan Kaufmann.

Tullis, T. S., & Stetson, J. N. (2004). A comparison of questionnaires for assessing website usability. In *Proceedings of the UPA International Conference* (pp. 1–12).

Tungare, M., Pyla, P. S., Glina, V., Bafna, P., Balli, U., Zheng, W., et al. (2006). Embodied data objects: Tangible Interfaces to Information Appliances. In *Proceedings of 44th ACM Southeast Conference (ACMSE)* (pp. 359–364).

U.S. Department of Health and Human Services. (2006). *Research-Based Web Design & Usability Guidelines*.

Usability Net. (2006). Questionnaire resources. http://www.usabilitynet.org/tools/r_questionnaire.htm. Last accessed 7/15/2011.

Venkatesh, V., Ramesh, V., & Massey, A. P. (2003). Understanding usability in mobile commerce. *Communications of the ACM, 46*(12), 53–56.

Vermeeren, A.P.O.S., Bouwmeester, K. D., Aasman, J., & de Ridder, H. (2002). DEVAN: A tool for detailed video analysis of user test data. *Behaviour & Information Technology, 21*(6), 403–423.

Vermeeren, A.P.O.S., van Kesteren, I. E. H., & Bekker, M. M. (2003). Managing the evaluator effect in user testing. In *Proceedings of the INTERACT Conference on Human-Computer Interaction* (pp. 647–654). Zurich, Switzerland.

Vertelney, L. (1989). Using video to prototype user interfaces. *SIGCHI Bulletin, 21*(2), 57–61.

Virzi, R. A. (1990). Streamlining the design process: Running fewer subjects. In *Proceedings of the Human Factors and Ergonomics Society Annual Meeting* (pp. 291–294).

Virzi, R. A. (1992). Refining the test phase of usability evaluation: How many subjects is enough? *Journal of the Human Factors and Ergonomics Society, 34*(4), 457–468.

Virzi, R. A., Sokolov, J. L., & Karis, D. (1996). Usability problem identification using both low- and high-fidelity prototypes. In *Proceedings of the CHI Conference on Human Factors in Computing Systems.* (pp. 236–243). British Columbia, Canada: Vancouver.

Wasserman, A. I. (1973). The design of 'idiot-proof' interactive programs. In *Proceedings of National Computer Conference* (pp. M34–M38).

Wasserman, V., Rafaeli, A., & Kluger, A. N. (2000). Aesthetic symbols as emotional cues. In S. Fineman (Ed.), *Emotion in Organizations* (pp. 140–165). London: SAGE.

Weiser, M. (1991). The computer for the 21st century. *Scientific American, 265*, 94–100.

Weiss, S. (2005). An alternative business model for addressing usability: Subscription research for the telecom industry. *interactions, 12*(4), 62–64.

Weller, H. G., & Hartson, R. (1992). Metaphors for the nature of human-computer interaction in an empowering environment: Interaction style influences the manner of human accomplishment. *Computers in Human Behavior, 8*(4), 313–333.

Westerman, S., Gardner, P. H., & Sutherland, E. J. (2006). *HUMAINE D9g, Taxonomy of Affective Systems Usability Testing (Workpackage 9 Deliverable)*. Information Society Technologies.

Whiteside, J. A., & Wixon, D. (1985). Developmental theory as a framework for studying human-computer interaction. In R. Hartson (Ed.), *Advances in Human-Computer Interaction* (Vol. 1, pp. 29–48). Norwood, NJ: Ablex Publishing.

Whiteside, J. A., Bennett, J., & Holtzblatt, K. (1988). Usability engineering: Our experience and evolution. In M. Helander (Ed.), *Handbook of Human-Computer Interaction* (pp. 791–817). Elsevier Science.

Whiteside, J. A., Jones, S., Levy, P. S., & Wixon, D. (1985). User performance with command, menu, and iconic interfaces. In *Proceedings of the CHI Conference on Human Factors in Computing Systems* (pp. 185–191). San Francisco, CA.

Wiklund, M., Thurrott, C., & Dumas, J. S. (1992). Does the fidelity of software prototypes affect the perception of usability. In *Proceedings of the Human Factors and Ergonomics Society Annual Meeting* (pp. 399–403). Santa Monica, CA.

Wildman, D. (1995). Getting the most from paired-user testing. *interactions, 2*(3), 21–27.

Williges, R. C. (1982). Applying the human information processing approach to human/computer interactions. In W. C. Howell & E. A. Fleishman (Eds.), *Information Processing and Decision Making* (Vol. 2., p. 83). Hillsdale, NJ: Lawrence Erlbaum.

Williges, R. C. (1984, May). Evaluating human-computer software interfaces. In *Proceedings of the International Conference on Occupational Ergonomics* (pp. 81–87), Toronto, Canada.

Wilson, C. (2011, March). Perspective-Based Inspection (Method 10 in 100 User Experience Design and Evaluation Methods for Your Toolkit). http://dux.typepad.com/dux/2011/03/. Last accessed 7/15/2011.

Wilson, C. E. (2007). Please listen to me!: Or, how can usability practitioners be more persuasive? *interactions, 14*(2), 44–45, 55.

Winchester, W. W., III, (2009). Catalyzing a perfect storm: Mobile phone-based HIV-prevention behavioral interventions. *interactions, 16*(6), 5–12.

Winograd, T., & Flores, F. (1986). *Understanding Computers and Cognition: A New Foundation for Design.* Norwood, NJ: Ablex Publishing Co.

Wixon, D. (2003). Evaluating usability methods: Why the current literature fails the practitioner. *interactions, 10*(4), 28–34.

Wixon, D., & Whiteside, J. A. (1985). Engineering for usability (panel session): Lessons from the user derived interface. In *Proceedings of the CHI Conference on Human Factors in Computing Systems* (pp. 144–147). San Francisco, CA.

Wood, S. (2007). CHI '07 Course: Building Affinity Diagrams to Reveal User Needs and Engage Developers. Unpublished CHI '07 course notes.

Wright, P. K. (2005). Rapid prototyping in consumer product design. *Communications of the ACM, 48* (6), 36–41.

Wright, P., Lickorish, A., & Milroy, R. (1994). Remembering while mousing: The cognitive costs of mouse clicks. *SIGCHI Bulletin, 26*(1), 41–45.

Ye, S. X., & Qiu, R. G. (2003). Global identification code scheme for promptly retrieving the pertinent information of a worldwide uniquely identifiable object. In *Proceedings of the International Conference on Control and Automation (ICCA)* (pp. 1000–1004).

Young, R. M., Green, T. R. G., & Simon, T. (1989). Programmable user models for predictive evaluation of interface designs. In *Proceedings of the CHI Conference on Human Factors in Computing Systems* (pp. 15–19).

Zhang, P. (2009). Theorizing the relationship between affect and aesthetics in the ICT design and use context. In *Proceedings of the International Conference on Information Resources Management,* Dubai: United Arab Emirates.

Zhang, P., & Li, N. (2004). Love at first sight or sustained effect? The role of perceived affective quality on users' cognitive reactions to information technology. In *Proceedings of the International Conference on Information Systems (ICIS)* (pp. 283–296). Washington, DC.

Zhang, P., & Li, N. (2005). The importance of affective quality. *Communications of the ACM, 48*(9), 105–110.

Zhang, Z., Basili, V., & Shneiderman, B. (1999). Perspective-based usability inspection: An empirical validation of efficacy. *Empirical Software Engineering, 4*(1), 43–69.

Zieniewicz, M. J., Johnson, D. C., Wong, D. C., & Flatt, J. D. (2002). The evolution of army wearable computers. *IEEE Pervasive Computing, 1*(4), 30–40.

Exercises

Active Learning

The best way to learn the processes described in this book is by doing them! We have organized your participation in the process at three levels: examples for you to follow in the text, a more or less parallel set of exercises to do on your own, and a set of extensively specified team project assignments (on the book Website).

Pointers to the exercises are indicated within many of the chapters, often right after a similar example in the text. Those pointers refer to the exercise descriptions here. The location of each forward reference is where you should consider doing the exercise before moving on, but we have put the exercise descriptions here so as not to interrupt the flow of the rest of the text in the chapters. Finally, a comprehensive set of team project assignments is available in the Instructor's Guide, available to instructors from the publisher. The exercises require medium-level engagement, somewhere in between the in-text examples and full project assignments.

Within the broader audience of this book, individual readers are encouraged to follow the examples and undertake the exercises on their own. Groups of readers, whether within classes taking the material as a course or within organizations that wish to acquire competency in these processes, will benefit even more from carrying out the exercises as a team. You should be able to figure out, from each exercise description, how to pursue the exercise either as an individual or as a team.

The exercises are for learning, not for producing a product, so you do not have to complete every detail if you think you have gotten what you need to out of each one. You should be able to learn most of what you can get from most exercises in an hour or so. In the case of a team within a classroom setting, this means that you can do the exercises as in-class activities, breaking out into teams and working in parallel, and possibly finishing the exercise as homework before the next class. This has the advantages of working next to other teams with similar goals and problems and of having an instructor present who can move among teams as a consultant and mentor. We recommend that student team deliverables be prepared in summary form for presentation to the rest of the class so that each team can learn from the others.

Choosing a Target Application System

Your choice of a target application system should be gauged toward the goal of learning, not producing a product. That means choosing something the right size. Avoid applications that are too large or complex; choose something for which the semantics and functionality are relatively easy to understand. However, avoid systems that are too small or too simple because they may not support the process activities very well. The bottom line: Choose something broad enough so that you can use the same system in all the exercises, each time building on your previous experience.

The criterion for selection here is that you will need to identify at least a half-dozen somewhat different kinds of user tasks. That usually means, for example, that a Website used only for information seeking is not a good candidate because information seeking is only a single type of task and often does not involve enough differences in the kinds of interaction. You should also choose a system that has more than one class of user. For example, an e-commerce Website for ordering merchandise will have users from the public doing the ordering and employee users processing the orders.

For practitioner teams in a real development organization, we recommend against using a real development project for these exercises. There is no sense in introducing the pressure to produce a real design and the risk of failure into this learning process.

Because many parts of these processes are best learned by interacting with a "user," "customer," or "client," it helps to choose an application for which you can find (among friends, family, or fellow students or practitioners) or simulate these roles, for example, for contextual inquiry interviews.

CHAPTER 3 EXERCISES

Exercise 3-1: System Concept Statement for a System of Your Choice

Goal: Get practice in writing a concise system concept statement.

Activities:

- Write a system concept statement for a system of your choice.
- Iterate and polish it. The 150 or fewer words you write here will be among the most important words in the whole project; they should be highly polished, which means that

you should spend a disproportionate amount of time and energy thinking about, writing, reading, editing, discussing, and rewriting this system concept statement.

Deliverables: Your "final" system concept statement.

Schedule: Given the simplicity of the domain, we expect you can get what you need from this exercise in about 30 minutes.

Exercise 3-2: Contextual Inquiry Data Gathering for the System of Your Choice

Goal: Get practice in performing contextual inquiry.

Activities:

- The best conditions for this exercise are to work as a team and have a real client, as you would in a team project, for example, in a course.

- If you are working with a team but do not have a real client, divide your team members into users and interviewers and do a role-playing exercise. If you are working alone, invite some friends over for one of your famous pizza-and-beer-and-contextual-inquiry parties and have them play a user role while you interview them. We have found that you get the best results if you follow this order: eat the pizza, do the exercise, drink the beer.

- Do your best to suspend disbelief and pretend that you and your users are in a real situation within the context of your domain of investigation.

- Interviewers each take their own transcripts of raw data notes as you ask questions and listen to users talk about their work activities in this domain.

- Preface each note with the user ID, for example, U3, of the user from whom the note is derived.

Deliverables: At least a few pages of raw contextual inquiry data transcript, hand written or typed, for the investigations you conducted for your example system. Include a few interesting examples (something unexpected or unique) from your notes to share.

Schedule: Given the simplicity of the domain, we expect this exercise to take about 1 to 2 hours.

CHAPTER 4 EXERCISES

Exercise 4-1: Flow Model Sketch for Your System

Goal: Get practice in making an initial flow model sketch for the work practice of an organization.

Activities:

- For your target system sketch out a flow model diagram, in the same style as our flow model sketch for MUTTS, shown in Figure 4-3, showing work roles, information flow, information repositories, transactions, etc.

- Draw on your raw work activity data and construct a representation of the flow of data, information, and work artifacts.

- Even if there is no existing automated system, you should capture the flow of the manual work process.
- Start with representing your work roles as nodes, add in any other nodes for databases and so on.
- Label communication and flow lines.
- If you do not have enough contextual data from your limited data-gathering exercise, make some up to make this work.

Deliverables: A one-page diagram illustrating a high-level flow model for the existing work process of your target system.

Schedule: Given the simplicity of the domain, we expect this exercise to take about an hour.

Exercise 4-2: Work Activity Notes for Your System

Goal: Get practice in synthesizing work activity notes from your contextual data.

Activities:

- If you are working alone, it is time for another pizza-and-beer-and-contextual-analysis party with your friends.
- However you form your team, appoint a team leader and a person to act as note recorder.
- The team leader leads the group through raw data, synthesizing work activity notes on the fly.
- Be sure to filter out all unnecessary verbiage, fluff, and noise.
- As the work activity notes are called out, the recorder types them into a laptop (preferably with a screen projector so that the group can see the work in progress).
- Everyone in the team should work together to make sure that the individual work activity notes are disambiguated from context dependencies (usually by adding explanatory text in italics).

Deliverables: At least a few dozen work activity notes synthesized from your raw contextual inquiry data transcript for your system, hand written or typed into a laptop. Highlight a few of your most interesting synthesized work activity notes for sharing.

Schedule: Based on our experience with these activities, we expect this to take you an hour or two.

Exercise 4-3: WAAD Building for Your System

Goal: Get practice in building a work activity affinity diagram to sort and organize contextual data.

Activities:

- If you are working alone, it is time for yet another pizza-and-beer-and-contextual-analysis party with your friends (the last time you have to buy pizza, at least in this chapter).

- However you assemble your team, using all the work activity notes created from the contextual inquiry investigations you did in the previous exercise, do your best to follow the procedure we have described in this chapter for WAAD building.
- Take digital photographs of your work process and products, including the full WAAD, some medium-level details, and some close-ups of interesting parts.
- Hang them on your fridge with magnets.

Deliverables: As much of the full WAAD for your system as you were able to produce. It is probably best to keep it rolled up into a bundle for safe keeping unless you have the luxury of being able to keep it taped to the wall. You should also have the digital photos you took of your WAAD. If you are working in a classroom environment, be prepared to share the photos in a narrated slide show and to discuss your WAAD and the process of building it with other teams in the class.

Schedule: This is one of the more time-consuming exercises; expect it to take 4 to 6 hours.

CHAPTER 5 EXERCISES

Exercise 5-1: Extracting Requirement Statements for Your System

Goal: Get some practice with requirements extraction.

Activities:

- Assemble a team per the preparation guidelines in this chapter.
- Choose a leader and recorder.
- Get together with your team where you have hung your WAAD for the Ticket Kiosk System or hang it back up again if you had to take it down before.
- Number all the WAAD nodes and notes with a structured set of ID markers.
- Do a careful walkthrough, traversing the WAAD.
- For each work activity note in the WAAD, work as a team to:
  - Deduce user need(s) and interaction design requirements to support the need(s).
  - As you go, have the recorder capture requirements in the format of Figures 5-4 and 5-5, including extrapolation requirements and rationale statements, where appropriate.
  - In the process, also make notes and lists about:
    - Questions about missing data
    - Software requirements inputs
    - System support needs
    - Marketing inputs
    - Ways to enhance the overall user experience
    - Information about design-informing models
    - Future features and issues

- To speed things up, have each person be responsible for writing the requirement statements extracted from a different sub-tree in the WAAD structure. Set aside any work activity notes that require additional thought or discussion to be dealt with at the end by the team as a whole.
- If time permits, have the whole team read all requirement statements to assure agreement.

Deliverables:

- A requirements document covering at least one subtree of the WAAD for your system.
- Notes and lists of the other kinds of information (above bullets) that come out of this process.

Schedule: We expect that this exercise could take at least a couple of hours. If you simply do not have that kind of time to devote to it, do as much as you can to at least get a flavor of how this exercise works.

Exercise 5-2: Constraints for Your System

Goal: Get a little experience in specifying constraints for system development.

Activities: Extract and deduce what you can about development and implementation constraints from contextual data for the system of your choice.

Deliverables: A short list of same.

Schedule: A half hour should do it.

CHAPTER 6 EXERCISES

Exercise 6-1: Identifying Work Roles for Your System

Goal: Get a little practice at identifying work roles from your contextual data.

Activities: By now you should be pretty certain about the work roles for your system.

- Using your user-related contextual data notes, identify the major work roles for your system.
- Write the major ones in a list.
- For each role, add explanatory notes describing the role.
- For each role, add a description of the major task set that people in that role would be expected to perform.

Deliverables: A written list of work roles you identified for your system, each with an explanation of the role and a description of the associated task set.

Schedule: A half hour should do it.

Exercise 6-2: User Class Definitions for Your System

Goal: Get practice in defining user classes for work roles.

Activities:

- Using your user-related contextual data notes, create a few user class definitions to go with the work roles definitions you created in the previous exercise.
- For each of the work roles that you identified in the previous exercise, draw on your user-related contextual data notes to define one or two corresponding user classes, describing the characteristics of each.

Deliverables: A few user class definitions to go with the work roles identified for the system of your choice.

Schedule: A half hour to 45 minutes should be enough to get the most out of this assignment.

Exercise 6-3: A Social Model for Your System

Goal: Get a little practice in making a social model diagram.

Activities:

- Identify active entities, such as work roles, and represent as nodes in the diagram.
- Include groups and subgroups of roles and external roles that interact with work roles.
- Include system-related roles, such as a central database.
- Include workplace ambiance and its pressures and influences.
- Identify concerns and perspectives and represent as attributes of nodes.
- Identify social relationships, such as influences between entities, and represent these as arcs between nodes in the diagram.
- Identify barriers, or potential barriers, in relationships between entities and represent them as red bolts of lightning ($\mathcal{N}$).

Deliverables: One social model diagram for your system, with as much detail as feasible.

Schedule: This could take a couple of hours.

Exercise 6-4: A Social Model for a "Smartphone"

Sketch out an annotated social model for the use of an iPhone or similar smartphone by you and your friends.

Exercise 6-5: Creating a Flow Model for Your System

Goal: Get a little practice in creating a flow model for an enterprise.

Activities:

- Follow up on your flow model initial sketch that you did in Exercise 4-1.
- Again represent each work role or system entity as a node in the diagram.

■ Use arcs between nodes to show all communication and coordination necessary to do the work of the enterprise.

■ Use arcs to represent all information flow and flow of physical artifacts.

■ Include all forms of communication, including direct conversations, email, phones, letters, memos, meetings, and so on.

■ Include both flow internally within the enterprise and flow externally with the rest of the world.

Deliverables: One flow model diagram for your system, with as much detail as feasible.

Schedule: This could take a couple of hours.

Exercise 6-6: Hierarchical Task Inventory for Your System

Goal: Get some practice creating a hierarchical task inventory diagram.

Activities: Using your task-related contextual data notes, make a simple hierarchical task inventory diagram for your system.

Deliverables: Simple HTI diagram(s) for the system of your choice.

Schedule: An hour should be enough to get what you need from this exercise.

Exercise 6-7: Usage Scenarios for Your System

Goal: Get some practice in writing usage scenarios.

Activities:

■ Select one or two good representative task threads for the most interesting user class, for example, the customer.

■ Write a couple of detailed usage scenarios, referring to user roles, tasks, actions, objects, and work context.

■ Work quickly; you can clean it up as you go.

Hints and cautions: Do not worry too much about the design yet; we will get to that.

Deliverables: A few usage scenarios to share and discuss.

Schedule: An hour should be enough time for this one.

Exercise 6-8: Design Scenarios for Your System

Goal: Get some practice in writing usage scenarios.

Activities:

■ For the same usage scenarios you wrote in the previous exercise, write a couple of detailed design scenarios, again referring to user roles, tasks, actions, objects, and work context.

■ Make up anything you need about the design on the fly.

■ Do this quickly; you can clean it up as you go.

Deliverables: A few design scenarios to share and discuss.

Schedule: An hour should be enough time for this one.

Exercise 6-9: Identifying Information Objects for Your System

Goal: Get a little practice in identifying information objects for a system.

Activities:

■ Review the ontology of your system.

■ Identify the entities within your application that are operated on by users—searched and browsed for, accessed and displayed, modified and manipulated, and stored back again.

■ Sketch an outline or list of these information objects, their attributes, and the relationships among them.

Deliverables: The list just described.

Schedule: A half hour should do it.

CHAPTER 7 EXERCISES

Exercise 7-1: Creating a User Persona for Your System

Goal: Get some experience at writing a persona.

Activities:

■ Select an important work role within your system. At least one user class for this work role must be very broad, with the user population coming from a large and diverse group, such as the general public.

■ Using your user-related contextual data, create a persona, give it a name, and get a photo to go with it.

■ Write the text for the persona description.

Deliverables: One- or two-page persona write-up

Schedule: You should be able to do what you need to learn from this in about an hour.

Exercise 7-2: Practice in Ideation and Sketching

Goal: To get practice in ideation and sketching for design.

Activities:

■ Doing this in a small group is strongly preferable, but you can do it with one other person.

■ Get out blank paper, appropriate size marking pens, and any other supplies you might need for sketching.

■ Pick a topic, a system, or device. Our recommendation is something familiar, like a dishwasher.

■ Start with some free-flow ideation about ways to design a new and improved concept of a dishwasher. Do not limit yourself to conventional designs.

■ Go with the flow and see what happens.

■ Remember that this is an exercise about the process, so what you come up with for the product is not that crucial.

- Everyone should make sketches of the ideas that arise about a dishwasher design, as you go in the ideation.
- Start with design sketches in the ecological perspective. For a dishwasher, this might include your dining room, kitchen, and the flow of dishes in their daily cycle. You could include something unorthodox: sketch a conveyor belt from the dinner table through your appliance and out into the dish cabinets. Sketch how avoiding the use of paper plates can save resources and not fill the trash dumps.
- Make some sketches from an interaction perspective showing different ways you can operate the dishwasher: how you load and unload it and how you set wash cycle parameters and turn it on.
- Make sketches that project the emotional perspective of a user experience with your product. This might be more difficult, but it is worth taking some time to try.
- Ideate. Sketch, sketch, and sketch. Brainstorm and discuss.

Deliverables: A brief written description of the ideation process and its results, along with all your supporting sketches.

Schedule: Give yourself enough time to really get engaged in this activity.

Exercise 7-3: Ideation and Sketching for Your System

Goal: More practice in ideation and sketching for design. Do the same as you did in the previous exercise, only this time for your own system.

CHAPTER 8 EXERCISES

Exercise 8-1: Conceptual Design for Your System

Goal: Get a little practice in initial conceptual design.

Activities:

- Think about your system and contextual data and envision a conceptual design, including any metaphors, in the ecological perspective. Try to communicate the designer's mental model, or a design vision, of how the system works as a black box within its environment.
- Think about your system and contextual data and envision a conceptual design in the interaction perspective. Try to communicate the designer's mental model of how the user operates the system.
- Finally, think about your system and contextual data and envision a conceptual design in the emotional perspective. Try to communicate a vision of how the design elements will evoke emotional impact in users.

Deliverables: Brief written descriptions of your conceptual design in the three perspectives and/or a few presentation slides of the same to share with others.

Schedule: You decide how much time you can afford to give this. If you cannot do this exercise in all three perspectives, just pick one, perhaps the ecological perspective.

Exercise 8-2: Storyboard for Your System

Goal: Get a little practice in sketching storyboards.

Activities:

- Sketch storyboard frames illustrating narrative sequences of action in each of the three perspectives.
- Include things like these in your storyboards:
  - Hand-sketched pictures annotated with a few words
  - All the work practice that is part of the task, not just interaction with the system, for example, include telephone conversations with agents or roles outside the system
  - Sketches of devices and screens
  - Any connections with system internals, for example, flow to and from a database
  - Physical user actions
  - Cognitive user actions in "thought balloons"
  - Extra-system activities, such as talking with a friend about what ticket to buy
- For the ecological perspective, illustrate high-level interplay among human users, the system as a whole, and the surrounding context.
- In the interaction perspective, show screens, user actions, transitions, and user reactions.
- Use storyboards in the emotional perspective to illustrate deeper user experience phenomena such as fun, joy, and aesthetics.

Schedule: You decide how much time you can afford to give this. If you cannot do this exercise in all three perspectives, just pick one, perhaps the ecological perspective.

CHAPTER 9 EXERCISES

Exercise 9-1: Intermediate and Detailed Design for Your System

Goal: Get some practice in developing a few parts of the intermediate and detailed design.

Activities:

- If you are working with a team, get together with your team.
- Choose just one principal work role for your system (e.g., the customer).
- Choose just one key task that work role is expected to perform.
- For that work role and task, make a few illustrated scenarios to show some of the associated interaction.
- Sketch some screen layouts to support your scenarios, along with some representation of the navigational structure.
- Go for a little depth, but not much breadth.
- Make a few annotated wireframes for the same scenarios.

Hints, cautions, and assumptions:

- Do not get too involved in design guidelines issues yet (e.g., icon appearance or menu placement).
- Control time spent arguing; learn the process!
- Base your screen designs on the contextual analysis and design you have done so far.

Deliverables: Just the work products that naturally result from these activities.

Schedule: Whatever you can afford. At least give it an honest try.

CHAPTER 10 EXERCISES

Exercise 10-1: Identifying User Experience Goals for Your System

Goal: A little experience in stating user experience goals.

Activities: Review the WAAD and user concerns in the social model for the system of your choice, noting user or customer concerns relating to user experience goals.

Deliverables: A short list of user experience goals for one user class of the system of your choice.

Schedule: A half hour or so (it should be easy by now).

Exercise 10-2: Creating Benchmark Tasks and UX Targets for Your System

Goal: To gain experience in writing effective benchmark tasks and measurable UX targets.

Activities:

- We have shown you a rather complete set of examples of benchmark tasks and UX targets for the Ticket Kiosk System. Your job is to do something similar for the system of your choice.
- Begin by identifying which work roles and user classes you are targeting in evaluation (brief description is enough).
- Write three or more UX table entries (rows), including your choices for each column. Have at least two UX targets based on a benchmark task and at least one based on a questionnaire.
- Create and write up a set of about three benchmark tasks to go with the UX targets in the table.
  - Do NOT make the tasks too easy.
  - Make tasks increasingly complex.
  - Include some navigation.
  - Create tasks that you can later "implement" in your low-fidelity rapid prototype.

■ The expected average performance time for each task should be no more than about 3 minutes, just to keep it short and simple for you during evaluation.

■ Include the questionnaire question numbers in the measuring instrument column of the appropriate UX target.

Cautions and hints:

■ Do not spend any time on design in this exercise; there will be time for detailed design in the next exercise.

■ Do not plan to give users any training.

Deliverables:

■ Two user benchmark tasks, each on a separate sheet of paper.

■ Three or more UX targets entered into a blank UX target table on your laptop or on paper.

■ If you are doing this exercise in a classroom environment, finish up by reading your benchmark tasks to the class for critique and discussion.

Schedule: Work efficiently and complete in about an hour and a half.

CHAPTER 11 EXERCISES

Exercise11-1: Building a Low-Fidelity Paper Prototype for Your System

Goal: To obtain experience with rapid construction of a low-fidelity prototype for early stages of user interaction design and to have a real paper prototype to generate lots of critical incidents later in your evaluation exercise.

Activities: This should be one of your most fun exercises, but it can also be a lot of work.

■ Following the guidelines for paper prototype construction given in Section 11.6.5, build a paper prototype for your system or product design.

■ Make sure that the prototype will support at least the benchmark tasks, descriptions for which you wrote in the previous exercise.

■ Add in some other "decoy" interaction design "features," widgets, and objects so that the prototype does not look tailored to just your benchmark tasks.

Hints and cautions:

■ It is normal for you to have to do more design work during this exercise, to complete details that were not fully designed in previous exercises.

■ Remember: You are learning the process, not creating a perfect design or prototype.

■ Assuming you are doing this as a team: Get everyone on your team involved in drawing, cutting, taping, and so on, not just one or two people.

■ You will be done much faster if everyone pitches in.

- This is not art class so do not worry too much about straight lines, exact details, etc.
- Pilot test to be sure it will support your benchmark tasks for evaluation.

Deliverables: A right smart "executable" paper prototype that will support your benchmark tasks in user experience testing, and your pilot tests passed with flying colors (no monochromatic flying).

Schedule: Just git 'er done. It could take several hours, but it is essential for all the exercises that follow.

CHAPTER 13 EXERCISES

Exercise13-1: Formative UX Inspection of Your System

Goal: Get a little practice in doing a UX inspection.

Activities:

- Unless you have another prototype, use the paper prototype you built in the previous exercise. If your paper prototype is not suitable for an effective exercise in UX inspection, select an application or appropriate Website as the target of your inspection.
- Perform a UX inspection as described in Chapter 13.
- If you are working with a team, use the team approach described in Chapter 13.

Deliverables: A list of UX problems identified by your UX inspection.

Schedule: An hour and a half.

CHAPTER 14 EXERCISES

Exercise 14-1: Formative UX Evaluation Preparation for Your System

Goal: To get some practice in preparation for a simple empirical evaluation.

Activities:

- If you are working with a team, get together with your team.
- Decide roles for team members. Include at least a facilitator and a prototype executor, plus a quantitative data recorder and one or more critical incident recorders.
- In addition, if you are doing this exercise in a classroom with other teams, assign two team members as participants to trade to another team when you start data collection in the next exercise.
- The prototype executor should get out the paper prototype you made in Exercise 11-1 and make sure the prototype works without breaking.

■ If you developed a programmed prototype, everything will be the same except that you will not need an interface executor. You will, instead, need someone to make sure the prototype hardware and software are set up, installed, and running properly for evaluation.

■ This activity works well for a team of about four. If you have more or fewer members in your team, it is easy to make adjustments. If there are only two of you, for example, one person can be the executor and the other person can record critical incidents and time the benchmark tasks. If there are four or five of you, the extra people will be valuable in helping record critical incidents. If you have been working alone on all the previous exercises, you may want find a couple of other people to help you run the evaluation. In addition and in any case, you need to recruit two people to serve as participants to evaluate your prototype.

■ Get out the UX target table you made in Exercise 10-2.

■ Have at least two benchmark tasks that you created in Exercise 10-2, each written on a separate piece of paper.

■ Assuming you used a questionnaire for subjective data in your evaluation session, get out copies of the questionnaire, one for each participant you will be using, and circle the questions you want participants to answer.

■ Review your evaluation protocols.

Deliverables: Just have everything just mentioned ready for the next exercise, data collection.

Schedule: It should not take too long to get ready for evaluation.

CHAPTER 15 EXERCISES

Exercise 15-1: UX Evaluation Data Collection for Your System

Goal: To get a little practice in the data collection part for a very simple formative UX evaluation using a paper prototype.

Activities: This is perhaps the most fun and most rewarding of all the exercises when you finally get to see some users in action with your interaction design.

■ New team formation:

■ This is described in terms of multiple teams in a classroom setting. For other setups, make appropriate adjustments.

■ After all the teams are gathered and sitting around a table, make the switch of participants with another team.

■ You send the two people in the participant role from your team to another team. Curb the potential confusion here by doing the swap in an orderly circular fashion among the teams.

- You will now have new participants from a different team who are unfamiliar with your design. These new participants are now permanently on your team, for the rest of these exercises, including data collection, analysis, and reporting.
- As an alternative, if you do not have multiple teams, try recruiting a couple of co-workers or friends as participants.
- Sitting together in your newly formed teams, get out your UX target table form, your benchmark task descriptions, and your questionnaires.
- Dismiss your two participants (the new team members you just got) to the hallway or other waiting area.
- Data collection:
  - Assemble and boot up your prototype, per the instructions in Section 15.3.6.
  - Call in your first participant into the "lab," greet the participant, and explain the evaluation session.
  - Have this first participant perform your first benchmark task for your objective UX targets.
    - Have the participant read the first benchmark task aloud.
    - Ask the participant to perform that task while thinking aloud.
    - The executor moves prototype parts in response to participant actions.
    - The facilitator directs the session and keeps it moving.
    - Timer(s) writes down or enters timing and error count data as indicated in UX targets as the user performs the task (do not count participant's reading aloud of task in task timing).
    - Everyone else available should be used to take notes on critical incidents and UX problems.
    - Remember the rules about not coaching or anticipating user actions. And the computer may not speak!
  - Have this first participant perform your second benchmark task for your objective UX targets.
    - Have the participant read the second task aloud and perform it while thinking aloud.
  - How much data to collect?
    - You need to collect a dozen or more critical incidents in this overall exercise (i.e., from both participants doing both benchmark tasks).
    - If you do not get at least a half dozen from each participant, continue with that participant doing exploratory use of your prototype until you get enough critical incidents.
    - For example, have them browse through each screen, looking at each object (button, menu, etc.), commenting on and giving their opinion about the quality of the user experience relating to various features.

- Have this participant complete your questionnaire and then give them their "reward."
- Keep your first participant as a new member of the rest of the team to help with observations.
- Bring in the second participant and perform the same session again.

Deliverables: All your data.

Schedule: Complete by end of class (about an hour and a half, if you are efficient).

CHAPTER 16 EXERCISES

Exercise 16-1: UX Data Analysis for Your System

Goal: To get some practice with the analysis part of a very simple formative UX evaluation.

Activities:

- If you are working with a team, get together with your team, including any new participants you picked up along the way.
- Fill in the UX target table "Observed results" column.
- Together, your team compiles and compares the quantitative results to determine whether UX targets were met.
- Review your raw critical incident notes and write a UX problem list.
- Organize the UX problem list and perform cost-importance analysis.
    - Using a paper cost-importance table or laptop spreadsheet, list a dozen or more UX problems from critical incidents.
    - Assign an importance (to fix) rating to each observed problem.
    - Propose solutions (without doing all the work of redesign).
    - Group together any related problems and list as single problem.
    - Assign cost values (in person-hours) to each solution.
    - Compute priority ratios.
- Compile your results:
    - Move your "Must fix" problems to the top of your cost-importance table.
    - Sort the remaining problems by decreasing priority ratios to determine the priority rank of UX problems.
    - Fill in the cumulative cost column.
    - Assume a hypothetical value for available time resources (something to make this exercise work).
    - Draw the cutoff, line of affordability.
    - Finalize your "management" decisions (resolution) about which changes to make now and in the next version.

Deliverables:

- Summary of quantitative results, written in "Observed results" column in your UX target table form (for comparison with UX targets).

- List of raw critical incidents.
- Cost-importance table form containing three UX problems selected as interesting to present to class or your work group (complete across all three rows).
- Choose someone to give brief a report on your evaluation results.

Schedule: Given the simplicity of the domain, we expect this exercise to take about 30 to 60 minutes.

CHAPTER 17 EXERCISES

Exercise 17-1: Formative Evaluation Reporting for Your System

Goal: Write a report of the formative UX evaluation you did on the system of your choice.

Activities:

- Report on your informal summative evaluation results using a table showing UX targets, benchmark tasks, questionnaires, and so on used to gather data, along with target values and observed values.
- Add brief statements about whether or not each UX target was met.
- Write a full report on a selected subset (about half a dozen) of UX problems found in the qualitative part of your formative UX evaluation. Follow the guidelines in this chapter regarding content, tone, and format, being sure to include redesign proposals for each problem.
- Report on the results of your cost-importance analysis, including problem resolutions, for all the problems you reported previously and, if appropriate, some others for context.

Deliverables: Your formative evaluation report.

Schedule: We expect this exercise to take about an hour.

Index

Note: Page numbers followed by *b* indicate boxes, *f* indicate figures and *t* indicate tables.

A